ISBN 978-1-330-70889-7
PIBN 10095225

1 MONTH OF
FREE
READING

at

www.ForgottenBooks.com

By purchasing this book you are eligible for one month membership to ForgottenBooks.com, giving you unlimited access to our entire collection of over 700,000 titles via our web site and mobile apps.

To claim your free month visit:
www.forgottenbooks.com/free95225

Similar Books Are Available from
www.forgottenbooks.com

BIOGRAPHICAL HISTORY

OF

GONVILLE AND CAIUS COLLEGE

Volume IV

CAMBRIDGE UNIVERSITY PRESS

London: FETTER LANE, E.C.

C. F. CLAY, Manager

Edinburgh: 100, PRINCES STREET
Berlin: A. ASHER AND CO.
Leipzig: F. A. BROCKHAUS
New York: G. P. PUTNAM'S SONS
Bombay and Calcutta: MACMILLAN AND CO., Ltd.

DR CAIUS

BIOGRAPHICAL HISTORY

OF

GONVILLE AND CAIUS COLLEGE

VOLUME IV

IN CONTINUATION OF VOLUMES I—III

COMPILED BY

JOHN VENN, Sc.D., F.R.S., E.S.A.

SENIOR FELLOW AND PRESIDENT

PART I

ADMISSIONS SINCE JANUARY 1, 1899

EDITED BY

E. S. ROBERTS, M.A., Master

PART II

CHRONICLE OF THE COLLEGE ESTATES

COMPILED BY

E. J. GROSS, M.A.

SENIOR FELLOW AND FORMERLY BURSAR

CAMBRIDGE:
AT THE UNIVERSITY PRESS
1912

Cambridge:
PRINTED BY JOHN CLAY, M.A.
AT THE UNIVERSITY PRESS

PREFACE

THE first volume of the *Biographical History of Gonville and Caius College*, published in 1897, contained an *Introduction* by Dr Venn and the record of individual admissions, fragmentary to the year 1559, and continuous from 1559 to 1713. The second volume, published in 1898, continued the record of admissions from 1713 to 1898. The third volume, published in 1901, completed the History of the College as originally designed. The delay in publication made it possible to include in an appendix the record of admissions for the three years 1899—1901. For the initiative, the plan, and the detail of the first three volumes Dr Venn was wholly responsible. It is not out of place here to note that the College, in recognition of the immense benefit conferred upon the College by the patient labour of Dr Venn, and his prolonged and accurate research, which has resulted in the production of this *History*, paid him the compliment of placing his coat of arms in a window of the Hall which contains those of the " Benefactors."

The record of admissions has proved to be a source of unfailing interest and practical usefulness. The Governing Body of the College accordingly sanctioned the compilation and publication of the record from the year to which it had been carried in Volume II to the present date (1911). Further the Chronicle of the College Estates, drawn up by Mr E. J. Gross, Bursar from 1876 to 1886, was approaching completion. It was therefore resolved to include in a fourth volume not only the continuation of the Admission Record and the Chronicle of the Estates, with appropriate maps and illustrations, but also an account of the Mastership of Dr Norman Macleod Ferrers, 1880—1903, *Addenda* and *Corrigenda* to Volume II, illustrations of the antiquities of the College, records of the donations and benefactions received by the College during the last ten years, and a description of new buildings or restorations of old buildings.

This Volume contains two Parts, each with its own Index and pagination. Part I contains the Admission Record and Appendices; Part II the Chronicle of the Estates.

The title "Biographical History," though not wholly accurate, is convenient and has been retained for this fourth volume. Even in the third there was much matter which could hardly be described as "biographical." But the design of the work has been in the past, and will be as regards continuations in the future, mainly concerned with the life-history of those whose names through the successive generations are enrolled in the Admission Registers of the College. All else, if important, is incidental.

E. S. ROBERTS,

E. J. GROSS.

December, 1911.

CONTENTS

PART I

PART II

CHRONICLE OF THE ESTATES

PLATES AND ILLUSTRATIONS

PART I

Goodall, Charles Cunliffe: son of the Rev. Charles Goodall, M.A., Vicar of High Lane, near Stockport, Cheshire; and Ruth Cunliffe. Born at High Lane Vicarage, Cheshire, 25 Feb. 1890. Schools: Wensleydale School, Aysgarth, Yorkshire, under J. Houfe, M.A.; and Trent College, under the Rev. J. S. Tucker, M.A. Admitted 1 Oct, 1909.

PLATES AND ILLUSTRATIONS

PART I

PART II

BIOGRAPHICAL HISTORY

OF

GONVILLE AND CAIUS COLLEGE.

ADMISSIONS SINCE JANUARY 1, 1899.

JANUARY 1899 TO MICHAELMAS 1899.

(Tutors: Mr Roberts, Mr Gallop, and Mr Knight.)

Widdicombe, Edward Parnell: son of James Widdicombe, farmer, of The Avenue, Cambridge; and Mary Sparke Hannaford. Born at Wickaborough, Berry Pomeroy, Devon, 17 June 1876. School: Higher Grade, Cambridge, under Mr J. W. Iliffe, M.A. Admitted 3 Jan. 1899, as Salomons Engineering Scholar.
> B.A. 1900. Mech. Sci. Tripos, Part I, Class 1. Assistant Engineer on the East Indian Railways 1900– .

Goode, Samuel Walter: son of William Goode, merchant, of Port Pirie, South Australia; and Marion Jones. Born at Port Pirie, 25 Nov. 1878. School: Way College, Adelaide, under Mr W. G. Tow, LL.D. Admitted 19 April 1899.
> B.A. 1901. Class. Tripos, Part I, Class 1, 1901. Exhibitioner, 1900; Scholar, 1901–1902. I.C.S. 1902; Assistant Magistrate and Collector, Bengal.

Rittenberg, Max Mark Lion: son of Benjamin Rittenberg, commercial agent, of 23, Earl's Court Gardens, London, S.W.; and Lily Moss. Born at Sydney, Australia, 18 April 1880. School: Tonbridge, under the Rev. Joseph Wood, D.D. Admitted 19 April 1899.
> B.A. 1902. Nat. Sci. Tripos, Part I, Class 1, 1901. Entrance Exhibitioner, 1899; Scholar, 1900–1902. Editor of "The Organiser" (1909).

Eberhardt, Frederic Charles (Fritz in certificate of birth): son of Charles Leopold Eberhardt, of 54, Avenue de la Toison d'Or, Brussels, deceased; and Mary Barlow. Born at 17, Abbey Road, London, N.W., 17 Feb. 1879. Schools: The Public School, Wiesbaden, and Private School, Wiesbaden. Admitted 19 April 1899.
> Resided two terms.

C IV 1

Jones, William Arthur: son of Rev. Alfred Jones, Nonconformist minister, of the Manse, Littleborough, near Manchester; and Helen Jane Jolly. Born at Pimlico, London, 2 Nov. 1873. Educated at University College of North Wales, under Principal Reichel, and at The Owens College, Manchester, under Principals Ward and Hopkins. Admitted as an Advanced Student in Classics, 4 May 1899.
> B.A. 1901. In the Methodist Ministry (1909).

Yapp, Richard Henry: son of Richard Keysall Yapp, farmer and landowner, of Orleton, Herefordshire, deceased; and Jane Gammidge. Born at Orleton, 8 Oct. 1871. School: Hereford County College, under the Rev. T. A. Stoodley, M.A. Admitted as Frank Smart Student, 19 June 1899; previously at St John's College.
> B.A. 1898. Nat. Sci. Tripos, Part I, Class 1, 1898; Part II, Class 1, 1899. Member of the Skeat Scientific Expedition to Malay, 1899–1900. Professor of Botany, University College, Aberystwith (1909).

MICHAELMAS 1899 TO MICHAELMAS 1900.

(Tutors: Mr Roberts, Mr Gallop, and Mr Knight.)

Alexander, William Arthur: son of Thomas Arthur Alexander, physician and surgeon, of Clematis House, Walton, Norfolk; and Ann Oldfield. Born at Walton, Norfolk, 1 March 1880. School: The Grammar School, Wellingborough, under Dr H. E. Platt. Admitted 2 Oct. 1899.
> B.A. 1902. Nat. Sci. Tripos, Part I, Class 2, 1902. In medical practice (1909).

Atkin, Eric Edwin: son of Edwin Aaron Atkin, gentleman, of Ravenswood, Surrey Road, Bournemouth; and Sophia Harrison. Born at 23, Braithwaite Road, Birmingham, 31 May 1881. Schools: Blundell's, Tiverton, under Mr Francis, and High School, Bournemouth. Admitted 2 Oct. 1899.
> B.A. 1902; M.B. 1907. Nat. Sci. Tripos, Part I, Class 3, 1902. Fishmongers' Research Scholar, 1907.

Beaton, Edwin: son of Edwin Beaton, naval architect, of 6, The Parade, H.M. Dockyard, Portsmouth; and Rebecca Murrell. Born at 9, Rush Hill Road, Battersea, 22 Nov. 1881. School: Portsmouth Grammar School, under Mr J. C. Nicol, M.A. Admitted 2 Oct. 1899.
> B.A. 1902; M.B., B.C. 1909. Nat. Sci. Tripos, Part I, Class 1, 1902; Part II, Class 2, 1903. Exhibitioner, 1902.

Braithwaite, Philip Pipon: son of the Rev. Philip Richard Pipon Braithwaite, of the Vicarage, Andover; and Jessie Beatrice Mackenzie Douglas. Born at Abbotsham, North Devon, 3 July 1880. School: Felsted. Admitted 2 Oct. 1899. Brother of William, II. 542.
> B.A. 1902. Hist. Tripos, Part I, Class 3, 1901; Part II, Class 2, 1902. Captain of University Association Football. Inspector in the Indian Education Service, Madras (1909).

Bulcraig, Herbert Henry, solicitor: son of Henry Bulcraig, solicitor, of Clapham, S.W.; and Mary Ann Carter. Born at 20, Lydon Road, Clapham, 10 Nov.

1878. School: Clapham High School, under Mr H. R. Hind and Mr E. M. Elligott, M.A. Admitted 2 Oct. 1899.

    B.A., LL.B. 1902. Law Tripos, Part I, Class 2, 1901; Part II, Class 2, 1902. Scholar, 1902. Died in 1905.

Burgess, Robert: son of Henry Burgess, gentleman, of Middleton, Market Harborough; and Kate Elizabeth West. Born at Middleton, 14 Dec. 1881. School: Oakham, under Mr E. V. Hodge. Admitted 2 Oct. 1899.

    B.A. 1902; B.C. 1908; M.B. 1910.

Chamberlain, Percy Garratt: son of Arthur Garratt Chamberlain, chemist, of 45, Church Street, Rugby; and Margaret White. Born at Rugby, 21 Sept. 1880. Schools: Oakfield, Rugby, under Mr T. A. Wise, and Rugby School, under the Rev. Dr James. Admitted 2 Oct. 1899.

    B.A. 1902; M.A. 1906. Nat. Sci. Tripos, Part I, Class 2, 1902. In chemical business at Rugby (1909).

Cooke, Arthur Ingram: son of the Rev. Frederic Cooke, of Westbury Rectory, Shrewsbury; and Ada Florence Bradford. Born at Church Preen, Shropshire, 31 July 1881. School: Shrewsbury, under the Rev. H. W. Moss. Admitted 2 Oct. 1899. Brother of William, IV. (1) 45.

    B.A. 1902; B.C. 1907; M.A., M.B. 1909.

Corry, Harry Barrett: son of William Longman Corry, of Woodside House, Woodside Park, London, N.; and Annie Longman. Born at The Gardens, East Dulwich, Surrey. School: Reading, under the Rev. W. Eppstein. Admitted 2 Oct. 1899.

    B.A. 1902. Captain of the College Cricket Club, 1901. In medical practice (1909).

Cox, Reginald Charles: son of Charles Cox, bookseller, of Courtlands, Archer's Road, Southampton; and Rosa Bartlett. Born at Southampton, 15 July 1880. School: Dean Close Memorial School, Cheltenham, under Rev. W. H. Fletcher, M.A., D.C.L. Admitted 2 Oct. 1899.

    B.A. 1902; M.A. 1906. Mech. Sci. Tripos, Part I, Class 2, 1902. Exhibitioner, 1900; Scholar, 1901. A.M.I.C.E. 1905. Civil Engineer in India to the firm of Marsland, Price & Co., Mazapore, Bombay.

Crean, Theodore: son of Richard Crean, physician and surgeon, of Montagu House, Higher Broughton, Manchester; and Lucy Bolongaro. Born at 26, Bury New Road, Cheetham, Manchester, 23 Oct. 1880. School: Stonyhurst College, under the Rev. Fathers Walmesley, and Browne, S.J. Admitted 2 Oct. 1899.

    Kept three terms. 2nd Lieut. 6th Batt. Lancashire Fusiliers, 1900; West African Regt. 1906.

Crosby, Josiah: son of Josiah Porter Crosby, master mariner, of 16, West Parade, Newcastle-on-Tyne; and Christina Addicoat. Born at Falmouth, Cornwall, 25 May 1880. School: Royal Grammar School, Newcastle-on-Tyne, under Mr S. C. Logan, M.A. Admitted 2 Oct. 1899.

    B.A. 1902. Med. and Mod. Lang. Tripos, Class 1, Special distinction in German, 1902. Entrance Scholarship for Modern Languages, 1899; Scholar, 1899–1902. Student Interpreter, 1904; Acting Vice-Consul at Nakawn Lampang, 1907– .

Davies, John Rhys: son of John Davies, retired merchant, of Hints Manor, Tamworth; and Katherine Pendered. Born at Oakham, 17 Nov. 1879. School·Aldenham, under the Rev. J. Kennedy. Admitted 2 Oct. 1899.
    B.A. 1902. Class. Tripos, Part I, Class 2, Division 2, 1902. Entrance Scholarship, 1899; Scholar, 1899–1902. Master at Lexden House School, Seaford (1909).

Day, Bernard: son of Francis Day, brewer, deceased; and Emma Ellen D'Eyncourt Wood, of 16, Cleveland Gardens, Hyde Park, London, W. Born at 89, Harley Street, London, W., 9 Feb. 1881. Educated at Font Hill, East Grinstead, Sussex, under Mr W. W. Radcliffe, and Haileybury College, under the Hon. and Rev. E. Lyttelton. Admitted 2 Oct. 1899. Brother of Edward, II. 526.
    B.A. 1902; M.B., B.C. 1909. In practice at Kuala Lumpur, Straits Settlements (1910).

Dickinson, Benjamin: son of Benjamin Dickinson, India merchant, deceased; and Adeline Fanny Allen, of Delaford, Iver, Bucks. Born at The Elms, Bourne End, Woburn, Bucks., 30 June 1880. Schools: King Edward's, Birmingham, under the Rev. A. R. Vardy, M.A., and Giggleswick, under the Rev. G. Style. Admitted 2 Oct. 1899.
    Resided one year.

Forsyth, Gerald: son of William Frederic Forsyth, surgeon dentist, of 24, George Street, Hanover Square, London, W.; and Marian Ada Brown. Born at 28, George Street, Hanover Square, London, 20 April 1881. School: Winchester College, under the Rev. Dr Fearon. Admitted 2 Oct. 1899. Brother of Lennard, II. 531.
    B.A. 1903; M.A. 1908. Architect in London (1909).

Gamlen, Robert Long: son of Leonard Blagden Gamlen, J.P., gentleman, of East Emlett, Morchard Bishop, N. Devon; and Selina Emma L. Brailey. Born at East Emlett, 2 March 1881. School: Monckton Combe, near Bath, under the Rev. R. G. Bryan, and Mr W. E. Bryan, M.A. Admitted 2 Oct. 1899.
    B.A. 1903; M.A., M.B., B.C. 1908. Nat. Sci. Tripos, Part I, Class 2, 1903. In the Indian Medical Service.

Gandhi, Nadirshaw Hormazshaw: son of Hormazshaw Dinshaw, head clerk of Customs Department, Jodhpore; and Goolbai Hormazshaw. Born at Surat, 17 May 1878. School: Proprietary High School, Bombay, under Mr H. J. Taleyarkhan. Admitted 2 Oct. 1899.
    B.A. 1902. Nat. Sci. Tripos, Part I, Class 2, 1902. In medical practice.

Garrett, Joseph Hugh: son of Joseph Payne Garrett, solicitor, of 94, Hazelville Road, Hornsey Lane, London, N.; and Eleanor Adelaide Hope. Born at 9, Blythwood Road, Crouch Hill, London, N. School: Highgate, under the Rev. A. E. Allcock, M.A. Admitted 2 Oct. 1899.
    B.A. 1902. Class. Tripos, Part I, Class 1, Division 3, 1902. Entrance Scholarship, 1899; Scholar, 1899–1902. In the Indian Civil Service, 1903– .

Greene, Gerald Edward: son of Edward Mackenzie Greene, solicitor, of 177, Loop Street, Maritzburg, Natal; and Maude Nourse. Born at Maritzburg, 1 July 1881. School: Lancing College. Admitted 2 Oct. 1899.
    B.A. 1903. Called to the Bar, Inner Temple, 26 Jan. 1904; practising at Maritzburg, Natal.

Hallowes, Vernon Buxton: son of William Alexander Tooke Hallowes (of the College, II. 355), solicitor, of Heath Fern Lodge, Heathside, Hampstead, N.W.; and Louise Minns. Born at 161, Gloucester Road, Regent's Park, London, 14 Sept. 1880. School: Heath Mount School, Hampstead, under the Rev. C. F. Walker and Mr J. S. Granville Grenfell, M.A. Admitted 2 Oct. 1899.

     Resided four terms. Theological Student at King's College, London (1909).

Harris, George Woodrouffe: son of Vincent Dormer Harris, M.D., F.R.C.P., of 22, Queen Anne Street, Cavendish Square, London, W.; and Agatha Morgan. Born at 23, Upper Berkeley Street, London, W., 6 Aug. 1880. School: Uppingham, under the Rev. E. C. Selwyn, M.A. Admitted 2 Oct. 1899.

     B.A. 1905. Class. Tripos, Part I, Class 2, 1901. Entrance Exhibitioner, 1899; Exhibition, 1899–1901.

Hill, Richard Athelstane Parker: son of Arthur James Hill, chartered accountant, of St Keverne, Harrow-on-the-Hill; and Fanny Catherine Hingston. Born at 36, Lansdowne Road, London, W., 11 Sept. 1880. School: Harrow, under the Rev. J. E. C. Welldon and the Rev. Dr Wood. Sayer Scholar. Admitted 2 Oct. 1899.

     B.A. 1902; M.B. 1909. Nat. Sci. Tripos, Part I, Class 1, 1902; Part II, Class 2, 1903. Union Medical College, Peking (1910).

Hoffmeister, Cyril John Roby: son of John Bates Hoffmeister, physician, of 3, The Parade, Cowes, Isle of Wight; and Fanny Georgiana Roby. Born at 8, Cambridge Road, Hove, Brighton, 15 Sept. 1881. School: Epsom College, under the Rev. W. Hart Smith. Admitted 2 Oct. 1899.

     B.A. 1902. Chapel clerk, 1901. In medical practice at Ramsgate (1909).

Horner, Norman Gerald: son of Arthur Claypon Horner, M.R.C.S., L.R.C.P., deceased; and Frances Cooper, of 137, High Street, Tonbridge. Born at Tonbridge, Kent, 1 Jan. 1882. School: Tonbridge, under the Rev. Dr Wood and the Rev. C. C. Tancock. Admitted 2 Oct. 1899.

     B.A. 1902. Nat. Sci. Tripos, Part I, Class 3, 1902. In medical practice (1909).

Jones, Thomas Arthur: son of Edward Jones, colliery proprietor, of Snatchwood House, Pontypool; and Susan Williams. Born at Snatchwood House, Pontypool, 5 Feb. 1881. School: Clifton College, under the Rev. G. M. Glazebrook. Admitted 2 Oct. 1899. Brother of Edward, IV. (1) 41.

     B.A. 1902. Nat. Sci. Tripos, Part I, Class 3, 1902.

Leite, Hubert Marie Joseph François-de-Paul Pinto: son of Joaquim Pinto Leite, merchant, of Antwerp House, Victoria Park, Manchester; and Sophie Pinto Havenith Pauwels. Born at Antwerp House, Wilbraham Road, Fallowfield, Manchester, 22 Sept. 1879. Educated at Beaumont College, Old Windsor, under the Rev. G. Tarleton, S.J., and Stonyhurst College, under the Rev. Pedro C. Gordon, S.J. Admitted 2 Oct. 1899.

     B.A. 1902. Nat. Sci. Tripos, Part I, Class 3, 1902.

L'Estrange, Julian: son of William L'Estrange, deceased; and Marian de Soyres, of 22, Horbury Crescent, London, W. Born at Weston-super-Mare, 6 Aug.

1880. School: King's School, Canterbury, under the Rev. A. J. Galpin. Admitted 2 Oct. 1899.

Resided one term. In the dramatic profession.

Lewis, Ernest Isaac: son of Charles Lewis, oil merchant, of 22, Fort Crescent, Margate; and Frances Elizabeth Impett. Born at Margate, 29 Dec. 1875. School: Apsley House School, Margate, under Mr J. Stokes, J.P. Admitted 2 Oct. 1899.

     B.A. 1902. Nat. Sci. Tripos, Part I, Class 1, 1902. Scholar, 1901–1903. Assistant Master at Felsted School; Assistant Master at Oundle School (1909). Author, *Inorganic Chemistry*.

Lloyd, Harold Rhys: son of John Lloyd, cashier and secretary, of Claremont, Cheadle Hulme; and Mary Esther Southworth. Born at Cheadle Hulme, Cheshire, 29 Oct. 1879. School: King William's College, Isle of Man, under the Rev. F. P. Walters. Admitted 2 Oct. 1899. Brother of Idwal, II. 553, and of Alan, IV. (1) 23.

     B.A. 1902. Math. Tripos, Part I (bracketed 18th Wrangler), 1902; Mech. Sci. Tripos, Class 1, 1903. Entrance Scholarship, 1899; Scholar, 1899–1903. Engineer, with Hans Renold, Ltd., Manchester (1909).

Lumb, Thomas Fletcher: son of William Wilkin Lumb, solicitor, deceased; and Jane Macpherson, of Mockerkin, Bays Hill, Cheltenham. Born at White-haven, 26 Nov. 1880. School: Cheltenham College, under the Rev. R. S. de C. Laffan. Admitted 2 Oct. 1899.

     Resided three years. Medical Officer in Uganda, 1909– .

Master, Dudley Cyril: son of Henry Hugh Master, surgeon and physician, of Melbourne, Australia; and Alice Ella Coats. Born at Ixworth, Suffolk, 8 May 1882. Schools: Hurstleigh, Tunbridge Wells, under Mr R. Buston, and Haileybury College, under the Hon. and Rev. E. Lyttelton. Admitted 2 Oct. 1899.

     B.A. 1902. Medical Officer B.S.A. Company, Fort Jameson, N.E. Rhodesia (1909).

Mowatt, Osmond: son of James Mowatt (of the College, II. 365), barrister, of Kingswood Firs, Shottermill, Haslemere; and Fanny Louisa Akroyd. Born at 5, Notting Hill Square, Kensington, 24 May 1880. Educated at home. Admitted 2 Oct. 1899.

     B.A. 1904; M.A. 1907. Left in Feb. 1901 to serve in the South African War, as Lieut. in the 17th Batt. Imperial Yeomanry. Wounded at Plessisdam, July 1901, and Tweefontein, Christmas 1901. Member of Lloyd's.

Nicholls, Stanley Harold: son of Thomas Arthur Nicholls, underwriter, of Laurieston, Woodside Park, London, N.; and Florence Rosa Thompson. Born at 8, Woodberry Grove, London, N., 19 Sept. 1880. School: Oundle, under Mr F. W. Sanderson. Admitted 2 Oct. 1899.

     B.A. 1902. Math. Tripos, Part I, *jun. opt.* 1902. Entrance Scholarship, 1899; Scholar, 1899–1901. Chartered Accountant.

Noyes, Harry Francis Golding: son of the Rev. Henry Edward Noyes, D.D., Chaplain to H.B.M. Embassy, Paris, of 103, Rue de la Boétie, Paris; and of Catherine Barton. Born at Kingstown, Ireland, 13 Oct. 1879. School: South

Eastern College, Ramsgate, under Mr F. W. Tracy, M.A. Admitted 2 Oct. 1899.
> B.A. 1902; M.B., B.C. 1907. Nat. Sci. Tripos, Part I, Class 3, 1902.

Owen, Albert Harold: son of Hugh Owen, late manager National Provincial Bank of England, Bala, of Bryn Hyfryd, Conway; and Mary Elizabeth Brindley. Born at Lampeter, 14 March 1880. School: Llandovery College, under the Rev. W. W. P. Hughes. Admitted 2 Oct. 1899. Brother of Hugh, II. 553.
> B.A. 1902. Nat. Sci. Tripos, Part II, Class 3, 1902.

Parker, Owen Fortrie: son of Orfleur Parker, late Lieut. 60th Rifles; and Delia Jane Minet. Born in New Zealand, 24 Aug. 1879. School: Newton College, S. Devon. Admitted 2 Oct. 1899.
> B.A. 1902; M.A. 1906. In Upper Egypt with the Dareheib and African Syndicate, Ltd., 1905–

Paul, Arthur Edward: son of Robert Macleane Paul, solicitor, of Southleigh Truro; and Blanche Amy Price. Born at Southleigh, 2 June 1880. School: Rugby, under the Rev. Dr James. Admitted 2 Oct. 1899.
> B.A. 1903. Assistant Engineer on the permanent staff of the South Indian Railway (1909).

Pocock, Henry Willmer: son of the Rev. Thomas Willmer Pocock, Minister of Religion (retired), of Fort Beaufort, Cape Colony; and Fanny Matilda Kidwell. Born at Burghersdorp, Cape Colony, 5 Sept. 1880. School: Kingswood College, Grahamstown, S. Africa, under Mr E. G. Gane, M.A. Admitted 2 Oct. 1899.
> B.A. 1904.

Pring, John Grattan: son of Arthur Henry Pring, deceased; and Lucy Jane Barnsly Reid. Born at Belfast, 7 March 1881. Schools: Highgate, under the Rev. A. E. Allcock, and Clifton House School, Eastbourne, under Mr J. Winder. Admitted 2 Oct. 1899.
> B.A. 1903.

Ransome, John Theodore: son of Arthur Ransome, M.D., F.R.C.P., F.R.S. (Hon. fell. of the College, II. 312), of Sunnyhurst, Dean Park, Bournemouth; and Lucy Elizabeth Fullarton. Born at Bowdon, Cheshire, 7 Nov. 1878. Schools: Hinckley Grammar School, under the Rev. A. L. Wotherston, and Repton School, under the Rev. W. M. Furneaux. Admitted 2 Oct. 1899. Brother of Herbert, II. 454, and Arthur, II. 492.
> Resided one year.

Rosser, Holbein John: son of John Holbein Rosser, colliery proprietor, of Dysgwylfa, Sketty, Glamorganshire; and Catherine Elizabeth Price. Born at 14, Somerset Place, Swansea, 4 March 1882. ·Educated at St Andrew's College, Swansea, under Mr G. G. Sutherland, M.A.: Christ's College, Blackheath, under the Rev. F. W. Aveling, M.A.: Technical School, Swansea, under G. S. Turpin, M.A., D.Sc. Admitted 2 Oct. 1899. ·
> Resided two terms. Died by accidental poisoning at Sketty, 1901.

Shettle, Philip Shakespeare: son of Thomas William Shettle, of Chandos Lodge, Eye, Suffolk; and Anne Frances Goasdill. Born at Bradford, near Wimborne,

Dorset, 23 Feb. 1880. School: Oundle, under Mr F. W. Sanderson. Admitted 2 Oct. 1899.
  B.A. 1902. Class. Tripos, Part I, Class 1, Division 2, 1902. Entrance Scholarship, 1899; Scholar, 1899–1902. I.C.S. 1903; Assistant Magistrate and Collector, Bengal.

Simpson, John Basil: son of John Millington Simpson, solicitor, of 65, Spilsby Road, Boston; and Emilie Mary Jackson. Born at Skirbeck, Lincolnshire, 6 Sept. 1880. School: Boston Grammar School, under Mr W. White. Admitted 2 Oct. 1899. Grandson of John S. Jackson, Fellow, II. 280.
  B.A. 1902; M.A. 1906. Math. Tripos, Part I, *jun. opt.* 1902. Ordained deacon (London), 1903; priest, 1904. Curate of All Saints, Poplar, 1903–   Missionary in Japan, 1910–

Sisterson, George Edward: son of Edward Sisterson, iron merchant, of Woodley Field, Hexham; and Mary Jane Murton. Born at West End Terrace, Corbridge, 31 Aug. 1880. Schools: Rydal Mount, under Mr T. G. Gordon; Uppingham, under the Rev. E. C. Selwyn; and the Leys School, Cambridge, under the Rev. W. T. A. Barber. Admitted 2 Oct. 1899.
  B.A. 1903; M.A. 1906. Address (1909), The Towers, Alnmouth, Northumberland. In business as an iron and steel merchant, Newcastle-on-Tyne.

Smith, Arthur Lionel Hall: son of Solomon Charles Smith, physician, of Four Oaks, Walton-on-Thames; and Mary White. Born at Halifax, Yorkshire, 16 Feb. 1874. Educated at Oakham, under the Rev. E. V. Hodge, and Halifax Grammar School, under Mr A. W. Reith. House Physician at Addenbrooke's Hospital, 1899. Admitted 2 Oct. 1899.
  M.B., B.C. 1908. Served as Civil Surgeon in the South African War, 1900. In practice in London (1909).

Smith, Laurence Willoughby: son of William Oliver Smith, electrical engineer, of 5, South Row, Blackheath, S.E.; and Evelyn Easum. Born at Norwood, 6 Aug. 1880. School: Blackheath School, under Mr H. R. Woolrych, M.A. Admitted 2 Oct. 1899.
  B.A. 1903. Electrical Engineer, with Elliott Brothers, Lewisham (1909).

Smith, Percival Frere: son of Charles Thomas Smith (of the College, II. 264), late Senior Puisne Judge of the Supreme Court of the Cape of Good Hope, of the Oaks, Rosebank, near Cape Town; and Julia Emily Greathead. Born at Grahamstown, S. Africa, 8 Sept. 1877. School: Diocesan College, Rondebosch, near Cape Town, under the Rev. Canon Brooke, B.A. Admitted 2 Oct. 1899.
  B.A., LL.B. 1902. Law Tripos, Part I, Class 2, 1901; Part II, Class 2, 1902. Called to the Bar, Inner Temple, 17 Nov. 1902; in practice at Johannesburg, Transvaal (1909); author (joint), 1909, *A Digest of South African Case Law.*

Somers-Clarke, Geoffrey: son of George Somers Leigh Clarke, architect, deceased; and Louisa Harker Williamson. Born at Chislehurst, 6 Oct. 1878. Schools: Marlborough, under the Rev. G. C. Bell; Agricultural College, Cirencester. Admitted 2 Oct. 1899.
  B.A. 1902. Assistant Engineer on the Bengal Nagpur Railway (1909). English address, North Lew, Ashtead, Surrey.

Stallard, Philip Lechmere: son of Jonah Valentine Stallard, merchant, of South-wick Lodge, Lower Wick, Worcester; and Katharine J. Sutton. Born at Worcester, 20 May 1880. Educated at May Place, Malvern Wells, under Mr Tillard, and Sedbergh School, under Mr H. G. Hart. Admitted 2 Oct. 1899.
B.A. 1902; M.A. 1909. Nat. Sci. Tripos, Part I, Class 2, 1902; Part II, Class 1, 1903. Diploma in Sanitary Science, 1909.

Strickland, Cyril: son of Frank Strickland, dental surgeon, L.D.S., R.C.S. Eng., late of S. Africa; and Alice Esse. Born at Port Elizabeth, S. Africa, 29 Sept. 1881. Educated at St Andrew's College, Grahamstown, S. Africa, under the Rev. Canon Espin, M.A., and Oundle School, under Mr F. W. Sanderson. Admitted 2 Oct. 1899.
B.A. 1902; M.A. 1911. Nat. Sci. Tripos, Part I, Class 1, 1902. Exhibitioner, 1901. Assistant to the Quick Professor of Biology (1910).

Stuart, Athol Alexander Paul Rees: son of Montague Pelham Stuart, of Steynton, Surbiton; and Mary Rees. Born at Kingston-on-Thames, 25 May 1881. School: Cheltenham College, under the Rev. R. S. de C. Laffan. Admitted 2 Oct. 1899.
Resided two terms. Lieut. 6th Batt. Manchester Regt. 1900; served in the South African War.

Suhr, Alfred Christopher Hermann: son of Johann Georg Suhr, merchant, of 82, Palace Road, Tulse Hill, London, S.W.; and Johanna Charlotte Wilhelmine Wehncke. Born at 41, Wiltshire Road, Brixton, London, 27 Aug. 1881. School: Dulwich College, under Mr A. H. Gilkes. Admitted 2 Oct. 1899.
B.A. 1902; M.B., B.C. 1907. In the Army Medical Service.

Symonds, John Ashby: son of John Fish Symonds, solicitor, of 20, Hertford Street, Chesterton, Cambridge; and Gertrude Catharine Whitehead. Born at Cam-bridge, 1 June 1882. Educated at the Perse School, Cambridge, under Mr H. C. Barnes-Lawrence, and Ripon Grammar School. Admitted 2 Oct. 1899. Brother of Frederic, IV. (1) 76.
B.A. 1903; M.A. 1906. Solicitor in Cambridge (1910).

Talbot, Stafford Cecil: son of Gerald Francis Talbot, colonel, of the Carlton Club, London, and 42, St George's Square, S.W.; and Henrietta Clarissa Bradhurst, of New York. Born in London, 3 May 1880. School: Cheltenham College, under the Rev. R. S. de C. Laffan. Admitted 2 Oct. 1899. Brother of Gerald, IV. (1) 26.
Resided seven terms. Entrance Exhibition, 1899; Russian Scholarship, 1901. For some time editor of an illustrated paper in Moscow.

Thompson, Tom: son of Thomas Thompson, merchant, of 38, Carson Road, Dulwich; and Elizabeth Bell. Born at 93, St James's Street, Burnley, 29 June 1880. School: City of London, under Mr A. T. Pollard. Admitted 2 Oct. 1899.
B.A. 1902; M.A. 1906. Class. Tripos, Part I, Class 1, Division 1, 1902. Entrance Scholarship, 1899; Scholar, 1899–1902. In his father's business in London, 1902– . Resident (1909) at St Anselm's, Cambridge.

Thompson, Thomas William: son of the Rev. John Thompson, Wesleyan minister, of Cottenham, Cambridgeshire; and Emma Jane Hipkins. Born at Chaxhill, Westbury-on-Severn, 28 Jan. 1880. Educated at Thetford Grammar School, under the Rev. B. Reed, B.A., and The Leys, Cambridge, under the Rev. W. T. A. Barber. Admitted 2 Oct. 1899.
B.A. 1902; M.A. 1906. In the Wesleyan Ministry, 1907– .

Thornton, Francis John: son of John Thornton, woollen manufacturer, of Castle
Hill House, Rastrick, Brighouse, Yorkshire; and Elizabeth Seppington.
Born at Rastrick, 28 June 1880.   School: Giggleswick, under the Rev.
G. Style.   Admitted 2 Oct. 1899.
    B.A. 1902; M.A., M.B., B.C. 1906.   Nat. Sci. Tripos, Part I, Class 2, 1901.
    Scholar, 1900–1902.   In medical practice.

Vernon, Rupert John: son of Arthur Vernon, architect, of Borshams, High
Wycombe; and Elizabeth Rutty.   Born at Borshams, 3 Dec. 1880.   School:
Uppingham, under the Rev. E. C. Selwyn.   Admitted 2 Oct. 1899.
    B.A. 1903.   In medical practice.

Watermeyer, Ernest Frederick : son of Christian Johannes Watermeyer, farmer, of
Euboniesplaats, Graaf Reinet, Cape Colony; and Caroline Agnes Maria de
Graeff von Polsbroek.   Born in Graaf Reinet, Cape Colony, 12 Oct. 1880.
School: Bath College, under Mr T. W. Dunn and the Rev. W. Y. Faussett.
Admitted 2 Oct. 1899.   Brother of Herbert, IV. (1) 77.
    B.A. 1902; LL.B. 1903.   Math. Tripos, Part I, *jun. opt.* 1902; Law
    Tripos, Part II, Class 3, 1903.   Entrance Scholarship, 1899; Scholar,
    1899–1901.   Captain of the Boat Club; Captain of C Company,
    C.U.R.V.   Called to the Bar, Inner Temple, 27 April 1904; in practice
    at Cape Town.

Webb, Gilbert Lowell: son of Albert Webb, hair cloth manufacturer, of The Fort
Royal, Worcester; and Mary Elizabeth Horne.   Born at Worcester, 17 May
1881.   Educated at Worcester Cathedral King's School; and King Henry
VIII School, Coventry, under the Rev. C. R. Gilbert, M.A.   Admitted
2 Oct. 1899.
    B.A. 1902; B.C. 1906; M.B. 1907.   Nat. Sci. Tripos, Part I, Class 3.

Williams, Milbourne Bransby: son of Morgan Bransby Williams, J.P., M.I.C.E.
of Killay House, Killay, Glamorgan; and Margaret Brock.   Born at
Brynsyfi, Mount Pleasant, Swansea, 29 June 1880.   School: Malvern College,
under the Rev. S. R. James.   Admitted 2 Oct. 1899.   Brother of Morgan,
II. 438 and Caryl, IV. (1) 45.
    B.A. 1903.   Studying at Freiburg for Mining, 1905.   Mining Engineer
    in Wales (1909).

Wyman, Henry Norman: son of Henry Wyman, brewer, deceased; and Marion
Steer, of 17, Beaconsfield Road, Clifton, Bristol.   Born at Hemel Hempstead,
15 Oct. 1881.   School: Clifton College, under the Rev. M. G. Glazebrook.
Admitted 2 Oct. 1899.   Brother of Bernard, IV. (1) 37.
    B.A. 1902.   Nat. Sci. Tripos, Part I, Class 3, 1902.   Died 15 Aug. 1909
    in the Argentine.

Curtis, Lewis: son of Henry Curtis, mason, of Church Road, Westbury-on-Trym,
Bristol; and Eliza Partridge.   Born at Westbury-on-Trym, 5 March 1878.
Educated at the Bristol Pupil Teacher Centre.   Admitted 2 Oct. 1899;
previously kept six terms as a Non-Collegiate student.
    B.A. 1900; M.A. 1904.   Moral Sci. Tripos, Part I, Class 2.   Cusack
    Institute, Moorfields, London, E.C.

MICHAELMAS 1900 TO MICHAELMAS 1901.

(Tutors: Mr Roberts, Mr Gallop, Mr Knight, and Mr Hardy.)

Lester, Charles Valentine: son of the Rev. Edward Augustus Lester, M.A., Vicar of Bishop's Nympton, near South Molton, Devon; and Mary Frideswide Standish. Born at Kingsbridge, 2 April 1877. Educated at Kelly College, Tavistock, under the Rev. W. H. David. Admitted 1 Oct. 1900; previously kept three terms as a Non-Collegiate student. Brother of Augustine, II. 532.

> B.A. 1902. Chapel Clerk, 1901. Ordained deacon (Gloucester), 1904; priest, 1905. Resident in Canada (1910).

Hayward, Frank Herbert: son of John Hayward, of 56, Seymour Road, Bristol; and Anne Lydiard. Born at Wootton under Edge, Gloucestershire, 16 Dec. 1872. Admitted as an Advanced Student, 1 Oct. 1900; previously kept three terms as a Non-Collegiate student.

> B.A. 1901 on a certificate of research in Moral Sciences. Moral Science Prize, 1901. Lecturer at the Cambridge Training College, 1899. Inspector of Schools under the London County Council (1909).

Ashcroft, William: son of Charles Wesley Ashcroft, flour miller, of 16, Waterford Road, Oxton, Birkenhead; and Alice Muson Hutchinson. Born at 15, Derby Lane, Stoneycroft, Liverpool, 27 July 1881. Educated at Liverpool College Upper School, under the Rev. F. Dyson, and Birkenhead School, under Mr F. Griffin, M.A. Admitted 1 Oct. 1900. Brother of Harold, IV. (1) 46, and Alec, IV. (1) 67.

> B.A. 1903; M.A. 1907. Law Tripos, Part I, Class 3, 1902; Part II, 1903. Law Entrance Exhibition, 1900. Solicitor in Liverpool, 1909– .

Atkinson, Edward William: son of Joseph Atkinson, surgeon, of Romaldkirk, Darlington; and Elizabeth Georgiana Berridge. Born at Egglesthorpe Terrace, Eggleston, Durham, 30 Sept. 1881. Educated at Startforth, Barnard Castle, under the Rev. Hartley Jennings, Epsom College, and Denston College, under the Rev. D. Edwardes. Admitted 1 Oct. 1900.

> B.A. 1903.

Bailey, George Frederick Selborne: son of George Frederick Bailey, surgical instrument maker, of Towalla, Langley Road, Watford; and Alice Broad. Born at 125, Coningham Road, Shepherd's Bush, London. Educated at St Paul's Preparatory School, under Mr Brewsher, and St Paul's School, under Mr F. W. Walker. Admitted 1 Oct. 1900.

> B.A. 1903; B.C., M.B. 1907; M.D. 1910. Nat. Sci. Tripos, Part I, Class 2, 1903. Entrance Scholarship, 1900; Scholar, 1901–3.

Beesley, Lawrence: son of Henry Beesley, bank manager, of Bank House, Wirksworth; and Annie Maria James. Born at Steeple Grange, Wirksworth, Derbyshire, 31 Dec. 1877. Educated at Wirksworth Grammar School, under Mr Alfred Berridge, M.A., and Derby School, under Mr J. R. Sterndale Bennett, M.A. Admitted 1 Oct. 1900.

> B.A. 1903. Nat. Sci. Tripos, Part I, Class 1, 1903. Assistant Master at Dulwich College (1909).

Bickford-Smith, John Clifford: son of William Bickford-Smith (deceased), land-owner, of Trevarno, Helston, Cornwall; and Anna Matilda Bond. Born at Trevarno, 24 Dec. 1881. School: The Leys, Cambridge, under the Rev. W. T. A. Barber. Admitted 1 Oct. 1900. Brother of William (below).

> B.A. 1905. Manufacturer.

Bickford-Smith, William Noel : brother of above. Born 24 Dec. 1881. Educated at the same school as his brother. Admitted 1 Oct. 1900. Brother of John (above).
> Resided nine terms.

Binning, Stevenson : son of James Stevenson Binning, flour miller, of 101, Shooters Hill Road, Blackheath ; and Emily Anne Hone. Born at 49, Upper Tollington Park, Hornsey, London, 19 Sept. 1881. School : City of London, under Mr A. T. Pollard. Admitted 1 Oct. 1900.
> B.A. 1903. Nat. Sci. Tripos, Part I, Class 3, 1903. Studied in Germany after graduating. Chemist to the Ilford Gas Company (1909).

Black, James Gavin: son of James Gordon Mitchell Black, ironfounder (deceased); and Margaret Thompson. Born at Down Hill, West Boldon, Durham, 20 Jan. 1882. Educated at Corchester School, under the Rev. J. A. Scott, and Cheltenham College, under the Rev. R. S. de C. Laffan and the Rev. R. Waterfield. Admitted 1 Oct. 1900.
> B.A. 1908. Class. Tripos, Part I, Class 2, 1902. Entrance Scholarship, 1900. Kept three terms. Admitted as Non-Collegiate student in fourth term. Master at a School for some years. Readmitted 1907 for study in Geology. In scholastic work (1909).

Blew, Charles Leslie : son of Alfred Jesse Blew (deceased) ; and Clara Elizabeth Wood, of Trefnant, Denbighshire. Born at Hafod Lodge, Trefnant, 27 Sept. 1881. School : Uppingham, under the Rev. Dr Selwyn. Admitted 1 Oct. 1900.
> B.A. 1904. Bombay and Burmah Trading Company ; returned invalided 1905.

Bousfield, William Eric : son of William Robert Bousfield (of the College, II. 406), Q.C., M.P., of St Swithin's, Hendon ; and Florence Maria Elizabeth Kelly. Born at Cricklewood, London, N.W., 21 Nov. 1881. Educated at St Andrew's, Southborough, under the Rev. R. A. Bull, and Rugby School, under the Rev. Dr James. Admitted 1 Oct. 1900. Brother of Robert, IV. (1) 56.
> B.A. 1903. Math. Tripos (br. 12th Wrangler), 1903 ; Mech. Sci. Tripos, Part I, Class 1, 1904. Entrance Scholarship, 1900 ; Scholar, 1901–4. Called to the Bar, Inner Temple, 17 Nov. 1905 ; practising in London.

Brown, Anthony William Scudamore : son of William Charles Brown, of Penchirche, Oaklands Road, Bromley ; and Catherine Cecilia Ellen Scudamore (deceased). Born at Bromley, Kent, 24 Nov. 1880. School : Uppingham, under the Rev. Dr Selwyn. Admitted 1 Oct. 1900. Brother of Harold, IV. (1) 68.
> B.A. 1903 ; M.A. 1907. Class. Tripos, Part I, Class 1, Division 2, 1903. Entrance Scholarship, 1900 ; Scholar, 1901–3. Assistant Master at Trinity College, Glenalmond to 1908 ; at Uppingham School, 1908–10. Head Master of Michaelhouse School, Pietermaritzburg, Natal, 1910–

Clayton, Edward Bellis : son of Charles Houghton Clayton, solicitor, of Hillside, Ditton, Surrey ; and Lydia Mary Hare. Born at " Rydal," Surbiton Hill Park, Surbiton, 2 Nov. 1882. Educated at Hurst College, near Hastings, under Mr Lloyd Griffiths ; and Cheltenham College, under the Rev. R. S. de C. Laffan, and the Rev. R. Waterfield. Admitted 1 Oct. 1900.
> B.A. 1903 ; M.B., B.C. 1910. Nat. Sci. Tripos, Part I, Class 3, 1903.

Cockin, Maurice Stanley: son of John Cockin, estate agent (deceased), of " Whinny-royd," The Park, Hull; and Ann Maria Roberts. Born at Hull, 23 Dec. 1881. School: Hymers College, Hull, under Mr C. H. Gore. Admitted 1 Oct. 1900. Brother of Reginald, II. 557.
> B.A. 1904; M.A. 1907. Assistant District Commissioner in Southern Nigeria (1910).

Coward, Charles Ernest: son of Henry Coward, Mus.Doc. Oxon., Professor of Music, of 286, Western Bank, Sheffield; and Mary Elizabeth Best. Born at Nether Hallam, 23 Dec. 1880. School, Wesley College, Sheffield, under the Rev. V. W. Pearson, B.A. Admitted 1 Oct. 1900.
> B.A. 1903. Math. Tripos (br. 18th Wrangler), 1903. Entrance Scholar-ship, 1900; Scholar, 1901–3. In Somerset House (1909), Home Civil Service.

Cox, Douglas Howard : son of Robert Cox (deceased), formerly M.P., manufacturer; and Harriett Bennett. Born at Nice, France, 6 Feb. 1882. Educated at Cargilfield, Edinburgh, under the Rev. C. Darnell, Rugby School, under the Rev. Dr James, and Heidelberg College, Germany. Admitted 1 Oct. 1900.
> B.A. 1903. Nat. Sci.Tripos, Part I, Class 3, 1903. Farming in Ireland (1909).

Dick, John Bernard Goodrich : son of Charles Baker Goodrich Dick, Lieutenant-Colonel Royal Marines, of 80, Durnford Street, Plymouth; and Katherine Anna Kingsford. Born at the Royal Marine Barracks, Plymouth, 10 Oct. 1881. Schools: Exeter, under Mr W. A. Cunningham, and Mannamead College, Plymouth, under Mr F. H. Colson, M.A. Admitted 1 Oct. 1900.
> B.A. 1903. Med. and Mod. Lang. Tripos, Class 3, 1903. Assistant Master at Bradfield College, 1908–   .

Drummond, James Francis Montagu : son of James Ramsay Drummond, of H.M. Indian Civil Service, Deputy Commissioner of Gondarpur, Punjab; and Elizabeth Helen Montagu Campbell. Born at Lahore, India, 30 April 1881. Educated in Westphalia, and at King's College, London. Admitted 1 Oct. 1900.
> B.A. 1904. Nat. Sci. Tripos, Part I, Class 2, 1902; Part II, Class 1, 1904. Entrance Exhibition, 1900. Lecturer in Botany at Armstrong College, Newcastle-on-Tyne (1909).

Dryland, Gilbert Winter : son of John Winter Dryland, surgeon, of High Street, Kettering; and Susanna Adella Stephenson. Born at 47, High Street, Kettering, 29 Dec. 1881. School: Uppingham, under the Rev. Dr Selwyn. Admitted 1 Oct. 1900.
> B.A. 1903. Nat. Sci. Tripos, Part I, Class 3, 1903. University Hockey team, 1904. In medical practice.

Edge, Charles Noel: son of Hall Travers Edge, solicitor, of Clenthynt, Meadow Road, Edgbaston; and Jane Barrows. Born at St Augustine's Road, Edgbaston, Birmingham, 31 Dec. 1881. School: Clifton College, under the Rev. M. G. Glazebrook. Admitted 1 Oct. 1900.
> B.A. 1903. Mech. Sci. Tripos, Class 1, 1903. Entrance Scholarship, 1900. Engineer (at Shanghai, 1909).

Ellison, Harold Blades : son of Thomas Ellison, cotton broker, of Hoscote, West Kirby, Cheshire; and Anne Mary Blades. Born at Moor Lane, Great Crosby, near Liverpool, 14 Oct. 1880. School: Shrewsbury, under the Rev. H. W. Moss. Admitted 1 Oct. 1900.
> B.A. 1903; M.A. 1910.

Emrys-Jones, Mansel Franklin : son of Abraham Emrys-Jones, M.D., of Brynderu,
Fallowfield, Manchester; and Mary Kate Franklin Mew.   Born at 10, St John
Street, Manchester, 5 Dec. 1882.   Educated at Rugby, under the Rev. Dr
James.   Admitted 1 Oct. 1900.
   B.A. 1903.   Nat. Sci. Tripos, Part I, Class 3, 1903.   In medical practice.

Fancourt, William : son of Thomas Fancourt, Archdeacon of Wellington, New
Zealand ; and Elizabeth Emma Robinson.   Born at Lower Hutt, Wellington,
8 March 1879.   Educated at Woodcote House School, under Mr C. L.
Gardiner, and Wanganui Collegiate School, New Zealand, under Mr W.
Empson.   Admitted 1 Oct. 1900.
   B.A. 1903; M.A. 1907.   Hist. Tripos, Part I, Class 3, 1902; Part II,
   Class 2, 1903.   Ordained deacon (Liverpool), 1904; priest, 1905.   Curate at
   Liverpool, 1904-1906 ; at St Thomas's, Wellington South, New Zealand,
   1907-

Findlay, Henry Alexander : son of Archibald Findlay, merchant (deceased); and
Mary Hooper, of Arbroath, Musgrave Road, Durban, Natal.   Born at Durban,
6 April 1881.   Educated at High School, Durban, under Mr W. H. Nicholas,
and at Michaelhouse, Pietermaritzburg, under the Rev. Canon Todd.   Admitted
1 Oct. 1900.   Brother of Archibald, II. 555.
   B.A. 1903.   In legal practice at Durban (1909).

Fry, Lucius George Pownall : son of the Rev. Lucius George Fry, M.A., of St James's
Vicarage, Upper Edmonton ; and Jane Amelia Pownall.   Born at Snell's
Park, Edmonton, 15 May 1881.   Educated at Glengorse, Eastbourne, under
Mr J. Watson Willis, and St John's, Leatherhead, under the Rev. A. F. Rutty.
Admitted 1 Oct. 1900.
   B.A. 1903.   Math. Tripos, 1903, *jun. opt.*   Choral Exhibition, 1900.
   Master at Orley Farm School, Harrow, to 1908.   Ordained deacon
   (Jerusalem), 1908.   Assistant Chaplain at St Mark's, Alexandria, 1908.

Gow, Alexander : son of John Gow, engineer, of 51, Shrewsbury Road, Harlesden,
London ; and Mary Kelly.   Born at Wolverton, Bucks, 15 May 1869.
Educated at the Presbyterian School, Crewe, under Mr W. Dishart, and
Borough Road Training College, London, under Principal Barnett.   Admitted
1 Oct. 1900.
   B.A. 1903; M.A. 1907.   Nat. Sci. Tripos, Part I, Class 1, 1902; Part II,
   Class 1, 1903.   Scholar, 1901-3.   Director of the Imperial Institute of
   Technology, South Kensington, 1908-   .

Hardy, Francis Kyle : son of Frederick Hardy, Major-General (retired), of
Fairleigh, Shawford, Hants; and Kate Cotter Kyle.   Born at Fairleigh
Pontefract, Yorkshire, 24 Aug. 1881.   School : Shrewsbury, under the Rev.
H. W. Moss.   Admitted 1 Oct. 1900.
   Resided six terms.   Lieutenant 2nd Batt. York and Lancaster Regt.
   (1909).

Hathorn, Alexander Anthony Roy : son of Kenneth Howard Hathorn, solicitor,
of Pietermaritzburg ; and Agnes Elizabeth Blaikie.   Born at Pietermaritzburg,
Natal, 1 Jan. 1882.   School : Lancing College, under the Rev. Dr Wilson.
Admitted 1 Oct. 1900.

B.A. 1903. Law Tripos, Part I, Class 3, 1902; Part II, 1903. Lieutenant
C Company, C.U.R.V. Called to the Bar, Inner Temple, 26 Jan. 1904.
In practice at Pietermaritzburg (1909).

Hollis, Percy Ainslie: son of George Hollis, of 47, Dartmouth Park Hill, N.W. ;
and Susannah Smith. Born at 47, Dartmouth Park Hill, London, N.W.,
22 May 1881. School: Highgate, under the Rev. A. E. Allcock. Admitted
1 Oct. 1900.
Entrance Scholarship, 1900. Died in College 25 Oct. 1900.

Hope, Stephen Jervis: son of George Palmer Hope (of the College, ii. 367),
stockbroker, of Havering Grange, near Romford; and Aline Jervis White
Jervis. Born at Chase Cross, Romford, Essex, 10 Aug. 1881. School: Eton,
under the Rev. Dr Warre. Admitted 1 Oct. 1900. Brother of George,
iv. (1) 22.
Resided three terms. Farming.

Jobson, Richard Fitton: son of the Rev. Edward Jobson, Vicar of Brierfield,
Burnley; and Sarah Jane Fitton. Born at Heyside, near Oldham, 25 March
1881. School: Rossall, under the Rev. J. P. Way. Admitted 1 Oct. 1900.
B.A. 1903. Class. Tripos, Part I, Class 2, Division 1. Entrance Exhibi-
tion, 1900. Ordained deacon (Sarum), 1904; priest, 1905. Curate of
Buckland Newton, 1904-7; in charge of Kinnerton, Chester, 1907-

Kingsford, Guy Thornhill: son of the Rev. Frederick Williams Kingsford (deceased);
and Emma Elizabeth Sadler. Born at 67, Clapton Common, London, N.E.,
4 June 1881. School: Merchant Taylors', under the Rev. Dr Baker. Admitted
1 Oct. 1900.
B.A. 1903; LL.B. 1904. Law Tripos, Part I, Class 3, 1902; Part II,
1903. Solicitor in London, 1906-   .

Medley, Robert Percival: son of Gerald Morse Medley, of Christchurch Road,
Birkenhead; and Sarah Rosanna Birkett. Born at 9, Beresford Road,
Birkenhead, 22 April 1881. Schools: Birkenhead, under the Rev. Arthur
Sloman; and Rossall, under the Rev. J. P. Way. Admitted 1 Oct. 1900.
B.A. 1903; M.A. 1907. Class. Tripos, Part I, Class 2, Division 2, 1903.
Entrance Exhibition, 1900. Assistant Master at Felsted School
(1909).

Newbold, Charles Joseph: son of William Newbold (deceased); and Eleanor Isabel
Fergusson. Born at 7, Broadwater Down, Tunbridge Wells, 12 Jan. 1881.
Schools: Rose Hill School, Tunbridge Wells, under the Rev. A. R. Cronk;
and Uppingham, under the Rev. E. C. Selwyn. Admitted 1 Oct. 1900.
B.A. 1903. Nat. Sci. Tripos, Part I, Class 2, 1903. University (Rugby)
Football player, 1903. Brewer, in Guinness's, Dublin (1909).

Norton, Gilbert Paul: son of George Pepler Norton, chartered accountant, of
Birkby Lodge, Huddersfield. Born at 37, Trinity Street, Huddersfield,
17 Aug. 1882. School: Shrewsbury, under the Rev. H. W. Moss.
Admitted 1 Oct. 1900.
B.A. 1903; M.A. 1907. Captain of the Boat Club, 1902-3. Chartered
Accountant.

Prince, Louis Perrott: son of James Perrott Prince, Doctor of Medicine, of Durban, Natal; and Malvina Louise Mansergh O'Leary. Born in London, 21 Feb. 1883. Educated at Hilton College, High School, Durban, and Michaelhouse, Pietermaritzburg, under the Rev. Canon Todd. Admitted 1 Oct. 1900. Resided one year.

Pytches, George Julian: son of John Thomas Pytches, of Little Grange, Wood-bridge; and Mary Elizabeth Dickinson. Born at Melton, Suffolk, 21 Dec. 1880. Schools: Eaton House, Aldeburgh, under Dr Wilkinson; and Oundle School, under Mr F. W. Sanderson. Admitted 1 Oct. 1900.
　　Entrance Scholarship, 1900. Kept three terms. Completed time with Ransom, Simms & Jefferies, Engineers, 1905. Master at Trinity College, Glenalmond (1909). Readmitted Oct. 1910.

Rae, Arthur Joseph: son of William Maples Rae (deceased); and Ellen Maria Ray. Born at Cheltenham, 18 Feb. 1879. Educated at Cheltenham College under the Rev. Dr James and the Rev. R. S. de C. Laffan. Admitted 1 Oct. 1900.
　　B.A. 1903.

Raymond, Cuthbert: son of Walter Raymond, novelist, of Sutherland House, Preston, Yeovil; and Mary Elizabeth Johnston. Born at Hendford Hill, Yeovil, Somerset, 2 Sep. 1881. Schools: Highfield Preparatory School, Southampton, under Mr E. A. Wells, M.A.; and Blundell's School, Tiverton, under Mr A. L. Francis. Admitted 1 Oct. 1900.
　　B.A. 1903.

Scougal, Henry James: son of Andrew Edward Scougal, H.M. Chief Inspector of Schools, of 14, Kelvin Drive, Kelvinside, N. Glasgow; and Annie H. Cowan. Born at Melrose, Scotland, 20 Nov. 1880. Educated at Aird House School, Edinburgh, under Mr Jas. J. Muir, and George Watson's College, Edinburgh, under George Ogilvie, D.D. and Mr W. L. Carrie, M.A. Admitted 1 Oct. 1900.
　　B.A. 1903. Med. and Mod. Lang. Tripos, Class 2, 1903. Died in Edin-burgh, 6 July 1907.

Smale, Oswald Ridley: son of John Smale, silk manufacturer, of the Brooklands, Macclesfield; and Sarah Alice Edwards. Born at Macclesfield, 21 Jan. 1882. Educated at Locker's Park School, under Mr Draper, and Rugby School, under the Rev. Dr James. Admitted 1 Oct. 1900.
　　B.A. 1903; M.B., B.C. 1909.

Sommer, John William Ernest: son of the Rev. John James Sommer, Wesleyan Minister, of 72, East India Road, Poplar, London; and Zilla Elizabeth Barratt. Born at Stuttgart, Germany, 31 March 1881. Educated at Kingswood School, Bath, under Mr W. P. Workman, M.A., and Rydal Mount, Colwyn Bay, under Mr T. G. Osborn, M.A. Admitted 1 Oct. 1900.
　　B.A. 1903. Med. and Mod. Lang. Tripos, Class 1, 1903. Missionary, Turkey in Asia, under the "Deutscher Hülfsbund für christliches Liebeswerk im Orient" (1909).

Spearman, William: son of William Taylor Spearman, Colonel of Volunteers (retired), of Briar Tor, Yelverton, S. Devon; and Mary Hannah Leake. Born at Yelverton, 20 Sep. 1881. School: Blundell's, Tiverton, under Mr A. L. Francis. Admitted 1 Oct. 1900. Brother of Robert, II. 545, and Barugh, II. 550.
　　B.A. 1903; M.A. 1907. Law Tripos, Part I, Class 3, 1902; Part II, 1903. Solicitor at Plymouth (1906).

Stewart, Francis Hugh: son of Richard Morris Stewart, landed proprietor, of 7, Hope Street, St Andrews; and Sarah Armstrong. Born in 1879. School: the Oratory School, Edgbaston, under the Rev. John Norris. Admitted as an Advanced Student 1 Oct. 1900.

     Kept three terms. Captain Indian Medical Service (1909).

Svensson, Robert: son of Anders Gillis Svensson, analytical chemist, of 1, Nelson Terrace, Coatham, Redcar; and Isabella Jane Tomlinson. Born at Redcar Yorks, 18 May 1883. School: Sir William Furner's Grammar School, Coatham, under Mr A. Pryce, M.A. Admitted 1 Oct. 1900. County Council Exhibitioner.

     B.A. 1903. Nat. Sci. Tripos, Part I, Class 3, 1903. In medical practice.

Taylor, Alfred Rickard: son of Francis James Taylor, solicitor, of Overdale, Bakewell; and Emily Rickard. Born at Bakewell, Derbyshire, 24 Sept. 1882. Educated at St Anselm's, Bakewell, and at Derby School, under Mr P. K. Tollit. Admitted 1 Oct. 1900.

     B.A. 1904. Assistant Master at Dulwich College (1909).

Tillyard, Henry Julius Wetenhall: son of Alfred Isaac Tillyard, M.A., newspaper proprietor, of Fordfield, the Avenue, Cambridge; and Catharine Sarah Wetenhall. Born at Station Road, Cambridge, 18 Nov. 1881. School: Tonbridge, under the Rev. Dr Wood and the Rev. C. C. Tancock. Admitted 1 Oct. 1900.

     B.A. 1904; M.A. 1910. Class. Tripos, Part I, Class 1, Division 2, 1902; Part II, Class 1, 1904. Entrance Scholarship, 1900; Scholar, 1901–4; Research Student, 1905–6 at the British School of Archaeology, Athens; Prince Consort Prize, 1908. Assistant-Lecturer in Greek at Edinburgh University (1909).

Vickers, Stansfeld: son of Charles William Vickers, surgeon, of Roseneath, Paignton, Devon; and Annie Stansfeld. Born at 94, East India Road, Poplar, London, E., 13 June 1881. School: Blundell's, Tiverton, under Mr A. L. Francis. Admitted 1 Oct. 1900.

     B.A. 1903. Solicitor at Paignton (1909).

Wegg, Hugh Neville: son of William Wegg, M.D. Cantab., of 15, Hertford Street, Mayfair, W. (formerly of the College, II. 242); and Mary Ann Rickards. Born at 15 Hertford Street, Mayfair, London, W. Educated at Waynflete, Clifton; and Marlborough College, under the Rev. G. C. Bell. Admitted 1 Oct. 1900. Brother of William, II. 545.

     B.A. 1904. Solicitor in London (1909).

Williams, Cecil: son of John Rowland Williams, of Crathorne, East Finchley, London, N.; and Agnes Fanny Charsley. Born at Montem, Salt Hill, Slough, 29 Nov. 1881. School: Merchant Taylors', under the Rev. Dr Baker. Admitted 1 Oct. 1900.

     B.A. 1903; M.A. 1907. Oriental Lang. Tripos, Class 3, 1903. Theol. Tripos, Part II, Class 2, 1904. Entrance Exhibition, 1900. Entered Ridley Hall. Ordained deacon, 1905 (Ely); priest, 1906. Curate of Deal, 1908– .

Wilson, John Dover: son of Edwin Wilson, scientific artist, of Cherryhinton Road, Cambridge; and Elizabeth Dover. Born at 10, St Leonards, Mortlake,

13 July 1881. Educated at Kenley School, under the Rev. S. Shilcock; and Lancing College, under the Rev. Dr Wilson. Admitted 1 Oct. 1900. B.A. 1903; M.A. 1908. Hist. Tripos, Part I, Class 2, 1902; Part II, Class 2, 1903. Entrance Scholarship, 1900. Members' Prize for English Essay, 1903; Harness Prize, 1905. Master at Whitgift School, Croydon, 1904. Lecturer in English at Helsingfors. Lecturer in English at the Goldsmiths' College, New Cross (London University), 1909– .

Wilson, James Vernon: son of Edward Thomas Wilson, M.B., Oxon., F.R.C.P. Lond., of Westal, Montpellier Parade, Cheltenham; and Mary Agnes Whishaw. Born at Cheltenham, 29 Jan. 1881. Educated at Brandon House, Cheltenham, under Mr Haskoll, and Cheltenham College, under the Rev. R. S. de C. Laffan and the Rev. R. Waterfield. Admitted 1 Oct. 1900. Brother of Edward, II. 523.

B.A. 1903; M.A. 1907 Ordained deacon (Lichfield), 1904; priest, 1906. Curate at Stoke-on-Trent, 1909

Wood, Ravenshaw William Bodkin Cecil: son of the Rev. William Cecil Wood (deceased), late Head Master of Epsom College; and Ellen Sophia Bodkin. Born at Wellington College, Sandhurst, 8 March 1882. School: Felsted, under the Rev. H. A. Dalton. Admitted 1 Oct. 1900.

B.A. 1903. Nat. Sci. Tripos, Part I (*aegrotat*), 1903. Director of Agriculture, Coimbatore, Madras (1909).

MICHAELMAS 1901 TO MICHAELMAS 1902.

(Tutors: Mr Roberts, Mr Gallop, Mr Knight, and Mr Hardy.)

Barker, Ronald William: son of the Rev. Conrad Robert Barker (deceased), of the College, II. 389; and Edith Mary Millington, who married, secondly, the Rev. J. P. A. Fletcher (of the College, II. 371). Born at Parry House, Leamington, 20 Sept. 1883. School: St John's School, Leatherhead, under the Rev. A. F. Rutty. Admitted 1 Oct. 1901.

B.A. 1904. 2nd Lieut. 43rd Burma Infantry (1909).

Bayer, Sidney Francis: son of Charles Bayer, dry goods manufacturer, of Tewkesbury Lodge, Forest Hill, S.E.; and Fanny Craft. Born in London, 16 April 1882. School: Dulwich College, under Mr A. H. Gilkes. Admitted 1 Oct. 1901.

B.A. 1904. Med. and Mod. Lang. Tripos, Class 3, 1904. Entrance Scholarship, 1901. Member of Lloyd's (1909).

Biedermann, Cecil Clare Reginald: son of Conrad Biedermann, of Villa Hedwig, Arco, South Tyrol, Austria, gentleman; and of Hedwig Lang. Born at Trieste, 16 March 1883. School: Cheltenham College, under the Rev. R. S. de C. Laffan and the Rev. R. Waterfield. Admitted 1 Oct. 1901. Kept three terms.

Blake, William Twynam: son of William Henry Blake, M.B., of Bowers House, Harpenden, Herts; and Elizabeth Alice Twynam. Born at Harpenden, Herts, 20 April 1882. School: Aldenham, under the Rev. J. Kennedy and the Rev. A. H. Cooke. Admitted 1 Oct. 1901.

B.A. 1904. Class. Tripos, Part I, Class 2, Division 1, 1904. Entrance Scholarship, 1901. Of the Indian Civil Service. Died at Jubbulpore on 9 Jan. 1907 (*Caian*, XVI. 97).

Boys-Stones, William : son of the Rev. George Boys-Stones, of Garstang, Lancs.;
and Kate Susanna Lawden. Born at Garstang, 4 Jan. 1882. School:
Rossall, under the Rev. Dr Way. Admitted 1 Oct. 1901.
B.A. 1904.

Brinton, Cecil Charles : son of John Brinton, J.P., D.L., of Moor Hall, Stourport;
and Mary Chagter. Born at Kensington, 25 April 1883. School : Cheltenham
College, under the Rev. R. S. de C. Laffan and the Rev. R. Waterfield.
Admitted 1 Oct. 1901.
B.A. 1904; M.A. 1908. Mech. Sci. Tripos, Part I, Class 3, 1904. Salomons
Engineering Scholarship, 1901. In business as carpet-manufacturer.
Address (1909), The Hostel, Kidderminster.

Burwell, William Keith: son of William Burwell, retired seed-crusher, of Southfield,
Hessle, Yorks; and Elizabeth Mackie. Born at Hull, 23 March 1882.
School : Giggleswick, under the Rev. G. Style. Admitted 1 Oct. 1901.
B.A. 1904. Nat. Sci. Tripos, Part I, Class 2, 1904. Under-manager in
the Hayfield Printing Company, Hayfield, near Stockport (1909).

Cane, Howard James Barrell : son of Howard Cane, Doctor of Medicine, of Belvedere, Kent; and Alice Jane Barrell. Born at Belvedere, 9 April 1883.
School : Bradfield College, under the Rev. H. B. Gray, D.D. Admitted
1 Oct. 1901.
B.A. 1904. Nat. Sci. Tripos, Part I, Class 3, 1904.

Cardwell, William : son of John Henry Cardwell (of the College, II. 354), clerk in
Holy Orders, rector of St Anne's, Soho Square, W.; and Elizabeth Barnes.
Born at West Kensington, 22 Jan. 1882. Schools : Haileybury, under the
Hon. and Rev. E. Lyttelton; and St Paul's, under Mr F. W. Walker.
Admitted 1 Oct. 1901. Brother of Percy, II. 525, and Cyril, IV. (1) 79.
B.A. 1906; M.A. 1909. Entrance Scholarship, 1901. Assistant Master
at Merchant Taylors' School; Assistant Master at a Preparatory School
(Mr J. Roscoe), Harrogate (1909).

Cave, William Thomas Charles : son of William John Cave, silk agent and
merchant, of Bromley, Kent; and Eleanor Flogg. Born at Rockbourne,
Fox Lane, Upper Norwood, 24 Nov. 1882. School : Tonbridge, under the
Rev. Dr Wood and the Rev. Dr Tancock. Admitted 1 Oct. 1901.
B.A., LL.B. 1904. Law Tripos, Part I, Class 3, 1903; Part II, Class 3,
1904. Captain, Rugby Football, 1903-4; in University team, 1903;
International player, 1903. Solicitor in London.

Chan, Sze Pong, son of Fook Nyan Chan, civil servant, Malay States, of 109, High
Street, Kuala Lumpur, Malay States; and Nyat Jin Cheang. Born August
1884, at Sarawak, East Indies. School : The Raffles Institution, Singapore,
under Mr R. W. Hullett, M.A. Admitted 1 Oct. 1901.
B.A. 1906; B.C. 1907; M.B. 1908. Nat. Sci. Tripos, Part I, Class 2,
1904. Practising at Singapore, 1910.

Colledge, Lionel : son of John Colledge, late major, Bengal Staff Corps, of Cheltenham; and Jane Mackenzie Inglis. Born at Lauriston House, Bayshill,
Cheltenham, 5 Oct. 1883. School : Cheltenham College, under the Rev. B. S.
de C. Laffan and the Rev. R. Waterfield. Admitted 1 Oct. 1901.
B.A. 1904 ; M.A. 1910. Nat. Sci. Tripos, Part I, Class 3, 1904. In
medical practice.

Collinge, Robert Maurice : son of John Sutcliffe Collinge, J.P., cotton manufacturer, of Park House, Burnley; and Mary Ann Allen. Born at Burnley, 9 May 1883. Schools: Giggleswick, under the Rev. G. Style; and Shrewsbury, under the Rev. H. W. Moss. Admitted 1 Oct. 1901.
> B.A. 1904. Died in London 2 Jan. 1907, at the King's Cross Hotel.

Cooper, Charles Robert Plant : son of John Capps Cooper (deceased), draper's counting-house manager, of 6, Sussex Place, Cheltenham; and Jane Hannah Plant. Born at Cheltenham, 26 April 1882. School: Bath College, under Mr T. W. Dunn and the Rev. W. Y. Fausset. Admitted 1 Oct. 1901.
> B.A. 1904. Class. Tripos, Part I, Class 1, Division 3, 1904. Entrance Scholarship, 1901. Scholar, 1902–4. Stewart of Rannoch Scholarship for Classics, 1901. President of Musical Society, 1905–6. I.C.S. 1905. Assistant Commissioner, Burma.

Davy, Gerald Henry : son of David Henry Davy, surgeon, of 84, Beverley Road, Hull; and Mary Jane Field. Born at Hull, 7 April 1883. School: Hymers College, under Mr C. H. Gore, M.A. Admitted 1 Oct. 1901.
> B.A. 1904; M.B. 1909. Nat. Sci. Tripos, Part I, Class 1, 1904.

Dearden, Harold : son of Jonathan Dearden, cotton manufacturer, of Holly Bank, Bromley Cross; and Frances Goldsmith. Born at Bolton, 13 Dec. 1882. School: Bromsgrove, under Mr H. M. Millington. Admitted 1 Oct. 1901.
> B.A. 1904. Nat. Sci. Tripos, Part I, Class 3, 1904.

Dietrichsen, Frederick Christian : son of James Mark Dietrichsen, manufacturer, of The Pollards, Loughton; and Elizabeth Consa Connell. Born at Buckhurst Hill, Essex, 30 Oct. 1882. School: Chigwell Grammar School, under the Rev. R. D. Swallow. Admitted 1 Oct. 1901.
> B.A., LL.B. 1904. Law Tripos, Part I, Class 3, 1903; Part II, Class 3, 1904. Called to the Bar, Inner Temple, 12 June 1907; practising at Nottingham (1909).

Dixon, William Scarth : son of David Watson Dixon, mining engineer, of Brotton Hall, Yorks; and Mary Ann Moffatt. Born at Brotton, 4 May 1883. School: Sir W. Turner's School, Coatham, Redcar. Admitted 1 Oct. 1901.
> B.A. 1904. President of Musical Society, 1903–4; Stewart of Rannoch Scholarship for Music, 1905. Assistant Master at Twyford School, Winchester (1909).

Douglas, Cecil Howard : son of William Thomas Parker Douglas, M.B. (of the College, II. 369), of Holmby Speen, Newbury, Berks; and Agnes Maria Shaw. Born at Newbury, 24 Nov. 1882. School: Marlborough College, under the Rev. G. C. Bell. Admitted 1 Oct. 1901.
> Kept four terms. Died early.

Ebden, James Wylde : son of Edward James Ebden, of the College, II. 357, Indian Civil Service (retired), of 3, Downfield Road, Clifton; and Mary Bullock. Born at Bandra, Bombay, 6 Feb. 1882. School: Clifton College, under the Rev. M. G. Glazebrook. Admitted 1 Oct. 1901. Brother of William, IV. (1) 69.
> B.A. 1904. Class. Tripos, Part I, Class 2, Division 2, 1904. Entrance Scholarship, 1901. Assistant-Accountant-General, Rangoon, 1909- .

Eisdell, Hubert Mortimer: son of John Arthur Eisdell (deceased), solicitor; and Mary Mortimer, of 4, Windmill Hill, Hampstead, N.W. Born at Hampstead, 21 Sept. 1882. School: Highgate School, under the Rev. A. E. Allcock, M.A. Admitted 1 Oct. 1901.
> B.A. 1904. Choral Entrance Exhibition, 1901. President of Musical Society, 1904-5. In profession as a singer.

Elger, Thomas Gwyn: son of Thomas Gwyn Empey Elger, civil engineer (deceased); and Fanny Edith Gissing, of 13, Wilton Road, Bexhill-on-Sea, Sussex. Born at Kempston, Beds, 22 Aug. 1883. School: Bedford Grammar School, under Mr J. S. Phillpotts. Admitted 1 Oct. 1901.
> B.A. 1904. Nat. Sci. Tripos, Part I, Class 3, 1904.

Elton, Henry Brown: son of Charles Tierney Elton, G.J.P.R.Y. Bombay, civil engineer; and Mary Higgs. Born in Ceylon, 18 Aug. 1882. School: Sherborne, under the Rev. F. B. Westcott. Admitted 1 Oct. 1901.
> B.A. 1905; M.B., B.C. 1909.

Esdaile, Everard George Kennedy: son of James Kennedy Esdaile, J.P., of Horsted Keynes, Sussex; and Florence Crawshay. Born at East Grinstead, 29 May 1882. School: Lancing College, under the Rev. Dr Wilson. Admitted 1 Oct. 1901.
> B.A. 1904. Class. Tripos, Part I, Class 2, Division 3, 1904. Entrance Scholarship, 1901. Scholar, 1902-4. Captain, Association Football, 1903-4. Ordained deacon (Southwark), 1907; priest, 1908. Curate of All Saints, Battersea Park, London, S.W., 1907- .

Fearfield, Joseph: son of John Piggin Fearfield, lace manufacturer, of Stapleford, Notts (deceased); and Mary Dalley, of 176, Derby Road, Nottingham. Born at Stapleford, 18 Dec. 1883. School: Dean Close Memorial School, Cheltenham, under the Rev. W. H. Flecker, D.C.L. Admitted 1 Oct. 1901. Brother of Cecil, IV. (1) 113.
> B.A. 1904. Mech. Sci. Tripos, Part I, Class 3, 1904. Assistant Engineer, Jodhpur Bihaner Railway (1909). English address (1909), Parkside, Nottingham.

Gillies, Harold Delf: son of Robert Gillies, surveyor and landowner, of Auckland, New Zealand; and Emily Street. Born at Dunedin, N.Z., 17 June 1882. Schools: Private School, Warwickshire, under Mr Lea; and Collegiate School, Wanganui, under Mr Epsom. Admitted 1 Oct. 1901. Brother of Charles, II. 512.
> B.A. 1904. Nat. Sci. Tripos, Part I, Class 2, 1904. Exhibitioner, 1903. Holden Research Scholarship, St Bartholomew's Hospital, 1910. Captain, Boat Club, 1903-4. University Oar, 1904.

Glanville, Walter Josolyne: son of George Glanville, gentleman, of Ashley House, Tunbridge Wells; and Ellen Mary Josolyne. Born at Tunbridge Wells, 16 Jan. 1881. School: Tonbridge Grammar School, under the Rev. Dr J. Wood. Admitted 1 Oct. 1901.
> B.A. 1904. Mech. Sci. Tripos, Part I, Class 2, 1904. Assistant Engineer P.W.D., Amritsar, India, 1905-10. In the office of the Perfector Building and Constructions Co., Bristol (1910).

Hale, Herbert Edward: son of the Rev. George Hale, rector of Swanscombe, Greenhithe, Kent; and Mary Jane Hooper. Born at 121, Chesterton Road, Cambridge, 2 July 1882. Schools: Blundell's School, under Mr A. L. Francis; and Dulwich College, under Mr A. H. Gilkes. Admitted 1 Oct. 1901.
> B.A. 1904; M.A. 1910. Class. Tripos, Part I, Class 2, Division 1, 1904. Entrance Scholarship, 1901. Assistant-Master at Grove House, Leighton Park School, Reading.

Hall, John Percy: son of John Percy Hall, engine-works manager, of "Carville," Laurie Park Road, Sydenham, S.E.; and Georgina Clavering. Born at Jarrow-on-Tyne, 6 Oct. 1882. School: Dulwich College, under Mr A. H. Gilkes. Admitted 1 Oct. 1901.

> B.A. 1904. Mech. Sci. Tripos, Part I, Class 3, 1904. In the engineering firm of J. P. Hall and Sons, Peterborough.

Herbert, Philip Lee William: son of William Dickes Herbert, of the Civil Service, of 15, Ladbroke Gardens, W.; and Bessie Florence Clark. Born at Witham House, New Barnet, Herts, 31 Oct. 1882. School: Wellington College, under the Rev. B. Pollock. Admitted 1 Oct. 1901.

> Kept three terms. Lieut. 2nd Battalion Sherwood Foresters (1909).

Hoffmann, Geoffrey: son of Gustavus Hoffmann, merchant, of Rookwood, Bradford; and Anne Avery Law. Born 31 March 1882. School: Giggleswick, under the Rev. G. Style. Admitted 1 Oct. 1901.

> B.A. 1904. Nat. Sci. Tripos, Part I, Class 3, 1904.

Hope, George Meredyth: son of George Palmer Hope (of the College, II. 367), stockbroker, of Havering Grange, near Romford; and Aline Jervis White-Jervis. Born at Romford, 9 Oct. 1883. School: Eton, under Dr Warre. Admitted 1 Oct. 1901. Brother of Stephen, III. 403 and IV. (1) 15.

> B.A. 1905. On the Stock Exchange.

Humphrys, Herbert Edward: son of Charles Beyer Humphrys, physician and surgeon, of Eagle House, Blandford, Dorset; and Kate Ellen Robinson. Born at Northam, North Devon, 22 Feb. 1883. Schools: Malvern College, under the Rev. S. R. James; and Milton Abbas Grammar School, Blandford, under the Rev. E. Mears, M.A. Admitted 1 Oct. 1901.

> B.A. 1904; B.C. 1910.

Hutchinson, Char.es Hilton: son of the Rev. C. P. Hutchinson, of the College, II. 392, of Kent House, Eastbourne; and Eleanor Taylor. Born at Beckenham, Kent, 10 Jan. 1882. School: Kent House School. Admitted 1 Oct. 1901.

> B.A. 1904. Associate Member Inst.C.E. Civil Engineer.

Ingleby, Bertram Edward: son of Edward Francis Ingleby, stockbroker, of The Manor House, North Ferriby, East Yorks; and Alice Mary Lawson. Born at Hull, 17 Feb. 1882. Schools: Ripon Grammar School, under the Rev. W. Yorke Fausset; Hymers College, Hull, under Mr C. H. Gore; and Giggleswick School, under the Rev. G. Style. Admitted 1 Oct. 1901.

> B.A. 1904. Nat. Sci. Tripos, Part I, Class 3, 1904. Died 24 Feb. 1907 at Higham's Park, Essex.

Jewson, Norman: son of John William Jewson, timber merchant, of Hill House, Thorpe Hamlet, Norwich; and Henrietta Catt. Born at Thorpe Hamlet, Norwich, 10 Feb. 1884. School: St Aubyn's, South Lowestoft, under Mr J. Bruce-Payne. Admitted 1 Oct. 1901.

> B.A. 1906. In practice as an architect.

Kohan, Robert Mendell : son of Mendel Kohan, commission agent and shipper, of 11 Strada Zimbrului, Galatz, Roumania; and Rebecca Blumenfeld. School · Manchester Grammar School, under Mr J. E. King, M.A.
    B.A. 1904. Med. and Mod. Lang. Tripos, Class 2, 1904. Vice-Consul at Zanzibar, 1908.

Little, Harold Norman : son of James Little, of Normanhurst, Strood, Rochester; and Agnes Maude Matthews. Born at Strood, 13 Aug. 1883. School : Epsom College, under the Rev. T. N. Hart-Smith. Admitted 1 Oct. 1901.
    B.A. 1904 ; B.C. 1908 ; M.A. 1909.

Mair, Gilbert Robertson : son of Charles Mair, retired merchant, of The Grange, Keith, N.B.; and Mary Robertson. Born at Grange, Banffshire, N.B., 2 Aug. 1877. Educated at Keith School and Aberdeen University. Admitted 1 Oct. 1901. Brother of Alexander, II. 532.
    B.A. 1904. Class. Tripos, Part I, Class 1, Division 3, 1904.

Markham, Richard George : son of Henry William Markham, merchant, of Sydenham, Kent, and Cape Town; and Emily Jacob. Born at Green Point, Cape Town, 12 Aug. 1882. Educated at Dale College School, King William's Town, under the Rev. S. Sutton; South African College School, Cape Town, under Mr J. Russell; and Berkhamstead School, under the Rev. Dr Fry. Admitted 1 Oct. 1901. Brother of Frank, IV. (1) 42.
    B.A. 1904; M.B., B.C. 1907. Nat. Sci. Tripos, Part I, Class 2, 1904.

Marklove, John Carrington : son of Maurice William Carrington Marklove, schoolmaster (deceased); and Fanny Catherine Taylor, of 7, Lansdown Crescent, Cheltenham. Born at 113, Victoria Street, London, S.W., 5 Oct. 1882. School : Cheltenham College, under the Rev. R. S. de C. Laffan and the Rev. R. Waterfield. Admitted 1 Oct. 1901.
    B.A. 1904. In medical practice.

* Mawer, Allen : son of George Henry Mawer, secretary to Religious Society, of 10, Tredegar Road, Bow; and Clara Isabella Allen. Born at Bow, 8 May 1887. Schools : Prisca, Coborn Foundation School and Coopers' Company's School. Admitted 1 Oct. 1901.
    B.A. 1904; M.A. 1908. Med. and Mod. Lang. Tripos, Class 1, 1904. Drosier Fellow, 1905-9. Supernumerary Fellow, 1909- . Lecturer in English Literature, University of Sheffield, to 1908; Professor of English Literature at Armstrong College, Newcastle-on-Tyne, 1908-

North, Walter Grosvenor Bertie : son of Walter Meyrick North, stipendiary magistrate of Merthyr Tydfil (deceased); and Earle Ada Butts, of The Steps, Brecon, S. Wales. Born at Wallington, Surrey, 12 Jan. 1882. Educated at Llandaff Cathedral School, under the Rev. E. Owen; and Cheltenham College, under the Rev. R. S. de C. Laffan and the Rev. R. Waterfield. Admitted 1 Oct. 1901.
    B.A. 1904. Class. Tripos, Part I, Class 2, Division 3, 1904. Entrance Exhibition, 1901. Exhibitioner, 1902-4. In scholastic work at Cairo, 1910.

Oats, Wilfrid: son of Francis Oats, mine-owner, of Carn House, St Just,
Cornwall; and Elizabeth Anne Olds.   Born at St Just, 2 July 1883.
Educated at Clifton College under the Rev. M. G. Glazebrook.   Admitted
1 Oct. 1901.
    B.A. 1907.

Pearman, James O'Hara: son of the Rev. W. D. Pearman, head-master of Potsdam
School, Jamaica; and Florinda O'Hara.   Born at Beckbury, Shifnal, Salop,
29 Dec. 1881.   Educated at Potsdam, under the Rev. W. D. Pearman.
Admitted 1 Oct. 1901.
    B.A. 1904; M.A. 1908.   Class. Tripos, Part I, Class 2, Division 1, 1904.
    Master at Wakefield Grammar School to 1908; at Huddersfield, 1909– .

Perrin, Walter Sydney: son of Walter Perrin, of 31, Halford Road, Richmond;
and Harriet S. Savage.   Born at 50, Camberwell Road, Camberwell, 25 April
1882.   Educated at Wilson Grammar School, under Mr McDowell; Richmond
Hill School, under Mr Whitbread; and City of London School, under Mr A. T.
Pollard.   Admitted 1 Oct. 1901.
    B.A. 1904; M.A. 1908.   Nat. Sci. Tripos, Part I, Class 1, 1903; Part II,
    Class 1, 1904.   Tancred Studentship, 1901.   Shuttleworth Studentship,
    1905–7.

Phillips, Oscar Frederick: son of Arthur F. Phillips, civil engineer, of High Croft,
St Albans; and Jane Elizabeth Harris.   Born at St Albans, 7 Jan. 1882.
School: Uppingham, under the Rev. E. C. Selwyn.   Admitted 1 Oct. 1901.
    Kept two terms.   Solicitor at St Albans (1909).

Platt, Arthur Hardwicke: son of William H. Platt, surgeon (deceased), of
St James's Lodge, West End Lane, W. Hampstead; and Kate Ellen Winn,
of 8, Weech Road, W. Hampstead.   Born at Hampstead, 30 March 1883.
Educated at Streete Court, Westgate-on-Sea, under Mr J. V. Milne; and
Epsom College, Surrey, under the Rev. T. N. Hart-Smith.   Admitted 1 Oct.
1901.
    B.A. 1904.   In medical practice.

Priest, Robert Cecil: son of Thomas Priest, collector of taxes, of 379, Hagley
Road, Edgbaston; and Louisa Read.   Born at Harborne, Stafford, 5 Nov.
1882.   Educated at King Edward VI. School, Birmingham, under the Rev.
H. R. Vardy and Mr R. C. Gilson.   Admitted 1 Oct. 1901.
    B.A. 1904; M.B., B.C. 1908.   Nat. Sci. Tripos, Part I, Class 1, 1904;
    Part II, Class 2, 1905.   Scholar, 1904.

Pringle, Kenneth Douglas: son of Henry Turnbull Pringle, M.D., of Angelton,
Bridgend, Glamorgan; and Jessie Isabella Smith (deceased).   Born at Angelton,
20 Jan. 1883.   Educated at May Place, Malvern Wells, under Mr A. E.
Tillard; and Linton House, Notting Hill, under Mr James Hardie.   Admitted
1 Oct. 1901.
    B.A. 1904; M.B., B.C. 1908.   Nat. Sci. Tripos, Part I, Class 3,
    1904.

Radford, Archibald Campbell: son of Walter Thomas Hindmarsh Radford, East
India merchant, of Hillside, Hendon; and Ann Louisa Maria Wulff.   Born at
Hendon, 8 Dec. 1882.   Educated at Eastbourne College, under the Rev. M. E.
Bayfield.   Admitted 1 Oct. 1901.
    B.A. 1906.   Tutor in the family of Sir Solomon Diaz, Ceylon (1910).

Sephton, Ralph: son of Robert Sephton, surgeon, of The Manor House, Atherton; and Eliza Poole. Born at Atherton, 8 Nov. 1882. Educated at St John's School, Leatherhead, under the Rev. A. F. Rutty. Admitted 1 Oct. 1901.

> B.A. 1904. On works at Goodwick Harbour (1905); on S. W. Railway (1906); Assistant Engineer, G. W. Railway (1909).

Shann, Samuel Edward Thornhill: son of Thomas Thornhill Shann, merchant, of Meadow Bank, Heaton Norris, near Stockport; and Hannah Sutcliffe (deceased). Born at The Hollies, Heaton Norris, near Stockport, 20 Oct. 1882. School: Cheltenham College, under the Rev. R. S. de C. Laffan. Admitted 1 Oct. 1901.

> B.A. 1904; M.B., B.C. 1909; M.A. 1910. Nat. Sci. Tripos, Part I, Class 3, 1904.

Sharp, Leonard Whittaker: son of John Sharp, gold thread manufacturer, of West Cliff House, Preston; and Elizabeth Sharp. Born at Preston, 27 Nov. 1882. School: Cheltenham College, under the Rev Dr James, the Rev. R. S. de C. Laffan, and the Rev. R. Waterfield. Admitted 1 Oct. 1901.

> B.A. 1904; B.C. 1909; M.A. 1910. Nat. Sci. Tripos, Part I, Class 3, 1904.

Sheringham, Horace Valentine: son of Herbert Valentine Sheringham, farmer, of South Creake, Fakenham; and Louisa Tanner. Born at South Creake, 21 April 1884. School: Mill Hill, under Dr McClure. Admitted 1 Oct. 1901. Diploma in Agriculture, 1904.

Siddle, George Ludorf: son of George Siddle, merchant, of Klerksdorp, Transvaal, South Africa; and Josephine Ludorf. Born at Potchefstrom, Transvaal, South Africa, 6 Oct. 1881. Educated at Blairlodge School, Perthshire, under Mr F. H. Matthews. Admitted 1 Oct. 1901.

> B.A. 1904. Nat. Sci. Tripos, Part I, Class 1, 1904. Captain, C Co., C.U.R.V., 1903. Died 24 Sept. 1908, at the London Hospital (*Caian* XVIII. 3). The George Ludorf Siddle Prize founded in his memory by his father, 1908 (*Caian* XVIII. 5).

Small, Walter Joseph Tombleson: son of Walter Thomas Small, draper, of Bargate Lodge, Boston; and Emily Faith Tombleson. Born at Boston, 4 July 1883. Educated at Boston Grammar School under Mr W. White, M.A. Admitted 1 Oct. 1901.

> B.A. 1904; M.A. 1908. Math. Tripos, Part I (br. 7th Wrangler), 1904; Theol. Tripos, Part I, Class 1, 1906. Principal of Richmond College, Galle, Ceylon (1909).

Smith, Ernest Whately: son of the Rev. Granville V. V. Smith, vicar of Swaffham, Norfolk (of the College, II. 336); and Sarah G. Frost. Born at Ipswich, 19 Aug. 1882. Educated at St George's, Windsor, under Mr Deane; and Felsted, under the Rev. H. A. Dalton. Admitted 1 Oct. 1901.

> B.A. 1904. Choral Entrance Exhibition, 1901. Ordained deacon, 1907 (Norwich); priest, 1908. Curate at Aldeburgh, 1907–9. Master at a Preparatory School, Roydon Hall, Diss, 1909–10; at Dover College, 1910– .

Snell, Henry Cecil: son of Simeon Snell, surgeon, of Lynwood, Broomhall Park Sheffield; and Amie Christiana Woodley. Born at Sheffield, 5 May 1882. School: Uppingham, under the Rev. E. C. Selwyn. Admitted 1 Oct. 1901. Brother of John, IV. (1)

> B.A. 1904; M.A. 1908. Nat. Sci. Tripos, Part I, Class 2, 1904. In medical practice.

Spence, Richard Bennett: son of James Beveridge Spence, M.D., of Burntwood, near Lichfield; and Elizabeth Roebuck Bennett. Born at Burntwood, 8 March 1882. Educated at Southlea, Malvern, under the Rev. S. Latham; and Haileybury College, under the Hon. and Rev. E. Lyttelton. Admitted 1 Oct. 1901.

    Kept three terms. Lieut. Indian Army, 96th Berar Infantry (1909).

Stagg, Cecil: son of Walter Stagg, wool merchant, of Rose Hill, Bobbing, Sittingbourne; and Rose Richardson. Born at Milton, Kent, 23 April 1882. School: Clifton, under the Rev. M. G. Glazebrook. Admitted 1 Oct. 1901.

    B.A. 1904; M.A. 1908. Class. Tripos, Part I, Class 1, Division 3, 1904. Captain, Cricket Club, 1903–4. Master at Marlborough College (1909).

Stirling, Ernest Morgan: son of Hugh Auchincloss Stirling (deceased), metal merchant, Liverpool; and Louise Wilder Sheffield. Born at Liverpool, 12 April 1881. Educated at Sedbergh, under Mr Hart; and Brighton College, under the Rev. A. F. Titherington. Admitted 1 Oct. 1901.

    B.A. 1904. In the Richard Brazier motor firm at Dublin (1905).

* Stratton, Frederick John Marrian: son of Stephen Samuel Stratton, Professor of Music, of "Raymead," 14, Harborne Road, Edgbaston; and Mary Jane Marrian. Born at Edgbaston, 16 Oct. 1881. School: King Edward's Grammar School, Five Ways, under the Rev. E. J. MacCarthy; and Mason University College. Admitted 1 Oct. 1901.

    B.A. 1904; M.A. 1908. Math. Tripos, Part I (3rd Wrangler), 1904; Part II, Class 1, Division 2, 1905. Entrance Scholarship, 1901; Scholar, 1902–5; Isaac Newton Studentship, 1905; Tyson Medal, 1905; Smith's Prize, 1906; Drosier Fellow, 1906– ; Assistant-Demonstrator in Astrophysics at the Observatory, 1909– ; Steward of the College, 1910– ; Lecturer, 1910– ; Officer in the Communication Company, C.U.O.T.C.

Talbot, Gerald Francis: son of Gerald Francis Talbot, colonel, of the Carlton Club, London; and Henrietta Clarissa Noyes Bradhurst. Born in London, 21 Aug. 1881. School: Cheltenham College, under the Rev. R. S. de C. Laffan and the Rev. R. Waterfield. Admitted 1 Oct. 1901. Brother of Stafford, iv. (1) 9.

    Entrance Exhibition, 1901. Kept three terms.

Taylor, Charles Henry Shinglewood: son of Henry Shinglewood Taylor, M.D., J.P., of Ficksburg, Orange River Colony; and Beatrice Aletta Bell. Born at Thlotse Heights, Basutoland, 8 Nov. 1882. Schools: Bilton Grange, near Rugby; and Rugby, under the Rev. Dr James. Admitted 1 Oct. 1901.

    B.A. 1904; M.A. 1910; M.B., B.C. 1910. Nat. Sci. Tripos, Part I, Class 2, 1904. University Oar, 1905.

Teichmann, Erik: son of Emil Teichmann, merchant, of Sitka, South Hill, Chislehurst; and Mary Lydia Schroeter. Born at Eltham, Kent, 16 Jan. 1884. School: Charterhouse, under the Rev. Dr Haig Brown and the Rev. G. H. Rendall. Admitted 1 Oct. 1901. Brother of Oskar, ii. 559.

    B.A. 1904. Changed his name to Eric Teichman. Student Interpreter at Pekin (1909).

Treves, Wilfred Warwick: son of Edward Treves, surgeon, of 2, The Drive, Hove, Brighton; and Mary Warwick. Born at Hove, 8 Feb. 1883. School: Marlborough College, under the Rev. G. C. Bell. Admitted 1 Oct. 1901.

    B.A. 1904; M.B., B.C. 1909. Army Medical Service.

Turner, Sidney: son of Charles Turner, of 4, Agamemnon Road, W. Hampstead; and Ada Minnie Croxon. Born at Finchley, 18 Jan. 1882. School: Sherborne, under the Rev. F. B. Westcott, M.A. Admitted 1 Oct. 1901.
B.A. 1904. Math. Tripos, Part I (br. 10th Wrangler), 1904. Entrance Scholarship, 1901. In the India Office (1909).

Twigg, Garnet Wolseley: son of Henderson James Twigg, sheepfarmer, of Petane, Hawke's Bay, New Zealand; and Elizabeth Mary Torr. Born at Petane, 28 Nov. 1882. School: Napier Boys' High School, under Mr W. Wood. Admitted 1 Oct. 1901.
B.A. 1904; M.B., B.C. 1910. Nat. Sci. Tripos, Part I, Class 3, 1904.

Viney, Francis Henry: son of Henry Viney, gentleman, of The Mount, Stechford; and Sarah Edwards. Born at Stechford, 17 Oct. 1882. School: King Edward's School, Birmingham, under the Rev. A. R. Vardy and Mr R. C. Gilson. Admitted 1 Oct. 1901.
B.A. 1905; M.A. 1909. Class. Tripos, Part I, Class 2, Division 2, 1904. Entrance Exhibition, 1901.

Vivian, Charles St Aubyn: son of Richard Thomas Vivian, medical practitioner of Roseville, Winchmore Hill, London, N.; and Annie Maria Sugden. Born at Southgate, Middlesex, 25 July 1882. School: Epsom College, under the Rev. T. N. Hart-Smith, M.A. Admitted 1 Oct. 1901.
B.A. 1904. Nat. Sci. Tripos, Part I, Class 3, 1904. In medical practice.

Walker, Kenneth MacFarlane: son of William James Walker, South African merchant, of 90, Amhurst Park, Stamford Hill, N.; and Isabella MacFarlane Currie. Born in London, 6 June 1882. School: The Leys School, Cambridge, under the Rev. W. T. A. Barber. Admitted 1 Oct. 1901.
B.A. 1904; M.A. 1908; M.B., B.C. 1909. Nat. Sci. Tripos, Part I, Class 1, 1904. Exhibitioner, 1903–4.

Whitehead, Charles Ernest: son of Elihu Theophilus Whitehead, surgeon, of 118, Lavender Hill, S.W.; and Frances Capeling. Born at 10, Winders Road, Battersea, 11 Feb. 1883. School: Battersea Grammar School, under Mr W. H. Bindley. Admitted 1 Oct. 1901.
B.A. 1904. Nat. Sci. Tripos, Part I, Class 1, 1903; Part II, Class 2, 1904. Entrance Scholarship, 1901. Scholar, 1902–4. In medical practice.

Whitty, Hamlin Nowell: son of William John Sympson Whitty, clerk in Holy Orders, formerly solicitor, of St Philip's Vicarage, Arlington Square, Islington; and Dorothea Nowell Wallingford. Born at Westbury-on-Trym, 7 June 1883. School: Merchant Taylors', under the Rev. W. Baker, D.D. Admitted 1 Oct. 1901.
B.A. 1904; M.A. 1908. Oriental Lang. Tripos, Class 3, 1904. Entrance Scholarship, 1901. Scholar, 1902–4. Stewart of Rannoch Scholarship for Hebrew, 1901.

Winter, William Henry: son of Herbert Charles Winter, clerk in Holy Orders; and Mary Clarke Lowe, of Stoneydale, Christleton, Chester. Born at Hotsmonden, Kent, 1 April 1881. Schools: Christ's Hospital, under the Rev. R. Lee; and St John's College, Hurstpierpoint. Admitted 1 Oct. 1901.
B.A. 1904. Tancred Student, 1902– . In the Auditor's Department, Local Government Board (1909).

Wordsworth, John Lionel: son of John Wordsworth (deceased), of Black Gates, near Wakefield, landowner; and Caroline Elizabeth Bates, of Glen Park, Scalby, Yorks. Born at Bradford, 21 April 1882. Educated privately. Admitted 1 Oct. 1901.

> Resided three years. Lieut. 5th Lancers; Aide-de-camp to the General Officer Commanding in Chief at York (1909).

MICHAELMAS 1902 TO MICHAELMAS 1903.

(Tutors, to Easter 1903: Mr Roberts, Mr Gallop, Mr Hardy; from Easter 1903: Mr Gallop, Mr Buckland, Mr Hardy.)

Ashcroft, John Myddleton: son of William Ashcroft, gentleman, of Croydon; and Edith Blanche Rayner. Born at West Wickham, Kent, 28 Dec. 1882. School: Felsted, under the Rev. H. A. Dalton. Admitted 1 Oct. 1902.

> B.A. 1905. Hist. Tripos, Part I, Class 3, 1903; Part II, Class 3, 1905. Exhibitioner, 1902. Chapel Clerk, 1904. Address (1907), M. A. O. College, Aligarh, U. P., India.

Aurelius, Thomas: son of Joshua Aurelius, gentleman, of Treharris, Glamorgan; and Jane Hopkins. Born at New Tredegar, 24 June 1881. School: Penarth, under Mr D. C. Jones. Admitted 1 Oct. 1902. Brother of Joshua (below).

> B.A. 1905.

Aurelius, Joshua: son of Joshua Aurelius, gentleman, of Treharris, Glamorgan; and Jane Hopkins. Born at New Tredegar, 14 Oct. 1882. School: Penarth, under Mr D. C. Jones. Admitted 1 Oct. 1902. Brother of Thomas (above).

> B.A. 1906. Ordained deacon (Llandaff), 1910. Curate of St Margaret's, Mountain Ash, 1910– .

Barrett, Rollo Samuel: son of Charles Rollo Barrett, mining engineer, of White-hill Hall, Chester le Street; and Mary Delmar Barry. Born at Seaham Colliery, Co. Durham, 28 April 1883. School: Rossall, under the Rev. Dr Way. Admitted 1 Oct. 1902.

> B.A. 1905. Nat. Sci. Tripos, Part I, Class 3, 1905. In profession as a mining engineer (1909).

Bickerdike, Robert Brian: son of William Edward Bickerdike, chemical manu-facturer, of Bryer's Croft, Wilpshire, near Blackburn; and Bessie Eccles. Born at The Grange, Clayton le Dale, 11 July 1883. School: Cheltenham College, under the Rev. R. Waterfield. Admitted 1 Oct. 1902.

> B.A. 1905. Nat. Sci. Tripos, Part I, Class 1, 1904; Part II, Class 3, 1905. Entrance Scholar, 1902. Scholar, 1903–5. In his father's business (1909).

Blandy, Raleigh Evelyn: son of Richard Redpath Blandy, gentleman, of Kensington; and Ada Elizabeth Penfold. Born at Funchal, Madeira, 22 May 1884. School: Tonbridge, under the Rev. C. C. Tancock. Admitted 1 Oct. 1902.

> B.A. 1906. University Commission in the Indian Army, 1907.

Cam, Walter Holcroft : son of the Rev. William Herbert Cam, M.A., of Birchanger Rectory, Bishop's Stortford ; and Kate Scott. Born at Dudley, 24 June 1883. School : Marlborough, under the Rev. G. C. Bell. Admitted 1 Oct. 1902.
>B.A. 1906. Nat. Sci. Tripos, Part I, Class 1, 1905. Scholar, 1905.

Carver, Alfred Edward Arthur: son of Rev. Arthur Wellington Carver, of Langton Vicarage, Wragby ; and Katharine Jane Tregarthen. Born at Rosario, Argentine Republic, 29 April 1883. Educated at Trent College, under the Rev. J. S. Tucker ; and at Lausanne, under Pasteur P. Vallotton. Admitted 1 Oct. 1902.
>B.A. 1905 ; M.A. 1910. Nat. Sci. Tripos, Part I, Class 2, 1905.

Chaplin, Percy Frank Plunkett: son of William Henry Chaplin, merchant, of Penywern Road, London, S.W.; and Mary Timms. Born at Penywern Road, Brompton, 28 July 1883. School : Bradfield College, under the Rev. Dr H. B. Gray. Admitted 1 Oct. 1902.
>B.A. 1905. In his father's business, 1908- .

Churchill, Arnold Robertson : son of Augustus Churchill, publisher, of Fairhaven, Putney Heath ; and Eleanor Cox. Born at Fairhaven, Putney Heath, 4 March 1883. School : Harrow, under the Rev. J. E. C. Welldon and the Rev Dr Wood. Admitted 1 Oct. 1902.
>B.A., LL.B. 1905. Law Tripos, Part I, Class 3, 1904; Part II, Class 3, 1905. Sayer Scholar. President of the Athletic Club, 1904. University athlete, 1904. Called to the Bar (Inner Temple), 1907.

Clarke, James Bertram : son of Joseph Bennett Clarke, solicitor, of Handsworth; and Maria Brown. Born at Endwood Court, Handsworth, 31 July 1882. School : Bromsgrove, under Mr H. Millington, M.A. Admitted 1 Oct. 1902. Resided three terms. In South Africa (1909).

Cloudsley, Hugh : son of John Leslie Cloudsley, manufacturer, of Willesden ; and Elizabeth Smith. Born at Stonebridge Park, Willesden, 6 Sept. 1883. School : Berkhamstead, under the Rev. Dr Fry. Admitted 1 Oct. 1902.
>B.A. 1905 ; LL.B. 1907. Law Tripos, Part I, Class 3, 1904. Called to the Bar at the Inner Temple, 18 Nov. 1907. Address (1909), 5, New square, Lincoln's Inn.

Cocksedge, Thomas Abraham Bryan Cocksedge : son of Thomas Abraham Jerningham Cocksedge (of the College, II. 342), surgeon, of Kilnaborris, Banagher, Ireland ; and Eva Margaret Craig. Born at Waterbeach, Cambridgeshire, 10 Aug. 1883. School : Shrewsbury, under the Rev. H. W. Moss. Admitted 1 Oct. 1902.
>Resided four terms.

Cox, Ralph : son of William Cox, merchant, of Mayflower, Devonshire, Bermuda; and Norah Jane Cox. Born at Bermuda, 24 Oct. 1884. Schools: Saltus, Bermuda ; and Bromsgrove, under Mr H. Millington, M.A., and Mr F. J. R. Hendy, M.A. Admitted 1 Oct. 1902.
>B.A. 1905 ; M.B., B.C. 1909. Nat. Sci. Tripos, Part I, Class 2, 1905.

Deck, Samuel Frederick : son of Frederick Seaman Deck, agricultural agent, of Beccles; and Sarah Elizabeth Howes. Born at Westleton, Suffolk,

4 May 1883. School: Felsted, under the Rev. H. A. Dalton. Admitted 1 Oct. 1902.

B.A. 1906. Hist. Tripos, Part I, Class 2, 1904; Part II, Class 2, 1905. Entrance Scholar, 1902. Scholar, 1903-5. Assistant Collector in British East Africa, 1907- . Address (1908), Naiwasha.

Duke, Herbert Lyndhurst: son of Surgeon-Col. Joshua Duke, Indian Medical Service, of Kashmir; and Fanny Harriet Hall. Born at Lyndhurst, Hampshire, 31 Aug. 1883. School: Eastbourne, under Mr H. R. Thomson. Admitted 1 Oct. 1902.

B.A. 1905; M.B., B.C. 1910. Nat. Sci. Tripos, Part I, Class 1, 1905. Entrance Scholar, 1902. Scholar, 1903-5. Research Student, 1906. Captain of Lawn Tennis Club, 1904.

Ellis, John Henry: son of George William Ellis, L.R.C.P., L.R.C.S., of Bishop Auckland; and Rosa Shafto Stratton. Born at High Bondgate, Bishop Auckland, 15 July 1883. School: Sherborne, under the Rev. F. B. Westcott. Admitted 1 Oct. 1902.

B.A. 1905; M.A. 1910. Clergy Training School, 1905. Ordained deacon (York), 1906; priest, 1909. Curate of Campsall, 1906-9; of Stokesley, 1909-

Ezechiel, Victor Gerald: son of Captain James Aloysius Ezechiel, Indian Army, of Wandsworth Common; and Scholastica Rosa Fernandez. Born at Poona, India, 31 Oct. 1883. Educated at King's College School, Wimbledon, under the Rev. C. W. Bourne, M.A. Admitted 1 Oct. 1902.

B.A. 1905. Math. Tripos, Part I (br. 1st Jun. Opt.), 1905. Exhibitioner, 1902. Eastern Cadetship, 1907. A remarkable violinist.

Finlay, Richard Vary Kirkman: son of Kirkman Finlay, East India merchant, of Ealing; and Jane Vary Campbell. Born at Helensburgh, Scotland, 12 May 1883. Educated at the University College School, London, under Mr J. L. Paton, M.A. Admitted 1 Oct. 1902.

Resided ten terms.

Fitzgerald, Harold Snowdon: son of Durham Walker Fitzgerald, shipbuilder, of Wood Terrace, South Shields; and Mary Agnes Foreman. Born at Westoe, South Shields, 27 June 1884. School: Durham, under the Rev. W. Hobhouse and the Rev. A. E. Holland. Admitted 1 Oct. 1902.

B.A. 1907. In banking business (1907) at Riding Mill, Northumberland.

Flint, Charles Nigel: son of Arthur Flint, M.D., surgeon, of Westgate-on-Sea; and Amy Fox. Born at Westgate-on-Sea, 14 Aug. 1883. School: Winchester, under the Rev. Dr Fearon. Admitted 1 Oct. 1902.

Resided three terms. Farming in Queensland (1908).

Forsyth, James Peters: son of John Forsyth, clerk, of Lancaster; and Margaret Peters. Born at Victoria Road, West Cowes, 22 April 1883. School· Lancaster, under the Rev. G. A. Stocks, M.A. Admitted 1 Oct. 1902.

B.A. 1905. Math. Tripos, Part I (br. 8th Wrangler), 1905. Entrance Scholar, 1902. Scholar, 1903-5. Clerk in Somerset House, 1906- .

Glaisyer, Henry Ernest: son of Henry Glaisyer, solicitor, of Edgbaston; and Edith Glaisyer. Born at George Road, Edgbaston, 27 Nov. 1882. School:

King Edward's, Birmingham, under Mr R. Cary Gilson, M.A. Admitted
1 Oct. 1902.
> LL.B. 1905. Law Tripos, Part I, Class 1, 1904 ; Part II, Class 2, 1905.
> Called to the Bar, Lincoln's Inn, 28 Jan. 1907.

Gray, Henry Malcolm Franklin : son of Arthur Gray, Fellow of Jesus College,
Cambridge; and Alice Honora Gell. Born at Cambridge, 28 June 1883.
School: Aldenham, under the Rev. J. Kennedy, M.A., and the Rev. A. H.
Cooke, M.A. Admitted 1 Oct. 1902. Brother of William, IV. (1) 48.
> B.A. 1905. Class. Tripos, Part I, Class 3, 1905. Exhibitioner, 1902.
> Master at the Public School, Shanghai, 1907–

Hallowes, Basil John Knight: son of the Rev. John Francis Tooke Hallowes
(of the College, II. 367), congregational minister, of Cambridge; and Frances
Sarah Knight. Born at Huddersfield Road, Barnsley, 27 Aug. 1884. Edu-
cated at King Edward's School, Birmingham ; Wesley College, Sheffield ; and
Mill Hill School, under J. D. McClure, LL.D. Admitted 1 Oct. 1902.
Brother of Kenneth, II. 558.
> B.A. 1905. Hist. Tripos, Part I, Class 2, 1904 ; Part II, Class 2, 1905.
> Selected Candidate for I.C.S., 1908. Appointed to Upper Bengal,
> 1909.

Harding, Edmund Wilfrid: son of George Robinson Harding, art dealer, of
Beckenham ; and Mary Ann Wareham. Born at Wimbledon, 20 Feb.
1883. School: Merchant Taylors', under the Rev. Dr Baker and the Rev.
J. A. Nairn, B.D. Admitted 1 Oct. 1902.
> B.A. 1905. Nat. Sci. Tripos, Part I, Class 3, 1905.

Hargreaves, Arthur Gerard: son of James Hargreaves, J.P., corn merchant,
of Heasandford, Burnley ; and Rachel Jane Strachan. Born at Burnley,
30 Jan. 1882. School : Denstone College, under the Rev. D. Edwardes, M.A.
Admitted 1 Oct. 1902.
> Resided seven terms.

Hatten, Geoffrey: son of Charles Edward Hatten, solicitor, of Gravesend ; and
Florence Esther Elizabeth Lawson. Born at Park Hill, Richmond, Surrey,
20 May 1884. School: Tonbridge, under the Rev. Dr C. C. Tancock.
Admitted 1 Oct. 1902.
> B.A., Mus.Bac. 1905. Musical Scholar, 1902 ; Stewart of Rannoch
> Scholarship for Sacred Music, 1903. Solicitor (1908), at Gravesend.

Heald, Charles Brehmer: son of Walter Heald, railway secretary, of Bromley ;
and Emily Isabel Krabbe. Born at Bowden, Cheshire, 3 Dec. 1882.
School: Tonbridge, under the Rev. Dr C. C. Tancock. Admitted 1 Oct. 1902.
Brother of Walter, IV. (1) 48.
> B.A. 1905 ; M.A. 1910. Nat. Sci. Tripos, Part I, Class 2, 1905.
> Captain, C Co., C.U.R.V., 1906. In medical practice.

Heurtley, Walter Abel : son of Rev. Charles Abel Heurtley, Rector of Ashington,
Sussex ; and Mary Elizabeth Brown. Born at Ashington, 24 Oct. 1882.
School: Uppingham, under the Rev. Dr E. C. Selwyn. Admitted 1 Oct.
1902.
> B.A. 1905. Class. Tripos, Part I, Class 2, 1905. Entrance Scholar, 1902.
> Scholar, 1903–5 Master at the Oratory School, Birmingham, 1907– .

Higgin, Robert Francis : son of James Walter Higgin, gentleman, of Oban, N.B.;
and Sarah Emma Roberts. Born at Oban, 10 Dec. 1884. School:
Giggleswick, under the Rev. George Style, M.A. Admitted 1 Oct. 1902.
B.A. 1905.

Hills, Arthur Hyde: son of Walter Hills, pharmaceutical chemist, of Primrose
Hill Road, London; and Louisa Woods. Born at Park Village West,
London, 26 Oct. 1882. School: Aldenham, under the Rev. J. Kennedy and
the Rev. A. H. Cooke. Admitted 1 Oct. 1902.
B.A. 1905. Class. Tripos, Part I, Class 2, 1905. Exhibitioner, 1902. In
the firm of J. Brinton, carpet manufacturers, Stourport, 1907–

Hollis, Walter: son of Walter Dawson Hollis, auctioneer, of Whitekirk, near Leeds;
and Mary Ellen Woodhead. Born at Garforth, near Leeds, 22 Sept. 1883.
School: Felsted, under the Rev. H. A. Dalton. Admitted 1 Oct. 1902.
B.A. 1906. Ordained deacon (Southwark), 1908; priest, 1910. Curate
at Caterham, 1908– .

Horsfall, John : son of Joseph John Mendelssohn Horsfall, merchant, of Den-
holme, Wimbledon; and Thirza Sophia Skinner. Born at The Downs,
Wimbledon, 26 Sept. 1883. School: Tonbridge, under the Rev. C. C. Tancock,
D.D. Admitted 1 Oct. 1902.
B.A. 1906. Chapel Clerk, 1904. University football player (Rugby), 1903.
In the firm of J. Brinton, carpet manufacturers, Stourport, 1907–8.

Howlden, Richard Cyril: son of Herbert Linley Howlden, managing director,
of Renishaw Hall, Chesterfield (afterwards, 1907–, of Park Grange, Sheffield);
and Mary Florence Foster. Born at Sheffield, 18 June 1883. School:
Cheltenham College, under the Rev. R. Waterfield. Admitted 1 Oct. 1902.
Resided three terms. In business as railway contractor and general export
merchant (1908).

Johnson, Harold Cecil John : son of Arthur John Johnson, gentleman, of Rayne,
Essex; and Alice Dickinson. Born at Bolton-le-Sands, 28 April 1883.
School: Felsted, under the Rev. H. A. Dalton. Admitted 1 Oct. 1902.
B.A. 1906.

Khan, Framjee Pestonjee : son of Bhikhajee Khan, merchant, of Bombay. Born
at Bombay, 1 Dec. 1883. Schools: St Xavier's, Bombay; and Dulwich
College, under Mr A. H. Gilkes, M.A. Admitted 1 Oct. 1902.
B.A. 1905 ; M.A. 1909. Pupil of Messrs Baker & Shelford, civil engineers
(1907).

Kitching, Cecil Ross : son of Lieut.-Col. Charles William Ross Kitching, of
Birkenhead; and Florence Jeannette Bell. Born at Walmer, 11 Nov.
1883. Educated under Rev. T. L. Tudor Fitzjohn, at Cardington Vicarage.
Admitted 1 Oct. 1902.
B.A. 1905; M.A. 1909. Theol. Tripos, Part I, 1905. Ordained deacon
(Meath), 1907; priest, 1908. Curate of Athlone, 1907–10; of Castle-
knock, 1910– .

Lander, Harold Drew : son of Frederick Charles Lander, gentleman, of St Minver,
Cornwall; and Elizabeth Drew Cock. Born at Bodmin, Cornwall, 4 Jan.
1884. Educated at Kelly College, Tavistock, under the Rev. W. H. David.
Admitted 1 Oct. 1902.
B.A. 1906.

Langley, Frederick Owen: son of Frederick Theobald Langley, solicitor, of Tettenhall, Wolverhampton; and Eleanor Marianne Owen. Born at Tettenhall Road, Wolverhampton, 9 May 1883. School: Uppingham, under the Rev. E. C. Selwyn. Admitted 1 Oct. 1902.
    B.A., LL.B. 1905. Law Tripos, Part I, Class 2, June, 1904; Part II, Class 2, 1905. Entrance Scholar, 1902. Scholar, 1903-5. Called to the Bar, Inner Temple, 21 Apr. 1907. On the staff of "Punch."

Lauderdale, Edward Maitland: son of the Rev. Edward Lauderdale, of St Mark's Vicarage, Lincoln; and Mary Jane Brown. Born at Great Grimsby, 28 July 1883. School: Lincoln, under Mr F. H. Chambers, M.A. Admitted 1 Oct. 1902.
    B.A. 1905. Nat. Sci. Tripos, Part I, Class 2, 1905. In medical practice.

Leach Lewis, William: son of William Leach Lewis, J.P., headmaster of Margate College, of St Peter's, Isle of Thanet; and Anna Jane Masters. Born at Margate, 15 Oct. 1880. School: Aldenham, under the Rev. J. Kennedy, M.A. Admitted 1 Oct. 1902.
    Resided six terms. Master, with his brother, of Margate College (1908).

Ledeboer, John Henry: son of Herman Arnold Ledeboer, calico printer, of Fallowfield; and Bernardina Antonia Cornelia Van der Linden. Born at Fallowfield, Manchester, 27 Nov. 1883. School: Tonbridge, under the Rev. C. C. Tancock. Admitted 1 Oct. 1902.
    B.A. 1905. Med. and Mod. Lang. Tripos, Class 1, 1905. Entrance Scholar, 1902. Scholar, 1903-5. Captain of Rugby Football Club, 1904. Journalist and author.

Leney, Ronald John Barcham: son of Augustus Leney, brewer, of Wateringbury, Kent; and Kate Green. Born at Tovil House, Maidstone, 8 Aug. 1883. School: Uppingham, under the Rev. E. C. Selwyn, D.D. Admitted 1 Oct. 1902.
    B.A. 1905. Nat. Sci. Tripos, Part I, 1905.

Lewin, William George: son of Frederick Dealtry Lewin, merchant, of Folkestone; and Christina Hutchinson. Born at Kidbrook, 6 Jan. 1883. School: Oundle, under Mr F. W. Sanderson, M.A. Admitted 1 Oct. 1902.
    Entrance Scholar, 1902. Resided four terms. Theol. Assoc. of King's Coll., London. Ordained deacon (London), 1908; priest, 1909. Curate of St John on Bethnal Green, 1908- .

Lloyd, Alan Hubert: son of John Lloyd, merchant, of Cheadle Hulme; and Mary Esther Southworth. Born at Cheadle Hulme, 30 Aug. 1883. School: King William's College, Isle of Man, under the Rev. E. H. Kempson, M.A. Admitted 1 Oct. 1902. Brother of Idwal, II. 553, and of Harold, IV. (1) 7.
    B.A. 1905. Class. Tripos, Part I, Class 1, 1905. Entrance Scholar, 1902. Scholar, 1903-5. Members' Latin Essay Prize, 1905. I.C.S. 1907 (Burmah). Bhaonagar Medallist, 1907.

Loram, William Carpenter: son of Albert Edmund Loram, accountant, of Maritzburg, Natal; and Alice Hipkiss. Born at Pietermaritzburg, 5 May 1883. Educated at Pietermaritzburg College, under Mr R. D. Clarke, M.A. Admitted 1 Oct. 1902.
    Resided three terms. Returned to Natal.

Macquarrie, Edmund Jeffrey: son of Charles John Macquarrie, merchant, of Georgetown, British Guiana; and Florence Jeffrey. Born at Georgetown, British Guiana, 28 Dec. 1883. Educated at Stanley House, Bridge of Allan; and Queen's College, Georgetown, under Mr J. A. Potbury, M.A. Admitted 1 Oct. 1902.

    B.A., LL.B. 1905. Law Tripos, Part I, Class 2, 1904; Part II, Class 2, 1905. Called to the Bar (Inner Temple), 1906. Practising at Belize, British Guiana.

Martin, Walter Baird: son of John Martin, sheep farmer, Puruatanga Station, Martinborough, Wellington, New Zealand; and Henrietta Louisa Collins. Born at Huangarua, near Martinborough, N.Z., 31 July 1883. Educated at Wanganui College, N.Z., under Mr W. Simpson, B.A. Admitted 1 Oct. 1902.

    B.A. 1905. LL.B. 1906. Law Tripos, Part I, Class 3, 1904; Part II, Class 2, 1906. Called to the Bar (Inner Temple), 1907. Returned to New Zealand, 1908.

Mayhew, Arthur Farr: son of Arthur Farr Mayhew, stockbroker, of Portinscale Road, E. Putney; and Louisa Tickner. Born at Balham, London, 19 Aug. 1883. School: St Aubyn's, Lowestoft, under Mr J. Bruce Payne, M.A. Admitted 1 Oct. 1902.

    B.A. 1906; M.A. 1909. Ordained deacon (St Albans), 1907; priest, 1908. Curate at Walthamstow, 1907– .

Messiter, Cyril Cassan: son of Matthew Arden Messiter, surgeon, of Dudley; and Isabella Houghton. Born at Dudley, 23 May 1884. School: Repton, under the Rev. L. Ford, M.A. Admitted 1 Oct. 1902.

    B.A. 1906.

Mitchell, Alec Lea: son of William Mitchell, cotton spinner, of Sutton, Macclesfield; and Jessie Froane. Born at The Hockley, Sutton, 12 April 1883. Educated at Sutherland House, Folkestone; and by private tutors. Admitted 1 Oct. 1902.

    B.A. 1905. Mech. Sci. Tripos, Part I, Class 2, 1905. In the engineering profession; with Douglas, Fox and Co., Westminster (1910).

Nicholson, Cuthbert John: son of Cuthbert Ismay Nicholson, merchant, of Devizes; and Louisa Alexandrina Turner. Born at Grove Road, Sutton, Surrey, 21 June 1884. School: Charterhouse, under the Rev. Dr Rendall. Admitted 1 Oct. 1902.

    B.A. 1905.

Oke, Robert William Leslie: son of Alfred William Oke, solicitor, of Cumberland Place, Southampton; and Katherine Coldcall Unwin. Born at Beacondale Road, Norwood, 12 Feb. 1884. Schools: Highfield, Southampton; Sherborne; and Rugby, under the Rev. H. A. James, D.D. Admitted 1 Oct. 1902.

    Resided one term. Admitted 1904 at Corpus Christi College. B.A. 1908.

Parsons, Harold: son of John Parsons, timber merchant, of Lewes; and Mary Matilda Madgwick. Born at Priory Crescent, Lewes, 24 Feb. 1884. Schools: Mill Hill; and Bradfield College, under the Rev. H. B. Gray, D.D. Admitted 1 Oct. 1902.

    B.A. 1905; M.B., B.C. 1910. Nat. Sci. Tripos, Part I, Class 2, 1905. In the Federated Malay States (1911).

Peshall, Samuel Frederick : son of the Rev. Samuel Peshall, Rector of Oldberrow-cum-Morton Bagot ; and Constance Eyre. Born at Oldberrow Rectory, 18 Nov. 1882. School : Rossall, under the Rev. J. P. Way, D.D. Admitted 1 Oct. 1902.
> B.A. 1905. Class. Tripos, Part I, Class 2, 1905. Entrance Scholar, 1902. Captain, Association Football Club, 1904. In calico-printing business (the Gartside Co., of Manchester), 1908- .

Priestley, Reginald Fawcett : son of James Henry Priestley, schoolmaster, of West Monmouthshire School, Pontypool ; and Mary Rogerson. Born at Baylie Street, Stourbridge, 22 June 1885. School : West Monmouthshire County School, under Mr J. H. Priestley, B.A. Admitted 1 Oct. 1902.
> B.A. 1905 ; M.B., B.C. 1909. Nat. Sci. Tripos, Part I, Class 2, 1905. Exhibitioner, 1904.

Randles, James Gilbert Heighway : son of James Randles, gentleman, of Pietermaritzburg, Natal ; and Mary Heighway. Born at Sydenham, Natal, 5 Aug. 1876. Educated at Leamington College, under Dr Wood ; and Maritzburg College (Natal), under Mr R. D. Clarke, M.A. Admitted 1 Oct. 1902.
> B.A. 1905. Law Tripos, Part I, Class 3, 1904 ; Part II, 1905. Called to the Bar (Inner Temple), 19 Nov. 1906. Returned to South Africa.

Rayner, Arthur Errington : son of Henry Rayner, physician, of Hampstead ; and Rosa Field. Born at Hanwell, Middlesex, 6 Nov. 1883. School : Marlborough College, under the Rev. G. C. Bell. Admitted 1 Oct. 1902. Brother of Edwin, IV. (1) 51.
> B.A. 1905. Nat. Sci. Tripos, Part I, 1905. In medical practice.

Rhodes, William Atkinson : son of William Atkinson Rhodes, dentist, of Selwyn Gardens, Cambridge ; and Kate Louise Palmer. Born at Trumpington Street, Cambridge, 28 July 1884. Educated at Perse School, Cambridge, and Weymouth College, under Mr H. C. Barnes-Lawrence. Admitted 1 Oct. 1902. Brother of Sidney, IV. (1) 96.
> B.A. 1905 ; M.A. 1910. Solicitor in Cambridge (1911).

Ripley, Henry Edward : son of Henry Ripley, J.P., of Donabate, Cheltenham ; and Emma Alice Seaton. Born at Rawdon, Yorkshire, 7 Jan. 1884. School : Charterhouse, under Dr Rendall. Admitted 1 Oct. 1902.
> B.A. 1905. In motor-car business at Gloucester, 1908.

Romer, Carrol : son of Edgar Romer, stockbroker, of Elvaston Place, London ; and Blanche Mandoline Clark. Born at Gloucester Terrace, London, 20 Jan. 1883. School : Eastbourne, under Mr H. R. Thomson. Admitted 1 Oct. 1902.
> B.A. 1905 ; M.A. 1909. Mech. Sci. Tripos, Part I, Class 2, 1905. Entrance Scholar, 1902. In the Egyptian Civil Service, 1906–7. Admitted at the Inner Temple, 5 March 1908.

Ross, Nigel Douglas Carne : son of Joseph Carne Ross, physician, of Withington ; and Kate Selwyn. Born at Shian Lodge, Penzance, 21 Dec. 1882. School : Uppingham, under the Rev. E. C. Selwyn, D.D. Admitted 1 Oct. 1902.
> B.A. 1905. Captain of the Cricket and Hockey Clubs, 1901–5. Master at Stoke House School, Stoke Poges (1910).

Routh, Laurence Melville: son of Alfred Curtis Routh, surgeon, St Leonards-on-Sea; and Annie Julia Adèle Routh. Born at 33, Marina, St Leonards-on-Sea, 28 July 1883. School: Tonbridge, under the Rev. J. Wood, D.D., and the Rev. C. C. Tancock, D.D. Admitted 1 Oct. 1902.
> B.C. 1910; M.B. 1911.

Sargeaunt, George Montague: son of Colonel Charles Chester Sargeaunt, of Granville Park, Lewisham; and Rosa Powell. Born at Waterfield Terrace, Blackheath, 4 May 1883. School: Shrewsbury, under the Rev. H. W. Moss, M.A. Admitted 1 Oct. 1902.
> B.A. 1905; M.A. 1909. Class. Tripos, Part I, Class 1, 1905. Entrance Scholar, 1902. Master at St Edward's School, Oxford (1909).

Tapp, Theodore Arthur: son of Charles James Tapp, stockbroker, of The Hill, Bromley; and Olga Henriette Marie Andreae. Born at Scott's Lane, Shortlands, Kent, 5 April 1883. School: Rugby, under the Rev. H. A. James, D.D. Admitted 1 Oct. 1902.
> Resided four terms. On the Stock Exchange.

Tidman, Oscar Paul: son of Paul Frederick Tidman, C.M.G., East India merchant; and Frances Amelia Kershaw. Born at Blackheath, 30 Nov. 1876. Schools: Rugby, under the Rev. Dr Percival and the Rev Dr James; and Redburn, Eastbourne. Admitted 1 Oct. 1902.
> B.A. 1906. Chapel Clerk, 1904. Assistant Master at St Christopher's School, Eastbourne (1909).

Vicary, Ronald Herbert: son of Robert Vicary, merchant, of Churchills, Newton Abbot; and Harriet Palmer. Born at Churchills, Newton Abbot, 12 March 1884. Educated at Newton College; Bradworthy School; and at Wintercroft, Moretonhampstead, under Mr R. Courtland, M.A. Admitted 1 Oct. 1902.
> Resided three years.

von Kaufmann, Günther Jacob Ferdinand: son of Baron Ludwig Merz Josef von Kaufmann, of Villa Colombaia, Bello Sguardo, Florence; and Bianca Landau. Born at Viktoria Strasse 8, Berlin, 20 June 1884. Educated at Villa Longchamp, Lausanne, under the Rev. Paul Kummer; and with le Pasteur Springer, Wundersleben, Germany. Admitted 1 Oct. 1902.
> Resided three terms.

Wedd, Edward Parker Wallman: son of Edward Arthur Wedd, J.P., of Great Wakering, Essex; and Katherine May. Born at Whitehall, Great Wakering, 1 Sept. 1883. School: Cheltenham College, under the Rev. R. Waterfield. Admitted 1 Oct. 1902.
> B.A. 1906. Captain of the Boat Club, 1904–5. Rowed in the University Boat, 1905. 2nd Lieut. Essex Yeomanry (1908).

Whitworth, John: son of William Whitworth, of Lapworth, near Birmingham; and Grace Appleyard Holdsworth. Born at Snitterfield, Warwickshire, 31 May 1882. Educated at Malvern College, under the Rev. St J. Grey and the Rev. S. R. James; and at Wellingore, near Lincoln, under Mr F. Adams. Admitted 1 Oct. 1902.
> Resided five terms. Farming (1908).

Williams, Arthur Donald John Bedward : son of Arthur Evan Williams, civil engineer, of Hammersmith Road, London; and Eleanor Martha Bedward. Born at Bollingham House, Eardisley, Herefordshire, 10 Jan. 1883. School: St Paul's, under Mr F. W. Walker. Admitted 1 Oct. 1902.
B.A. 1905. In medical practice.

Williams, Arthur John : son of Egbert Williams, L.R.C.P., M.R.C.S., of Bridgend, Glam.; and Annie Williams. Born at Llandovery, 27 March 1885. School: Felsted, under the Rev. H. A. Dalton, M.A. Admitted 1 Oct. 1902.
B.A. 1905. Master at a Preparatory School, Freshfield, 1907- .

Williams, Joseph Coryton Stanley: son of Captain George Stanley Williams (10th Hussars), of Kirkby Mallory (deceased); and Adelaide Elizabeth Manders. Born at Kirkby Mallory, 10 March 1884. Educated at Temple Grove, East Sheen; at Harrow, under Dr Welldon and Dr Wood; and at Redburn, Eastbourne, under Mr P. J. Vinter. Residing with his uncle and guardian, J. G. Williams, Pendley Manor, Tring. Admitted 1 Oct. 1902.
Resided eight terms.

Williams, Richard Gregson : son of John Williams, surgeon, of Bryn Castell, Carnarvon; and Mary Gregson. Born at Castle Square, Carnarvon, 24 June 1883. Schools: Arnold House, Llandulas, under the Rev. J. C. C. Pipon; and Rossall, under the Rev. J. P. Way, D.D. Admitted 1 Oct. 1902.
B.A. 1905. Nat. Sci. Tripos, Part I, Class 3, 1905. Mining engineer, Mysore Gold Mines, India (1908).

Wilson, Philip Frederick : son of Brigade-Surgeon Frederick Robert Wilson; and Anna Lyons. Born at Perth, N.B., 14 Feb. 1884. Schools: Gisburne House, Watford, under Mr W. H. Wright, M.A.; and Aldenham, under the Rev. A. H. Cooke. Admitted 1 Oct. 1902.
B.A. 1905; B.C. 1911. Nat. Sci. Tripos, Part I, Class 2, 1905.

Wood, Norris Ramsden : son of William Edward Ramsden Wood, M.D., of Uplyme, Devon; and Alice Louisa Henry. Born at Bethlem Royal Hospital, London, 14 Jan. 1883. School: Bradfield, under the Rev. H. B. Gray, D.D. Admitted 1 Oct. 1902.
Resided two terms. Farming at Bulwer, Canada (1908).

Wyman, Bernard : son of Henry Wyman, brewer, of Hemel Hempstead; and Marion Steer. Born at Hemel Hempstead, 4 Aug. 1883. School: Clifton College, under the Rev. Canon Glazebrook. Admitted 1 Oct. 1902. Brother of Henry, IV. (1) 10.
B.A. 1905. Nat. Sci. Tripos, Part I, Class 3, 1905. Master at Bradfield College, 1907. Chemist, with Messrs Brunner, Mond & Co. (1909).

Binns, Cuthbert Charles Harber : son of George Jonathan Binns, mining engineer, of Duffield, Derby; and May Constance Smith. Born at Dunedin, New Zealand, 3 March 1884. School: Repton, under the Rev. W. M. Furneaux, the Rev. H. M. Burge and the Rev. L. G. B. Ford. Admitted 8 Jan. 1903.
B.A. 1905. Nat. Sci. Tripos, Part I, Class 3, 1905. In medical practice.

MICHAELMAS 1903 TO MICHAELMAS 1904.

(Tutors: Mr Gallop, Mr Buckland and Mr Hardy.)

Adams, James Wilmot: son of James Adams, M.D., F.R.C.S., of Eastbourne;
and Eliza Anne Lowry. Born at Ashburton, Devon, 9 Feb. 1884. Schools:
Eastbourne, under the Rev. C. Crowden, D.D., and the Rev. A. Bayfield, M.A.;
and Tonbridge, under the Rev. C. C. Tancock, D.D. Admitted 1 Oct. 1903.
B.A. 1906. Nat. Sci. Tripos, Part I, Class 2, 1906.

Alderson, Gerald Graham: son of John Alderson, timber merchant, of Grosvenor
Villas, Newcastle; and Jane Isabella Rennoldson. Born at Loraine
Crescent, Newcastle-on-Tyne, 18 July 1884. Schools: St George's, Gosforth,
Newcastle; and Durham, under the Rev. W. Hobhouse, M.A., and the Rev.
A. E. Holland, M.A. Admitted 1 Oct. 1903.
B.A. 1906; B.C., M.B. 1910. Nat. Sci. Tripos, Part I, Class 1, 1906 ·
Part II, Class 2, 1907. Scholar, 1906.

Arnot, David William: son of William Joseph Arnot, schoolmaster, of Edgbaston;
and Louise Marie Charpentier. Born at York Road, Edgbaston, 11 Feb.
1884. School: King Edward VI, Birmingham, under the Rev. A. R. Vardy
M.A., and Mr R. Cary Gilson, M.A. Admitted 1 Oct. 1903.
B.A. 1906. Math. Tripos, Part I (br. 31st Wrangler), 1906. Entrance
Scholar, 1903. Scholar, 1904–6. Eastern Cadetship, 1907.

Atkins, Basil Sydney: son of Sydney George Atkins, farmer and valuer,
of Wymondham; and Katherine Hotblack. Born at Park Farm, Kimberley,
Norfolk, 4 April 1885. School: St Aubyn's, Lowestoft, under Mr J. Bruce
Payne, M.A. Admitted 1 Oct. 1903.
Resided four terms. 2nd Lieut. Suffolk Regt.; serving in 11th Rajputs
(1908).

Barker, Robert Lewis: son of John Barker, officer in H.M. Mint, Victoria,
Australia; and Christine Leslie Russell. Born at St Hilda, Melbourne,
Australia, 13 Oct. 1885. Educated at The Wick School, Brighton, under
Mr L. S. Thring; and Bradfield College, under the Rev. H. B. Gray, D.D.
Admitted 1 Oct. 1903.
B.A. 1906; B.C. 1911. Nat. Sci. Tripos, Part I, Class 3, 1906.

Batterbury, Geoffrey Richard: son of George Henry Batterbury, M.D., of
Codford, Wimborne, Dorset; and Jessie Flower. Born at West Borough,
Wimborne, 21 April 1884. Schools: Wimborne, under Mr E. Fynes-Clinton;
and Felsted, under the Rev. H. A. Dalton. Admitted 1 Oct. 1903.
B.A. 1906; M.A. 1911. Nat. Sci. Tripos, Part I, Class 3, 1906. Master of
Preparatory School (Rokeby, The Downs, Wimbledon), 1909– .

Bewley, Edward Neville: son of Frank Bewley, chartered accountant, of Teaveley,
Ashbourne; and Sarah Ann Davies. Born at Liverpool, 2 Feb. 1885.
Schools: Birkenhead, under the Rev. A. Sloman; and Ashton, Dunstable,
under Mr L. R. C. Thring, M.A. Admitted 1 Oct. 1903.
B.A. 1906. Law Tripos, Part I, Class 1, 1905; Part II, Class 2, 1906.
Scholar, 1905.

Billing, Edward: son of the Rev. George Billing, M.A., of Platt Vicarage, Borough Green; and Caroline Flora Gabbett. Born at Park Road, West Dulwich, 24 Nov. 1884. Educated at Dover College, under the Rev. W. C. Compton, M.A. Admitted 1 Oct. 1903.
> B.A. 1906. Nat. Sci. Tripos, Part I, Class 2, 1906. Tancred Student, 1903–

Birks, Alan Herrenden: son of Thomas Birks, maltster, of Oakleigh, Worksop; and Emily Isabel Lenton. Born at Potter Street, Worksop, 1 Dec. 1883. School: Repton, under the Rev. L. Ford. Admitted 1 Oct. 1903.
> B.A. 1906. Captain, Association Football, 1906–7; University player, 1906.

Blaikie, Cuthbert James: son of James Andrew Blaikie, M.A., civil servant, formerly Fellow of the College, of Lancaster Road, West Norwood; and Georgina Jane Dunbar. Born at Edinburgh, 22 Oct. 1884. School: Dulwich College, under Mr A. H. Gilkes, M.A. Admitted 1 Oct. 1903.
> B.A. 1906. Nat. Sci. Tripos, Part I, Class 2, 1906. Entrance Scholar, 1903. Scholar, 1904–6. In medical practice.

Bromley, Lancelot: son of John Bromley, civil servant, of Elsham Road, Kensington; and Marie Louise Bowman. Born at Coverdale Road, London, 18 Feb. 1885. School: St Paul's, under Mr F. W. Walker, M.A. Admitted 1 Oct. 1903.
> B.A. 1906; M.B., B.C. 1911. Nat. Sci. Tripos, Part I, Class 3, 1906. Captain of the Cricket Club, 1905–6. In medical practice.

Cawston, Frederick Gordon: son of Samuel Cawston, stockbroker, of Bromley Hill, Kent; and Agnes Isabella Boys. Born at Bromley Hill, 23 Jan. 1885. School: South Eastern, Ramsgate, under the Rev. T. W. Tracy and Mr C. Morris, M.A. Admitted 1 Oct. 1903.
> B.A. 1906; M.B., B.C. 1910. Nat. Sci. Tripos, Part I, Class 3, 1906.

Chick, Herbert George: son of Alfred Chick, of Foots Cray; and Elizabeth R. Hamp. Born at Foots Cray, Kent, 19 Nov. 1882. Schools: Marlborough House, Sidcup, under Mr E. Hawkins, M.A.; and Tonbridge, under the Rev. Joseph Wood, D.D., and the Rev. C. C. Tancock, D.D. Admitted 1 Oct. 1903.
> Resided six terms as Exhibitioner and Student Interpreter. Russian Scholar, 1904. Student Interpreter in Persia (1905).

Compton, Albert George William: son of George William Compton, gentleman, of Cleveland Road, Ealing; and Rosina Vicary. Born at De Beers, Kimberley, South Africa, 30 Sept. 1885. Schools: Kent House, Eastbourne, under the Rev. C. P. Hutchinson; and Bradfield College, under the Rev. H. B. Gray, D.D. Admitted 1 Oct. 1903.
> B.A. 1906.

de Saram, Richard Frederick Henry Shelton: son of Richard F. de Saram, proctor and notary, of Colombo, Ceylon; and Louise Selina Dickman. Born at Colombo, 25 Sept. 1876. School: St Thomas', Colombo, under the Rev. C. F. Miller, M.A. Admitted 1 Oct. 1903.
> Resided six terms. Admitted at the Inner Temple.

Dodd, Walter Edward Fagan : son of the Rev. Edward Sutton Dodd, M.A., Vicar of Milton Ernest, Bedfordshire; and Harriette Agnes Georgiana Fagan. Born at Milton Ernest, 30 July 1883. School: St Edward's, Oxford, under the Rev. T. W. Hudson, M.A. Admitted 1 Oct. 1903.
  B.A. 1906. Theol. Tripos, Part I, 1906. Choral Exhibitioner, 1903, Cuddesdon Theological College, 1906. Ordained deacon (Birmingham), 1907; Curate of St Hilda's, Marlowe Woods, 1907–

Franklin, Cecil Douglas Gilbey : son of Douglas Thomas Franklin, estate agent, of Thaxted, Essex; and Florence Newport Mossman. Born at Thaxted, 10 Nov. 1885. School: Saffron Walden Grammar, under Mr H. B. Stanwell, M.A., and the Rev. A. D. Perrott, M.A. Admitted 1 Oct. 1903.
  Resided seven terms.

Gosse, Alfred Hope : son of John Gosse, M.R.C.S., of Wallaroo, S. Australia ; and Mary Bennet. Born at Wallaroo, 27 Aug. 1882. School: Saint Peter's Collegiate, Adelaide, under the Rev. H. Girdlestone. Admitted 1 Oct. 1903. Brother of Reginald, iv. (1) 114.
  B.A. 1906; M.A. 1910. Nat. Sci. Tripos, Part I, Class 3, 1906. Captain of the Boat Club, 1905.

Gray, Douglas Leslie : son of John Selby Gray, coal merchant, of West Hampstead ; and Alice Markham Bradley. Born at Acol Road, West Hampstead, 8 Aug. 1884. Schools: Henley House, Kilburn, under the Rev. H. V. Goudby, M.A.; and Felsted, under the Rev. H. A. Dalton, M.A. Admitted 1 Oct. 1903.
  B.A. 1906. Captain of the Cricket Club, 1905

Greatrex, Ferdinand Cecil : son of Major Ferdinand William Greatrex, Royal Dragoons, of Marine Parade, Brighton ; and Florence Manuelle. Born at Queen's Gate, London, 12 July 1884. School: Haileybury College, under Canon the Hon. E. Lyttelton. Admitted 1 Oct. 1903.
  B.A. 1906. Med. and Mod. Lang. Tripos, Class 2, 1906. Entrance Scholar, 1903. Scholar, 1904–5. Student Interpreter in Japan, 1907– .

Gunter, William Hector : son of the Rev. William Gunter, Rector of Abberton, near Colchester ; and Elizabeth Rockett. Born at Little Sampford Rectory, near Saffron Walden, 25 July 1883. School: Framlingham, Suffolk, under the Rev. O. D. Inskip, M.A., LL.D. Admitted 1 Oct. 1903.
  B.A. 1906. Chapel Clerk, 1904. Ordained deacon (York), 1907; priest (Newcastle), 1909. Curate of Benwell, Newcastle-on-Tyne, 1907– .

Harrison, Cecil Cantilupe : son of Edward Tom Harrison, miller, of Lincoln ; and Elena Luisa Francesca Hillingford. Born at Lincoln, 17 March 1884. School: Sherborne, under the Rev. Canon F. B. Westcott. Admitted 1 Oct. 1903.
  B.A. 1907.

Hewett, Cecil Douglas : son of Robert Douglas Hewett, colonial civil service, of Kwala Lumpur, Selangor, Straits Settlements; and Sophie Gray. Born at Teluk Anson, Perak, 18 Aug. 1884. Schools: Bedford Grammar, under Mr J. S. Philpotts ; Hart House, Burnham, under the Rev. J. S. Thompson ; and Chigwell, under the Rev. R. D. Swallow. Admitted 1 Oct. 1903.
  Resided three terms.

Higgins, Sydney James : son of Thomas James Higgins, M.D., of Louth, Lincolnshire; and Hannah Riggall Foster. Born at Louth, 22 March 1884.
Schools : Louth Grammar, under the Rev. W. W. Hopwood, M.A.; and
Pocklington Grammar, under the Rev. C. F. Hutton, M.A. Admitted
1 Oct. 1903. Brother of Thomas, II. 539, and William, II. 548.
> B.A. 1906. Nat. Sci. Tripos, Part I, Class 3, 1906. In medical practice.

Holman, Charles Colgate : son of Thomas Holman, surgeon, of Gate House, East
Hoathly ; and Sylvia Lodge. Born at East Hoathly, Sussex, 18 Sept.
1884. School : Eastbourne College, under the Rev. M. A. Bayfield and
Mr H. B. Thomson. Admitted 1 Oct. 1903.
> B.A. 1906; M.B., B.C. 1909. Nat. Sci. Tripos, Part I, Class 2, 1905.
> Entrance Scholar, 1903. Scholar, 1904–6.

Holmes, Geoffrey : son of Godfrey Booker Holmes, banker's clerk, of Ashgate
Road, Chesterfield ; and Kate Elizabeth Hoskin. Born at Brampton
St Thomas', Derby, 2 June 1886. School : Chesterfield Grammar, under
Mr James Mansell, B.A. Admitted 1 Oct. 1903.
> B.C. 1910; M.B. 1911.

Hutchence, William Gordon : son of William Atkinson Hutchence, brick manu-
facturer, of Thorncliff, Saltburn, Yorkshire; and Mary Elizabeth Levick.
Born at Southfield, Northallerton, 12 July 1885. Educated at Middlesbrough
High School, under Mr Sewell ; and Coatham Grammar School, under Mr A.
Pryce, M.A. Admitted 1 Oct. 1903. Brother of Byron, IV. (1) 82.
> B.A. 1906; M.A. 1910. Law Tripos, Part I, Class 3, 1905; Part II,
> Class 3, 1906. Captain of Association Football Club, 1905.

Jones, Edward Hubert Gunter : son of Edward Jones, colliery proprietor, of
Snatchwood Park, Pontypool; and Susan Williams. Born at Snatchwood
Park, Pontypool, 11 March 1885. School : Clifton College, under the Rev.
M. G. Glazebrook. Admitted 1 Oct. 1903. Brother of Thomas, IV. (1) 5.
> B.A. 1906. Law Tripos, Part I, Class 3, 1905; Part II, Class 3, 1906.
> Called to the Bar at the Inner Temple, 13 May 1908.

Keir, James Laurence Young : son of William Ingram Keir, F.R.C.S., of Melksham,
Wiltshire; and Emily Elizabeth Mary Young. Born at Melksham, 7 Feb.
1886. Schools : Bath ; Weymouth College, under Mr J. Miller; and Warwick,
under the Rev. W. T. Keeling. Admitted 1 Oct. 1903.
> B.A. 1906; M.A. 1910. Law Tripos, Part I, Class 3, 1905; Part II,
> Class 3, 1906. Called to the Bar at the Inner Temple, 27 Jan. 1908.

Koop, Gerard Godfrey (Gerhard Gottfried) : son of Paul Koop, merchant, of Forest
Hill; and Anna Lange. Born at Rangoon, 11 Sept. 1884. School : Tonbridge, under the Rev. C. C. Tancock, D.D. Admitted 1 Oct. 1903.
> B.A. 1906. Law Tripos, Part I, Class 3, 1906. President of the Athletic
> Club, 1905. University (Rugby) Football player, 1906. Called to the
> Bar at the Inner Temple, 17 Nov. 1908.

Lea, Max : son of Arthur Sheridan Lea, Sc.Doc., F.R.S., Physiologist, Fellow
of the College, of Sunnyside, Sidcup; and Mary Henwood. Born at Ennis
Road, Hornsey, 14 Feb. 1884. Schools : Highgate, under Dr McDowell
and Dr Allcock; Little Appley, Ryde, under Mr R. W. Philpott; and
Tonbridge, under Dr Tancock. Admitted 1 Oct. 1903.
> Resided six terms. Choral Exhibitioner, 1903. Motor Car Engineer
> (1910).

Lindenbaum, John Benjamin: son of Moses Lindenbaum, pearl merchant, of Hampstead; and Caroline Weil. Born at 19, Canonbury Villas, London, 14 Sept. 1884. School: Harrow, under the Rev. Dr Wood. Admitted 1 Oct. 1903.
> B.A., LL.B. 1906; M.A., M.L. 1910. Law Tripos, Part I, Class 1, 1905; Part II, Class 1, 1906. Entrance Scholar, 1903. Scholar, 1904–6. Called to the bar at Inner Temple, 17 Nov. 1909; Cert. of honour, 1907.

Lloyd-Jones, Percy: son of Edward Lloyd-Jones, mining engineer, of Plasisa, Rhosymedre; and Jane Frances Puleston. Born at Plasisa, Rhosymedre, 8 Feb. 1885. Schools: Crescent House, Brighton, under Mr A. H. Thomas, M.A.; and Bromsgrove, under Mr H. Millington, M.A., and Mr F. J. R. Hendy, M.A. Admitted 1 Oct. 1903.
> B.A. 1906.

Mappin, Frank Crossley: son of Samuel Wilson Mappin, farmer, of Pembroke Road, Clifton; and Laura Morton. Born at Scampton, near Lincoln, 15 Aug. 1884. School: Felsted, under the Rev. H. A. Dalton. Admitted 1 Oct. 1903.
> Resided ten terms. Resides (1909) at Auckland, New Zealand.

Markham, Frank Reynolds: son of Henry William Markham, merchant, of Sydenham; and Emily Jacobs. Born at Capetown, South Africa, 1 Nov. 1884. Schools: South African College, Capetown; and Berkhamsted, under the Rev. Dr Fry. Admitted 1 Oct. 1903. Brother of Richard, iv. (1) 23.
> Resided three terms. Returned to South Africa.

Marsden, Tom: son of William John Marsden, solicitor's managing clerk, of Gainsborough; and Ann Spilman. Born at Gainsborough, Lincolnshire, 28 March 1884. Schools: Gainsborough, under the Rev. J. R. U. Elliott, M.A.; and Oundle, under Mr F. W. Sanderson, M.A. Admitted 1 Oct. 1903.
> B.A. 1906. Class. Tripos, Part I, Class 1, 1906. Entrance Scholar, 1903. Master at Pontefract School, 1907–8. Clergy Training School, Cambridge, 1908. Theological Exhibitioner, 1909. Ordained deacon (Wakefield), 1910; priest, 1911. Curate of Illingworth, 1910– .

Mattingly, Harold: son of Robert Mattingly, J.P., of Sudbury; and Gertrude Emma Mattingly. Born at Sudbury, 24 Dec. 1884. School: The Leys, Cambridge, under the Rev. Dr W. F. Moulton and the Rev. Dr W. T. A. Barber. Admitted 1 Oct. 1903.
> B.A. 1906; M.A. 1910. Class. Tripos, Part I, Class 1, 1906; Part II, Class 1, 1907. Entrance Scholar, 1903; Battie University Scholar, 1905; Craven University Scholar, 1906; Senior Chancellor's Medallist for Classics, 1907; Research Student, 1907; Craven Student, 1908; Thirlwall Prize, 1909. Drosier Fellow, 1909– . Assistant in the British Museum, 1910– . Author: *The Imperial Civil Service of Rome*, 1910.

Mills, Kenneth Laurence: son of Harry Mills, solicitor, of Stourbridge; and Jane Elizabeth Nash. Born at Stourbridge, 8 June 1884. Schools: King Edward's, Stourbridge, under Mr R. Deakin, M.A.; and Royal Grammar, Guildford, under Mr J. C. Honeybourne, M.A. Admitted 1 Oct. 1903. Brother of Gerald, ii. 544.
> Captain of the Lawn Tennis Club, 1905–6. University Lawn Tennis Team, 1906. In the Bombay-Burma Trading Corporation service, 1907–

Moore, Charles Gordon Holland : son of William Henry Moore, solicitor, of Upton-on-Severn ; and Mary Braddon. Born at Upton-on-Severn, 6 Dec. 1884. Schools : May Place, Malvern Wells, under Mr A. E. Tillard ; and Sherborne, under the Rev. F. B. Westcott. Admitted 1 Oct. 1903.
> B.A. 1906. Nat. Sci. Tripos, Part I, Class 3, 1906. In medical practice.

Muir, Romney Moncrieff Pattison : son of Matthew Moncrieff Pattison Muir, Fellow of the College, of Brookside, Cambridge ; and Florence Haslam. Born at 8, Brookside, Cambridge, 25 April 1885. School : Sherborne, under the Rev. F. B. Westcott. Admitted 1 Oct. 1903. Brother of Clive, II. 533.
> B.A. 1906. Hist. Tripos, Part I, Class 2, 1905 ; Part II, Class 2, 1906. Theological Exhibitioner, 1906, 1907. Clergy Training School, 1906. President of the Union Society, 1908. Ordained deacon (Winchester) 1908 ; priest, 1909. Curate of Farnham, 1908 .

Nicoll, Henry Maurice Dunlop : son of William Robertson Nicoll, journalist, of Frognal, Hampstead ; and Isa Dunlop. Born at Kelso, 19 July 1884. School : Aldenham, under the Rev. J. Kennedy and the Rev. A. H. Cooke. Admitted 1 Oct. 1903.
> B.A. 1906. Nat. Sci. Tripos, Part I, Class 1, 1906. Scholar (elected, but not admitted), 1906. In medical practice.

O'Brien, John Cooke Power : son of Brigade-Surgeon Thomas Butler Power O'Brien, Hon. Lieut.-Col. Army Medical Staff ; and Marion Crooke. Born at Peshawur, Punjab, India, 26 Jan. 1885. School : Wellington, under the Rev. B. Pollock.
> B.A. Dec. 1906 ; M.A. 1910. University Commission in the Army, 2nd Lieut. Royal Irish Fusiliers, 1907.

Padfield, Francis Joseph : son of the Rev. Joseph Edwin Padfield, of Pathfield Road, Streatham ; and Rosa Sophia Denham. Born at Masulipatam, Southern India, 25 Oct. 1883. School : Merchant Taylors', under the Rev. Dr Baker and the Rev. J. A. Nairn. Admitted 1 Oct. 1903.
> B.A. 1906 ; M.A. 1910. Oriental Lang. Tripos, Class 2, 1906. Entrance Scholar in Hebrew, 1903 ; Stewart of Rannoch Scholarship for Hebrew, 1904. Student at Ridley Hall, 1906–7. Tyrwhitt Scholar, 1908. Ordained deacon (York), 1908 ; priest, 1909. Curate of Attercliffe, Sheffield, 1908– .

Page, John : son of Martin Fountain Page, merchant, of Blakeney, Norfolk ; and Emma Eliza Salmon. Born at Blakeney, Norfolk, 9 April 1885. School : St Aubyn's, Lowestoft, under Mr J. Bruce Payne, M.A. Admitted 1 Oct. 1903. Brother of Martin, IV. (1) 61, and Dennis, IV. (1) 83.
> B.A. 1906. In profession as an architect.

Pickett, Alfred Cleveland : son of Alfred John Pickett, merchant, of Keswick Lodge, East Putney ; and Helen Cleveland Peters. Born at Brighton, 4 July 1883. Schools : St George's, Ascot, under Mr C. G. Shackle ; and Wellington College, under the Rev. B. Pollock. Admitted 1 Oct. 1903.
> B.A. 1908.

Price, Lloyd Owen Lloyd: son of Meredydd Lewes Willy Lloyd Price, solicitor, of Bryn Cotta, Nantgandy, S. Wales; and Frances Margaret Lloyd. Born at Castle Pigyn, Abergwilly, S. Wales, 30 July 1884. School: Bedford, under Mr J. S. Philpotts and Mr J. E. King. Admitted 1 Oct. 1903.
B.A. 1906. Mining Engineer in the Transvaal (1910).

Rix, Reginald George Bertram: son of Henry William Rix, gentleman, of Lee, Blackheath; and Mary Ellen Arkwright. Born at Leamington, 6 Dec. 1883. Schools: Dover, under the Rev. W. C. Compton; and St Aubyn's, Lowestoft, under Mr J. Bruce Payne, M.A. Admitted 1 Oct. 1903.
Resided five terms. Master at a Preparatory School (1907).

Robson, William Newby: son of Frederick Robson, solicitor, of Stockton-on-Tees; and Jane Nattrass. Born at Hardwick Terrace, Stockton-on-Tees, 31 Dec. 1883. Educated at Stockton Grammar School, under Mr E. J. Vie, B.A.; and Yorkshire College, Leeds. Admitted 1 Oct. 1903.
B.A. 1906; M.A. 1910. Law Tripos, Part I, Class 1, 1905; Part II, Class 2, 1906. Scholar, 1905. Solicitor (1911), Sunderland.

Saner, John Godfrey: son of Charles Taylor Saner, planter, of Johannesburg, Natal; and Mary Blaine. Born at Southburn, Victoria County, Natal, 31 May 1885. School: St Andrew's, Grahamstown, Cape Colony, under the Rev. J. Espin, D.D., and the Rev. S. McGowan. Admitted 1 Oct. 1903.
B.A., B.C. 1910. Nat. Sci. Tripos, Part I, Class 2, 1906. Captain of Rugby Football Club, 1905; in the University Team, 1905.

Savill, Philip Robin Lydall: son of Philip Savill, gentleman, of Chigwell Row; and Nina Sophia Womersley. Born at Chigwell Row, Essex, 11 June 1885. Schools: Eastbourne; and Harrow, under the Rev. Dr Wood. Admitted 1 Oct. 1903.
Resided six terms.

Seiler, Gerhard Jan Chandler: son of Godfried Benjamin Jan Karl Seiler, doctor of medicine, of Paramaribo, Dutch Guiana; and Johanna Margareth Elizabeth Chandler. Born at Paramaribo, 6 Oct. 1879. Educated at the High-Burghal School of Amersfoort; and Het Christelijk Gereformeerd Gymnasium te Zetten, under Dr Kramer, M.A. Admitted 1 Oct. 1903.
Resided one term.

Smith, William d'Alton: son of William John Smith, merchant, of Parco Margherita, Naples; and Laura d'Alton. Born at Naples, 11 Nov. 1884. Schools: The International, Naples; and Clifton College, under the Rev. M. G. Glazebrook, M.A. Admitted 1 Oct. 1903.
B.A. 1908. Med. and Mod. Lang. Tripos, 1908 (aegrotat). Entrance Exhibition, 1903.

Speakman, Laurence Arthur: son of Murray Mackenzie Speakman, stock and share broker, of Knutsford; and Emily Welsh. Born at Rowley Brow, Knutsford, 25 Nov. 1883. Schools: Arnold House, Llandulas, under the Rev. J. C. C. Pipon; and Haileybury College, under the Rev. and Hon. E. Lyttelton. Admitted 1 Oct. 1903.
B.A. 1906; M.A. 1910. Med. and Mod. Lang. Tripos, Class 2, 1906. Entrance Exhibition, 1903. Exhibitioner, 1904-6. Captain, Hockey Club, 1905. Master at Haileybury College, 1908- .

Sykes, Stanley William : son of Frederick William Sykes, manufacturer, of Lindley, Huddersfield; and Catherine Whitley. Born at Green Lea, Lindley, 17 May 1884. Schools: Huddersfield College School, under Mr H. Wild, B.A.; privately; and Clifton College, under the Rev. M. G. Glazebrook, M.A. Admitted 1 Oct. 1903.

> B.A. 1906; M.A. 1910. Med. and Mod. Lang. Tripos, Class 3, 1906. Entrance Exhibition, 1903. Admitted at the Inner Temple, 29 Oct. 1907.

Tillard, Philip John Berkley : son of John Tillard, H.M. Inspector of Schools, of Ipswich Road, Norwich; and Mabel Katherine Berkley. Born at Broomfield Crescent, Kirkstall, Leeds, 15 Nov. 1883. Schools: Norwich Grammar, under the Rev. E. F. Gilbard; and Aldenham, under the Rev. A. H. Cooke, M.A. Admitted 1 Oct. 1903.

> B.A. 1906; M.A. 1910. Class. Tripos, Part I, Class 2, 1906. Entrance Exhibition, 1903. Tutor on Russian Man-of-War, 1906–7. English Lektor at Posen, 1907–8. Master at a Preparatory School, Bengeo, Hertford (1909).

Tremearne, Thomas Fitzalan: son of Shirley Tremearne, newspaper proprietor, of Calcutta, India; and Norah Emily Dundas Wollen. Born at Allahabad, India, 20 Oct. 1884. Educated at Darjeeling, Calcutta; Moravian School, Neuwied am Rhein; and Chateau de Lancy, Lancy, Switzerland. Admitted 1 Oct. 1903.

> Resided three terms. Called to the Bar at Lincoln's Inn, 1907. Returned to India.

Tweedie, James Moore: son of the Rev. Archibald George Tweedie (of the College, II. 426), of Selby Vicarage, Yorkshire; and Katherine Eliza Hall. Born at Ranmoor, Sheffield, 13 June 1884. Schools: Leamington College; and Rossall, under the Rev. J. P. Way, D.D. Admitted 1 Oct. 1903.

> B.A. 1906. University Commission in the Army Service Corps, 1907.

Usher, Reginald Nevile: son of the Rev. William Nevile Usher (of the College, II. 395), Vicar of Wellingore, Lincoln; and Margaret Louisa Stapylton Barnes. Born at Lansdowne Crescent, Edinburgh, 11 March 1886. School: Marlborough College, under the Rev. G. C. Bell. Admitted 1 Oct. 1903.

> B.A. 1906; M.A. 1910. Hist. Tripos, Part I, Class 3, 1905; Part II Class 3, 1906. Chapel Clerk, 1905; Theological Exhibitioner, 1906. Wells Theological College, 1908. Ordained deacon (Winchester), 1909; priest, 1910. Curate at Shanklin, 1909– .

Webb, Thomas Langley: son of Henry Langley Webb, M.R.C.S., of Lulworth House, Cheadle; and Jeanette Docksey. Born at Cheadle, 21 Oct. 1884. Schools: Bilton Grange, near Rugby; and Cheltenham College, under the Rev. R. Waterfield. Admitted 1 Oct. 1903. Brother of Henry, IV. (1) 121.

> B.A. 1906. Solicitor at Cheadle, Staffordshire (1910).

Williams, Caryl Bransby : son of Morgan Bransby Williams, J.P., D.L., of Killay, Glamorgan; and Margaret Brock. Born at Killay House, Swansea, 14 May 1884. Schools: Malvern Wells, under Mr A. H. Stahle; and Malvern College, under the Rev. S. R. James. Admitted 1 Oct. 1903. Brother of Morgan, II. 438; and Milbourne, IV. (1) 10.

> Resided six terms.

Willink, Herman James Lindale: son of the Rev. Arthur Willink, of Nackington Vicarage, Canterbury; and Margaret Dickson. Born at Lindale in Cartmel, N. Lancashire, 14 Sept. 1884. School: Tonbridge, under the Rev. Dr Wood and the Rev. C. C. Tancock. Admitted 1 Oct. 1903.
>   B.A. 1906. In the paper-manufacturing business at Burneside Mills, near Kendal (1908).

Woodward, Frank James: son of John Woodward, messenger of the House of Commons, of Ducie Street, Clapham; and Emily Mary Kenney. Born at Ebury Square, Pimlico, 11 Sept. 1884. Schools: Hosebrigge Higher Grade School, Clapham; and Dulwich College, under Mr A. H. Gilkes, M.A. Admitted 1 Oct. 1903.
>   B.A. 1906. Math. Tripos. Part I (br. 29th Wrangler), 1906. Entrance Scholar, 1903. Scholar, 1904–6. Selected Candidate, I.C.S., 1908. Appointed to Upper Bengal, 1909.

Cooke, William Seymour: son of the Rev. Frederic Cooke, M.A., of Westbury Rectory, Shrewsbury; and Ada Florence Bradford. Born at the Rectory, Clungunford, Shropshire. School: Shrewsbury, under the Rev. H. W. Moss. Admitted 1 Oct. 1903. Brother of Arthur, iv. (1) 3.
>   Resided five terms. Ranching in Canada, 1908.

MICHAELMAS 1904 TO MICHAELMAS 1905.

(Tutors: Mr Buckland, Mr Hardy, and Mr Cameron.)

Ashcroft Harold: son of Charles Wesley Ashcroft, flour miller, of Waterford Road, Oxton; and Alice Mason Hutchinson. Born at Greenfield Road, Stoneycroft, Liverpool, 11 May 1884. School: Birkenhead, under Mr F. Griffin, M.A. Admitted 1 Oct. 1904. Brother of William, iv. (1) 11, and Alec, iv. (1) 67.
>   B.A. 1907; M.A. 1911. Hist. Tripos, Part I, Class 3, 1906. Wesleyan Methodist Mission, Madras, 1908– .

Bennett, Arthur Russell: son of Courtenay Walter Bennett, consul-general, San Francisco; and Edith Russell Leay. Born at 8, Oxford Terrace, Cheltenham, 13 May 1885. Schools: Brandon House, Cheltenham, under Mr T. S. F. Haskoll; and Clifton College, under Canon M. G. Glazebrook. Admitted 1 Oct. 1904.
>   B.A. 1907. Med. and Mod. Lang. Tripos, Class 2, 1907. Entrance Scholar, 1904. In the Indian Customs Department, Calcutta (1910).

Bentall, Charles Edward: son of Edmund Ernest Bentall, mechanical engineer, of The Towers, Heybridge; and Maude Alice Miller. Born at Liverpool, 4 Dec. 1885. Educated at Bilton Grange, Rugby, under the Rev. W. Earle; Wellington College, under the Rev. B. Pollock; and privately. Admitted 1 Oct. 1904.
>   Resided three years.

Berrington, Leslie George: son of Richard Evans Willoughby Berrington, C.E., of Graiseley, Wolverhampton; and Emily Anne Leslie Clunes. Born at Penn Fields, near Wolverhampton, 21 April 1886. Schools: Lindley Lodge, Nuneaton, under Mr R. S. Lea; and Repton, under the Rev. L. G. Ford. Admitted 1 Oct. 1904.
>   Resided three terms. Ordained deacon (Worcester), 1910. Curate of Dunchurch, 1910– .

Bonhote, Thomas Edward: son of Frederic Bonhote, merchant (deceased), of Batavia, Java; and Eugènie Charlotte Ten Brinck. Born at Sourabaya, Java, 26 June 1885. School: Tonbridge, under the Rev. Dr Tancock. Admitted 1 Oct. 1904.
  B.A. 1907. Med. and Mod. Lang. Tripos, Class 2, 1907. Entrance Exhibition, 1904. In profession as a singer.

Brown, Hubert Horan: son of James William Henry Brown, M.B., of Roundhay; and Henrietta Horan. Born at Ripley House, Holbeck, Leeds, 28 March 1886. School: Epsom College, under the Rev. T. N. Hart-Smith-Pearce, M.A. Admitted 1 Oct. 1904.
  B.A. 1907. Nat. Sci. Tripos, Part I, Class 3, 1907.

Chittick, Hubert Stanley: son of Charles Chittick, C.E., of Shooters Hill Road, London; and Amelia Edith Davis. Born at St Mary's Road, London, 6 June 1885. School: Rugby, under the Rev. Dr James. Admitted 1 Oct. 1904.
  B.A. 1908; M.A. 1911. Math. Tripos, Part I, Sen. Op., br. 40 (= 7th), 1906. Mech. Sci. Tripos, 1908 (*aegrotat*). Salomons Engineering Scholarship, 1904. Engineer on the staff of the General Post Office, 1908– .

Cory, Robert Francis Preston: son of the Rev. Charles Page Cory, of Cantonment Parsonage, Budd Road, Rangoon, Burma; and Grace Margaret Gross. Born at Antananarivo, Madagascar, 3 Sept. 1885. School: Sedbergh, under Mr C. Lowry. Admitted 1 Oct. 1904. Brother of Charles, IV. (1) 69.
  B.A. 1907. Nat. Sci. Tripos, Part I, Class 2, 1907.

Couchman, Hugh John: son of Robert Edward Couchman, land agent and surveyor, of Vicarage Road, Edgbaston; and Frances Louisa Goodman. Born at Highfield Road, Edgbaston, 25 April 1886. School: Marlborough College, under the Rev. G. C. Bell and Mr F. Fletcher. Admitted 1 Oct. 1904.
  B.A. 1907. Nat. Sci. Tripos, Part I, Class 3, 1907.

Cullimore, James: son of John Cullimore, solicitor, of Christleton, Chester; and Mary Elizabeth Dale. Born at Christleton, 28 Sept. 1886. School: Rugby, under the Rev. Dr James. Admitted 1 Oct. 1904. Brother of William, IV. (1) 69, and Charles, IV. (1) 103.
  B.A. 1907; M.A. 1911. Mech. Sci. Tripos, Part I, 1907. In the engineering profession.

Debailleul, Alexandre: son of Alexandre Debailleul, coal merchant, of Rue de Wattignies, Paris; and Berthe Dubois. Born at Paris, 29 Feb. 1880. Educated at the Sorbonne. Admitted as an Advanced Student, 1 Oct. 1904. Admitted to the College as Lector in French on the recommendation of the French Ministry of Education.
  Resided six terms. Professeur at the Lycée, Dijon, 1906– .

Denning, Howard: son of Henry Denning, merchant, of Redland Grove, Bristol; and Hannah Pollard. Born at Bristol, 20 May 1885. School: Clifton College, under the Rev. M. G. Glazebrook. Admitted 1 Oct. 1904.
  B.A. 1907. Math. Tripos, Part I (br. 10th Wrangler), 1907. Entrance Scholar, 1904. Scholar, 1905–8. Selected Candidate, I.C.S., 1908. Appointed to Bombay, 1909.

Faulkner, Alfred Mortland : son of Charles Irvine Faulkner, physician, of Escrick,
York; and Alice Tickell.   Born at North Richmond Street, Dublin,
21 July 1885. School: Pocklington, under the Rev. C. F. Hutton, M.A.
Admitted 1 Oct. 1904.
    Resided three terms. Studying engineering in London (1908).

Francis, Guy Lancelot Brereton : son of George Carwardine Francis, solicitor,
of St Tewdric, near Chepstow; and Catherine Lilian Peach. Born at The
Mead, Tidenham, Gloucestershire, 4 Aug. 1886. School: Rugby, under the
Rev. Dr James. Admitted 1 Oct. 1904.
    B.A. 1907. Solicitor at Chepstow.

Fryer, John Claud Fortescue : son of Herbert Fortescue Fryer, farmer, of The
Priory, Chatteris; and Mary Katherine Terry. Born at The Priory,
Chatteris, 13 Aug. 1886. School: Rugby, under the Rev. H. A. James, D.D.
Admitted 1 Oct. 1904.
    B.A. 1907. Nat. Sci. Tripos, Part I, Class 1, 1907; Part II, Class 1,
    1908. Exhibitioner, 1906 ; Scholar, 1907. Shuttleworth Student, 1908.
    Balfour Student, 1910. Walsingham Medal, 1910. Went on scientific
    expedition to the Seychelles and Aldabra, 1908.

Fullagar, Leo Alfred : son of the Rev. Hugh Scales Fullagar, M.A. (of the College,
II. 315), Rector of Melton Constable; and Mary Louisa Pryme Hawkes.
Born at Hunworth, Norfolk, 3 April 1883. School: Framlingham, under
the Rev. O. D. Inskip, M.A., LL.D. Admitted 1 Oct. 1904.
    B.A. 1907. Mech. Sci. Tripos, Part II, Class 2, 1907. Exhibitioner,
    1905 ; Scholar, 1906. In the engineering profession ; with the British
    Cyanides Co., Birmingham (1910).

Garrett, Gerald William Blackman: son of Frederick Garrett, of Westfield,
Stanmore; and Ellen Blackman. Born at Fountayne Road, Stamford
Hill, Middlesex, 18 Feb. 1885. School: Highgate. Admitted 1 Oct. 1904.
    B.A. 1907. Nat. Sci. Tripos, Part I, Class 3, 1907.

Gaye, Alan Willis: son of the Rev. Robert Edward Gaye, Rector of Skeyton,
Swanton Abbot; and Maria Elizabeth Willis. Born at Skeyton Rectory,
23 Dec. 1885. School : St John's Foundation, Leatherhead, under the Rev.
A. F. Rutty. Admitted 1 Oct. 1904.
    B.A. 1907. Nat. Sci. Tripos, Part I, Class 2, 1907. Tancred Student, 1904.

Goodwin, Ernest St George Sagar: son of George Goodwin Goodwin, engineer
commander, R.N. ; and Mary Jane Sagar. Born at The Parade, St John's
Road, Battersea, 10 Feb. 1887. School: Dulwich. Admitted 1 Oct. 1904.
    B A. 1907 ; M.A. 1911; M.B., B.C. 1911. Nat. Sci. Tripos, Part I, Class 1,
    1907. Exhibitioner, 1906.

Gray, William Athelstan : son of Arthur Gray, Fellow and Senior Tutor of Jesus
College, Cambridge ; and Alice Honora Gell. Born at North House, Jesus
College, 1885. School : Aldenham, under the Rev. A. H. Cooke. Admitted
1 Oct. 1904. Brother of Henry, IV. (1) 31.
    B.A. 1907. Class. Tripos, Part I, Class 1, Div. 3, 1907. Entrance Scholar,
    1904. Scholar, 1905-7. Captain of the Cricket Club, 1906-7. In the
    Burma Oil Company, Rangoon (1910).

Grazebrook, Owen Francis : son of Francis Grazebrook, iron-master and colliery proprietor, of Himley House, near Dudley; and Isabella Mary Grazebrook. Born at Queen's Cross, Dudley, 11 Nov. 1884. School: Marlborough, under the Rev. G. C. Bell. Admitted 1 Oct. 1904.
> B.A. 1907. President of the Union Society, 1907. In business with his father.

Greenough, Thomas Rigby: son of Thomas Rigby Greenough, auctioneer and valuer, of Leigh, Lancashire; and Annie Knowles. Born at Leigh, 12 April 1885. Educated at the University School, Southport. Admitted 1 Oct. 1907.
> B.A. 1907. Nat. Sci. Tripos, Part I, Class 3, 1907. Analytical chemist.

Hare, Samuel Henry: son of Charles Edward Hare, bank manager, of The Gables, Kibworth, Leicester; and Agnes Marian Isabella Pruen. Born at Priory Terrace, Stamford, 14 Oct. 1884. School: Stamford, under the Rev. Dr Barnard. Admitted 1 Oct. 1904.
> B.A. 1908. Theol. Tripos, Part I, Class 2, 1907. Choral Exhibitioner, 1904; Yatman Exhibitioner, 1906; Exhibitioner, 1907. Master in the Lower School at Uppingham, 1907–8. Ordained deacon (Lichfield), 1908; priest, 1909. Curate of Stoke-on-Trent, 1908– .

Harper, Edward Russell: son of Robert Russell Harper, surgeon, of Holbeach, Lincolnshire; and Marian Sutcliffe. Born at Littlebury House, Holbeach, 1 July 1886. Schools: Marlborough, under the Rev. G. C. Bell; and King Edward VII, King's Lynn, under the Rev. W. Boyce.
> Resided six terms.

Hartree, Raymond: son of William Hartree, engineer, of Havering, Tunbridge Wells; and Una Kathleen Brocklebank. Born at Blackheath, 14 Dec. 1885. School: Charterhouse, under the Rev. Dr G. H. Rendall. Admitted 1 Oct. 1904. Brother of Cyril, II. 553, and Kenneth, IV. (1) 94.
> B.A. 1907. Mech. Sci. Tripos, Part I, Class 3, 1907. In the engineering profession.

Heald, Walter Marsden: son of Walter Heald, railway secretary, of Bromley, Kent; and Emily Isabel Krabbè. Born at Ford Bank, Hale, Cheshire, 3 Nov. 1885. School: Tonbridge, under the Rev. Dr C. C. Tancock. Admitted 1 Oct. 1904. Brother of Charles, IV. (1) 31.
> B.A. 1908; M.A. 1911. Law Tripos, Part I, Class 3 (br. 27–29), 1907.

Heard, Alexander St John: son of Rev. Henry James Heard, M.A. (of the College, II. 447). Rector of St Michael's, Bath; and Maud Jervis Bannatyne, deceased. Born at Woodsdown, Limerick, Ireland, 8 October 1885. School: Clifton College, under the Rev. Canon M. G. Glazebrook. Admitted 1 Oct. 1904. Brother of Henry, IV. (1) 94.
> B.A. 1907; M.A. 1911. Hist. Tripos, Part I, Class 3, 1906; Part II, Class 3, 1907. Ordained deacon (London), 1909; priest, 1910. Curate of Stanmore, 1909–11. Curacy in Queensland, Australia, 1911–

Little, James Armstrong: son of Rev. George Little, Vicar of St John's, Monk Hesleden, Castle Eden, R.S.O.; and Elizabeth Armstrong. Born at Brasfort House, Wigton, Cumberland, 16 March 1885. Educated at Dulwich College, under Mr A. H. Gilkes. Admitted 1 Oct. 1904.
> B.A. 1907; M.A. 1911. Ordained deacon (Chester), 1909. Curate of Tarporley, 1909– .

Lluellyn, Raymond Chester: son of Richard Lluellyn, deceased, late Lieut.-Col. of Durham Light Infantry; and Amy Hawkins Chester. Born at 4, Grange Road, Upper Norwood, 14 Jan. 1882. School: Wellington College, under the Rev. B. Pollock. Afterwards at Christ Church, Oxford, 1 year. Resided two terms.

Lock, Norman Francis: son of Rev. John Bascombe Lock, Fellow and Bursar of the College (p. 383); and Emily Baily. Born at Cambridge, 18 March 1885. Schools: King's Choir School, Cambridge; Aysgarth; and Charterhouse, under the Rev. Dr Rendall. Admitted 1 Oct. 1904.
B.A. 1908. Nat. Sci. Tripos, Part I, Class 1, 1906; Part II, Class 1, 1908. Exhibitioner, 1905. Scholar, 1906-8. Elected to Research Studentship, 1908.

Lowson, Kenneth John: son of David Lowson, surgeon, of 15, Albion Street, Hull; and Elizabeth Brown. Born at Wycliffe House, Anlaby Road, Hull, 6 March 1885. Educated at St Paul's School, under Mr F. W. Walker, M.A. Admitted 1 Oct. 1904.
B.A. 1907. Hist. Tripos, Part I, Class 3, 1906; Part II, Class 3, 1907. Entrance Exhibitioner, 1904.

Lunniss, Sydney Frederick: son of Fred Lunniss (deceased), director of companies, of Stutton, Ipswich, Suffolk; and Anna Maria Bucke. Born at 269, Goldhawk Road, Hammersmith, 21 March 1880. Schools: Chatham House, Ramsgate; and Uppingham, under the Rev. Dr Selwyn. Admitted 1 Oct. 1904.
Resided six terms. Captain, Hockey Club, 1906. Cultivator of fruit and narcissus at Standford, Hants.

McQuistan, Dougald Black: son of Alexander McQuistan, baker, of Inverkip, Scotland; and Agnes Leitch. Born at Inverkip, Renfrew, Scotland, 12 July 1879. Schools: Whitehill Public School, under Mr James Henderson, M.A.; and University of Glasgow. Admitted as Advanced Student, 1 Oct. 1904. Resided six terms.

Milsom, Ernest: son of William Hallifax Milsom, boot dealer, of 52, Kirkgate, Wakefield; and Maria Ellen Taylor. Born at Wakefield, 5 April 1885. Schools: Wakefield Cathedral; Wakefield Grammar, under Mr M. H. Peacock, M.A., B.Mus. Admitted 1 Oct. 1904.
B.A. 1907. Math. Tripos, Part I, Sen. Opt., 1907. Entrance Scholarship, 1904. Scholar, 1905-7. Appointed to the Indian Civil Service, 1909.

More, Thomas: son of Francis More, chartered accountant, of 59, Fountainhall Road, Edinburgh; and Jessie McCartney. Born at 5, Fountainhall Road, Edinburgh, 11 April 1885. Educated at Morelands School, Grange, Edinburgh, under Mr W. E. Anderson, M.A.; and privately. Admitted 1 Oct. 1904. Resided nine terms.

Morgan, Ernest Charles: son of Rev. Ernest Augustus Morgan, Rector of Scole Norfolk; and Julia Sarah Charles. Born at the Rectory, Ilketshall St John Suffolk, 25 Jan. 1886. Schools: Packwood Haugh, Hockley Heath, Warwickshire; Clifton College; and St Aubyn's, Lowestoft, under Mr J. Bruce Payne. Admitted 1 Oct. 1904.
B.A. 1907. Ordained deacon (Birmingham), 1909; priest, 1910. Curate of Oldbury, Birmingham, 1909- .

Neame, Thomas: son of Frederick Neame, land agent, of Luton, near Faversham; and Kathleen Stunt. Born at Macknade, Preston, Faversham, 23 Dec. 1885. Schools: St Michael's, Westgate-on-Sea; and Cheltenham College, under the Rev. R. Waterfield. Admitted 1 Oct. 1904.
> B.A. 1907. Entrance Exhibitioner, 1904. Captain, Rugby Football, 1906–7. Lieut. "C" Co., C.U.R.V., 1905. In dyeing business; with Brinton and Co., Stourport (1909).

Opie, Philip Adams: son of Ernest Opie, commission merchant, of Woodcock's Well, Cullompton, Devon; and Mary Adams. Born at Hayesleigh, Compton Gifford, Plymouth, 7 Jan. 1886. School: Blundell's, Tiverton, under Mr A. L. Francis, M.A. Admitted 1 Oct. 1904.
> B.A. 1907; B.C. 1911. Nat. Sci. Tripos, Part I, Class 2, 1907.

Pawle, Hanbury: son of George Strachan Pawle, senior partner in Campion & Co., Stock Exchange, of Widford, Ware, Herts; and Clotilda Agatha Hanbury. Born at Widford, Herts. School: Haileybury College, under the Hon. and Rev. Canon E. Lyttelton. Admitted 1 Oct. 1904.
> Resided nine terms. On the Stock Exchange.

Pollak, Harry: son of Joseph Pollak, stockbroker, of 12a, Kensington Palace Gardens, London, W.; and Emma Jane Goldmann. Born at 10, Greville Place, Marylebone, London, 18 July 1885. Schools: Eton College, under Rev. Dr Warre; and Heidelberg College, under Dr Holzberg and Mr A. B. Catty. Admitted 1 Oct. 1904.
> Resided five terms. Afterwards resided in South Africa.

Powys-Jones, William Richard: son of Thomas Jones, M.A. (T.C.D.), H.M. Inspector of Schools, of Glanbaiden, Abergavenny; and Mary Harry. Born at St Andrew's Major, Glamorganshire, 1876. Educated privately. Admitted 1 Oct. 1904.
> Resided seven terms.

Raven, Charles Earle: son of John Earle Raven (of the College), Barrister at Law, of 7, Durham Terrace, Bayswater, London, W.; and Alice Comber. Born at Paddington, 4 July 1885. Schools: Gloucester House Preparatory School, Paddington; and Uppingham, under the Rev. Dr Selwyn. Admitted 1 Oct. 1904.
> B.A. 1907; M.A. 1911. Class. Tripos, Part I, Class 1, Div. 2, 1907. Theol. Tripos, Part II, Class 1, 1908. Entrance Scholar, 1904. Scholar, 1905–8. Research Student, 1908–9. Schuldham Plate, 1908. George Williams Prize, 1908. Editor of the *Caian* and the *Granta*, 1907. Ordained deacon (Ely), 1909; priest, 1910. Elected Fellow and Dean of Emmanuel College, 1909.

Rayner, Edwin Cromwell: son of Henry Rayner, physician, of Upper Terrace House, Hampstead, London, N.W.; and Rosa Field. Born at Hanwell, Middlesex, 1 Feb. 1886. Schools: Grove House, Boxgrove, Guildford; and Marlborough College, under Rev. Dr Bell. Admitted 1 Oct. 1904. Brother of Arthur, IV. (1) 35.
> B.A. 1907. Captain of the Boat Club, 1906–7.

Richards, Crosland Smith: son of Samuel Smith Crosland Richards, C.B., of Falconhurst, Maison Dieu Road, Dover; and Josephine Rogers Thomson. Born at 36, Bedford Square, London, W.C., 7 May 1886. School: Dover College, under the Rev. W. C. Compton. Admitted 1 Oct. 1904. Brother of Frederick, IV. (1) 74.
> B.A. 1907. Mech. Sci. Tripos, Part I, Class 3, 1907. In the engineering profession (Dock Construction, Southampton, 1910).

Robinson, Austen Quinton: son of Rev. William Robinson, Rector of Eggesford, Devon; and Dora Harriet Oldfield. Born at Quinton Rectory, Worcestershire, 5 April 1885. Schools: St Ronan's, Worthing; and Marlborough College, under the Rev. Dr Bell and Mr F. Fletcher, M.A. Admitted 1 Oct. 1904.
> B.A. 1907. Class. Tripos, Part I, Class 2, Div. 1, 1907. Entrance Scholar, 1904–7. Scholar, 1905–7.

Salomons, David Reginald Herman Philip Goldsmid-Stern: son of Sir David Lionel Goldsmid-Stern-Salomons (of the College, II. 391), Baronet, M.A., barrister and engineer, of Broomhill, Tunbridge Wells; and Laura Stern. Born at Broomhill, Tunbridge Wells, 13 Oct. 1885. Educated at Eton College, under the Rev. Dr Warre. Admitted 1 Oct. 1904.
> B.A. 1907; M.A. 1911.

Smith, Everard: son of Sir Clarence Smith, Knt., retired stockbroker, of Falconwood, Shooter's Hill, Kent; and Mary Webster. Born at "Hawthorns," Chislehurst, Kent, 2 March 1885. Educated at The Leys School, Cambridge, under the Rev. W. T. A. Barber, M.A., D.D. Admitted 1 Oct. 1904. Brother of Kenneth, IV. (1) 102.
> B.A. 1907; M.A. 1911. Class. Tripos, Part I, Class 2, Div. 3, 1907. Ordained deacon (Ely), 1908; priest, 1909. Curate of St Luke's, Chesterton, 1908– .

Smith, John Hughes Bennett: son of William Charles Smith, K.C., M.A., LL.B. (Edinb.), of 6, Darnaway Street, Edinburgh; and Lucy Margaret Bennett. Born at Edinburgh, 7 June 1885. Educated at Edinburgh Academy, under Mr R. J. Mackenzie and Mr R. C. Carter. Admitted 1 Oct. 1904.
> Resided five terms; migrated to St Catharine's College.

Stevens, Leicester Bradney: son of Leicester Bradney Stevens, railway signal and gas engineer, of Knapdale, Upper Tooting, S.W.; and Julia Diggles. Born at East Hill Lodge, Wandsworth, Surrey, 24 April 1884. Schools: Beaumont Lodge, Old Windsor; and Eastman's, Southsea, under Mr H. E. Caldecott (Gonv. & Cai. II. 456). Admitted 1 Oct. 1904. Brother of Rutland (below).
> B.A. 1907; M.A. 1911. In the engineering profession.

Stevens, Rutland Duel: son of Leicester Bradney Stevens, railway signal and gas engineer, of Knapdale, Upper Tooting, London, S.W.; and Julia Diggles. Born at East Hill Lodge, Wandsworth, Surrey, 14 April 1886. Schools: Beaumont Lodge, Old Windsor; and Eastman's, Southsea, under Mr H. E. Caldecott. Admitted 1 Oct. 1904. Brother of Leicester (above).
> B.A. 1907; M.A. 1911. Captain, Lawn Tennis, 1906–7. In the engineering profession.

Sutcliffe, Joseph Hedley: son of Joseph Sutcliffe (deceased), merchant, of Bradford; and Edith Marion Pain. Born at Bradford, 21 April 1885. Educated at Cheltenham College, under the Rev. R. Waterfield. Admitted 1 Oct. 1904.
> B.A. and LL.B. 1907; M.A. 1911. Hist. Tripos, Part I, Class 3, 1906; Part II, Class 3, 1907. Entrance Exhibitioner, 1904. Solicitor.

Symns, James Llewellyn Montfort: son of the Rev. John Edward Symns, M.A., of Bancroft's School, Woodford Green, Essex; and Mary Corser. Born at Bancroft's School, Mile End Road, London, E., 11 April 1885. School: Aldenham, Herts, under the Rev. J. Kennedy and the Rev. A. H. Cooke. Admitted 1 Oct. 1904. Brother of John, II. 559.
B.A. 1907.

Thomas, Gwilym Ewart Aeron: son of John Aeron Thomas, solicitor, M.P. for West Glamorgan, of West Cross, Glamorgan; and Eleanor E. Lewis. Born at 196, St Helen's Road, Swansea, 5 Nov. 1885. Educated at Llandovery; and Clifton College, under the Rev. Canon M. G. Glazebrook. Admitted 1 Oct. 1904.
B.A. 1907. Nat. Sci. Tripos, Part I, Class 3, 1907. Law Tripos, Part II, Class 3, 1908. Admitted at the Inner Temple, November 1906.

Todhunter, John Reginald Arthur Digby: son of John Todhunter, M.D., of Orchardscroft, Bedford Park, Acton, London, W.; and Dora Louisa Digby. Born at Orchardscroft, Bedford Park, Acton, London, W., 14 Feb. 1885. Educated at Aldenham School, under the Rev. J. Kennedy and the Rev. A. H. Cooke. Admitted 1 Oct. 1904.
B.A. 1907. Nat. Sci. Tripos, Part I, Class 2, 1907. Entrance Scholar, 1904.

Townsend, Aubrey Lewis Hume: son of the Rev. John Hume Townsend, D.D., of St Mark's Vicarage, Broadwater Down, Tunbridge Wells; and Amelia Dorothea Harriet Joy. Born at Herne Lodge, Frant Road, Frant, Sussex, 2 Jan. 1885. Schools: Tonbridge, under Dr Wood and Dr Tancock; and Eastbourne College, under Mr W. H. Thomson. Admitted 1 Oct. 1904.
B.A. 1907. Class. Tripos, Part I, Class 2, Div. 1, 1907. Entrance Exhibitioner, 1904. Exhibitioner, 1905–7. Master at the Wells House School, Malvern, 1909– .

Tucker, Ernest Edwin George: son of Edwin Tucker, cattle dealer, of Alphington, Exeter; and Elizabeth Channon. Born at 182, Coswick Street, St Thomas', Exeter, 19 Aug. 1885. Schools: East Devon County School, Sampford Peverill, near Tiverton; and Queen Elizabeth's Grammar School, Crediton, under Mr J. E. Burton. Admitted 1 Oct. 1904.
B.A. 1907. Med. and Mod. Lang. Tripos, Class I, Section E, 1907; Class I, Section F, 1908. Entrance Scholar, 1904. Scholar, 1905–8. In the Reform Club Library (1910).

van Schalkwijk, Johannes: son of Andries Albertus van Schalkwijk, general agent, of South Africa; and Martha Maria Susanna Louisa Swart. Born at Bloemfontein, South Africa, 26 Feb. 1884. Educated at Victoria College, Stellenbosch, S. Africa. Admitted 1 Oct. 1904.
B.A. 1906; M.A. 1911; B.C. 1911. Nat. Sci. Tripos, Part I, Class 2, 1906; Part II, Class 3, 1907. Exhibitioner, 1905–6. Captain, Athletic Club, 1906–7. University (Rugby) Football team, 1907.

Watson, Francis Herbert: son of Walter Herbert Watson, worsted manufacturer, of 28, Blenheim Road, Bradford; and Annie Jowett. Born at 9, Valley View Grove, Bradford, 7 July 1885. Educated at Bradford School, under the Rev. W. H. Keeling, M.A. Admitted 1 Oct. 1904. Brother of Walter, IV. (1) 64.
B.A. 1907; B.C. 1911.

Wilks, William Arthur Reginald: son of Arthur Wilks (deceased), mining engineer, of 50, Stowheath Lane, Priestfield; and Catherine Alice Grove. Born at Merthyr Tydvil, 24 March 1885. Educated at Coseley Church School; and Wolverhampton Grammar School, under Mr J. H. Hichens, M.A. Admitted 1 Oct. 1904.

> B.A. 1907; M.A. 1911. Nat. Sci. Tripos, Part I, Class 1, 1906; Part II, Class 1, 1908. Entrance Scholarship, 1904. Scholar, 1905-8. Wiltshire Prize, 1906. Research Studentship, 1908-10. Drosier Fellow, 1910- .

Wilson, Harold Crewdson: son of Thomas Crewdson Wilson, retired woollen manufacturer, of Castle Lodge, Kendal; and Anna Mary Braithwaite. Born at "Elmhurst," Kendal, 26 Jan. 1885. Educated at Kendal Grammar School; and The Leys School, Cambridge, under the Rev. W. T. A. Barber. Admitted 1 Oct. 1904.

> B.A. 1907. Nat. Sci. Tripos, Part I, Class 1, 1906; Part II, Class 1, 1907. Scholar, 1905-7. Research Student, 1907. In chemical business, Kendal (1910).

Winterbotham, Frederick Page: son of William Howard Winterbotham, solicitor, of 6, Ladbroke Terrace, Notting Hill, London; and Elizabeth Micklem. Born at 6, Ladbroke Terrace, Notting Hill, London, 9 Aug. 1885. Educated at St Paul's School, London, under Mr F. W. Walker, M.A. Admitted 1 Oct. 1904.

> B.A. 1907. Math. Tripos, Part I, 22nd Wrangler, 1907. Entrance Scholarship, 1904. Scholar, 1905-8.

Worsley-Worswick, Christopher Francis Aloysius: son of William Worsley-Worswick, major in the army, of Ashman's Hall, Beccles; and Ellen Jane Moody. Born at Sarnesfield, Herefordshire, 18 June 1884. Educated at Downside School, Bath, under Rev. H. W. M. Howlett and Rev. H. L. Ramsey; and privately, under the Rev. Allan Coates, Rector of Barsham. Admitted 1 Oct. 1904.

> B.A. 1907.

Gordon, Geoffrey: son of Alexander Gordon, Principal of the Unitarian Home Missionary College, Memorial Hall, Manchester, formerly Minister of the first Presbyterian Church, Belfast; of 15, York Place, Manchester; and Clara Maria Boult. Born at 9, Upper Crescent, Belfast, 15 Oct. 1881. Educated at Grafton House, Manchester, under Mr N. Notman. Admitted 20 Oct. 1904.

> Selected candidate for the Indian Civil Service, 1904. Appointed to the Indian Civil Service, 1905.

Jones, Samuel: son of William Jones (deceased), draper's assistant; and Elizabeth Reeves (deceased). Born at 30, Ashford Road, Maidstone, 27 March 1867. Educated at the Grammar School, Maidstone, under the Rev. G. M. Gould, M.A., and the Rev. S. M. Crosthwaite, M.A. B.A. London, 1889. Wycliffe Hall, Oxford, 1890-1. Ordained deacon, 1892; Priest, 1893. Curate of St Clement's, Ipswich, 1892-6; of St Mary's, Bury St Edmund's, 1897-1905. Admitted 27 April, 1905.

> Resided three terms. Secretary to the Bible Society for Cambridge District, 1905-6. Curate of St Clement's, Ipswich, 1906-

Stitt, Samuel Stewart: son of Colonel Samuel Stitt, J.P., of Holmfield, Birkenhead; and Ruth Abraham Medder. Born at Birkenhead, 21 May 1866. Educated at Birkenhead Grammar School, under the Rev. J. T. Pearse, and the Rev. W. Cecil Wood. Admitted as a Member of the College, 11 August, 1905.

B.A. (Pembroke College), 1889; M.A. (Pemb.), 1903. Ordained deacon (Ely), 1890; Priest, 1891. Curate of St Mary the Great, Cambridge, 1890-1. Tutor of St Aidan's College, Birkenhead, 1891-2. Curate of Tring, 1892-4, of St Helier, Jersey, 1894-7. Acting Chaplain to the Forces at Cork, 1897-9; Chaplain at Aldershot, 1899-1901. Chaplain in the South African War, 1901-2, medal and five clasps. Chaplain of the College, 1903-4. Vicar of St Michael's, Cambridge, 1903-6; of Stretham, Ely, 1906- . Author.

MICHAELMAS 1905 TO MICHAELMAS 1906.

(Tutors: Mr Gallop, Mr Buckland and Mr Hardy.)

Alexander, Edward: son of William Harvey Alexander, cotton broker, of Eton House, Bidston Road, Birkenhead; and Edith Ganthony. Born at Eton House, Bidston Road, Birkenhead, 6 June 1887. Educated at Birkenhead School; and Uppingham School, under the Rev. E. C. Selwyn. Admitted 1 Oct. 1905.

B.A. 1908. Mech. Sci. Tripos, Class 3, 1908. In the Indian Public Works Department (1910).

Andrews, Walter Scott; son of Walter Scott Andrews, lawyer; and Irene Fittsch. Born at 38, East Twentieth Street, New York, U.S.A., 7 Nov. 1886. Educated at Heidelberg College, under Mr A. B. Catty, M.A. Cantab. Admitted 1 Oct. 1905.

Law Tripos, Part I, Class 3, 1907. Entrance Scholarship, 1905, for Modern Languages. In University Lawn Tennis team, 1906.

Attwood, Herbert Clifton: son of Matthew Attwood, solicitor, of Westleigh, Derby; and 'Alice Flora Whitworth. Born at 24, Bass Street, Derby, 29 Aug. 1886. Educated at Haileybury College, under the Hon. and Rev. Canon E. Lyttelton. Admitted 1 Oct. 1905.

B.A. 1908. Nat. Sci. Tripos, Part I, Class 3, 1908.

Bevan, John Maybery: son of Isaiah Bevan, chemical manufacturer (deceased), of Calffynon, Llanelly, S. Wales; and Caroline Edith Bishop. Born at Greenfield Villa, Llanelly, S. Wales, 12 Sept. 1886. Educated at Clifton College, under the Rev. M. G. Glazebrook. Admitted 1 Oct. 1905.

B.A. 1908.

Bigland, Alfred Douglas: son of Alfred Bigland, merchant, of Bigland Hall, near Ulverston; and Emily Jane Arkle. Born at 84, Shrewsbury Road, Birkenhead, 15 Jan. 1887. Educated at Birkenhead School, under Mr F. Griffin, M.A. Admitted 1 Oct. 1905.

B.A. 1908. Nat. Sci. Tripos, Part I, Class 2, 1908. Captain, Athletic Club, 1907-8.

Bousfield, Robert Bruce: son of William Robert Bousfield (of the College), K.C., M.P., of St Swithin's, Hendon, London, N.W.; and Florence Maria Elizabeth Kelly. Born at Westbury Villa, Cricklewood, London, N.W., 25 Oct. 1886. Educated at St Andrew's, Southborough; and Malvern College, under the Rev. Dr James. Admitted 1 Oct. 1905.
  B.A. 1908. Master at St Lawrence College, Ramsgate, 1909-11.

Bradfield, Richard: son of Edward James Bradfield, miller, of Oaklands, Warminster; and Agnes Amelia Prior. Born at Boreham, Warminster, 10 Oct. 1887. Educated at Lord Weymouth's Grammar School, Warminster, under Mr W. F. Blaxter, M.A. Admitted 1 Oct. 1905.
  B.A. 1908. Mech. Sci. Tripos, Class 2, 1908. Engineer in the General Post Office.

Brisley, Cuthbert Everard: son of George Charles Brisley (deceased); and Ella Marie Gahagan. Born at The Pines, Umzimkulu, Griqualand, Cape Colony, July 1886. Educated at Lancing College, under Dr A. J. Wilson and Mr H. B. Tower. Admitted 1 Oct. 1905. Brother of Gerald, iv. (1).
  B.A. 1910. Captain, Association Football, 1907-8. President, University Association Football, 1908.

Brown, Arthur Anthony: son of John Brown, gentleman, of The Close, Purton, near Swindon; and Amelia Mitchell. Born at Chilhampton, near Salisbury, 30 April 1886. Educated at Abingdon School, under the Rev. T. Layng. Admitted 1 Oct. 1905.
  Resided nine terms.

Bulmer, David George: son of the Rev. George Frederick Bulmer, Vicar of Canon Pyon, Herefordshire; and Caroline Gwendoline Thomas. Born at Canon Pyon Vicarage, Herefordshire, 19 Aug. 1887. Educated at Collingwood House, Exeter; and Marlborough College, under the Rev. G. C. Bell and Mr F. Fletcher. Admitted 1 Oct. 1905.
  B.A. 1908.

Burnet, John Rudolph Wardlaw: son of George Wardlaw Burnet (deceased), Sheriff-Substitute of Aberdeen, Kincardine and Banff; and Mary Crudelius. Born at 6, West Circus Place, Edinburgh, 31 Dec. 1886. Educated at Fettes College, Edinburgh, under the Rev. W. A. Heard, LL.D. Admitted 1 Oct. 1905.
  B.A. 1908. Nat. Sci. Tripos, Part I, Class 2, 1908.

Buswell, Henry Leslie Farmer: son of Charles Buswell, merchant, of 169, Queen's Gate, South Kensington; and Caroline Croft. Born at The Priory, Richmond, Surrey, 3 Dec. 1887. Educated at Temple Grove, East Sheen; and Winchester College, under the Rev. Dr Burge. Admitted 1 Oct. 1905.
  B.A. 1908. Nat. Sci. Tripos, Part I, Class 3, 1908.

Campbell, William Hastings: son of John Davies Campbell, of Howden Court, Tiverton; and Jennie Maria Hastings. Born at 27, Pembridge Square, London, W., 15 Aug. 1886. Educated at Farnborough Park; and Cheltenham College, under the Rev. R. Waterfield. Admitted 1 Oct. 1905.
  B.A. 1908. Captain of the Boat Club, 1907-8. In Nitrate of Soda Works, Iquique, Chile (1910).

Cannington, Arthur Shelmerdine: son of Arthur Kershaw Cannington (deceased), glass manufacturer; and Lucy Shelmerdine (deceased). Born at Blundellsands, near Liverpool, 12 April 1887. Educated at The Leys School, Cambridge, under the Rev. W. T. A. Barber, D.D. Admitted 1 Oct. 1905.
Resided eight terms.

Compton, Robert Harold: son of Robert Ernest Compton, managing clerk, of Oldbury House, Tewkesbury; and Eleanor Wilkes Fluck. Born at Oldbury House, Tewkesbury, 6 Aug. 1886. Educated at Abbey House School, Tewkesbury; and Mill Hill School, under Mr J. D. McClure, M.A., LL.D. Admitted 1 Oct. 1905.
B.A. 1908. Nat. Sci. Tripos, Part I, Class 1, 1907; Part II, Class 1, 1909. Entrance Exhibition, 1905. Scholar, 1906–9. Frank Smart Prize, 1907. Schuldham Plate, 1909. Frank Smart Student, 1909. Frank Smart (University) Prize, 1910. Frank Smart (University) Student, 1910.

Crompton, James: son of Henry Dickinson Crompton, solicitor, of Wilton House, St James's Road, Edgbaston; and Annie Maud Starey. Born at 44, Beaufort Road, Edgbaston, Birmingham, 19 July 1886. Educated at Sedbergh School, under Mr H. G. Hart and Mr C. Lowry. Admitted 1 Oct. 1905. Brother of Kenneth, II. 537, and IV. (1) 92.
B.A. 1908. Theol. Tripos, Part I, Class 3, 1908. University Commission in the Army, 1909.

Dale, Hugh Frederick: son of Frederick Dale (of the College, II. 413), M.D., F.R.C.S., of Park Lea, Scarborough; and Katherine Maughan. Born at Park Lea, Scarborough, 24 Sept. 1886. Educated at Scarborough Preparatory School; and Haileybury College, under the Rev. Canon Lyttelton. Admitted 1 Oct. 1905.
B.A. 1910.

Davis, Frank Prosser: son of Edward Prosser Davis, engineer and ironmaster, of Oakhurst, 17, Lenton Road, The Park, Nottingham; and Mary Gent. Born at Beeston, Nottinghamshire, 18 June 1886. Educated at Rugby School, under the Rev. Dr James. Admitted 1 Oct. 1905.
B.A. 1908. In the engineering profession.

Dawson, Ernest Edward: son of Edward Dawson, iron founder, of Southfield Grove, Middlesbrough; and Annabella Stark Kirkwood. Born at Southfield Grove, Middlesbrough, 2 May 1886. Educated at Coatham Grammar School; and Shrewsbury School, under the Rev. H. W. Moss. Admitted 1 Oct. 1905.
B.A. 1908. Mech. Sci. Tripos, Class 2, 1908.

Duncan, Joseph Hugh: son of John Duncan, newspaper proprietor, of 105, St Mary Street, Cardiff, and Dros-y-Mor, Penarth; and Mary Stowe. Born at Cardiff, 27 Feb. 1887. Educated at Rugby School, under Rev. Dr James; and privately under the Rev. E. Skrimshire, Minor Canonries, Llandaff. Admitted 1 Oct. 1905.
B.A. 1908.

Dunlop, John Gunning Moore; son of Archibald Dunlop, M.D. (deceased); and Bessie Moore, of St Helens, Holywood, Belfast. Born at Holywood, Co. Down, 14 Nov. 1885. Educated at Summerfields, Oxford; and Charterhouse, under the Rev. G. H. Rendall. Admitted 1 Oct. 1905.
B.A. 1909. Nat. Sci. Tripos, Part I, Class 1, 1907; Part II, Class 1, 1909. Scholar, 1906–9. Research Studentship, 1909.

Dyas, George Eldridge: son of Robert Dyas, auctioneer, of Blyth Wood, Bromley, Kent; and Ellen Eldridge. Born at Avoca, Blyth Wood, Bromley, Kent, 12 Aug. 1886. Educated at Winchester House School, Hastings; and Lancing College, under Dr Wilson and Mr B. H. Tower. Admitted 1 Oct. 1905. B.A. 1908. Nat. Sci. Tripos, Part I, Class 3, 1908.

Emmett, William Gidley: son of William Gidley Emmett, lace curtain manufacturer, of 10, Burns Street, Nottingham; and Annie Maria Gibbs. Born at Beeston, Nottinghamshire, 21 Aug. 1887. Educated at Nottingham High School, under Dr James Gow and Dr Turpin. Admitted 1 Oct. 1905. B.A. 1909. Nat. Sci. Tripos, Part I, Class 1, 1907; Part II, Class 2, 1909. Entrance Scholar, 1905. Scholar, 1906–9. Chemist in the Chilworth Powder Co. (1910).

Ewald, Peter Paul: son of Dr Ewald, Privatdozent at Berlin (deceased). Born at Berlin, 23 January 1888. Educated at Königliches Victoria Gymnasium at Potsdam. Admitted 1 Oct. 1905. Resided two terms.

Felton, Duncan George William: son of Henry James Felton, manufacturer, of 4, Beach Mansions, Southsea; and Mary Page. Born at "Hornden," Bromley, Kent, 27 July 1887. Educated at Eastman's, Southsea; and Portsmouth Grammar School, under Mr J. C. Nicol, M.A. Admitted 1 Oct. 1905. Resided six terms. Re-admitted Jan. 1910.

Formoy, Ronald Ralph: son of James Arthur Formoy, oil expert and chemist, of Chestham, Sutton, Surrey; and Emily Ann Reid. Born at Lothair Villa, Barry Road, Camberwell, 24 July 1883. Educated at Dulwich College, under Mr A. H. Gilkes. Admitted 1 Oct. 1905. B.A., LL.B. 1910; Law Tripos, Part I, Class 2, 1907; Part II, Class 3 (br. 36th), 1910. Called to the Bar at the Inner Temple, 1911.

Forster, Charles Michael: son of Michael Seymour Forster, M.A., B.C.L. (Oxon.), B.Sc. (London), Bursar of Wellington College, of Woodside, Crowthorne, Berks; and Elizabeth Humphrys. Born at Heatherside, Wellington College, Berks, 6 June 1888. Educated at Hartford House, Winchfield, Hants; and Wellington College, under the Rev. B. Pollock, D.D. Admitted 1 Oct. 1905. B.A. 1908. Nat. Sci. Tripos, Part I, Class 3, 1908.

France, Walter Frederic: son of George Thornton France (deceased), chemical manufacturer; and Harriet Lucy Stogdon, of The Old Vicarage, Heworth-on-Tyne. Born at Ford House, Gateshead-on-Tyne, 15 Feb. 1887. Educated at Newcastle Grammar School, under Mr S. C. Logan, M.A. Admitted 1 Oct. 1905. B.A. 1908. Archbishop of Canterbury's Missionary Exhibitioner, 1905. B.A. Exhibitioner, 1908. Ordained Deacon (Japan), 1910. Missionary in Japan, 1910.

George, Athelstan Key Durancé: son of Arthur Durancé George, bank manager, of Alderholt, West Cliff Road, Bournemouth; and Charlotte Ada Key. Born at Brixton, 24 March 1887. Educated at Tonbridge School, under the Rev. Dr C. C. Tancock. Admitted 1 Oct. 1905. Resided three terms. Lieut. Dorsetshire Regiment, 1910.

Glyn, John Paul: son of Henry Pettitt; and Bessie Finch (deceased). Born at St Leonards-on-Sea, 24 Feb. 1886. Educated at Edinburgh Academy, under Mr R. J. Mackenzie and Mr R. Carter. Took the name of Glyn. Admitted 1 Oct. 1904.
> B.A. 1908. Nat. Sci. Tripos, Part I, Class 3, 1908.

Greathead, James Henry: son of James Greathead (deceased), civil engineer, M.Inst.C.E.; and Blanche Emily Caldecott Coryndon, of Dewerstone House, Cheltenham. Born at 3, St Mary's Grove, Barnes, London, S.W., 5 May 1887. Educated at Streatham College Preparatory School; and Marlborough College, under the Rev. Canon G. C. Bell and Mr F. Fletcher, M.A. Admitted 1 Oct. 1905.
> B.A. 1908. Captain, Cricket Club, 1907–8. Sudan Irrigation Service (1911).

Growse, Robert Henry: son of Edward Frederick Growse, I.C.S., of Cuttack, Oussa, Bengal; and Emily Ousely Sherlock. Born at Buxar, India, 22 March 1887. Educated at Lindley Lodge, Nuneaton; and Cheltenham College, under the Rev. R. Waterfield. Admitted 1 Oct. 1905
> B.A. 1910. University Commission in the Army Service Corps, 1910.

Hawes, Bertram Lowth: son of Major-General William Harington Hawes (deceased), of the Indian Army; and Mary Lyne Bicknell. Born at 19, The Barons, Twickenham, 30 March 1887. Educated at Dover College, under the Rev. W. E. Compton, M.A. Admitted 1 Oct. 1905.
> B.A. 1908. Mech. Sci. Tripos, Class 2, 1908. Master at the High School, Newcastle-under-Lyme (1910).

Hereford, James Cecil: son of George Hereford (late H.M. Civil Service), of Lingfield, New Malden, Surrey; and Salome Alexander. Born at 20, Lingfield Road, Wimbledon, Surrey, 3 May 1886. Educated at the Proprietary School, Ealing; and Felsted School, under the Rev. H. A. Dalton, M.A. Admitted 1 Oct. 1905.
> B.A. 1908.

Hudson, Robert James: son of George Matthews Hudson (deceased), merchant; and Rosa Sophia Crozier, of 8, Blakeley Avenue, Ealing, London, W. Born at Mossel Bay, Cape Colony, 15 May 1885. Educated at the Diocesan College, Cape Town, under the Rev. Owen Jenkins, M.A. (Oxon.). Admitted 1 Oct. 1905.
> B.A. 1908. Law Tripos, Part I, Class 2, 1907; Part II, Class 3, 1908. Captain, Lawn Tennis Club, 1907–8. Called to the Bar at the Middle Temple, 26 Jan. 1909. Returned to South Africa.

Jenkinson, Stanley Noel: son of Alexander Dixson Jenkinson, glass manufacturer, of 4, Carlton Terrace, Edinburgh; and Edith Telford. Born at 13, Cobden Crescent, Edinburgh, 7 Dec. 1886. Educated at the Edinburgh Academy; and Trinity College, Glenalmond, under the Rev. John Huntley Skrine and the Rev. Archibald F. Hyslop. Admitted 1 Oct. 1905.
> Resided nine terms. In the Edinburgh and Leith Flint Glass Company, Norton Park, Edinburgh (1909).

Jeppe, Theodor Julius Juta: son of Carl Theodor Ludowig Abraham Jeppe (advocate), of Wynberg, near Cape Town, South Africa; and Marie Albertina Offers Juta. Born at Pretoria, Transvaal, 9 Dec. 1886. Educated at Forest Hill House School; Diocesan College School, Rondebosch; and South African College School, under Mr H. B. Stanwell, M.A. Admitted 1 Oct. 1905.
> Resided nine terms.

Kennedy, Anthony: son of Thomas John Kennedy, I.C.S., of Umballa City,
Punjaub, India; and Edith Ellen Elliott. Born at Montgomery, Punjaub,
India, 20 Feb. 1888. Educated at Marlborough College, under the Rev.
Canon G. C. Bell and Mr F. Fletcher. Admitted 1 Oct. 1905.
    B.A. 1908. Nat Sci. Tripos, Part I, Class 3, 1908.

King, George Charles: son of Richard Thacker King, M.D., of Sandfield House,
West Kirby, Cheshire; and Mary Louisa Felton. Born at 118, Mount
Pleasant, Liverpool, 24 March 1886. Educated at St Columba's, Dublin;
The Mount, West Kirby; and privately, under John Sanger, Esq., The Little
Hermitage, Rochester. Admitted 1 Oct. 1905.
    B.A. 1910.

Knight, Henry Foley: son of John Henry Knight, landowner, of Barfield, Farn-
ham, Surrey; and Elizabeth Bligh Foley. Born at Farnham, 19 Jan. 1886.
Educated at Pembroke House Preparatory School, Hampton; and Haileybury
College, under the Hon. and Rev. Canon E. Lyttelton. Admitted 1 Oct. 1905.
    B.A. 1908. Class. Tripos, Part I, Class 2, Division 1, 1908. Entrance
    Scholarship, 1905. Scholar, 1906–8. Captain, Hockey Club, 1907–8.
    Editor of the *Caian*. In the Indian Civil Service, 1910.

La Fontaine, Sydney Hubert: son of Sydney James William La Fontaine,
merchant, of Bournabat, Smyrna, Asia Minor; and Edith Amelia Whittall.
Born at Smyrna, 2 Dec. 1885. Educated at Uppingham School, under the
Rev. Dr Selwyn. Admitted 1 Oct. 1905.
    B.A. 1908. Class. Tripos, Part I, Class 2, Division 2, 1908. Entrance
    Scholarship, 1905. Scholar, 1906–8. Captain, Rugby Football, 1907–8.
    In the Asiatic Petroleum Company (1909). Assistant District Collector,
    British East Africa, 1910 .

Lane, Henry John: son of Frederick Lane, ship-broker, of Chestnuts, Sydenham
Hill, London; and Elizabeth Sarah Hall. Born at 24, Copleston Road,
Camberwell, London, 25 Sept. 1886. Educated at Sydenham School; and
Uppingham School, under the Rev. Dr Selwyn. Admitted 1 Oct. 1905.
    Resided nine terms.

Leete, William John Hurstwaite: son of William Chambers Leete, town clerk of
Kensington, of 48, Holland Road, Kensington; and Alice Eugenie Pippin
(deceased). Born at Highbury, London, 27 Aug. 1886. Educated at Berkhamsted School, under Dr T. C. Fry. Admitted 1 Oct. 1905.
    B.A. 1908. Math. Tripos, Part I, 29th Senior Optime, 1908. Entrance
    Scholarship, 1905. Scholar, 1906–8. In the Asiatic Petroleum Company.

Little, John Caruthers: son of Charles William Little, sub-manager of the Scottish
Australian Investment Co., Ltd., of Sydney, Australia; and Minnie Mary
Morgan. Born at Rockhampton, Queensland, Australia, 21 April 1887.
Educated at Marlborough College, under Canon G. C. Bell and Mr F. Fletcher.
Admitted 1 Oct. 1905.
    Resided two years. Returned to Australia.

Macfarlane, Charles Bate: son of James Golder Macfarlane, merchant, of 16,
Fitzjohn's Avenue, Hampstead, London, N.W.; and Mary Anderson Bate.
Born at 2, Western Road, Port Elizabeth, South Africa, 11 Oct. 1886.
Educated at Clifton Bank School, St Andrews, N.B.; and Clifton College,
under The Rev. Canon M. G. Glazebrook. Admitted 1 Oct. 1905.
    B.A. 1908.

Mackintosh, Leslie Parkin Fraser : son of the Rev. Alexander Mackintosh, Vicar of Hamble, near Southampton ; and Constance Whiteway (deceased). Born at Northampton, 17 June 1886. Educated at Laleham School, Staines ; and Eton College, under Dr Warre. Admitted 1 Oct. 1905. Resided two years.

Macleod, Douglas Noël : son of Neil Macleod, physician, of Fairview, Shanghai, China ; and Jessie Menzies McClure. Born at Shanghai, China, 25 Dec. 1886. Educated at Bromsgrove School, under Mr H. Millington and Mr F. J. R. Hendy. Admitted 1 Oct. 1905.
     Nat. Sci. Tripos, Part I, Class 2, 1907. Entrance Scholarship, 1905. Scholar, 1906–8.

Norton, David George : son of George Pepler Norton, chartered accountant, of Birkby Lodge, Huddersfield ; and Julia Ann Slade. Born at Queen's Road, Edgerton, Huddersfield, 27 July 1886. Educated at Shrewsbury School, under the Rev. H. W. Moss. Fifteen months at Zürich. Admitted 1 Oct. 1905.
     B.A. 1908. In the engineering profession.

Norton, William John : brother of the above. Born at Queen's Road, Edgerton, Huddersfield, 25 Sept. 1887. Educated at Shrewsbury School, under Rev. H. W. Moss. Admitted 1 Oct. 1905.
     B.A. 1908. In the engineering profession.

Page, Martin Fountain : son of Martin Fountain Page, merchant (deceased) ; and Emma Eliza Salmon, of Blakeney, Norfolk. Born at Blakeney, Norfolk, 2 May 1886. Educated at St Aubyn's, Lowestoft, under Mr J. Bruce Payne, and The School, Bishop Stortford. Admitted 1 Oct. 1905. Brother of John, IV. (1) 43, and Dennis, IV. (1) 84.
     B.A. 1908. Ordained Deacon (Liverpool), 1911.

Pageot, René Emile Joseph : son of Eugène Pageot, iron merchant, of 21, Rue de Lamoricière, Nantes, France ; and Lucie Baboneau. Born at Nantes, 1 June 1880. Educated at Lycée de Nantes ; Faculté de Droit de Paris. Diplomé de l'Ecole des Sciences Politiques de Paris. Admitted 1 Oct. 1905.
     Admitted as an Advanced Student in Law. Resided one term.

Parish, George Woodbyne : son of Arthur Woodbyne Parish, gentleman, of Sellarsbrook, Monmouth ; and Beatrice Upton Cottrell Dormer. Born at Urmston Lodge, Urmston, Lancashire, 4 June 1887. Educated at Monmouth Grammar School ; Bradley Court, Mitcheldean, under Mr W. Hunter Gandy. Admitted 1 Oct. 1905. Resided four terms.

Peck, John Norman : son of Alfred Peck, of 3, Rawlinson Road, Southport ; and Hannah Bradbury. Born at Southport, 5 Feb. 1887. Educated at Mintholme, Southport ; Preparatory School, Sedbergh ; Sedbergh School, under Mr C. Lowry. Admitted 1 Oct. 1905.
     B.A. 1908. Mech. Sci. Tripos, Class 3, 1908. In the engineering profession.

Percival, Andrew Francis: son of John Andrew Percival, solicitor, of Ashfield, Peterborough; and Catherine Hogg Kirkwood. Born at Peterborough, 14 June 1887. Educated at Uppingham School, under the Rev. Dr Selwyn. Admitted 1 Oct. 1905.
  B.A. 1908. Class. Tripos, Part I, Class 2, Division 2, 1908. Entrance Exhibition, 1905. Exhibitioner, 1906–8. Solicitor at Peterborough.

Pope, Herbert Barrett: son of Henry Pope, surgeon, M.R.C.S., L.R.C.P. (Lond.), of Gathorne House, Roundhay Road, Leeds; and Sarah Barrett. Born at Roomfield House, Todmorden, 8 May 1887. Educated at Leeds Grammar School, under the Rev. J. R. Wynne-Edwards. Admitted 1 Oct. 1905.
  B.A. 1908. Nat. Sci. Tripos, Part I, Class 2, 1908.

Pratt, Cecil John Charles: son of Lord Charles Robert Pratt, Lieut.-Col. late Oxfordshire Light Infantry (retired) (deceased), of Hilden Oaks, Tonbridge; and Florence Maria Stevenson. Born at The Palace House, Burnley, Lancashire, 27 Aug. 1886. Educated at Tonbridge School, under the Rev. Dr Wood and the Rev. Dr Tancock. Admitted 1 Oct. 1905. Brother of Ronald, IV. (1) 74.
  B.A. 1908. Med. and Mod. Lang. Tripos, Class 2, 1908. Entrance Scholarship, 1905. Scholar, 1906–8. Ordained deacon (Newcastle), 1909; priest, 1910. Curate at Newcastle, 1909– .

Prestige, Sydney Ernest: son of Sydney Prestige, civil engineer, Assoc.M.Inst.C.E., of Aberdeen House, Blackheath Park, London, S.E.; and Alice Emma Worringham. Born at Homeleigh, Sunderland Road, Forest Hill, Kent, 8 Sept. 1886. Educated at Blackheath School, under Mr Herbert R. Woolrych, M.A. Admitted 1 Oct. 1905. Brother of Arthur, IV. (1) 117.
  B.A. 1908. In the engineering profession.

Prior, Herman Brooke: son of the Rev. Charles Herman Prior, M.A. (deceased), Tutor of Pembroke College, formerly Scholar of Gonville and Caius College (II. 386); and Margaret Westcott. Born at 4, Bene't Place, Cambridge, 9 July 1886. Educated at Goodchild's School, Cambridge; Mason's School, Rottingdean; and Harrow School, under the Rev. Dr Wood. Sayer Scholar. Admitted 1 Oct. 1905.
  B.A. 1908. Class. Tripos, Part I, Class 2, Division 2, 1908. Entrance Scholarship, 1905. Scholar, 1906–8. In the Bombay-Burma Trading Corporation service, Rangoon (1910).

Pritchard, David: son of David Pritchard, of 23, Priory Avenue, Hastings; and Kathleen Hamilton. Born at Solis Villa, Westbourne Road, Forest Hill, London, S.E., 10 March 1885. Educated at Hastings Grammar School, under Mr W. H. La Touche. Admitted 1 Oct. 1905.
  B.A. 1909. Student at Ridley Hall, 1908–9.

Pye-Smith, Talbot Edward Baines: son of Arnold Pye-Smith, manufacturer, of 27, Park Hill Rise, Croydon; and Alice Mary Taunton. Born at 16, Fairfield Road, Croydon, 26 Oct. 1887. Educated at St Anselm's, Bakewell; and Mill Hill School, under Mr J. D. McClure. Admitted 1 Oct. 1905.
  B.A. 1908. Law Tripos, Part I, Class 3, 1907; Part II, Class 3, 1909.

Ramsay, Robert Anstruther: son of Robert Anstruther Ramsay (deceased), Advocate, of Montreal, Canada; and Katherine Hamilton Duff. Born at Montreal, Canada, 18 Feb. 1887. Educated at Wellesley High School, Wellesley, Mass., U.S.A.; and Les Charmettes, Lausanne, under M. Ami Simond. Admitted 1 Oct. 1905.
  B.A. 1908. Nat. Sci. Tripos, Part I, Class 1, 1908.

Richards, Francis Shakspeare: son of Robert Richards, butcher, of 157, High Street, Burton-on-Trent; and Frances Shakespear. Born at 157, High Street, Burton-on-Trent, 27 March 1886. Educated at the Grammar School, Burton-on-Trent, under Mr R. T. Robinson. Admitted 1 Oct. 1905.
  B.A. 1908. Math. Tripos, Part I (br. 12th Wrangler), 1908. Nat. Sci. Tripos, Part I, Class 2, 1909. Entrance Scholarship, 1905. Scholar, 1906–9. In the Egyptian Survey Department, 1909– .

Rogers, George Swire De Moleyns: son of Alfred Tom Rogers (deceased), solicitor; and Harriet Georgina Strickland, of Frenchgate, Richmond, Yorks. Born at The Hermitage, Richmond, Yorks, 1 July 1887. Educated at Richmond School, Yorks, under Mr D. R. Smith and Mr J. M. Furness. Admitted 1 Oct. 1905.
  B.A. 1908. Math. Tripos, Part I (br. 30th Sen. Opt.), 1908. In the Burma Oil Company, Rangoon (1910).

Rolston, Arthur Comyn: son of John Restarick Rolston, surgeon, of 14, The Crescent, Plymouth; and Rose Margaret Comyn. Born at Devonport, 5 April 1885. Educated at Kelly College, Tavistock, N. Devon, under Mr W. H. David. Admitted 1 Oct. 1905.
  B.A. 1909.

Scrimgeour, Geoffrey Cameron: son of the Rev. Ronald Cameron Scrimgeour, Vicar of Sibton, Yoxford, Suffolk; and Lucy May Barrow. Born at Easthampstead, Berkshire, 14 March 1887. Educated at Suffield House, Cromer; and Rugby School, under Dr James. Admitted 1 Oct. 1905.
  B.A. 1908.

Sparrow, Geoffrey: son of Benjamin Sparrow, lime and stone merchant (deceased); and Mary Hutchings, of 15, Rue Armand, Camperhout, Brussels. Born at Greenwood Villa, Ivybridge, Exmington, 13 July 1887. Educated at Alton School, Plymouth; and Kelly College, Tavistock, under the Rev. W. H. David. Admitted 1 Oct. 1905.
  B.A. 1908. Nat. Sci. Tripos, Part I, Class 2, 1908.

Stradling, Arthur Renny: son of Arthur William Stradling, medical practitioner, of 6, Manor Grove, Tonbridge; and Emmaline Isabelle Rennie. Born at 28, Station Road, Watford, 22 June 1885. Educated at Marlborough House, Reading; and Tonbridge School, under the Rev. C. C. Tancock, D.D. Admitted 1 Oct. 1905.
  B.A. 1908. Admitted at the Inner Temple, 1907.

Strickland, Alan Faulkner: son of Peter Strickland (deceased; of the College, II. 394), colonial broker; and Helena Nessie Brown, of The Lodge, Wimbledon. Born at The Lodge, South Side, Wimbledon Common, 6 Jan. 1886. Educated at Stoke House, Slough; Charterhouse, under Dr Rendell. Admitted 1 Oct. 1905.
  B.A. 1908. In the engineering profession.

Stringer, Harold : son of Frederick Septimus Stringer, bank manager, of 3, The Villas, Stoke-on-Trent; and Eliza Sarah Eyre. Born at Lord Street, Basford, Stoke-on-Trent, 3 Sept. 1883. Educated at The High School, Newcastle-on-Tyne, under Mr G. W. Rendall. Admitted 1 Oct. 1905.
B.A. 1908. Railway engineer in China (Nanking), 1910.

Tewson, Edward George : son of Edward Arthur Tewson, land agent (retired), of 14, Molyneaux Park, Tunbridge Wells; and Fides Grimwood. Born at Delamere, Hagger Road, Walthamstow, 17 April 1886. Educated at Malvern College, under the Rev. S. R. James. Admitted 1 Oct. 1905.
Choral Entrance Exhibition, 1905. Resided one year.

Treadgold, Harry : son of John Reckerby Treadgold, grocer, of Birklands, Christchurch Road, Bournemouth; and Marie Balls. Born at Ivy Dene Southcote Road, Bournemouth, 11 Nov. 1886. Educated at the Boys' High School, Bournemouth; and Leys School, Cambridge, under the Rev. Dr Barber. Admitted 1 Oct. 1905.
B.A. 1908. Hist. Tripos, Part I, Class 3, 1907; Part II, Class 2, 1908.

Wainwright, Charles Barron : son of Musson Wainwright, wholesale merchant, of Hamilton, Bermuda; and Janie McEwan Barron. Born at Bermuda, 12 June 1885. Educated at Saltus Grammar School, Bermuda; and Felsted School, under the Rev. H. A. Dalton. Admitted 1 Oct. 1905.
B.A. 1908. Nat. Sci. Tripos, Part I, Class 2, 1908.

Watson, Walter Geoffrey : son of Walter Herbert Watson, gentleman, of The Acacias, Old Chesterton, Cambridge; and Annie Jowett. Born at 9, Valley View Grove, Bradford, 26 Sept. 1886. Educated at Bradford Grammar School, under the Rev. W. H. Keeling. Admitted 1 Oct. 1905. Brother of Francis, iv. (1) 53.
B.A. 1909.

Watt, George Townsend Candy : son of Arthur Chorley Watt (deceased), judge, East Indian Civil Service; and Henrietta Vary Hunter. Born at 61, Picton Road, Wavertree, 3 April 1886. Educated at Clifton College, under the Rev. Canon M. G. Glazebrook. Admitted 1 Oct. 1905.
B.A. 1908. Entrance Exhibition, 1905. Master at Wixenford Preparatory School, Wokingham (1911).

Weeks, Llewellyn McIntyre : son of Richard Llewellyn Weeks, mining engineer, of Willington House, Willington, co. Durham; and Susan Helen Walker McIntyre. Born at Burn House, Helmington Row, co. Durham, 9 June 1887. Educated at The Mount, Northallerton; and Charterhouse, under Dr Rendell. Admitted 1 Oct. 1905. Brother of Ronald, iv. (1) 119.
B.A. 1908. Nat. Sci. Tripos, Part I, Class 3, 1908.

Wigmore, James Buckley Aquilla : son of James Wigmore, M.D., of 26, Green Park, Bath; and Catharine Elizabeth Brown. Born at Twerton Villa, Twerton-on-Avon, Bath, 31 Oct. 1887. Educated at the Hermitage School, Bath; and Bath College, under Mr Trice Martin. Admitted 1 Oct. 1905.
B.A. 1908. Nat. Sci. Tripos, Part I, Class 2, 1908.

Whitley, Herbert: son of Edward Whitley, solicitor (deceased), formerly M.P. for Liverpool; and Elizabeth Eleanor Walker. Born at Halewood, near Liverpool, 2 Jan. 1886. Educated at Liverpool College; Clifton College; and Bromsgrove School, under Mr H. Millington and Mr F. J. R. Hendy. Admitted 1 Oct. 1905.
Kept two terms.

Wilkinson, George Jerrard: son of the Rev. Willoughby Balfour Wilkinson (of the College, II. 368), Vicar of Bishop's Itchington, near Leamington; and Amy Hale. Born at Pershore Road, Edgbaston, Birmingham, 16 Aug. 1885. Educated at Uppingham, under the Rev. Dr Selwyn. Admitted 1 Oct. 1905.
B.A. 1908. Musical Scholar, 1905–8.

Willcocks, Robert Waller: son of George Waller Willcocks, civil engineer, of Redthorn, Rodwey Road, Roehampton, London, S.E.; and Mary Escombe. Born at 3, Lisgar Terrace, West Kensington, 26 July 1887. Educated at Westminster School, under the Rev. Dr Rutherford and the Rev. Dr Gow. Admitted 1 Oct. 1905.
B.A. 1908. Nat. Sci. Tripos, Part I, Class 2, 1908.

Willey, Rupert Harold: son of Joseph Willey, draper, of Regent Terrace, Penzance; and Lydia James. Born at 12, Regent Terrace, Penzance, 20 June 1886. Educated at Probus School, Cornwall; and the Leys School, Cambridge, under the Rev. Dr Barber. Admitted 1 Oct. 1905.
B.A. 1908. Theol. Tripos, Part I, Class 1, 1908; Part II, Class 1 (a) (Hebrew Prize), 1909. Scholar, 1906–9. Open Stewart of Rannoch Scholarship in Hebrew, 1907. Carus Greek Testament Prize for Undergraduates, 1908. Tyrwhitt Hebrew Scholarship, 1909. Mason Prize for Biblical Hebrew, 1909. Schuldham Plate, 1909. Research Studentship, 1909.

Williams, Raymond Burke: son of John Richard Williams, merchant, of 11, West Hill, Highgate, London; and Edith Boxwell. Born at Glenville, Wexford, Ireland, 10 Jan. 1887. Educated at Cheltenham College, under the Rev. R. Waterfield. Admitted 1 Oct. 1905.
B.A. 1908.

Williams, Thomas Bowen: son of David Williams (deceased), merchant, of Dolgader House, Llanybyther, Carmarthenshire; and Anne Bowen. Born at Dolgader House, Llanybyther, S. Wales, 22 Jan. 1880. Educated at Llandovery College; Lampeter College, under the Rev. Principal Bebb. In Holy Orders. Admitted 1 Oct. 1905.
B.A. 1908. Nat. Sci. Tripos, Part I, Class 3, 1908. Curate at Harrogate, 1908–

Wimbush, Ronald: son of Charles Wimbush, director of Wimbush & Co., Ltd., of Netherelms, Woodside Avenue, N. Finchley; and Helen Stewart Robertson. Born at Newstead House, Finchley, 2 Jan. 1885. Educated at Merchant Taylors', under the Rev. Dr Nairn; and privately, under Mr Arthur Reynolds, Charterhouse, E.C. Admitted 1 Oct. 1905.
B.A. 1908. Ordained deacon (Southwark), 1909; priest, 1910. Assistant-Missioner at the College Mission, Battersea, 1909- ·

5

Woodruff, George Gould: son of William Herbert Woodruff, dental surgeon, of
6, Stratford Place, London, W.; and Jacquetta Southmead Gould.   Born
at 13, New Burlington Street, London, 31 July 1886.   Educated at Ascham
House, Eastbourne; and Rossall School, under the Rev. Dr Way.   Admitted
1 Oct. 1905.
    B.A. 1908.   Math. Tripos, Part I (br. 33rd Wrangler), 1908.   Entrance
    Scholarship, 1905.   Scholar, 1906-8.   In the Asiatic Petroleum
    Company at Yokohama, 1910- .

Yeats, Basil Edward: son of the Rev. George Yeats, M.A., Vicar of Heworth,
    York; and Rosa Bertha Walker.   Born at Heworth Vicarage, 6 Aug. 1887.
    Educated at St Peter's School, York, under the Rev. G. T. Handford and
    the Rev. E. C. Owen.   Admitted 1 Oct. 1905.
    B.A. 1908.   Master at Cargilfield School, Cramond Bridge, 1908- .

Bradfield, Linden Gordon: son of John Linden Bradfield, attorney (retired), of
    Indwe, Cape Colony; and Jeanie Shearer.   Born at Dordrecht, Cape Colony,
    10 March 1886.   Educated at the High School, Dordrecht; and South
    African College, under Mr H. B. Stanwell.   Admitted 1 Oct. 1905.
    B.A. 1908.

Candy, Edward Townshend; Knight Bachelor: son of Thomas Candy, C.S.I.,
    major, Indian Army (deceased); and Carolina Boyce.   Born at Mahabhesh-
    war, Bombay Presidency, India, 15 April 1845.   Educated at Cheltenham
    College, under the Rev. W. Dobson, the Rev. H. Highton, and the Rev. Dr
    Barry.   Admitted 21 Feb. 1906.
    M.A. (Hon.) 1908.   Deputy for the Reader in Indian Law, 1906.   Teacher
    in Indian Law, 1907- , and Teacher in Marathi, 1909-10, under the
    Board of Indian Civil Service Studies.

Clifford, Maurice William: son of Miller Hancorne Clifford, gentleman, of
    53, Canynge Road, Clifton, Bristol; and Louisa Mann Peterson.   Born at
    Dehra Dun, N. W. P., India, 10 Jan. 1886.   School: Clifton College, under
    the Rev. Canon M. G. Glazebrook.   Admitted 20 April 1906.
    Resided one term.

Oliver, Thomas Herbert: son of Thomas Andrew Oliver, lace manufacturer,
    of Moorside, Sidmouth, Devon; and Florence Herbert.   Born at 10, Ebury
    Road, New Basford, Nottingham, 31 Dec. 1887.   School: Rugby, under
    Dr James; and University College, Nottingham.   Admitted 9 June 1906.
    Brother of Harold, IV. (1) 95.
    B.A. 1909.   Nat. Sci. Tripos, Part I, Class 1, 1909.

Brooks, Frederick Tom: son of Edward Brooks, clerk of works, of 8, Davis
    Terrace, Wells, Somerset; and Ann Maria Downing.   Born at Wells,
    Somerset, 17 Dec. 1882.   School: Sexey's, Bruton, Somerset, under
    Mr W. A. Knight.   Previously four years at Emmanuel College.   Admitted
    July 1906, as Frank Smart Student.
    B.A. (1905) at Emmanuel College.   Senior Demonstrator of Botany,
    1911.

Johnson, Robert Harrington: son of Robert Sedgwick Johnson, estate agent's clerk, of Vron Deg, Upton Park, Chester; and !Alice Harrington. Born at 100, Garden Lane, Chester, 5 April 1887. Educated at the Technical School, Chester; and Strand School, King's College, London, under Mr W. Braginton. Previously kept three terms at Selwyn College. Admitted 1 Oct. 1906.

> B.A. 1908. Theol. Tripos, Part I, Class 3, 1908. Choral Exhibitioner, 1906–8. Ordained deacon (Truro) 1910; priest 1911. Curate of Par, Cornwall, 1910–

MICHAELMAS 1906 TO MICHAELMAS 1907.

(Tutors: Mr Buckland, Mr Hardy and Mr Cameron.)

Armstrong, John Cardew: son of Henry George Armstrong, medical officer to Wellington College, Berks; and Annette Ethel Cardew (deceased). Born at Wellington College, Berks, 3 June 1887. Schools: Crowthorne Preparatory School; and Wellington College, under Dr Pollock. Admitted 1 Oct. 1906.

> B.A. 1910. University Commission in the Army, 1910.

Arnfield, Gordon: son of Thomas Owen Arnfield, manufacturing engineer, of Redgate, New Mills, Stockport; and Julia Brayne. Born at New Mills, Stockport, 17 Aug. 1888. Schools: Dinglewood, Colwyn Bay, under J. and S. Wood. Admitted 1 Oct. 1906.

> B.A. 1909. Nat. Sci. Tripos, Part I, Class 3, 1909.

Aron, Frederick Adolph: son of Ludwig Aron, merchant, of South Villa, Victoria Park, Manchester; and Amélie Herz. Born at South Villa, Victoria Park, Manchester, 4 June 1888. School: Shrewsbury, under Mr Moss. Admitted 1 Oct. 1906.

> B.A. 1910. Nat. Sci. Tripos, Part I, Class 3, 1910.

Ascoli, George Hugh Daniel: son of Ephraim Ascoli, shipper, etc., of Brooklyn Lodge, Withington, Manchester; and Clementine Fleischmann. Born at Withington, Lancashire, 30 Mar. 1888. School: Manchester Grammar, under Mr J. L. Paton. Admitted 1 Oct. 1906.

> B.A. 1910.

Ashcroft, Alec Hutchinson: son of Charles Wesley Ashcroft, corn miller, of Waterford Road, Oxton, Birkenhead; and Alice Mason Hutchinson. Born at Liverpool, 18 Oct. 1887. School: Birkenhead, under the Rev. A. Sloman, and the Rev. F. Griffin. Admitted 1 Oct. 1906. Brother of William, IV. (1) 11; and Harold, IV. (1) 46.

> B.A. 1909. Class. Tripos, Part I, Class 1, div. 2, 1909; Hist. Tripos, Part II, Class 1, 1910. Entrance Scholarship, 1906. Scholar, 1907–10. University (Rugby) football player, 1908, 1909; International player, 1909. Master at Fettes College, Edinburgh, 1910– .

Atkin, Charles Sidney: son of Charles Atkin, F.R.C.S., of Endcliffe Croft, Sheffield; and Alice Brady. Born at 287, Glossop Road, Sheffield, 26 Feb. 1889. Educated at St Aurelius, Bakewell; Marlborough College, under Dr Bell and Mr Fletcher. Admitted 1 Oct. 1906.

> B.A. 1909. Captain, Hockey Club, 1908–9. Captain of University Hockey Club, 1909–10.

Avent, Mark: son of the Rev. John Avent (of the College, II. 329), Rector of Broughton, Lechlade, Glos.; and Alice Thornton. Born at Broughton-Pogis, Devon, 23 July 1888. Schools: Hunstanton and Hindhead; and Radley College, Abingdon, under the Rev. T. Field. Admitted 1 Oct. 1906. Brother of John, II. 518; and Ernest, II. 536.
B.A. 1910.

Barlow, Lancelot White: son of Alfred Barlow, gentleman, of Kelvedon, Bloem-fontein, South Africa; and Kate Brereton. Born at Bloemfontein, South Africa, 11 June 1887. School: Grey College School, Bloemfontein, under Dr J. Bull. Admitted 1 Oct. 1906.
B.A. 1910.

Bartlett, Harold Sloan: son of Felix Paul Bartlett, surgeon, of Raleigh House, Ottery St Mary, Devon; and Marian Sloan. Born at Cowra, New South Wales, 16 Sept. 1888. School: Blundell's, Tiverton, under Mr A. Francis. Admitted 1 Oct. 1906.
Resided three years. Farming in Australia (1910).

Beech, John: son of John Beech, bank cashier, of Glen Burn, Basford Park, Stoke-on-Trent; and Kate Davis. Born at Congleton, Cheshire, 1 July 1887. School: Newcastle-under-Lyme High School, under Mr G. W. Rundall and Mr F. Harrison. Admitted 1 Oct. 1906.
B.A. 1909. Nat. Sci. Tripos, Part I, Class 1, 1908. Math. Tripos, Part I, Class 1, 1909; Part II, Sen. Opt. 1910. Entrance Exhibition, 1906. Scholar, 1907–10. Eastern Cadetship, 1910.

Belfield, Stafford St George Conway: son of Henry Conway Belfield, J.P. (Colonial Civil Service, Resident, Selangor, Federated Malay States), of Cambridge Lodge, East Sheen, Surrey; and Florence Rathborne. Born at Shanklin, Isle of Wight, 20 Sept. 1887. Schools: Quebec House, St Leonards-on-Sea; and Eton College, under the Rev. E. Warre. Admitted 1 Oct. 1906.
B.A. 1909.

Boyson, John Charles: son of John Alexander Boyson, East India merchant and banker, of 5, Durward House, Kensington Court, London; and Mary Josephine Bowen. Born at London, 1 Jan. 1888. School: The Oratory, Edgbaston, under the Rev. J. Norris. Admitted 1 Oct. 1906.
Kept seven terms.

Breach, Wilfred Norman: son of Charles Breach, solicitor, of Kitsbury Lawn Berkhamsted; and Edith Rachel Marshall. Born at 20, King's Road, Wimbledon, 5 Aug. 1887. School: Berkhamsted, under Dr Fry. Admitted 1 Oct. 1906.
B.A. 1910.

Brown, Charles Barrington: son of Charles Barrington Brown, geologist, of Cotinga, Harrowdene Road, Wembley, Middlesex; and Clara Mavor. Born at 77, Ladbroke Grove Road, Notting Hill, 10 March 1884. Schools: St Michael's College, N. Kensington; St Paul's School, under Mr Walker and Rev. A. E. Hillard; Royal School of Mines, S. Kensington. Admitted 1 Oct. 1906.
B.A. 1909. Nat. Sci. Tripos, Part I, Class 2, 1908; Part II, Class 3, 1909. Engaged in Commercial Geology, Peru (1910).

Brown, Harold Montagu: son of William Charles Brown, company director, of Penchirche, Oaklands Road, Bromley, Kent; and Catherine Cecilia Ellen Scudamore. Born at Penchirche, Oaklands Road, Bromley, Kent, 31 Dec. 1887. Schools: Streete Court, Westgate; and Uppingham, under the Rev. Dr Selwyn. Admitted 1 Oct. 1906. Brother of Anthony, IV. (1) 12.
B.A. 1909. Hist. Tripos, Part I, Class 3, 1908. Law Tripos, Part II, Class 3 (br. 7th), 1909.

Calderwood, John Lindow: son of George Calderwood, surgeon, of Beech House, Egremont, Cumberland; and Mary Eleanor Lindow. Born at 57, Main Street, Egremont, Cumberland, 22 Jan. 1888. School: St Bees Grammar, under the Rev. W. T. Newbold and the Rev. H. A. P. Sawyer. Admitted 1 Oct. 1906.
B.A., LL.B., 1909. Law Tripos, Part I, Class 3 (br. 3rd), 1908; Part II, Class 3 (br. 2nd), 1909.

Carey, Gordon Vero: son of Francis Carey, gentleman, of Lea Copse, Burgess Hill, Sussex; and Elizabeth Harrowell. Born at Sible Hedingham, Essex, 9 Oct. 1886. Schools: King's College Choir, Cambridge; and Eastbourne College, under Mr H. R. Thomson. Admitted 1 Oct. 1906.
B.A. 1909. Class. Tripos, Part I, Class 2, Division 1, 1909. Entrance Scholarship, 1906. Scholar, 1907-9. Chapel Clerk (Choral), 1908-9. Captain, Rugby Football, 1908-9; University player, 1908. Master at Eastbourne College, 1909-10; at Trinity College, Glenalmond, 1911- .

Cooke, William Ingram: son of Joseph Cooke, newspaper proprietor, of 94, West Street, Boston; and Laetitia Walker. Born at Boston, 21 May 1886. School: Boston Grammar, under Mr W. White. Admitted 1 Oct. 1906.
B.A. 1909. Math. Tripos, Part I, 64 (Junior Optime), 1909.

Cory, Charles Woolnough: son of the Rev. Charles Page Cory, of Rosedale, Maymye, Burma, India; and Grace Gross. Born in Madagascar, 10 Nov. 1887. School: Sedbergh, under Mr C. Lowry. Admitted 1 Oct. 1906. Brother of Robert, IV. (1) 47.
B.A. 1909.

Cullimore, William: son of John Cullimore, solicitor, of Christleton, Chester; and Mary Elizabeth Dale. Born at Christleton, Chester, 20 May 1888. School: Shrewsbury, under the Rev. H. W. Moss. Admitted 1 Oct. 1906. Brother of James, IV. (1) 47, and Charles, IV. (1) 103.
B.A. 1909. Nat. Sci. Tripos, Part I, Class 2, 1909.

Darley, Cecil Barrington: son of Cecil West Darley, I.S.O., M.Inst.C.E., of 34, Campden Hill Court, Kensington, W.; and Constance Leila Annette Campbell. Born at Sydney, New South Wales, 22 July 1887. Schools: The Grammar School, Sydney; Haileybury College, under the Hon. and Rev. E. Lyttelton; and King's College School, under the Rev. C. W. Bourne. Admitted 1 Oct. 1906.
Kept nine terms.

Dawes, Henry Franklin: son of Maurice Dawes, retired merchant, of Woodstock, Ontario, Canada; and Catherine Stewart. Born at Paisley, Ontario, Canada, 15 Oct. 1881. Schools: Woodstock Collegiate Institute, Canada; Toronto University. M.A. of Toronto University. Admitted as an advanced Student, 1 Oct. 1906.
Wollaston Studentship, 1906-8. Professor of Physics at the McMaster University, Toronto (1911).

Ebden, William Sydenham: son of Edward James Ebden, I.C.S. (retired) of 17, All Saints' Road, Clifton, Bristol; and Mary Anne Bullock. Born at Kirkee, Bombay, India, 3 Oct. 1887. School: Clifton College, under the Rev. Canon M. G. Glazebrook and Rev. A. A. David. Admitted 1 Oct. 1906. Brother of James, IV. (1) 20.

   B.A. 1909. Class. Tripos, Part I, Class 2, Division 1, 1909. Entrance Exhibition, 1906. Exhibition, 1907–9. Eastern Cadetship, 1911.

Eley, Henry Gerard: son of Henry Eley (retired captain H.M.S.), of Altyre House, Great Horkesley, Colchester; and Kathleen Smyth. Born at 12, Herbert Place, Dublin, 19 Nov. 1887. Schools: Rolstead Hall; and Charterhouse, under the Rev. Dr Rendall. Admitted 1 Oct. 1906. Kept three terms.

Ewing, William Turner: son of James Laidlaw Ewing, manufacturing chemist, of Derreen, Murrayfield, Midlothian; and Mary Turner. Born at 18, St Catherine's Place, Edinburgh, 15 Dec. 1887. School: Edinburgh Academy; and Trinity College, Glenalmond, under the Rev. W. Hyslop. Admitted 1 Oct. 1906.

   B.A. 1910. In his father's business.

Forman, Dudley Perry: son of James Forman, newspaper proprietor, of Cavendish Crescent North, The Park, Nottingham; and Ethel Perry. Born at 54, Forest Road, Nottingham, 13 May 1887. Schools: Arthur Street, Nottingham; Boxgrove, Guildford; and Rugby, under Dr James. Admitted 1 Oct. 1906.

   B.A. 1909. Hist. Tripos, Part I, Class 1, 1908; Part II, Class 1, 1909. Entrance Scholarship, 1906. Scholar, 1907–9. Colour-printer.

Graham, Lionel Augustine: son of George William Graham, L.R.C.P., M.R.C.S., L.S.A., of Camlough, Portarlington Road, Bournemouth, W.; and Susan Sarah Richardson. Born at Stoneleigh, Wimborne, Dorset, 21 Dec. 1887. School: Downside College, near Bath, under the Rev. H. L. Ramsay. Admitted 1 Oct. 1906.

   Captain, Lawn Tennis Club, 1909–10.

Grimwade, Edward Ernest: son of Sydney Richard Grimwade, earthenware manufacturer, of 29, Jackson's Lane, Highgate, London, N.; and Agnes Mary Ellis Illingworth. Born at Holders Lea, Blythe Bridge, near Stoke-on-Trent, Staffs, 16 Dec. 1885. Educated at Newcastle High School, Newcastle-under-Lyme; Dr Lange's Privat Realschule, Hamburg; The Swiss School at Neuchâtel. Admitted 1 Oct. 1906.

   B.A. 1909. Med. and Mod. Lang. Tripos, Class 2, 1909. With the Calcutta Port Commissioners (1910).

Hancock, Walter Raleigh: son of the Rev. Frederick Hancock, Vicar of Dunster Priory, Prebendary of Wells; of Dunster Priory, Somerset; and Baptista Josephine Wilson Woodhouse. Born at Selworthy, Somerset, 30 Oct. 1887. Schools: Walton Lodge, Clevedon; Charterhouse, under Dr Rendall; and privately. Admitted 1 Oct. 1906.

   Kept three terms. Tea-planting in Ceylon (1911).

Hickman, Christie William: son of Alfred William Hickman, ironmaster (deceased) of Golthorn Hill, Wolverhampton; and Mary Whitby Hickin (of Trunkwell House, near Reading). Born at Pennfields, Wolverhampton, 23 March 1888. School: Farfield, Malvern; and Marlborough College, under the Rev. G. C. Bell and Mr F. Fletcher. Admitted 1 Oct. 1906.

   B.A. 1909. Nat. Sci. Tripos, Part I, Class 3, 1909.

Hitchcock, Roger Knight: son of Charles Knight Hitchcock (of the College, II.
389), physician, of Bootham Park, York; and Alice Hailstone. Born at
Bootham Park, York, 19 June 1886. School: Giggleswick, under the
Rev. G. Style and Mr W. W. Vaughan. Admitted 1 Oct. 1906.
Resided three years. President of the Musical Society, 1908–9.

Hunkin, Joseph Wellington : son of Joseph Weston Hunkin, ship owner, coal and
cement merchant, of 16, The Parade, Truro, Cornwall; and Elizabeth Hockin
Wellington. Born at Truro, 25 Sept. 1887. Schools: Truro College; and
The Leys School, Cambridge, under the Rev. Dr Barber. Admitted 1 Oct.
1906.
> B.A. 1909. Math. Tripos, Part I (br. 12th Wrangler), 1908. Entrance
> Scholarship, 1906. Scholar, 1907–10. Schuldham Plate, 1910. Research
> Student, 1910. Carus Prize, 1910. Crosse (University) Scholar, 1910.
> At Headingly College, 1910–11.

Inman, Ernest Charles: son of Richard Inman, yeoman, of Low House, Garsdale
Sedbergh, Yorks; and Martha Mason. Born at Low House, Garsdale,
Sedbergh, Yorks, 26 March 1887. Schools: Garsdale National School; and
Sedbergh, under Mr Lowry. Admitted 1 Oct. 1906.
> B.A. 1909. Theol. Tripos, Part I, Class 2, 1909. Exhibition, 1907.
> Stewart of Rannoch Scholarship in Hebrew, 1908. President, Athletic
> Club, 1908–9. University athlete. Ordained deacon (Ripon), 1911.
> Curate of St John and St Barnabas, Holbeck, 1911– .

Irwin, Alfred Percy Bulteel : son of Alfred MacDonald Bulteel Irwin, C.S.I., of
5, Raglan Road, Dublin; and Alice Kathleen French. Born at Pegu, Burma,
30 Sept. 1887. School: Sedbergh School, under Mr C. Lowry. Admitted
1 Oct. 1906.
> B.A. 1910. University Commission in the Army, 1910.

Jarvis, Frederic : son of Ernest Frederic Jarvis (deceased); and Emma Green, of
Albert House, Cromer. Born at Cromer, 16 April 1885. School: Gresham's,
Holt, under the Rev. R. T. Roberts and Mr G. W. S. Howson. Admitted
1 Oct. 1906.
> B.A. 1910. Hist. Tripos, Part I, Class 3, 1908. Chapel Clerk, 1908–9.
> Captain of the Boat Club, 1908–9. Ordained deacon (Norw.), 1910.
> Curate of Blakeney, 1910– .

Kirk, Arthur: son of Samuel Kirk, commercial traveller, of 92, Bellott Street
Cheetham Hill, Manchester; and Sarah Ann Cooke. Born at 35, Cobden
Street, Nottingham, 12 Sept. 1887. Schools: Cheetham Higher Grade; and
Manchester Grammar, under Mr J. L. Paton. Admitted 1 Oct. 1906.
> B.A. 1910. Med. and Mod. Lang. Tripos, Class 1, with distinction, 1910.
> Entrance Scholarship, 1906. Scholar, 1907–10. Master at Bolton
> Grammar School, 1910–11.

Knox, William : son of Robert William Knox, J.P. (deceased), manufacturer; and
Jessie Fulton, of Moor Park, Kilbirnie, Ayrshire. Born at Moor Park,
Kilbirnie, Ayrshire, 9 April 1888. School: The Leys, Cambridge, under the
Rev. Dr Barber. Admitted 1 Oct. 1906.
> B.A. 1909.

Leak, Hector: son of Hector Leak, M.R.C.S., L.R.C.P., of Dingle House, Winsford, Cheshire; and Miriam Annie Bagott. Born at Dingle House, Winsford, Cheshire, 23 July 1887. School: Berkhamsted, under Dr Fry. Admitted 1 Oct. 1906.
> B.A. 1909. Math. Tripos, Part I, 9th Wrangler, 1908. Nat. Sci. Tripos, Part I, Class 2, 1909. Entrance Scholarship, 1906. Scholar, 1907–10. Home Civil Service, 1910– .

Lester, Ronald Kingsley: son of Henry Edward Lester, shipper (retired), of The Grange, Loughton, Essex; and Mary Johnson. Born at Leytonstone, Essex, 7 Dec. 1887. School: Mill Hill, under Dr J. D. McClure. Admitted 1 Oct. 1906.
> B.A. 1909.

Lewis, Trevor Edward: son of Henry Lewis, colliery proprietor, of Tynant, Taff's Well, near Cardiff; and Katherine Hannah Davies. Born at Tynant, Taff's Well, near Cardiff, 13 Oct. 1887. School: Clifton College, under the Rev. Canon M. G. Glazebrook. Admitted 1 Oct. 1906.
> B.A. 1909. Nat. Sci. Tripos, Part I, Class 2, 1908.

Lloyd, Arthur Cresswell: son of Philip James Lloyd, tea merchant, of 22, Hurle Crescent, Clifton, Bristol; and Emma Margaret Pierce. Born at Clifton, 10 July 1887. School: Clifton College, under the Rev. A. A. David. Admitted 1 Oct. 1906.
> Resided three terms.

MacDonald, John Norman: son of Ebenezer MacDonald (late banker); and Elizabeth Gray. Born at Sydney, Australia, 8 April 1888. Schools: St Andrews, Southborough; and Cheltenham College, under the Rev. R. Waterfield. Admitted 1 Oct. 1906.
> B.A. 1909. Lieut. in the King's Colonials (1910).

McGeagh, George Robert Denison: son of Robert Thomas McGeagh, M.D., of 15, Breeze Hill, Bootle, Lancashire; and Ida Charlotte Napier Morice. Born at Exeter, 12 Dec. 1887. School: Uppingham, under the Rev. Dr E. C. Selwyn. Admitted 1 Oct. 1906.
> B.A. 1909. Nat. Sci. Tripos, Part I, Class 3, 1909.

McNair, Arnold Duncan: son of John McNair, underwriting member of Lloyd's, of Glynde, Christchurch Park, Sutton, Surrey; and Jeanie Ballantyne. Born at Highbury, London, 4 March 1885. Educated at Sutton Preparatory School; Aldenham School, under the Rev. A. H. Cooke. Qualified Solicitor. Admitted 1 Oct. 1906.
> B.A., LL.B. 1909. Law Tripos, Part I, Class 1, 1908; Part II, Class 1, 1909. Scholar, 1907–9. President of the Union Society, 1909. Editor of *The Caian*, 1908–9. Solicitor in London (1910). Lecturer for the Incorporated Law Society (1911).

Malcolm, Alan Samuel Lack: son of William Aberdeen Malcolm, M.B., C.M. (Edin.), of Oak House, 421, Holloway Road, London, N.; and Helen Agnes Mason. Born at 421, Holloway Road, London, N., 5 April 1888. Schools: Highgate Preparatory; and Highgate School, under the Rev. A. E. Allcock. Admitted 1 Oct. 1906.
> B.A. 1910.

Mason, James Herbert: son of William Joshua Mason, engineer, of Woodville, Lovelace Road, Surbiton; and Eliza Emily Walters. Born at Holmleigh, The Avenue, Surbiton, 16 June 1887. Schools: Wellesley House, Broadstairs; and Haileybury College, under the Hon. Canon Lyttelton and the Rev. B. St J. Wynne Wilson. Admitted 1 Oct. 1906.
> B.A. 1910. Mech. Sci. Tripos (*aegrotat*), 1910. Entrance Scholarship, 1906. Scholar, 1907–9.

Meggeson, Richard Ronald Hornsey: son of Thomas Agar Meggeson, engineer, of Southlands, Sandon, Chelmsford; and Sarah Ann Masterman. Born at Middlesbrough, Yorks, 9 July 1887. Schools: Higher Grade School, Stockton-on-Tees; and High School, Middlesbrough, under Mr W. Edwards. Admitted 1 Oct. 1906.
> B.A. 1909. Math. Tripos, Part I (15th Wrangler), 1909. Entrance Exhibition, 1906. Scholar, 1907–9.

Melvill, Lionel Vintcent: son of Edward Harker Vintcent Melvill, surveyor, of Johannesburg, South Africa; and Johannah Elizabeth (Melvill). Born at Plumstead, near Cape Town, S.A., 7 Jan. 1888. Schools: St Andrew's, Grahamstown, S.A.; and Clifton College, under the Rev. M. G. Glazebrook. Admitted 1 Oct. 1906.
> B.A. 1909. Nat. Sci. Tripos, Part I, Class 2, 1908. Student of Mining at Freiberg (1910).

Metcalfe, George Christopher: son of John Hawbridge Metcalfe, J.P., company director, of Wood Close, Pateley Bridge, Yorks; and Adeline Walker. Born at Grassfield House, Bewerley, Pateley Bridge, 21 Dec. 1887. Schools: Oatlands, Harrogate; and Shrewsbury School, under the Rev. Preb. Moss. Admitted 1 Oct. 1906.

Metcalfe-Gibson, Arthur Edward: son of Thomas Atkinson Metcalfe-Gibson, gentleman, of Elm Lodge, Ravenstonedale, Westmoreland; and Mary Beck. Born at Ravensdale, 20 April 1888. School: Harrogate College, Yorkshire, under the late Mr G. M. Savery and Mr A. F. Gotch. Admitted 1 Oct. 1906.
> B.A. 1909.

Miller, Austin Timæus: son of Joseph Miller, J.P., surveyor, of 1, de Parys Avenue, Bedford; and Eliza Jane Timæus. Born at 1, de Parys Avenue, Bedford, 28 July 1888. School: Bedford Grammar School, under Mr J. S. Phillpotts and Mr J. E. King. Admitted 1 Oct. 1906.
> B.A. 1910. University Commission in the Army, 1910.

Milligan, Robert Alexander: son of Robert Gordon Milligan, merchant, of 86, Herne Hill, London, S.E.; and Margaret Beck. Born at 15, De Crespigny Park, Camberwell, London, 28 Jan. 1887. Schools: Dulwich College Preparatory; and Sedbergh, under Mr C. Lowry. Admitted 1 Oct. 1906.
> Kept six terms. Farming (1911).

Nangle, Edward Jocelyn: son of Edward Cuthbert Nangle, M.B., B.Ch., B.A., Dublin, of Grahamstown, East London; and Dorothy Bolland Brisco. Born at Alice, Cape Colony, 15 June 1888. School: St Andrew's College, Grahamstown, under Canon Espion and Dr McGowan; and Rhodes University, Grahamstown. Admitted 1 Oct. 1906.
> Nat. Sci. Tripos, Part I, Class 2, 1909.

Pearkes, André Mellard: son of Walter Pearkes, master draper, of Lulworth, Upton Road, Watford; and Catherine Mary Culshaw. Born at 28, St Albans Road, Watford, 10 May 1888. Schools: Milton House School, Watford; and Tonbridge School, under Dr C. C. Tancock. Admitted 1 Oct. 1906.

> B.A. 1909. Med. and Mod. Lang. Tripos, Class 1, 1909. Entrance Exhibition, 1906. Scholar, 1907–9.

Pendered, John Hawkes: son of John Pendered, auctioneer, valuer and estate agent, of The Wigwam, Hatton Park, Wellingborough; and Louisa Hawkes. Born at Harrowden Road, Wellingborough, 7 Sept. 1888. School: Wellingborough Grammar, under Mr H. E. Platt. Admitted 1 Oct. 1906.

> B.A. 1909. Nat. Sci. Tripos, Part I, 1909.

Pratt, Ronald Arthur Frederick: son of Lord Charles Robert Pratt (deceased); and Florence Maria Stevenson, of Hilden Oaks, Tonbridge. Born at Palace House, Burnley, Lancashire, 27 Aug. 1886. School: Tonbridge, under the Rev. Dr J. Wood and Dr C. C. Tancock. Admitted 1 Oct. 1906. Brother of Cecil, iv. (1) 62.

> B.A. 1909. Ordained deacon (London), 1910. Curate of Emmanuel Church, West Hampstead, 1910–

Raimes, Lancelot: son of Frederick Raimes, J.P., general merchant, of Hartburn Lodge, Stockton-on-Tees; and Maria Dresser. Born at 2, Westbourne Street, Stockton-on-Tees, 2 April 1887. School: The Leys School, Cambridge, under the Rev. Dr Barber. Admitted 1 Oct. 1906.

> B.A. 1909. Med. and Mod. Lang. Tripos, Class 2, 1909.

Ramsay, Alexander: son of the Rev. Alexander Ramsay, M.A., B.D., Presbyterian minister, of 15, Cromwell Place, Highgate, London, N.; and Ella Euphemia Barbara Clark. Born at Coatbridge, Lanarkshire, N.B., 9 Aug. 1887. School: City of London, under Mr A. T. Pollard and the Rev. A. Chilton. Admitted 1 Oct. 1906.

> B.A. 1909. Class. Tripos, Part I, Class 1, Div. 2, 1909. Entrance Scholarship, 1906. Scholar, 1907–10. President of the Union Society, 1909. Junior Inspector in the Board of Education, 1911.

Reynolds, Ernest Percy: son of William George Reynolds, commercial traveller, of Longview, Harlow Moor, Harrogate; and Lucy Hooley. Born at Ebberstone, Franklin Road, Harrogate, 26 Oct. 1886. Schools: The College, Harrogate; and Clifton College, under the Rev. Canon M. G. Glazebrook and the Rev. A. A. David. Admitted 1 Oct. 1906.

> B.A. 1909; LL.B. 1910. Nat. Sci. Tripos, Part I, Class 1, 1908. Law Tripos, Part II, Class 2 (br. 7th), 1910. Entrance Scholarship, 1906. Scholar, 1907–10. Captain, Cricket Club, 1908–9. With Cookson and Co., Newcastle-on-Tyne.

Richards, Frederick Maurice Smith: son of Samuel Smith Crosland Richards, C.B., of Falconhurst, Maison Dieu Road, Dover; and Josephine Rogers Thomson. Born at Burbage House, Burbage, near Hinckley, Leicestershire, 14 April 1889. School: Dover College, under the Rev. W. C. Compton. Admitted 1 Oct. 1906. Brother of Crosland, iv. (1) 51.

> B.A. 1909. Hist. Tripos, Part I, Class 3, 1908. Chapel Clerk, 1908–9. Theological Exhibitioner, 1909.

Rigby, Francis John: son of John Richard Rigby, solicitor, of Ashbourne, Derbyshire; and Clara Jane Skewington. Born at St John Street, Ashbourne, Derbyshire, 31 Jan. 1888. Schools: Ashbourne Grammar; and Rugby, under Dr James. Admitted 1 Oct. 1906.
> B.A. 1909; LL.B. 1910. Law Tripos, Part I, Class 3 (br. 4th), 1908; Part II, Class 3 (br. 1st), 1910.

Riley, Charles Lawrence: son of The Right Rev. Charles Owen Leaver Riley (of the College, II. 412), Bishop of Perth, Western Australia, of Bishop's House, Perth, Western Australia; and Elizabeth Merriman. Born at St Paul's Vicarage, Preston, Lancashire, 10 Oct. 1888. School: the High School, Perth, Western Australia, under Mr F. C. Faulkner. Admitted 1 Oct. 1906.
> B.A. 1909; LL.B. 1910. Class. Tripos, Part I (aegrotat), 1909. Law Tripos, Part II, Class 2 (br. 1st), 1910. Theological Exhibitioner, 1909. Captain of "C" Company, C.U.R.V. and C.U.O.T.C., 1907–10.

Scott, Rupert Strathmore: son of the Hon. Robert Steele Scott, landowner and merchant, Member of the Legislative Council of Tasmania, of Launceston, Tasmania; and Alice Florence Tulloch. Born at Launceston, Tasmania, 4 June 1887. Schools: Church Grammar School, Launceston; and Wesley College, Melbourne, Australia, under Mr L. A. Adamson. Admitted 1 Oct. 1906.
> B.A. 1909. Nat. Sci. Tripos, Part I, Class 2, 1909.

Shelley, Lewis Wilton: son of Percy Shelley, bill-broker, of Coningsby, Shortlands, Kent; and Charlotte Agnes Solly. Born at Willowcroft, Chislehurst, 23 Mar. 1887. Schools: Marlborough College, under the Rev. G. C. Bell; and Oundle School, under Mr F. W. Sanderson. Admitted 1 Oct. 1906.
> B.A. 1910.

Sherman, Reginald: son of Arthur Sherman, insurance clerk, of 2, Gloucester Place, Greenwich, London, S.E.; and Marian Elizabeth Smith. Born at 8, The Circus, Greenwich, 4 Aug. 1887. School: Merchant Taylors', under Dr Baker, and Dr Nairn. Admitted 1 Oct. 1906.
> B.A. 1909. Nat. Sci. Tripos, Part I, Class 1, 1909.

Stallard, George Victor: son of John Stallard, solicitor, of Redland, Colwall, near Malvern; and Lilla Mary Thursfield. Born at Lower Wick, St John, near Worcester, 18 Aug. 1887. Schools: Hillside, West Malvern; and Malvern College, under the Rev. S. R. James. Admitted 1 Oct. 1906.
> B.A. 1909.

Stephenson, Humphrey Meigh: son of the Rev. John Stephenson, of Argyle House, Church Road, Upper Norwood; and Annie Meigh Peek. Born at St Saviour's Vicarage, Denmark Hill, London, 3 Aug. 1882. School: Harrow, under the Rev. J. E. C. Welldon. Admitted 1 Oct. 1906.
> B.A. 1909. Nat. Sci. Tripos, Part I, Class 3, 1909.

Stone, Gilbert: son of Richard Stone, contractor to H.M. Government, of Ferndale, Wellington, Salop; and Elizabeth Clift. Born at Ferndale, Wellington, Salop, 6 June 1886. School: Wellington College, Salop, under Mr J. Bayley. Admitted 1 Oct. 1906.
> B.A. LL.B. 1909. Law Tripos, Part I, 3rd in Class 1, 1908; Part II, Class 2 (br. 2nd), 1909. Scholar, 1907–9. Tancred Law Student, 1909. Called to the Bar at Lincoln's Inn, 1911.

Stretton, John Weston: son of John Lionel Stretton, surgeon, of 27, Church Street, Kidderminster; and Lucy Emma Houghton. Born at 27, Church Street, Kidderminster, 21 June 1888. School: Malvern College, under the Rev. S. R. James. Admitted 1 Oct. 1906.
> B.A. 1910.

Sutherland, James Fleming: son of Robert Mackay Sutherland, chemical manu-facturer, of Solsgirth, Dollar; and Isabella Fleming. Born at Wallside, Falkirk, 25 Aug. 1888. Schools: Cargilfield, Edinburgh; Trinity College, Glenalmond, under the Rev. A. R. Hyslop; Heriot Watt College, Edinburgh, under Principal A. P. Laurie. Admitted 1 Oct. 1906.
> B.A. 1909. Nat. Sci. Tripos, Part I, Class 3, 1909. University (Rugby) football player, 1908. In his father's business.

Sykes, Carrington: son of Matthew Carrington Sykes, M.D., of Sykeshurst, Barnsley, Yorks; and Annie Pickles. Born at Sykeshurst, Regent Street, Barnsley, 6 June 1889. School: Cherbourg, Malvern, under Mr Vines and Mr T. Coates. Admitted 1 Oct. 1906.
> Kept three terms.

Symonds, Frederic Cotton: son of John Fish Symonds, solicitor, of 54, Lensfield Road, Cambridge; and Gertrude Catherine Whitehead. Born at 20, Hertford Street, Cambridge, 10 March 1888. Schools: Mr Goodchild's, Trumpington Road, Cambridge; and Repton, under the Rev. L. Ford. Admitted 1 Oct. 1906. Brother of John, IV (1) 9.
> B.A. 1909.

Taylor, Cedric Rowland: son of the Rev. Robert Edward Taylor (deceased), Vicar of Cresswell, Morpeth, Northumberland; and Karen Fannie Nielsen. Born at Cresswell Vicarage, Northumberland, 20 Aug. 1888. School: St Edmund's School, Canterbury, under the Rev. A. W. Upcott and Mr E. J. W. Houghton. Admitted 1 Oct. 1906.
> B.A. 1909. Nat. Sci. Tripos, Part I, Class 3, 1909. Tancred Student, 1906– .

Tonks, John Wilson: son of Samuel Tonks, retired commercial traveller, of Bescot (Bascote); and Edith Jennie Ross Wilson. Born at 43, Oxford Street, Wednesbury, 14 Feb. 1888. School: Queen Mary's Grammar, Walsall, under Mr J. A. Alldis and Mr H. Bompas Smith. Admitted 1 Oct. 1906.
> B.A. 1909. Nat. Sci. Tripos, Part I, Class 1, 1908. Exhibitioner, 1907. Scholar, 1908–9.

Tottenham, Charles Edward Loftus: son of Henry Loftus Tottenham, East India merchant, of 1, The Boltons, London, S.W.; and Mary Elizabeth Barnwell. Born at Melksham House, Melksham, Wilts, 29 Oct. 1887. School: Harrow, under Dr Wood. Admitted 1 Oct. 1906.
> Kept eight terms.

Treffry, Thomas Justin: son of the Rev. Edward Lambert Treffry, Rector of Blankney, Lincoln; and Evelyn Pares. Born at Aswarby Rectory, Folking-ham, Lincolnshire, 31 March 1886. Schools: Uppingham, under the Rev. Dr E. C. Selwyn; Bradley Court, under Mr W. H. Gandy. Admitted 1 Oct. 1906.
> B.A. 1910.

Uhthoff, Roland King: son of John Caldwell Uhthoff, physician, of Wavertree House, Furse Hill, Brighton; and Elen Aston King. Born at 19, Brunswick Place, Hove, Brighton, 17 April 1888. School: Marlborough College, under Canon G. C. Bell and Mr Fletcher. Admitted 1 Oct. 1906.
B.A. 1909. Mech. Sci. Tripos, Class 2, 1909. Entrance Scholarship, 1906. Scholar, 1907–9.

Walford, Henry Howard: son of Howard Joseph Walford (Stock Exchange), of 47, Hamilton Terrace, London, N.W.; and Lucy Adeline Straus. Born at 37, Porchester Square, London, 19 Sept. 1888. School: Cheltenham College, under the Rev. R. Waterfield. Admitted 1 Oct. 1906.
B.A. 1909; LL.B. 1910. Law Tripos, Part I, Class 3 (br. 2nd), 1908, Part II, Class 3 (br. 2nd), 1910.

Warden, Arthur Reginald Stuart: son of Arthur Henry Warden, barrister, of Netherfield, Crowborough, Sussex; and Jenny Harriet Davies. Born at 56, Pain's Road, Southsea, 11 Dec. 1887. Schools: Cambridge House, Tunbridge Wells; Grange, Crowborough; Lancing College, under Mr B. H. Tower. Admitted 1 Oct. 1906.

Watermeyer, Herbert Arnold: son of Christian John Watermeyer, retired farmer, of Accarsane, Indian Road, Wynberg, Cape Town, S. Africa; and Carry Agnes Maria De Graeff. Born at Graaff-Reinet, Cape Colony, 8 May 1887. Schools: St Andrew's College, Grahamstown, under Canon Espion and Dr McGowan; Victoria College, Stellenbosch, under Mr Hofmeyer; Bath College, under Mr A. Trice-Martin. Admitted 1 Oct. 1906. Brother of Ernest, IV. (1) 10.
Nat. Sci. Tripos, Part I, Class 3, 1909.

Wells, Norman Lancaster: son of Charles Wells, quarry proprietor, of Richmond House, Burscough, Lancs; and Ann Shawe. Born at 13, St Edmond's Road, Bootle, 17 May 1888. Schools: Elleray Park School, Wallasey, under the Rev. I. M. Stuart Edwards; and Shrewsbury, under the Rev. H. W. Moss. Admitted 1 Oct. 1906.
B.A. 1909. In the Asiatic Petroleum Company at Yokohama (1910).

Wolff, Lucien: son of Emile Wolff, rentier, of 4, Rue Castex, Paris, France; and Ernestine Isaure de la Garde de Chambonas. Born at Paris, 23 Feb. 1880. Educated at Lyceè Janson, Paris; Faculté des Lettres de Paris. Admitted as an Advanced Student, 1 Oct. 1906.
B.A. 1910. French Lector, 1906–8. Professor at the Collège Rollin, Paris, 1909– .

Wright, Herbert Middleton: son of Peter Halliday Wright (deceased), M.A., of St John's College; and Caroline Rosita Chilton, of Lennel, Fleet, Hants. Born at Welshpool, Wales, 27 March 1888. Educated at Liverpool College: and privately by Mr Sangar, Little Hermitage, near Rochester. Admitted 1 Oct. 1906.
B.A. 1910.

Hughes, Evan: son of Evan Hughes, farmer, of Llwydiarth Hall, Llanfyllin, S.O., Montgomeryshire; and Elizabeth Ann Jones. Born at Waen Farm, Llansaintffraid, Montgomeryshire, 18 Jan. 1882. School: Deytheur Grammar School, Montgomeryshire; University College, Aberystwith. Has kept three terms as non-collegiate student. Admitted 1 Oct. 1906.
B.A. 1907. Economics Tripos, Part I, Class 2, Div. 2, 1906; Part II, Class 2, Div. 2, 1907. Assistant-Lecturer in Economics at Liverpool University, 1909– .

Perkins, Bertram Mark Nevill: son of Major-General John Perkins, of 13, rue Africaine, Brussels; and Marie Jackson. Born at Sandown, Isle of Wight, 2 April 1868. School: Wellington College, under the Rev. E. C. Wickham. Admitted as an Advanced Student 8 Jan. 1907.

> B.A. 1908. Passed Med. and Mod. Lang. Tripos, 1908, as Advanced Student. Lecturer in French at the Victoria University, Manchester, 1909– . Author.

MacRury, Evan: son of Brigade Surgeon-Lieut.-Col. Colin William MacRury, I.M.S. (retired), of 65, Earl's Court Road, London, W.; and Georgina Agnes Eliza Rose. Born at 6, Claverton Street, London, S.W., 29 Oct. 1883. Schools: Linton House Preparatory School, Holland Park Avenue; and St Paul's School, under Mr F. W. Walker. Admitted 8 Jan. 1907.

> B.A. 1909. Med. and Mod. Lang. Tripos, Class 3, 1909. Master at Bedford Grammar School (1910).

Gilliat-Smith, Bernard Joseph: son of Frederic Ernest Gilliat-Smith, of 4, Rue de la Soufrière, Bruges; and Ellinor Marie Cockerell. Born at Sevenoaks, 20 Oct. 1883. Educated at St Francis Xavier's College, Bruges; and privately, by Mr W. B. Scoones, 19, Garrick Street, London, W.C. Admitted as a Student Interpreter, 21 Jan. 1907.

> Kept six terms. Russian Scholarship, 1908. In the Levant Consular Service, 1909–

Born, Maximilian: son of Professor Doctor Gustav Born, of 5, Zimmerstrasse, Breslau V, Germany; and Bertha Lipstein. Born at Breslau, Germany, 11 Dec. 1882. Educated at König-Wilhelms Gymnasium, Breslau; Universities of Breslau, Heidelberg, Zürich, Göttingen. Admitted 4 May 1907, as an Advanced Student.

> Resided one term.

*Layton, Walter Thomas, B.A.: son of Alfred John Layton, musician, of Stanley House, Milner Street, Chelsea; and Mary Johnson. Born at 4, Milner Street, Chelsea, London, S.W., 15 March 1884. Schools: St George's Choir School, Windsor; King's College School, London; Westminster City School, under Mr R. E. H. Goffin. Trinity College, Cambridge, 1904–7. Admitted 19 July 1907.

> B.A. 1907 (Trinity). Econ. Tripos, Part I, Class 1, 1906; Part II, Class 1, 1907. Sir Thomas Gresham Student, 1907. Cobden Prize, 1907. Elected Drosier Fellow, 1909. Appointed by the Local Examinations Syndicate to lecture for the "Workers' Association," 1909. University Lecturer in Economics, 1911– Married, 2 April 1910, Eleanor Dorothea, daughter of Francis P. Osmaston, of Limpsfield.

MICHAELMAS 1907 TO MICHAELMAS 1908.

(Tutors: Mr Gallop, Mr Buckland, and Mr Hardy.)

Henry, Augustine: son of Bernard Henry (deceased), farmer, of Tyannee, County Derry, Ireland; and Mary McNamee. Born at Dundee, Scotland, 2 July 1857. Educated at the Academy, Cookstown, Tyrone; Queen's Colleges, Galway and Belfast. Admitted pensioner, Oct. 1907.

> M.A. (Hon.) 1908. Appointed University Reader in Forestry, 1907.

Arnell, Oliver Roach: son of William Thomas Arnell, J.P., mill owner, of Whitecliff, Sandown, Isle of Wight; and Henrietta Gibbings. Born at Whitecliff, Sandown, Isle of Wight, 26 Aug. 1888. School: Berkhamsted, under Dr T. C. Fry. Admitted 1 Oct. 1907.
> B.A. 1910. Math. Tripos, Part I, Class 1, 1908 ; Part I (br. 29th Wrangler), 1909. Entrance Scholarship, 1907. Scholar, 1908– .

Ballard, Edward: son of Edward George Ballard, H.M. Inspector of Alkali Works, of Greenfield, Hoole Village, Chester; and Catherine Eugenie Davidson. Born at Chester, 5 Sept. 1888. Schools: King's School, Chester; and St Paul's School, London, under Mr F. W. Walker and the Rev. A. E. Hillard. Admitted 1 Oct. 1907.
> B.A. 1910. Nat. Sci. Tripos, Part I, Class 3, 1910.

Bedford, Seaton Hall: son of Henry Hall Bedford, steel manufacturer, of Sharrow Hurst, Sheffield; and Lucy Danby. Born at Park Lane, Broomhall Park, Ecclesall Bierlow, 24 Jan. 1889. School: Uppingham, under the Rev. Dr E. C. Selwyn. Admitted 1 Oct. 1907.
> B.A., LL.B. 1910. Law Tripos, Part I, Class 3 (br. 4th), 1909 ; Part II, Class 3 (br. 14th), 1910

Bell, Aubrey Parker: son of the Rev. Colin Edward Beever Bell, vicar of St Mary, Whittlesey; and Katherine Henrietta Louisa Bradley. Born at Bedford Street, Liverpool, 17 June 1888. School: Magdalen College School, Oxford, under Mr C. E. Brownrigg. Admitted 1 Oct. 1907.
Choral Entrance Exhibition, 1907.

Besly, Edward Maurice: son of Edward Frederick Seymour Besly (deceased), clerk in Holy Orders, of Stokesley, York; and Evelyn Georgina Moore. Born at Normanby, R.S.O., Yorks, 28 Jan. 1888. Schools: High Croft, Wester-ham, Kent; and Tonbridge School, under Dr C. C. Tancock. Admitted 1 Oct. 1907.
> B.A. 1910. Class. Tripos, Part I, Class 2, 1910. Entrance Scholarship, 1907. Scholar, 1908–10. President of the Musical Society, 1909–10.

Boddam-Whetham, Gerald Avery: son of John Whetham Boddam-Whetham, gentleman, of Earlscliffe, Folkestone; and Harriett Matilda Manning. Born at Oddo House, Winster, Bakewell, 25 March 1888. School: Oundle, under Mr F. W. Sanderson. Admitted 1 Oct. 1907.
Lieutenant in "C" Company of the University Officers' Training Corps, 1908.

Broadmead, Harold Hamilton: son of the Rev. Philip Palfrey Broadmead (of the College, II. 416), of Olands, Milverton, Somerset; and Edith Birch. Born at Bradford Vicarage, near Taunton, 23 Jan. 1889. Schools: Naish House, near Bristol ; and Malvern College, under the Rev. S. R. James. Admitted 1 Oct. 1907.
> B.A. 1910.

Brockman, Ralph St Leger: son of the Rev. Ralph Thomas Brockman, of St John Baptist Vicarage, The Brook, Liverpool; and Anna Charlotte Sheldrake. Born at Blyth, Notts, 3 June 1889. School: Liverpool College, under Mr J. B. Lancelot. Admitted 1 Oct. 1907. Brother of William, IV. (1) 112.
> B.A. 1910. Nat. Sci. Tripos, Part I, Class 3, 1910.

Cardwell, Cyril Rowland: son of the Rev. John Henry Cardwell (of the College, II. 354), of 28, Soho Square, London, W.; and Elizabeth Barnes. Born at The Vicarage, St Andrew's Road, Fulham, 2 Feb. 1889. Schools: Merton House, Southwick; and St Mark's School, Windsor, under the Rev. C. N. Nagel. Admitted 1 Oct. 1907. Brother of Percy, II. 525; and William IV. (1) 19.

　　B.A. 1910. Med. and Mod. Lang. Tripos, Class 3, 1910. Master at Lancing College, 1910–

Chapman, George Martin: son of Frederick Revans Chapman, Justice of New Zealand Supreme Court, Wellington, New Zealand; and Clara Jane Cook. Born at 203, Leith Street, Dunedin, New Zealand, 26 March 1887. School: Waitaki Boys' School, Oamaru, New Zealand, under Dr J. R. Don. Admitted 1 Oct. 1907.

　　B.A. 1910. Nat. Sci. Tripos, Part I, Class 2, 1910. University (Rugby) football player, 1909.

Clarke, Guy Cuthbert: son of Lieut.-Colonel Thomas Sydenham Clarke, King's Royal Rifles (retired), of Sandown Lawn, Pittville, Cheltenham; and Jane Taylor. Born at Rookery Farm, Westcott, Dorking, 11 May 1887. Educated at Ovingdean, near Brighton; Marlborough College, under the Rev. G. C. Bell and Mr F. Fletcher; Neuchâtel; Frankfurt-am-Main. Admitted 1 Oct. 1907.

　　B.A. 1910. Med. and Mod. Lang. Tripos, Class 1, 1909 and 1910, with distinction. Exhibitioner, 1908. Scholar, 1909–10. Captain of the Hockey Club, 1909–10. In the service of the Asiatic Petroleum Company (1911).

Claye, Hugh: son of Edgar Havelock Claye, rolling stock manufacturer, of Darleyfields, Derby; and Mary Pickthall. Born at 114, Osmaston Road, Derby, 22 June 1889. Educated at Hinwick House; Heidelberg College; and Clayesmore School, Pangbourne, under Mr A. Levine. Admitted 1 Oct. 1907.

　　B.A. 1910. Econ. Tripos, Part I, Class 3, 1909; Part II, Class 2, 1910. In his father's business.

Coates, Vincent Hope Middleton: son of Charles Middleton Coates, medical practitioner, of Heathfield House, Creech St Michael, Taunton; and Janet Rae. Born at 2, Woodburn Terrace, Edinburgh, 2 Feb. 1889. Schools: Monkton Combe, Bath, under the Rev. J. W. Kearns; and Haileybury College, under the Hon. and Rev. Canon Lyttelton and the Rev. St J. B. Wynne Wilson. Admitted 1 Oct. 1907.

　　B.A. 1911.

Coyajee, Jehangirshah Cooverjee: son of Cooverjee Coyajee, of Bombay; and Manekbai Taleyarkhan. Born at Bombay, 11 Sept. 1875. Educated at Elphinstone College, Bombay, under Messrs Oxenham, Hathornthwaite and Macmillan. Professor at Wilson College, Chopata, Bombay. Admitted as Advanced Student, 1 Oct. 1907.

　　B.A. 1910. Research Studentship (Honorary) in Economics, 1910. Professor of Economics at Calcutta, 1910–

Creswell, Henry Edmund: son of Henry Thomas Creswell, retired merchant, of 19, Bedford Grove, Eastbourne; and Harriet Louisa Echalaz. Born at Gibraltar, 27 May 1889. School: St Edward's, Oxford, under the Rev. T. Hudson and Mr J. Millington Sing. Admitted 1 Oct. 1907.

　　B.A. 1910. Nat. Sci. Tripos, Part I, Class 3, 1910.

Day, Gilbert: son of Gilbert Morland Day (deceased), brewer (of Messrs Bass and Co.); and Elizabeth Annie Hutchinson Bell. Born at 14, Alexandra Road, Burton-on-Trent, 5 April 1888. Schools: Oxford Preparatory School; and Winchester College, under Dr H. M. Burge. Admitted 1 Oct. 1907. Brother of Francis, (IV) (1) 103.

> B.A. 1910. Math. Tripos, Part I, Class 1, 1908; Mech. Sci. Tripos, Class 1, 1910. Salomons Engineering Scholarship, 1907. In the service of the Asiatic Petroleum Company (1910).

Dobson, Gordon Miller Bourne: son of Thomas Dobson, M.D., of Knott End, Windermere; and Marianne Bourne. Born at Windermere, 25 Feb. 1889. Schools: Craig School, Windermere; and Sedbergh School, under Mr Thomas and Mr Lowry. Admitted 1 Oct. 1907.

> B.A. 1910. Nat. Sci. Tripos, Part I, Class 1, 1910. Exhibition, 1909. Research Studentship in Geography, 1911.

Dracup, Athelstane Hamleigh: son of John Wright Sandford Dracup, Presidency magistrate, Bombay, of 6, Club Road, Byalla, Bombay; and May Marie Clifford. Born at Gogo, India, 26 Oct. 1887. Educated at Bishop's High School, Poona; Education Society's School, Bombay; Wilson College, Bombay, under Mr D. Mackiehan; Wren's, London. Admitted 1 Oct. 1907. Kept four terms. Migrated to St Catharine's College. B.A. 1910. Hist. Tripos, Part I, Class 3, 1909; Part II, Class 3, 1910.

Drewry, George Hayward: son of Frank Drewry, estate agent, of Court Heath, Buxton, Derbyshire; and Lizzie Matilda Hayward. Born at Court Heath, Buxton, Derbyshire, 7 Jan. 1889. Educated at Stanmore Park; and Malvern College, under the Rev. S. R. James. Admitted 1 Oct. 1907.

> B.A. 1910.

Ewens, Bernard Creasy: son of Creasy Ewens, solicitor, of Hong Kong, and 8, Chepstow Villas, Bayswater, London, W.; and Harriet Cotton Crafer. Born at Magazine Gap, Hong Kong, 14 Dec. 1888. Schools: Park House, Southborough, Tunbridge Wells; and Rugby, under the Rev. Dr H. A. James. Admitted 1 Oct. 1907.

> B.A. 1910. Nat Sci. Tripos, Part I, Class 2, 1910.

Franklin, Hugh Arthur: son of Arthur Ellis Franklin, banker, of 29, Pembridge Gardens, London; and Caroline Jacob. Born at 28, Pembridge Villas, Kensington, London, 27 May 1889. Educated at Mr Wilkinson's, Orme Square; and Clifton College, under the Rev. Canon M. G. Glazebrook. Admitted 1 Oct. 1907.

> Kept eight terms.

Gell, William Charles Coleman: son of William James Gell, managing director, of 111, Gough Road, Edgbaston, Birmingham; and Catherine Coleman. Born at Birmingham, 10 July 1888 School: Malvern College, under the Rev. S. R. James. Admitted 1 Oct. 1907.

> B.A., LL.B. 1910. Law Tripos, Part I, Class 3 (br. 5th), 1909; Part II, Class 3 (br. 18th), 1910.

Getty, James Houghton: son of Frederick Getty, fruit-broker, of The Knoll, Hoylake, Cheshire; and Mary Smith. Born at Valencia, Spain, 29 Aug. 1888. School: Shrewsbury, under the Rev. H. W. Moss. Admitted 1 Oct. 1907.

> B.A. 1910. University Commission in the Army, 1911.

C IV 1

Hall, Leslie Mackinder: son of Townson Mackinder Hall, bank manager, of Bank House, Horncastle; and Emma Jane Truelove. Born at 25, High Street, Horncastle, 17 July 1888. Schools: Horncastle Grammar School; and King Edward VI Grammar School, Louth, under Mr A. H. Worrall. Admitted 1 Oct. 1907.
B.A. 1910.

Hatton, George Arthur Lyon: son of George Hatton, director of iron and steel works, of Saltwells House, Brierley Hill, Staffs; and Louisa Brinton. Born at Hagley, Worcestershire, 15 May 1888. School: Rugby, under Dr James. Admitted 1 Oct. 1907.
B.A. 1910.

Haydon, Arthur Dodsworth: son of Walter Dodsworth Haydon, schoolmaster, of The Schools, Shrewsbury; and Katharine Mary Salt. Born at Kingsland, Shrewsbury, 20 Sept. 1889. Schools: Hill House, St Leonards-on-Sea; and Winchester College, under Dr Burge. Admitted 1 Oct. 1907.
B.A. 1910. Nat. Sci. Tripos, Part I, Class 3, 1910.

Hislop, Thomas Charles Atkinson: son of Thomas William Hislop, barrister, Supreme Court, New Zealand, of Salamanca Road, Wellington, New Zealand; and Maria Annie Simpson. Born at Moturoa Street, Wellington, New Zealand, 29 Nov. 1888. School: Wellington College, New Zealand, under Mr J. P. Firth. Admitted 1 Oct. 1907.
Resided six terms.

Huelin, Edward Scotton: son of Edward Huelin (of the College, II. 407), County Court registrar, of 11, Elsham Road, Kensington; and Edith Theodora Eliza Francis. Born at 60, Portsdown Road, Paddington, 7 Aug. 1888. Educated at Westminster, under Dr Gow. Admitted 1 Oct. 1907.
B.A. 1910.

Hutchence, Byron Levick: son of William Atkinson Hutchence, merchant, of Thorncliffe, Saltburn-by-the-Sea; and Mary Elizabeth Levick. Born at Kirby in Cleveland, Yorks, 25 Oct. 1888. School: Durham, under the Rev. A. E. Hillard and the Rev. H. W. McKenzie. Admitted 1 Oct. 1907. Brother of William IV. (1) 41.
B.A. 1910. Nat. Sci. Tripos, Part I, Class 2, 1910.

Jephcott, Ernest Woodward: son of Richard Henry Jephcott, retired grocer, of Whernalls, Alcester; and Edith Annie Bomford. Born at High Street, Alcester, 12 May 1888. Schools: Alcester Grammar School; and King Henry VIII School, Coventry, under the Rev. C. R. Gilbert and the Rev. A. D. Perrott. Admitted 1 Oct. 1907.
B.A. 1910. Hist. Tripos, Part I, Class 3, 1909. Chapel Clerk, 1909–10. Theological Exhibitioner, 1910.

Knight, Edward Foley: son of John Henry Knight, landowner, of Barfield, Farnham, Surrey; and Eliza Bligh Foley. Born at Thumblands, Farnham, Surrey, 27 Jan. 1888. Schools: Holyrood House, Bognor; and Haileybury College, under Canon Lyttelton and the Rev. St J. B. Wynne Wilson. Admitted 1 Oct. 1907.
B.A. 1910. Mech. Sci. Tripos, Class 3, 1910.

Kr ge, Leo Jacobus: son of Jacob Daniel Krige, farmer, of "Libertas Parva," Stellenbosch, S. Africa; and Susanna Johanna Schabort. Born at Stellenbosch, S. Africa, 12 Aug. 1884. Educated at Victoria College, Stellenbosch. Admitted 1 Oct. 1907. Affiliated from the Cape of Good Hope University. B.A. 1911. Nat. Sci. Tripos, Part I, Class 2, 1911. Exhibitioner, 1910.

Lake, Walter Ivan: son of William Robert Lake, chartered patent agent and consulting engineer, of Alaska, Sutton, Surrey; and Maria Grant Williamson. Born at 80, Marine Parade, Brighton, 3 April 1888. School: Eastbourne College, under the Rev. M. A. Bayfield and Mr H. R. Thomson. Admitted 1 Oct. 1907.
B.A. 1910.

Leighton, Arthur Francis: son of the Rev. John Francis Leighton, of 56, Portland Road, Bishop Stortford; and Florence Mary Staunton. Born at Esk, Queensland, Australia, 6 Mar. 1889. Schools: St Peter's, Exmouth; and Bishop's Stortford School, under Mr J. Bruce Payne. Admitted 1 Oct. 1907. B.A. 1910. Chapel Clerk, 1909-10. University Hockey player, 1908-10.

Lescher, Frank Graham: son of Frank Harwood Lescher, East India drug merchant, of 31, Devonshire Place, London, W.; and Mary O'Conor Graham Grehan. Born at 149, Haverstock Hill, Hampstead, London, 19 May 1888. School: Stonyhurst College, under the Rev. Father I. Browne, S.J. Admitted 1 Oct. 1907.
B.A. 1910. Nat. Sci. Tripos, Part I, Class 2, 1910.

Lewis, Henry Howard: son of William Howard Lewis (deceased), tube manufacturer, of Penn Croft, Wolverhampton; and Henrietta Frances Anne Marten. Born at Goldthorn Hill, Wolverhampton, 25 Oct. 1888. Educated at Stubbington Naval School; and Cheltenham College, under the Rev. R. Waterfield. Admitted 1 Oct. 1907.
Resided one year. Re-admitted, October 1909. Left in 1910 for residence in Australia.

Lewis, William Hawthorne: son of Thomas Crompton Lewis (late Indian Government Service), of West Home, West Road, Cambridge; and Mary Olivia Hawthorne. Born at Kasauli, Lahore, India, 29 July 1888. School: Oundle, under Mr F. W. Sanderson. Admitted 1 Oct. 1907.
B.A. 1910. Classical Tripos, Part I, Class 2, 1910. Entrance Exhibition, 1907. Exhibitioner, 1908-10. Selected candidate for the I.C.S., 1911.

Lilly, George Austen: son of Charles Edward Lilly, merchant, of 2, Cambridge Place, Regent's Park, London, W.; and Sarah Anne Hinds. Born at 7, Rochester Square, London, N.W., 5 Jan. 1888. School: St Paul's, under Mr F. W. Walker and Dr Hillard. Admitted 1 Oct. 1907.
B.A. 1910. Nat. Sci. Tripos, Part I, Class 3, 1910.

Loveband, Francis Yerburgh: son of the Rev. Walter Loveband (of the College, II. 433), Vicar of Ifield, Crawley; and Lucy Isabel Yerburgh. Born at Ifield Vicarage, Crawley, 16 Jan. 1889. Educated at Eastbourne; St Paul's House, St Leonards-on Sea; privately, under Mr J. F. Richards, Bishopstone Manor, Lewes. Admitted 1 Oct. 1907.
B.A. 1910.

Lukis, Sydney: son of Charles Pardy Lukis, M.D., I.M.S., of the Medical College Calcutta, India; and Lilian Stewart. Born at Jhansi, India, 16 July 1887. Educated at Danecourt, Parkestone; and Dulwich College, under Mr A. H. Gilkes. Admitted 1 Oct. 1907.
B.A. 1910.

MacGregor, Malcolm: son of Peter MacGregor, F.R.C.S., of Rashcliffe, Huddersfield; and Sarah Florence Scholes. Born at Rashcliffe, Lockwood, Huddersfield 2 Sept. 1888. Schools: Huddersfield College School; and Rugby, under Dr James. Admitted 1 Oct. 1907.
B.A. 1910. Nat. Sci. Tripos, Part I, Class 2, 1910; Law Tripos, Part II, Class 3, 1911. Captain of Rugby Football, 1910. University player.

MacMullen, Alfred Robinson: son of William Francis MacMullen, merchant, of Rockcliffe, Blackrock Road, Cork, Ireland; and Barbara Grahame Ronalds (deceased). Born at North Mall House, Cork, 21 Nov. 1888. Schools· Mr Littlejohn's School, The Limes, Greenwich; and Clifton College, under Canon Glazebrook and the Rev. A. A. David. Admitted 1 Oct. 1907.
B.A. 1910. Nat. Sci. Tripos, Part I, Class 2, 1910.

Mayne, Cyril Frederick: son of Frederick Arthur Mayne, secretary to Committee of Classification, Lloyd's Register of Shipping, of 41, London Road, Forest Hill, London, S.E.; and Ida Shoosmith. Born at 38, Trossachs Road, East Dulwich, 19 July 1889. School: Merchant Taylors', under the Rev. Dr W. Baker and the Rev. Dr J. A. Nairn. Admitted 1 Oct. 1907.
B.A. 1910. Nat. Sci. Tripos, Part I, Class 2, 1909. Entrance Scholarship, 1907.

Morgan, Frederic James: son of the Rev. Ernest Augustus Morgan, Rector of Scole, Norfolk; and Julia Sarah Charles. Born at St John's Rectory, Ilketshall, Suffolk, 27 Sept. 1889. Educated at Packwood Haigh, Warwickshire; and Bishop's Stortford School, under Mr J. Bruce Payne. Admitted 1 Oct. 1907.

Page, Dennis Salmon: son of Martin Fountain Page (deceased), corn and coal merchant, of Blakeney, Norfolk; and Emma Eliza Salmon. Born at Blakeney, Norfolk, 27 Jan. 1888. Educated at Bishop's Stortford School, under Mr J. Bruce Payne; and at "Mayenfels," Pratteln, near Basel, Switzerland. Admitted 1 Oct. 1907. Brother of John iv. (1) 43; and Martin iv. (1) 61.
B.A. 1910. Nat. Sci. Tripos, Part I, Class 3, 1910.

Platts, Sydney Goodman: son of Arthur Platts (deceased), wholesale draper; and Julia Maria Hardy. Born at Gainsborough, 18 Sept. 1888. Schools: Gainsborough Grammar; and Oundle School, under Mr F. W. Sanderson. Admitted 1 Oct. 1907.
B.A. 1910. Nat. Sci. Tripos, Part I, Class 2, 1910.

Powell, George Gerald: son of Robert Leonard Powell, of Heatherbank, Chislehurst, Kent; and Bessie Constance Curwen. Born at Heylands, Hampstead, London, N.W., 17 July 1887. Schools: Mr W. R. Lee's Preparatory School, Ashdown, Kent; Uppingham, under the Rev. Dr E. C. Selwyn; and Loretto, near Edinburgh, under Mr H. B. Tristram. Admitted 1 Oct. 1907.
B.A. 1911.

Pye-Smith, Desmond Edward: son of Edward Foulger Pye-Smith, solicitor, of The Close, Salisbury; and Gertrude Elizabeth Taunton. Born at Lee Hurst, Milford, Alderbury, Wilts, 5 July 1887. School: Leighton Park School, Reading, under Mr J. Ridges. Admitted 1 Oct. 1907.
    B.A. 1910. Nat. Sci. Tripos, Part I, Class 3, 1910.

Pyman, Frederick Cresswell: son of Frederick Haigh Pyman, shipowner, of 82, Fitzjohn's Avenue, Hampstead; and Blanche Gray. Born at Raithwaite, Old Park Road, Enfield, 2 Jan. 1889. School: The Leys School, Cambridge, under the Rev. Dr W. T. A. Barber. Admitted 1 Oct. 1907.
    B.A. 1910. Econ. Tripos, Part I, Class 2, Div. 2, 1909; Part II, Class 2, Div. 2, 1910. Captain, Rugby Football, 1909–10. University (Rugby) Football player, 1908–9. In business at West Hartlepool (1911).

Raikes, William Oswell: son of the Rev. Walter Allan Raikes, Vicar of Ide Hill, Sevenoaks, Kent; and Catherine Amelia Oswell. Born at Ide Hill Vicarage, Kent, 3 Sept. 1887. Educated at 5 Clare, Walmer, under Mr A. E. Murray; and Charterhouse, under Dr Rendall. Admitted 1 Oct. 1907.
    B.A. 1910. Med. and Mod. Lang. Tripos, Class 2, 1909. Econ. Tripos (*aegrotat*), 1910. Captain of the Cricket Club, 1909–10. Assistant Master at Merchiston Castle School, Edinburgh, 1910–11. On the staff of *The Times* (1911).

Read, Ralph Irving: son of Ralph William Read, contractor, of 16, Widdrington Road, Coventry; and Elizabeth Graham Irving. Born at 29, Lord Street, Coventry, 14 May 1889. School: King Henry VIII School, Coventry, under the Rev. A. D. Perrott and the Rev. C. R. Gilbert. Admitted 1 Oct. 1907.
    B.A. 1910. Hist. Tripos, Part I, Class 3, 1909; Part II, Class 2, 1910.

Reynolds, Wilfred Thomas: son of Charles Partridge Reynolds (of Reynolds Bros., Ltd., sugar planters), of Esperanza, Natal, South Africa; and Lilian Julia Mary Barker. Born at Umzinto, Natal, South Africa, 14 Dec. 1888. Schools: Winton House, Winchester; and Cheltenham College, under the Rev. R. Waterfield. Admitted 1 Oct. 1907.
    B.A. 1910. University Commission in the Army, 1911.

Riddiford, Frederick Earle: son of Frederick Riddiford (deceased), sheep farmer, of Palmerston North, New Zealand; and Alice McGregor. Born at Hawera, New Zealand, 12 Dec. 1887. Educated at The Collegiate School, Wanganui, under Mr W. Empson. Admitted 1 Oct. 1907.
    Kept nine terms.

Roberts, Alan Dixon: son of Griffith Roberts (deceased), shipowner, of 7, Brandling Park, Newcastle-on-Tyne; and Elizabeth Annie Teasdale. Born at 7, Brandling Park, Newcastle-on-Tyne, 5 Dec. 1887. Schools: Newcastle Preparatory School; and Durham School, under the Rev. A. E. Hillard and the Rev. H. W. McKenzie. Admitted 1 Oct. 1907.
    B.A.; LL.B. 1910. Law Tripos, Part I, Class 2 (br. 4th), 1909; Part II, Class 3 (br. 1st), 1910.

Robinson, Gilbert Wooding: son of John Fairs Robinson (late secretary Wolverhampton Education Committee), of 52, Park Street, Wellington, Salop; and
Mary Emma Wooding. Born at 43, Waterloo Road, Wolverhampton, 7 Nov.
1888. Schools: Red Cross Street Board School, Wolverhampton; Miss
Belcher's Private School, Codsall; St Peter's Collegiate School, Wolverhampton; Wolverhampton Higher Grade School; Wolverhampton Grammar
School, under Mr J. H. Hichens and Mr W. Caldecott. Admitted 1 Oct.
1907.
> B.A. 1910. Nat. Sci. Tripos, Part I, Class 1, 1909. Entrance Scholarship,
> 1907. Scholar, 1908–

Robinson, Hugh Douglas: son of Arthur Samuel Francis Robinson, Assoc.M.
Inst.C.E., consulting engineer, of The White House, Barsham, Beccles, Suffolk;
and Eliza Fortunée Behrends. Born at Wantage, Berks, 12 Oct. 1889.
School: St Edward's, Oxford, under the Rev. T. W. Hudson, and Mr J.
Millington Sing. Admitted 1 Oct. 1907.

Roscoe, William: son of Richard Roscoe (deceased), solicitor; and Charlotte
Alicia Wickstead, of 16, Kemplay Road, Hampstead, London, N.W. Born
at 2, St Mark's Square, Regent's Park, London, 28 Jan. 1888. Schools:
Hampstead Preparatory; and Aldenham, under the Rev. A. H. Cooke.
Admitted 1 Oct. 1907.
> B.A., LL.B. 1910. Law Tripos, Part I, Class 2, 1909; Part II, Class 3
> (br. 40th), 1910. Entrance Scholarship, 1907. Scholar, 1908–10.

Rushforth, Frank Victor: son of Jesse Rushforth, education secretary, of
41, Pellatt Grove, Wood Green, London, N.; and Clara Thorn. Born at
102, Grafton Street, Hull, 7 Jan. 1888. Educated at Wood Green Higher
Grade School; Stationers' School, Hornsey; City of London School, under
Mr A. T. Pollard and the Rev. Dr Chilton. Admitted 1 Oct. 1907.
> B.A. 1910. Math. Tripos, Part I, Class 1, 1908; Wrangler, 1910.
> Entrance Scholarship, 1907. Scholar, 1908–10. In the Indian Finance
> Service (1911).

Russell, John Clement: son of John Russell, M.Inst.C.E., of Lexham Lodge,
Eastbourne; and Laura Clement Smith. Born at 53, Lexham Gardens,
Kensington, 6 April 1888. Schools: New Beacon, Sevenoaks; and Ton-
bridge School, under Dr Tancock. Admitted 1 Oct. 1907.
> Captain of the Boat Club, 1910.

Sanderson, Fred Borthwick: son of Frederick Reid Sanderson, of 12, Rothesay
Terrace, Edinburgh; and Alice Helen Scott. Born at Comrie, Perthshire,
15 June 1889. Schools: Routenburn School, Largs, Ayrshire; and Charterhouse, under Dr G. H. Rendall. Admitted 1 Oct. 1907.
> B.A. 1910. In business with his father (1911).

Scholfield, John Arthur: son of Arthur Beaumont Scholfield, of Winder, St Anne's-
on-Sea, Lancs; and Amy Smith. Born at St Anne's-on-Sea, 6 April 1888.
Schools: Arnold House, Llanddulas; and Sedbergh, under Mr C. Lowry.
Admitted 1 Oct. 1907.
> B.A. 1910. University (Rugby) Football player, 1909. In Insurance
> business (1911).

Sharp, John Edward: son of John Adolphus Sharp, surgeon, of Charnwood House, Derby; and Marian Isabelle Dumas. Born at 92, Osmaston Road, Derby, 4 Feb. 1888. Schools: Hurstleigh Preparatory School, Tunbridge Wells; and Bradfield College, under the Rev. Dr H. B. Gray. Admitted 1 Oct. 1907.
> B.A. 1910. Nat. Sci. Tripos, Part I, Class 3, 1910.

Smith, Samuel Harold: son of John Robert Smith, cotton spinner and manufacturer, of The Priory, Windermere; and Elizabeth Ann Hartley. Born at 67, Victoria Road, Fulwood, Preston, Lancs, 30 April 1888. Schools: Preston Grammar; and The Leys School, Cambridge, under the Rev. Dr Barber. Admitted 1 Oct. 1907.
> B.A. 1910. Hist. Tripos, Part I, Class 1, 1909; Part II, Class 1, 1910; Law Tripos, Part II, Class 1, 1911. Entrance Scholarship, 1907. Scholar, 1908–11. Ramadge Student, 1911.

Smith, Samuel Percy: son of Frederick Samuel Wilson Smith, solicitor, of Spring Vale, Walsall; and Beatrice Jane Cozens. Born at The Sycamores, Birmingham Road, Walsall, 14 Sept. 1889. School: Wolverhampton Grammar, under Mr T. H. Hichens and Mr W. Caldecott. Admitted 1 Oct. 1907.
> B.A., LL.B. 1910. Law Tripos, Part I, Class 3 (br. 5th), 1909; Part II, Class 3 (br. 40th), 1910.

Spackman, Harold Charles: son of Henry Charles Spackman, commercial traveller, of 20, Jedburgh Street, Clapham Common, London, S.W.; and Alice Brown. Born at Fulham, London, 17 June 1882. Educated at Balham School, under Mr Simpson. Admitted 1 Oct. 1907.
> B.A. 1910. Ordained deacon (Southwark), 1910. Curate of St Paul, Wimbledon Park, 1910– .

Squires, Charles Stephenson: son of Henry Charles Squires, solicitor, of Vale House, Cherryhinton Road, Cambridge; and Charlotte Elizabeth Todd. Born at Vale House, Cherryhinton Road, Cambridge, 4 Oct. 1888. School: Oundle, under Mr F. W. Sanderson. Admitted 1 Oct. 1907.
> LL.B. 1910. Law Tripos, Part I, Class 3, 1909; Part II, Class 2 (br. 12th), 1910.

Storey, Lewis Henry Tutill: son of Henry William Ernest Storey, silk manufacturer, of 29, City Road, London, E.C.; and Georgina Tutill. Born at Red House, Upton, Essex, 29 Jan. 1889. School: Mill Hill, under Dr McClure. Admitted 1 Oct. 1907.
> B.A. 1910. Econ. Tripos, Part I, Class 3, 1909.

Thurston, Edgar Hugh: son of Daniel Thurston, medical practitioner, of 7, Endsleigh Gardens, London, N.W.; and Isabella Brock. Born at 107, Chalton Street, London, N.W., 23 June 1887. School: University College School, Gower Street, London, under Dr H. J. Spenser. Admitted 1 Oct. 1907.
> Died on September 6, 1911, at his home.

Tisza, Count Stephan: son of Count Stephan Tisza, landowner, of Geszt, Bihar Megye, Hungary; and Ilona, his wife. Born at Geszt, Hungary, 28 Aug. 1886. Educated at Debreczin Gymnasium, and the Universities of Budapest, Leipzig, Berlin, and Heidelberg. Admitted 1 Oct. 1907.
> Resided five terms.

Titterton, Sidney John: son of Sidney Titterton, bank inspector, of Hazeldene, Strensham Hill, Moseley, Birmingham; and Margaret Elizabeth Johnson. Born at 6, Church Avenue, Penarth, Glamorgan, 4 Mar. 1888. School: Cheltenham College, under the Rev. R. Waterfield. Admitted 1 Oct. 1907.
    B.A. 1910.

Tweedy, Roger John: son of Sir John Tweedy, Fellow (late President) R.C.S.E., of 100, Harley Street, London, W.; and Mary Hillhouse. Born at 100, Harley Street, London, W., 16 Nov. 1887. Educated at Marlborough College, under the Rev. G. C. Bell and Mr F. Fletcher. Admitted 1 Oct. 1907.
    B.A. 1910. University Commission in the Indian Army, 1910.

Walton, George Warren: son of William Warren Walton, colliery owner, of Holcum, Ferryside, R.S.O., S. Wales; and Mary Beatrice Gott. Born at Bretton West, Yorkshire, 22 April 1887. School: Repton, under the Rev. Lionel Ford. Admitted 1 Oct. 1907. Brother of John, below.
    B.A. 1910.

Walton, John Humphrey: brother of the above. Born at Bretton West, Yorkshire, 4 April 1889. School: Repton, under the Rev. Lionel Ford. Admitted 1 Oct. 1907.

Walton, Richmond: son of the Rev. Octavius Frank Walton, Vicar of Leigh, Tonbridge; and Amy Catherine Deck. Born at St Thomas' Vicarage, Hoxby Road, Clifton, York, 16 May 1888. School: Wolverhampton Grammar, under Mr T. H. Hichens and Mr W. Caldecott. Admitted 1 Oct. 1907.
    B.A. 1910. Classical Tripos, Part I, Cl. 1, Div. 1, 1910. Entrance Scholarship, 1907. Scholar, 1908–10. Selected Candidate (5th) for the H.C.S., 1911. In the Admiralty.

Watkin-Jones, Nathaniel Thomas Howard: son of the Rev. Robert Watkin-Jones, Wesleyan Minister, of South Bank, S.O., Yorkshire; and Elizabeth Mary Hillman. Born at Ironbridge, Salop, 13 Aug. 1888. School: Kingswood School, Bath, under Mr W. P. Workman. Admitted 1 Oct. 1907.
    B.A. 1910. Hist. Tripos, Part I, Class 3, 1909; Part II, Class 3, 1910. Choral Entrance Exhibition, 1907.

Wetenhall, William Thornton: son of William James Wetenhall, J.P., of 8, Maitland Park Villas, Haverstock Hill, London, N.W.; and Mary Jane Thornton. Born at 2, Southampton Road, Haverstock Hill, London, 24 Jan. 1888. School: City of London, under Mr A. T. Pollard and Dr A. Chilton. Admitted 1 Oct. 1907.
    B.A. 1910. Med. and Mod. Lang. Tripos, Class 1, 1909, with distinction. Entrance Scholarship, 1907. Scholar, 1908–10. President of the Athletic Club, 1909–10. University Athlete, 1910.

Wheldon, Emrys John: son of Pierce Jones Wheldon, bank manager, of the National and Provincial Bank of England, Carmarthen: and Louisa Arnaud Mackenzie. Born at Brienton Villas, Rylands, Hereford, 13 Aug. 1886. Schools: Mr F. W. Byers' Preparatory School, Portsmouth; Portsmouth Grammar School; and Carmarthen Grammar School, under Mr E. S. Allen. Admitted 1 Oct. 1907.
    B.A. 1910. Mech. Sci. Tripos, Class 3, 1910. With the British and Colonial Aeroplane Co., Bristol (1911).

Whittall, Henry Cecil: son of Herbert Octavius Whittall, merchant, of Smyrna, Asia Minor; and Louisa Jane Maltass. Born at Smyrna, Asia Minor, 27 Jan. 1888. School: St Paul's, under Mr F. W. Walker and the Rev. A. E. Hillard. Admitted 1 Oct. 1907.
 B.A. 1910. Nat. Sci. Tripos, Part I, Class 2, 1910. Captain of the Boat Club, 1909. In the service of the Asiatic Petroleum Company (1910).

Williams, Alfred Gregson: son of John Williams, M.R.C.S., of Bryn Castell, Carnarvon; and Mary Gregson. Born at 37, Castle Square, Carnarvon, 29 Jan. 1890. School: Shrewsbury, under the Rev. H. W. Moss. Admitted 1 Oct. 1907.
 Nat. Sci. Tripos, Part I, Class 3, 1910. In the service of the Asiatic Petroleum Company (1910).

Wood, Cecil Shuckburgh: son of the Rev. Charles Robert Wood, Rector of Bredfield, Woodbridge, Suffolk; and Mary Frances Jones. Born at Bredfield, Woodbridge, Suffolk, 9 June 1888. Educated at Amberley, Gloucestershire; and Oundle School, under Mr F. W. Sanderson. Admitted 1 Oct. 1907.
 B A. 1910. Mech. Sci. Tripos, Part I, Class 2, 1910.

Woolf, Henry Mortimer Albert: son of Albert Morris Woolf, gentleman, of 52, Priory Road, London, N.W.; and Martha Isaacs. Born at 75, Boundary Road, London, N.W., 17 June 1889. School: Cheltenham College, under the Rev. R. Waterfield; and privately, under Mr F. W. Gilbert, Tunbridge Wells. Admitted 1 Oct. 1907.
 Resided two terms.

Woollcombe-Boyce, Kenneth Woollcombe: son of William Frederick Reynolds Woollcombe-Boyce, M.A., of Christowe, Minchinhampton, Glos; and Sarah Louisa Griffiths. Born at Warwick House, Maida Hill West, London, W., 11 July 1888. Educated at Radley College, under Dr Field. Admitted 1 Oct. 1907.
 B.A. 1910. Classical Tripos, Part I, Class 2, 1910. Entrance Scholarship, 1907. Scholar, 1908-10. Editor of *The Caian*, 1909-10.

Wynne-Yorke, Bulkeley Aneurin Yorke: son of Bulkeley Wynne Yorke Wynne-Yorke, gentleman, of Bryn Aled, Llanfair, Abergele, North Wales; and Annie Beatrice Crosby. Born at 77, Picton Road, Wavertree, Liverpool, 14 April 1889. School: Birkenhead, under Mr F. Griffin. Admitted 1 Oct. 1907.
 Resided three terms.

Anderson, James Drummond: son of James Anderson, M.D. (deceased), formerly Inspector-General of Hospitals in Bengal; and Ellen Garsten (deceased). Born at Calcutta, 11 Nov. 1852. Schools: Cheltenham College, under Dr A. A. Barry, 1862-6; and Rugby School, under Dr Temple and Mr Hayman, 1867-72. Entered the Indian Civil Service 1875 in Bengal. Retired in 1900 as magistrate and collector of Chittagong. Compiled vocabularies of the Lushai, Tipperah, Deori-Chutia and Aka languages and a collection of Kachari folk-tales.
 Teacher of Bengali for the Board of Indian Civil Service Studies 1907- .
 Honorary M.A. 1909.

Duisberg, Carl Ludwig : son of Professor Dr Carl Duisberg, director of the Elber-feld Chemical Works, of Elberfeld ; and Johanna Seebohm.   Born at Elber-feld, Germany, 18 July 1889.   Educated at Real-Gymnasium, Elberfeld, under Dr Booner.   Admitted 22 April 1908.
    Resided one term.

Foreman, Frederick William : son of Frederick William Foreman, bricklayer, of Grimston, near King's Lynn ; and Elizabeth Rudd.   Born at Grimston, near King's Lynn, 22 Sept. 1880.   Educated at King's Lynn Technical Institute, under Mr J. H. Haigh.   Admitted as a Research Student 23 April 1908.
    Diploma in Agriculture 1904.   B.A. (by Certificate of Research) 1910. Associate of the Institute of Chemistry.   Demonstrator in the School of Agriculture 1908–

Flecker, Herman Elroy : son of the Rev. William Herman Flecker, Head Master of Dean Close School, Cheltenham ; and Sarah Ducat.   Born at Lewisham, 5 Nov. 1884.   Educated at Uppingham School and at Trinity College, Oxford. Admitted 20 April 1908 as Student Interpreter.
    Appointed to Constantinople 1900.   Author.

Brooke, Zachary Nugent : son of George Brooke (deceased), of Somerset House (Inland Revenue Department), barrister-at-law of the Middle Temple ; and Alice Elizabeth Nicholas (deceased).   Born at Sutton, Surrey, 1 Feb. 1883. Educated at Artington House, Brighton ; and Bradfield College, under the Rev. Dr H. B. Gray.   Admitted as Drosier Fellow, 19 June 1908.
    Previously admitted at St John's College, Cambridge, 1902.   Scholar of St John's.   Class. Tripos, Part I, Class 1, Div. 2, 1905.   Hist. Tripos, Part II, Class 1, 1906.   Gladstone Prize, 1906.   Winchester Prize, 1906. Lightfoot Scholarship, 1907.   Lecturer in History at Gonville and Caius College from Michaelmas 1908.   B.A. 1905 ; M.A. 1909.

MICHAELMAS 1908 TO MICHAELMAS 1909.

(Tutors: Mr Gallop, Mr Buckland, and Mr Hardy.)

Arrowsmith, George Ernest : son of George Vernon Arrowsmith, gentleman ; and Isabella McKibbin.   Born at 17, Hamilton Road, Ealing, London, W., 17 July 1887.   School : University College School, London, under Mr J. L. Paton.   Admitted 1 Oct. 1908.
    B.A. 1911.

Arrowsmith, Walter Gordon : son of Walter Arrowsmith, gentleman, of Torwood Gardens, Torquay ; and Maria Morse Uphill.   Born at Loughton, Essex, 17 Sept. 1888.   School : Bishop's Stortford, under Mr J. Bruce Payne. Admitted 1 Oct. 1908.

Audra, Emile : son of Eugène Audra, Pasteur de l'Église Réformée, Président du Consistoire de Nantes (deceased) ; and Mary Hilliar.   Born at Angers, Maine et Loire, France, 5 March 1882.   Educated at Lycée David d'Angers ; Sorbonne, Paris ; École Pratique des Hautes Études.   Admitted as a Research Student and Lector in French 1 Oct. 1908.
    French Lector 1908–11.

Bache, Harold Godfrey : son of William Bache, solicitor (deceased); and Frances Mary Stamps. Born at Stakenbridge, Churchill, near Kidderminster, 20 Aug. 1889. School: King Edward's High School, Birmingham, under Mr R. C. Gilson. Admitted 1 Oct. 1908.

>Hist. Tripos, Part I, Class 3, 1910. Played in the University Association Football team 1909, 1910; University Lawn Tennis player 1910. Captain of the Association Football Club 1910–11; of the Cricket Club 1910–11; of the University Club 1910–11.

Back, Percy Robert Hatfeild : son of William Henry Back, solicitor, of Hurn House, Hethersett, Norfolk; and Marion Edith Browne. Born at Wentworth, Newmarket Road, Eaton, Norwich, 10 May 1889. School: Repton, under the Rev. L. Ford. Admitted 1 Oct. 1908.

>B.A. 1911.

Baynes, Frederic William Wilberforce : son of William Wilberforce Baynes, J.P., D.L., Manager of the "Star Life" (Assurance Co.), London (deceased); and Phebe Maria Knight, of Pickhurst Wood, South Hill, Bromley, Kent. Born at 21, Kensington Park Gardens, London, W., 4 Aug. 1889. Schools: Orley Farm, Harrow, under G. B. I. Hopkins, M.A.; Harrow, under Dr Wood. Sayer Scholar. Admitted 1 Oct. 1908.

>B.A. 1911. Class. Tripos, Part I, Class 2, 1911. Entrance Exhibition 1908. Scholar 1910–11. Editor of *The Caian*, 1910–11.

Beard, Cyril Godfrey: son of William Gascoyen Beard, barrister and solicitor, of Masterton, New Zealand; and Fannie Knight. Born at Masterton Wellington, New Zealand, 11 May 1888. Schools: Wellington College, New Zealand; and Wanganui Collegiate School, under Mr W. Epsom. Admitted 1 Oct. 1908.

>Resided three terms.

Bower, Cedric William: son of David Bower, M.D., of Springfield Cottage, Kempston, Beds; and Marian Le Lièvre Rider. Born at Kempston, Beds, 4 Feb. 1890. Schools: St Andrew's, Eastbourne; and Uppingham, under the Rev. Canon Selwyn. Admitted 1 Oct. 1908.

Brisley, Gerald Gahagan Vivian : son of George Charles Brisley, gentleman (deceased), of The Pines, Umzimkulu, South Africa; and Ella Marie Gahagan. Born at Umzimkulu, South Africa, 1888. Educated at Weston College, South Africa; and Lancing College, Shoreham, under the Rev. A. J. Wilson and Mr B. H. Tower. Admitted 1 Oct. 1908. Brother of Cuthbert, IV (1) 56.

>Resided three terms. Returned to South Africa 1909.

Brown, Thomas : son of Davis Brown, farmer, of Markham Hall, Downham Market, Norfolk; and Leonora Mary Coleman. Born at Markham, Norfolk, 27 April 1890. School: Wellingborough Grammar, under Dr H. E. Platt and Mr. P. A. Fryer. Admitted 1 Oct. 1908.

>B.A. 1911.

Buckell, Edward Ronald: son of Dr Edward Buckell, of Wykeham House, Romsey, Hants; and Emma Hillier. Born at Romsey, Hants, 8 April 1889. School: Bedales, Petersfield, under Mr J. H. Badley. Admitted 1 Oct. 1908.

>B.A. 1911. Nat. Sci. Tripos, Part I, Class 3, 1911. Captain of the Hockey Club 1910–11.

Bull, William Edward Hugh: son of William Henry Bull, F.R.C.S., of St Oswald's
House, Stony Stratford, Bucks; and Emma Elizabeth Cherry Garde. Born
at Stony Stratford, Bucks, 20 June 1889. Schools: The Philberds, Maiden-
head; Stubbington House, Fareham; and Lancing College, under Mr B. H.
Tower. Admitted 1 Oct. 1908.
    B.A. 1911. Nat. Sci. Tripos, Part I, Class 3, 1911.

Callaghan, Kenneth Ford: son of William Edmund Callaghan, optician (deceased),
of 13, Roland Gardens, Kensington, London; and Mary Ford. Born at
13, Roland Gardens, Kensington, 27 Feb. 1889. School: Stonyhurst College,
under the Rev. Joseph Browne. Admitted 1 Oct. 1908.
    B.A. 1911. Law Tripos, Part I, Class 3 (br. 13) 1910.

Carr, George D'Rastricke: son of George Frederick Carr, LL.D., Vicar of Amberley-
with-Houghton, Arundel; and Ella Louisa Saunders. Born at Hastings,
11 Sept. 1889. School: Marlborough College, under Mr Fletcher; Central
Technical College, S. Kensington, under Mr W. E. Dalby. Admitted
1 Oct. 1908.
    B.A. 1911. Nat. Sci. Tripos, Part I, Class 2, 1911.

Clarke, Roger Heine: son of Edward Nalder Clarke, gentleman (deceased), of
Colnbrook, Bucks; and Wilhelmina Sarah Heine. Born at Colnbrook,
Bucks, 16 Aug. 1890. School: Kelly College, Tavistock, under the
Rev. W. H. David and the Rev. E. I. A. Phillips. Admitted 1 Oct. 1908.
    B.A. 1911.

Claudet, Frederic Herbert Bontemps: son of Arthur Crozier Claudet, Assayer
to the Bank of England, of 12, Fitzjohn's Avenue, Hampstead, London, N.W.;
and Ethel Ada Cooper. Born at Hampstead, 13 Dec. 1889. Schools: Heddon
Court Preparatory, Hampstead; and Tonbridge, under Dr Tancock and
Mr C. Lowry. Admitted 1 Oct. 1908.
    B.A. 1911.

Costobadie, Lionel Palliser: son of Harry Alister Costobadie, manufacturer, of
Overdale, Mottram-in-Longdendale; and Christina Mary Black. Born at
Mottram-in-Longdendale, 25 Oct. 1889. Schools: Harrogate; Eastman's
Royal Naval College, Southsea; and Haileybury College, under the Rev.
Canon Lyttelton and the Rev. St J. B. Wynne-Willson. Admitted 1 Oct. 1908.
    B.A. 1911. Nat. Sci. Tripos, Part I, Class 1, 1911.

Crompton, Reginald: son of Henry Dickinson Crompton, solicitor (deceased),
of Edgbaston, Birmingham; and Annie Maud Starey. Born at 59, Beaufort
Road, Edgbaston, 6 May 1889. Schools: Dent-de-Lion, Westgate-on-Sea;
and Sedbergh School, under Mr C. Lowry and Mr F. B. Malim. Admitted
1 Oct. 1908. Brother of Kenneth, II. 537, and of James, IV. (1) 57.

Creed, John Martin: son of the Rev. Colin John Creed, Vicar of All Saints,
Leicester; and Etheldreda Wright Spackman. Born at Leicester, 14 Oct.
1889. School: Wyggeston, Leicester, under the Rev. J. Went. Admitted
1 Oct. 1908.
    B.A. 1911. Class. Tripos, Part I, Class 1, Div. 2, 1911. Entrance
    Scholarship, 1908. Scholar, 1909. Bell Scholar, 1909. Winchester
    Prizeman, 1911.

Crosse, Thomas Latymer : son of the Rev. Thomas George Crosse (of the College, II.
392), Vicar of Faversham ; and Fanny Marie Simpson. Born at Eastbridge,
Canterbury, 28 May 1889. Schools: King's School, Canterbury, under the
Rev. A. J. Galpin ; and St Lawrence College, Ramsgate, under Mr C. Morris
and the Rev. E. C. Sherwood. Admitted 1 Oct. 1908.
  B.A. 1911. Class. Tripos, Part I, Class 3, 1911.

Cursetjee, Heerajee Jehangir Manockjee : son of Jehangir Manockjee Cursetjee,
late Deputy-Collector, Government of Bombay ; and Rabanhai Dosabhoy
Cama. Born at Bombay, 14 Aug. 1885. Educated at Bishop's High
School, Poona ; and Grant Medical College, Bombay, under Lieut.-Col.
Dimmock, M.D. Admitted 1 Oct. 1908, as an Affiliated Student.

Curwen, Cecil Niel : son of Thomas Cecil Curwen, stockbroker, of 9, Oak Hill
Park, Hampstead, London, N.W. ; and Margaret Anderson. Born at 9, Oak
Hill Park, Hampstead, 27 Feb. 1889. Schools: Locker's Park, Hemel
Hempstead ; and Rugby, under Dr James. Admitted 1 Oct. 1908. Brother
of Brian, IV. (1) 103.
  B.A. 1911. Hist. Tripos, Part I, Class 3, 1910.

Davis, Frederick Mowbray : son of Felix Arthur Davis, barrister-at-law, of
12, Upper Hamilton Terrace, London, N.W. ; and Viola Maraquita Car-
lotta Marie Webber. Born at 33, Marlborough Hill, Marylebone, London,
23 April 1889. School : Harrow, under Dr Wood. Admitted 1 Oct. 1908.
Entrance Scholarship, 1908.

Evatt, James Millar : son of Edward Pratt Evatt, L.R.C.P., etc., of Waterbeach,
Cambridge ; and Elizabeth Millar. Born at 2, Beaconsfield Terrace, Hawick,
N.B., 22 May 1890. Schools: Perse School, Cambridge, under Dr Rouse ; and
St Albans School, under Mr E. Montague Jones. Admitted 1 Oct. 1908.
  B.A. 1911.

Fairbrother, James : son of Charles Fairbrother, farmer and landowner, of Scotia,
Preston Park, Brighton ; and Elizabeth Jane Kidman. Born at Waffenham,
Northamptonshire, 13 Feb. 1889. School : Oundle, under Mr. F. W. Sanderson.
Admitted 1 Oct. 1908.
  B.A. 1911. Nat. Sci. Tripos, Part I, Class 3, 1911.

Farr, Lawrance Ernest Augustus Bolton : son of Ernest Augustus Farr, M.R.C.S.,
L.R.C.P., J.P., of Heath House, Andover, Hants ; and Anne Lawrance
Augusta Mabel Bolton. Born at Lawrance House, Andover, Hants, 3 June
1890. Schools: Kingsgate House, Winchester ; and Marlborough College,
under Mr F. Fletcher. Admitted 1 Oct. 1908.

Fuchs, Harold Munro : son of Georg Friedrich Gotthilf Fuchs, retired army officer
(Prussian), of Berlin ; and Margaret Isabella Campbell Munro. Born at
34, Sisters Avenue, Clapham Common, London, 28 Sept. 1889. School :
Brighton College, under the Rev. A. F. Titherington and the Rev. W. R.
Dawson. Admitted 1 Oct. 1908.
  B.A. 1911. Nat. Sci. Tripos, Part I, Class 1, 1910 ; Part II, Class 2, 1911.
    Entrance Scholarship, 1908. Scholar, 1909-11. Frank Smart Prize,
    1909.

Game, Arthur Kingsley: son of James Aylward Game, merchant, of Yeeda Grange, Cockfosters, near New Barnet, Herts; and Charlotte Pearse. Born at Yeeda Grange, Cockfosters, Enfield, 8 Nov. 1890. Schools: Orley Farm, Harrow under Mr G. B. I. Hopkins; and Winchester College, under Dr Burge. Admitted 1 Oct. 1908.
    B.A., LL.B. 1911. Law Tripos, Part I (aegrotat), 1910; Part II, Class 2, 1911.

Gardner, Robert Cotton Bruce: son of Philip Thomas Gardner, gentleman, of Conington Hall, near Cambridge; and Emily Elizabeth Calland. Born at Conington Hall, near Cambridge, 3 Dec. 1889. Schools: St Faith's, Trumpington Road, Cambridge, under Mr Goodchild; and Oundle School, under Mr. F. W. Sanderson. Admitted 1 Oct. 1908.
    B.A. 1911.

Gimblett, Charles Leonard: son of Robert Wheddon Gimblett, retired Commander B.I.S. Nav. Co., of 6, Duchess Road, Clifton, Bristol; and Emmeline Ella Rawle. Born at Linden House, Apollo Bunder, Bombay, India, 19 June 1890. Schools: St Peter's, Weston-super-Mare; Elizabeth College, Guernsey; Stubbington, Fareham; and Clifton College, under the Rev. A. A. David. Admitted 1 Oct. 1908.
    B.A. 1911. Nat. Sci. Tripos, Part I, Class 2, 1911. Chapel Clerk, 1910–11.

Gimlette, Charles Hart Medlicott: son of Thomas Desmond Gimlette, Inspector-General of Hospitals and Fleets, R.N., of Normanhurst, Station Road, Chingford; and Mary Ann Nichols. Born at Ireland Island, Sandys, Bermuda, 5 Aug. 1889. School: Merchant Taylors', London, under Dr J. A. Nairn. Admitted 1 Oct. 1908.
    B.A. 1911. Nat. Sci. Tripos, Part I, Class 2, 1911.

Gingell, Walter Craven: son of John Gingell, landowner, of Elmwood, Epping; and Sophia Oakes Miller. Born at Theydon Bois, Essex, 5 April 1889. School: Bishop's Stortford School, under Mr J. Bruce Payne. Admitted 1 Oct. 1908.
    B.A., LL.B. 1911. Math. Tripos, Part I, Class 3, 1909; Law Tripos, Part II, Class 3, 1911.

Gooderham, Ernest John Robinson Briggs: son of Robinson Briggs, farmer (deceased); and Harriet Gooderham. Born at Bulcamp, Blyburgh, Suffolk, 23 Feb. 1889. Nephew and adopted son of the Rev. A. Gooderham (of the College, II. 356), Vicar of Eglingham. School: Durham School, under the Revs. A. E. Hillard, H. W. McKenzie, R. D. Budworth. Admitted 1 Oct. 1908.
    B.A. 1911. Theol. Tripos, Part I, Class 2, 1911.

Greenish, Frederick Harold Sellick: son of Frederick Robert Greenish, Doctor in Music (New College, Oxford), of The Grove, Haverfordwest; and Ellen Elizabeth Anne Sellick. Born at Haverfordwest, 31 March 1890. Schools: St Andrew's, Tenby; and Cheltenham College, under the Rev. R. Waterfield. Admitted 1 Oct. 1908.
    B.A. 1911.

Guinness, John Frith Grattan : son of Henry Grattan Guinness, M.D., of Harley House, Bow, London; and Annie Reed. Born at 51, Bow Road, Bow, London, 17 Dec. 1889. Schools : City of London, under the Rev. A. Chilton; The Leys School, Cambridge, under the Rev. Dr W. T. A. Barber. Admitted 1 Oct. 1908.
    B.A., LL.B. 1911. Hist. Tripos, Part I, Class 2, 1910 ; Law Tripos, Part II, Class 3, 1911.

Hardy, Jack : son of George Hardy, retired brewer (deceased), of Pickering Lodge, Timperley ; and Ada Elizabeth Asquith. Born at Pickering Lodge, Timperley, Cheshire, 22 Feb. 1890. School : Harrow, under Dr Wood. Admitted 1 Oct. 1908.

Hargreaves, Robert: son of Edmund Hargreaves, M.D., of 2, Eyre Street, Sheffield; and Elizabeth Feirn. Born at Sheffield, 10 Jan. 1890. School : Uppingham, under the Rev. Dr Selwyn. Admitted 1 Oct. 1908.
    B.A. 1911. Nat. Sci. Tripos, Part I, Class 3, 1911.

Hartree, Kenneth : son of William Hartree, engineer, of Havering, Tunbridge Wells ; and Una Kathleen Brocklebank. Born at Lewisham, 28 Oct. 1889. Educated at Hurstleigh, Tunbridge Wells ; and Bradfield College, under the Rev. Dr H. B. Gray. Admitted 1 Oct. 1908. Brother of Cyril, II. 553 ; and Raymond, IV. (1) 49.
    B.A. 1911.

Hawkins, Caesar Hugh George Wills : son of Caesar Hugh Hawkins, Commander R.N. (deceased); and Annie Beatrice Wills, who afterwards married C. H. B. Elliott (of the College, II. 397). Born at Stapleton, Bristol, 3 April, 1889. School : Charterhouse, under the Rev. G. H. Rendall. Admitted 1 Oct. 1908.
    Kept three terms.

Heard, Henry Fitzgerald: son of the Rev. Henry James Heard (of the College, II. 447), Rector of St Michael's, Bath ; and Maud Jervis Bannatyne. Born at 69, Victoria Park Road, South Hackney, London, 6 Oct. 1889. Schools: Lansdowne Proprietary, Bath; and Sherborne School, under the Rev. F. B. Westcott. Admitted 1 Oct. 1908. Brother of Alexander, IV. (1) 49.
    B.A. 1911. Hist. Tripos, Part I, Class 2, 1910; Part II, Class 2, 1911. Theological Exhibitioner, 1911

Hoff, Henry Gilson : son of Henry Hoff, yeoman, of Shouldham Thorpe, Downham Market ; and Alice Ada Clarke. Born at Wormegay, near King's Lynn, 12 June 1889. School : Marlborough College, under the Rev. Canon Bell and Mr F. Fletcher. Admitted 1 Oct. 1908.
    B.A. 1911.

Hunter, John Hubert : son of the Rev. Robert Alexander Hunter (deceased), Rector of St. John's, Maddermarket, Norwich ; and Eleanor Waring. Born at Heavitree, Exeter, Devon, 27 May 1885. School : Bedford Modern, under Mr Cecil W. Kaye. Admitted 1 Oct. 1908.
    B.A. 1911. Theol. Tripos, Part I, Class 3, 1911. Archbishop of Canterbury's Exhibitioner, 1908. Chapel Clerk, 1910–11. In the Burma Oil Company (1911).

Langley, Edward Ralph : son of the Rev. Edward Langley (of the College, ii. 371),
Vicar of Alveston, R.S.O., Glos ; and Alicia Brunshill Tagert. Born at
Lower Hazel, Olveston, 12 April 1889. School : Cheltenham College, under
the Rev. R. Waterfield. Admitted 1 Oct. 1908.
Kept seven terms. With Hoare, Miller and Co., Calcutta (1911).

Lovelock, Arthur Reginald : son of Arthur Samuel Lovelock, chartered accountant,
of Kirkalie, Darley Road, Eastbourne; and Janette Alexandrina Scott.
Born at Calcutta, India, 26 Feb. 1890. Schools : Dollar Institution ; and
Clifton College, under the Rev. A. A. David. Admitted 1 Oct. 1908.
Resided three terms.

Lowry, William Augustine Harper : son of William Buchanan Lowry, tea planter
(retired), of Manor Way Grange, Lee-on-the-Solent ; and Annie Sophia Bull.
Born at Calcutta, India, 21 Feb. 1890. Schools : St Andrew's, Southborough,
Tunbridge Wells ; and Cheltenham College, under the Rev. R. Waterfield.
Admitted 1 Oct. 1908.

McCaw, Osmond Calbraith : son of George Calbraith McCaw, printer and publisher,
of 177, Camden Road, London, N.W. ; and Emily Harriett Roads. Born at
238, Camden Road, London, N.W., 25 April 1889. School : Highgate, under
the Rev. A. E. Allcock. Admitted 1 Oct. 1908.
President of the Athletic Club, 1910–11.

Mahmoud Khan, Mirza : son of Mirza Ahmed Khan, Nassir-ed-Dauleh, Persian
Minister in Belgium. Born at Teheran, Persia, January 1890. School :
Harrow, under Dr J. Wood. Admitted 1 Oct. 1908.
Resided one term, but did not matriculate.

Manning, John Carlton : son of Samuel Manning, merchant, of Barbados; and
Alice Pitcher. Born at St Michael, Barbados, 4 Nov. 1888. Educated at
The Lodge School, Barbados ; and Dulwich College, under Mr A. H. Gilkes.
Admitted 1 Oct. 1908.
B.A., LL.B. 1911. Law Tripos, Part I, Class 3 (br. 13), 1910 ; Part II,
Class 2, 1911.

Maunsell, Frederick Wyndham : son of John Frederick Maunsell, sheep farmer, of
Masterton, New Zealand ; and Emma Louise Beauchamp. Born at Thorndon
Quay, Wellington, New Zealand, 10 Oct. 1888. School : Wanganui Collegiate
School, under Mr W. Empson. Admitted 1 Oct. 1908.
B.A. 1911. Nat. Sci. Tripos, Part I, Class 2, 1911.

Miskin, Geoffrey : son of William Miskin (deceased), member of Lloyd's ; and Ella
Harriette Kemp (who afterwards married the Rev. Henry Arthur Serres, of
the Vicarage, Birchington, Kent). Born at Fairhaven, Sidcup, Kent, 9 Jan.
1890. Educated at Eastman's, Southsea ; The Limes, Greenwich ; South
Eastern College, Ramsgate ; Loudwater, Westgate, under Mr P. B. Allen.
Admitted 1 Oct. 1908.

Nickels, Robert Norman : son of John Tetley Nickels, farmer, of The Day House,
Shrewsbury ; and Alice Mary Minton. Born at The Day House, Shrewsbury,
1 Nov. 1890. Educated at the School, Malvern Link ; and Repton School,
under the Rev. L. Ford. Admitted 1 Oct. 1908.
B.A. 1911. Mech. Sci. Tripos, Class 3, 1911.

Oliver, Harold Gordon : son of Thomas Andrew Oliver, lace manufacturer (retired), of Moorside, Sidmouth, Devon ; and Florence Herbert. Born at Ebury Road, Balford, Nottingham, 5 Feb. 1889. School : Rugby, under Dr James. Admitted 1 Oct. 1908. Brother of Thomas, IV. (1) 66.
> B.A. 1911. Nat. Sci. Tripos, Part I, Class 3, 1911.

Owen, Owen : son of Owen Owen, brigade surgeon, of Dan-y-Rallt, Cheltenham ; and Alice Augusta Walker. Born at Nicosia, Cyprus, 27 April 1884. Educated at Malvern College under the Rev. S R. James ; and at the Royal Military College, Sandhurst. Served in the Indian Army. Admitted 1 Oct. 1908.
> B.A. 1911.

Pentland, George Charles Croker : son of George Henry Pentland, J.P., landowner, of Black Hall, Drogheda, Ireland ; and Jessy Frances Barrington. Born at 58, Fitzwilliam Square, Dublin, 15 Feb. 1890. Educated at Oaklands Court, Broadstairs ; Malvern College, under the Rev. S. R. James ; and privately at Westgate-on-Sea, under Mr P. B. Allen. Admitted 1 Oct. 1908.
> B.A. 1911.

Peters, Rudolph Albert : son of Albert Edward Duncan Ralph Peters, physician and surgeon, of 24, High Street, Petersfield, Hants ; and Agnes Malvina Watts. Born at Kensington, 13 April 1889. Schools : Warden House, Upper Deal, Kent ; Wellington College, Berks, under the Rev. Dr B. Pollock ; and King's College, London. Admitted 1 Oct. 1908.
> B.A. 1911. Nat. Sci. Tripos, Part I, Class 1, 1910. Scholar, 1909– President of the Musical Society, 1910–11.

Pinkham, Charles : son of Charles Pinkham, J.P., builder (retired), of 7, Winchester Avenue, Brondesbury, London, N.W. ; and Margaret Mary Vine. Born at 1, Cromwell Terrace, Hazel Road, Kensal Green, London, N.W , 21 Jan. 1889. Schools : Brondesbury College ; and Leys School, Cambridge, under the Rev. Dr W. T. A. Barber. Admitted 1 Oct. 1908.
> B.A. 1911. Math. Tripos, Part I, Class 2, 1909. Econ. Tripos, Part I, Class 2, 1911. Played in the University Association Football team 1909, 1910, 1911 ; Rugby team 1910.

Porritt, Reginald Norman : son of Norman Porritt, L.R.C.P., M.R.C.S., consulting surgeon, Huddersfield Infirmary ; of 24, New North Road, Huddersfield ; and Sarah Ann Richardson. Born at New North Road, Huddersfield, 3 May, 1890. School : Epsom College, under the Rev. T. N. H. Smith-Pearse. Admitted 1 Oct. 1908.
> B.A. 1911. Nat. Sci. Tripos, Part I, Class 2, 1911.

Reid, Cedric Boileau : son of Frank Lumsden Reid (deceased) ; and Fanny Harriet Boys (who afterwards married Lieut. Sampson Sladen, R.N., of the London Fire Brigade). Born at 13, Old Cavendish Street, London, W., 27 July 1889. Educated at Hill Brow, Meads, Eastbourne ; Redburn, Eastbourne, under Mr J. Vinter. Admitted 1 Oct. 1908.
> Resided six terms.

Rhodes, Sidney Herbert : son of William Atkinson Rhodes, dentist, of " Brocodale," Selwyn Gardens, Cambridge ; and Kate Louise Palmer. Born at 53, Trumpington Street, Cambridge, 6 Oct. 1889. Schools : St Faith's, Cambridge ; and Weymouth College, under Mr H. C. Barnes-Lawrence. Admitted 1 Oct. 1908. Brother of William, IV. (1) 35.

C IV 1

Robathan, Kenneth Minshull : son of the Rev. Thomas Frederick Robathan, Rector of Harthill, Chester ; and Edith Jane Adcock. Born at Naini Tal, India, 1 Sept. 1889. Educated at Church Missionary School, Limpsfield, Surrey ; and Merchant Taylors' School, London, under the Rev. J. A. Nairn. Admitted 1 Oct. 1908.
> B.A. 1911. Or. Lang. Tripos, Class 1, 1911. Entrance Scholarship, 1908 ; Scholar, 1909. Stewart of Rannoch Scholarship, 1908.

Roberts, Walter Stewart : son of the Rev. Ernest Stewart Roberts, Master of Gonville and Caius College, Cambridge, of The Lodge, Gonville and Caius College, Cambridge ; and Mary Harper. Born at The Principal's Lodgings, Jesus College, Oxford, 24 March 1889. Schools : King's College Choir School, Cambridge ; Stoke House, Slough ; and Eton College, under the Rev. Dr E. Warre and the Hon. and Rev. E. Lyttelton. Admitted 1 Oct. 1908.
> B.A. 1911. Classical Tripos, Part I, Class 2, Div. 1, 1910 ; Med. and Mod. Lang. Tripos, Class 2, 1911. Entrance Scholarship, 1908 ; Scholar, 1910–11. Probationer for the Egyptian Civil Service, 1911.

Ross, Ivan Dingley : son of the Rev. Thomas Ross, Wesleyan minister, of 72, Thorne Road, Doncaster ; and Blanche Dingley. Born at Bromyard, near Worcester, 22 Dec. 1888. School : Kingswood School, Bath, under Mr W. P. Workman. Admitted 1 Oct. 1908.
> B.A. 1911. Math. Tripos, Part I, Class 1, 1909 ; Part II, Sen. Opt. 1911. Entrance Scholarship, 1908 ; Scholar, 1909–11. Master at Richmond College, Surrey (1911).

Rutherford, William McConnell : son of William Rutherford (deceased), commercial traveller (retired), of Belfast ; and Lilias Watt Adams. Born at 10, College Green, Belfast, Co. Antrim, Ireland, 4 Dec. 1881. Educated at Methodist College, Belfast ; Queen's College, Belfast ; and New College, Edinburgh, under President Dods. Admitted as Research Student, 1 Oct. 1908.
> B.A. 1910, by Certificate of Research.

Sanctuary, Campbell Thomas : son of Campbell Fortescue Stapleton Sanctuary, land agent, of Mangerton, Melplash, R.S.O., Dorset ; and Mary Eliza Glossop. Born at Mangerton, Melplash, R.S.O., Dorset, 31 July 1889. School : Sherborne, under the Rev. Canon Westcott. Surveyors' Institute Scholarship, 1908. Admitted 1 Oct. 1908. Brother of Arthur, IV. (1) 118.
> B.A. 1911. Nat. Sci. Tripos, Part I, Class 2, 1910. Diploma in Agriculture, 1911.

Schlesinger, Gerald Leonard : son of Leonard Bernhard Schlesinger, banker, of Brandon House, Kensington Palace Gardens, London ; and Mary Sophia Nathan. Born at London, 23 Nov. 1889. School : Clifton College, under the Rev. Canon Glazebrook and the Rev. A. A. David. Admitted 1 Oct. 1908.
> B.A. 1911.

Snell, John Aubrey Brooking : son of Simeon Snell, surgeon, of Moor Lodge, Sheffield (deceased) ; and Anne Christiana Woodley. Born at Sheffield, 13 May 1890. Schools : Holmleigh, Buxton ; and Uppingham, under Dr Selwyn. Admitted 1 Oct. 1908. Brother of Henry, IV. (1) 25.
> B.A. 1911.

Statham, Heathcote Dicken: son of Henry Heathcote Statham, F.R.I.B.A., editor of *The Builder*, of 1, Camp View, Wimbledon Common, London; and Florence Elizabeth Dicken. Born at 40, Gower Street, Bedford Square, London, 7 Dec. 1889. Schools: St Michael's College, Tenbury, Worcester; and Gresham's School, Holt, Norfolk, under Mr G. W. S. Howson. Admitted 1 Oct. 1908.

   Mus.Bac. 1911.   Musical Scholarship, 1908.

Stevens, Gilbert Henry: son of Charles Frederick Stevens, draper, of 20, High Street, Harlesden, London, N.W.; and Emily Emma Kate Tack. Born at 20, High Street, Harlesden, London, N.W., 20 Feb. 1889. Educated at Wimborne Grammar School; and Hartley University College, Southampton. Admitted 1 Oct. 1908.

   B.A. 1911.   Math. Tripos, Part I, Class 1, 1909; Part II, Wrangler, 1911.
   Entrance Scholarship, 1908; Scholar, 1909–

Sturgess, John: son of John Moore Sturgess, land agent, of The Mount, Penshurst, Kent; and Annie Shepherd. Born at Whitepost, Leigh, Kent, 13 Oct. 1889. Schools: Quebec House, St Leonards-on-Sea; and Tonbridge School, under Dr Tancock and Mr C. Lowry. Admitted 1 Oct. 1908.

Swaffield, Alfred Ronald Otway: son of Alfred Owen Swaffield, stockbroker, of 5, Lansdowne Square, Weymouth; and Amy Rose Dowding. Born at Worple Road, Wimbledon, Surrey, 27 Dec. 1889. Schools: Warden House, Deal; and Radley College, under the Rev. T. Field, D.D. Admitted 1 Oct. 1908.

   Choral Entrance Exhibition, 1908.   Migrated to King's, 1909, as Choral Scholar.

Swindlehurst, Joseph Eric: son of Joseph Eaves Swindlehurst, C.E., of Brantwood, Spencer Road, Coventry; and Elizabeth Isabella Artis. Born at 138, Alexandra Road, Winshill, Burton-on-Trent, 2 Aug. 1890. School · King Henry VIII School, Coventry, under the Rev. C. R. Gilbert and the Rev. A. D. Perrott. Admitted 1 Oct. 1908.

   B.A. 1911.

Sword, Arthur Nicholson: son of John Stevenson Sword, landed proprietor, of Sandhurst, Tunbridge Wells; and Florence Nicholson. Born at Rosario, Argentine Republic, 2 March 1889. Schools: St Andrew's School, Southborough, Tunbridge Wells; and Repton School, under the Rev. L. Ford. Admitted 1 Oct. 1908.

   B.A. 1911.   Nat. Sci. Tripos, Part I, Class 3, 1911.

Sykes, Ronald: son of Alfred Sykes, J.P., worsted manufacturer, of Woodville, Thongsbridge, near Huddersfield; and Sarah Jane Hirst. Born at Clare Bank, Clare Hill, Huddersfield, 19 Sept. 1889. School: Uppingham, under the Rev. Dr Selwyn. Admitted 1 Oct. 1908.

   B.A. 1911.   Nat. Sci. Tripos, Part I, Class 3, 1911.

Syme, Gordon Wemyss: son of John Wemyss Syme, of Hobart, Tasmania; and Jessie Gordon McHardy. Born at "Cascade," Hobart, Tasmania, 15 July 1890. Schools: St Bede's, Eastbourne; and Clifton College, under the Rev. A. A. David. Admitted 1 Oct. 1908.

Thomas, Duncan Collisson Willey: son of Lieut.-Colonel William Frederick
   Thomas, M.D., I.M.S.; and Jane Willey. Born at Quilon, India, 19 Nov.
   1890. Schools: Holm Leigh, Buxton; and Uppingham School, under the
   Rev. Dr Selwyn. Admitted 1 Oct. 1908.
      Resided three terms.

Turner, Arthur James: son of Alexander Abraham Turner, house decorator,
   of 5, Azenby Road, Peckham, London, S.E.; and Annie Maria Brown.
   Born at 14, Lyndhurst Grove, Camberwell, London, S.E., 30 Sept. 1889.
   Educated at Lyndhurst Grove School; and Wilson's Grammar School,
   Camberwell, under the Rev. F. McDowell, D.D. Admitted 1 Oct. 1908.
      B.A. 1911. Nat. Sci. Tripos, Part I, Class 1, 1910. Math. Tripos,
      Part I, Class 2, 1911. Entrance Exhibition, 1908; Scholar, 1909.

Tweedie, Leslie Kinloch: son of Alec Tweedie (deceased), shipbroker and underwriter at Lloyd's, of 30, York Terrace, Regent's Park, London, N.W.; and
   Ethel Harley. Born at 30, York Terrace, Regent's Park, London, N.W.,
   11 Jan. 1890. School: Harrow, under Dr J. Wood. Admitted 1 Oct. 1908.

Tweedy, Owen Meredith: son of Henry Colpoys Tweedy, M.D. (Dublin), of
   28, Clifton Park Road, Clifton, Bristol; and Alice Maud Meredith. Born
   at 2, Gardiner's Row, Dublin, 22 Oct. 1888. School: Clifton College, under
   the Rev. Canon Glazebrook and the Rev. A. A. David. Admitted 1 Oct.
   1908.
      B.A. 1911. Med. and Mod. Lang. Tripos, Section E, Class 2, 1910;
      Section C, Class 2, 1911. Entrance Scholarship, 1908; Scholar,
      1910–11.

Wallace, Robert William Joshua: son of William Dollin Wallace, gentleman, of
   Alyth, Woodside Lane, N. Finchley; and Eleanor Margaret Pedley. Born
   at Trafalgar House, Tottenham, Middlesex, 19 April 1889. School: Ashton
   Grammar, Dunstable, under Mr L. C. R. Thring. Admitted 1 Oct. 1908.
      B.A. 1911. In business in the Argentine Republic (1911).

Wedel, Hans Albrecht: son of Otto Wedel, Major; and Elisabeth Poppe. Born
   at Memel, Germany, 30 Nov. 1888. Educated at the Realgymnasium at
   Rixdorf, near Berlin; and at the University, Freiburg i. B. Admitted 1 Oct.
   1908.
      Resided two terms.

Wells-Cole, Gervas Charles: son of Gervas Frederick Wells-Cole, brewer, of Stones
   Place, near Lincoln; and Mary Beatrice Brook. Born at The Mount,
   St Peter's-at-Eastgate, Lincoln, 5 May 1889. Educated at Repton School,
   under the Rev. L. G. B. Ford. Admitted 1 Oct. 1908.
      B.A. 1911. Nat. Sci. Tripos, Part I, Class 3, 1911.

Williams, Philip Stanhope: son of Claude St Maur Williams, Assoc.M.Inst.C.E., of
   " Bellevue," Harrow-on-the-Hill; and Alice Frances Crofton. Born at Harrow-
   on-the-Hill, 7 July 1889. Schools: Orley Farm, Harrow-on-the-Hill, under
   Mr G. B. I. Hopkins; and Harrow School, under Dr Wood. Sayer Scholar,
   1908. Admitted 1 Oct. 1908.
      B.A. 1911. Class. Tripos, Part I, Class 1, Div. 3, 1911. Entrance Scholar-
      ship, 1908; Scholar, 1909– .

Williamson, John Maurice : son of Charles Henry Williamson, managing director of company, of Stanstead, Sutton, Surrey; and Mary Wright. Born at Eversley, Avenue Road, Grantham, 10 Jan. 1890. School : The Leys, Cambridge, under the Rev. Dr. Barber. Admitted 1 Oct. 1908.
> B.A., LL.B. 1911. Hist. Tripos, Part I, Class 3, 1910. Law Tripos, Part II, Class 3, 1911.

Wimbush, Gordon Stewart : son of Charles Wimbush, chairman and director of Wimbush and Co., of Netherelms, Woodside Avenue, N. Finchley; and Helen Stewart Robertson. Born at Newstead House, East Finchley, Middlesex, 3 Dec. 1889. School : Haileybury College, under the Rev. St J. B. Wynne-Willson. Admitted 1 Oct. 1908.

Wood, Eric Horace : son of John Horace Wood, school teacher, of Sholing, Southampton; and Mary Handy. Born at Sholing, Southampton, 26 June 1889. Educated at Hartley University College, Southampton, under Dr S. W. Richardson. Admitted 1 Oct. 1908, as an Affiliated Student.
> B.A. 1911. Med. and Mod. Lang. Tripos, Section C, Class 1, 1910; Section E, Class 2, 1911. Entrance Scholarship, 1908; Scholar, 1909–11. At the École Normale, Paris (1911).

Wright, Charles Seymour : son of Alfred Wright, manager of the London and Lancashire Fire Insurance Company, Toronto, of 60, Crescent Road, Toronto, Canada; and Kate Charlotte Kennedy. Born at 42, Harrison Street, Toronto, Canada, 7 April 1887. Educated at Upper Canada College; and at Toronto University. Admitted 1 Oct. 1908, as Wollaston Student.
> Wollaston Studentship, 1908–10. Joined the scientific staff of the Antarctic Expedition under Captain Scott, 1910.

Kennington, William Davy : son of Mr Kennington (deceased), retired wine-merchant; and Elizabeth Davy. Born at Great Coates, Lincolnshire, 3 May 1889. Schools : The Lower School, Uppingham; and Uppingham School, under the Rev. Dr E. C. Selwyn. Admitted 8 Jan. 1909.
> Kept one term.

Ern, Otto : son of Carl Friederich Ern, manufacturer of razors, of Solingen; and Auguste Kelk. Born at Wald, Rhenish Prussia, 6 April 1889. Admitted 23 April 1909.
> Resided one term.

Thomson, William : son of the Rev. James Laing Thomson, B.D. (deceased), Minister of Menmuir, of The Manse, Menmuir, Brechin; and Eliza Ann Laing (deceased). Born at The Manse, Menmuir, Brechin, 7 May 1885. Educated at Robert Gordon's College, Aberdeen; and at Aberdeen University. Admitted 1 Oct. 1909, as a Research Student.
> Kept one term as a Non-Collegiate Student. Resided one term.

MICHAELMAS 1909 TO MICHAELMAS 1910.

(Tutors : Mr Buckland, Mr Hardy, and Mr Cameron.)

Ainsley, Alan Colpitts : son of Thomas George Ainsley, M.D., of Greylands, West Hartlepool; and Wilhelmina Caroline Hill. Born at Hartlepool, 4 July 1890. Schools: Aysgarth School, R.S.O., Yorks; and Malvern College, under the Rev. S. R. James. Admitted 1 Oct. 1909.

Allen, Percy Herman Charles : son of Richard William Allen, solicitor (deceased) ; and Charlotte White, of 76, Paulet Road, Myatt's Park, London, S.E.   Born at 64 Geneva Road, Brixton, 9 April 1890.   Schools : Christ's Hospital under the Rev. R. Lee and the Rev. A. W. Upcott.   Admitted 1 Oct. 1909.
   Math. Tripos, Part I, Class 1, 1910.   Entrance Scholarship, 1909 ; Scholar, 1910-   .

Back, Hatfeild Arthur William : son of the Rev. Arthur James Back (of the College, II. 398), Rector of Carleton Rode, Norfolk ; and Ellen Harriett Bensly.   Born at Worstead, Norfolk, 23 Sept. 1890.   School : the Grammar School, Norwich, under the Rev. E. F. Gilbard.   Admitted 1 Oct. 1900.

Bailey, Thomas Burton : son of Alfred Albert Bailey, managing director of Bailey and White, Ltd., of The Thicket, Southsea ; and Alice Elizabeth Burton. Born at Southsea, 30 March 1891.   Schools : Portsmouth Grammar, under Mr J. C. Nicol ; and Cheltenham College, under the Rev. R. Waterfield. Admitted 1 Oct. 1909.

Baker, Stanley : son of Daniel Baker, architect and contractor (deceased) ; and Mary Gosling.   Born at 13, Copt Hall Gardens, Folkestone, 4 April 1890. Schools : Seabrook Lodge ; and Charterhouse, under Dr G. H. Rendall. Admitted 1 Oct. 1909.
   In University Association Football team, 1910.

Barraclough, Jack Norman : son of Norman Charles Barraclough, LL.B., solicitor (St John's College, Cambridge), of 11 Russell Road, Kensington, London, W. ; and Blanche Christiana Allen.   Born at 56, Rossetti Mansions, Chelsea, London, S.W., 14 June 1890.   School : Malvern College, under the Rev. S. R. James.   Admitted 1 Oct. 1909.

Batten, William Douglas Grant : son of John Kaye Batten, I.C.S., first additional Judicial Commissioner of the Central Provinces, Nagpur, India ; and Eva Muriel Elizabeth Ketchen.   Born at Calicut, district of Malabar, India, 9 July 1890.   School : Clifton College, under the Rev. A. A. David.   Admitted 1 Oct. 1909.
   Med. and Mod. Lang. Tripos, Section C, Class 2, 1911.   Entrance Scholarship, 1909 ; Scholar, 1910-   .   2nd Lieut. O.T.C. 1911.

Batty-Smith, Sydney Harry : son of Henry Batty-Smith, journalist, of " Round-wood," Windlesham, Surrey ; and Lilian Emily Kent.   Born at 93, Comeragh Road, West Kensington, London, W., 26 Oct. 1890.   Schools : Quernmore, Bromley, Kent ; and Bradfield College, under the Rev. Dr H. B. Gray. Admitted 1 Oct. 1909.
   Hist. Tripos, Part II, Class 2, 1911.   Entrance Scholarship (honorary), 1909.

Bell, John Dobrée : son of John Charles Bell (deceased) ; and Ethel Dobrée. Born at Great Ayton, Yorkshire, 28 Sept. 1887.   Schools : Mulgrave Castle, Whitby ; and Trinity College, Glenalmond, under the Rev. J. H. Skrine and the Rev. A. R. F. Hyslop.   Admitted 1 Oct. 1909.
   Med. and Mod. Lang. Tripos, Section E, Class 3, 1911.   Editor of The Caian.

Bonar, Thomas Lonsdale: son of Thomas Mitchell Bonar, surgeon, of Probus, Córnwall; and Maud Mary Lonsdale. Born at Gwĕl Marten, Probus, Cornwall, 30 July 1891. Schools: Probus School; and Exeter School, under Mr W. A. Cunningham. Admitted 1 Oct. 1909.

Bratton, Allen Basil: son of James Allen Bratton, M.A. (Cantab.), M.R.C.S., L.R.C.P. (London) (deceased), of College Hill House, Shrewsbury; and Vera Rose Matveieff, who afterwards married Cyril Wintle, of The Lodge, New Romney, Kent. Born at College Hill House, Shrewsbury, 11 Jan. 1890. Schools: St Ronan's, West Worthing; and Harrow, under Dr Wood. Admitted 1 Oct. 1909.
    Entrance Scholarship (honorary), 1909. In the University Shooting Eight, 1910, 1911. In the English "Twenty" Shooting team, 1911.

Brownsword, Douglas Anderson: son of Harry Anderson Brownsword, lace manufacturer, of Rollesby Hall, near Great Yarmouth; and Mabel Parr. Born at 5, Magdala Road, Basford, Nottingham, 11 Sept. 1892. School: Gresham's, Holt, Norfolk, under the Rev. G. Howson. Admitted 1 Oct. 1909.

Bull, Henry Cecil Herbert: son of William Henry Bull, physician and surgeon, of St Oswald's House, Stony Stratford; and Emma Elizabeth Cherry Garde. Born at St Oswald's House, Stony Stratford, Bucks, 27 April 1892. School: Wellington College, under the Rev. Dr Pollock. Admitted 1 Oct. 1909.

Cant, Frederick Vaudrey: son of Frederick Cant, surgeon, of Woodley House, Woodley, near Stockport; and Edith Howard Yeld. Born at Holly Bank Woodley, Bredbury, near Stockport, 1 March 1890. School: Shrewsbury, under the Rev. H. W. Moss. Admitted 1 Oct. 1909.

Christie, James Francis Alexander: son of the Rev. James Thomas Christie, of Les Fréesias, Petit Juas, Cannes; and Maria Antoinetta Felice Storoni Finocchi. Born at Via del Tritone 185, Rome, 18 April 1890. School: Clifton College, under the Rev. Canon M. G. Glazebrook and the Rev. A. A. David. Admitted 1 Oct. 1909.
    Entrance Scholarship, 1909. Kept one term.

Clarence Smith, Kenneth William: son of Sir Clárence Smith, of the White House, Woodford Common, Essex; and Mary Webster. Born at Hawthorns, Chislehurst, Kent, 6 April 1891. Schools: Laleham, Margate; and The Leys, Cambridge, under the Rev. Dr Barber. Admitted 1 Oct. 1909. Brother of Everard, IV. (1) 52.

Cockayne, Alan Andreas: son of Henry John Marsh Cockayne, director of a limited company, of Stand House, Broomhill, Sheffield; and Florence Titley Evans. Born at Hastings Road, Millhouses, Sheffield, 21 Sept. 1890. School: Charterhouse, under the Rev. Dr G. H. Rendall. Admitted 1 Oct. 1909.

Combe, Edmund Percy: son of Charles Thomson Combe (deceased), corn merchant, of 14, Clarendon Crescent, Edinburgh; and Margaret McBean Gibson. Born at 14, Clarendon Crescent, Edinburgh, 2 March 1891. School: the Edinburgh Academy, under Mr Mackenzie and Mr Carter. Admitted 1 Oct. 1909.

Costigan, Robert Hampton : son of Charles Edward Costigan, assistant super-intendent in the Post Office, Cambridge, of 11, Parker Street, Cambridge ; and Emma Maria Taylor. Born at 43, Victoria Road, Chesterton, Cambridge, 18 July 1890. School : The Perse, Cambridge, under Dr W. H. D. Rouse. Admitted 1 Oct. 1909.

Cottam, Horace Charles Bowman : son of Horace James Cottam, secretary, of 24, Harlesden Gardens, London, N.W. ; and Mary Bowman. Born at Langley Road, Watford, Herts, 5 Jan. 1891. School : Harrow, under Dr Wood. Admitted 1 Oct. 1909.

Cowie, Alexander Gordon : son of Alexander Hugh Cowie, Colonel, Royal Engineers, of Burgoyne House, Stanhope Lines, Aldershot ; and Katherine Elizabeth Ward. Born at Yeatton, Brockenhurst, Hants, 27 Feb. 1889. Schools : Summerfields, Oxford ; and Charterhouse, under Dr G. H. Rendall. Admitted 1 Oct. 1909.
(Honorary Entrance Scholarship, 1908.) University Cricketer, 1910.

Cross, Kenneth Mervyn Baskerville : son of Alfred William Stephens Cross (of the College, II. 525), M.A., F.R.I.B.A., architect, of 5, Palace Gardens Mansions, Linden Gardens, London, W. ; and Emily Thursfield. Born at 71, Parliament Hill Road, London, 8 Dec. 1890. Educated at Felsted School, under the Rev. Dr A. H. Dalton and the Rev. F. Stephenson. Admitted 1 Oct. 1909. Hist. Tripos, Part I, Class 3, 1911.

Cullimore, Charles : son of John Cullimore, solicitor, of Christleton, Chester ; and Mary Elizabeth Dale. Born at Christleton, Chester, 30 Sept. 1891. Schools : Arnold House, Chester ; and Marlborough College, under Mr F. Fletcher. Admitted 1 Oct. 1909. Brother of James, IV. (1) 47, and William, IV. (1) 69. Economics Tripos, Part I, Class 3, 1911.

Curwen, Brian Murray : son of Thomas Cecil Curwen, stockbroker, of 9, Oak Hill Park, Hampstead ; and Margaret Anderson. Born at 9, Oak Hill Park, Hampstead, 22 Jan. 1891. Schools : Lockers Park, Hemel Hempstead ; and Rugby, under Dr James. Admitted 1 Oct. 1909. Brother of Cecil, IV. (1) 92.
Hist. Tripos, Part I, Class 3, 1911.

Dannhorn, Theodore John : son of John Dannhorn, wine and spirit merchant, of 5, Surrey Square, London, S.E. ; and Jannett Mary Lavinia Kohlhausen. Born at Walthamstow, 25 June 1890. School : City of London, under Mr A. T. Pollard and Mr A. Chilton. Admitted 1 Oct. 1909.
Entrance Scholarship, 1909 ; Scholar, 1910–

Day, Francis Morland : son of Gilbert Morland Day (deceased), brewer ; and Elizabeth Annie Hutchinson Bell, of 4, Malvern Street, Burton-on-Trent. Born at 8, Alexandra Road, Burton-on-Trent, 25 May 1890. Schools: Oxford Preparatory ; and Repton, under the Rev. L. Ford. Admitted 1 Oct. 1909. Brother of Gilbert, IV. (1) 81.
Entrance Exhibitioner, 1909 ; Exhibitioner, 1910–   .

Dickson, Arthur Francis : son of Thomas Arthur Dickson, estate agent, of Sywell Hall, Northampton ; and Mary Frances Clay. Born at Sywell Hall, 29 Nov. 1890. Schools : Lindley Lodge, Nuneaton ; and Cheltenham College, under the Rev. R. Waterfield. Admitted 1 Oct. 1909.

Doak, James Kidd Robertson : son of the Rev. Andrew Doak (Free Church), of Carr Bridge, Inverness-shire ; and Agnes Elizabeth Thompson. Born at 15, Queen's Road, Aberdeen, 7 Dec. 1890. School : The Leys, Cambridge, under the Rev. Dr W. T. A. Barber. Admitted 1 Oct. 1909.
    Hist. Tripos, Part I, Class 3, 1911. University La Crosse player, 1911.

Dobson, Harry Desborough : son of Sir Benjamin Alfred Dobson (deceased), engineer, of Doffcockers, Bolton ; and Coralie Palin. Born at Doffcockers. Heaton, Bolton, 24 Feb. 1890. School : Clifton College, under the Rev. Canon Glazebrook and the Rev. A. A. David. Admitted 1 Oct. 1909. Brother of Darrell, ii. 557.

Drury, Alan Nigel : son of Henry George Drury, railway officer (retired), of St Oswald's, Downs Road, Clapton ; and Elizabeth Rose Seear. Born at 50, Bodney Road, Hackney, 3 Nov. 1889. School : Merchant Taylors', London, under the Rev. Dr Nairn. Admitted 1 Oct. 1909.
    Nat. Sci. Tripos, Part I, Class 1, 1911. Scholar, 1910– .

Eyre, Leonard Bucknall : son of Alfred James Eyre, Professor of Music, of Penybryn, Fox Hill, Upper Norwood, London, S.E. ; and Margaret Bucknall. Born at Melrose, The Avenue, Gipsy Hill, Norwood, London, S.E., 14 May 1890. Schools : St Paul's Cathedral Choir ; and Dulwich College, under Mr A. H. Gilkes. Admitted 1 Oct. 1909.
    Entrance Exhibition, 1909 ; Exhibitioner, 1910– . Chapel Clerk (Choral), 1911.

Faulkner, Odin Tom : son of William Henry Faulkner, clerk, of Glenside, Carlisle Avenue, St Albans ; and Sophia Grace. Born at Beacon Villa, Prospect Road, St Albans, 7 Aug. 1890. School : St Albans, under Mr E. Montague Jones. Admitted 1 Oct. 1909.
    Nat. Sci. Tripos, Part I, Class 1, 1911. Scholar, 1910–

Fisher, Ronald Aylmer : son of George Fisher, fine art expert, of 19, Tankerville Road, Streatham Common ; and Katie Heath. Born at The Uplands, East Finchley, 17 Feb. 1890. School : Harrow, under Dr J. Wood. Admitted 1 Oct. 1909.
    Math. Tripos, Part I, Class 1, 1910. Entrance Scholarship, 1909 ; Scholar, 1910–

Fitton, Richard : son of Walter Fitton, cotton spinner and manufacturer, of Birshaw House, Shaw, Lancs ; and Emma Taylor. Born at Birshaw House, Shaw, Lancs, 9 July 1890. School : Sedbergh, under Mr. C. Lowry and Mr F. B. Malim. Admitted 1 Oct. 1909.

Fruhe-Sutcliffe, Reginald : son of James Henry Fruhe (deceased), civil engineer, of Colwyn Bay ; and Adeline Eliza Sutcliffe, of Royd House, Heptonstall, Hebden Bridge, Yorks. Born in London, 2 Feb. 1890. School : Shrewsbury, under the Rev. H. W. Moss. Admitted 1 Oct. 1909.
    Exhibitioner, 1911.

Glasson, Joseph Leslie: son of Joseph Glasson, church organist and music teacher, of Kadina, South Australia; and Lucy Ware Langsford. Born at Adelaide, South Australia, 16 Sept. 1888. Educated at Prince Alfred College, Adelaide; and at the University of Adelaide. Admitted 1 Oct. 1909, as a Research Student.

Grantham-Hill, Clermont: son of Stanley Grantham-Hill, gentleman, of Twickenham, Wellington Road, Bournemouth; and Charlotte Augusta Barker. Born at Milford-on-Sea, Hants, 30 April 1891. School: Shrewsbury, under the Rev. Preb. Moss and the Rev. C. A. Alington. Admitted 1 Oct. 1909.

Gregory-Jones, Cecil: son of Frederick Gregory Jones, corn broker, of 5, Waterford Road, Oxton, Birkenhead; and Anne Frances Holden. Born at 24, Cearns Road, Oxton, Birkenhead, 11 July 1890. School: Birkenhead, under Mr F. Griffin. Admitted 1 Oct. 1909.

Hewitt, Rupert Conrad: son of David Basil Hewitt, physician and surgeon, of Grove Mount, Davenham, Cheshire; and Mary Alice Beare. Born at Oakleigh, Northwich, Cheshire, 8 Feb. 1891. School: Mostyn House, Parkgate, Chester; and Wellington College, under Rev. Dr Pollock. Admitted 1 Oct. 1909.

Hilpern, Wilfred Thomas Henry: son of David James Hilpern, divisional traffic inspector of Egyptian State Railways, of The Station, Egyptian State Railway, Beni-Souef, Upper Egypt; and Mary Erba. Born at Cairo, Lower Egypt, 22 April 1891. School: St Mark's, Windsor, under the Rev. C. N. Nagel. Admitted 1 Oct. 1909.

Hotblack, Gerald Vernon: son of Frederick Mills Hotblack, manufacturer, of 87, Newmarket Road, Norwich; and Mary Elliot Allnutt. Born at 67, Pitt Street, Norwich, 13 Feb. 1891. Schools: "Bracondale," Norwich; and Gresham's School, Holt, under Mr G. W. S. Howson. Admitted 1 Oct. 1909. Yatman Exhibitioner, 1909–   . Chapel Clerk, 1911.

Hutchison, John Colville: son of John Du Flon Hutchison, silk and tea merchant, of Hong Kong; and Helen Chalmers. Born at Hong Kong, 16 Oct. 1890. School: Malvern College, under the Rev. S. R. James. Admitted 1 Oct. 1909.

Jacob, Arthur Cecil: son of William Frederic Jacob, sheep farmer, of Kiwitea, near Feilding, New Zealand; and Henrietta Maria Wright. Born at Kiwitea, New Zealand, 1 Feb. 1890. School: Collegiate School, Wanganui, New Zealand, under Mr W. Empson. Admitted 1 Oct. 1909. Law Tripos, Part I, Class 3, 1911.

James, Edward Haughton: son of Richard Boucher James, gentleman, of Foxwold, Westward Ho, North Devon; and Sophia Margaret Charlewood (deceased). Born at Slapton, Bucks, 22 July 1890. School: Malvern College, under the Rev. S. R. James. Admitted 1 Oct. 1909.

Jasper, Reginald Frederic Tudor: son of Frederic Jasper, flour merchant, of The Firs, Bromley, Kent; and Grace Croneen. Born at Paddock Terrace, Chatham, on 21 June 1891. Schools: The Abbey School, Beckenham; and Charterhouse, under Dr Rendell. Admitted 1 Oct. 1909.

Kon, George Armand Robert: son of Isidor George Kon, inspector of the Russo-Chinese Bank, St Petersburg; and Mary Antoinette Fleuret. Born at St Petersburg, 18 Feb. 1892 (new style). Educated at home. Admitted 1 Oct. 1909.

Kutsuzawa, Senichiro: son of Jimbei Kutsuzawa, of Masuda, Akitaken, Japan, and of his wife, Take Kutsuzawa. Educated at the Tokyo Higher Commercial College, under Dr Matsuzaki. Admitted 1 Oct. 1909.

Lamb, Cecil Mortimer: son of Gerald Henry Lamb, who resides in the United States; and Jessie Mylne Rivington, of Sunnymead, St Matthew's Road, Worthing. Born at Elm Street, West New Brighton, Staten Island, New York, U.S.A., 14 June 1890. Schools: Simon Langton School, Canterbury; and Stationers' Company School, Hornsey, London, N., under Mr. H. Chettle. Admitted 1 Oct. 1909.
Chapel Clerk, 1911.

Langdale, Arthur Hugh: son of Arthur Carthew Langdale, builder, of Heathfield House, Heathfield, Sussex; and Annie Susan Miers. Born at 25, Pembroke Road, Kensington, London, 7 March 1890. Schools: Streete Court, Westgate-on-Sea; and Tonbridge School, under the Rev. C. C. Tancock and Mr C. Lowry. Admitted 1 Oct. 1909.

Leather, James Bertram: son of William Henry Leather, manufacturing jeweller, of The Beeches, 57, Heathfield Road, Handsworth, Birmingham; and Ellen Annie Copner. Born at Aston, Birmingham, 28 April, 1890. Schools: King Edward's, Five Ways, Birmingham; and King Edward's High School, Birmingham, under Mr R. Cary Gilson. Admitted 1 Oct. 1909.

Liang, Pao Kau: son of Yu Hao Liang, Chancellor of the Viceroyalty, Manchuria, of the Government House, Moukden; and his wife, Lu. Born in Korea, 20 Sept. 1890. Schools: The Anglo-Chinese College, Tien-tsin, China; Harrow, under Dr Wood; and Mill Hill, under Dr. J. D. McClure. Admitted 1 Oct. 1909.

Loo, Gee Liang (anglicised "Gerald Loo"): son of Lu Sum Chuan, retired, of Tien-tsin; and his wife, Ku. Born at Canton, 23 Aug. 1890. Schools: The Anglo-Chinese College, Tien-tsin, China; and Mill Hill School, under Dr J. D. McClure. Admitted 1 Oct. 1909.

Macgregor, Andrew Hamilton: son of Marcus Macgregor, gentleman, of 95, Crouch Hill, London, N.; and Elizabeth Hamilton. Born at Valparaiso, Chile, 31 March 1890. School: Mill Hill, under Dr J. D. McClure. Admitted 1 Oct. 1909.
Med. and Mod. Lang. Tripos, Section C, Class 2, 1911. Scholar, 1910-

Malden, Edmund Claud: son of Walter Malden, M.D., of 58, Lensfield Road, Cambridge; and Caroline Ada Chapman. Born at Stanmore Villa, Pembury Road, Tonbridge, 20 Aug. 1890. Schools: St Andrew's, Southborough; and Tonbridge, under the Rev. Dr C. C. Tancock and Mr C. Lowry. Admitted 1 Oct. 1909.
Tancred Student.

Marett-Tims, Ronald Douglas: son of Henry William Marett Tims, M.A. (Cantab.), M.D. (Edin.), Lecturer at the University of London, of Deepdene, Cavendish Avenue, Cambridge; and Alice Maud Mary Findlay. Born at 48, Lupus Street, St George's Square, London, S.W., 6 Oct. 1890. Schools: King's College Choir, Cambridge; and Gresham's School, Holt, under Mr G. W. S. Howson. Admitted 1 Oct. 1909.

Marshall, Arthur Raymond: son of Charles William Marshall, late manager of the Bengal Silk Co., of The Sycamores, Bathford, Bath; and Lucy Emma Georgina Guillebaud. Born at Mussooree, India, 3 Oct. 1890. Schools Ascham, St Christopher's, Eastbourne; and Marlborough College, under Mr F. F. Fletcher. Admitted 1 Oct. 1909.

Marten, Robert Humphrey: son of Robert Humphrey Marten, M.D. (of the College II. 474), of 12, North Terrace, Adelaide, South Australia; and Anne Ffrebairn Monteith. Born at North Terrace, Adelaide, South Australia, 14 June 1891. Schools: Cheltenham College, under Rev. R. Waterfield; and St Peter's College, Adelaide, under the Rev. H. Girdlestone. Admitted 1 Oct. 1909.
      Captain of the Cricket Club, 1911–

Maxwell, Noël: son of Robert Maxwell, private secretary (deceased), of Ashford House, Lanercost Road, Tulse Hill; and Lydia Christmas, of 6, Palgrave Mansions, Eastbourne. Born at 20, Thornton Avenue, Telford Park, Streatham, 26 March 1889. Schools: Horley Grammar; Whitgift Grammar; Oxford House School; and Eastbourne College, under Mr H. R. Thomson and Mr F. S. Williams. Admitted 1 Oct. 1909.
      Entrance Scholarship, 1909.

Methven, Malcolm David: son of David Methven, merchant, of Hollycroft, Forest Row, Sussex; and Amy Johnson Walsham. Born at Hampstead, 12 May 1891. Schools: Haddon Court, Hampstead, London; and Westminster, under Dr J. Gow. Admitted 1 Oct. 1909.
      Lieutenant, C.U.O.T.C., 1910. Captain of the Boat Club, 1911.

Milne, Herbert John Mansfield: son of John Milne, merchant (retired), of 73, Forest Road, Aberdeen; and Mary Anne Milne. Born at Fetterangus, Old Deer, Banffshire, N.B., 18 July 1888. Educated at Aberdeen Grammar School, and Aberdeen University. Admitted 1 Oct. 1909.
      Class. Tripos, Part I, Class 1, Div. 2, 1911. Scholar, 1910–

Mitchell, Alfred William Coutts: son of Alexander Forrest Mitchell, of 10, St Devenick Terrace, Cults, Aberdeen; and Isabella Robertson. Born at 21, Seamount Place, Aberdeen, 11 March 1887. Educated at Robert Gordon's College, Aberdeen; and Aberdeen University. Admitted 1 Oct. 1909.
      Math. Tripos, Part I, Class 1, 1910. Scholar, 1910–

Mogg, Albert Oliver Dean: son of Joseph William Mogg, J.P., estate owner, of Pretoria, South Africa; and Agnes Emma Johanna Krause. Born at Newcastle, Natal, South Africa, 27 April 1886. Educated at St Andrew's College, Grahamstown, South Africa; Merchant Venturers' Technical College, Bristol; Ontario Agricultural College, Guelph, Canada, under President G. C. Creelman. Admitted 1 Oct. 1909.

Montague, Paul Denys: son of Leopold Agar Denys Montague, J.P. (Devon), landed proprietor, of Penton, Crediton, N. Devon; and Amy Lind. Born at Penton House, Crediton, 19 March 1890. School: Bedales, Petersfield, under Mr J. H. Badley. Admitted 1 Oct. 1909.
Nat. Sci. Tripos, Part I, Class 2, 1911.

Mosse, Cotton Grimley Tenison: son of Lewis Tenison Mosse, clerk in the Bank of England, of Belmont Cottage, Surbiton; and Constance Mary Ebden. Born at 1B, Oxford and Cambridge Mansions, Marylebone, London, 29 April 1891. School: Marlborough College, under Mr F. Fletcher. Admitted 1 Oct. 1909.
Captain of the Lawn Tennis Club, 1911–

Muirhead, James Alexander Orrock: son of Lewis Andrew Muirhead, D.D., Minister, United Free Church of Scotland, of 9, Balgillo Crescent, Broughty Ferry, N.B.; and Lilias Jane Johnston. Born at East Wemyss, Fife, N.B., 11 Oct. 1889. Schools: Seafield House, Broughty Ferry; and Trinity College, Glenalmond, under the Rev. A. R. F. Hyslop. Admitted 1 Oct. 1909.
Entrance Scholarship, 1909. University Athlete, 1911. 2nd Lieut. O.T.C. 1911.

Myles, Herbert Blythe: son of Thomas Patrick Myles, M.B., C.M., medical practitioner (retired), of 1, Castle Street, Brechin, Scotland; and Euphemia Grace Whitson. Born at 1, Castle Street, Brechin, 26 Aug. 1891. School: The Leys School, Cambridge, under the Rev. Dr W. T. A. Barber. Admitted 1 Oct. 1909.

Neilson, Henry Vere: son of William Fitzroy Neilson, bank manager, of Sunnybank, Uppingham; and Anna Helen Hodge. Born at Cliftonville Avenue, Northampton, 4 March 1890. School: Oakham, under the Rev. E. V. Hodge and Mr W. L. Sargant. Admitted 1 Oct. 1909.
Entrance Scholarship, 1909; Scholar, 1910– .

Norsworthy, Edwal: son of William Milford Norsworthy, chartered accountant (deceased); and Henrietta Threlfall Wilson. Born at 15, Somers Place, Hyde Park, London, W., 7 May 1891. Schools: Hoe Preparatory School, Plymouth; and Sherborne School, under the Rev. Canon F. B. Westcott. Admitted 1 Oct. 1909.

Paget, Geoffrey Walter: son of Henry Marriott Paget, artist, of 76, Parkhill Road, Hampstead, London, N.W.; and Henrietta Farr. Born at Bedford Park, Acton, Middlesex, 12 March 1890. Schools: Heddon Comb Preparatory; Highgate Grammar; and St Paul's, under the Rev. A. Chilton. Admitted 1 Oct. 1909.
Nat. Sci. Tripos, Part I, Class 2, 1911. Entrance Exhibition, 1909; Exhibitioner, 1900

Pask-Hughes, Bernard: son of Thomas Pask-Hughes, merchant (retired), of Merriemont, Barnt Green, near Birmingham; and Laura Kate Merriott. Born at The Oaklands, Selly Oak, near Birmingham, 17 Aug. 1890. School: Cheltenham College, under the Rev. R. Waterfield. Admitted 1 Oct. 1909.

Pears, Robert: son of Andrew Pears, perfumer (deceased), of Mevagissey, Isleworth and The Wakes, Selborne, Hants; and Marian Pearson Hollingham. Born at Greenbank, Spring Grove, Heston, Middlesex, 15 May 1891. School: Clifton College, under the Rev. Canon M. G. Glazebrook and the Rev. A. A. David. Admitted 1 Oct. 1909.

Pike, Howard Hurstwood: son of James Pike, mohair merchant, of Hurstwood, Manningham, Yorks; and Jane Anne Pike. Born at Finchley, London, 10 March 1890. School: The Leys, Cambridge, under the Rev. Dr W. T. A. Barber. Admitted 1 Oct. 1909.

Playfair, Kenneth: son of George William Forbes Playfair (retired eastern banker), of Kelvedon, Essex; and Florence Emily Isabel Edwards. Born at Kingston, Surrey, 6 Sept. 1891. School: Fettes College, Edinburgh, under the Rev. W. Heard. Admitted 1 Oct. 1909.

Read, Henry Cecil: son of Edward Robert Read, brewer, of Craigholm, Foxrock Road, Co. Dublin; and Elizabeth Katherine Dickinson. Born at 20, Ailesbury Road, Dublin, 25 Dec. 1890. Schools: Tyttenhanger Lodge, St Albans; and Wellington College, Berks, under the Rev. B. Pollock. Admitted 1 Oct. 1909.
Entrance Scholarship, 1909; Scholar, 1910–   .

Richardson, Conrad: son of William James Richardson, chairman of public company, of Beech Knoll, Oxted, Surrey; and Marion Tilley. Born at Buckhurst Hill, Chigwell, Essex, 9 Sept. 1891. Educated at Clifton College; and privately. Admitted 1 Oct. 1909.

Robertson-Shersby, Robert: son of Thomas Harvie Shersby Robertson-Shersby, Commander R.N. (deceased), of St Michael's, Bedford; and Elizabeth Robertson. Born at Little Heath House, Charlton, 22 June 1890. Educated at Bedford Grammar School, under Mr J. E. King. Admitted 1 Oct. 1909.
Took the name Robertson-Shersby-Harvie, 1911.

Showell-Rogers, Eric Norman: son of William Showell-Rogers, M.A., LL.D., solicitor (Clare College, Cambridge) (deceased), of The Nook, 27, George Road, Edgbaston; and Sara Matilda Faire. Born at 27, George Road, Edgbaston, Birmingham, 13 Nov. 1890. Educated at Shrewsbury School, under the Rev. H. W. Moss and the Rev. C. A. Alington. Admitted 1 Oct. 1909.

Sanford, Dudley William: son of William Thomas Sanford, hotel proprietor (retired), of Botley House, Chiddingfold, Surrey; and Ada Jane Foster. Born at The Holme, Walton-on-Thames, 15 April 1890. School: Uppingham School, under the Rev. Dr E. C. Selwyn and the Rev. H. W. McKenzie. Admitted 1 Oct. 1909.
University Shooting Eight, 1910, 1911.

Sargant-Florence, Philip: son of Harry Smyth Florence (deceased), of Nutley, Essex County, New Jersey, U.S.A.; and Mary Sargant. Born at Nutley, Essex County, New Jersey, U.S.A., 26 June 1890. Educated at Windlesham House, Brighton; Rugby School, under Dr H. A. James. Admitted 1 Oct. 1909.
Entrance Scholarship, 1909; Scholar, 1910–   .

Singh, Labh : son of Sandar Sundar Singh, landowner, of Gujran Walla, Punjab,
India ; and Shri Mati Bhagwanti. Born at Gujran Walla, Punjab, India,
on 16 August 1887. Educated at Government High School, Gujran Walla ·
Forman Christian College, Lahore, Punjab ; Government College, Lahore
under Mr S. Robson. Admitted 1 Oct. 1909, as an Affiliated Student.
  LL.B. 1911. Mor. Sc. Tripos, Part I, Class 3, 1910 ; Law Tripos, Part II,
  Class 2, 1911.

Somervell, Theodore Howard : son of William Henry Somervell, leather merchant,
of Brantfield, Kendal ; and Florence Howard. Born at 9, Vicarage Terrace,
Nethergraveship, Kendal, 16 April 1890. Schools : The Leas, Hoylake ; and
Rugby, under the Rev. Canon H. A. James. Admitted 1 Oct. 1909.
  Nat. Sci. Tripos, Part I, Class 1, 1911. Entrance Scholarship, 1909.

Stafford, Harry Neville : son of William Stafford, medical practitioner, of 110,
Mansfield Road, Nottingham ; and Mary Emma Pollard. Born at 36, Mansfield Road, Nottingham, 21 Aug. 1890. School : Dean Close, Cheltenham,
under the Rev. Dr Flecker. Admitted 1 Oct. 1909.

Turcan, James Somerville : son of Charles Jameson Turcan, corn factor, of
19, Douglas Crescent, Edinburgh ; and Marion Alexandrina Somerville.
Born at 1, East Claremont Street, Edinburgh, 19 June 1888. School :
Edinburgh Academy, under Mr R. Carter. Admitted 1 Oct. 1909.

Vos, Philip : son of John Isidor Vos, manufacturer, of 292, Amherst Road, Stoke
Newington, London, N. ; and Rayner De Groot. Born at Wood Street,
London, 25 March 1891. Educated at Owen's School, Islington ; University
College, London ; and the London School of Economics. Admitted 1 Oct.
1909.
  Econ. Tripos, Part I, Class 1, 1911. Scholar, 1910–   .

Watson-Williams, Eric : son of Patrick Watson-Williams, physician, of 4, Clifton
Park, Bristol ; and Margaret Long Fox. Born at Clifton, Bristol, 18 Sept.
1890. School : Clifton College, under the Rev. Canon Glazebrook, and the
Rev. A. A. David. Admitted 1 Oct. 1909.
  Nat. Sci. Tripos, Part I, Class 2, 1911. Entrance Scholarship, 1909 ;
  Scholar, 1910–   .

Weeks, Ronald Morce : son of Richard Llewellyn Weeks, mining engineer, of
Willington House, Willington, Co. Durham ; and Susan Helen Walker
McIntyre. Born at Helmington Row, Co. Dublin, 13 Nov. 1890. Schools :
The Mount, Northallerton ; Aysgarth ; and Charterhouse, under the Rev. Dr
J. H. Rendall. Admitted 1 Oct. 1909. Brother of Llewellyn, IV. (1) 64.
  Nat. Sci. Tripos, Part I, Class 3, 1911. University Association Football
  team, 1910 ; Captain, University and College, 1911.

Wileman, Gerald Watkins Brett : son of John Watkins Brett Wileman (of the
College, II. 410), operative brewer (retired), of Sutton, Surrey ; and Harriet
Kate Turner. Born at The Lindens, Alton, Hants, 11 April 1890. Schools :
Cambridge House, Margate ; and Berkhamsted, under Dr T. C. Fry. Ad-
mitted 1 Oct. 1909.
  Choral Entrance Exhibition, 1909.

Wilkinson, Noël: son of Edward Robert Wilkinson, engineer, of Littlecroft, Oakleigh Park, Middlesex; and Mary Lake. Born at High Barnet, Herts, 25 Dec. 1890. School: Highgate, under the Rev. A. E. Allcock. Admitted 1 Oct. 1909.
Med. and Mod. Lang. Tripos, Section C, Class 2, 1911.

Williams, Oswald Temple: son of Thomas Sydney Williams, manager of sheep station, of Tuparoa, Gisborne, New Zealand; and Agnes Lydia Williams. Born at Pakaraka, Bay of Islands, New Zealand, 13 Feb. 1889. School: Wanganui Collegiate, New Zealand, under Mr W. Empson. Admitted 1 Oct. 1909.
Captain, Rugby Football, 1911.

Woolls, George Harman: son of George Harman Woolls, gentleman (deceased), of Elm Lawn, Hillingdon; and Alice Marshall. Born at Elm Lawn, Hillingdon, Uxbridge, Middlesex, 4 May 1890. Schools: Streete Court, Westgate-on-Sea; and Malvern College, under the Rev. S. R. James. Admitted 1 Oct. 1909.

Woolward, Arthur Trevor: son of the Rev. Spencer Alfred Woolward, Rector of Myddle, Shrewsbury; and Agnes Ethel Russell Davies. Born at Totternhoe Vicarage, Dunstable, Beds, 13 Feb. 1891. Schools: Brandon House, Cheltenham; Pelham House, West Folkestone; and Haileybury College, under the Hon. and Rev. Canon Lyttelton and the Rev. St J. B. Wynne-Willson. Admitted 1 Oct. 1909.

Yolland, Reginald Horace: son of John Horatio Yolland, surgeon, of 53, Bromley Common, Bromley, Kent; and Emily Constance Railton. Born at 38, Bromley Common, Bromley, Kent, 28 May 1891. Schools: Clare House, Beckenham; and Westminster, under Dr J. Gow. Admitted 1 Oct. 1909.

Reddaway, Harold: son of Frank Reddaway, merchant, of Didsbury Lodge, Manchester; and Elizabeth Baxter. Born at Southport, Lancs, 21 Dec. 1892. Schools: Bilton Grange; and Uppingham, under the Rev. E. C. Selwyn and the Rev. H. W. Mackenzie. Admitted 27 Jan. 1910.

Paul, Hamilton: son of Lewis Gordon Paul, public analyst, Huddersfield, of 22, Cleveland Road, Huddersfield; and Clara Alice Halstead. Born at 29, Clara Street, Huddersfield, 7 April 1891. Schools: The Ryleys, Alderley Edge; and Oundle School, under Mr F. W. Sanderson. Admitted 15 April 1910.

MICHAELMAS 1910 TO MICHAELMAS 1911.

(Tutors: Mr Buckland, Mr Hardy, and Mr Cameron.)

Adams, Eustace Victor: son of Rev. Henry Walter Adams (deceased), Clerk in Holy Orders, of Pretoria; and Jamima Amelia Melville. Born at Barberton, South Africa, 19 June 1888. Schools: Diocesan School, Pretoria; and Dulwich College, under Mr Gilkes. Admitted 1 Oct. 1910.

Back, Gilbert Alfred: son of Herbert Hatfield Back, M.B., of Acle, Norfolk; and Mabel Helen Graham Gilbert. Born at Reepham, 17 March 1892. School: Sherborne, under Canon Westcott and Mr Howell Smith. Admitted 1 Oct. 1910.

Ball, Cyril Francis: son of Percy Marshall Ball, barrister-at-law, of Agra, India; and Frances Mary Moore. Born at Agra, 16 July 1891. Schools: The Modern School, Mussoorie, India; and Sherborne, under Mr Nowell Smith. Admitted 1 Oct. 1910.

Bannatyne, Edgar James: son of Alexander Edmund Bannatyne (of the College, II. 454), gentleman, of Glenbeavan, Croom, Co. Limerick; and Alice Maude Phelps. Born at Woodsdown, Co. Limerick, 7 Feb. 1891. Schools: Arnold House School, Llandulas; and Wellington College, under Rev. Dr Pollock. Admitted 1 Oct. 1910.

Barnett, Sydney Herbert: son of John Barnett, merchant, of Antofagasta, Chile; and Margarita O'Shea. Born at the British Vice-Consulate, Antofagasta, 6 Dec. 1891. School: Shrewsbury, under the Rev. H. W. Moss and the Rev. C. A. Alington. Admitted 1 Oct. 1910.

Barron, George Desmond: son of Albert Henry Barron, Superintending Engineer, Public Works Department, India (retired), of Beechfield, Balcombe, Sussex; and Georgina Alma Russell. Born at Meerut, India, 7 Jan. 1891. School: Berkhamsted, under the Rev. Dr Fry. Admitted 1 Oct. 1910.
Math. Tripos, Part I, Class 2, 1911. Entrance Scholarship, 1910.

Benest, Edward Ernest: son of Edward Benest Shaw Benest, engineer, of Rio de Janeiro, S. America; and Annie Sophia Ripper. Born at Kensington, 9 Oct. 1891. Schools: Thames Nautical Training College; and Bishop's Stortford School, under Mr Bruce-Payne. Admitted 1 Oct. 1910.

Berry, Henry Vaughan: son of John Henry Berry (deceased), stockbroker, of Manor House, Koyenbedon, Madras; and Eva Maria Williams. Born at Madras, India, 28 March 1891. Schools: St Anne's, Redhill; and City of London School, under Dr Chilton. Admitted 1 Oct. 1910.
Entrance Exhibition, 1910. Scholar, 1911–

Bharucha, Navroji Maneckji: son of Maneckji Sheriarji Bharucha, land manager, of 182, Chira Bazaar, Bombay, India; and Avanbai. Born at Broach, India, 29 June 1890. Educated at Elphinstone College, Bombay, under Principal Covernton. Admitted 1 Oct. 1910.
Math. Tripos, Part I, Class 2, 1911.

Boardman, John Hopwood: grandson of John Hopwood Boardman (Fellow of the College, II. 263) and son of John Hopwood Boardman, solicitor (deceased), of 41, John Dalton Street, Manchester; and Emily Cox. Born at Cheetham Hill, Manchester, 16 Sept. 1891. Schools: St Lawrence House, St Anne's-on-Sea; and Haileybury College, under the Rev. E. Lyttelton and the Rev. St J. B. Wynne-Willson. Admitted 1 Oct. 1910.

Bradbury, Norman : son of Harry Frederick William Bradbury (deceased), of the Bengal Civil Service; and Margaret Crawford Fraser. Born at Calcutta, 1 May 1892. School: Edinburgh Academy, under Mr R. Carter. Admitted 1 Oct. 1910.
Math. Tripos, Part I, Class 2, 1911.

Bradley, Stanley Blackall : son of Walter Frederick Blackall, Clerk in Holy Orders; and Lilian Elizabeth Samuel. Born at 108, Old Meeting Street, West Bromwich, 8 Oct. 1887. School: Cranleigh, Surrey, under the Rev. G. C. Allen. Three years in Railway Works at Crewe. Admitted 1 Oct. 1910.

Brittain, Edward Samuel : son of Samuel Swan Brittain, landed proprietor, of Orient Lodge, Buxton; and Emma Evans. Born at Alexandria, Egypt, 13 April 1892. School: University School, Hastings; and Clifton College, under the Rev. Canon M. G. Glazebrook and the Rev. A. A. David. Admitted 1 Oct. 1910.

Brockman, William Dominic : son of Rev. Ralph Thomas Brockman, vicar of The Brook, Liverpool, of St John's Vicarage, The Brook, Liverpool; and Anna Charlotte Sheldrake. Born at Cowley Road, Cowley St John, Oxford, 19 July 1891. School: Liverpool College, under the Rev. J. B. Lancelot. Admitted 1 Oct. 1910. Brother of Ralph, iv. (1) 79.

Broughton, Alfred Delves : son of Alfred Delves Broughton, colonial civil servant; and Mary Florence Louise Rosenzweig. Born at 1, Wells Villas, Whittingdon Road, Wood Green, London, N., 28 March 1891. Schools: Rosehill, Banstead, Surrey; and Charterhouse, Godalming, under Dr G. H. Rendall. Admitted 1 Oct. 1910.

Candy, Kenneth Edgerley : son of Sir Edward Townshend Candy, K.C.S.I., Indian civil servant, retired, of Whitefield, Great Shelford, Cambridge; and Constance Mary Harrison. Born at Bombay, 29 Dec. 1890. School: Rugby, under Dr James and the Rev. A. A. David. Admitted 1 Oct. 1910.

Cave, Harvard Wells : son of William John Cave, of Beechfield, Bromley, Kent; and Eleanor Hogg. Born at Belmont, Caterham Valley, Surrey, 29 Feb. 1892. School: Tonbridge, under Mr C. Lowry. Admitted 1 Oct. 1910. Brother of William, iv. (1) 19.

Chapman, James Crosby : son of Rev. James Chapman, Wesleyan minister, of Southlands College, Battersea, London, S.W.; and Annie Thompson. Born at Nottingham, 23 July 1889. Educated at City of London School, under Mr A. T. Pollard; and King's College, London. Admitted 1 Oct. 1910.
Research Studentship, 1910.

Cheffaud, Paul Harry Martin : Licencié ès Lettres, son of Jean Baptiste Cheffaud, civil servant under the French Government, of 38, Rue de Tourtille, Paris; and of Juliette Nez. Born at Paris, 13 July, 1888. Educated at Lycée Louis le Grand (Paris); École Normale Supérieure, Paris, under M. Lavisse. Admitted as Research Student, 1 Oct. 1910.
Resided one year.

Coates, Norman Henry : son of Charles Middleton Coates, medical practitioner, of Heathfield House, Creech, near Taunton ; and Janet Rae. Born at Edinburgh, 21 Sept. 1891. Schools : Monkton Combe School ; and Haileybury, under the Rev. St J. B. Wynne-Willson. Admitted 1 Oct. 1910.

Cochrane, Kenneth Alexander Basil : son of Charles Basil Cochrane, of 57, Bird-hurst Rise, Croydon ; and of Maude Dowse Collins. Born at 20, Marlborough Road, London, N.W., 3 Mar. 1891. School : Tonbridge School, under Dr Tancock and Mr C. Lowry. Admitted 1 Oct. 1910.
    Math. Tripos, Part I, Class 3, 1911.

Davidson, George Frederick : son of James Madgwick Davidson, bank manager, of Bank of New South Wales, South Brisbane, Queensland ; and Lucy Cribb. Born at Brisbane, Queensland, 18 April 1886. School : Brisbane Grammar, under Mr R. H. Roe, M.A. Admitted as Research Student, 1 Oct. 1910.

Dendy, Edward Herbert : son of Edward Evershed Dendy, metal manufacturer, of Wealey Park Road, Selly Oak, Birmingham ; and of Edith New. Born at Frederick Road, Selly Oak, Birmingham, 17 May, 1891. Schools : West House School, Edgbaston ; and Shrewsbury School, under the Rev. H. W. Moss and the Rev. C. A. Alington. Admitted 1 Oct. 1910.

Duckworth, Leslie : son of William Duckworth, manufacturing chemist, of Ribby Hall, Kirkham, Lancs ; and Emily Blackburn. Born at Moss Grove, Urmston, near Manchester, 29 Nov. 1891. School : Sedbergh, under Mr C. Lowry and Mr F. B. Malim. Admitted 1 Oct. 1910.

Everitt, Humphrey Leggatt : son of Thomas Everitt, farmer, of North Creake, Norfolk ; and Maud Helen Leggatt. Born at North Creake, 15 Nov. 1892. School : Norwich Grammar, under the Rev. E. F. Gilbard. Admitted 1 Oct. 1910.

Fairrie, James Leslie : son of James Fairrie (junior), sugar refiner, 253, Vauxhall Road, Liverpool ; and Amelia Brereton. Born at Aigburth, Liverpool, 29 Sept. 1889. School : Shrewsbury, under the Rev. H. W. Moss. Three years in engineering works. Admitted 1 Oct. 1910.

Fawcett, Richard Wilfrid : son of Charles Fawcett (deceased), wool merchant, of Hamilton Cottage, Rawdon, Yorks ; and Arabella Mary Prest Wightman. Born at Hamilton Cottage, Apperley Bridge, near Leeds, 21 Dec. 1891. Schools : Wharfedale School, Ilkley ; and Haileybury College, under the Rev. St J. B. Wynne-Willson. Admitted 1 Oct. 1910.

Fearfield, Cecil John : son of John Piggin Fearfield, lace manufacturer, of 176, Derby Road, Nottingham ; and Mary Dalley. Born at Stapleford, Notts, 4 Jan. 1891. School : Dean Close Memorial, Cheltenham, under the Rev. Dr Flecker. Admitted 1 Oct. 1910. Brother of Joseph, III. 408 and IV. (1) 21.

Filandi, Rodolfo : son of Ignazio Filandi, of Venice ; and Maria Fanton, both deceased. Born at Venice, 3 Feb. 1888. Guardian : Icilio Filandi, of Treviso. Educated at Collegio Provinciale, Verona ; Collège Latin, Neuchâtel ; and Drei-Konig-Schule, Dresden, under Professor Dr O. Stange. Admitted 1 Oct. 1910.

Fowler, Tracy Grant: son of Aplin Grant Fowler, M.Inst.C.E., F.R.A.S., and F.R.G.S., civil engineer, of Sea View, Isle of Wight; and Ellen Bell Lomax. Born at 1, Agincourt Villas, London Road, Kingston, 22 Feb. 1892. Schools: Elm House, Surbiton; and Eastbourne College, under the Rev. F. S. Williams. Admitted 1 Oct. 1910.

Freeman, George Cyril: son of George Freeman, stockbroker, of Ricketts, Horley, Surrey; and Charlotte Amelia Burrell. Born at 142, Norwood Road, West Norwood, 9 Oct. 1890. Schools: Burstow Preparatory, near Horley; and Tonbridge, under Dr Tancock and Mr C. Lowry. Admitted 1 Oct. 1910.

Gabb, James Desmond: son of James Percy Alwyne Gabb, M.D., surgeon, of Poyle Mount, Guildford; and Emma Ada Price. Born at Copthorne, Epsom Road, Guildford, 16 Aug. 1891. Schools: Edgeborough, Guildford, under Mr W. E. Terry; and Epsom College, under Rev. T. N. H. Smith-Pearse. Admitted 1 Oct. 1910.

Gardiner, Henry Hamilton: son of Henry Lawrence Gardiner, Colonel R.A., of Shoeburyness; and Isobelle Violet Dunlop. Born at Edinburgh, 27 Nov. 1890. Schools: Temple Grove, East Sheen; and Haileybury College, under the Rev. St J. B. Wynne-Willson. Admitted 1 Oct. 1910.
Entrance Scholarship, 1910. Scholar, 1911–

Goodbody, Arthur Brand: son of Thomas Henry Goodbody, merchant, of Bellfield Park, Drumcondra, Co. Dublin; and Margaret Brand Paterson. Born at Kincora, Temple Gardens, Dublin, 30 May 1882. Schools: Monkstown Park School, Dublin; and Monkton Combe, near Bath, under the Rev. J. W. Kearns. Admitted 1 Oct. 1910.

Goodchild, Edward Lionel: son of Herbert Goodchild, solicitor, of Chestnuts, Unthank Road, Eaton, Norwich; and Harriet Boorne. Born at 7, West Parade, Norwich, 31 Dec. 1890. School: Norwich Grammar, under the Rev. E. F. Gilbard. Admitted 1 Oct. 1910.

Goolden, George Anthony: son of Edwin Richardson Goolden, solicitor, of Cookham Grove, Berks; and Eva Sophia Massey. Born at 11, Southwick Place, Hyde Park, London, 25 Jan. 1891. School: Bradfield College, under the Rev. Dr Gray. Admitted 1 Oct. 1910.

Gosse, Reginald Wilkes: son of John Gosse, M.R.C.S., L.R.C.P. (deceased); and Mary Bennett. Born at Wallaroo, S. Australia, 12 May 1891. Schools: Beechmont, Sevenoaks; and Charterhouse, Godalming, under Dr G. S. Rendall. Admitted 1 Oct. 1910. Brother of Alfred, iv. (1) 40.

Gotch, Duncan Hepburn: son of Davis Frederic Gotch, Assistant Secretary for Education for Northants, of Bassingbourne, Abington, Northants; and Ethel Hepburn. Born at Kettering, 25 Aug. 1891. School: Oundle, under Mr F. W. Sanderson. Admitted 1 Oct. 1910.
Entrance Scholarship, 1910.

Green, Samuel Arnold Collier : son of Professor Samuel Walter Green, of 9, Bellasis Avenue, Streatham Hill, London, S.W. and Regent's Park College, London ; and Elizabeth Clara Hemming. Born at Streatham, 29 May 1891. School : Dulwich College, under Mr A. H. Gilkes. Admitted 1 Oct. 1910. Entrance Scholarship, 1910.

Haines, Frederick Edward Church : son of the Rev. Frederick William Haines of Hazeldene, Pembury, Kent, Clerk in Holy Orders ; and Anna Elizabeth Grahame Church. Born at Holy Trinity Vicarage, Bromley Common, 18 Aug. 1891. School : Malvern College, under the Rev. S. R. James. Admitted 1 Oct. 1910. Resided one year.

Haines, Robert Thomas Moline : son of Lieut.-Col. Robert Lewis Haines, late R.A., of 1, Alexandra Road, Clifton, Bristol ; and Amy Marion Moline. Born at Lydd, Kent, 5 July 1891. School : St Ives ; and Clifton College, under the Rev. M. G. Glazebrook, the Rev. A. A. David and Mr King. Admitted 1 Oct. 1910. Entrance Scholarship, 1910.

Hamblin, Edward Charles Clifford : son of Edward Hamblin, bookbinder, of Kimberley, Green Lanes, Palmer's Green, London, N. ; and Elizabeth Emily Hoelen. Born at London, 6 Oct. 1890. Schools : Stationers' Company School ; and City of London School, under Dr Chilton. Admitted 1 Oct. 1910.

Hare, Adrian Church : son of Alfred Thomas Hare, M.A. (Oxon.), Principal of the Law Courts Branch, Treasury Solicitors' Department, of The Orangery, St Margaret's, Twickenham ; and Florence Edith Church. Born at Neston Lodge, Sandycombe Road, Twickenham, 28 July 1891. School : St Paul's, under Mr Walker and Mr A. E. Hillard. Admitted 1 Oct. 1910.

Hazeldine, Donald : son of Francis Hazeldine (deceased), railway waggon builder ; and Agnes Grimwade. Born at 6, Clarendon Terrace, Brighton, 2 June 1891. School : Brighton College, under the Rev. A. F. Titherington and the Rev. W. R. Dawson. Admitted 1 Oct. 1910.

Hulbert, John Norman : son of Henry Harper Hulbert, M.A. (Oxon.), M.R.C.S., L.R.C.P., of 6, Weymouth Court, Portland Place, London, W. ; and Lilian Mary Hinchliff. Born at Ely, 24 April 1892. School : Westminster School, under the Rev. Dr Gow. Admitted 1 Oct. 1910.

James, Charles Kenneth : son of Charles Alfred James, physician and surgeon, of Ebor House, Stamford Hill, London, N. ; and Annie Lucy Philipson. Born at 24, Cazenove Road, London, 19 Jan. 1892. Schools : Orley Farm School ' and Cheltenham College, under the Rev. R. Waterfield. Admitted 1 Oct. 1910. Entrance Scholarship, 1910. Scholar, 1911- .

Landau, Henry : son of Charles Landau, merchant, of Standerton, Transvaal ; and of Christina Smith. Born at "Rotterdam," Bethal District, Transvaal, 7 March 1892. Educated at Durban High School, under Mr W. H. Nicholas ; and at the School of Agriculture, Potchefstroom, under Mr Alex. Holm. Admitted 1 Oct. 1910.

Lang, Horace: son of Lawrence McDonald Lang, foreman of engineers, of 2, Genesta Road, Plumstead; and Alice Mary Chaplin. Born at 24, St James's Place, Plumstead, 18 Jan. 1891. School: Christ's Hospital, under the Rev. Dr Upcott. Admitted 1 Oct. 1910.

    Math. Tripos, Part I, Class 1, 1911. Entrance Scholarship, 1910. Scholar, 1911   Barnes University Scholar, 1911.

Leacock, David John: son of John Milberne Leacock, merchant, of Las Palmas, Madeira; and Mary Silence Erskine. Born at Madeira, 10 June 1890. Schools: Lindisfarne, Blackheath; Wellington College, Berks, under the Rev. B. Pollock; and Central Technical College, S. Kensington. Admitted 1 Oct. 1910.

Lewtas, Frederick George: son of John Lewtas, M.D., Lieut.-Col. I.M.S., (retired), of 27, Redcliffe Gardens, London, S.W.; and Annie Chambers Wilson. Born at Simla, India, 11 Dec. 1890. Schools: Mr Goodchild's Preparatory Cambridge; and St Paul's School, under Mr Walker and the Rev. Dr Hillard. Admitted 1 Oct. 1910.

MacCombie, William John: son of John MacCombie, M.D., of Bartram Lodge, Hampstead, London, N.W.; and Emily Finn. Born at South-Eastern Hospital, Deptford, London, 19 Aug. 1891. School: Oundle School, under Mr F. W. Sanderson. Admitted 1 Oct. 1910.

McKerrow, George: son of George McKerrow, physician, of 7, Barns Street, Ayr, N.B.; and Jessie Highet. Born at 7, Barns Street, Ayr, 26 May 1892. Schools: Cargilfield, Cramond, Midlothian, N.B.; and Clifton College, under the Rev. A. A. David. Admitted 1 Oct. 1910.

    Math. Tripos, Part I, Class 1, 1911. Salomons Scholarship, 1910.

Malet, Hugh Arthur Grenville: son of Allan Arthur Grenville Malet, M.Inst.C.E., engineer inspector, Local Government Board; and Elizabeth Anne Lysaght. Born at Dugirala, Kistna District, Madras Presidency, India, 22 Sept. 1891. Educated at Harrow School, under Dr Wood. Admitted 1 Oct. 1910.

    Math. Tripos, Part I, Class 3, 1911.

Marshall, Douglas: son of the Rev. Walter Marshall, of 8, Montpellier Villas, Brighton, Clerk in Holy Orders; and Leonora Hemery. Born at Windsor Castle, 22 May 1891. Schools: St George's Choir, Windsor Castle; and Lancing College, under Mr B. H. Tower and the Rev. H. T. Bowlby. Admitted 1 Oct. 1910.

    Kept two terms. Choral Entrance Exhibition, 1910.

Mason, John Walton: son of Harry Walton Mason, medical practitioner, of Tumut, New South Wales; and Gertrude Beck. Born at Tumut, New South Wales, 4 June, 1892. School: Clifton College, under the Rev. A. A. David. Admitted 1 Oct. 1910.

Matheson, Charles Frederick: son of Charles Louis Matheson, K.C., Irish Bar, of 20, Fitzwilliam Square, Dublin, and Nirvana, Greystone, Co. Wicklow; and Elinor Tuthill. Born at 20, Fitzwilliam Square, Dublin, 9 Aug. 1892. School: Aldenham, under the Rev. A. H. Cooke. Admitted 1 Oct. 1910.

Morrison, Edward Oliver : son of Alexander Morrison (deceased), linen merchant, of Park View, Harrogate; and Annie Oliver. Born at Park View, Harrogate, 16 Dec. 1891. School : Sedbergh, under Mr Lowry and Mr Malim. Admitted 1 Oct. 1910.

Paige, John Friend : son of Henry Paige, solicitor, of Trengweath House, Redruth. and Mary Philippa Grylls. Born at Trengweath, Redruth, 31 July 1892. Schools : Upcott House, Okehampton ; and Rugby, under the Rev. Dr James and the Rev. A. A. David. Admitted 1 Oct. 1910.

Pank, Philip Edmond Durrell : son of Philip Durrell Pank, Lieut.-Col. Indian Medical Service; and Elizabeth Crane. Born at Jaipur, Rajputana, India, 22 April 1892. Schools : Boxgrove, Guildford ; and Wellington College, under the Rev. B. Pollock. Admitted 1 Oct. 1910.

Perry, Edward William : son of William Payne Perry, War Office official, of Glendower, Belmont, Surrey ; and Constance Gower McLaren. Born at 82, Abbeville Road, North Clapham, 12 June 1891. School : St Paul's, under Dr Hillard. Admitted 1 Oct. 1910.
Entrance Scholarship, 1910. Scholar, 1911–

Pickering, Bernard Milner : son of the Rev. Arthur Milner Pickering, of the Rectory, Woolwich ; and Louisa Mills. Born at Wimbledon, 6 April 1891. Schools : King's College School, Wimbledon ; and Merchant Taylors', London, under the Rev. Dr Nairn. Admitted 1 Oct. 1910.
Entrance Scholarship, 1910. Scholar, 1911– .

Platts, Arthur Leslie, son of Arthur Platts (deceased), draper, of Gainsborough ; and Julia Maria Hardy. Born at Morton Terrace, Gainsborough, 14 July 1891. Educated at King's College School, Wimbledon ; and at Oundle School, under Mr F. W. Sanderson. Admitted 1 Oct. 1910. Brother of Sydney, IV. (1) 84.

Powell, Ashley : son of the Venerable Dacre H. Powell, D.D., Archdeacon of Cork and Rector of St Mary, Shandon, Cork, of the Rectory, St Mary, Shandon, Cork ; and Edith Louisa Cummins. Born at Cork, 7 Oct. 1885. Educated at Llandaff Cathedral School, under Rev. E. Owen, Dover College, under Rev. W. E. Compton, and Dublin University. Admitted 1 Oct. 1910, as Egyptian Civil Service Probationer.
Resided one year. In the Egyptian Civil Service (1911).

Prestige, Arthur Reginald : son of Sydney Prestige, Assoc. M.Inst. C.E., of Berners-mede, Blackheath Park, London, S.E.; and Alice Emma Worringham. Born at 137, Sunderland Road, Forest Hill, 28 Oct. 1891. School : Harrow, under the Rev. Dr Wood. Admitted 1 Oct. 1910. Brother of Sydney, IV. (1) 62.

Rattray, Ian Maxwell : son of James Clerk Rattray (deceased), doctor of medicine; and Jessie Louisa Stuart. Born at 61, Grange Loan, Edinburgh, 12 Jan. 1899. Educated privately at Harriston, Moffat, N.B.; the British Chaplain's, Neuchâtel ; and Giggleswick. Admitted 1 Oct. 1910.

Renton, Thomas : son of James Renton, engineer, of 46, Lavington Road, Ealing ; and Isabella Margaret Mackenzie. Born at 62, Albert Road, Jarrow-ou-Tyne, 10 Dec. 1891. School : Latymer Upper School, Hammersmith, W., under the Rev. C. J. Smith. Admitted 1 Oct. 1910.
Entrance Scholarship, 1910.

Rentrop, Carl Hermann : son of Carl Rentrop (deceased), landed proprietor; and Clara Noell (deceased). Born at Werdohl, Westphalia, 15 April 1890. Educated at The Gymnasium at Herford, under Dr Windle. Kept one term as Non-Collegiate Student. Admitted 1 Oct. 1910.
    Kept two terms.

Richardson, Francis Krüger : son of Charles Richardson (deceased), provision merchant, of Drewton Manor, East Yorks ; and Marion Eliza Krüger. Born at 98, Beverley Road, Hull, 28 Feb. 1891. Schools : Hymers College, Hull ; and the Leys School, Cambridge, under the Rev. Dr Barber. Admitted 1 Oct. 1910.

Rogers, Esmond Hallewell : son of Sir Hallewell Rogers, knight, director of public companies, of Greville Lodge, Edgbaston ; and Lydia Watton Smith. Born at Greville Lodge, Sir Harry's Road, Edgbaston, 22 June 1891. Schools : West House School, Edgbaston ; and Shrewsbury, under the Rev. H. W. Moss and the Rev. C. A. Alington. Admitted 1 Oct. 1910.

Sanctuary, Arthur George Everard : son of Campbell Fortescue Stapleton Sanctuary, land agent, of Mangerton, Melplash, R.S.O., Dorset ; and Mary Eliza Glossop. Born at Mangerton, Melplash, 8 Nov. 1891. Educated at Sherborne School, under the Rev. Canon F. B. Westcott, the Rev. C. H. T. Wood and Mr N. C. Smith. Admitted 1 Oct. 1910. Brother of Campbell, iv. (1) 97.
    Ackroydkin Scholarship, 1911.

Saunder, Douglas Arthur : son of Samuel Arthur Saunder, Assistant Master at Wellington College, of Fir Holt, Crowthorne, Berks ; and Alice Duthoit. Born at Wellington College, 18 March 1891. School : Marlborough College, under Mr F. Fletcher. Admitted 1 Oct. 1910.
    Math. Tripos, Part I, Class 2, 1911. Entrance Exhibition, 1910. Scholar, 1911–

Schäfer, Thomas Sydney Hermann : son of Edward Albert Schäfer, professor of physiology, University of Edinburgh, of Marly Knowe, North Berwick ; and Maud Dixey. Born at Little Gillions, Croxley Green, Rickmansworth, 20 May 1891. Schools : Stanmore Park, under the Rev. Vernon Royle ; and Edinburgh Academy, under Mr R. Carter. Admitted 1 Oct. 1910.
    Entrance Exhibition, 1910.

Schoell, Frank Louis : Licencié ès Lettres, son of Théodore Louis Schoell, professeur, of 22, Faubourg de la Grappe, Chartres, France ; and Berthe Goetschy. Born at Amiens, 19 Aug. 1889. Educated at the Lycée, Rennes ; Lycée Louis-le-Grand, Paris ; École Normale Supérieure, Paris, under M. Lavisse. Admitted as a Research Student, 1 Oct. 1910.
    Resided one year.

Silburn, Laurence : son of John Henry Silburn, solicitor, of Savile Chambers, College Street, Newcastle-on-Tyne; and Emma Bolleter. Born at 62, Jesmond Road, Newcastle-on-Tyne, 2 Sept. 1890. Schools : The Abbey School, Beckenham ; and Uppingham School, under the Rev. Dr Selwyn. Admitted 1 Oct. 1910.

Simonds, Charles Cabourn Bannister : son of William Turner Simonds, gentleman, of 99, Albemarle Road, Beckenham ; and Laura Beatrice Bannister. Born at Ivy House, Skirbeck Quarter, Boston, 31 May 1891. Schools : Stanmore, under Rev. Vernon Royle, M.A. ; and Harrow, under the Rev. Dr Wood. Admitted 1 Oct. 1910.

Skinner, John Adrian Dudley : son of John Allan Cleveland Skinner, of the Indian Civil Service ; and Augusta Beatrice Newman. Born at Hornsea, near Hull, 2 Sept. 1891. Schools : Sussex House, Seaford ; and Wellington College, under the Rev. B. Pollock. Admitted 1 Oct. 1910.

Smith, Eric Percival : son of Rev. Harry Percival Smith, Rector of Ridlington, of Ridlington Rectory, Uppingham ; and Eliza Marion Parker. Born at 22, Queen Anne Terrace, Battersea, 1 Oct. 1890. School : Tonbridge, under Rev. Dr C. C. Tancock. Admitted 1 Oct. 1910.
Entrance Scholarship, 1910.

Smith, Harry Edgar : son of Harry Edward Smith, M.A., M.B. (of the College, II. 461), of Gleneagle House, Streatham, S.W. ; and Maud Mary Hutchings. Born at 11, Riggindale Road, Streatham, 5 Oct. 1891. Schools : New Beacon, Sevenoaks ; and Marlborough College, under Mr F. Fletcher. Admitted 1 Oct. 1910.

Stein, Philip : son of Solomon Stein, trader and farmer, of Milner Villa, Koeberg Road, Maitland, Cape Colony : and Sarah Leah Malag. Born at Schwekshna, Government of Kovno, Russia, 25 Jan. 1890. Educated at Normal College School, under Mr J. R. Whitton ; and South African College, Cape Town. Government Scholar. Admitted 1 Oct. 1910.
Math. Tripos, Part I, Class 2, 1911. Exhibitioner, 1911.

Stokoe, Frank Woodyer : son of Paul Henry Stokoe (deceased), M.D., B.A. ; and Alice Ruth Woodyer. Born at Wycombe Court, Lane End, Great Marlow, Bucks, 21 Oct. 1882. Educated at College de St Antoine, Geneva. Admitted 1 Oct. 1910.
Scholar, 1911–   .

Stuart, Robert Spurrell Dacre : son of Robert Edward Stuart, solicitor, of Stroud, Gloucestershire ; and Frances Dacre Spurrell. Born at Stroud, Gloucestershire, 13 Aug. 1890. Schools : Streatham House, Blackheath, under Mr Chitty ; and Bradfield College, under Dr Gray. Admitted 1 Oct. 1910.

Sturge, Paul Dudley : son of Theodore Sturge, land agent and surveyor, of Fern Hollow, Stoke Bishop, Bristol ; and Jane Gripper. Born at Clyde Park, Bristol, 1 July 1891. Educated at Clifton College, under the Rev. A. A. David. Surveyors' Institution Scholarship, 1910. Admitted 1 Oct. 1910.
Entrance Exhibition, 1910. Scholar, 1911–

Summers, Geoffrey : son of Henry Hall Summers, ironmaster, of Cornist Hall, Flint, North Wales ; and Minnie Gertrude Brattan. Born at Greenfield, Yorkshire, 2 Sept. 1891. Schools : The Mount School, West Kirby ; and Uppingham, under Rev. Dr E. C. Selwyn and Mr H. W. Mackenzie. Admitted 1 Oct. 1910.

Taylor, George Hebb: son of George Taylor, groom, of 20, Panton Street, Cambridge; and Elizabeth Hebb. Born at 13, Coronation Street, Cambridge, 31 Oct. 1890. School: The Cambridge and County School, under the Rev. C. J. N. Child, M.A. Admitted 1 Oct. 1910.
Choral Entrance Exhibition, 1910.

Thomas, John Glyndor Treharne: son of David John Thomas, surgeon, of Brynbedw, Nantymore, near Bridgend; and Catherine Elizabeth Treharne. Born at Nantymore, 21 May 1892. Schools: Christ's College, Brecon, under Rev. R. H. Chambers; and Clifton College, under Rev. A. A. David. Admitted 1 Oct. 1910.

Thompson, Oswald Stuart: son of Sydney Thompson, solicitor, of Farnaby, Sevenoaks; and Catherine MacNicol. Born at Wood Dene, Oak Hill Road, Sevenoaks, Kent, 21 Nov. 1892. Schools: Rottingdean, near Brighton; and Winchester, under Dr Burge. Admitted 1 Oct. 1910.

Threlfall, Richard Evelyn: son of Richard Threlfall, F.R.S. (of the College, II. 446), chemical manufacturer, of Oakhurst, Church Road, Edgbaston; and Evelyn Agnes Baird. Born at Sydney, New South Wales, 8 Oct. 1891. Schools: West House School, Edgbaston; and Oundle, under Mr F. W. Sanderson. Admitted 1 Oct. 1910.

Topham, Denis Bevan: son of Alfred George Topham (of the College, II 447), of 20, Barkston Gardens, London, S.W.; and Constance Sophia Bevan. Born at 20, Barkston Gardens, 19 Jan. 1890. Educated at Harrow, under Dr. Wood; privately; and abroad. Admitted 1 Oct. 1910
Resided one year.

Tween, Alfred Stuart: son of Alfred Augustus Tween, architect and surveyor, of Havering-atte-Bower, near Romford; and Phoebe Alice Jones. Born at Woodford, Essex, 19 Sept. 1891. School: Chigwell, under Canon Swallow, M.A. Admitted 1 Oct. 1910.

Vyvyan, Maurice Courtenay: son of the Rev. Thomas Grenfell Vyvyan, M.A. (formerly Fellow of the College, II. 324), licensed preacher in Natal; and Edith May Man. Born at Charterhouse, Godalming, 24 May 1891. Educated at home. Admitted 1 Oct. 1910.

Watkins, William Bertram: son of Henry Horatio Watkins, solicitor, of "Cynghordy," Mumbles, Glamorgan; and Elizabeth Esther Saunders. Born at Swansea, 22 Aug. 1892. Schools: Llanyre Hall, Llandrindod Wells; and Charterhouse, under Dr Rendall. Admitted 1 Oct. 1910.

Webb, Henry John: son of Henry Langley Webb, M.R.C.S. (deceased), of Cheadle, Staffordshire; and Jannette Docksey. Born at High Street, Cheadle, 14 March 1886. School: Cheltenham College, under Rev. R. Waterfield. Admitted 1 Oct. 1910.
Resided one year.

Wilcockson, William Howson: son of the Rev. John Howson Wilcockson, M.A. (of the College, II. 438), of Tarvin Vicarage, Chester; and Helena Mary Jackson. Born at Weston Point, Chester, 15 April 1891. School: Repton, under Rev. Lionel Ford. Admitted 1 Oct. 1910.

Williams, Geoffrey Commeline: son of Lionel Henry Williams, M.D. (Durham), of Oriel House, Thornbury, Gloucestershire; and Edith Emily Commeline. Born at Thornbury, 5 June 1892. School: Clifton College, under the Rev. A. A. David. Admitted 1 Oct. 1910.

Williams, John Lias Cecil: son of John Cadwaladr Williams, physician, of 30, Connaught Street, London, W.; and Catherine Thomas. Born at 30, Connaught Street, W., 14 Oct. 1892. School: City of London, under Rev. Dr A. Chilton. Admitted 1 Oct. 1910.

Williams, Ulric Gaster: son of Rev. Alfred Owen Williams, Clerk in Holy Orders of Putiki, Wanganui, New Zealand; and Alice Gaster. Born at Wanganui, New Zealand, 22 May 1890. School: Wanganui Collegiate, New Zealand, under Mr W. Empson, B.A. Admitted 1 Oct. 1910.

Wilson, William: son of William Wilson, clerk, of 4, Ash Grove, Victoria Park, Manchester; and Jane Whittingham. Born at 43, Ripton Street, Preston, Lancs, 29 March 1887. Educated at Manchester Grammar School, under Mr J. E. King, and Mr J. L. Paton; and at Manchester University. Admitted 1 Oct. 1910.
 Wollaston Student, 1910–   .

Woodsend, Philip Duncan: son of Thomas Woodsend, South American merchant, of Holme Hey, Croxteth Drive, Liverpool; and Isabel Jane Duncan. Born at Valparaiso, Chile, 29 November 1890. Schools: Greenbank School, Liverpool; and Uppingham School, under the Rev. Dr Selwyn, and the Rev. H. W. McKenzie. Admitted 1 Oct. 1910.
 Resided one year.

Ashton, Harry: son of Edwin Ashton, schoolmaster, of Bury, Lancashire; and Priscilla Wrigley. Born at Bury, Lancashire, 31 Jan. 1882. Educated at the Grammar School, Bury, under the Rev. W. H. Howlett, M.A.; the Worcester, Lichfield and Hereford Diocesan Training College, under the Rev. F. W. Burbidge, M.A.; and the University of Paris. Admitted 20 April 1911 as a Research Student.

Smith, Thomas: son of Thomas Smith (deceased 1886), works manager at Birmingham; and Mary Louisa Grigg. Born at King's Norton, Worcestershire, 23 Dec. 1884. Schools: King's Norton Elementary School, under Mr J. C. Burraston; Birmingham Blue Coat School, under Mr J. Irving. Kept six terms as a Non-Collegiate Student. Admitted 1911.
 Choral Exhibitioner, 1911.

APPENDIX I

ADDENDA TO VOLUME II

290 Hooper, D. Died in London, Nov. 24, 1908.

290 Ayerst, W. Invited, 1902, to be Bishop of "The Church of England in Natal." Died in London, April 6, 1904. *Caian*, XIII. 140.

291 Johnson, A. C. Died at Briersfield, Dartmouth, March 13, 1909. *Caian* XVIII. 198.

291 Matthews, T. R. Died Jan. 1910.

292 Bowen, C. C. Knighted, 1910.

292 Symonds, W. Donor of the Advowson of Stockport Rectory, 1910.

293 Scott, T. Resigned the Rectory of Lavenham, 1906.

294 Gabb, J. Died May 17, 1900.

294 Heard, J. B. Died Feb. 29, 1908. *Caian*, XVIII. 1.

295 Tanner, J. V. Died at Chawleigh, Devon, April 14, 1903. *Caian*, XII. 161, XIII. 1.

296 Kennedy, C. M. Died at Exmouth, Oct. 25, 1908. *Caian*, XVIII. 16 (portrait), 111.

296 Hose, T. C. Died at Lowestoft, Aug. 4, 1903.

296 Jones, W. S. Died March 10, 1910.

297 Nash, W. Died June 3, 1905.

297 Stokes, H. Resigned his cure, 1902. Died at Crowthorne, Berkshire, Aug. 1904. *Caian*, XIV. 2.

297 Brown, W. H. Died at Oxburgh, Nov. 24, 1905. *Caian*, XV. 2.

299 Girling, J. C. Died about 1907.

299 Nottidge, G. S. Died at Muggrudorf, Bavaria, June 6, 1908.

299 Malden, B. S. Died about 1906.

300 Thursfield, R. Died at Worcester, July 20, 1906.

300 Beck, A. Died at Gorefield, Wisbech, June 13, 1902.

300 Hunnybun, J. Died at Cambridge, Aug. 17, 1899.

300 Drummond, M. *Add* "Captain of the Boat Club." Died March 23, 1898.

301 Henty, G. A. Died on his yacht in Weymouth Harbour, Nov. 16, 1902. *Caian*, XII. 24.

302 Kelly, H. P. Resigned his cure, 1902.

303 Du Port, J. M. Died at Denver, Feb. 21, 1899. *Caian*, VIII. 217.

303 Bousfield, H. B. Died at Cape Town, Feb. 10, 1902. *Caian*, XI. 49.

304 Spencer, M. T. Resigned his cure, 1891. Died at Worcester, Jan. 23, 1904.

306 Payne, A. D. Died July 19, 1904.

306 Southey, H. W. P.C. of St Mary's, Hatfield, 1900. Rector of St Paul's, New Cross, Manchester, 1900–

308 Thompson, W. H. "Of Dennington, Swymbridge, N. Devon." Died March 17, 1908.

309 Slocock, S. Died Dec. 20, 1902.

309 May, F. S. Died at High Laver, April 6, 1909.

310 Willis, E. C. Treasurer of the Inner Temple, 1907.

310 Monro, C. H. Died at Eastbourne, Feb. 13, 1908. Left his estate to the College. *Caian*, XVII. 79, 161 (portrait).

311 Gould, J. Resigned his cure, 1903. Died at Ealing, May 22, 1908.

311 Beedham, M. J. Died in 1902.

312 Holloway, E. J. Died at Hereford, June 25, 1908.

312 Shaw, J. A. Died about 1903.

314 Sharp, J. P. Died at Longstow, Jan. 1, 1906.

314 Ashley, J. M. Died at Malvern Link, Sept. 10, 1909.

315 Mansell, J. Died in Guernsey, April 23, 1899. *Caian*, IX. 6.

316 Cowan, C. E. R. Rector of Kyre-Wyard, Herefordshire, 1902.

316 Swete, H. B. One of the first Fellows of the British Academy. Hon. D.D. Glasgow, 1901; Hon. Litt.D. Oxon., 1911.

318 Deer, T. G. P. Resigned his cure, 1905. Died at Bedford, Oct. 1, 1906.

318 Leighton, E. T. Died March, 1903.

318 Andrew, W. W. W. Died at Hendon, Aug. 6, 1908, from gnat-stings.

C IV 1

409   Atkinson, E. D.   Archdeacon of Dromore, 1905- .
410   Knight, E. F.   On the staff of the *Morning Post*.
410   Dalton, E. S.   Chaplain of Hastings and E. Sussex Hospital, 1909-
412   Thurtell, W. E.   Resident in the Argentine.
413   Baggallay, F.   Hon. Canon of Peterborough, 1903-5. Rector of Pulborough, Sussex, 1904
413   Fenwick, G. B.   Rector of Nympsfield, 1902-4.
413   Lodge, J. W.   Served in the South African War.   Colonel.
414   Carpenter, E. W.   Rector of Boothby Pagnell, Lincolnshire, 1907- .
415   Joseph (Watkin), T. M.   M.A. 1907.
416   Robson, W. S.   Solicitor-General, 1905.   Attorney-General, 1908.   Hon. D.C.L. Durham.
        Representative at the Hague Arbitration on Newfoundland Fisheries, 1910. Lord of
        Appeal, 1910 (Lord Robson of Jesmond).   Hon. Fellow, 1910.   G.C.M.G. 1911, in
        recognition of his services at the Hague.
416   Loveband, M. T.   Died at Burrington, Devon, April 26, 1903.
416   Broadmead, P. P.   Resigned his cure, 1899.
417   Coombe, W.   Rector of Oxburgh with Foulden, 1906- .
417   Jepson, G.   Curate of All Saints with Holy Trinity, Wandsworth, 1907-
417   Carr, R. G.   Ordained deacon (Exeter), 1899; priest, 1900. P.C. of North Nibley,
        Gloucestershire, 1906- .
418   Judkins, E.   Rector of Holy Trinity, Winchester, 1907- .
418   Atherton, T. J.   Lieut.-Col. (retired).   C.B.
419   Grane, W. L.   Vicar of Cobham, 1903- .   Select Preacher, 1904-5.
419   Boyd, F. L.   Select Preacher, 1907.   Vicar of the Church of the Annunciation (Quebec
        Chapel), Marylebone, 1908; of St Paul's, Knightsbridge, 1908-
420   Gulliver, C. H.   Vicar of Lambley, Northumberland, 1898- .
421   Jolley, S. B.   Died at Sydenham, Dec. 10, 1909.
421   Cobbold, R. F.   Rector of Beachampton, Bucks, 1903- .
421   Bangham, T. K.   Migrated to Jesus.
421   Winslow, R.   Died 1892.
421   Knaggs, R. L.   Professor of Surgery at the University of Leeds.
422   Whittam, W. G.   Rector of Hartley Wespall, Hants, 1905- .
422   Steel, J. E. P.   Died in London, March 19, 1907.
423   Fowler, J. K.   Dean of the Faculty of Medicine, Univ. of London.   K.C.V.O. 1910.
423   Wallis, F. C.   Knighthood, 1911.
424   Collisson, R. K.   Rector, Christ Church, Mt Gambier, S. Australia, 1908. R.D. of South
        East, 1908.
424   Clarke, F. J.   Speaker of the House of Assembly, Barbados.   K.C.M.G. 1911.
425   Nettlefold, E.   Died at Harborne, April 11, 1909.   *Caian*, xviii. 199.
426   Tweedie, A. G.   Vicar of Ruswarp, Yorkshire, 1904-7. Rector of Lavenham, Suffolk, 1908.
426   Welsford, J. W. W.   Author: *The Strength of England* (published 1910).   Died at Harrow,
        April 29, 1909.   *Caian*, xviii. 200.
427   Darrell, J. F.   Rector of Monk Soham, Suffolk, 1899- .
428   Apcar, A. T.   Died in London, Sept. 2, 1906.
429   Bolton, W. W.   Warden of University School, Victoria, B.C.
429   Tata, D. J.   Knighted, 1910.
429   Bendall, C.   Professor of Sanskrit, 1903.   Honorary Fellow.   Died at Liverpool, March 14,
        1906. Officier de l'Académie (posthumous). Left to the College in charge for the Uni-
        versity his students' working library of Oriental literature.
429   Niven, G.   Died in Manchester, Feb. 7, 1901.
429   Ley, H.   Curate of St Matthias, Earl's Court, London, 1900-
430   Payne, J. Bruce.   Head-master of Bishop's Stortford School.
430   Collins, F.   Head-master of Alleyn's School, Dulwich, 1903-

450 Ince, J. B. C. Vicar of All Souls, Cheriton Street, Kent, 1900-1. Curate of Aldington, Sussex, 1902- .

450 Hopkins, W. B. L. Secretary of the Church Building Society, 1899-1907. Rector of Lavenham, 1907- .

451 Pemberton, M. J.P. for Suffolk. Author, Novels.

451 Dickinson, W. L. Died at Tintagel, Sept. 6, 1904. *Caian*, xiv. 4.

452 Mais, H. A. Vicar of Burpham, Sussex, 1903-

452 Buckland, W. W. Tutor of the College, 1903- . Praelector. Author: *The Roman Law of Slavery*.

452 Hosgood, S. Vicar of Lockington, Leicestershire, 1898- .

453 Page, F. G. J. Head-master of Ascham School, Bournemouth, and afterwards of St Christopher's School, Eastbourne. Vicar of Mountfield, Sussex, 1910-

453 Leigh-Lye, A. Rector of Thurloxton, Som., 1909- .

453 MacFarland, R. A. H. Head-master, Campbell College, Belfast, 1907-

454 Farthing, J. C. Bishop of Montreal, 1909- .

455 Mariette, F. A. Head-master of St Alban's School, Lyme Regis.

455 Stewart, D. A. Rector of Long Stratton, Norfolk, 1906-

455 Giles, P. Litt.D. 1910. Master of Emmanuel College, 1911-

455 Edkins, J. S. Sc.D. 1910.

456 Macklin, A. R. Revising barrister, Cambridgeshire (1911)

456 Carnegie, D. J. Died at Darlington, Oct. 1, 1909. Author. *Caian*, xix. 4.

456 Daniell, A. E. Died Dec. 15, 1901.

456 Caldecott, H. E. Died 1910.

456 Russell, A. Principal of Faraday House, 1910- .

457 Southby, W. P. Died Aug. 27, 1906.

459 Boyd, G. K. Vicar of St Andrew's, Worthing, 1905- .

459 Pughe, T. St George Parry. *For* " St George " *read* " St John." Vicar of Hursley, Hants, 1909- .

460 Colclough, W. F. M.A., M.D. 1902.

460 Heawood, E. Librarian, Royal Geographical Society.

460 Roberts, H. A. Secretary to the Board of Indian Civil Service Studies, the Appointments Board, and the Cambridge University Association.

460 Conway, R. S. Professor of Latin, and Dean of the Faculty of Arts, University of Manchester.

460 Barry, G. D. Rector of Denver, 1905- .

461 Edgeworth, F. H. M.D. 1908. Professor of Medicine, University of Bristol.

461 Jameson, R. B. Diocesan Inspector of Schools, Chichester, 1909- .

461 Mathieson, J. F. Publisher in London.

462 Stuart, H. V. Rector of Stoke-on-Trent, 1904- . Prebendary of Lichfield, 1905 Select Preacher, 1906.

462 Berkeley, G. H. A. C. M.A., M.D. 1911. Obst. Phys. Middlesex Hospital.

463 Bodington, A. E. M.D. 1903.

464 Buncombe, T. Rector of Black Torrington, Devon, 1907- .

464 Cavell, H. T. P.C. of All Saints, Woodford Wells, Essex, 1903- .

464 Norman, W. H. Vicar of St Barnabas, Cambridge, 1907- .

465 Purvis, J. H. Special Service Mounted Infantry, South African War, 1901.

465 Nurse, E. J. Rector of Windermere, 1904- .

466 Robinson, E. F. M.A. 1905.

466 Day, A. W. Died at Brighton, Nov. 11, 1902. *Caian*, xiii. 3.

466 Kelly, E. O'F. Died Aug. 10, 1897.

466 Williams, C. E. M.A. 1904; M.D. 1905.

466 Harris, W. B. Married Lady Mary Savile, daughter of the Earl of Mexborough, 1898.

467 Riches, T. H.   Gave £1000 towards the re-decoration of the Hall.

467 Sidebotham, F. W. G.   Vicar of Petham, Kent, 1901- .

468 O'Neill, B. P.   In medical practice in London.

468 Bayly, E. W.   Rector of Watlington, Norfolk, 1899- .

468 Whittam, M.   Master at the Acton County School.

469 Stephens, J. W. W.   M.D. 1898.   Walter Myers Lecturer in Tropical Medicine, University of Liverpool.

470 Ashwin, C. M.   Rector of Poyntington, Dorset, 1901- .

470 Anderson, H. K.   College Lecturer in Physiology.   University Lecturer in Physiology. F.R.S. 1907.   Member of the Council of the Senate, 1910- .

470 Lindley, T.   LL.D. 1903.

470 Wickham, P. R.   Precentor and Minor Canon of Winchester Cathedral, 1906–

470 Mitchell, W. G.   Died at Vancouver, Jan. 14, 1905.

470 Sladen, E. S. St B.   John Lucas Walker Student, 1901.   Served in the Prahsu Expedition; *Caian*, x. 51.   Lt.-Colonel of the 4th Batt. S. Wales Borderers at the time of its disbandment.   Mayor of Tunbridge Wells, 1910.

471 Craig, M.   Physician for Mental Diseases, Guy's Hospital.

471 Hall, A. J.   M.D. 1905.   Lecturer on Practical Medicine, University of Sheffield.

472 Hardy, W. B.   Tutor in Natural Science, 1898.   Tutor, 1903.   F.R.S. 1902.   Thruston Prizeman, 1900.   Croonian Lecturer, 1905.

473 Smith, H. N.   Curate of Walkley, Sheffield, to 1901.   Joined the Roman Catholic Church.

473 Thornhill, C. B.   Indian Staff Corps, 1892.   Canton magistrate at Agra to 1904.   Died at Agra, Oct. 5, 1904.   *Caian*, xiv. 5.

473 Bartley, G. H. C.   Vicar of Sacriston, Durham, 1900- .

474 Marten, R. H.   M.D. 1905.

474 Stretton, W. S.   Died in London.

475 Beaumont, W. N.   Till 1902 in scholastic work.   Fruit-farmer.

475 Box, R. D.   Vicar of St Paul's, Haggerston, London, 1904- .

475 Martyn, A. J. K.   Ordained deacon (Ripon), 1911.

475 Tennant, F. R.   B.D. 1903; D.D. 1907.   Student in Philosophy.   Rector of Hockwold, Norfolk, 1903- .   Select Preacher, Cambridge, 1899; Oxford, 1907–8.   Hulsean Lecturer, 1901.   University Lecturer in the Philosophy of Religion, 1907–

475 Still, G. F.   Professor in the Diseases of Children, King's College, London.

476 Hargrave, A. B.   M.A. 1901.   Vicar of Long Sutton, Hants, 1903–

477 Townsend, A. H.   Curate of St Alban's, Streatham Park, London, 1907–

477 Calthrop, H. G.   Died at Hong Kong, Nov. 5, 1909.   *Caian*, xix. 120.

478 Grimsdale, H. B.   Ophthalmic Surgeon, St George's Hospital.

479 Croft, W. B.   Vicar of Wombridge, Salop, 1905- .

480 Thorne, H. A.   Died at Sierra Leone, July 20, 1903.   *Caian*, xiii. 2.

481 Billington, C.   Vicar of Audenshaw, Lancashire, 1900–11; of St Audries, Bridgwater, 1911.

482 Euan-Smith, E. M.   Solicitor in London, 1900.   In 1909 took the surname "Maclaurin."

482 Gilbert, H. E.   M.A. 1906.   Master at Aldenham School.

482 Goldsmith, G. H.   M.D. 1902.

482 Hawthorn, John.   Curate of Wensley, Yorkshire, 1901- .

483 Jerrard, J. H. F.   M.B., B.C. 1899.

483 Kempson, F. C.   Author.

483 McConnel, E. W. J.   M.A. 1904.   Vicar of Khandallah, Wellington, New Zealand, 1906–

484 Miller, F. T.   Head-master (1901) of the Grammar School, Townsville, Queensland; afterwards of the Grammar School, Mudgee, N.S.W.   Died Jan. 1898.

484 Monro, C. G.   Ordained deacon (Calcutta), 1903; priest (Durham), 1905.   C.M.S. Missionary at Doyabari, Diocese of Calcutta.

484 Morrell, R. S.   Fellow till 1904.   Chemist (1905) with Mander and Co., Wolverhampton.

484   Neill, C. Ordained deacon (Durham), 1903; priest, 1904. Curate of Haughton-le-Skerne, 1903–4. Missionary at Ranaghat, India, 1906–7. Curate of Liskeard, 1907–8; of Cheltenham, 1908–9. Organising Sec. C.M.S. Dio. Gloucester and Worcester, 1909– .

484   Pawson, A. P.C. of St James's, Scarborough, 1910–

485   Phillips, H. D. Organist at Baltimore, U.S.A.

485   Pooley, G. H. B.A. 1907. Lecturer on Ophthalmology, University of Sheffield.

485   Stewart, H. G. Tutor (1909) to the children of the Grand Duke Alexander Michailowitch, The Palace, Gatchino, Russia.

486   Stutter, W. O. M.A. 1905. Ordained priest (Newcastle), 1899. Rector of Kirstead, Norfolk, 1910– .

486   Trevellick, H. G. Assumed the title Marquis de Trèvelec.

486   Walford, W. S. Curate of Monk Sherborne, Hants, 1909– .

486   Watts, T. J. M.A. 1910. Vicar of St Mary's, Wellingborough, 1905– .

486   Wells, M. C. Vicar of Sittingbourne, 1903–9.

487   Wright, W. C. Vicar of Rocester, Staffordshire, 1907–

487   Beresford, G. Rector of Beaford, Devon, 1898– .

487   Milner-Barry, E. L. Professor of German in the University of N. Wales, Bangor.

488   Bertram, T. A. Attorney-General, Bahamas. Puisne Judge, Cyprus. Attorney-General, Ceylon (1911).

488   Christopherson, J. B. Director of Hospitals, Khartoum and Omdurman.

489   Fenton, W. J. M.D. 1909. Medical Tutor, Charing Cross Hospital.

490   Gardner, J. E. G. Barlow Lecturer on Dante at University College, London, 1910.

490   Grünbaum, A. S. F. Professor of Pathology, University of Leeds.

490   Irving, W. In practice at Christchurch, New Zealand.

491   Latham, H. G. D. Dean of Perth, Western Australia, 1906–11. Vicar of St George's, Camberwell, 1911.

491   Peters, E. A. M.D. 1900.

491   Pim, G. Died a few years after his degree.

492   Rice, A. C. Vicar of Tywardreath, Cornwall, 1905– .

492   Slipper, T. A. C. Vicar of Kinver, Staffordshire, 1900–

493   Harper-Smith, A. R. Chaplain (Missions to Seamen) for Valparaiso, 1908

493   Spender, A. H. Engaged in literary work; mainly at Venice (1910).

493   Staats, C. W. O. Returned to residence as a Non-Collegiate Student, B.A. 1899. Classical Tripos, Class I, Div. 2. Died three or four years later.

493   Sumner, C. P. M.A. 1899. Private Tutor at Cambridge.

493   Trethewy, A. Resident Medical Officer at Haileybury College. Died there, May 4, 1903. *Caian*, xii. 163, 213.

493   Tripp, G. D. In Insurance business at Johannesburg, South Africa.

494   Wicks, S. In practice at Kimberley, South Africa.

494   Willis, R. B.A. 1907. H.B.M. Acting Consul-General, Mukden (1911).

494   Wilson, H. L. Formerly vicar of Abbotsley. Joined the Roman Catholic Church. In educational work at Preston (1910).

494   Wood, T. B. Elected to a Monro Fellowship, 1908. Professor (afterwards Drapers' Professor) of Agriculture, 1907– . *Caian*, xvii. 7.

494   Woodhouse, A. J. Vicar of Werneth, Lancashire, 1903– .

495   Inagaki, M. Japanese Minister at Madrid. Died there Nov. 26, 1908.

495   Kermode, R. D. Vicar of Maughold, 1898–1908; of St George and All Saints, Douglas, Isle of Man, 1908– .

495   Groom, P. Professor of Forest Botany at Cooper's Hill College till its close in 1906.

496   Alexander, E. C. Vicar of Edington, Wilts, 1911.–

496   Aston, R. L. M.A. 1905.

496   Bardsley, C. C. B. Vicar of St Helens, Lancashire, 1901– .

496 Bardsley, J. U. N. Vicar of Lancaster, 1909- .

496 Beard, W. F. M.A. 1903. For some years master at a school in Melbourne, Australia. Master at Wakefield Grammar School (1910).

497 Burkill, I. H. Government Botanist at Calcutta.

497 Carter, E. B. Served in the South African War. In the library of the *Daily Express* Office, 1906-

497 Dickinson, J. H. Rector of St Juliot, Cornwall, 1906-

497 Donaldson, A. H. M.A. 1902. Qualified, but not in practice.

497 Donne, C. E. Rector of Keele, Staffordshire, 1905-

498 Evershed, F. T. P. Vicar of South Bersted, Sussex, 1909- .

498 Hadow, G. E. Died in 1900.

498 Hawthorn, James. Ordained deacon (Exeter), 1903 ; priest, 1904. Master and Chaplain at Newton Abbot College, 1903-4. Master at Loughborough Grammar School, 1906-8 ; at The Cedars School, Ealing (1910).

499 Hersch (Herschkowitz), I. H. Master at the Perse School, Cambridge.

499 Higson, G. H. Served in the South African War.

499 Jeffcoat, W. F. H. Ordained deacon (London), 1903 ; priest, 1904. Curacies, 1903-10. Rector of North Stoke, Som., 1910-

500 Long, S. H. M.D. 1903.

500 Mayfield, E. Resident in Australia (1910).

501 Murphy, J. K. M.D. 1899. M.C. 1904.

501 Pochin, E. C. Master at a preparatory school, Seafield, Lytham.

502 Srawley, J. H. B.D. 1903 ; D.D. 1907. Tutor of Selwyn College, 1907   Examining Chaplain to the Bishop of Lichfield, 1905- .

502 Stephenson, R. C. Teacher of voice-production in London.

502 Sugden, C. G. Farming.

502 Sutthery, H. M.A. 1899. Master at Blundell's School, Tiverton, 1900-1 ; Chaplain of Arnold House School, 1901-3. Curate of Rickinghall, Norfolk, 1903-5. Vicar of Warden, Northumberland, 1905- .

502 Terry, C. J. Vicar of All Souls, South Hampstead, 1909- .

502 Trayes, F. E. A. Vacated fellowship, 1899. H.M. Inspector of Schools, 1905- .

502 Turnbull, C. C. I. Resident Medical Officer, Italian Hospital, Queen Square, London, W.C.

503 Venn, H. S. In the United States Civil Service. Died at Washington, U.S.A., Jan. 1908.

503 Welton, J. Professor of Education, University of Leeds.

503 Whitestone, R. A. W. Master at a preparatory school, Ealing.

503 Winkfield, T. H. Served in the South African War. Died at Johannesburg in the winter of 1903-4 of typhoid fever.

503 Gerold, G. L. Ordained deacon (Hereford), 1898 ; priest, 1900. Curate of Thruxton, 1898-1901. Vicar of Easthope (Salop), 1901- .

503 Towers, R. M. Died at Cambridge, April 16, 1907. *Caian*, XVI. 161.

503 Goodchild, E. Acting Chaplain at the Embassy, Constantinople, 1905-6. Chaplain of Long Grove Asylum, Epsom, 1907-

504 Mitchell, A. Canon of St Mary's Cathedral, Edinburgh ; Pantonian Professor.

504 Wood, C. Hon. LL.D. Leeds, 1904.

504 Gallop, E. G. Tutor in Mathematics, 1901-3. Tutor, 1903-9. Registrary, 1900-1904. Praelector 1894-1900.

505 Atkins, G. E. Rector of Scole, Norfolk, 1900-1 ; of Tibshelf, Derbyshire, 1901- .

505 Bagshawe, A. W. G. D.P.H. 1908. Director of the Sleeping Sickness Bureau, Royal Society ; seconded from the Uganda Medical Service.

505 Bland, G. I. Died at Cannes, Feb. 23, 1903.

505 Bousfield, S. M.A. 1899 ; M.D. 1910.

505 Buck, G. M. Died Oct. 1899. *Caian*, VIII. 17.

506 Fuhrken, G. E.   Lector, University of Upsala, 1901.

507 Hayward, M. C.   M.A. 1898; M.B., B.C. 1903.

507 James, E. B.   M.A. 1902.   Curate of St Michael's, Gloucester, 1901–4.

507 Keeble, F. W.   Sc.D. 1906.   Professor of Botany, University College, Reading.

507 Lea, John.   M.A. 1907.   Assistant Registrar for Extension Lectures, University of London.

508 Legg, S. C. E.   Sub-Warden of King's College Hostel, London.

508 Maturin, F. H.   M.B., B.C. 1899.

508 May, E. G.   Curate of N. Mundham, Sussex, 1908–11.   Rector of Wiarton, Canada, 1911.

508 Mercer, J. W.   M.A. 1903.   Master at Osborne Naval College; and Dartmouth Naval College (1910).

509 Oelsner, H.   Professor of Romance Philology, Oxford.

509 Panton, D. M.   Pastor at Norwich, 1910.

509 Perrott, A. D.   Head-master of Saffron Walden School, 1901–2; Master at Cheltenham College, 1903–5; Head-master of King Edward VII School, Coventry, 1905–10. Duncombe Lecturer at Kingsbridge, 1910–

509 Phillips, Ll. C. P.   M.D. 1903.   Professor at the School of Medicine, Cairo.

509 Priddle, A. E.   M.R.C.S., L.R.C.P. (London); not in practice.   Served in the South African War.

510 Smith, F. B.   Died Dec. 13, 1902, at Berrow, Somerset.

510 Stanbrough, M. H.   Master at preparatory schools.   Died at Hildersham House, St Peter's, Kent, in 1904.

510 Tubbs, L.   M.A. 1902.

510 Tuckett, J. E. S.   Master at Marlborough College, 1902– .

511 Willis, J. C.   Sc.D. 1905.   Hon. Sc.D. Harvard.   Korresp. Mitglied, Deutsche botanische Gesellschaft.

511 Brooks, A.   P.-in-c. of St Matthew's, Abbey Hill, Edinburgh, 1909– .

512 Bull, G. V.   M.B., B.C. 1901.

512 Collingwood, B. J.   B.C. 1900; M.B. 1905; M.D. 1906.

512 Fletcher, W.   M.D. 1910.   Medical Officer in the Federated Malay States (1910).

512 Gillies, C. E. S.   Died at Auckland, N.Z., 1905.

513 Goode, G. E.   M.R.C.S., L.R.C.P. London, 1894.   In practice at Shanghai.

513 Grimston, H. D. K.   For some time in the dramatic profession.

513 Halliday, J. W. G.   M.A. 1899.   Master at Oakham School till 1902.   Ordained deacon (Exeter), 1902; priest, 1903.   Curate of Bradninch, 1902–6; of St Mary Major, Exeter, 1906–8.   Rector of Selworthy, Som., 1908.

513 Hirosawa, K.   Count.   Vice-Speaker in the House of Lords, Japan, 1904.

513 Hughes, J. B.   M.B., B.C. 1898.

513 Ilott, C. H.   M.A. 1902.   For some time Master at the Northampton County School.

514 Johnson, A. M.   Vicar of Masterton, N.Z., 1905–8; of St Mark's, Wellington, N.Z., 1908–

514 Miller, W. G. D.   Died May, 1902.

514 Myers, W.   *Caian*, x. 74, 84.   The Walter Myers Lectureship in Tropical Medicine at the University of Liverpool was founded in memory of him.

515 Owen, E.   Master of Birkdale Preparatory School, Southport.

515 Parker, R. D.   M.A., M.D. 1901.   In practice at Caledon, South Africa.   Served in the South African War.

515 Phillipps, H. V.   Called to the bar at Lincoln's Inn, Jan. 27, 1908.

515 Powell, H. T.   M.A. 1898.   B.D. Durham, 1907.   Ordained deacon (Carlisle), 1900; priest, 1901.   Curate of Ulverston, 1900–4; Assistant Diocesan Inspector, Liverpool, 1904–6.   Diocesan Inspector of Schools, Rochester, 1906–

515 Rawling, L. B.   Assistant-Surgeon, St Bartholomew's Hospital.

515 Rigby, J. C. A.   M.B., B.C. 1900.   In practice in South Africa.

516 Rösing, A. H.   In profession as a singer.

516 Scowcroft, H. E. M.A. 1900. Served in the South African War.

516 Sharples, J. (Percival). In medical practice.

516 Smith, M. Died April, 1898.

516 Solberg, C. N. A. Electrician in London. Died in Norway, May, 1908. *Caian*, XVIII. 3.

516 Stephenson, P. T. Master at the Mercers' School, Holborn, London, 1899; at Berkhamsted School (1910).

517 Swatman, M. S. Curate of St Mark's, Kennington, 1899–1906; Kelshall, Herts, 1906–9. Rector of Kelshall, 1909–

517 Walker, J. Curate of Eketahuna, N.Z., 1898–1902. Vicar of St Thomas's, Wellington, N.Z., 1902– .

517 Ware, F. Master at St Peter's College, Adelaide, S. Australia.

517 Ware, J. *Dele* "Master at St Peter's College." *Add* "Master at the County School, Kilburn, London."

517 Woolley, E. J. M.D. 1907.

517 Young, H. W. P. M.D. 1902.

518 Sturrock, P. S. In practice in Scotland.

518 Sulley, A. Master at the High School, Middlesbrough.

518 Paget, O. F. M.D. 1905.

518 Abercrombie, R. G. M.B. 1902; M.D. 1910.

518 Avent, J. T. Warden of the College Mission at Battersea, 1906–8. Rector of Dowdeswell, Gloucestershire, 1908–

518 Burkill, H. J. M.A. 1899. Stockbroker in London.

519 Carsberg, A. E. M.B., B.C. 1899.

519 Charles, J. R. M.A., M.D. 1901. Physician Royal Infirmary, Bristol.

519 Cook, S. A. M.A. 1899. Drosier Fellow to 1907. Assistant Lecturer in Hebrew.

519 Duval, H. P. LL.M. 1906.

519 Ellis, F. H. M.B., B.C. 1899.

519 Borradaile, B. W. G. M.A.

519 Gardiner, J. S. Balfour Student, 1899–1901. Conducted and organised an Expedition to the Maldive Islands, 1899; Indian Ocean Expedition, 1905; Seychelles, 1908. Dean of the College, 1903–9. Lecturer on Oceanography, 1908–9. Professor of Zoology, 1909– F.R.S. 1908. On the Council of the R. Geogr. Soc. 1906–8. Author.

520 Hancock, W. C. Analytical Chemist in London.

520 Hill, J. P. M.A. 1898. In medical practice.

520 Hill, P. A. M.A. 1901. Master of St Andrew's Preparatory School, Bromley, Kent.

520 Jeffcoat, R. Rector of Littleton-on-Severn, 1910.

520 Keeling, G. S. M.B., B.C. 1900; M.D. 1907.

520 Martin, F. R. Served in the South African War. In practice in South Africa.

521 Myers, C. S. M.A. 1901; M.D. 1902; Sc.D. 1910. Thruston Prize, 1902. Professor of Psychology, Univ. of London (1909). Univ. Lecturer in Experimental Psychology.

521 Paton, L. J. B.C. 1900; M.B. 1902. F.R.C.S. Eng. 1902. Assistant Ophthalmic Surgeon, St Mary's Hospital.

521 Pollard, S. P. M.B., B.C. 1900; M.A., M.D. 1905. Horton-Smith Prize, 1905.

521 Quin, W. T. Died at Guildford, Feb. 17, 1899.

521 Richardson, G. A. In business at Swatow, China.

521 Sangster, F. H. Vicar of St John's, Dewsbury, 1908– .

522 Shillito, A. M.A. 1906. Warden of the College Mission, Battersea, 1899–1905. Organising Secr. S.P.C.K. 1905.

522 Hart-Smith, H. M. M.B., B.C. 1899. For some time Surgeon R.N. Retired 1901. In practice at Brockley.

522 Thoseby, A. E. V. M.A. 1910. Master at the Grammar School, Dudley, 1902; at the Municipal Day School, Harrogate (1906).

522 Tucker, W. E. M.B., B.C. 1902. In practice at Hamilton, Bermuda.

522 Walder, E. M.A. 1907. Head-master of Ockbrook (Moravian) School. Contributor to Vol. V of the *Cambridge History of Literature*.

522 Warren, S. P. Vicar of St Chad's, Longsdon, Staffordshire, 1906–

522 Watts-Silvester, T. H. E. M.A. 1900. B.C. 1904.

523 Wilson, E. A. M.B. 1900. Medical Officer, Zoologist and Scientific Artist on the Antarctic Expedition under Captain R. F. Scott, 1901–4. Head of the Scientific staff on Captain Scott's second Expedition, 1910.

523 Knight, A. M. Fellow till 1903. D.D. 1903. Bishop of Rangoon, 1902–1910. Warden of St Augustine's College, Canterbury, 1900– . *Caian*, XII. 96.

523 Shutte, M. W. M.A. 1898. M.R.C.S., L.R.C.P. London, 1904.

523 Symonds, W. N. In legal practice at Hankow, China.

523 Ingoldby, T. E. Electrician with Messrs Siemens & Co., London.

524 Barham, G. F. B.C. 1902; M.B. 1903.

524 Bowen, F. G. Died at Fort Jameson, Rhodesia, Feb. 21, 1905. *Caian*, XIV. 172.

524 Bradley, H. P. M.A., M.B. 1902. Died at Nottingham, June 16, 1905. *Caian*, XV. 83.

525 Brunner, F. E. Died at Hillingdon, Middlesex, June 15, 1901.

525 Cardwell, P. B. M.A. 1905. Farming in Kent. Previously in scholastic work.

525 Clarke, H. N. Died Aug. 4, 1900.

525 Clarke, J. S. M.A., M.B. 1902; B.C. 1901.

525 Clarke, T. W. K. Assistant Engineer on the "Bakerloo" Railway. Served in the Imperial Yeomanry in the South African War; wounded. Designer of aeroplanes at Kingston, Surrey.

525 Cox, E. M.B., B.C. 1900. Surgeon R.N. 1901.

525 Cross, A. W. S. M.A. 1903.

525 Cross, W. E. M.A. 1909. Master at Geelong School, Australia; at Crewkerne; at Felsted; at Whitgift's School, Croydon. Head-master of King's School, Peterborough, 1909– .

526 Donaldson, E. A. M.A. 1899. Curate of Black Torrington, 1900–4. Rector of Pyworthy, Devon, 1904– .

526 Fraser, A. T. B.C. 1900; M.B. 1901. In practice at Pietermaritzburg, Natal.

526 Jeffries, F. J. M.A. 1907; LL.M. 1909.

526 Hay, K. R. M.A., M.B. 1902.

526 Heilborn, W. E. M.B., B.C. 1898.

527 Marshall, G. E. Private Tutor at Hastings (1909).

527 Matheson, F. M. B.A. 1900. M.R.C.S., L.R.C.P. 1903.

527 Orme, G. E. M.A., M.B., B.C. 1901.

527 Scott, H. C. Called to the bar at Lincoln's Inn, Jan. 26, 1900. On the South-Eastern Circuit.

527 Sephton, R. M.R.C.S., L.R.C.P., London, 1905.

527 Stiff, H. H. M.B., B.C. 1902.

528 St Leger, A. Y. In medical practice at Cape Town.

528 Taylor, E. J. Davis. M.B., B.C. 1905.

528 Todd, A. F. M.A. 1899. Lieut. in Roberts's Horse, South African War; wounded.

528 Vivian, G. T. In Johannesburg, S.A., 1902.

528 Wilkinson, J. A. In the Education Department, Johannesburg, S.A.

528 Wilson, A. G. M.B., B.C. 1899; M.C. 1907. F.R.C.S. Tutor in Surgery, University of Sheffield.

529 Wright, J. H. In business at Warrington.

529 Wyatt, H. S. M.A. 1899. Curate of St Mary's, Southampton, 1902–4. Rector of St Mary Major, Exeter, 1904.

529 Wiltshire, F. Curate-in-charge, St Simon's, Plymouth, 1900–3. Vicar of Bude Haven, Cornwall, 1903– .

140   APPENDIX I

539 Menzies, W. R. Ordained deacon (Rochester), 1899; priest, 1901. Assistant-Missioner at
     the College Mission, Battersea, 1899–1903. Curate of All Saints, Newton Heath, Man-
     chester (Rossall Mission), 1903–6. S.P.G. Missionary, Toungso, Burma, 1906– .
539 Moxon, R. S. M.A. 1901; B.D. 1908. Ordained deacon (Chester), 1899; priest, 1900.
     Master at Warrington Grammar School, 1899–1905. Curate of Stockton Heath, 1899–1902;
     of Northenden, 1899–1905. Master at King's School, Canterbury, 1905– .
539 Pridmore, C. A. M.A. 1901. Master at Rochester Grammar School. Died at Edinburgh,
     Sept. 4, 1905.
539 Punnett, R. C. M.A. 1902. Assistant to Professor Mackintosh at St Andrew's, 1899.
     Walsingham Medal, 1900. Thruston Medal, 1908. Demonstrator in Zoology. Super-
     intendent of the Museum of Zoology, 1909. Professor of Biology, 1910– .
539 Rogers, R. A. M.A. 1902. Solicitor at Bristol.
540 Simpson, P. B. M.A. 1902. Master at Chigwell School; at Merchant Taylors' School.
540 Sparenborg, H. A. Commission in King's Own R. Lancaster Regiment, 1900, on the nomi-
     nation of the Vice-Chancellor, during the South African War.
540 Spurrier, H. M.B., B.C. 1905.
540 Taylor, H. M.A. 1901. Ordained deacon (Ely), 1897; priest, 1898. Curate of Lavenham,
     1897–1900 and 1901–7; of St James's, Bury St Edmunds, 1900–1. Vicar of Great Barton,
     Suffolk, 1907–
540 Telford, E. D. M.A. 1902; B.C. 1903; F.R.C.S. Eng. 1903; M.R.C.S., L.R.C.P. 1900.
     Hon. Assistant Surgeon, Manchester Infirmary.
540 White, G. F. M.A. 1908. Master at St Clare's School, Walmer.
540 Wiener, H. M. M.A. 1901. Whewell Scholar, 1899. Called to the bar at Lincoln's Inn,
     May 1, 1901; Equity Draughtsman and Conveyancer.
540 Williams, L. In the Hand in Hand Life Office, 1900– .
540 Williams, R. F. M.B., B.C. 1901. Served in the South African War (Queen's Medal and
     five clasps; mentioned in Despatches, 1902). On the medical staff, North Nigeria.
540 Willoughby, W. M. M.B., B.C. 1900; M.D. 1904. D.P.H. 1902.
541 Wilson, T. E. M.A. 1904. Ordained deacon (Oxon.), 1900; priest, 1901. Assistant
     Chaplain of Bradfield College, 1900–9; Head-master of the Junior School, 1909– .
541 Winder, J. F. E. Master at his father's school, Eastbourne, 1900; at Stourbridge
     Grammar School, 1910.
541 Wolfe, E. D. C. Eastern Cadetship, 1897. In business at Canton, 1900.
541 Armbruster, H. E. H. B.A. 1901; M.A. 1910. District Resident, British Central Africa,
     1900– .
541 Ashton, R. Ll. Private Tutor in Paris. For a time Master at Blundell's School, Tiverton.
     Master at Camberwell Grammar School, 1910.
541 Barker, B. T. P. B.A. 1899; M.A. 1902. Nat. Sc. Tripos, Pt. II, Cl. 2, 1899. Walsingham
     Medal, 1902. Professor of Botany, University of South Wales.
541 Barker, L. E. H. R. M.B., B.C. 1903.
541 Blume, L. Admitted at one of the Inns of Court. Died in London, March 12, 1902.
541 Bradley, A. S. M.B., B.C. 1902; M.A. 1904. Surgeon R.N.
542 Braithwaite, W. D. In business at Calcutta. Previously organist at Bishop Cotton
     School, Simla.
542 Browne, G. B. Served in the South African War, with the Lancashire Fusiliers (Com-
     mission given by Lord Roberts: previously in Ceylon M.I.). Taken prisoner.
542 Bruce, T. Assistant to Professor Harrower at Aberdeen. Dele "At Ridley Hall,
     1898."
542 Bruce-Payne, O. D. B.A. 1898; M.A. 1902. Ordained deacon (Cant.), 1899; priest, 1900.
     Curate of Walmer, 1903–6; of St George the Martyr, Deal, 1906– .
542 Burlingham, R. E. M.A. 1902. Ordained deacon (Durham), 1899; priest, 1900. Curate
     at South Shields, 1899–1904; Halifax, 1904–9. Vicar of Holy Trinity, Ossett, Yorkshire,
     1909– .

546 Hall, A. L. B.A. 1899. Nat. Sc. Tripos, Pt. II, Cl. 1. Scholar, 1899. Harkness Scholar-
       ship, 1899. Master at Dulwich College, 1900. On the Geological Survey, Transvaal.
546 Biffen, R. H. Professor of Agricultural Botany, 1908.
546 Iles, J. H. M.A., M.B., B.C. 1907.
546 Stote, A. W. M.A. 1903. Ordained priest (Durham), 1899. Curate at Bournemouth,
       1900–5 ; Wimborne Minster, 1905–8. Vicar of Holy Trinity, Trowbridge, 1908–
546 Ackroyd, H. B.A. 1899 ; M.A. 1904 ; B.C. 1903 ; M.B. 1904 ; M.D. 1910. Nat. Sc. Tripos,
       Pt. I, Cl. 2, 1899. Research Scholar, B.M.A. Thruston Medal, 1911.
546 Balfour, A. M.D. Edin. (Gold Medal), 1898. Director of the Research Laboratory,
       Gordon College, Khartoum.
547 Beamish, R. de B. B.A. 1901. Called to the bar at Lincoln's Inn, Jan. 26, 1909.
547 Boardman, T. B. Served in the South African War.
547 Brackenbury, G. H. (Prendergast). B.A. 1899 ; M.A. 1905. Med. and Mod. Lang. Tripos,
       Cl. 2, 1899. Master at Hymers College, Hull, 1903 ; at Godolphin School, Hammer-
       smith ; at the Khedive's Schools, Cairo (1910).
547 Cardwell, L. W. Private tutor in Paris.
547 Carpenter, S. C. B.A. 1899 ; M.A. 1906. Class. Tripos, Pt. I, Cl. 2, 1899. Theol. Tripos,
       Pt. I, Cl. 1 (Distinguished), 1901. Carus Prize, 1902. Curate of St Paul, Newington,
       1902–4. Sub-Warden, Queen's College, Birmingham, 1904–6. Vice-Principal, Clergy
       Training School, Cambridge, 1906–8. Examining Chaplain to the Bishop of Manchester,
       1906–8. Select Preacher, 1907. Chaplain to Jesus College, 1907–8. Warden of the
       College Mission, Battersea, 1908– .
547 Chessex, R. E. A. B.A. 1899. Med. and Mod. Lang. Tripos, Cl. 2, 1899. Master at
       New College, Eastbourne ; at Park Holm, Buxton ; at the R.N. College, Dartmouth.
547 Clark, G. W. B.A. 1901 ; M.A. 1910. University athlete, 1899, 1900. For some years
       farming in Rhodesia.
547 Davidson, G. E. B.A. 1899 ; M.A., M.B., B.C. 1904.
548 Dodd, S. B.A. 1899 ; M.A. 1905 ; B.C. 1903 ; M.B. 1904. Nat. Sc. Tripos, Pt. I, Cl. 3,
       1899.
548 Donnell, J. H. B.A. 1899 ; M.B., B.C. 1903. Nat. Sc. Tripos, Pt. I, Cl. 3, 1899.
548 Fraser, D. Hammand (not Hammond). B.A. 1900 ; M.A. 1905 ; M.B., B.C. 1904.
548 Furber, L. G. H. In medical practice in London.
548 Gardner, E. B.A. 1899 ; M.B., B.C. 1904. Nat. Sc. Tripos, Pt. I, Cl 2, 1899.
548 Gretton, G. F. 7th Hariana Lancers, India.
548 Gubbay, M. M. S. B.A. 1899. Entered the I.C.S. 1899.
548 Harper-Smith, G. H. B.A. 1899 ; M.A. 1909. In medical practice.
548 Higgins, W. R. B.A. 1899 ; M.A. 1906 ; M.B., B.C. 1905.
548 Hignett, G. D. B.A. 1899. Master at Naish House Preparatory School, Somerset, 1900.
       Private Secretary to Lord Ampthill, 1906– .
548 Hirst, G. G. B.A. 1899. Indian Medical Service.
548 Hunter, H. M. B.A. 1899. In brewing business at Burton.
549 Jones, C. S. B.A. 1899 ; M.A. 1905. Ordained deacon (Bristol), 1902 ; priest, 1903.
       Curate at Swindon, 1902–4 ; Bath, 1904–7 ; Assistant Chaplain at Nice, 1907–8. Rector
       of Nettleton, Wilts, 1908–
549 Lillie, E. B.A. 1899. In business in New York.
549 Littlejohns, A. S. B.A. 1899. R.A.M.C.
549 Lowe, W. (Pickering Lowe). B.A. 1900 ; B.C. 1905 ; M.B. 1906. Nat. Sc. Tripos, Pt. II,
       Cl. 1, 1900. Shuttleworth Scholar, 1900.
549 MacBean, W. R. B.A. 1900. Math. Tripos, br. 9th Wrangler, 1900. Chartered accountant,
       Aberdeen and Buenos Ayres.
549 McCaskie, H. B. B.A. 1899 ; M.A. 1904 ; M.B. 1903 ; M.D. 1909. M.R.C.S., L.R.C.P.
       London, 1903.

549 Makin, E. Ll. B.A. 1899. 2nd Lieut., Manchester Regiment, 1900; afterwards 99th, Duke of Edinburgh's Regiment. Captain. Passed into the Staff College, 1910.
549 Marshall, F. Commission in the Army, 1900, on the nomination of the Vice-Chancellor, during the South African War.
549 Moore, A. R. B.A. 1899; M.A. 1905; M.B., B.C. 1904.
549 Morris, A. B.A. 1900. In medical practice.
549 Parry, C. F. B.A. 1899. Served in the South African War. Mine-Captain, Simmer and Jack Gold Mining Co., Germiston, Transvaal.
549 Payne, R. B.A. 1899. Nat. Sc. Tripos, Pt. I, Cl. 3, 1899. LL.B. 1900. Law Tripos, Pt. II, Cl. 3, 1900. On the staff of the South Indian Railway.
549 Pirie, R. S. Died at Richmond, Surrey, Oct. 26, 1905.
550 Porter, F. B.A. 1899; M.A. 1904. Math. Tripos, br. 19th Wrangler, 1899. Incorporated as B.A. at Worcester College, Oxford. Entered the Home Civil Service. In the Admiralty.
550 Reid, C. H. B.A. 1899. Math. Tripos, br. 12th Wrangler, 1899. 54th in the Open Competition I.C.S. 1900. Entered the I.C.S. 1901.
550 Russell, E. C. B.A. 1899. Class. Tripos, Pt. I, Cl. 2, 1899. For some time solicitor in London.' In the Asiatic Petroleum Company, Shanghai (1910).
550 Sington, H. S. In medical practice.
550 Spearman, B. B.A. 1899; M.A. 1907; M.B., B.C. 1902. Nat. Sc. Tripos, Pt. I, Cl. 2, 1899.
550 Thompson, T. W. B.A. 1899; M.A. 1906. In the engineering profession.
550 Thresher, W. H. B.A. 1899; M.A., B.C. 1905; M.B. 1906.
550 Thurlow, B. L. B.A. 1899; M.B., B.C. 1902; M.D. 1906.
550 Toppin, S. M. B.A. 1899. Commission in the Royal Artillery, 1900, on the nomination of the Vice-Chancellor, during the South African War.
550 West, P. C. In medical practice in Assam (1911).
550 Wicks, C. A. B.A. 1903; M.A. 1906. Nat. Sc. Tripos, Pt. 1, Cl. 2, 1899. Held Masterships at Penang; Chelmsford Grammar School (1903); in Ceylon (1911).
550 Williams, E. K. B.A. 1900. In medical practice.
551 Lancelot, R. L. B.A. 1898.
551 Akerman, C. B.A. 1900; M.A., M.B., B.C. 1906.
551 Andrews, S. H. B.A. 1901. Captain of the C.U.R.V. Shooting Eight.
551 Baker, F. R. B.A. 1901. In legal practice at Kokstad, Cape Colony.
551 Banks, J. H. B.A. 1900. Masterships at South-Eastern College, Ramsgate (1900); at Chigwell (1901); at Northampton (1909). Ordained deacon (Peterborough), 1909; priest, 1910. Curate of St Michael, Northampton, 1909– .
551 Blakelock, T. L. S. B.A. 1900; M.A. 1905. Solicitor at Rochdale. Died at Littleborough, Aug. 17, 1908.
551 Blakemore, T. R. B.A. 1900.
551 Chisholm, D. C. H. Commission in the Worcestershire Regiment, 1900, on the nomination of the Vice-Chancellor, during the South African War. On the Stock Exchange (1911).
551 Clarke, S. H. B.A. 1900; M.A 1906; M.B., B.C. 1905; M.D. 1910. Nat. Sc. Tripos, Pt. I, Cl. 3, 1900.
551 Cleminson, F. J. B.A. 1901; M.A. 1904; B.C. 1909. Shuttleworth Scholar, 1901. For some years took pupils in Cambridge.
552 Compton, G. C. Died May 6, 1899. *Caian*, VIII. 226.
552 Crowther, G. B.A. 1900.
552 Croysdale, J. H. B.A. 1901; M.A. 1905. Called to the bar at the Inner Temple, June 24, 1903. On the North-Eastern Circuit.
552 Daukes, S. H. B.A. 1900. M.B., B.C. 1905. Nat. Sc. Tripos, Pt. I, Cl. 2, 1900.

552   Dragten, F. R.   Law Tripos, Pt. I, Cl. 2, 1899 ; Pt. II, Cl. 2, 1900.   Held a Mastership.
      Called to the bar at Gray's Inn, 1907.   In legal practice in British Honduras.
552   Engleheart, P.   B.A. 1900.   Mech. Sc. Tripos, Pt. I, Cl. 2, 1900.   In the engineering
      profession.
552   Fagan, C. H. J.   B.A. 1900.   In medical practice.
552   Ferrers, E. B.   Scottish Rifles since 1899.   Wounded at Spion Kop, Natal, 1900.   Captain.
552   Fletcher, N. H.   Served in the South African War.
552   French, E. N.   Captain of the Boat Club, 1899.   Served in the South African War,
      Lincoln Regiment, 1900.
552   Gaskell, J. F.   B.A. 1900 ; M.A. 1904 ; M.B., B.C. 1907.   D.P.H. 1909.   Math. Tripos,
      Sen. Opt. 1900.   Elected to a Beit Research Fellowship, 1910.
552   Gordon, D'A. J.   For a short time Master at Parkgates School, Cheshire.
552   Gould, L. M.   B.A. 1900.   For some time Master at Parkgates School, Cheshire.   Editor
      of a newspaper in British Columbia (1910).
552   Haigh, B.   B.A. 1902.   In medical practice.
552   Hale, R. E. V.   B.A. 1901.
553   Hartree, C.   B.A. 1900.   Class. Tripos, Pt. II, Cl. 2, 1900.   Law Tripos, Pt. II, Cl. 2, 1901.
      Captain of the Boat Club, 1900.   Called to the bar at Lincoln's Inn, June 24, 1903.
      At the Chancery bar.
553   Ker, J. C.   B.A. 1900.   Math. Tripos, Sen. Opt. 1900.   Entered the I.C.S. 1902.
553   Kidd, E. S.   B.A. 1900 ; M.A. 1905.   Class. Tripos, Pt. I, Cl. 1, Div. 3, 1900.   Master at
      Bolton Grammar School, 1900–
553   Lloyd, I. G.   B.A. 1900.   Class. Tripos, Pt. I, Cl. 2, 1900.   Exhibitioner, 1899.   Entered
      the I.C.S. (Burma), 1902.
553   Marris, H. F.   B.A. 1900 ; M.A. 1904.   In medical practice.
553   Moorhouse, S.   Commission in the 21st Lancers, 1900, on the nomination of the Vice-
      Chancellor, during the South African War.
553   Owen, H. B.   B.C. 1906 ; M.B. 1907.   Medical Officer in Uganda.
553   Phillips, T. H. B.   Held tutorships.
553   Poignand, R. N.   B.A. 1900 ; M.B., B.C. 1905.
553   Rieu, H.   B.A. 1900 ; M.A. 1904.   Med. and Mod. Lang. Tripos, Cl. 3, 1900.   Master at
      Chigwell School ; at Merchant Taylors' School (1910).
553   Rigg, R.   B.A. 1900.   Law Tripos, Pt. I, Cl. 3, br. 15th, 1899.   M.P. for North Westmor-
      land, 1900 (youngest member of the House).   Resigned before the end of the session.
      Called to the bar at the Inner Temple, Jan. 26, 1899 (Irish Bar, Middle Temple,
      1902).   J.P.
553   Roberts, F. P.   B.A. 1900.
554   Sachse, F. A.   B.A. 1900.   Class. Tripos, Cl. I, Div. 3, 1900.   Entered the I.C.S.
      1902.
554   Simpson, W. H.   Kept eleven terms.   Poultry-farming (1910).
554   Tate, R. F.   B.A. 1900.   Med. and Mod. Lang. Tripos, Cl. 3, 1900.   Correspondent at
      Rome of the *Morning Leader*, 1901– .
554   Taylor, S. H. S.   B.A. 1900.   Nat. Sc. Tripos, Pt. I, Cl. 3, 1900.   In medical practice.
554   Ware, J.   B.A. 1900.   Class. Tripos, Pt. I, Cl. 1, Div. 3, 1900.
554   Warner, M.   B.A. 1902 ; M.A. 1905.   Ordained deacon (Ripon), 1903 ; priest, 1904.
      Curate at Laithkirk, 1903–4 ; Folkestone, 1904–5 ; Chaplain and Bursar, Ely Theol.
      College, 1905–8.   Mission priest in New Zealand, 1908– .   Served in the South African
      War as a member of the C.U.R.V. ; medal with clasps.
554   Wimpfheimer, M.   LL.B. 1900.   Law Tripos, Pt. I, Cl. 3, 1899 ; Pt. II, Cl. 3, 1900.
      Called to the bar at the Inner Temple, June 24, 1903.   On the Northern Circuit.
554   Woods, F. L.   B.A. 1900 ; M.B., B.C. 1905.
554   Jones, F. J.   B.A. 1903 ; M.A. 1906.

554   Guest, S. A.   B.A. 1900.   Math. Tripos, Sen. Opt. 1900.   Called to the bar at the Inner Temple, May 17, 1905.   On the South-Eastern Circuit.

555   Fitzjohn, T.   Kept four terms.   Worcestershire Regiment.   Captain.   Served in the South African War.

555   Keyser, L. E.   B.A. 1900.   Class. Tripos, Pt. II, Cl. 2, 1900.   In the Consular service.

555   Graham, C.   Admitted Jan. 8, 1898.   B.A. 1901; M.A. 1905.   Ordained deacon (Rochester), 1902; priest, 1903.   Curate of Gravesend, 1902-5.   Head-master and Assistant Chaplain R. Masonic School, 1905-6.   Chaplain R. N. 1906-

555   Findlay, A.   B.A. 1901.   Law Tripos, Pt. I, Cl. 2, 1900; Pt. II, Cl. 2, 1901.   In legal practice at Durban, Natal.

555   Pearson, H. H. W.   M.A. 1900; Sc.D. 1907.   Walsingham Medal, 1899.   In the Indian Department, Kew Gardens.   Professor of Botany at the South African College, Cape Town.

555   Simpson, J. C.   B.A. 1903 (as Research Student); M.A. 1907.   Previously M.D. Edin.   In practice at Cambridge.

555   Wimperis, H. E.   B.A. 1900 (through the Mechanical Sciences Tripos).   Hon. Mention for Smith's Prize, 1902.   Salomons Scholarship.   Enquirer to the Crown Agents for the Colonies, Downing Street.

555   Thomas, P. G.   B.A. 1900; M.A. 1904.   Med. and Mod. Lang. Tripos, Cl. 1 (with distinction in English), 1900.   Scholar, 1899.   Lecturer in English at Bedford College, University of London, 1906- .

555   Alexander, G. D.   B.A. 1903; B.C. 1908.

555   Barris, J. D.   B.A. 1901.   Nat. Sc. Tripos, Pt. I, Cl. 2, 1901.   In medical practice.

556   Bateman-Champain, J. N.   B.A. 1902; M.A. 1907.   Ordained deacon (Bristol), 1903; priest, 1904.   Curate of St Mary Redcliffe, Bristol, 1903-8.   Vicar of Germiston, Transvaal, 1909- .

556   Black, P.   B.A. 1901.   In medical practice.

556   Blanchard, N.   B.A. 1901; M.A. 1905.   Math. Tripos, 16th Wrangler, 1901.   In Assurance business in London.

556   Bottomley, C. C.   B.A. 1901.   Class. Tripos, Pt. I, Cl. 3, 1901.   Chapel Clerk, 1900-1.   Master at Louth Grammar School, 1901.   Ordained deacon (Newcastle-on-Tyne), 1904.   Curate of Benwell, 1904-5.   Died at Benwell, Sept. 29, 1905.

556   Braithwaite, C. F.   B.A. 1901.   Law Tripos, Pt. I, Cl. 3, 1900; Pt. II, Cl. 3, 1901.   In legal practice in Demarara.

556   Bright, W. A.   B.A. 1901.   Class. Tripos, Pt. I, Cl. 2, 1901.   Solicitor in London.

556   Broadbent, E. R.   Resided two terms.   Served in the South African War.   Commission in 8th Hussars, 1902.   Ranching in North America.

556   Brown, A.   B.A. 1901.   Math. Tripos, Pt. I, Senior Wrangler, 1901.   Scholar, 1898-1902.   Professor of Mathematics, South African College, Cape Town.

556   Brown, H. A.   B.A. 1901.   Math. Tripos, Pt. I, 3rd Wrangler, 1901.   Scholar, 1899-1902.   Scholar as select candidate for I.C.S. 1902.   College Prize for I.C.S.   Entered the I.C.S. 1903.   Bhaunagar Medal.

556   Bull, D. W. A.   B.A. 1901; M.B., B.C. 1908.   Nat. Sc. Tripos, Pt. I, Cl. 3, 1901.

556   Burgess, A. S.   B.A. 1901; M.A. 1907; M.B., B.C. 1909.   Nat. Sc. Tripos, Pt. I, Cl. 3, 1901.

557   Burne, B.   B.A. 1901; M.A. 1911.   Nat. Sc. Tripos, Pt. I, Cl. 2, 1901.   Exhibitioner, 1900.   Ph.D. Heidelberg.   Master at Holt Secondary School, Liverpool, 1907; at Coatham Grammar School, 1908- .

557   Burnell, E. W.   B.A. 1901.   Math. Tripos, Pt. I, Jun. Opt., 1901.   Ordained deacon (Manchester), 1902; priest, 1903.   Curate at Bury, 1902-7.   Domestic Chaplain to the Bishop of Wakefield, 1907-9.   Curate of Swinton, Lancashire, 1909- .

557   Chamberlain, D. A.   B.A. 1901.   In medical practice.

557 Cockin, R. P. B.A. 1901; M.A., M.B., B.C. 1906. Nat. Sc. Tripos, Pt. I, Cl. 3, 1901. Medical Officer in Nigeria; served in the Munshi Campaign, 1909; at Nicosia, Cyprus, 1910; in Southern Nigeria, 1910- . Brother of Maurice, IV (1) 13.

557 Cook, E. B. B.A. 1901. Nat. Sc. Tripos, Pt. I, Cl. 3, 1901.

557 Coulson, R. N. B.A. 1901; M.A. 1907. Nat. Sc. Tripos, Pt. I, Cl. 3, 1901. Captain "C" Company, C.U.R.V. In business.

557 Cunningham, N. R. B.A. 1901. In medical practice at Boksburg, Transvaal.

557 Dixon, F. N. B.A. 1901. Hist. Tripos, Pt. I, Cl. 1, 1900; Pt. II, Cl. 1, 1901. Scholar, 1899-1901. In the Exchequer and Audit Department.

557 Dobson, D. R. B.A. 1902; M.A. 1908. Acting Inspector of Cattle diseases, Egypt, 1905.

557 Dunn, T. W. N. B.A. 1902; M.A., M.B., B.C. 1906. Captain of the Boat Club, 1900-1.

557 Escolme, J. B. B.A. 1906. In scholastic work.

557 Fielding, E. F. B.A. 1901. Law Tripos, Pt. I, Cl. 3, 1900; Pt. II, Cl. 3, 1901. Solicitor at Bath.

557 Foster, B. le N. B.A. 1901; M.A. 1906. Nat. Sc. Tripos, Pt. I, Cl. 2, 1900. Scholar, 1899-1901. In business with his father.

557 Garnsey, E. B.A. 1901; LL.B. 1910. Nat. Sc. Tripos, Pt. I, Cl. 1, 1901. Exhibitioner, 1900; Scholar, 1901. Master at Merchant Taylors' School, 1901-3. Inspector for the Board of Agriculture, 1903- .

558 Hallowes, K. A. K. B.A. 1901. Nat. Sc. Tripos, Pt. I, Cl. 2, 1901; Pt. II, Cl. 3, 1902. On the Geological Survey of India.

558 Hewett, F. S. M.B., B.C. 1906; M.D. 1911.

558 Ilott, C. H. T. B.A. 1901; M.A. 1909; M.B., B.C. 1908.

558 Jackson, H. S. Commission in the Royal Artillery, 1900, on the nomination of the Vice-Chancellor, during the South African War.

558 Jones, A. S. Duncan. B.A. 1901; M.A. 1905. Or. Lang. Tripos, Cl. 2, 1901. Scholar, 1899-1901. Stewart of Rannoch Scholarship for Hebrew, 1899. Tyrwhitt Scholarship, 1902. Ordained deacon (Ely), 1904; priest, 1905. Chaplain and Lecturer, 1904. Fellow and Junior Dean, 1906- . Examining Chaplain to the Bishop of Lincoln, 1910- .

558 Keighley, W. G. M. Migrated to Trinity Hall. B.A. 1901.

558 Lee, C. S. B.A. 1905. In medical practice.

558 Lock, R. H. B.A. 1902; M.A. 1905; Sc.D. 1910. Nat. Sc. Tripos, Pt. I, Cl. 1, 1900; Pt. II, Cl. 1, 1902. Frank Smart Studentship, 1902-4. Drosier Fellow, 1904-10. Assistant Director of the Royal Botanical Garden, Peradeniya, Ceylon, 1908- . Married Bella, eldest daughter of the late Sidney Woolf, Q.C., July 7, 1910. Author.

558 Macfie, J. W. Scott. B.A. 1901. Nat. Sc. Tripos, Pt. I, Cl. 1, 1901; Pt. II, Cl. 1, 1902. Scholar, 1899-1902. B.Sc., M.B., Ch.B. Edin. (Honours). In medical practice.

558 Mackintosh, H. B.A. 1901. Class. Tripos, Pt. 1, Cl. 3, 1901.

558 McLean, D. B.A. 1901.

558 McLean, H. B.A. 1901. Nat. Sc. Tripos, Pt. I, Cl. 3, 1901.

558 Macpherson, D. G. B.A. 1901; M.A. 1906. Ordained deacon (Rochester), 1903; priest, 1904. Assistant Missioner at the College Mission, 1903-6. Curate of St Mary Redcliffe, Bristol, 1906-8. Vicar of Knighton, Herefordshire, 1908- .

558 Monro, H. E. B.A. 1901. Med. and Mod. Lang. Tripos, Cl. 3, 1901. Author: poems.

559 Palmer, C. E. B.A. 1901; M.A., M.B., B.C. 1905. Nat. Sc. Tripos, Pt. I, Cl. 2, 1901. Indian Medical Service.

559 Parkinson, P. R. B.A. 1901; M.B., B.C. 1907. Nat. Sc. Tripos, Pt. I, Cl. 3, 1910. Died at Burnley, May 23, 1910.

559 Phillips, M. B.A. 1901; M.A., M.B., B.C. 1909.

559 Poignand, C. W. B.A. 1901; M.A. 1907. Theol. Tripos, Pt. I, Cl. 3, 1901. Ordained deacon (York), 1903; priest, 1904. Curate at Whitby, 1903-9. Chaplain R.N. 1909- .

MASTERS

(Continued from Volume III)

NORMAN MACLEOD FERRERS

NORMAN MACLEOD FERRERS, thirty-second master (1880—1903), was the son and only child of Thomas Bromfield Ferrers[1], stockbroker, of London, and Lavinia, daughter of Alexander Macleod, of Harris. He was born Aug. 11, 1829, at Prinknash Park, Gloucestershire, a house at that time in occupation or possession of some member of his mother's family. He was educated at Eton for three years. Before entering as a freshman in 1847 he lived as a private pupil for about a year in the house of the Rev. Harvey Goodwin. Mr Goodwin had been a fellow of our College, but marrying early and thus losing his fellowship he settled in the town and soon became a distinguished private tutor. He was at the time vicar of St Edward's, Cambridge, but was best known as the author of a work on Elementary Mathematics, composed to meet the requirements of the new examination system. He was afterwards Dean of Ely, and Bishop of Carlisle. Mr Ferrers always retained an affectionate remembrance of the Bishop's personal character and intellectual powers.

Of his early College life no traditions seem to survive beyond a mere recollection of his remarkable powers of memory, as handed down by some of his contemporaries. He graduated in 1851 as senior wrangler; being also first Smith's prizeman of his year. Almost immediately after this he left Cambridge and went to London to study the Law. Apparently his ambition was to follow the precedent of a number of other senior wranglers of the old *régime* and become a judge. If so, he might very likely have succeeded, as he had in a high degree some of the qualifications for professional success at the English Bar.

---

[1] Thomas Bromfield Ferrers was son of Thomas Ferrers, of Westminster, and fifth in descent from William Ferrers, of Taplow Court, who seems to have been himself descended from Edmund Ferrers, 5th Baron, of Chartley. A full pedigree and account of the various descents is given in the *Ferrers Family History* (by Cecil S. F. Ferrers). The well-known economist, Henry Dunning Macleod, was a nephew of Mr T. B. Ferrers.

He remained in London for some years, and was actually called to the Bar in 1855 as a member of Lincoln's Inn.   But in 1856 changes had occurred in College which gave him the opportunity of ensuring an income at once, besides prospects for the future.   When he had been elected to a fellowship in 1852 there was at the time no opening for him in College.   But in the course of 1855 the two principal mathematical lecturers, Mr Croker and Mr Mackenzie, were preparing to leave, the one for a College living, the other for missionary work in Africa; and the Master, Dr Guest, thought it a good opportunity to secure the services of the man who was by far the best mathematician in the College.   This at once fixed his career for life.

He held the following College offices : Mathematical Lecturer, 1856—1880 ; Dean, 1860—1865 ; Tutor, 1865—1880.   In University business he was for many years very active.   He was a member of the Council of the Senate for 23 years, serving on various Boards and Syndicates, and he frequently examined for the Mathematical Tripos.   He was Vice-Chancellor 1884 and 1885.   In 1876 he was appointed a Governor of St Paul's School, and in 1885 a Governor of Eton College. In 1877 he was elected a Fellow of the Royal Society, and in 1883 received from the University of Glasgow the honorary degree of LL.D.   To the Cambridge degree of D.D. he proceeded in 1881, soon after he became Master.   On April 3, 1866, he married Emily, daughter of the Very Reverend John Lamb, D.D., Dean of Bristol and Master of Corpus Christi College.

Such in brief outline is the history of Dr Ferrers's academic life.   To characterise the man himself is a more difficult matter.   The impressions he left upon the members past and present of his own College, as well as upon other members of the University, were very various.   To the undergraduates in the Chapel on the day following his death a few telling words were spoken by the Bishop of Wellington, New Zealand, a Fellow of the College and one who had been undergraduate and Dean under Dr Ferrers as Tutor or Master, and these words may form a fitting preface to the remarks which follow : " I am permitted," said Bishop Wallis, " to speak a few sentences of the loss which our College is mourning to-day. It is hardly possible that many of you, my younger brothers, knew our late Master at all intimately; for you have seen him only in great bodily weakness.   To some even of us older men he was not well known, for his early days were lived in a time when it was held, whether rightly or wrongly I will not attempt to discuss, that the supreme ruler of a College, to whom was entrusted the discipline alike of teachers and of taught, ought not to come into close relations with those over whom he might some day be called to sit in judgment.   And further, his intense hatred of what was unreal or extravagant led him often to repress sternly any expression of his strongest feelings.   But there are among us those who knew and loved him—to me and to my father, with whom he was contemporary, he was always a true friend.   We who knew him in the hour of trouble, and saw how deeply he could grieve, were then able to discover his great tenderness of heart. He was a very just man, incapable of a mean or paltry act.   Above all, he was intolerant, in himself as in others, of pretentiousness and artificiality.   So we learned to honour him as one of the great teachers of this place who have tried to lead us, both by word and example, to speak and do only that which is true. He had great intellectual gifts, but he had also a child-like reverence for all that is unselfish and generous ; and he had the simple faith and trust of a child in God, whom he feared and for whom he wrought."

Others again of those who were in close touch with him were struck by the two intellectual gifts which he possessed in a high degree—the power of mathematical analysis and his remarkably retentive memory. Of his mathematical powers, so far as original work is concerned, more will be said presently. His memory for names and facts and the details of English literature, both in poetry and in prose, was quite astonishing. If, for instance, any quotation from Shakespeare were ventured upon in his presence, it would first, as a rule, be corrected, and then, if desired, the full context of it would be given. It seemed to his friends a matter of regret that, though he was in possession of such a magnificent mental instrument, the main work of his life—pure mathematics—should be just that in which memory was least of all required. Had he undertaken to write the history of any branch of mathematics, he would have found, in comparison with other writers, the prodigious advantage of being able to recall instantly and accurately the problems discussed by every previous author. He seemed, for instance, familiar with every problem and example which had ever been set in Cambridge.

He was singularly precise and conscientious in all matters of official routine, and never neglected to be present at committees or other meetings of which he was a member. He ranked through most of his College life as a reformer, and certainly was so in comparison with the seniors of his time. The first thing he did on returning to College was to reorganise the mathematical examinations on the plan of the Tripos. Every paper was carefully scrutinised by two examiners at a succession of meetings before it was finally passed. As a consequence the standard of the papers set in the College under his superintendence was considered to be high; so that it was generally worth while for a student to consult them as a source of good questions from which something out of the common could be learnt. As a lecturer he was simply admirable. By his clear and vivid exposition he let it be seen what a real difference there might be between a live lecturer and a printed text-book. A long series of pupils testified to his originality, his zeal which bred zeal, and his helpfulness. The ordinary undergraduate mathematical scholar gave them the highest praise of which his vocabulary would admit in saying that attendance at these lectures at any rate was as good as going to a private tutor. And there will be those who will recall gratefully the ungrudging pains with which as a work of love he forwarded their progress towards high wranglerships by his Long Vacation informal lectures. But all good things have their end; and whether it was that new generations have new shibboleths, or that the consciousness of a decline, however slight, in physical strength, deprived his work of some of its old vigour, it is certain that the time came when former Caians revisiting the College heard with blank astonishment that the mathematical scholars of the day did not go with the same enthusiasm to those lectures which in their time were reputed to be of the best in the University.

As a reformer in academic matters he was a typical representative of his era. He was keen for the removal of abuses, but seemed to care little for the preservation of the historic element in our ancient Colleges. As many have found in later days, what might once have been "conserved" it has been necessary in various ways, partially and expensively, to "restore." The old scholarship system had of course become by lapse of time seriously defective. Many of the endowments were confined, in accordance with ancient practice and sentiment, to Norfolk, as the native county of the donors. The most distinguished student of his year therefore did not always obtain the most valuable scholarship. The existence of grievances of this kind, with which perhaps he was not personally untouched, led Dr Ferrers to acquiesce in the action of the University Commissioners in 1860, by which all historic connexion of scholarships with the names of their founders was swept away. There is reason to believe that at a later stage of his life he came to sympathise with the tendency to reverse the previous policy and to value and respect the association of founders' names with the benefactions which they had created.

He also favoured and promoted other of the typical mid-Victorian reforms:— abolition of tests, universal extension of free competition and so forth. But beyond this he did not seem prepared to go. Like many reformers he was much of a conservative within his own domain. To him, as to many other prominent mathematicians, the Mathematical Tripos seemed the supreme glory of Cambridge, and to touch it was to lay one's hand on the Ark. The place therein assigned to any man was (except so far as the claims of the Classical Tripos were admitted) the necessary and sufficient test for election to a fellowship, and no further consideration of exceptional cases was to be admitted. It was not by his support, and probably against his will, that the principle was gradually established according to which distinction in any subject of academic study was in itself ground for recognition. At the same time, but in due subordination, he was willing to admit other subjects into the curriculum. It was, for instance, with his hearty co-operation that a permanent lectureship in the Moral Sciences, first held by Mr John Venn, President of the College from 1903, was established in the College in 1862. The scheme indeed found hardly any other supporters than himself at the time.

The important part which he played in University politics fell within a period which included some momentous changes in the history of the University. Like most reformers he had occasionally to experience rebuffs. He first came on to the Council of the Senate at a chance vacancy in 1865, but at the regular election in November 1866 he failed to secure election. The question of the admission of Nonconformists to Fellowships had in the meantime become prominent, and his liberal views on that subject were not acceptable to the majority of the electoral roll. This question formed the subject of active discussion during the following years, but the controversy was finally closed by the passing of the Tests Act in

1871. He was again rejected at the election of 1868, but in 1872 the position had changed and he was elected for a full period. Finally, in 1878, he was placed at the head of the poll and retained his seat for sixteen years, when his increasing illness obliged him to decline re-election.

The following account of his mathematical work is taken from the obituary notice contributed to the *Proceedings of the Royal Society* (Volume LXXV) by his friend, Dr E. J. Routh:

"His first book was called *Solutions of the Cambridge Senate House Problems for the Four Years* 1848—1851. In this he was assisted as joint author by J. S. Jackson, another Caius man and fifth wrangler in his own year.

Ferrers was also the author of a treatise on *Trilinear Co-ordinates*, published in 1861. These co-ordinates seem first to have been brought into notice in the University by some chapters in Salmon's *Conics*, but there was no regular treatise on the subject. Ferrers' book at once became one of the text-books much used for the Tripos examination. There was a second edition in 1866, and a third in 1876. The subject is, however, not now studied to the same extent.

At the request of the Master and Fellows of Caius College, Ferrers edited the *Mathematical Writings of George Green*, a man of consummate genius who was fourth wrangler in 1837, and afterwards Fellow of his own College. This important work was published in 1871, and rendered generally accessible a series of memoirs which have remained of fundamental importance in both pure and applied mathematics. These writings have also a special interest as the work of an almost untaught mathematician; a glance at the contents of the volume shows how much of the after progress of discovery had been anticipated by him, or has its roots in his work.

His treatise on *Spherical Harmonics*, published in 1877, presented many original features. The theory of ellipsoidal harmonics was first studied by Green and Lamé, who used different methods. In his last chapter Ferrers gives an account of these functions, using both methods and adding things of his own. He also illustrates their application by the problem of the attraction of a heterogeneous ellipsoid.

One of his early memoirs was on Sylvester's development of Poinsot's representation of the motion of a rigid body about a fixed point by means of a *material ellipsoid* whose centre is fixed and which rolls on a rough plane. This paper was read to the Royal Society in 1869, and printed in the *Transactions*. He investigates expressions for the pressure and friction, and arrives at a treatment of the problem different from that of Sylvester, in the course of which some other theorems presented themselves which were not without interest.

His contributions to the *Quarterly Journal* are too numerous to be discussed at any length. A complete list of his papers may be found in the Royal Society's *Catalogue of Scientific Papers*. We may, however, mention the headings of a few, to show the varied nature of his writings. In 1861 and 1862, he has a series of notes on trilinear and quadriplanar co-ordinates, the latter being probably preparatory to a treatise on *Quadriplanar Co-ordinates*, which he once informed the present writer he intended to publish. Then, in 1867, he investigates the envelope of the Simson or pedal line of a triangle, and shows that it is a three-cusped hypocycloid. In 1873, he has an extension of Lagrange's equations. In 1875, he has two good papers on hydro-dynamics. In the first, he supposes that a cylindrical vessel is constrained to move in a given manner with fluid inside and outside. He compares the problem to find the motion of the fluid with that to determine the potential of an attracting film, and finally uses the known results of the second problem to solve the first. In the second paper, he solves the same problem when the cylinder is replaced by an ellipsoidal vessel. The manner in which he treats this problem is different from and simpler than that of his predecessors Green and Clebsch in the same work.

These hydro-dynamical researches were allied to the theory of attractions, and accordingly we find him writing on the latter subject in 1877. The components of the attraction of a solid ellipsoid, whose strata of equal density were similar to the boundary, had been investigated by Poisson. Ferrers gave a method of deducing from these the potential of a solid ellipsoid whose density varies as $x^f y^g z^h$, which is easily applied when the integers f, g, h, are not large. He also explains a new device by which the potential of an ellipsoidal shell may be deduced from that of the contained solid.

Lastly, in 1882, he applied himself to study Kelvin's investigation of the law of distribution of electricity in equilibrium on an uninfluenced spherical bowl. In this he made the important addition of finding the potential at any point of space in zonal harmonics."

The period of his greatest vigour, in the College and in the University, was that which included the first ten years of his Tutorship, from 1865. In the winter of 1879 he felt the beginning of those symptoms of the rheumatoid arthritis which afterwards made him a complete cripple. He thought nothing of them at the time, but no remedies could stop the steady progress of the disease. In his later years he had lost the power of locomotion. He spent his vacations mainly at the Heacham residence, left by Dr Davy, Master 1803—1839, for the use of his successors in office. After he had held the laborious office of Vice-Chancellor in 1884 and 1885, his initiative in College business sensibly decreased, and the administration and direction of the College devolved almost wholly upon his colleagues. It was characteristic with him most loyally to support their policy and action. He died in Cambridge on January 31, 1903, at the age of 73. The burial service was read in the Chapel on February 4. After the service the body was, according to ancient custom, borne round the court headed by the choir and followed by members of the College and University. On arriving a second time at the Gate of Honour the choir parted on either side and sang softly the *Nunc Dimittis* while the body of the late Master passed through. His cremated remains were afterwards deposited beneath the floor of the Ante-chapel.

With the mastership of Dr Ferrers a new era had begun; the College was shortly to be governed under statutes differing in many important respects from those which they supplanted in 1882. A brief summary of the changes which came into operation by the statutes of 1882, followed by amendments in 1892 and 1897, is given in the *Biographical History*, Volume III, 153—4.

———————————

Dr Ferrers was succeeded by the Reverend ERNEST STEWART ROBERTS, M.A., who was elected on February 16, 1903.

The vacancy in the office of President was filled by the appointment of JOHN VENN, Sc.D. The appointment was made under the statutes previous to 1904, and the office is tenable by him till the next vacancy in the mastership. By the statutes of 1904 the appointment is made by a General Meeting for a period of three years.

APPENDIX III

ILLUSTRATIONS OF CERTAIN ANTIQUITIES AND PORTRAITS

PLATE.

In Vol. III. pp. 301—305 will be found a description and enumeration of the most interesting of the pieces of plate belonging to the College. The illustrations given in this volume are as follows:

Plate II.   *The cocoa-nut cup described in Vol. III. p. 302, No. 1.

Plate III.   *The cocoa-nut cup described in Vol. III. p. 302, No. 2.

Plate IV.   Dr Caius's *caduceus*, with the *pulvinar reverentiae*, described in Vol. III. p. 302, No. 3.

Plate V.   (a)   Archbishop Parker's Chalice and Cover. Described in Vol. III. p. 302, No. 4.

            (b)   Archbishop Parker's Flagon: Silver-gilt, 1571. Described in Vol. III. p. 303, No. 5.

            (c)   Flagon, silver-gilt, 1609. Presented by Richard Branthwaite and William Webb, nephews of Dr Branthwaite, the Master. Described in Vol. III. p. 303, No. 6.

            (d)   A sister flagon to the above.

Plate VI.   Lord Hopton's Camp plate, described in Vol. III. p. 303, No. 8.

In addition to the College Plate described in Vol. III. as being of chief interest, presentations have been made in recent years by the following: Mr J. Stanley Gardiner, Fellow, Dr A. M. Knight, late Fellow, Bishop of Rangoon, Dr A. S. F. Grünbaum, Mr H. T. Francis, late Fellow, the Rev. J. B. Lock, Bursar, Mr R. H. Lock, Fellow, Mrs Ferrers, widow of the late Master, Professor T. B. Wood, Fellow, Mr M. M. P. Muir, Fellow, Mr J. F. Cameron, Fellow, Mr T. H. Riches, Mr H. C. Haslam, Sir David Salomons, the Rev. A. G. Day, formerly Fellow and President, and Lord Robson of Jesmond, Honorary Fellow. Of these pieces of plate perhaps the most notable are the Rosewater Dish and Ewer, presented by the Rev. J. B. Lock and his son Mr R. H. Lock, both being Fellows at the same time, and the Silver-gilt Cup presented by Sir David Salomons, originally a wedding present made by the late Queen Victoria to the Duke of

---

* Not improbably the gift of Bishop Goldwell, of Norwich, who died in 1498.

Sussex. In 1909 Mr E. G. Gallop, Fellow, presented to the Combination Room a handsome grandfather clock.

THE ASTROLABES.

Plate VII.   The older Astrolabe, exterior.

Plate VIII.   do.   do.   interior.

Plate lX.   The leather case containing it.

Plate X.   The later Astrolabe, exterior.

Plate XI.   do.   do.   interior.

These, the first of which may be the oldest of our possessions, are described in Vol. III. p. 194 sq., and, also by Dr Venn, in the *Caian*, Vol. VI. pp. 34 sqq.

PICTURES.

The portraits in the possession of the College to 1901 were enumerated and described in Vol. III. pp. 291—297, according to their place in the Lodge, the Hall, the Combination Room, the Staircase and the Library respectively. As they have recently been rearranged and are liable to rearrangement in the future, no account is here taken of their present position.   In Vol. III. are given a reproduction of the portrait of Dr Caius in the Hall (p. 294, No. 30) and a photograph of Dr John Venn (frontispiece).   In the present Volume are added :

Plate   I   (Frontispiece). The portrait of Dr Caius in the Lodge (Vol. III. p. 291, No. 1).

Plate XII.   The portrait of Robert Trapps (Vol. III. p. 294, No. 37).

Plate XIII.   The portrait of Joan Trapps (Vol. III. p. 295, No. 39).

Plate XIV.   The portrait of Joyce Frankland (Vol. III. p. 295, No. 39).

Plate XV.   The portrait of William Harvey (Vol. III. p. 292, No. 17).
    Accompanying this is

Plate XVI.   A facsimile of the admission register of William Harvey in 1593, which may serve as a type of the entries at that period. The text (expanded) is

Gul(ielmus) Harvie filius Thomæ Harvie, yeoman, Cantua-
rius ex oppido Folkestone, educat(us) in ludo l(it)erario Cantuaren(si)
ann(os) nat(us) 16. Admissus est Pensionarius minor [in] Com(meatu)
Scholar(ium) ult(imo) die Maii 1593 sub tutela M(a)g(ist)ri Geo(rgii)   iij[s] iiij[d]
Estey Coll(eg)ii socii, qui pro eo fidejubet   *Solvit*   x
pro ingressu suo in Collegium——

Next follow three portraits by distinguished artists :

Plate XVII.   Dr John Smith, Master : by Sir Joshua Reynolds (Vol. III. p. 292, No. 11).

Plate XVIII.   Dr Belward, Master : by Opie (Vol. III. p. 292, No. 12).

Plate XIX.   Dr Davy, Master : by Opie (Vol. III. p. 292, No. 13).

Since 1899 the following have been added :

Portrait of the Rev. E. S. Roberts, Master, painted in 1904 by Arthur Hacker, A.R.A., and presented to the College by William Munro Tapp, LL.D.

Portrait of the Rev. H. B. Swete, D.D., Fellow, Regius Professor of Divinity, painted in 1906 by Hugh Rivière, and presented to the College by subscribers.

Portrait of T. Clifford Allbutt, M.D., F.R.S., Regius Professor of Physic, painted in 1907 by Sir George Reid, P.R.S.A., and presented to the College by subscribers.

Portrait of Francis Glisson, M.D., Regius Professor of Physic, 1636–77. A copy of the original in the Royal College of Physicians : presented by the President and Fellows of the Royal College of Physicians in 1911.

A crayon portrait by Strang of Henry Thomas Francis, late Fellow.

A crayon portrait by Stevenson, a Danish artist, of the Rev. A. G. Day, formerly Fellow and President, bequeathed by him to the College.

A bust of John Hookham Frere (see Vol. II. 114) has also been added and is placed in the Library.

APPENDIX IV

NEW BUILDINGS, RESTORATIONS, AND ALTERATIONS SINCE THE PUBLICATION OF VOL. III. IN 1901

St Michael's Court (Plates XX, XXI).

In Vol. III. p. 148 sq., was recorded the acquisition by purchase of the south side of Rose Crescent and its conversion into College Rooms in the year 1887. The number of sets obtained was about forty-eight. The old doors of the separate houses on the Rose Crescent side were blocked up and seven entrances to staircases were made on the churchyard side, opening into a continuous gangway. At the Trinity Street end there was a Porter's Lodge. The external appearance of the very unattractive houses remained practically unaltered. The object of the alterations was to make the building serviceable until the time should have arrived for rebuilding and it was contemplated that about twenty years would pass before there would be a reasonable prospect of placing on the site a new building worthy of the traditions of the College. But towards the end of the last century, opinion took shape very decidedly in favour of rebuilding at the earliest possible opportunity, and the demolition of the old buildings was begun in 1901, fourteen years after their conversion for College purposes. The architect was Mr (now Sir) Aston Webb, with whom was associated his partner, Mr Ingress Bell. Mr Webb had good reason to be satisfied with his first piece of University work. The contractors were Messrs Kerridge and Shaw.

Mr Webb had a peculiarly difficult problem to solve. He was desired to respect ancient rights of light enjoyed by the neighbouring properties, and it was deemed necessary that, with the exception of a strip of ground about 18 inches broad along the Trinity Street frontage, sacrificed to the widening of the street, the ground-plan of the old Rose Crescent houses should be almost exactly adhered to. It demanded, as was remarked in Vol. XI. of the *Caian,* some patient ingenuity to make the most of this irregular figure in fitting the requirements of the College to its shape. But, in compensation, the elevations of the new block have received a variety of treatment which adds naturally and materially to its picturesqueness. The photograph (Plate XX) shows the lofty tower-like end of the range abutting on Trinity Street. The design generally follows that development of the later native Gothic, which is traditionally associated with collegiate buildings and which admirably meets their requirements. The sixteenth century originals have not been however mechanically followed, but an attempt has been made to imprint upon their general form and character a distinctive treatment marking them as the work of the twentieth century.

As regards the internal planning and arrangement of the rooms the task of the architect was materially lightened by the thoughtful care and ingenuity of the Bursar, the Rev. J. B. Lock. In fact the whole design of the interior may be said to be his. The plans of College buildings of various periods had been studied with a view to avoiding the repetition of errors in the new building. And the smooth working of the whole undertaking was due in great measure to his unremitting zeal and watchfulness.

Access to the sets of rooms is given by six staircases (see Plan, Plate XXI). The entrance to each has a character of its own and some of them lend themselves to varieties of carved adornment. The spectator is struck at once by the absence of anything that savours of stencil-work or monotonous repetition. There is an abundant display of heraldic devices, of which a detailed account is given in the *Caian*, Vol. XVII. pp. 94—106, 181—9. All the sitting-rooms face south or west; bedrooms and staircases are on the Rose Crescent side. The treatment of that portion of the building which faces Rose Crescent is singularly successful. At the corners in the Trinity Street front are niches containing statues of Sir Thomas Gresham, founder of the Royal Exchange, and William Harvey, discoverer of the circulation of the blood; a third niche facing the porch of St Michael's Church contains a statue of Archbishop Colton of Armagh, the first Master of Gonville Hall. Over the entrance in Trinity Street is the following inscription, taken from the Grant of Arms made to Dr Caius:

Ex prudentia et litteris virtutis petra firmatis immortalitas: "*that is to say, by wisdome & lerning graffed in grace & vertue men cum to immortalite.*"

On the roof over the entrance is a flag-staff supported by an open cupola of oak. This addition has been freely criticised, but we may be content to think that in this matter the judgment of the architect, who has been so eminently successful in the general design, will not be found to have erred.

The builders' contract for the rebuilding was £26,400.

A brief account of the purchase of the other property adjoining the churchyard of St Michael's, and the use which has been made of it, will be found in Part 2 of this Volume.

The New Combination Rooms (Plate XXII).

Between the Old Combination Room over the vestibule in the Gonville Court and the Master's Lodge, the building contains a ground floor, a first floor and an attic floor. The vicissitudes in the history of this block are sufficiently described in Vol. III. pp. 188 sqq., 195 sq. The later history may be briefly summed up as follows.

Ground floor. In connexion with the extension of the Lodge westward in 1853–4 the ground floor of the block, which had been used as an occasional dining-room of the Lodge, was given up and converted into two sets of chambers for students. In 1896 the southern of these sets was adapted for a Bachelors' Combination Room. In 1909 the whole of the ground floor was cleared and made into a single room to be used as a Junior Combination Room. It is decorated with the panelling removèd in 1908 from the Hall. In the south-west corner is a hinged panel arranged to show an old pointed doorway (which had been plastered up in 1853–4) leading to the turret staircase demolished in the alterations of 1795.

First floor. This floor contained the ancient Library dating from 1441, and it was approached both from the Lodge by the turret staircase alluded to above and from the Combination Room (see Vol. III. pp. 188 sqq.). In 1854, when the books were removed to the newly-built Library in the north-west corner of the College, this floor was utilised by the construction of two sets of students' rooms. In 1868 these were incorporated in the Lodge. In 1891 the northern set was converted into an additional Combination Room for the Fellows; and finally in 1905 the southern set also was added to the Combination Room and the whole area appropriated for this purpose under the direction of Mr Arnold Mitchell as architect. The ancient beams and joists forming the ceiling, most of which were of chestnut, had been obscured by a plaster ceiling in 1854 and were again exposed and carefully restored and strengthened. Two of the principal crossbeams are of oak and are moulded in the style of the fifteenth century; these are probably the main timbers in the ceiling of the Library of 1441, for they divide the ceiling into three equal portions. The additional chestnut beams may have been added by Dr Caius, as there is evidence that alterations in the attics above the Library were made at the time of the building of the Caius Court. The design of the fireplaces was copied from that of one discovered in an attic of the Lodge in the Caius building. The panelling, the gift jointly of the Rev. J. B. Lock, Bursar, and Dr H. K. Anderson, is of seasoned oak, procured by the contractor, Mr Sindall, from the Duke of Wellington battleship, the flagship in the Baltic during the Crimean War; and a new floor of polished oak was laid down.

Attic. The Attic floor had been used up to 1903 for servants' bedrooms in the Lodge. On a change in the Mastership in that year they ceased to be used for this purpose and the space was taken over by the College. The roof was raised without altering the appearance from the Court and a commodious set of rooms was constructed, the approach being from the upper landing of the Fellows' approach to the Hall. When the Combination Room below was enlarged, in 1905, the rooms in the Attic were again transferred to the Lodge for guest chambers.

The cost of the alterations of this portion of the building was £996.

THE HALL (PLATES XXIII, XXIV).

In 1908 it was decided to make very considerable alterations in the internal decoration of the Hall, which had been built in 1853–4 from the plans of Mr Salvin. It had been felt for some years past that the internal decoration was hardly worthy of the College. Accordingly five distinguished architects were invited to give advice and in the end the designs of Mr Edward Warren, F.R.I.B.A., were selected. In arriving at a final decision the Governing Body of the College were much impressed and encouraged by the liberality of former members who had unasked contributed £1700, since increased to £2000, towards the cost of the proposed decoration.

The alterations effected may be briefly described thus. The sills of the windows on each side and at the south end were raised, so that the length of the windows was diminished by one-third. The panelling of 1854 was replaced by English oak panelling of a more dignified height; the large oriel window at the south-west was altered; the tops and the mouldings of all the windows were improved in appearance; and a fine carved screen, with a gallery, was erected at the north end. The interspaces of the roof, between the principals, were boarded, and subdivided by broad ribs, with carved bosses at their inter-sections; the panels thus formed were painted white. On the roof-timbers, on the panelling at the south end, and on the gallery are placed heraldic shields. Beneath the gallery is an inscription EX DONO THOMAE HENRICI RICHES, A.M. In the south window are two rows of heraldic shields, the upper representing the coats of arms of five bishops, the lower those of five judges. Some of the windows on the west side also contain coats of arms[1].

Some of the shields on the roof-timbers call for a special note. While the Hall was being thus decorated, the wish was naturally felt to revive, as far as possible, some of the old associations in the way of heraldic decoration. One

[1] The following, to be added to as opportunity occurs, are the persons whose arms have so far (1911) been placed in the windows: William Lyndwood, Bishop of St David's, 1442—6; Jeremy Taylor, Bishop of Down and Connor, 1661—7; John Cosin, Bishop of Durham, 1660—72; Thomas Gooch, Master, Bishop of Ely, 1748—54; Harvey Goodwin, Bishop of Carlisle, 1869—91; Richard Baggallay, Lord Justice of Appeal, 1875—88; William Baliol Brett, Viscount Esher, Master of the Rolls, 1883—97; Edward Thurlow, Lord Chancellor, 1878—92; Henry Bickersteth, Master of the Rolls, 1836—51; Edward Hall Alderson, Baron of the Exchequer, 1834—57; Sir Richard Malins, Vice-Chancellor, 1866—82; Sir John Pearson, Chancery Judge, 1882—6; Sir Matthew Ingle Joyce, Chancery Judge, 1900— ; William Hamilton Yatman (M.A. 1844), Benefactor; Francis Gray Smart (M.A. 1870), Benefactor; Charles Henry Monro, Fellow, Benefactor, died 1908; Sir David Salomons, Bart. (M.A. 1877), Benefactor; John Venn, President, 1903— ; John Lyon, Founder of Harrow School; Francis Glisson, R.P.P., 1636—77.

Among the contributors to the cost of this work are (1) the living representatives of Bishop Goodwin, Lord Justice Baggallay, Baron Alderson, Vice-Chancellor Malins, Mr Justice Pearson; (2) Mr Justice Joyce, Mr Yatman, Mr Smart, Sir D. Salomons, Dr H. K. Anderson, Professor J. Stanley Gardiner.

obstacle here, of course, was the change of destination of some of the buildings concerned. The ancient Library had been converted into a Combination Room : the ancient Hall into a Library : the existing Hall was an entirely new building. It was decided that the actual purpose to which the room was devoted should decide the selection, rather than the site or former usage. Accordingly the names of the donors of windows, as well as of those who aided in the building of the ancient Hall, have been as far as possible preserved in the recent decoration of the present Hall.

The principle on which they have been arranged is as follows. On the tie-beams, at the top of the roof, there is a double row, one set facing to the north, the other to the south. The former comprise the names Sponne, Clynt, Warner, Crouch, Busby, Barwick. It will be noticed that these display merely names, without armorial bearings. They commemorate former fellows and others, who, as far as can be ascertained, had no right to arms. The first four were donors of windows in the ancient Hall, as Dr Caius records. Busby and Barwick are remembered as having been, with Bishop Shaxton, the first to provide funds for warming the building (see III. 108).

Facing to the south, we have, in the same order, the coats of arms of Boleyn, Shaxton, Paston, and Guest, and two scrolls for Chapman and Wortley. Shaxton, Bishop of Salisbury, contributed to the warming of the building: Sir Will. Paston gave £100 in 1606 towards rebuilding the Hall : Dr Chapman and Dr Guest, successively Masters of the College, contributed generously towards the erection of the existing building : Mr Wortley, former fellow, left a large sum, which was employed partly in refacing the side facing the court.

More will be found about all these benefactors in the previous volumes of the *Biographical History*. There are various other coats of arms on the walls of the Hall. But as the benefactors and celebrities thus recorded are not, like the preceding, in any special way connected with the history of the building they hardly need special enumeration here.

The cost of the alterations in the Hall was £3800.

APPROACHES TO THE HALL.

The vestibule entrance from the Gonville Court was panelled with oak in 1909. An unsightly projection of wall separating the fellows' stairway from that of the undergraduates was removed. The steep stone staircases leading to the two ends of the Hall were demolished and teak staircases of an easier gradient substituted, the walls from bottom to top being panelled with oak and the shape of the windows altered. A new butler's pantry was constructed on the first landing and the old pantry on the north side of the vestibule remodelled for a set of student's rooms.

The history of the ancient Hall of 1441, occupying the space between the Combination Room and Trinity Lane on the west side of the Gonville Court, is given by Dr Venn in Vol. III. pp. 176 sqq. An account of the restoration of this Hall and its dedication for the purposes of Library extension, the most interesting of all the alterations of this period, was contributed to *The Caian*, Vol. XIX. pp. 239—244, by the Bursar, the Rev. J. B. Lock, whose description furnishes the substance of the following remarks.

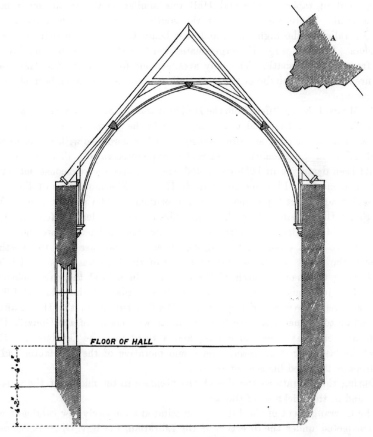

FLOOR OF HALL

From Vol. III. p. 148 it will be seen that the Tutor's House, provided in 1886 by the absorption and reconstruction of certain sets of rooms, occupied part of the space on which stood the ancient Hall, dismantled in 1854-5 and converted into dwelling rooms. The munificent bequest made to the College in 1909 by Charles Henry Monro, Senior Fellow, who died in 1908, made it possible to carry out a scheme for the much needed extension of the Library. Mr Monro's bequest was not fettered by any conditions, but it was known that he had expressed the wish that the College Library should benefit by his gift. Accordingly it was decided to enlarge the existing Library by the addition to it of the restored Hall and to defray the cost in large part from the Monro benefaction, the extension bearing the name of the "Monro Library."

The Hall then which has been restored was 48 feet long, 24 feet wide, and about 17 feet high to the cornice of the ceiling[1]. The floor was on arches, and was about 5 feet above the ground level. Under the Hall was a cellar about 7 feet high, used as a Buttery and Store room for sedge. It is worthy of record that the arrangement of tables in the Old Hall was similar to the arrangement in the present Hall. There was a dais at the south end on which was the Fellows' Table; parallel to the high Table and just below the dais was a shorter table for Bachelors. The tables for Undergraduates were in three rows running down the Hall from north to south. The only arrangement for warming the Hall was an open fireplace in the middle of the west wall, which is said to have been singularly ineffective.

The Monro Library differs from the Hall as it was in 1853 in having the principals and purlins of the roof exposed, thus going back to the roof as it was before the year 1763, when a plaster waggon ceiling was inserted in accordance with the taste of the period. Four of the principals of the roof were restored *in situ*. The fact that they had not been destroyed in 1853 was noted when the attics were reconstructed in the adaptations made in 1886 for the Tutor's House. The mouldings of the cornice and purlins are exact reproductions of the originals. The present floor is 5 feet higher than the old stone floor. The old stairs to the Hall leading from the north-west corner of the Gonville Court were of stone and consisted of two short flights of about five steps each. A door opened from the staircase into the north-east corner of the Hall. In the north-west corner of the Hall was a door which led to the kitchen; traces of the arch of the door remain behind the new bookshelves. A new door just south of this connects the two portions of the enlarged Library. Of three other new doors one opens on to the first landing of the Hall staircase; a second on to the new staircase from the north-west corner of the Gonville Court, which also serves as access to rooms; and a third into the Combination Room. Above the last door is an inscription commemorative of the Benefactor and over the fireplace is placed his coat of arms.

During the alterations the flue of the fireplace in the middle of the west wall was found in the thickness of the wall.

The rearrangement of the Library necessitated an entirely new catalogue which was completed under the direction of the Librarian, the Rev. G. A. S. Schneider, assisted by members of the staff of the University Library. A new edition of the Catalogue of Manuscripts had been generously undertaken and finished in 1908 by Dr M. R. James, the learned Provost of King's College.

---

[1] By kind permission of the Syndics of the University Press a section is given on p. 165 of Gonville Hall measured and drawn by Professor Willis.

The total cost of the reconstruction of the approaches, and of the Library extension was £9283. The expenses of the general catalogue amounted to £300 and of publishing the manuscript catalogue to £340.

The work was carried out under the direction of Mr Warren, previously mentioned in connexion with the re-decoration of the Hall built by Salvin in 1854.

BATHS AND HEATING APPARATUS.

In 1904 hot and cold baths were constructed in a basement in the rebuilt St Michael's Court. A further set of baths was made in 1907 under Staircase N in the Tree Court; and in 1909 a third set in the basement at the north-west corner of the Gonville Court. In the same year, in an excavated space beneath the vestibule was installed a furnace for supplying hot water to radiators for warming the Library, the Lodge and the Chapel.

ADDITIONAL ROOMS IN TRINITY STREET.

In 1910 eight additional sets of rooms were provided by adapting the first and upper floors of the two houses in Trinity Street fronting the Porter's Lodge. Behind these are the Bendall Library (installed in the Lecture Room purchased from Trinity College in 1894; see IV (2)) and two Lecture Rooms purchased in 1909. Below these are basements used for the storage and cleaning of bicycles, and approached by a sloping passage.

THE CHAPEL.

While the panelling was temporarily removed in 1909 for the insertion of radiators, remains were discovered of the sills of the original windows (see Vol. III.) at a lower level than those of the existing windows, and on the south side just west of the monument of Dr Legge was found the remains of the ancient piscina, which thus marks the beginning of the sanctuary as it was before the lengthening described in Vol. III. p. 161.

Brasses in memory of the following have been placed in the ante-chapel: the Rev. B. H. Drury (*Biogr. Hist.* II. 235); R. L. Bensly (II. 301); N. M. Ferrers, our late Master; and C. H. Monro (see IV (1) 166).

APPENDIX V

Frederick Benjamin D'Elwood Ramadge, Barrister at Law, formerly Fellow of the College, who died on April 15, 1902, bequeathed to the College the sum of £2000, which was appropriated for the purpose of establishing the Ramadge Studentship intended primarily for the encouragement of research in Legal History.

Christopher James, Barrister at Law, formerly Fellow of the College, in 1904 gave anonymously to the College the sum of £2000, which has since been set apart as the 'Christopher James Fund' for the purposes of the Studentship Fund. Before his death in December, 1910, he gave to the College £500 for the erection of a clock with bells.

William Hamilton Yatman, M.A., of St George's, West Cliff, Bournemouth, in 1905 gave to the College £1000 for the establishment of the Yatman Exhibition, to be awarded to candidates for Holy Orders.

Among the contributors to the re-decoration of the Hall were Mr T. H. Riches, who gave £1000 and Sir Dorab Tata, who gave £500. Mr Francis G. Smart and Sir David Salomons, Bart., were also substantial contributors both to this object and to the Library Extension.

Mr George Siddle, of Klerksdorp, Transvaal, gave £100 to found a prize in memory of his son George Ludorf Siddle, B.A., who died on September 24, 1908, in London.

Charles Henry Monro, Senior Fellow of the College, who died on February 13, 1908, left his estate to the College. By his benefaction it has been possible to create a fellowship, to establish a Lectureship in Celtic of the annual value of £100, and to carry out the extension of the Library described on p. 165 sq. The sum of £1000 also was presented to the Squire Law Library to form a "Monro Fund" for the purpose of purchasing foreign Law works.

Mrs Marke Wood of Liverpool in 1909 gave £300 to provide an annual Medal for an Essay on a military subject in memory of her son James Marke Wood, B.A., who died on May 14, 1903.

The Reverend William Symonds, Honorary Canon of Chester Cathedral, and Rector of Stockport, in 1910, through a Bill promoted by the Ecclesiastical Commissioners, presented to the College, subject to the right reserved to him or his family to make the next presentation, the advowson of the Rectory of Stockport.

Plate II

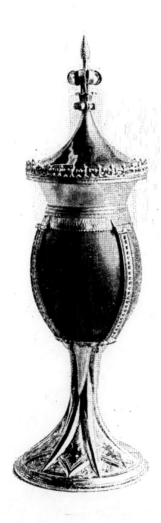

Cocoa-nut cup

Plate III

Cocoa-nut cup

Plate IV

D · Caius's *caduceus* and the *pulv nar reveren iae*

Plate V

(a)   (b)   (c)   (d)

(a) Archbishop Parker's Chalice and Cover   (b) Archbishop Parker's Flagon

(c) Branthwaite and Webb Flagon   (d) A sister Flagon to the above

Plate VI

Lord Hopton's Camp p ate

Plate VII

The Older Astrolabe, exterior

Plate VIII

The Older Astrolabe, interior

Plate IX

The leather case containing the Older Astrolabe

Plate X

The later Astrolabe, exterior

Plate XI

The later Astrolabe, interior

Plate XII

ROBERT TRAPPS

Plate XIII

JOAN TRAPPS

Plate XIV

JOYCE FRANKLAND

Plate XV

WILLIAM HARVEY

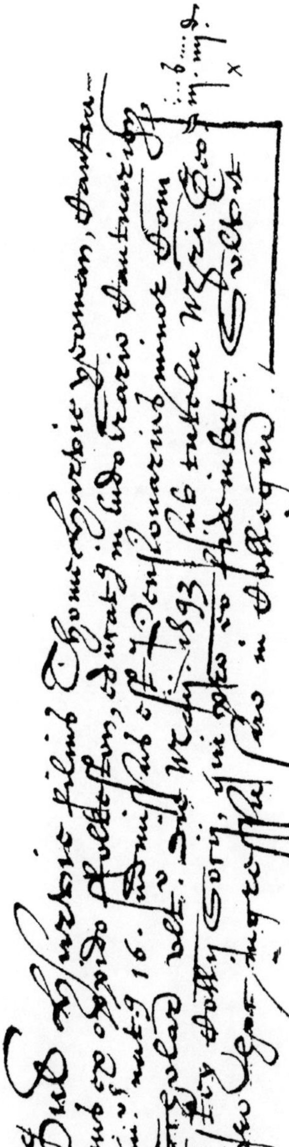

Plate XVI

Facsimile of adm ss on register of William Harvey n 1593

Plate XVII

JOHN SMITH,
Master, by Sir Joshua Reynolds, P.R.A.

Plate XVIII

DR BELWARD, ·
Master, by John Opie, R.A.

Plate XIX

DR DAVY,

Master, by John Opie, R.A.

St Michael's Court

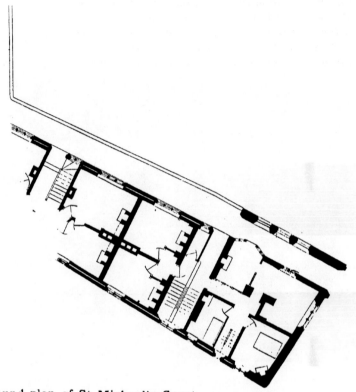

Ground-plan of St Michael's Court

Plate XXII

The new Fellows' Comb nat on Room

Plate XXIII

The Hall, looking South

Plate XXIV

The Hall, looking North

Plate XXV

The Monro Library

INDEX TO VOL. IV, PART 1

PART II

CHRONICLE OF THE ESTATES

OF

GONVILLE AND CAIUS COLLEGE

COMPILED BY

EDWARD J. GROSS, M.A.,

SENIOR FELLOW AND FORMERLY BURSAR

" Mony littles mak a muckle."

HISLOP.

PREFACE

I have to acknowledge much assistance from the Master and many of the Fellows: especially has Dr Venn been ever ready to give his advice and decipher ancient documents, and Mr Buckland to render help on legal and historical points such as that in the footnote on page 80. For an account of the legislation in 1391 referred to on page 45 I am indebted to the late Professor Maitland. From the late Dr W. Bensly I received various pieces of information derived from the Registry of the Norwich Diocese. Similar matter was obtained through the Incumbents of the College Livings from their Parish records, especially the terriers presented at the Visitations of the Bishops of Norwich.

Outside the documents and books in the College Treasury my principal sources of information have been the Tithe and Enclosure Awards in the Parishes in which our property is situated.

INTRODUCTION

As explained by Dr Venn in his chapter on the College Records (Vol. III, pp. 265–268) the materials for an account of the management of the estates of the College during the first 250 or 300 years of its existence are but scanty.

We have the conveyances to the College and other evidences of title conveniently arranged in the Treasury and admirably summarised and catalogued in the *Registrum Magnum*.

The *Bursar's Indentures* (Venn, Vol. III, p. 266) were drawn up half-yearly by the Master, as Bursar, and each gives the debts owed by and to the College on the day on which it was drawn up. They are thus the exact complement of the Bursar's Books, which give the sums actually paid by and to the College during each half-year.

In the *Bursar's Books*, beginning with 1609, we have a list each half-year of the various estates of the College. At first they were arranged somewhat in the order in which they came into the possession of the College—a very interesting arrangement,—the later estates being added at the end. In the year 1697 they come in the alphabetical order of the tenants' names. This system, happily, was soon (1727) changed, and that at present in use was adopted, of giving the estates in the alphabetical order of the names of the places, in which they were situated.

Benefactions. Certain estates given by particular benefactors (after the time of Dr Caius) were not thus entered, but had account books of their own, in which were set out the receipts from them and the expenditure on account of them. These Benefactions usually had conditions as to how the receipts were to be employed—generally in fixed payments. So that, when the annual receipts increased, the balances in these rolled up considerably and formed part of our present " Reserve Fund."

In the *Gesta* (Venn, Vol. III, p. 264), of which the clearly written copies begin at 1650, are found all orders of the College relating to the acquisition of the estates and to any alterations respecting them.

Lease Books. We have copies of all leases of estates from 1579 onwards, and of several leases granted in previous years in the reigns of Henry VIII, Mary and Elizabeth.

C IV 2

Various *Survey Books* give the particulars of the several estates at different times. Two systematic sets of surveys were compiled by Dr Brady, Master, and J. Smith, at first Bursar and afterwards Master. All other surveys were made by professional surveyors at irregular intervals as occasion required.

An inspection of the Bursar's Indentures shows that before the Mastership of Caius the College had no working cash balance at its command. It generally happened that at the dates, on which these indentures were drawn up, several tenants still owed money, &c., to the College and, in consequence, the College was unable at the moment to discharge its own debts. The payments due to the Master and Fellows for their stipends and allowances, though small, were often two or three years in arrear, the money laid out by the Master on the repairs of buildings on the College estates could not be repaid to him, and the College had had to borrow from "bursa Magistri Albon" and "cista de Ayleward" (Venn, Vol. III, pp. 284 and 285). This is evidence of the deplorable state in which Caius says he found the College upon his election to the Mastership (Venn, Vol. III, p. 42).

Soon after Caius's accession to the Mastership all this was changed. As before, money might be owed to the College, but now it had sufficient funds to keep itself out of debt.

Length of Leases. Originally colleges had the power of granting leases for any number of years, and we find our College granting leases for different terms up to 99 years.

In 1571 an Act was passed restraining colleges from granting leases for longer terms than 21 years (or than three lives); but the next year they had leave to grant them for 40 years, if the property was situated in a town and did not contain more than 10 acres and the tenant undertook all repairs, thus allowing colleges to grant Building Leases.

Also in 1572 an Act deprived colleges of the power to grant a lease in reversion, *i.e.* after the expiration of an existing lease, should the latter have more than three years to run.

These three Acts and that of 1567 relating to Corn Rents (to be noticed presently) were the principal Acts governing the management of college estates up to the passing of the Universities and College Estates Act, 1858 (*see* p. vii).

By the 86th of Caius's statutes our College was prohibited from granting leases for longer terms than 20 years, and for this period our agricultural leases were usually granted after Caius's time. The custom was that, after a few years of a lease had expired, the tenant surrendered it and took out another for a further period of 20 years, and so on. At first the time at which the old lease was surrendered was very uncertain; but by the end of the 17th century the custom was established of a new lease being granted when seven years of the old lease had expired, and after the end of the 17th century it is the exception to find a new lease granted at any other time.

To a person accustomed to the management of estates in the latter half of the 19th century the most surprising feature in the records of earlier times is the constancy of the annual rents.

These rents remained the same for very many years. Caius, as he says in his 89th statute, had raised some, and others were increased, later, in the 16th century, in accordance with this statute—which, by the way, prohibited the further increase of any rent which he had himself raised[1]. Except for these few increases, the rents of our estates remain the same for hundreds of years. Even when a portion is detached and let separately (as of Wilton Rectory in 1646 and, notably, of Mortimer's Manor at Newnham, Cambridge, at many different times in the 19th century) the annual rent of the remainder is unaltered. Thorold Rogers, in his work on Prices, often refers to this constancy of rents and ascribes it to the absence of improvement in the practice of agriculture. Whatever the cause, our predecessors in the 17th and 18th centuries had become less accustomed to a change in the rent of an estate than we are to a change in the rate of interest on Consols. When the annual value of an estate varied, it was the *fine* on the renewal of the lease (as explained later) which varied and not the annual rent.

It will be seen that both Caius and Perse direct their executors to purchase lands of *definite yearly rentals*, just as anyone now, wishing to found an annual school prize, might purchase Consols sufficient in amount to bring in the required income.

This fixed rent of an estate, excluding the increase (if any) made in the second half of the 16th century, is called "thaccustomed rent" in the Act of 1571, to which we have referred, and "the olde rent" in the Corn Act of 1576.

It must be remembered that the tenants, paying these small fixed rents, paid in addition for all repairs and also all rates and taxes and other outgoings: so that, when (1799–1801) the College had redeemed the land taxes on most of its estates, the tenants paid them to the College, instead of to the Government, till their tenancies were rack-rented.

Corn Rents. Rogers says that colleges began early, before the Corn Act of 1576, to take their rents partly in corn; but no trace of such a practice is found in the early leases of our College. The Bursar's Indentures, indeed, show that certain tenants owed corn to the College; but how this came about I have been unable to find out. These Indentures also show that the College owned corn stored in its granaries on its estates. Thus in the Indenture dated 16 October, 1491, we have "Robertus Orwell de Aylysham, firmarius de Totyngton debet 6ˣˣ (six score) et 12 combes brasil (brank)." Again, on 21 October, 1497, "Wilhelmus Leverton, firmarius de Totyngton debet pro anno Doin¹ 1496 pro 4 cumbes frumenti, pro 5ˣˣ cumbes hordei et 3ˣˣ cumbes avenarum et pro 10 cumbes de brank solvendis secundum inten

[1] "Quem nos auximus redditum, non amplius augebitis, sed eo censu retinebitis."

tionem suae indenturae." Also, on 16 October, 1499, "dominus Hugo
Randole cum suis sociis debet pro granis isto anno apud Matsale in horreatis
15 libras."

In 1576 was passed the "Corn Act" promoted by Sir T. Smith[1] for the
Maintenance of Colleges. By this it was enacted that, in all new leases
granted by a college, "one-third of the 'Old Rent' shall be reserved in good
wheat after 6s. 8d. the quarter or under and good malt after 5s. the quarter
or under to be delivered yearly at the college on a certain day or, in default, to
pay in money after the rate as the best wheat and malt in the market of
Cambridge shall be sold at the next market-day before the rent is due; the
wheat and malt, or money coming of the same, to be expended to the use of
the relief of the commons and diet of the college."

For example, at Caxton, upon the first renewal of the lease, the old rent
of £10 was converted into a money rent of £6. 13s. 4d. and a corn rent of
5 qrs. of wheat and 6 q. 5 b. 1 p. of malt.

Thus, however high the price of wheat and malt might be—whether
in consequence of bad harvests, or of depreciation of the currency, or of
increased demand for corn on account of an increase in population or a
change in its habits—the College would be sure of a supply of corn or its
value.

Further, in 1575 the average prices of wheat and malt, as given by Rogers,
are 15s. 11d. and 10s. 10d.; in 1576 they are 22s. 2d. and 14s. 7d. a quarter.
Also the average price of wheat had not been as low as 6s. 8d. since 1547
(when it was 4s. 11d.) and that of malt had not been as low as 5s. since 1543
(when it was 4s. 8d.). It would seem therefore that, besides securing to the
College due provision for its members, however high prices might rule, the
Legislature, by fixing such low values at which the change from "money-
rents" to "corn-rents" was to be calculated, showed its intention of bringing
about an automatic rise in the annual rents. Certainly this increase in the
annual rent would mean generally a diminution in the "fines" paid on
renewals of leases—to these reference will be made later.

For a few tenancies the rent was increased, as we have seen, when the
opportunity occurred, in the second half of the 16th century. Thus Caius, in
his 91st statute (Venn, III, p. 383) says he has increased the rent of Rickmansworth from the Old Rent (£15. 7s. 0d.) to £40. In such a case it is
only the "old rent" of which the third had to be converted into corn: the
increase (£24. 13s. 0d.) was paid wholly in money.

Again, in accordance with the first paragraph of the same statute, the rent
of Runcton was increased in 1582 to £40; but no part of the increase was
converted into a corn rent. Also at Barningham there was in 1579 an increase
of £5, all of which was paid in money.

---

[1] Mullinger's *The University of Cambridge*, Vol. II, pp. 374, &c.

The first lease affected by this Act was that of Gaye's land at Hinton granted in 1579. It is significant that in this year (Venn, III, p. 69) the College decided to make its own bread and proceeded to construct an oven. It would seem therefore that at first the grain of the corn rents was actually brought to the College; and probably from the first it was appropriated by the Master and the 12 (Senior) Fellows (Venn, III, p. 217).

Judging from the arrangements made in later years the Master and Seniors paid the Bursar the third part of the "old rent" (see p. iii) to make up, with the money rent paid by the tenant, the full "old rent"; for this always appears in the Bursar's Accounts, where no hint is to be found of the receipt of the corn.

On a fly-leaf of the earliest extant Bursar's Book—beginning with 1609—we find a memorandum that 23 tenancies had then come under the Act, the tenants of which paid half-yearly

£82. 15s. 5d. in wheat,
39 q. 4 b. 0 p. in wheat,
46 q. 0 b. 2½ p. in malt,

and that £107. 0s. 6d. was carried into the Bursar's Book.

Thus the Master and Seniors probably took the corn and paid £24. 5s. 1d. into the Bursar's Book.

The fact that the tenants' payments in money amounted to *more* than double the payments in money by the Master and Seniors is accounted for by the increase in some of the money rents as explained above.

How long the corn rents continued to be received in kind I do not know; but by the year 1717 (*Absence Book*, Venn, III, p. 266) the practice of receiving their money values, according to the alternative provided by the Corn Act, had been established. The Master took ⅛th, and the remainder was divided equally amongst the Seniors in residence during the preceding half-year.

With the year 1732 our earliest *Corn Book* begins. In this book is given in different columns:

(1) The amount of money-rent payable for each tenancy, (2) the amount of wheat, and (3) its value according to the price on the previous Cambridge market-day, (4) the amount of malt, and (5) its value, (6) the sum of (3) and (5), then (7) the third part of the "old rent" to be deducted from (6) and handed over for the Bursar's Book, (8) the remainder to be divided between the Master and resident Seniors, (9) the sum of (1) and (7) to be entered in the Bursar's Book, and (10) the sum of (1) and (6) to be found by the tenant.

The College originally calculated the corn rents by the Common Bushel, "the capacity of which : to the Winchester Bushel :: 67 : 54." In 1826 the College adopted "the Imperial Bushel which : Winchester Bushel :: 1 : ·969447," and the numbers of bushels of wheat and malt in the Rents were altered in accordance with the new arrangements.

At Lady Day, 1832, there were 28 tenancies for which corn rents were payable. For these the half-yearly money rents amounted to £54. 9s. 6d., and the values of 51 q. 5 b. 0 p. of wheat and 58 q. 7 b. 3 p. of malt to £172. 18s. and £157. 5s. respectively, and the total amount carried into the Bursar's Book was £73. 11s. 8d., whilst £304. 1s. 2d. was divided amongst the Master and Seniors.

In 1800 the College sold two of these tenancies (at Hockwold and Morden); but till 1832 it continued to allow the Master and Seniors the money for corn, which they would have received from the tenants had these sales not taken place.

Early in the 19th century, for various periods, the receipt of corn rents for a few estates was dropped; but the College always allowed to the Master and Seniors what would have been the value of the corn rent above the third of the old rent, and the same practice was retained when the corn rents were gradually and permanently given up. The last money for corn actually paid by a tenant was in 1885 for the Foulden Rectory. After Lady Day, 1887, in accordance with the Statutes of 1860, the calculation of the half-yearly allowance based on the value of corn was dropped and each Senior Fellow in residence, holding his Fellowship under the Statutes of 1860 or previous Statutes, has from that date received £50 a year in lieu thereof.

This series of Corn Books, from 1732 to 1887, gives an unbroken record of the prices of wheat and malt in the Cambridge market every half-year for 155 years. They also give the price of barley at Michaelmas for each of these years.

Fines. These were payments, other than annual rents, made to the College by their tenants.

The occasions on which they were made were of four kinds.

I. For copyholds of inheritance—in all the Manors owned by the College in the Eastern Counties.

Whenever a new tenant of one of those copyholds required "admission," *i.e.* that his name should be entered on the rolls of the Manor Court as the owner of the copyhold, he paid a "fine," which in all our Manors was at first "arbitrary" (*i.e.* it was settled by the will of the Lords of the Manor), but was gradually required by the Courts of Law to be not more than two years' gross annual value.

II. For renewal of agricultural leases under which the annual rent was less than the annual value—called *beneficial* leases.

In the 16th century the annual value which a tenant was willing to pay for a farm was probably not much in excess of the "old rent," which he had to pay every year, so that the amount he would pay for an extension of his 20 years' lease, of which some years had expired, was small.

Rogers says (Vol. IV, p. 29) that in Mary's reign "the practice of taking fines on leases had certainly begun ; but the fines, originally a present, perhaps a mere handsel, to those who granted the lease had not become large as yet."

In 1617 (Venn, *Annals*, p. 269) the (Senior) Fellows were able to speak of such fines as merely "the tenants' benevolences for their leases."

In the 17th and still more in the 18th century the difference between the annual value and the annual rent, even when increased by the automatic action of the Corn Act of 1576, became greater and greater—so that, as will be seen on reference to the accounts of any of the estates, the fines became larger and larger.

It has been already mentioned that the practice was gradually established of renewing these leases every seven years. It might then be said that the tenant paid a half-yearly rent due at the end of each half-year and a septennial rent paid at the beginning of each seven years.

III. For copyholds for lives, without right of renewal.

This was the tenure upon which the lands were held in our two Manors in Dorset—Bincombe and Oborne. The annual rent of each tenancy was exceedingly small and, not being affected by the Corn Act of 1576, remained so: the tenancy was held for "three lives." When one life had died out the tenant, or his heir, applied to have a new life admitted and of course for this he was willing to pay a fine. In fact such fines formed the real value of the Manor to the College. As will be seen in the accounts of Bincombe and Oborne, the fines ceased when the College, in the first part of the 19th century, bought up or ran out the interests of the tenants in their estates.

IV. For renewals of building leases.

By the Act of 1572 the College had power to grant them for 40 years but not for longer. When a few years of such a lease had expired, the tenant renewed his lease, and thus he obtained an annuity to commence at the end of his former 40 years—consisting of the annual value of the house, *less* the amount he had to pay for repairs and insurance and for the ground rent reserved to the College—this annuity to continue till the end of the new 40 years. For this annuity he would, of course, be willing to pay the present value, which was in fact the fine.

Before the year 1799 very little of our land was held on building leases —just that in Philip Lane, London, and one or two bits in the King's Parade, Cambridge, and a little in Norwich.

Since 1799, as explained under the heads of Newnham and Mortimer's Manor, such tenancies have become numerous.

By the Act of 1858 the College obtained the further power of letting for 99 years, but without the power of renewal; and upon this tenure almost all the building leases granted since 1858 are held.

Since 1880 the College has not taken fines for renewing the 40 years' building leases, and has substituted an increase of ground rent, the increase being the annuity for 40 years which is the equivalent of the fine.

The payments under I and III were received by the Bursar and accounted for in the yearly or half-yearly accounts in the Bursar's Book.

Some of the money thus obtained was laid out from time to time, as opportunity offered, in buying new estates (*e.g.* Shelford), or in adding to our existing estates. The annual rents of the new purchases were carried into the Bursar's Book, and, when one was large enough, a small addition was made to the stipends (originally small) of the Master and Seniors—on the principle that the increase of the Master's stipend was double that of each Senior's. A similar addition was made after purchases of Stock in the Public Funds had begun to be made in 1766.

No part of the receipts of the Bursar's Book was expended on the Master and Fellows except these fixed stipends and the payments for *livery* (Venn, III, p. 205, note) and commons.

Here is a statement of the amounts paid to a Senior Fellow out of the Bursar's Book at Lady Day in a year between 1782 and 1786 (as given in two MSS. in the College Library, viz. No. 61, p. 55 and No. 621, p. 252).

	£	s.	d.
Pro Stipendio (2 terms)	2	13	4
Pro Liberatura ⌠		6	8
⌡ Caian Fellow		13	4
In Distributionibus		3	0
From purchase at Shelford in 1614	2	10	0
From purchase at Weeting in 1632	2	10	0
From Nunn's Barn at Foulden and from purchase at Runcton in 1665		10	0
From purchases at Runcton and Weeting in 1673		10	0
From purchase of Aynells in 1681		15	0
From purchase at Hockwold in 1682 ...	1	5	0
From purchase at E. Dereham in 1703	1	0	0
From purchases at Runcton and Foulden in 1703		10	0
From purchase at Bassingbourne in 1734		10	0
From purchase at Cowling in 1748	1	0	0
From purchase of Public Funds in 1782 ...	2	10	0

After the middle of the 18th century the receipts under the head of III, from Dorset, increased considerably, and their accumulation was used partly for the large repairs to the College buildings at the end of that century and partly in running out the old 20 years' leases as explained later, and in buying up the interests of the tenants for lives of the estates in Dorset. Also the Stocks of the Public Funds purchased by the Bursar's Book between 1766 and 1860 formed a large part of our present Reserve Fund; the remainder being the Stocks which had been bought from time to time with the accumulations in the Books of the various Benefactions, notably the Halman Book (*see* MEPAL).

The amounts under II and IV were recorded in the Gesta Book as they became payable.

The receipts from them up to 1857, except from estates belonging to the different special Benefactions, were divided into 14 parts, of which two were paid to the Master and one to each Senior Fellow—probably by the Registrary.

This practice seems to have been a direct violation of Caius's 95th statute, which says (Venn, Vol. III, p. 384): "Fines autem collegii esse volumus, non magistri et sociorum, praeterquam fines et amerciamenta maneriorum nostrorum de Roughton, Crokesley et Snellschall, quae custodi dedimus in augmentum salarii sui sub ea conditione, ut in collegio resideat."

It is this practice that is complained of by some of the Fellows in 1617 (Venn, *Annals*, p. 267, No. 1).

The theory which underlay this practice seems to have been as follows: when a Benefactor desired to make a fixed annual payment to a Scholar or the Porter or for the Common Fire or for any other purpose within the College, the College undertook to make it for him, and received from him certain lands, of which the (fixed) annual rent was sufficient to enable them to make the payment every year, and any further proceeds, such as fines, which the Members of the College (the Master and Seniors in our case) could obtain from the lands, belonged to them personally for the time being (*Annals*, p. 270, No. 9). It was, no doubt, a theory which always had its opponents (Mullinger's *Cambridge*, Vol. II, pp. 377, &c.).

After the practice of renewing the 20 years' leases every 7th year had been established as the general rule, if in any particular case the lease was not renewed at the 7th year, the College advanced for division amongst the Master and (Senior) Fellows, out of the Bursar's Book, some sum in lieu of the fine, which the tenant should have paid, and the Book was recouped when the tenant did pay and did renew his lease, or else when, the lease having been run out, the tenancy was relet at a Rack Rent; and the same thing happened at the 14th year. As soon as a lease had expired and the estate had been rack-rented and the Book had in consequence been recouped, some addition was made to the stipends of the Master and Seniors out of the rack rent at which the tenancy had been relet. Thus an increase of stipend was gradually substituted for the division of the fines by the Master and Seniors. In this way during the first half of the 19th century most of the 20 years' leases were run out.

In 1791 the 20 years' lease of Wilton Rectory ran out, and the College let it on an increased annual rent. The additional rent above the old rent, which the tenant had to pay, was just the actuarial yearly equivalent of the "septennial rents," which would have been paid under the old system.

Runcton (with Wiggenhall) was the first estate, for which the old beneficial 20 years' lease was given up and for which a rack rent based on the estimated annual value was substituted. This was in 1816.

In this year (October 30) the College passed the following order: After a leasehold estate falls in, the increase of the stipend resulting from the new rent shall continue for three years from the expiration of the old lease to be paid to the Master and Fellows (or their heirs) who would have been entitled to the fine paid after the usual manner.

In 1831 (May), from the increase in the rents, £200 a year had been added to the stipend of the Master and £100 to that of each Senior; and for this reason it is resolved in January 1834 that the advance (to the Master and Fellows) for the fine of Wilton Rectory be discontinued.

The following list of all the renewals of the 20 years' leases after 1848 will show how nearly by that time the old system had been discontinued.

1851   Tuttington, fine £550 and an additional annual rent of £60.
1854   Shelford Farm, fine £800.
       Teversham (Manor Farm), fine £570.
1855   Shelford Mill, fine £808.
       Haddenham, fine £400.
       Norwich (Houses), fine £80.
1858   Tuttington, no fine but additional rent.
1861   Shelford Farm, no fine but additional rent.

Thus the last beneficial agricultural lease ran out in 1881.

In 1857 (*Gesta*, December 15) it was resolved that the practice of dividing fines (from II and IV) be discontinued and that the stipend of a Senior Fellow be fixed at £300 a year.

From this year, till their cessation in 1880, the fines from IV were carried into the Bursar's Book.

A general description of the system of managing College Estates before 1858 will be found in *The Universities and College Estates Acts*, 1858 *to* 1880, by C. S. Shadwell, D.C.L., Oxford, 1898.

CHRONICLE OF THE COLLEGE ESTATES

ACLE (NORFOLK).

1441 Three roods of land—called "Gonvile half-acre"—"apud Ocle, *alias* Acle, in Hundreida de fflegge"—were conveyed to the College by W. Tweight, together with the patronage of S. Michael's, Coslany, in Norwich.

In the deeds it is always found as passing with the patronage of this living.

In a conveyance of the property in 1395 the land is called "Gunnelde's half-acre"; and in that in 1441 as "Gonneley's." Blomefield says that in 1304 W. Overdane presented to S. Michael's, Coslany, in right of "Gundelf's half-acre." It appears therefore that the name, Gonville half-acre, was not derived from its connection with the College, but was a college corruption of its previous name.

The annual rent at first was 1s. In 1731 the *half*-yearly rent is stated to be 4d. in money and 1 peck of malt. About 1742 the annual rent was changed to 7s. 8d. (and the 2 pecks of malt) and in 1808 to 19s. 8d. (and the 2 pecks). After 1831 the malt was dropped and the money rent set at £1.

The rents were paid at very irregular intervals; thus, in 1622, for 19½ years; in 1751, at Lady Day, for nine years, and, at Michaelmas, for one year; in 1828 for 11 years.

We have two leases—one in 1568 and one in 1626—from the Master and Fellows.

In later times the management of this estate seems to have been unique.

At one time it is said (*Reg. Mag.*) to be held on a lease for 20 years from 1656; at another time, for 20 years from 1751. I cannot find, in the *Gesta*, any trace of these leases having been sealed; nor of any fines having been set for them or at any other times.

Nor is there any order for either of the two changes in the annual rent mentioned above.

The *Registrum Magnum* says of the lease from Michaelmas, 1751, that it was "from the Bursar."

It would seem therefore that the management was entirely in the hands of the Bursar, without reference to the Master and Fellows.

1861 This year the property was sold—and for this there was a College order—to H. N. Burroughes for £31. 10s. 0d.

ASHDON (ESSEX). *Advowson of the Rectory.*

1708 The Patronage was bought of T. Baker, the then Rector, for £925 paid by the executors of Stephen Camborn (Venn, I, p. 395 and III, p. 281), as approved by the Master in Chancery.

1801 The land tax (£28. 12s.) was purchased for £953. 6s. 8d. Consols. The money for this, as well as for the land taxes on other College Livings, was found by the Wortley Benefaction, which therefore received the land taxes paid by the various Rectors in subsequent years.

1845 The apportionment of the Tithe Rent Charge is £910. 16s. 0d.

The glebe lands consist of 59 a. 2 r. 35 p., including the Rectory House and Grounds (Nos. 167, 231–7, 239–43 and 195 on the Tithe Map), also of the Old Vicarage House and Yard (No. 447), 1 r. 5 p., and School House and Garden (No. 314), 1 r. 10 p.; and School and Cottage, 2 r. 15 p.

The Rector owns the Manor of Ashdon Rectory. The average of the fines
for the seven years preceding 1888 was £6. 17s. 0d. The Governors of Q.A.B.
hold £317. 18s. 5d., derived from enfranchisements in this Manor. For it is
paid an annual Fee Farm Rent to Mr E. Reeves.

1909   This advowson was exchanged for that of the Vicarage of Chatteris.

Saltier's Lands.

1791   N. Saltier, Rector of Ashdon, devised certain lands to the College in trust
for the future Rectors of Ashdon (Venn, II, p. 13 ; III, p. 287).
These lands are in two parcels ; one contains 39 a. 1 r. 38 p. with house and
buildings, called Ryland's Farm (Nos. 667, 721–5, 733–8, 778 on the Tithe
Map) ; the other lies between the Rectory House and the Church, and was
left for the use of the Rectors, specially "for the conveniency of a road leading
through them to the Church and for collecting the tithes arising within the
parish with greater ease and expedition."

Chapman's Land.

1851   B. Chapman, Master of the College and Rector of Ashdon, devised two
allotments, containing 6 a. 0 r. 15 p., W. of the high road from Ashdon to
Bartlow, to the Master and Fellows, in trust :
    (1) To repair the organ in Ashdon Church.
    (2) ,,   ,,   National School House in Ashdon.
    (3) To place out with the residue poor children in the said National
        School.
The College may employ the Rector as their Agent.
The Ashdon Enclosure Award was settled in 1851—not long before
Dr Chapman's death. By it these two pieces were allotted to him in lieu
of the lands, which he had previously owned in Bartlow.

Mitchell's Farm and Woods.

1759   The original part of this—250 a. 2 r. of Farm and 42 a. of Wood—was
bought of Mrs M. King for Mr Wortley's Benefaction—price £4136. 10s.—
and £74. 10s. 6d. was spent on Manor Fines and Fees.
It is in the parishes of Little Walden and Ashdon. The Messuage, with
34 a. 1 r. of arable, and pasture, and 10 a. of woodland were copyhold of the
Manor of Chipping Walden : the rest was freehold.

1761   The College, with Mr Wortley's money, bought of Mrs M. King, for £452,
18 acres of woodland, all freehold, namely, Seven Ash Wood, Nunn's Wood
and Nunn's Valley Wood.

1799   The land tax was redeemed—£13. 8s. 0d. in Walden for £491. 6s. 8d.
Consols, £6. 8s. 0d. in Ashdon for £234. 13s. 4d. Consols.

1815   The rectorial tithes, commuted at £20, on the Walden portion (158 a.
0 r. 20 p.) were bought of Lord Braybrooke for £490. 16s. 2d. and law
expenses £30. 2s. 0d.

1833   Shortly before this the public road in front of the farmhouse was changed
from one side to the other of the plot of ground on which the College built
the cottages in 1871.

1864   The copyhold portion was enfranchised for £371. 12s. 2d., and a free rent
of 14s. 8d. was redeemed for £20. 10s. 8d.

1865   Mr Gibson was allowed to straighten a water-course and make it run at
the bottom of Chapel Field.

1868   Several bits of wood were stubbed up.

1869 There was an exchange with Mr Gibson costing £23 for expenses. The College gave up:

	a.	r.	p.
Ashwell's—Arable	15	0	26
„ Woodland	4	1	30
A projecting piece of Old Chapel Field—Arable	0	2	20
Total	20	0	36

and £20; and received in exchange

	a.	r.	p.
Two pieces to N.E. of Old Chapel Field	2	1	20
Piece to N.W. of new road, behind the land on which the cottages were built in 1872	14	0	0
Total	16	1	20

Ashwell's was to E. of the Brook, beyond the Street Farm, about a mile S.W. of Mitchell's Farmhouse. After the exchange the College threw into one field Jenny's Garden (2 a. 1 r. 20 p.), the two pieces acquired by exchange, Chapel Field and the remainder of Old Chapel Field, making in all 27 a. 1 r. 16 p.

1871 Nunn's Grove was stubbed up and Cow Shadows planted instead.

1872 The block of four cottages was built for £400.

1891 Additional farm buildings were built for £120.

1909 The piece of 14 acres acquired in 1869 was sold to Sir J. Mackay for £900.

1910 The College is arranging to sell the remainder of the farm and the woods to Sir J. Mackay for £9825 together with the value of the timber.

The Street Farm.

1863 The College bought, of P. Pegg and M. L. Pegg, 17 a. 3 r. 17 p., partly copyhold of the Manor of Ashdon Hall, for £600, which had been received for lands taken by various Railway Companies, paying £50 for admission to the copyholds;

1864 also, of John Miller and his brothers, 48 a. 3 r. 21 p., including house and farm buildings, partly copyhold of the same Manor, for £1750, which had been received partly from Railway Companies and partly for enfranchisements of copyholds in manors belonging to the College, paying also £25 for timber.

1867 The farm buildings were burned down and the house was scorched and injured.

1868 The buildings, except the barn, were rebuilt, on a smaller scale, at a cost of £279.

1869 The copyhold portions of the farm were enfranchised for £281. 7s. 8d.

1870 The barn was rebuilt for £105.

ATHERINGTON (DEVON). Boreat's Farm and Mill.

1749 Bartholomew Wortley, Rector of Bratton Fleming and formerly Fellow of the College, died in May; and by will, dated April 30, 1742, left to the College all his money, bonds, mortgages, debts and securities to the amount of more than £7000, and also his estates in Fakenham, Elmham and Gateley in Norfolk, and his estates in High Bray and Bratton in Devon.

The Accounts of the executors begin with the entry "May 12. Paid for flesh for ye Funeral 11s."

At his death, amongst his mortgages was one for £1100 on the estate called Boreat's in Atherington, formerly owned by one T. Ley, then deceased. Ley had left Boreat's to E. Law and after her death to J. Law, whom he also appointed executrix and executor of his will. Before 1749 his widow, J. Ley, had claimed dower out of this estate and had therefore exhibited a bill in Chancery.

1750　To stay J. Ley's suit in Chancery an agreement was come to between her, E. and J. Law, and Mr Wortley's executors to allow her ⅓ of the net rent of Boreat until it was sold and ⅛ of the purchase money and her legal expenses.

1752　Mr Wortley's executors acquired for £106 a further mortgage on the estate for that amount: they also conveyed to the College the mortgages and other securities.

The College purchased of J. Ley for £200 her right to the ⅛ of the purchase money of the estate.

After this the estate remained in the possession of the College.

The acreage was said to be 172 a. : the rental was £68 for the farm and £7 for the mill grounds.

For the barton (or homestead) a chief rent of 10s. is paid to the Lord of the Manor of Umberleigh.

1753　The sum of £84. 8s. 6d. was paid from the Wortley Book for a License of Mortmain, which had been obtained (March 5, 1748) for the College to possess estates of £500 a year and had been previously charged for in the Bursar's Book.

1756　The rent of the farm was reduced from £68 to £56.

1758　J. Ley's law charges—£33. 16s. 0d.—were paid.

1766　In a survey of the estate we find the following concise description of it.

"The lands of this estate lie together and cover the top of a Hill which falls quick to the S. and W. They produce good wheat and clover; but being cold are not favourable for barley. Oaks, of which there are many in Hedge and Coppice, thrive pretty well. The Moor is wet and coarse."

The mill is said to be an over-shot one.

1799　The land tax (£7. 8s. 9d.) was redeemed. £544. 16s. 1½d. Consols were given for it and the land taxes on our property at High Bray and Bratton Fleming.

1823　The mill is stated to have a single pair of stones.

1839　The Tithe Map gives the acreage of the farm as 210a. 0r. 26p.

1845　It is stated that the grist mill has two pairs of stones driven with one wheel and that the cottage is a very poor one.

1877　The mill and cottage had been dismantled for some years and the ground was included in the farm.

Before the end of the 18th century the rent had risen to £78; early in the 19th it was £115; in 1821 it was £150. In 1832 it was £110, at which it has remained, except between 1876 and 1884, when it was £120. Since 1902 the College has paid the tithe.

The apportionment of the tithe on Boreat's Farm is £20. 12s. 2d.

BARNBY (SUFFOLK).

1431–4　The Rectory, in the gift of the Priory of Buttele (Butley, Suffolk), was consolidated with the Vicarage of Mutford, the College and the Priory having alternate presentations.

1454　An agreement was made between T. Attwood, then Master of the College (and Vicar of Mutford), and the Prior of Butley, whereby the Priory was to give to the College 3 roods of land in Barnby (the patronage land, *i.e.* land to which the patronage was appendant, not glebe), together with their rights of presentation, in exchange for a room in College for the use of a 'Canon' from Butley.

No trace of this agreement is found amongst the documents in the

Treasury and we should not have known of it had it not been the subject of the litigation in 1470 mentioned below.

1465 We have in the Treasury (v, 13 *a—d*) a conveyance of the 3 roods and right of presentation from the Priory to the College.

1470 Some account of a lawsuit between the College and the Priory will be found in an article by Mr W. W. Buckland in the *Caian* for 1895 (v, p. 14).

In this suit it was alleged that, whereas it was essential to the validity of the exchange of 1454 that both parties should enter personally, Attwood had not entered on the land when he died (in 1456, Venn, III, p. 16).

1471 By this year the Priory had apparently acknowledged the right of the College to present. *See* Venn, Vol. III, p. 315.

From this time till 1583 the presentations to Mutford and Barnby are separate.

1542 After the Priory had surrendered its estates to the Crown in 1538, the Crown revived the claim to present to Barnby alternately with the College, and litigation ensued, and this year the King did actually present (R. Brandon); but this presentation was never enrolled on the Patent Rolls, and subsequently the Crown appears to have been satisfied as to the right of the College to present.

The rent of the 3 roods was 10*d.* I do not find that it was ever paid, except in 1628, when 18*s.* 4*d.* was paid for 22 years. After 1681 it ceases to be entered in the Bursar's Book as due.

1799 The land tax of £2. 6*s.* 0*d.* payable by the Rector was bought by the College from the Government (*see* MUTFORD).

BARNINGHAM (SUFFOLK).

1478 Stephen Smith, *alias* Tostock, Rector of Blonorton, in Norfolk, gave his lands and tenements (in Barningham) to the College.

The annual rent was then £4.

1538 The College bought of W. Buckenham (previously Master till 1536) two closes called Linton's Overyard and Netheryard. He had bought these closes 19 years before of J. Griffin and G. Bokenham. Their acreage is set down in the valuation in 1776 as 3a. 1r. 26p. R. Bauldry had previously disputed Buckenham's right to them and now released them to the College for 4 marks.

An out-rent of 1*s.* 4½*d.* is payable to the Manor of Bardwell Hall.

1558 This is the date of the first extant lease of this estate. It is granted for 21 years at a yearly rent of £5.

1579 In the lease granted this year, for 20 years, the rent is £10.

1599 This year the rent is set at £8. 6*s.* 8*d.* in money, together with 2½ quarters of wheat and 3 qrs. 3 bush. of malt.

There seems to have been great uncertainty as to the acreage of this estate. Dr Brady's survey put it at 92a. 1r.; Mr Smith's (1754) at 67a. 1r. 20p.; Bradfield's (1776) 86a. 1r. 18p.

Even after the Enclosure it was found difficult to arrive at the exact figures. Custance (1800) found the estate to contain 91a. 20p.; but was not certain about two or three pieces. Later (1807) he made the total acreage 89a. 0r. 30p.

In 1814 Day found that a piece (2a. 2r. 0p.), which did not belong to us, had been entered in the survey of 1807 and that three small pieces, containing in all 2a. 0r. 30p., had been omitted, thus finally settling the acreage at 88a. 3r. 22p.

1799 (May 10) The land tax (£2. 16s. 0d.) on the whole estate was redeemed for £102. 13s. 4d. Consols.

The enclosure of the parish took place this year. Three pieces, containing 10 a. 1 r. 5 p., were allotted to the College. In exchange with J. Lock the College gave up a piece, 3 r. 5 p., and took a piece of 3 r. 11 p., and in exchange with H. Patteson the College gave up four pieces, containing 2 a. 1 r. 2 p., and took five pieces, containing 2 a. 1 r. 32 p. The total costs of the enclosure were £1092. 12s. 0d., of which the College paid £24.

1808 (Jany 13) The tenant was allowed to break up 23 acres, for which the rent was increased by £5. 15s.

                "Pro 23 acris hodie aratis   ...   £5. 15s. 0d."

was the constant entry amongst the rents in the Bursar's Book for many subsequent years.

1817 The College bought, of G. Walton, Hole's Acre (0 a. 3 r. 38 p.), for £50 and legal expenses amounting to £7. 10s. 8d. For this the tenant subsequently paid £2. 2s. 0d. a year.

1819 The College bought of J. Walton two pieces, Upper Long Hedges (2 a. 2 r. 20 p.) and Long Hedges (4 a. 0 r. 30 p.) for £305; the expenses of the purchase were £14. 17s. 10d.

The tenant paid a rent of £12. 11s. 0d. for these two pieces—being about 4°/₀ on the money laid out. In the three years to Mich^s, 1822—24, the College accepted 3°/₀ (£9. 8s. 3d.) instead of the 4°/₀.

The following are some of the fines paid for the renewal of the 20 years' lease:

1655	7 years expired	...	...	...	£42.
1722	,,	,,	...	...	...	£37.
1777	8 years	,,	...	...	...	£94. 10s.
1793	7 years	,,	...	...	...	£76.
1807	,,	,,	...	...	...	£190.
1828	,,	,,	...	...	...	£220.

After this the lease was not renewed, and £180 were paid in 1835 and £150 in 1842 from the Bursar's Book for division amongst the Master and Senior Fellows in lieu of fines.

1847 The farm was let on a lease for 12 years for £134 a year and the old corn rent. The tenant was allowed to break up 14 a. 3 r. 29 p., "provided he keep the buildings in repair."

1850 The College bought of Margaret, widow of J. Thruston, Roselands, 8 a. 1 r. 35 p., for £400, received from various Railway Companies for lands taken by them. The bargain had been struck in J. T.'s lifetime. The land was let with our farm for £17. 8s. 3d.

1859 By the lease granted this year the whole estate was let for £166. 10s. 0d., the old corn rents being given up, the addition in consequence to the money rent being the average of the corn rents for the preceding 12 years.

1871 A survey of the estate was made when the acreage was returned at 104 a. 3 r. 32 p., and the Tithe Rent Charge Apportionment at £35. 4s. 0d.

1872 The College exchanged 27 a. 3 r. 1 p. (including the purchase of 1850) for 29 a. 2 r. 12 p. previously belonging to Mr C. Fison.

1897 In exchange with Mr A. J. Fison the College gave up one acre and took 1 r. 36 p. with a stable thereon, but paid £70. 10s. 0d. for equality of exchange.

1903 The rent was £80, out of which the College paid the tithe.

BARRINGTON (CAMBS). *Rent Charge.*

1560 T. Wendy, M.D., devised by will to the College—after the death of his wife, who died in 1570—his Rectory of Haslingfield, on condition that the College should let it in fee farm, together with the patronage of the Church, to his heir-at-law for ever, reserving £10 a year out of it for a Fellowship (Venn, III, p. 217).

1609 No annuity having been paid and the arrears amounting to £380, the College came to an agreement with the heir-at-law, whereby he made his lands at Barrington chargeable with 20 marks a year (£13. 6s. 8d.), the Rectory of Haslingfield being discharged of the rent charge of £10 (Venn, *Annals*, pp. 217–223).

BASSINGBOURNE (CAMBS). *Land and Two Cottages.*

1626 Martin Perse (executor of Dr S. Perse) conveyed 77 acres, estimated at the annual value of £21. 2s. 0d., to the Perse Feoffees, to make up—with the estates bought for the purpose in Frating and adjoining parishes—the annual rental of £250, as required by Dr Perse's will.

It is interesting to note that, when this property was conveyed to M. Perse in the previous year, one of those who joined in the conveyance was Sir Oliver Cromwell. The land had belonged to W. Linne (or Lynne), who left it to his widow Elizabeth (*née* Steward), afterwards married to Robert Cromwell, Esq. Robert was the brother of Sir Oliver Cromwell. Robert and Elizabeth were the parents of Oliver Cromwell, the Protector (*see* Mark Noble's *Memoirs of the House of Cromwell*, 1787, pp. 82–90).

1627 The College bought, of Martin Perse, a tenement with an orchard of half an acre and 26 acres 4 feet, for £180. Of this sum £100 was the gift of Dr Hervey, Master of Trinity Hall, 1555–84, for founding a Scholarship. Therefore it was agreed that, out of the rent, the sum of £4. 10s. 0d. was to be paid annually to Dr Hervey's Scholar (Venn, III, p. 231).

The two properties were let as one to the same tenant; but the rent was carried partly to the General College Account and partly to the Perse Account.

The rent of the College portion was always taken at £10: that of the Perse portion was frequently changed.

At first (1626) the rent of the latter was £21. 2s. 0d. a year: in 1686 it was £14. 0s. 6d. The last time it appears in the Perse Book—at Lady Day, 1734 —the half-year's rent to that date was £8. 6s. 8d.

After the amalgamation mentioned below the rent for the half-year to Michaelmas, 1734, is entered in the Bursar's Book at £12. 10s. 0d.

The annual rent was shortly after raised to £27, and at this it remained till the enclosure of the parish.

1729 Mr Lightwine, President of the College, died and left his estate at West Dereham, of the annual value of £50, to the same uses to which Dr Brady had before given his estate at Denver.

1733 It was thought much more convenient that the land applied to the purposes of Mr Lightwine's will should be adjacent to those left by Dr Brady, being both for the same purposes and under the same management (that of the Master directly).

Accordingly the lands at Denver left by Mr White in 1728 and those bought of Wilkinson in 1729 were applied to the purpose of Mr Lightwine's Trust and were afterwards called Mr Lightwine's lands; and, in their stead, the lands at West Dereham were taken for the general purposes of the College.' The College then exchanged the West Dereham lands for the 77 acres at Bassingbourne, held since 1626 for the Perse Trust (valued at £333. 6s. 8d., the rent being £16. 13s. 4d.), and £739. 16s. 10½d. paid in cash by the Perse Managers to the College.

Thus all the lands at Denver then owned by the College were concentrated into the management of the Master, and all those at Bassingbourne into the management of the Bursar for the General College Account.

No part of the rents of the Bassingbourne lands was at any time reckoned in corn and no fine was ever paid for a lease.

The lands were tithe free.

1801   The land tax, £4. 6s. 0d., was redeemed for £157. 13s. 4d. Consols.

At this time the estate consisted of half an acre of land, containing a house, garden and orchard, and 69 strips lying in the three open common fields, containing altogether about 99½ acres, but each acre contained only about 3 roods.

"The strips in the common fields lay not only much dispersed, but a considerable distance from the town, a great part not less than three miles, and that in the poorest part of the parish, and very little nearer than two miles."

1804   At the enclosure of the parish, in lieu of their lands in the common fields and two common rights for cows, the College had allotted to them seven allotments, containing about 56½ acres, lying immediately behind the house and garden.

The College paid £129. 6s. 6d. for the expenses of the enclosure and subsequently, in two years, £128. 7s. 0d. for fencing.

After that the farm was let for £75, and in 1866 for £100. In 1906 the rent was £58.

BEACHAMPTON (BUCKS). *Advowson of the Rectory.*

1818   This was bought—for the Wortley Benefaction—of the Rev. W. J. Palmer, free of land tax, for £2400.

1838   An agreement was made between the Rector and the Landowners of the parish to put the Tithe Apportionment at £354, of which £9 were on the Glebe.

1839   An exchange was agreed on between the Rector and J. Walker, by which the former gave up various pieces of Glebe lying away from the Parsonage House, amounting to 4a. 0r. 27p., and took two strips, one on each side of the Parsonage Garden, amounting to 2a. 3r. 1p.

1904   The Glebe consisted of 23a. 1r. 10p., let for £44, and 4a. 2r. 11p. occupied by the Rector.

BINCOMBE (DORSET).

1570   The College bought, of Clement Syseley,

The Manor of Bincombe for	£309
,, ,, Oborne for	260
and the Rectory (Advowson) of Bincombe for	20
Total.....................	£589 ;

all in reversion after the death of Lady Margaret Allington, who died in 1592.

The money was found as follows:	£	s.	d.
Abp. Parker's Gift	60	13	4
P. Hewet's Gift	180	0	0
Dr Byshby's Gift..	40	0	0
The College Chest[1]	308	6	8
Total	£589	0	0

The annual values of the Manors were:			
Of Bincombe	15	9	0
Of Oborne	14	7	8
Total........................	£29	16	8

This sum was distributed as follows:			
To Hewet's three Scholars	8	0	0
„ Dr Byshby's Scholar	1	15	0
„ the Abp.'s Scholar.............................	3	0	8
Remainder to College Chest	17	1	0
	£29	16	8

1667 The "extended" rent of Bincombe was estimated at £311. 16s. 8d. The annual rent paid to the College was £15. 19s. 3½d.

1683 One of the tenancies, called Nossiter's, was held by a widow named Ashe, and was bought up by the College for £200, which had been just before paid to the College as the fine for the first lease of the demesne lands of the Manor of Carles in Wilton—(College Library, MS 621, p. 245). While it was let as an annual tenancy Nossiter's brought to the Bursar's Book the annual rent of £22.

In 1691 it was let out again to the two sons of the widow Ashe for their two lives on a fine of £170, paid in five different instalments varying from £80 to £5. 10s., as shown by the extraordinary receipts in the Bursar's Book for the years following 1690.

From the time when the College acquired the parish till the year 1825 little or no change seems to have been made in the "estates," or "livings," into which the parish was divided, or in the conditions on which they were hired from the College.

The tenants held originally by copy of the Rolls of the Manor Court—for three lives, with widowhood.

In 1753 the College substituted the practice of granting leases under the seal, but still for three lives. The College at first intended to grant the leases for terms of years, but was advised that the tenancies would become chattels only, instead of freeholds (and thus would not have given a vote for a Member of Parliament).

For each estate a nominal fixed rent of a few shillings (or pence) was paid; and upon the death of the tenant one or two of his best beasts or goods accrued, as a heriot, to the landlord. When a new life was introduced a new copy, or lease, was granted and a varying fine was paid.

Thus the estate, let in 1762 to G. Pashen for three lives—with fine of £200 is let in 1797 to W. Pashen for three lives, with fine £42.

An "estate" consisted of

(1) one or more tenements, with garden and outbuildings;

(2) a few enclosed meadows and arable fields;

(3) a large number of strips in the common meadow and common (arable) fields;

[1] It will be remembered that this had recently been replenished by the liberality and prudent management of Dr Caius (Introduction, p. ii, and Venn, III, p. 42).

(4) a right to run a certain number of sheep and horses over the Down, which lay all along the hill to the north of the village, and over the fallow fields;

(5) a right to run a certain number of cows on the "Cow Pasture."

In the survey of 1752 there is a note that "the arable land is almost altogether manured by the sheep, which is the chief benefit the tenants receive from them. They are maintained by the Down and fallow fields."

Sometimes an estate was simply a cottage and thus consisted of (1) only.

1794 The extended rent of the College land and the Glebe was estimated at £453. 9s. 6d., the actual annual rent paid to the College being £15. 12s. 8d.

The following is an account of all the "estates" and the Glebe in this year:

es of Tenants	Copy or Lease	Names of Estates	Customary Acres	Commons for			Extended Yearly Value			Rents		
				Hor.	Cows	Sheep	£	s.	d.	£.	s.	d.
ey, J.	C	Cottage & Garden	¼				2	0	0		1	0
er, H.	L	Kitcherman's	37¼	2	5½	105	29	10	6	1	3	4
	C	Dircott's Cottage	¼				5	0	0		5	0
ne, S.	L	Hewlett's	57¼	3	7	140	45	17	9	1	9	9
per, R.	L	Ashe's	39⅓	2	5½	105	32	9	0	1	3	3
	C	Talbot's Cottage					2	0	0			6
	C	Pupler's Cottage										2
	C	A new Cottage									1	0
cott, J.	L	Day's & Tean's	⎫ 128¼ 1/10	6	16½	315	100	16	6	2	4	3
	L	Nossiter's & Read's	⎭							1	10	5
ns, M.	C	Cott. & Garden									1	0
ks, T.	L	Upper Tenement	40¾ ⅓	1	4	70	27	10	3		19	9
	C	Read's Cottage						15	0		1	0
drich, R. C.	L	late Tibbs'	31¼	2	4	70	25	14	3		12	0
, H.	L	Lower Livings	40	2	5½	105	30	6	8	1	3	3
eless, W.	L	Samway's	52⅔	2	5½	105	38	5	1	1	9	6
rce, W.	L	,,	27⅓	1	4	70	21	16	6		17	3
, W.	L	Sherring's	27	1	4	70	21	15	6		17	5
Hand	C	Three Placeholds	43	2	5½	105	34	6	6	1	3	7
lidge, R.	C	House & Orchard					5	0	0		1	6
, E.	C	A Placehold	14¼	1	1½	35	11	18	0		6	0
J.	C	Dearing's Cottage	¼				1	10	0		1	3
er, H. C.		Cottage										6
tor	C	Glebe	19⅓	1	4	70	16	18	0			
		Total	558¾	26	72½	1365	453	9	6	15	12	8

Clapcott's two estates contained seven enclosed meadows of 10½ acres, one enclosed arable field of 3 acres, 24 strips of the common (i.e. unenclosed) meadow and 131 strips of the common arable fields. They had been united in the same person for many years and occupied together, so that the lands belonging to each could not then be ascertained. They were however held by two separate leases. In them J. Clapcott is described as of Winterbourn, Whitechurch, in Dorset, Gentleman. He probably sublet our estates.

1796 The estate in hand in 1794 was let on a lease for three lives to Robert Cooper. He was a victualler living at Ridgeway, in the parish of Upwey.

The two larger estates thus let to R. Cooper and his three cottage estates probably formed the nucleus of the West Farm; just as the old-standing double tenancy of J. Clapcott was probably the nucleus of the East Farm, which was formed in 1826, when, as shown below, the concentration of the land into the hands of a few tenants was more fully carried out.

1823   A piece of land and cottages were bought of T. Hawkins for £30. Probably it was a small encroachment on the waste of the Manor.

About the year 1825 the arrangement and conditions of the tenancies was completely reorganized.

1824   An Act was passed to enclose the whole parish.

1826   The College bought up the interests of ten of the tenants. For most they paid in cash, apparently, £10,357. 3s. 11d. But two tenants preferred annuities. W. and J. Pearce had an annuity of £40, which came to an end in 1837. T. Fooks and his wife had an annuity of £30 and retained their old dwelling for their lives: they had both died by Lady Day, 1842. Two tenants, S. Baker and G. Pashen, ran their leases out: they terminated respectively in 1845 and 1862.

For the purpose of facilitating the enclosure, the parties interested in it, namely, the College, the Parson, S. Baker and G. Pashen, brought under the Award several of their old enclosures, in addition to the Downs and Cow Pasture and the open fields and meadows.

The Commissioners put up the fences between the new allotments. For the purpose of paying for this work and for all the other expenses of the enclosure they set aside two allotments, namely, 36 a. 2 r. 19 p. and 46 a. 1 r. 26 p. which they sold to the College for £2,759.

By the Award, dated April, 1828, the other allotments were as follows:

To the Parish Surveyor, for stone and gravel, two allotments containing 2 a. 2 r.;

For supplying fuel to the poor, 21 a.;

To the College, as Lords of the Manor, for their interest in the soil of the common and waste lands, 27 a. 3 r. 14 p.;

To the Rector, for Glebe, five enclosures, containing 28 a. 1 r. 21 p.;

To the College, for its interests in the commons and common fields, purchased of the ten tenants, and for the old enclosures, belonging to the College, brought under the Award, 12 allotments containing in all 640 a. 1 r. 22 p. and four old enclosures containing 7 a. 1 r. 32 p.;

To S. Baker, with reversion to the College at the end of his lease, one allotment containing 35 a. 3 r. 0 p., and five old enclosures containing 5 a. 3 r. 31 p.;

To G. Pashen, with reversion to the College, three old enclosures containing 42 a. 3 r. 7 p.

The College let their lands, other than Baker's and Pashen's, as follows:

To W. Read, East Farm, 344 a. 0 r. 3 p., Rent £318 after 1st two years.
,,   J. Galpin, West Farm, 458 a. 3 r. 19 p.,   ,,   £422   ,,   ,,   ,,
,,   J. Roper, Lime Kilns and 4 acres,   ,,   £21.

The College in several subsequent years bought up various cottages, or the leases remaining on them.

1829   There was a purchase of cottages for £70.

1832   Cooper's cottage was bought for £120, and Thorne's for £15. 15s. 0d.

1838   For Tithe Commutation, see Advowson.

1845   Baker's lease fell in, the tenancy was added to the East Farm at a rent of £66 a year.

For £1770 the College sold to the Wilts., Somerset and Weymouth Railway

Company 11a. 2r. 3p., tithe and land tax free, and the use of 5a. 0r. 4p. up to the opening of the line and for five years afterwards, and the right of tunnelling under 1a. 3r.

1861   Two cottages were built on the West Farm for £254. 2s. 0d.

1862   Pashen's lease fell in; the tenancy was let to the son of the late tenant at a rent of £40 a year.

1865   There was a fire at Ridgeway.   After it the site was let on a building lease to G. and S. Groves.

1870   A site for a School-house and £100 were given by the College: the convey-ance was sealed on March 19, 1872.

1873   Two cottages were built for about £250.

1878   The house and buildings of the East Farm were burnt down.   The house was rebuilt on the hill to the south for £1843. 17s. 3d.

1903   Extensive alterations were carried out at the Royal Oak Inn at a cost of £445.

In recent years the agricultural rents have been set as follows; £1007 in 1875; £571 in 1895; £646 in 1905; the College always paying the tithe.

1906   For £536 the College bought, from A. Drake, Hill House and garden, with an allotment adjoining and containing 2 acres, copyhold of the Manor of Wyke Regis and Elwell.   This property is in the parish of Upwey.

1908   The property bought in 1906 was enfranchised for £39. 7s. 5d.

BINCOMBE AND BROADWAY (DORSET).   *Advowsons of the Rectories.*

1570   For the purchase of the reversion of the Advowson of the Rectory of Bincombe for £20, *see* under BINCOMBE.

1692   The Advowson of the Rectory of Broadway was bought from T. Dassell for £200, obtained as follows:

Legacy of J. Robinson in 1674 for purchase of Advowsons	£50
Legacy of E. Gelsthorpe in 1678 for purchase of Advowsons	50
Gift of J. Ellis	50
Part of Legacy of W. Blanks to the College Chest...	50
Total......................	£200

1738   The Rectories of Bincombe and Broadway were consolidated.

1752   In the Survey of Bincombe it is stated that the Parson received a composition of £55. 15s. 0d. for Great and Little Tithes.
The Glebe of Bincombe consisted of: 3a. of enclosure; 1a. 3r. of meadow; 14a. 1r. of arable; a house, garden and orchard containing one acre; also a right of keeping six cows in the Cow Pasture, and one horse and as many sheep as each of the tenants of the seven larger "Livings."

1799   For £524. 6s. 8d. Consols the College acquired the land taxes, amounting to £15. 14s. 7d., payable out of the two Rectories.

1826   By the Bincombe Enclosure Award five pieces were assigned to the Rector, containing 28a. 1r. 21p., in addition to the Churchyard (1r. 14p.) and the barn, yard, and close, previously belonging to the Rector (1a. 0r. 15p.).
The Broadway Glebe amounted to 18a. 3r. 3p.

1839   The apportionment of the Tithe Rent Charge of Bincombe was fixed at £186, of which £6 was on the Glebe; that for Broadway at £292. 15s. 0d., of which £2. 5s. 0d. was on the Glebe.

1846 and 1853   The Railway Co. (now G.W.R.) took 3 r. 24 p. of Broadway Glebe and paid £72, which the College took, and, in consequence, reduced the land tax on the Rectory by £2. 5s. 6d., that being the interest of £72 at the then price of Consols.   The land tax thus became £13. 9s. 1d.

1901   £5 of the land taxes payable out of the Rectories was redeemed for £165, thus leaving £8. 9s. 1d. payable annually.

About the same time £6. 14s. 0d. of the Broadway Tithe Apportionment was redeemed for £167. 10s. 0d.   From the investment of this sum the Rector derives an income (through Q.A.B.) of £5. 0s. 6d.

BLOFIELD (NORFOLK).   *Advowson of the Rectory.*

1736   This was bought of T. Heath for £805. 5s. 0d., and 10 guineas were paid to our agent for his trouble in the matter.

Mr Camborn's executors paid £429 of the purchase money.   They obtained £359 of this contribution by the sale of their estate at Lawshall to Dr Perse's Benefaction.

1753   The terrier shows that the Glebe lay in 40 different parcels, containing in all 52 a. 1½ r.

1805   The enclosure of the parish took place.   The charge to the Rector for his share of the expenses connected with it was £8. 12s. 0d.

The effect of this enclosure is shown by the following schedule of the Glebe extracted from the latest terrier :

		a.	r.	p.
1.	Site of old Rectory with Churchyard and meadow	7	2	11
2.	Present Rectory House	5	2	1
3.	Arable, received under the Award for a part of the old Glebe	4	2	14
4.	Slackham Pightle	1	3	38
5.	Arable, partly old Glebe and partly land received in exchange for old Glebe under the Award	6	1	25
6.	Allotment in lieu of old Glebe lands in open fields and other lands given up in exchange to different persons	25	2	38
7.	An allotment of the old heath to the Rectory	10	0	15

The terrier further states that the tithes of the parish, except the tithe (10s. Apportionment) on 1 a. 0 r. 33 p. payable to the Rector of Strumpshaw, belong to the Rector, as also the tithe of 2 a. in the parish of Strumpshaw.

There are also two moduses of 3s. and 3s. 6d. respectively, payable to the Rector for two marshes in Wickhampton.

The apportionment of the tithe payable to the Rector is £972. 15s. 6d., and 6s. is now paid for the two moduses from Wickhampton and 16s. is paid as a modus in lieu of the tithe on the two acres in Strumpshaw.

Bratton Fleming (Devon). *Advowson of the Rectory.*

1667   Mr Gascoigne Canham (Rector of Arlington) gave the Advowson to the College.

1749   Mr B. Wortley (Rector) left for the Rector the interest of £100, to be paid by the College; and also his furniture, plate and books.

1781   At the death of Mr Bringloe (Rector), it having been found that little or none of this furniture was in being, the College ordered that £10 a year be allowed out of Mr Wortley's Fund—to commence from Mr Bringloe's death for the then and all future Rectors.

1799   The land tax on the Rectory and Glebe (£26. 10s. 0d.) was bought for £883. 13s. 4d. Consols.

1837   The tithe was commuted at £435.

1840   The accounts of Mr Wortley's Benefaction show that £209. 13s. 6d. was spent on books for the Rectory House, and, in the following year, £70 on plate.

1841   At the enclosure, 40 acres of Bratton Down were allotted to the Glebe, which after that contained 257a. 3r. 18p.—of which 28 acres were wood— and a good homestead.

1890   In the eight previous years several small parcels of land were sold off; and the Glebe then consisted of 243 acres, of which 20 acres were wood, and all but the wood and two or three acres near the house were let in two farms, the smaller one containing 45 acres, having a small homestead lately provided.

About £20 a year was the result of investments of the money paid for the various sales of land.

The gross rent of the two farms was £300.

1909   There have been repeated sales of small building plots lately.

Kippiscombe.

1749   The estate—called Kippiscombe or Northlands—was devised to the College by Mr B. Wortley.

It was estimated to contain 80 acres of arable and pasture on the S.E. side of the road to Lynton. It carried the right of keeping 100 sheep, six horses and six bullocks on Bratton Downs (to the N.W. of the Lynton Road).

When it first came to the College there was a lease on it—dated Nov. 7, 1712—for two lives, at a rent of £2 and a capon.

This lease was run out in accordance with a direction in a codicil to Mr Wortley's will.

1772   The estate was let on a new lease for 14 years at a rent of £30.

1799   A land tax of £2, together with those on Boreat (Atherington) and Fullover (Bray), was redeemed for £544. 16s. 1½d. Consols—being £36. 13s. 4d. for every £1 of land tax.

1813   The rent was changed this year to £52. 10s. and in 1821 to £50.

1832   The enclosed land was divided up by hedges at a cost to the College of £65.

1839   The enclosure of the town took place, and the College received two allotments, 9a. 2r. 2p. and 50a. 3r. 4p., on the N.W. side of the Lynton Road, and paid £94. 10s. 2d. and a further £26 for fencing and draining.

1844   The Tithe Apportionment was fixed at £6, at a cost to the College of £5. 5s. 4d.

1845   The old enclosures were found to contain 85a. 3r. 36p.

1846   The rent was reset at £60.

1863   The stream was straightened between our land and Mr Bassett's.

1909   The present rent is £62.

BRAY, OR HIGH BRAY (DEVON). *Fullaford, or Fullover.*

1749   This farm—called Fullaford, or Fullover—was devised to the College by Mr B. Wortley (Rector of Bratton), along with Kippiscombe, in Bratton. He had given £1095 for the two in 1719.

Fullaford then—as now—consisted almost entirely of grass land. It was estimated to contain 93 a. 2 r. 20 p.; and to it belonged a sheep-walk for 160 sheep on Fullover Down, with a right of turbary and of taking stone from the quarries for the repair of fences on the farm: it also carried the right of feeding 70 sheep on the Down called Showlesbury Castle.

The rent was then £39. It was raised in 1800 to £45; in 1813 to £87, and dropped in 1823 to £80.

1799   A land tax of £5. 8s. 6d., together with those on Boreat (Atherington) and Kippiscombe (Bratton), was redeemed for £544. 16s. 1½d. Consols.

1837   The tithe was commuted for £13. 10s. 0d.

1845   The acreage of the enclosed land was put at 125 a. 3 r. 20 p.

This year it was let to a new tenant for £117.

1846   The College made an addition to the house and built a shed at a cost altogether of £411. 3s. 10d., and the tenant paid £15 additional rent.

1850   Fullover Down was enclosed. The College received two allotments, 35 a. 1 r. 20 p. and 24 a. 2 r. 0 p., and paid for its share of the expenses £376. 6s. 8d. These allotments were, soon after, drained at a cost of £90.

1853   In consequence of these improvements the rent was raised, the total rent being £150; but in 1862 it was reduced to £142; in 1895 it was £157.

1870   Showlesbury Castle Down was enclosed. The College received an allotment of 25 a. 0 r. 24 p., and paid £128. 4s. 5d. as its share of the expenses; and in consequence £8 was added to the rent.

1879   A chief rent of 6s. a year, payable to the Lord of the Manor of High Bray, was redeemed by the payment of £6 to Sir T. D. Acland.

1890   A cottage was built at a cost of £174. 7s. 5d.

1895   A water-wheel was put up at a cost of £85.

BROADWAY (*see* BINCOMBE AND BROADWAY).

BURNHAM (NORFOLK). *The Manor of Burnham Thorpe, or Wyndhams.*

1557   Dr Caius gave this to the College.

It included ordinary copyholds, and the "Scite of the Manor (yᵉ place where yᵉ barne stood)," containing 1½ acres, and also various lands lying in a field called the Fold Course, containing in all 100 acres, subject to a sheep-walk over them.

The Manor had been bought by Dr Caius of Philip and Mary, and before the dissolution had been enjoyed by the Abbey of Wymondham.

When the Manor was sold to Caius there was a lease on it, granted by the Abbey in 1539 for 80 years, held by Sir R. Southwell, who made it over to Sir C. Cornwallis. Our lands were so mixed up with those of Sir C. C. that on the expiration of the lease in 1619 a great suit in Chancery arose. The result was a decree in Chancery in 1620 setting out to the College the "scite" of the Manor and 100 acres, with their abuttals and bounds. One part (called

Wyndhams) of the 100 acres was really meant to contain 50 acres, but was so abuttaled and bounded in the decree as to contain 100 acres of strict measure. Mr Soame, the occupier of the neighbouring land, commenced an action against Mr Pedder, the tenant of the College, when he began to plough beyond the 50 acres; though, while the ground had been fed only, neither did much regard his exact bounds. In this suit Mr Pedder was cast in 1655.

Under the 80 years' lease the rent had been £6. It seems to have been paid most irregularly. Thus, by one entry in the Bursar's Book, we find as many as 11 years' rent being paid at one time.

1619 The 101½ acres were let on a 20 years' lease for £8 wholly in money—at which sum it remained till 1866.

In thus letting the land wholly for a money rent the College seems to have disregarded the Corn Act of 1576. One would have expected that £2, one-third of the "old rent," would have been converted into a wheat and malt rent. May it not have been that, as no part of the land was then under the plough, the Corn Act was not considered to apply?

I have not been able to find out the amounts of the free and quit rents payable in the Manor, when it first passed to the College; but in 1751 they are stated to be £2. 7s. 7½d.

1795 The average value of the field lands was estimated at 7s. 6d. an acre, being reduced by 1s. 6d. an acre on account of the right of sheep-walk over them.

The 20 years' lease used to be renewed before 1768 at very irregular intervals.

							£	s.	d.
In 1675, when 9	years were expired, the fine was						14	0	0
1707	,, 14	,,	,,	,,	,,	,,	26	0	0
1761	,, 5	,,	,,	,,	,,	,,	9	6	0
1768	,, 7	,,	,,	,,	,,	,,	21	10	0
1804	,, 7	,,	,,	,,	,,	,,	45	0	0
1811	,, 7	,,	,,	,,	,,	,,	250	0	0
1839	,, 7	,,	,,	,,	,,	,,	300	0	0

The lease was renewed for the last time in 1846, when, seven years being expired, the fine was £260.

1853 The sum of £260 was paid from the Bursar's Book for division amongst the Master and 12 (Senior Fellows) in lieu of a fine.

1866 The lands were relet at a rack rent of £101. 10s.

1876 There was an exchange with the trustees of H. Blyth, and the College gave up all their lands except Wyndhams, amounting to 50 a. 3 r. 1 p., and took three pieces abutting on Wyndhams and containing 51 a. 2 r. Thus the land now belonging to the College forms a single compact piece of 101½ acres.

The rent was £92 in 1885; £60 in 1895; £55 in 1905; the College paying tithe in 1895 and 1905.

The apportionment in lieu of tithe on our land is £13. 12s. 6d. payable to the Vicar and £13. 12s. 6d. to Christ's College.

The 16 Quarters of Barley.

1572 Nicolas Mynne conveyed to the College 16 quarters of barley a year, payable out of the tithes of the Rectory of Burnham Overy, called the Manor of Lathes. In consideration for so doing he received from the College, "sine fine ut vocant," a lease for 21 years of our Manor of Burnham Wyndhams at an annual rent of £8. He was also to wage law with Sir R. Southwell and make null the lease of the Manor granted to him in 30th Hen. VIII.

1656   The 16 quarters had been rented of the College for many years at £8 a year. The owner of the Rectory now pretended that it was only a rent charge of £8. Upon this a suit arose between the College and him, and the 16 quarters were decreed to the College.

They were then let to the tithe owner on a 20 years' lease at a rent of £8 a year.   The rent of £8 was always carried into the Corn Book, and thus was divided amongst the Master and twelve Fellows.

The lease was renewed, at first at very irregular periods, and afterwards, generally, every seven years.   Like most other renewal fines they were divided amongst the Master and twelve Fellows.

The following are some of the fines paid for renewals of the lease:

					£	s.	d.
1687	20	years	expired	....	35	0	0
1704	17	,,	,,	....	15	0	0
1715	11	,,	,,	....	9	0	0
1729	14	,,	,,	....	20	0	0
1736	7	,,	,,	....	6	6	0
1792	7	,,	,,	....	10	0	0
1800	8	,,	,,	....	21	12	0
1807	7	,,	,,	....	39	12	0
1827	20	,,	,,	....	160	0	0

After this year there were no more renewals.

In 1814, when there was no renewal, the sum of £45. 7s. 6d. was advanced by the Bursar's Book for division amongst the Master and twelve Fellows in lieu of the fine.

Similarly in 1821 £47. 3s. 6d. was advanced; in 1834 £48, and in 1841 £43.

Out of the fine of £160 paid in 1827 the sum of £129 was taken to recoup the Bursar's Book for the advances in 1814 and 1821.

After 1847, when the last lease ran out, the tithe owner had to pay annually to the College the exact value of the 16 quarters.

At first this was paid to the Bursar's Book, from which only the £8 was paid to the Corn Book until it was considered—I suppose—that the Bursar's Book had been reimbursed for the sums advanced by it in lieu of the fines in 1834 and 1841.

From 1856 the full annual value was carried direct into the Corn Book until the Book was given up in 1883.

CAMBRIDGE.   *Barnwell Estate.*

In early times this estate consisted of five pieces of arable in the Barnwell fields and formed part of the demesne lands of the Manor of Mortimer's in Newnham (*q.v.*).   One piece, of 8 acres, lay in the North Field on the E. side of the New River; one piece, of 10 acres, lay in the Middle Field, and three pieces, containing, respectively, 9, 14 and 7 acres, were in Bradmore Field.   They were always let under one lease with all the other demesne lands.   The acreage here given was *by estimation* only and probably exceeded the actual contents.   Thus, the 14 acres was thought by one surveyor to contain only 10 acres.

1801   The land tax on them and the rest of the demesne lands was redeemed.

1807-11   At the Barnwell Enclosure the College received, in lieu of these five pieces, the two following allotments:

(a) In Middle Field, 13 a. 1 r. 27 p.   This consisted, roughly, of the land now bounded by Gonville Place, Hills, S. Paul's and Gresham Roads, with two plots beyond these limits, namely,

(a) the plot between the S. end of Queen Anne's Terrace and the Gresham Road, and extending along this road to the wall of the University Cricket Ground, and

(b) the plot between S. Paul's Walk and S. Paul's Road, extending along this latter road from the Hills Road to Gresham Road, but not (see 1862) extending quite up to where Cambridge Place is now situated.

(β) In Bradmore Field, 11 a. 1 r. 30 p.   This is the property to the N. of the Mill Road (of which part was sold in 1907 to the County Council for a school).

The share of the expenses of the enclosure, paid by the College, was £147. 8s. 2d.

1809   The College bought 36 a. 1 r. 0 p. for £3459 (and auction duty £60) from Lord Gwydir and the other successors in title of the late T. Panton, then recently deceased.   Part of the purchase money was the sum paid by Downing College for our rights over Pembroke Leys (see p. 20).

The purchase consisted of Lots 3–9 and 14 at a sale by auction on November 9 and following days under the provisions of the Act for the enclosure of Barnwell, the Award for which was then proceeding.

The sale was recognized by the Award: so that the 36 a. 1 r. 0 p. appear in it as the (γ) 3rd (18 a. 1 r. 26 p.), (δ) 4th (7 a. 0 r. 29 p.), and (ε) 5th (10 a. 2 r. 25 p.) allotments to Caius College.   They are therein said to lie in Middle Field and to have been purchased by the College from the estate of the late T. Panton.

These 3rd and 4th allotments together, Lots 3–9, extended from the Mill Road, with a frontage along it not quite (see 1865) so far E. as at present, up to the present Gresham Road and round the end of the present Cambridge Place (which occupies part of Lot 2) and on the other side of it, along both sides of the present Glisson Road to the Hills Road and then for some distance along the present Lyndewode Road on both sides of it, but not (see 1841) up to the present Tenison Road.

The 5th allotment, Lot 14, was the rectangular piece through which the S. Barnabas Road was afterwards carried.

The two manorial allotments continued to be let under the same lease with the Newnham Mill as part of the Manor till 1826, when they were let, separately, to the tenant of the Manor for one year at the rent of £60.

The three purchased allotments were let for the rent of £125 on a lease for eight years, from Michaelmas, 1811.

1827   The College began letting plots in this estate on building leases.   The plots were taken up slowly, just on the frontage to Gonville Place and Hills Road, as far as the present S. Paul's Road—the last plot being taken up in the year 1869.   It must be remembered that, until the year 1858, the College had no power to grant a lease for a longer period than 40 years.   Such a lease would be renewed every 14 years.   At first the renewals were for fines and later for an increase of the rent.

1852   Part of the 3rd and 4th allotments was let to Fenner for a cricket ground (now part of the University Cricket Ground).   He had occupied it for some years previously as a subtenant.

The remainder, together with the 5th allotment, continued to be let, partly for gardens, but mostly as a farm, up till 1873, after which they were gradually taken and built over, beginning with bits adjoining the Mill Road.

At different times the College has bought various bits adjoining the large

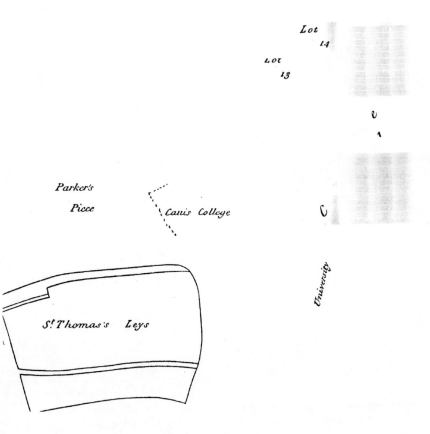

Bradmoor and Middl Fields

Part of the estate of the late Mr Panton, sold by auction, 9 Novemb

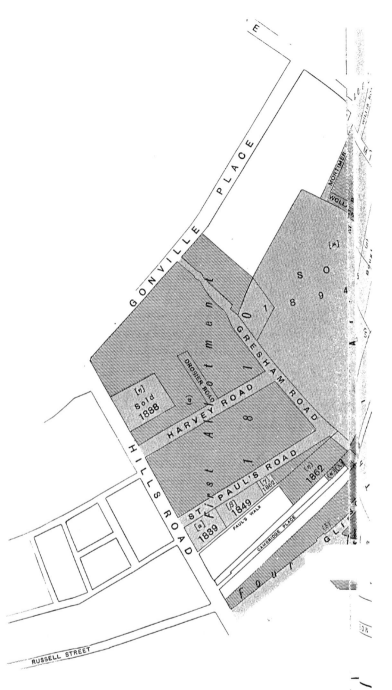

MAP OF THE 3ᴿᴰᵉ

The lighter shadings indicate the prᵗ...

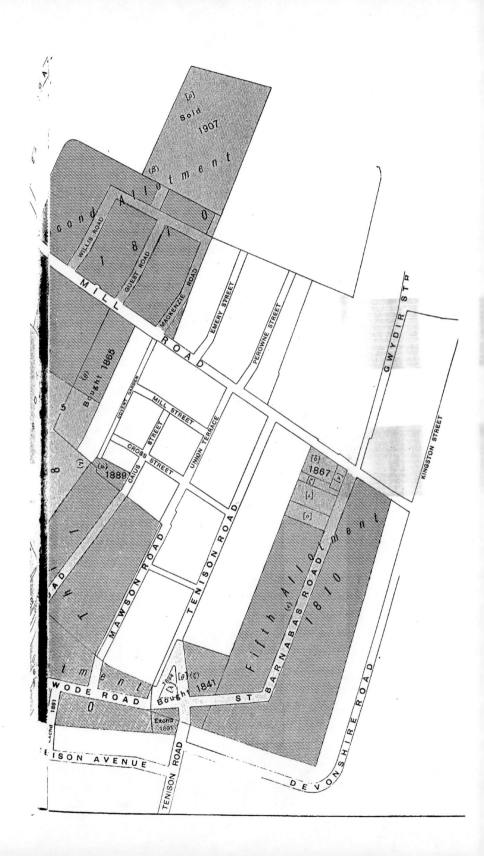

block bought at the auction in November, 1809, all of which were lots, or parts of lots, then sold.

The following are particulars of these various purchases:

1841.   (ζ) Part of Lot 13.   An acre and half, of Mr Humfrey, for £350. This plot connects the two blocks bought in 1809, and across it Tenison Road was carried in 1889.   But for it we could not have connected Lyndewode and S. Barnabas Roads.

1862.   (η) N.W. strip of Lot 2.   Three roods, of W. E. Lilley and H. Gotobed, for £350, with £21. 15s. 6d. for expenses.   This plot lies between Cambridge Place and the E. side of the land (b) allotted to us in 1810.

The money for this was part of the price paid for land taken by the Watford and Rickmansworth Railway Company.

1865.   (θ) Lot 10 and about half of Lot 11.   An orchard, containing three acres, for £3136. 8s. 0d., with £97. 11s. 8d. for expenses.

This land extended along Mill Road and lay to the E. of the third allotment of 1810—between it and Covent Garden (the other half of Lot 11).

The three following bits were parts of Lot 2 and were situated in Cambridge Place.

1876.   (ι) Seven cottages across the end, bought of R. Sayle, for £400.

1878.   (κ) Two cottages on the N. side, of W. H. Jarrold, for £150.

1882.   (λ) The Bell and Crown Public-house on the N. side (next the seven cottages bought in 1876), of Messrs Phillips, for £260.

1889.   (μ) Part of Lot 12 and a bit of Lot 11.   A plot of ground in (the then) Caius Street and Covent Garden, with Burchardt House, in Caius Street and a cottage behind, in Covent Garden, of G. Clark, for £500.   The greater part of this money was the price paid by the Improvement Commissioners for land taken for Tenison Road across the 1½ a. bought in 1841.

The land taxes on portions of these purchases had not been redeemed, consequently the following redemptions have been carried out:

1868, of £1. 5s. 4d. for £35. 17s. 7d.

1871, of 12s. 6d. for £17. 6s. 6d.

1896, of 4s. 10d. on Burchardt House, &c., for £8. 14s. 10d.

1877   Up to this year the plots let on building leases were all abutting on the existing public roads.   Now the College began to develop the interior of the estate and for this purpose to construct roads through it.   These were afterwards handed over to the public.   By the year 1893 £8300 had been spent on them.

The gross rental of the estate, not taking in the large portions sold in 1894, 1895 and 1907, is now (1910) about £3330.

At various times the College has parted with portions of this estate, as follows:

1839.   [a] The site for S. Paul's Church—frontage to Hills Road 90 feet and depth 120 feet—price £350.

1849.   [β] The site for S. Paul's Parsonage House—one-third of an acre— price £175.

1862.   [γ] The site, 392 square yards, beyond S. Paul's Parsonage House, appropriated to the Ely Almshouse Trust.   Upon this were built the Almshouses in 1865 for £505. 12s. 7d., i.e. the College took the site (98 square yards) of the old houses in Trinity Lane, and built the new houses and handed them over to the Trust.

1867.   [δ] A quarter of an acre was given as the site for S. Barnabas Church.

1872.   [ε] An encroachment by the tenant of Mr J. Eaden, in Covent Garden, was sold to Mr Eaden for £32. 5s. 0d.

1876.   [ζ] The site for S. Barnabas School—¼ acre—was sold for £80, but the College subscribed £50 to the building fund.

1888. [η] The site in Hills Road for the Perse (Boys') School—was sold for £4500.

1889. [θ] Tenison Road was carried across our land and the Improvement Commissioners paid us £488. 8s. 0d.

1891. [ι] One-third of an acre was given as the site for S. Barnabas's Vicarage House.

This year there was a rectification of the boundaries, with Jesus College, near the junctions of Lyndewode Road with Tenison Road and with a road (Tenison Avenue) made to lead out of Lyndewode Road to the property of Jesus College, which paid £62 for equality of exchange.

1894. [λ] The triangular piece of land (now a public garden) at the junction of Tenison and Lyndewode Roads was dedicated to the Public and £473 was charged to the Corporation; but was allowed back to the Corporation as a consideration for taking over the Glisson, Lyndewode and S. Barnabas Roads.

[μ] Fenner's Ground, with a portion of a garden adjoining, was sold to the University Cricket and Athletic Clubs for £13,500.

1895. [μ] A further piece of land (2½ acres) was sold to the same Club for £4000.

1898. [ν] A site at the E. end of S. Barnabas Church was given for the Parish Institute.

1904. [o] A piece of land next the Parsonage House of S. Barnabas Parish was sold for £420, as a garden for the Parsonage House.

1907. [ρ] A plot of ground, 4 a. 0 r. 12 p., to the N. of Collier Road was sold to the Cambs. County Council for £4078 as the site for a school.

Upon 28 pieces of this estate there are tithes (of S. Rhadegund) payable to Jesus College, of which the Apportionments amount to £5. 2s. 6d.: their total area is 16 a. 0 r. 4 p.

S. Thomas's (or Pembroke) Leys—anciently. called Swine's Croft—the present site of Downing College (see Vol. II of Willis and Clark's History).

In these Leys our College originally owned 9 acres. They formed part of the Manor of Mortimer's, and up to 1806 were let to our tenant with the other demesne lands.

1801 An Act for enclosing the Leys was passed.

1803 The Enclosure Award allotted to us 7 a. 2 r. 36 p., extending along Lensfield Road from Tennis Court Road to the waste grounds next S. Andrew's Street.

1804 The College paid £137. 1s. 4d. as our share of the expenses connected with the enclosure.

1807 Our allotment was sold to Downing College for £618. 8s. 1¾d. + £62. 10s. 9d.

Scroope House and Terrace.

The greater part of the site of these houses—called Gravel Pit Close—was part of the demesne lands of the Manor of Mortimer's, with which it was originally let. It was always *estimated* to contain 4 acres: the more accurate *measurement* was 4 a. 2 r. 29 p., as shown on the map accompanying the Enclosure Award of Pembroke Leys.

1804 The College paid £37. 4s. 2d. as the Commissioners' Rate for enclosing Gravel Pit Close, and £99. 17s. 2d. for extinguishing the rights of common over it.

1808 The tenant of Mortimer's surrendered this Close to the College, and on two small portions a house, &c., and a cottage, &c., were built.

1809 A lease, to terminate at Michaelmas, 1848, was granted for the first of these portions. The annual rent was 10s. for the first 11 years and £5. 5s. afterwards.

1810 The College bought of Mr P. Musgrave, for £240, a slip of land at the E. end of the Close (expenses, £8. 9s. 6d.); and granted a lease, to terminate at Michaelmas, 1848, of the portion on which the cottage had been built, together with the purchased slip, at a rent of £10; also a lease of the remainder of the Close, at a nominal rent, to terminate at Michaelmas, 1819.

1820 The College bought of the Rev. T. Musgrave, for 30 guineas, a piece of land, 18 feet long, adjoining the land purchased in 1810.

These two purchases made up, together, one rood, lying between the Gravel Pit Close and the present Trumpington Street.

After this, £10 a year was paid for the long leaseholds together, and £15 for the annual tenancy of the remainder of the Close together with the 18 feet purchased this year.

1837 The two building leases were bought for an annuity of £85 for the next 12 years.

The house (Gonville Cottage), with its gardens, &c., was let at a rack rent. It was situated at the S. end of the Close. The remainder of the frontage to Trumpington Street, to a depth of 180 feet, was reserved for houses.

The remainder, at the back (3 acres), was let on a building lease for 40 years—several times since renewed—and on this Scroope House was erected.

1839 The front land was let on building leases for 40 years and the first seven houses of Scroope Terrace were erected.

1864 Gonville Cottage was pulled down and the materials sold.

The last five houses of Scroope Terrace were built by the College at a total cost of £8704. 15s. 9d., provided as follows:

	£	s.	d.
From the Stokys Book (see DILHAM)	5210	15	2
From the Halman Book (see MEPAL)	990	0	0
From old materials sold	176	11	6
From the Reserve Fund	2327	9	1
Total	£8704	15	9

Pease Hill.

1534 This property, together with a portion of that at Haddenham (q.v.), was bought of W. Buckenham for £300, part of the gift of Dr Baily.

The rent was always £2. 3s. a year.

The following are some of the fines for renewals of the 21 years' lease of the property:

			£	s.	d.
1655	7 years expired		6	13	4
1670	8 ,, ,,		8	10	0
1720	7 ,, ,,		10	0	0
1746	3 ,, ,,		4	5	0
1794	7 ,, ,,		13	0	0

A rent charge of 3s. a year was payable to Jesus College out of this property.

1762 Mr J. Smith surveyed it and describes it as having a frontage of 12 feet to the Pease Market on the east, a depth of 41½ yards from E. to W. and a width of 46 feet at the back. Along the greater part of the W. end it abutted on the "Eagle and Child."

There were then on it a tenement in front and two cottages in the yards at the back.

1803 The whole property was sold to —. Brown for £347. 11s. 6d., invested in £512. 15s. 0d. Consols.

King's Parade.

1626 Dr Gostlin (Master of the College) devised to the College "a house or houses, called the 'Rose and Crown.'" He had bought it in 1622 for £280.

For a note on the penny payable annually out of this property to Corpus College, *see* p. 82 of Dr Venn's Vol. III.

At first the Bursar appears to have collected the rents from the various occupants of the different houses on the property, and entered in his Book each half-year the somewhat varying amount of the rents which he had obtained.

In March, 16$\frac{57}{58}$, we have in the *Gesta* orders to arrest one of the tenants and to seize the goods of another "for rent behind."

From Lady Day of this year it was let on a lease for 20 years to Alderman Blackley at a rent of £18; and at this figure it remained till 1839.

In 1690 the property was let on a lease for 20 years; and in 1693 it was relet on a 40 years' lease, the tenant undertaking to spend £100 on it within the next two years.

In 1707, when the lease for 40 years was renewed, no fine was taken, "only Registers Fees."

The fines at subsequent renewals were as follows:

		£	s.	d.
1721	....	5	0	0
1735	14 years expired, fine	20	0	0
1756	21 ,, ,, ,, ...	27	0	0
1775	19 ,, ,, ,, ...	25	0	0
1789	14 ,, ,, ,, ...	16	0	0
1803	14 ,, ,, ,, ...	16	10	0

The money spent by the tenant in 1693–5 was probably applied to alterations in the house on the N. side—as the house on the S. side was replaced by two a century later. Possibly the alterations may have amounted to re-building the present chemist's shop—as the College, in 1707, by taking no fine for renewal, showed that the tenant was thought not to have recouped himself for his outlay, and even in 1721 the fine was only £5.

1762 In Smith's *Survey* the property is described as a tenement, with the appurtenances, the side against Trumpington Street being 15 yards and the depth 20 yards—"called formerly the 'Rose and Crown' now the 'Six Bells.'" It is said to abut south (partly) and east on the "Eagle and Child," which thus separated it from our property on Pease Hill.

The lease of 1775 describes the property as "a messuage or tenement called the Mitre, in High Street; also another tenement, fronting the same street, with the stables and houses thereto belonging; likewise several (four) tenements lying behind."

In 1804 the description of the property is the same as in 1775.

In 1824 a survey of the property says that it consists of *three* houses *next* the street and three at the back, and puts the gross annual value of the whole at £193.

In 1829 the College grants a license of alienation, in which leave is given to split the tenancy into two and the houses on one (evidently the southern) portion are spoken of as having been *recently rebuilt,* and two cottages are said to lie at the back of the other (the northern) portion. Evidently the two houses on the southern portion had been rebuilt between 1804 and 1824.

At the split the rent for the northern portion is put at £6, that of the southern portion at £12.

In 1839 the old lease was surrendered and the northern portion was relet on a 14 years' lease for £46 a year, and the southern for £72.

In 1853 the rents of the two portions were £80 and £115.

In 1890 the rents were £100 for the house on the northern side and £125 for the southern portion.

1893   The southern portion was conveyed to Trinity College, with the "Blue Boar" property in Trinity Street, in the exchange noted below.

Trinity Street—opposite the College.

In 1893 our College had an exchange of property with Trinity College, by which we acquired one house, with a shop, and two dwelling-houses in Trinity Street to the south of S. Michael's Churchyard, of which the annual rental was £282. 10s. The land taxes on them amounted to £6. 1s. 10d.

There is also an approach to this property from S. Mary's Court.

The total area is 5776 sq. ft., and the frontage to Trinity Street 72 feet.

In the exchange we gave up to Trinity College the "Blue Boar," in Trinity Street, a house and part of our laboratory in Gifford Place, two houses in King's Parade and £1500.

1909   The College bought of Messrs Carter Jonas and Sons, for £1500, a building behind No. 3 Trinity Street, intending to use it for a lecture-room.

1910   The land tax on the property acquired in 1893 was redeemed for £182. 15s.

Rose Crescent.

1887   The College bought Nos. 7 and 8 Trinity Street and Nos. 14–23 Rose Crescent from W. Clayden for the sum of £17,100, and £257 for expenses. These houses lay on the N. and E. of the Churchyard of S. Michael's, between it and the Rose Crescent.

The houses were turned into chambers for students at a cost of £5722 and formed "S. Michael's Court."

The Court was rebuilt in 1901 and 1902 for £19,523.

1905   The College bought a house on the north side (No. 3) of the Rose Crescent from A. C. Newman for the sum of £1225, and £37 for expenses.

Trinity Street and Gifford Place.

1864   The College bought this property of Dr Whewell, the Master of Trinity College, for £3200.

It consisted of the following three freeholds:

    The "Blue Boar" Inn and premises, annual rent .   £115,

    Two tenements (being the portions of a tall red-
      brick house), annual rent £20,

    Two other tenements, annual rent £16;

and a house held on a lease for 40 years from 1841 of the Vicar of Effingham and let at the annual rent of £110, raised in 1878 to £150. Of course the latter passed from the College in 1881. The sum paid for the freehold portion was £2367. The legal expenses of the purchase were £51. 6s. 7d., of which the Salisbury and Yeovil Railway Company paid £41. 6s. 7d. for reinvestment of money paid for land taken at Oborne.

1869–70   Stables and a coach-house for the use of the Fellows were built on a portion of the "Blue Boar" premises, next Gifford Place, at a cost of £315.

1871   The billiard-room of the " Blue Boar " was turned into a laboratory at a cost of £260.

1878   The stables, &c., were converted into a lecture-room at a cost of £280.
Considerable alterations and additions to the laboratory accommodation have subsequently been made from time to time.

1893   The conditions of the exchange with Trinity College of part of this property, &c., for houses in Trinity Street, opposite the College, have been already explained (p. 23).

1909   The remainder of this property was sold to Trinity College for £4000.

Mill Lane.

1896   For £2150 the College bought, of the trustees under the will of C. M. Bidwell, a dwelling-house, with yards and stables, abutting on Mill Lane, with an access from Granta Place.
The rent was £105. The land tax on the ground was £2. 9s. 6d.

Fairclough's Holt (Coe Fen).

1692   The executors of Mr S. Fairclough (Venn, Vol. i, p. 379, and Vol. iii, p. 235), in accordance with his will, renewed the lease of this holt for 40 years from the Corporation of Cambridge at the rent of £4 and assigned it to the College.
The holt lay a little above the King's Mill, between the river and Coe Fen.
The College sublet it for 39 years, with a covenant that every 14 years the College would renew the lease from the Corporation and its own lease to the subtenant, he finding the money for whatever reasonable fine the Corporation might require for the renewal.
In 1754 Smith's *Survey* describes the property as consisting of
(1) A tenement, with garden of ½ acre, abutting W. on river, E. on Coe Fen in part and passage to Coe Fen in part, and N. on continuation of street from Little S. Mary's Church to river, and S. on Coe Fen in part and on (2) in part.
(2) A meadow of two acres, abutting W. on river and E. on Coe Fen.
In 1770 the fine for renewal paid to the Corporation was £21; in 1784 £26. 5s.
At the first the rent paid to the College was £7; but in 1784 it was raised to £10.
In 1790 the College sold its interest in the property to the subtenant for £80, with which the College bought £100 Consols, which were held up to 1806; but after that date they do not appear in our accounts.
The accounts for this Benefaction were evidently kept in a separate book, which I have been unable to find.

Newnham (Manor of Mortimer's).

1498   Lady Anne Scroop (Venn, iii, p. 215) devised this Manor to the College.
(In some of our documents and books we find the medieval Latin equivalent, de Mortuomari, for Mortimer's. The propriety of this equivalent is discussed on p. 506 of Vol. i of the 8vo. edition of Blomefield's *Norfolk*.)
Lady Anne Drury gave £40 " for the procuring of it in mortmain."
The license for this was obtained from the King.

1501–2   The Mayor, Bailiffs and Burgesses of Cambridge gave their license to the trustees of Lady A. Scroop to assign the Manor to the College. The demesne of the Manor is therein said to consist of
The Newnham Mill, with one close adjoining; one close, called Newnham Close; and 99 acres in the town and fields of Cambridge.

The whole property is said to be held of the Corporation "in burgage." All rents, &c., and other things arising to the Corporation are reserved (Cooper's *Annals*, Vol. I, p. 257).

1506–7 A composition was made between the Corporation and College respecting this Manor, said to be held of the Corporation as of their highgable, providing for the payment of 18s. a year to the Corporation and for the conditions under which the mill might be run, as explained by Dr Venn (Vol. III, p. 23).

The 18s. is still paid : it was said in the indenture to be a " highgable rent." It was, probably, one of the " Hagabul" payments with which the greater part of the houses in Cambridge were charged in 1278, as stated in the information supplied to the King's Commissioners in that year (Cooper's *Annals*, Vol. I, p. 60. See also pp. 18, n. 4, and 227).

Highgable was a municipal house tax. Maitland, in his *Township and Borough*, calls it "Hawgafol."

1507 The College leased the Manor to the Corporation for 99 years at the rent of 20 marks (£13. 6s. 8d.).

1515 The accounts of the treasurers of the town show that the mill and lands were relet for £18 a year.

1545 A report to the King (Venn, Vol. III, p. 339) gives the rent of Newnham as £15. 8s. 0d. The difference between this sum and the rent of the demesne lands would be made up by the quit rents, which then therefore amounted to £2. 1s. 4d.

1605 The lease to the Corporation being about to expire (1606) the Corporation obtained letters from the King commanding the College to renew it ; but, on the College addressing His Majesty, the mandate was withdrawn and they had liberty to grant a lease to whom they pleased (Cooper's *Annals*, Vol. III, p. 19).

The new lease was granted to W. Paget for the use of Dr Legge (then Master of the College) for 20 years, from Michaelmas, 1605—one year before the old lease expired.

In consequence of the Act of 1571 (p. ii) the College could not give a lease for longer than 21 years.

In accordance with the Corn Act of 1576 the annual rent was set at £8. 17s. 8d. in money, with 6 qrs. 6 bush. of wheat and 8 qrs. 7 bush. of malt. At these figures it remained till 1858.

1606 Upon the expiration of the old lease it was found that some of the rights and possessions of the College were confused with those of the Corporation and were thus lost to the College (*Annals*, Venn's edition, p. 212). The then Fellows were anxious that this should be recorded in the *Annals*, that their successors might understand how it happened that the rights of the College had been curtailed.

1607 Dr Legge died and left to the College his interest in this lease. It was vested in feoffees for the College, viz. Perse, Drisborough and Batchcroft.

At or before this time the whole property had been sublet in four different holdings :

(1) The mill and adjoining grass close, let for £48 a year (after Mids^r, 1618, at £44).
(2) Butchers' Closes for   8
(3) Part of the arable for 17
(4) Remainder of arable for· 17

Total £90

Apparently the custom was for the Bursar to collect half-yearly (quarterly from the Miller) the rents due to the feoffees, and, after deducting the "old rent" for the Bursar's Book and the corn money for the Master and (12) Fellows, to carry the "overplus" up to the Treasury, as shown by the book called "*Status Collegii*," in which are recorded the various withdrawals from and additions to the hoard in the Treasury.

In some memoranda at the end of the Bursar's Book are given the prices of wheat and malt used each half-year in calculating the corn rents between 1616 and 1619.

Thus, at Michaelmas, 1617, the 3 qrs. 3 bush. of wheat, at 5s. 7d. a bushel, came to £6. 15s., and the 4 qrs. 3 bush. 2 pecks of malt, at 2s. 4d. a bushel, came to £4. 2s. 10d.—total, £10. 17s. 10d., of which, after deducting £2. 4s. 6d. for the Bursar's Book, £8. 13s. 4d. was handed over for division amongst the Master and (12) Fellows for "their commons and diett."

By Michaelmas, 1619, there had been thus brought up to the Treasury the sum of £646. 10s. 5d. as Legge's Gift.

The lease held by the feoffees had still six years to run, but a new lease was then granted to a man named Woolfe, the feoffees apparently surrendering their lease and £140 being brought up and added to Legge's Gift—which thus amounted to £786. 10s. 5d. From it was taken the £660 required in 1618 and 1619 to pay for the building then erected next Trinity Street, to the north of the Gate of Humility, and hence called Legge's Building. It is for this reason that the letters T. L. (for Thomas Legge) have been carved over the entrance to the present staircase P.

The £140 mentioned above as compensation for the surrender of the lease was no doubt taken out of the "fine" paid by Woolfe for the lease granted to him. The remainder of the fine would be divided between the Master and (12) Fellows.

The grant of the lease in 1605 for the use of one who was then Master of the College excites surprise. No doubt the College was anxious to obtain a tenant at once, for fear it should be further pressed by the King or Corporation, and at the same time to have the property retained in friendly hands— but, as the money obtained from Legge's bequest of his interest in the lease is always spoken of as his absolute gift and the building was called after him, we must conclude that he paid to the Master and Fellows the usual "fine" for his lease, as any other lessee would have done.

1667   The following is a summary of the acreage of these lands, as given in the terrier :

	a.	r.	p.
Mill, house and close	1	2	0
Meadow adjoining, called Mill Piece	1	2	0[1]
Butchers' Close	7	0	0
On the W. side of Cambridge :			
In Middle Field	20	0	0
In Howe Field	15	2	0[2]
In College Field	6	0	0
On E. side of river :			
In S. and E. Fields	5	0	0[3]
In Forth Field	8	0	0[4]
In Swinescroft	9	0	0[5]
In Middle Field	10	0	0
In Bradmore Field	30	0	0[6]
Total	113	2	0

[1] Called in 1778 A Midsummer Piece.
[2] Of these, five acres, in 1778, are said to be Beyond Trinity Conduit Head.
[3] Four acres only in 1778, and in 1751 called "A Lammas Enclosure behind Peterhouse Gardens." Afterwards called Gravel Pit Close—*see* Scroope Terrace.
[4] In 1751 said to abut on the New River.
[5] Also called S. Thomas's, or Pembroke Leys,—now part of the site of Downing College.
[6] In 1799 this was thought to be over-estimated by four acres.

In a folio MS in the College Library (No. 733, p. 50) we have a statement of the actual annual value of this estate in or a little before 1682. It was then sublet in five different tenancies and brought in a total rent of £105. 18s. 0d. to the beneficial leaseholder.

1751   A careful survey of the whole Manor was made by J. Smith, Bursar. The schedule of lands agrees with that of 1667. He gives a list of the quit rents due to the College. They were as follows ·

	s.	d.
From Jesus College	16	6
„ Trinity College, for Bold's Gift	0	10
(Both these are still paid.)		
For four acres in Barnwell Field	3	0
(Paid by Mrs Ayre in 1850 for the last time.)		
For a house and barn near Mill Close, formerly Wendy's	1	0
(Overlooked after 1858, when the demesne was rack-rented.)		

It is also stated that five other quit rents were payable, amounting to 15s. 6d. : they were however no longer received. It may have been the loss of them of which the Fellows complained in the *Annals* for 1606.

We saw that in 1545 the quit rents amounted to £2. 1s. 4d. One of the quit rents (1s.) was said to have been for a house in Preacher's Street, opposite to the Convent of Preachers, now Emmanuel College.

In addition to the above there was also another quit rent of 10d., paid by Peterhouse, for seven selions of land at Hinton, in the Cambridge Field : this was redeemed by Peterhouse in 1871 for £1. 6s. 8d.

The whole of the demesne being let on a lease for 20 years, the following are some of the fines paid for its renewal :

				£	s.	d.
1664	7	years expired		63	0	0
1673	9	„	„	95	0	0
1721	6	„	„	70	0	0
1736	7	„	„	105	0	0
1764	7	„	„	95	0	0
1778	7	„	„	148	10	0
1799	7	„	„	240	0	0

1799   From this year onwards portions of the lands originally let with "the Scite of the Manor and the Mills" were gradually withdrawn from the successive leases of the mills, &c., and built upon, the rent of the mills, &c., remaining at the same figure till 1858.

At first Butchers' Piece was the only land excepted from the lease, and on this occasion the tenant paid a fine of £240.

Butchers' Piece, one of the closes abutting on (the present) Queens' Road, containing about one acre, was let to Mr Wilkins (probably the father of the Fellow, Venn, Vol. II, p. 130). Upon it he had built his house (now Newnham Cottage). The lease was for 40 years and the rent was at first 10s.

[As this was our earliest building lease it will be of interest to trace the way in which it was dealt with by the College, as an illustration of the methods pursued in similar cases. It will be remembered that it was not till 1858 that the College obtained power to grant building leases for periods longer than 40 years.

Soon after the lease was first granted the rent was raised to 18s. in consequence of the imposition of the land tax.

1813   Upon the renewal of the lease the tenant paid a fine of £125, which was divided amongst the Master and (12) Fellows, and, as it was found that the tenant had built beyond his leasehold, the boundaries were refixed and the new lease was made to include the whole of the land on which the buildings stood and the new rent was set at £2.

1827   The fine was £150.

1841   The fine was again £150 and the rent was set at £5.

1855   Fine £90 ; new rent £10.
       After 1857 fines for renewals of leases were not given to the Master and (12) Fellows for division, but were entered in the Bursar's Book.

1869   Fine £140 ; rent £10.
       After 1879 the College ceased to accept fines for renewals of leases, but increased the reserved rents.

1883   The rent was set at £24. 18s. 0d.

1907   At this renewal it was £64. 3s. 0d.]

1801   The land tax on the whole Manor was redeemed for £828. 9s. 5d. Consols.

1804–5   The enclosure of S. Giles's parish took place.
       The College paid £84. 15s. towards the expenses of it ; and received the three following allotments :
       (1)   12 a. 2 r. 11 p., abutting E. on Butchers' Closes and N. on (the present) West Road.
       (2)   7 a. 3 r. 9 p., abutting N. on the S. Neots Road.
       (3)   2 r. 32 p., exchanged under the Award with Corpus Christi College for 3 r. lying next to, and afterwards thrown into, the Newnham Closes. (*See* Wortley Purchase, p. 29.)
       The map attached to the Award shows that Butchers' Closes made up the pieces abutting on the present Queens' Road and extending from the present Sidgwick Avenue to West Road.

1806   It was arranged that only the "Scite of the Manor," the mill and 3 acres of meadow adjoining and the allotment on the S. Neots Road should be let for 20 years, and that the tenant should give up the remainder in 1819, when the lease of 1799 would have run out.
       The new lease was made out accordingly and the tenant paid a fine of £170 only, the Bursar's Book paying £120 to the Master and (12) Fellows in lieu of the remainder of the fine, which would have been paid by the tenant, if the whole had been relet for 20 years.

1809   The leaseholder, having assigned his interest in Gravel Pit Close to one Brown, and having surrendered his lease, had a fresh lease granted to him for 20 years as from Michaelmas, 1806, the terms being exactly the same as in the lease surrendered, except that the Gravel Pit Close was not included.
       The College at the same time agreed to give Brown or his nominees leases of the different parts of Gravel Pit Close (*see* Scroope House and Terrace).

1811   The effect of the Enclosure Award, as regards the portions in the Barnwell Fields, has been already explained (p. 18).

1813   Upon the renewal of the lease the tenant paid a fine of £270, and the Bursar's Book £396, for division between the Master and (12) Fellows. The lease was for 20 years, but only the mill and the 3 acres of meadow were to be held for the whole period ; it being agreed that all the other lands should be given up in 1820, except the allotment on the S. Neots Road, which was to be held till 1826.

1820 Upon renewal the tenant paid the fine of £280, and the Bursar's Book £233, for division. Only the mill and the 3 a. were to be held for 20 years; the three allotments, viz., the 7 a. 3 r. 9 p. on the S. Neots Road, the 13 a. 1 r. 27 p. in Middle Field, and the 11 a. 1 r. 30 p. in the Bradmore Field in Barnwell were to be given up in 1826.

This left the pieces next the present Queens' and West Roads to let separately. They have since been gradually let on building leases, except the pieces nearest to the mill, viz., 1 a. 0 r. 17 p. in S. Giles's parish and 2 r. 23 p. in S. Mary the Less, which now form the Fellows' Garden.

1827 The new lease related to the mill and 3 acres only. The tenant paid a fine of £360, and nothing was paid by the Bursar's Book, for division.

The allotment on the S. Neots Road was then let separately, and now (since 1903) forms the second cricket field.

The way in which the *Barnwell* portion was subsequently dealt with has been already explained (pp. 18–20).

1838 The fine for renewal was £480.

1854 The mill was burnt down and rebuilt in the following year.

1858 When the old beneficial lease at last ran out, the mill and the 3 acres of meadow were relet at a rack rent of £220.

1893 The Corporation paid £420 and took $814\frac{1}{2}$ sq. yds. and $127\frac{2}{3}$ sq. yds. to form part of Sidgwick Avenue, giving up to the College $57\frac{2}{3}$ sq. yds., which till then formed part of the footpath called Pightle Walk, the remainder being absorbed into Sidgwick Avenue.

1901 For £300 Selwyn College Public Hostel bought 1160 sq. yds. lying next the College and abutting on Grange Road.

In Maitland's *Township and Borough* will be found many references to this Manor, especially at pp. 179 and 180, §§ 104–6.

Wortley Purchase in Trinity Street, Newnham, and Grantchester.

1782 With £1700 belonging to the Wortley Benefaction the College bought of T. Lombe the reversion (after the death of C. Finch) of

(1) Certain tenements at the S.E. corner of the College;
and of several closes, namely,

(2) Slegg's Closes of 6 acres in Grantchester (*q.v.*);

(3) A close of Lammas land, estimated as containing $1\frac{1}{2}$ acres, extending from the E. side of the Newnham Way to our Mill Piece;

(4) Newnham Closes, estimated at 10 acres, on the W. side of Newnham Way—opposite to (3).

In the same year, with a further sum of £100 belonging to the Wortley Benefaction, the College bought of J. Simpson his reversionary interest in

(5) a house holden by lease of Trinity Hall for 40 years from 1783.

(1) and (5) formed the block of buildings pulled down in 1868, when the present staircases, N, O and P, were built on the site.

The fact of the site having been bought with Wortley money is commemorated by the statue of Wortley at the W. end of this building and by the letters B. W. (for Bartholomew Wortley) carved over the entrance to the staircase N.

1789 A plan drawn this year shows that (4) consisted of four closes, containing in all 8 a. 2 r. It will be remembered that in 1805 the 2 r. 32 p., obtained from Corpus College under the Enclosure Award of S. Giles's parish, were added to these closes. (*See* p. 28.)

In this year the row of elms by the W. side of the pathway through these closes was planted.

1791   For £20. 4s. 6d. the College redeemed the annual payment of 14s. to the
Crown for these lands—probably (4).

1797   This year, for a fine of £22. 10s. 0d., Trinity Hall renewed the lease of (5) to
our College; and in 1800 the freehold was bought for £200 under the Act for
the redemption of land taxes, for which purpose Trinity Hall used the purchase
money.

1799   The land taxes, amounting to £15. 10s. 6d., on these houses and on the
Newnham lands were redeemed for £569. 5s. 0d. Consols.

1802   The Newnham Closes were exonerated from tithe at a cost of £105. 16s. 2d.

1872   The College took part of the closes for a cricket ground; and subsequently,
for the same purpose, took all the remaining parts lying to the west of the
pathway through them.

1899   Clare College, desiring to develop their land beyond the N.W. corner of our
Cricket Ground, purchased from our College, for £200, a strip of land containing 660 square yards and lying along the greater part of the N. side of
our ground, and covenanted to make a road along the N. side within 10 years
—we undertaking, as soon as the road was made, to fence it on our side.

1909   The road not having been made and Clare College having sold their land
to Newnham College, the latter College agreed to make the road within the
next 10 years or to reconvey the strip to our College.

CAPEL (SUFFOLK).

1354   For the consideration of £200 Sir John Fitzralph conveyed the Advowson
of three-parts of the Church of Capel, near Braham (? Barham), in Suffolk,
to John Tyrington, Master of the College, and Walter Elveden, one of the
Fellows—evidently feoffees for the College.

   Thence there were conveyances to other feoffees at very short intervals—
sometimes in successive years, and in one year there were two conveyances;
till at length in 1468 and again in 1472 the last feoffees conveyed to the College.

   At first, in 1354, it seems to have been thought that Sir J. Fitzralph was
possessed of and conveyed to the feoffees the whole of the patronage, but it
was always the three-parts which subsequently each successive set of feoffees
conveyed to the next set.

1479   Sir R. Chamberlaine, having married Elizabeth, the sole heir of Sir J.
Fitzralph, claimed the right of presentation, and the Bishop accepted and
instituted his nominee. The Master of the College commenced an action but
was non-suited.

   After this time the College, at different vacancies, tried to get their nominee
instituted—notably in 1503, 1623 and 1631; but on his arrival on the spot he
found the nominee of the successor of Sir R. Chamberlaine already instituted,
and was told by the Bishop "Ecclesia est plena."

   There is no record of any presentation having been made by the College
since that in 1631.

CAUSTON OR CAWSTON (NORFOLK).

1493   Lady Elizabeth Clere gave (amongst many other things, Venn, Vol. III)
£40 to buy farms at Causton.

1540   These were sold and the purchase money was applied to buy certain lands
in Newnham and certain lands in Cowling (p. 35) and Cartling, called
Bansteds (see Annals, Venn, p. 11).

   It does not appear where these "lands in Newnham" were situated and what
was afterwards done with them.

CAXTON (CAMBS).

Dr Caius left directions in his will to purchase lands to the annual value of £10, that those of his foundation should be free from the charge of firing, and that the Porter should have £2. 13s. 4d. a year.

1574 His executors accordingly bought for £240 all the lands and tenements called Swannesley Manor, in Caxton, late part of the possessions of the Monastery of S. Neots, then of the yearly value of £10 and a brawn or 13s. 4d. in lieu thereof. In the deed conveying the property to the College it is stated to consist of "two messuages, seven tofts, one dovecote, two gardens, two orchards, 160 acres of land, 30 acres of meadow, 300 acres of pasture, 10 acres of wood, 160 acres of furze and heath, and common of pasture for 24 oxen, one bull, 10 cows, 400 sheep and 40 pigs with their young with their appurtenances."

It will be noticed that the above acreage is much greater than that of the farm as given at subsequent surveys, e.g. in 1762. Possibly the above is the acreage of the whole Manor, whereas it was only the demesne lands which the College actually acquired.

1632 The College bought of R. Levett, for £3, one acre, in the middle of our lands, which they let for 3s. 4d. with the farm.

1762 A survey of the estate was made by Mr J. Smith, President.

The acreage was put at 172 a. 2 r. One part of this was a pasture called Broad Close, near the Church, put down as 7 acres, but thought by Mr Smith to contain more. In it was formerly a messuage—at the S.W. angle—mentioned in Dr Legge's *Survey* in 1579. The remainder consisted of several pieces larger in size and therefore less numerous than the usual components of farms at that time; but from the description they must have lain widely apart and at some distance from the village.

In a close of arable land, called Swannesley Hill, containing 80 acres or more, at the S.E. corner, there stood then a brick barn, the only building on the estate. Near this barn, in Dove House Close, stood at one time the messuage which Dr Legge, in his *Survey*, calls a new building.

The arable land was then valued at 6s. an acre, and the pasture at 12s.

The tenant kept a flock of 400 sheep.

1777 The acreage was put at 163 a. 1 r. 3 p., the annual value at £49. 5s., and the annual value of the sheep-walk at £5.

1801 The land tax of £6. 19s. 0d. was redeemed for £254. 16s. 8d. Consols.

1803 For £107. 19s. 2d. the College bought, of J. Godfrey, half an acre, containing house, barn and pightle, in the village, and let it to the tenant of the Manor for £4. 4s.

1805 The Manor is said to consist of:

	a.	r.	p.
A barn, and dove house and close adjoining (the site of the Manor)	3	0	0
A close (apparently the piece near the Church and called Broad Close)	8	0	0
Lands lying in the common fields, viz.:			
In Swannesley, or Wood, Field	110	2	0
In Mill Field	30	0	0
In Stow Field	21	2	0

There was also a sheep-walk for 152 sheep—i.e. 14 sheep for every 20 acres of common field land, or 112 sheep, and 40 sheep in addition for the Manor.

It will be noticed that statements of area given at different times (1574, 1762, 1777, 1805) vary considerably. This is partly due to the fact that the acreage of fields was formerly settled by "estimation" and not by measurement, and that surveyors often reckoned only three roods to the acre. (*See* p. 34.)

1824	The College bought for £94. 5s. 3d. a house, yard, garden and close containing 2 r. 10 p., let for £10 a year.

This property was not added to the farm.

The *Registrum Magnum* speaks of 3 acres of pasture as having been bought at this time and added to Broad Close; but I cannot find any other trace of such an addition.

About £140 was spent this year in building a "cottage" on the farm.

1827	Some planting (of trees) was effected at an expense of £20.

1830	At the enclosure all the land in the parish was carefully measured and a considerable area was allotted to the tithe owners in lieu of tithe, thus rendering all the parish tithe-free.

The Award states that the exact measurements of the pieces retained by the College were as follows:

		a.	r.	p.
1	Wood Close	13	0	19
2	Swannesley Close	3	2	11
3	House and garden	0	1	20
4	Swannesley farmhouse and garden	0	1	13
108	Close	0	1	17
109	House, yard and garden	0	0	33
157	Broad Close	9	3	11

The College gave up a strip of land containing 3 r. 10 p. (probably that purchased in 1803) and received the following allotments:

		a.	r.	p.
1st	In Swannesley Hill Field	102	2	33
2nd	In Wood Field and Cow Common	30	2	35
3rd	On the Green	0	1	22
4th		1	0	33

The 4th was bounded on the N. by the brook, but on all other sides by Broad Close, to which it was added, together with the 3rd allotment, which lay just to the W. of Broad Close.

The old enclosures, Nos. 1–4, with the 1st and 2nd allotments, formed one continuous area and, with Broad Close, formed the farm.

The College contributed £145 towards the expenses of the enclosure; and

1835	there is a record of £243. 2s. 0d. being paid for fencing, draining and planting woods on the farm.

1861	The barn was blown down and rebuilt at a cost of £145. 7s. 0d.

1877	The College bought, for £2, of the Old North Road Turnpike Trustees, 6 poles of land, part of the site of the toll-gate house and garden.

1899	All the farm, except Broad Close, (150 a. 3 r. 11 p.) was sold to the nominee of Mrs Hooley (the wife of the well-known financier) for £2500.

When the farm came into our possession in 1574 the annual rent was £10 and a boar. In 1576 the Corn Act was passed, and accordingly at the first subsequent reletting the £10 was changed to £6..13s. 4d. in money together with 5 quarters of wheat and 6 q..5 b. 1 p. of malt or their value in money, and it is in this shape that the rent appears in our earliest records, except that £2 had to be paid in default of the boar, and, in 1632, 3s. 4d. was added to the rent for the acre bought that year, and, in 1803, £4. 4s. 0d. for the tenement then added to the holding.

As usual the farm was let on a 20 years' lease, which was renewed—with fair regularity—every seven years.

The earlier fines for renewal are generally about £25; but after 1760 they increased. In 1798 the fine was £53.

The lease granted in this latter year was run out, and in 1807 and 1812 the sums of £60 and £113 were paid from the Bursar's Book to the Master and (12 Senior) Fellows in lieu of the fines which they would have received had the lease been renewed in 1805 and 1812.

In 1818 the farm was let to a new tenant for nine years at an annual rent of £70 for the first three years, and £80 for the next three years and £90 for the last three years. By Lady Day, 1823, the tenant had not paid more than £48 in all: so that we are not surprised to find an order in March of this year empowering the Master and Residents to relet the farm. However the then tenant was kept on and paid £30 in 1824, £50 in 1826 and £50 in 1827.

From 1818 till 1826 there was paid from the Bursar's Book to the Corn Book—for division between the Master and 12 Seniors—whatever in each year would have been the value of the old corn rent above £3. 6s. 8d., as well as the £2 for the boar.

In 1826 the farm was let on a lease for 20 years to a new tenant, and it was agreed that he should pay the old annual rent of £6. 13s. 4d. with the corn rent and boar or their value, and that in each of the first three years he should pay an additional rent of £115. This last condition is unique, so far as I know. It is possible that it was actually a fine paid for the lease in three annual instalments. They were duly received and entered amongst the rents in the Bursar's Book.

After the enclosure an additional rent was paid by the tenant.

The lease was not renewed, but in 1834 the sum of £150 was advanced from the Bursar's Book in lieu of the fine for its renewal.

In 1844 a new lease is granted for 16 years for the old annual corn rents together with £26. 13s. 4d. in the first year and £74 in each of the last 15 years.

In 1861 a lease was granted for 8 years at the money rent of £110 without any corn rent.

In 1875 the rent was £150; in 1885, £81; in 1895, £45; in 1898, £70.

In 1900 the rent of Broad Close, the portion retained after the sale in the preceding year, was settled at £20.

CHATTERIS (CAMBS). *Advowson of the Vicarage.*

1909   This was obtained, in exchange for the advowson of Ashdon, from the Rev. C. H. Brocklebank.

The glebe, including the site of the Vicarage House and buildings, contains 279 a. 2 r. 20 p.

The Vicar receives the interest on £576 Leicester Corporation stock, bought, in 1902, for £576, the proceeds of the sale of 56 a. 2 r. 35 p. of glebe.

He also receives in lieu of tithes a corn rent created under the Enclosure Award in 1819, which is the value of 3117·693 bushels of wheat. The price per bushel is the average price of wheat at Wisbech Market for the preceding 7 years as fixed from time to time by Quarter Sessions. The average was last fixed, in 1896, at 3s. 4¾d.

CHESTERTON (CAMBS).

1503   W. Batesford devised by will his lands in Chesterton to our College (if we refused, to Clare) for the maintenance of a priest (to sing for him) in Chesterton, giving him nine marks a year.

     These lands were by force detained by one E. Batesford, a kinsman of W. B., and do not appear to have ever passed to the College.

1507   William Sigo (Venn, III, p. 225) gave his house at Castle End, in Cambridge (called the " Maid's Head "), and his lands in the fields of Cambridge, Chesterton, Histon, Girton and Coton (*i.e.* in the open fields between these five places)—late John Rawlins'—" to the maintenance of 20*s.* a year for a Bible clerke."

     He also gave £21. 13*s.* 4*d.*, the proceeds of the sale of his lands at Ikworth, (? Ickworth) in Suffolk.

     The house and 5 a. 1 r. of the land was at one time let for 16*s.* 4*d.* a year; but the house is said to have been alienated by John Skippe (Master) in 1540.

     Of some of his property W. Sigo appears at the time of his gift to have been only the equitable owner. For we have immediately afterwards a conveyance to the College by Margaret Rawlins (widow) of a tenement at Castle End and 7½ acres and ½ rood of land in Cambridge and Chesterton.

1541   The whole, or part, of Sigo's lands was copyhold of the Manor of Chesterton. With the Lord of this Manor the College agreed in 1541 to pay a quit rent of 5*s.* a year, and, in lieu of fines, 13*s.* 4*d.* upon the election of a Master.

     Sigo's and the Ely Almshouse lands in Chesterton, from 1671, were always let to the same tenant under one lease.

     The "old rent" of Sigo's land was 25*s.* a year.

1604   The "old rent" was converted, in accordance with the Corn Act of 1576, into 16*s.* 8*d.* in money and a corn rent of 1 quarter of wheat and 4 bush. of malt.

     The tenant had also to bring a couple of capons at Christmas or 3*s.* 4*d.*, and a wether at Easter or 6*s.* 8*d.*

1754   The whole of the land at Chesterton was valued at 7*s.* an acre and was said to be not more than 3 rood land, *i.e.* land reputed to measure an acre actually measured only 3 roods.

1833   The acreage and valuation of all our lands in Chesterton was as follows:

	a.	r.	p.		£	s.	d.
East Field	2	1	0	at 28s.	3	3	0
Middle Field	11	0	20	at 20s.	11	2	6
West Field	20	1	0	at 15s.	15	3	9
Total	33	2	20		£29	9	3

1840   The Enclosure Award allotted 34 a. 1 r. 22 p. (all freehold) in one allotment to Caius College, of which ⅛th has ever since been regarded as belonging to the Ely Trust.

     The following are some of the fines paid for the renewal of the 20 years' lease:

				£	s.	d.
1671	13 years	expired	....	20	0	0
1691	20	,, ,,	....	50	0	0
1706	7	,, ,,	....	7	0	0
1797	7	,, ,,	....	12	13	0
1806	7	,, ,,	....	20	0	0

In 1813 and 1820 the lease was not renewed, and the Bursar's Book advanced £54 and £56 for division amongst the Master and (Senior) Fellows.

1825 This year the fine was £250.

After this the lease was not renewed for a fine, and in 1832, and again in 1839, £50 was advanced for division.

In 1832 the College allowed £100 towards the roof of the barn.

1845 The whole of our land in Chesterton, *i.e.* the allotment of 1840, was let at a rack rent of £46 a year. In 1885 it was £55; in 1895, £42. 10s. 0d., College paying tithe.

The Apportionment of the tithe rent charge on the whole allotment is £8. 16s. 3d.

Boat House.

1878 The Boat Club bought the site for £450. It had a frontage of 122 feet to the river on the south and adjoins the Ferry Path on the east.

1903 The Club bought for £75 an additional triangular piece, containing 17 square yards, on the east of the site. It was conveyed at once to the College.

1905 The original site was conveyed to the College by the trustees, who had up till then held it for the Club (*see* Venn, Vol. III, pp. 307 and 308).

CHILTON (DURHAM).

1669 Bp. Cosin (of Durham) gave us £28 a year out of his lands at Chilton (Venn, III, p. 232).

He also gave to Peterhouse £58 a year issuing out of the same lands, so Peterhouse now collects our annuity for us.

COWLING (SUFFOLK). *Manor of Bansteds, &c.*

It is not clear how we came by this Manor. Caius in the *Annals* (p. 30) says it was bought with part of the money obtained from the sale of the land at Causton.

1505 He also says (*Annals*, Venn's edition, p. 22), that the Manor was acquired from W. Gale of Eye in Suffolk for £96 previously given us by him. It was of the annual value of £4. 10s. 0d. [Gale also gave to the College his lands in Hinxton, of the annual value of £4.]

1540 T. Atkyn, Vicar of Mutford, and Margary Hore, of the same place, each gave £48, with which were bought certain possessions in Cowling and Cartling, of the annual value of £4. [T. Atkyn gave us also Payne's Close, in Worlingham.]

But John Skippe, Master, was compelled by E. North (afterwards Lord North and Baron Cartling) to sell to him these estates, with our lands at Hinxton, for £300, with which was bought (1540) the Manor of Aynells, in Westoning, of the annual value of £14.

Rent Charge.

1712 A rent charge of £40, issuing out of the Manor of Caldebecks in Cowling, was bought for £860—Francis Dickyns contributing £400, to enjoy the rent charge for his life; the College contributing £460, to have the reversion.

1748 F. Dickyns died and the rent charge fell to the College.

1800 The land tax of £5. 10s. 0d. was redeemed for £201. 13s. 4d. Consols.

1889 As in the original deed, securing the rent charge, the lands subject thereto were described by the occupation of the then tenants, the exact delimitation of the lands had become practically impossible; and the owner, wishing to deal with them, at his own cost and with the consent of the College, executed a new deed charging certain definite lands with the rent charge.

DENVER (NORFOLK). *Dr Brady's and Mr Lightwine's Benefactions.*

1700   Dr Brady (Master) by will, dated Aug. 25, 1694, devised to the College (a collection of books, valued at £300, and) his estate, 186 acres, at Denver, leased for £130 a year.

     Out of this, annuities, amounting to £50, were to be paid and £500 to be raised to buy two Rectories, whereof Denver was to be one, if possible. After these payments had been made, the produce of the estate was to be divided into 10 "portions," of which the Master was to receive two, the President and the Frankland Fellows one each, and the College chest one.

1718   Before this year Mr Lightwine, the executor, had laid out £324 in building the house.

1721   The "portions" were first paid. Each was £6.

1723   The annuity of £40 to Mrs Fuller, which had to be paid out of the estate, came to an end and the value of each portion rose to £10.

1728   N. White, Rector of Denver (*see* under *Advowson*), devised by will, proved Sept. 14, 1728, an estate, containing 58 a. 2 r. and having many oaks and ashes growing on it, of the annual value of £40, the College to pay £800 in legacies within six months of his death.

1729   The College bought 4 acres of meadow land for £100 from R. Wilkinson and Mary, his wife, of the annual value of £4. It lay to the south of part of Mr White's land.

     Mr Lightwine (President) devised to the College by will, dated Dec. 19, 1723, his estate at W. Dereham, of the annual value of £50, to be applied to the same uses as Dr Brady's Benefaction.

1732   In consequence each portion was raised to £14.

1733   The College exchanged with the Benefaction the land, left by Mr White and that purchased of Wilkinson, for Mr Lightwine's at W. Dereham; but reserved to itself all the timber arising from the estate left by Mr White (*see* under BASSINGBOURNE). [From the receipts in subsequent years, as noted below, from sales of timber, it would appear that the timber formed a considerable part of the value of an estate at Denver.] Thus Mr White's and Wilkinson's lands came to be called Mr Lightwine's land, and all the land then owned at Denver was kept for the same uses and under the same management (viz. the Master's and not the Bursar's).

     Before the exchange the Denver rent for the Brady Benefaction had been £130, and that of W. Dereham £50: after the exchange the Denver rent became £160.

     After tithes, taxes and repairs had been allowed for, there remained each year not quite enough to pay the £140 for the 10 portions, and the balance in the hands of the Master, which had been recruited (1739 and 1749) by the sale of timber for about £125, was gradually drawn upon, and

1756   the College lent, without interest, £300 to the Benefaction, which then purchased, for £500, Old South Sea Annuities amounting to £556. 11s. 6d., and thus increased its income by about £19. Sir James Burrough was then Master.

1763   At his death he devised to the College an estate at Wilton for the use of this Benefaction. This estate was let for £28. 10s. 0d. a year, out of which the College allowed tithes, taxes and repairs.

1766   There was a sale of 78 oaks for £278, and the Benefaction bought £100 Old South Sea Annuities for £89. 5s. 0d.

1767 Again an equal quantity of Annuities was bought for £86. 17s. 6d.

1771 Again an equal quantity of Annuities was bought for £85. 2s. 0d.

1778 It was agreed to repay to the College the loan of £300, lent in 1756, by handing over to the College Sir J. Burrough's estate at Wilton and the clear produce of it from 1764 to Michaelmas 1776, the date to which the rent had then been paid.

1780 Seventy-three oaks were sold for £320; a barn was built for £280; the rent was reset at £180, and £200 Reduced Bank Annuities were bought for £118.

1785–99 £800 Reduced Bank Annuities were bought at prices varying from £68 to £97 per cent.

1791 The value of each "portion" was raised to £17.

1799 £614. 3s. 4d. Reduced Bank Annuities were expended on the redemption of the land tax amounting, in Denver parish, to £16. 8s. 0d., and, in Fordham, to 7s. a year. This left £385. 16s. 8d. Reduced Bank Annuities, as well as £866. 11s. 6d. Old S. S. Annuities.

We sold 2 a. 3 r. 10 p. in Fordham and I r. 26 p. in Denver to E. R. Pratt for £150 and £15 interest, as the payment was not made till 1801, when £214. 3s. 4d. Reduced Bank Annuities were bought for £143.

The rent was set at £240.

1800 The value of each of the 10 portions was raised to £24.

1802 The £866. 11s. 6d. O. S. S. Annuities were sold for £586, and £900 Reduced 3 per cents. were bought for £624.

Thus the amount of Stock then belonging to the Benefaction was £1500 Reduced 3 per cents.

1819 The estate was divided into two holdings.

1827 The rents, which had fluctuated in several previous years, were settled at £327. 10s. and £45.

Timber was sold for £108.

1834–5 There was a sale of 62 oaks for £260, of which £172 was spent on claying the land.

1840 The sum of £16. 11s. 6d. was paid as the College share of the expenses of the commutation of the tithe.

1841–2 £600 was spent on the buildings: and a bill for repairing the pew at Church for £1. 11s. 4d. was paid.

1843 There was a sale of 83 loads of stone, which produced £9.

1846 The Ely and Lynn Railway Company, crossing Old Dikes, took 1 a. 1 r. 16 p. and paid into the Court of Chancery £226, which was invested in £255. 1s. 5d. Consols.

The interest on this investment (£3. 14s. 3d.) was received for the half-year to July, 1847. I cannot find that the Benefaction received any subsequent dividend.

1860 The estate was merged in the general College property. The rents were then £327 and £45. The Benefaction had rolled up £5600 Reduced 3 per cents. and a cash balance of £350, and had been paying since 1817 £40 a year on each of the 10 equal portions.

Comparing the map, of which a copy is annexed, with the careful surveys made by Mr John Smith, Bursar, of Lightwine's (White's and Wilkinson's) lands in 1752 and of Brady's in 1754, we can make out whence each piece was obtained by the College.

Brady's lands (marked with a B on the map) consisted of:

(1) All the land S.W. of the Church, containing the house and homestead, to which two common rights are attached;

(2) Two pieces W. of the Church—down Dunster Lane: the further of these is now laid to one of Lightwine's lands;

(3) Old Dikes, containing 46 acres (estimated at 40 in 1754) before the 1 a. 1 r. 16 p. were taken for the railway, and stretching from Sluice Common to Middle Drove;

(4) South Fen, above Denver Sluice, containing 47 acres (estimated at 43 in 1754) and stretching from the Old Bedford River ("10-mile Bank") to the New Bedford River ("100 foot"). It is shewn in the in-set on the map. It lies nearly a mile above the Sluice.

Lightwine's lands (marked with an L on the map)—partly left by White and partly bought from Wilkinson—consisted of

(1) Nightingale's, a close of 5 or 6 acres, N.E. of the Church;

(2) Six pieces, containing 53½ acres (estimated at 56 in 1752) lying in pairs and approached by the three lanes called Pokam, Dunster and Crow Hall.

The 4 acres bought from Wilkinson lie in the S.E. corner of the piece at the end of Crow Hall Lane.

Advowson of the Rectory.

1705 Mr Lightwine—Dr Brady's executor—bought, for himself, the two medieties of the Rectory of Denver for £521. 10s. 0d., of which Mr Jenny, the then Rector, contributed £150 on the understanding that his Curate, Mr Nicholas White, should succeed to the Rectory, which he did in 1715, Mr Jenny dying April 10.

1715 Mr Jenny, by will dated 7 March, 1714, devised to the College, in trust for the Rector, four closes, adjoining the house, containing 15 a. 1 r. 17 p.

1716 Mr Lightwine sold the Advowson to Dr Brady's Benefaction, of which he still had the management, for £500.

This sum he gave to the College to be laid out in repairing and adorning the Chapel.

1753 There was an exchange of 3 roods 9 perches of Glebe, formerly Jenny's, for 2 a. 0 r. 34 p. of Mr Thurlow Stafford's lands.

1791 There was another exchange of 4 a. 3 r. 28 p. of Glebe for 5 a. 1 r. 28 p. of John Thurlow Dering's land.

1799 The land tax on the Rectory was bought by the Wortley Trust for £520. 13s. 4d. Consols.

1900 The Glebe contains 94 acres, and the tithe rent charge is apportioned at £911.

The Rector also owns two common rights, of which one was let in 1900 for 30s.

Smith's Lands and New Purchases in Middle Drove.

1852 S. Coleby Smith, Rector of Denver, by will dated June 23, 1851, devised to the College two farms, containing together 141 a. 2 r. 18 p., one between the Middle Drove and S. John's Eau, and the other (called Tallymore) between S. John's Eau and the River Ouse, below the Sluice. These are marked by X on the map.

Mr Smith in his lifetime had cut off 2 acres of the most northerly of his grounds in Tallymore, leaving its acreage as 13 a. 2 r. 10 p. instead of 15 a. 2 r. 10 p., and had added them to the Glebe to the S. of this ground.

This was to compensate for a diminution by 2 acres which the Glebe had suffered in his time.

1868 The College bought, for £100, of O. Blower, 2 acres between Middle Drove and S. John's Eau. This piece is farther from the Middle Drove homestead than any of Mr Smith's grounds, except the one with which it is now united— the ditch between them having been filled in. This is marked by Y on the map. For this a free rent of 1s. is paid to the Manor of West Hall.

1872 The College bought, of — Beton, 14 acres for £840, part of the money paid by the Dereham and Wells Railway Company for land taken at Elmham and Fakenham. This piece is the first—counting from the homestead—of the grounds which extend in one piece (*i.e.* without a cross ditch) from the Middle Drove to S. John's Eau. This is marked by Z on the map.

1898 Mr Coleby Smith also devised to the College the reversion, after the death of his nephew (F. Smith), which took place in 1898, of his farm (late Hutson's), containing about 36 acres and extending from the Middle Drove, nearly opposite to our last piece, across the railway up to the west side of the only piece of Lightwine's land which lies to the west of Pokam's Lane. This farm is marked by U on the map.

1900 The College bought, for £580, of S. H. Smith, 11 a. 3 r. 18 p., with 2 cottages thereon, between Sluice Common and Middle Drove. The expenses of the purchase were £27. 16s. 0d.

The part of this land which was copyhold of the Manor of West Hall was enfranchised at a total cost of £29. 6s. 8d. This land is marked by V on the map.

The apportionment of tithe rent charge on the whole of our estate in this parish is £78. 13s. 6d.

So much of our lands as lie west of the Ely-Lynn railway, including South Fen, is subject to drainage taxes. They lie some in one and some in another, and some in more than one, of four drainage districts which overlap each other. In three of these districts the taxes vary considerably from year to year. The total taxes average £78. 7s. 8d. a year on the 254·398 a., of which 46·592 acres are in South Fen.

The College has always paid part, and in some years all, of the Drainage Taxes; and in later years the tithe.

In 1875 the whole rental of our agricultural property in the parish was £645; in 1885 (part being unlet) £193, College paying tithe; in 1895, £289; in 1905 (after additions to the property), £420.

Schoolhouse.

1903 The executors of Sir Geo. Gabriel Stokes, Bart. conveyed to the College the site of the Schoolhouse, in accordance with arrangements made by Sir George in his lifetime. He was the brother of W. H. Stokes, a former Rector.

1907 Mrs E. de V. Beechey conveyed to the College a strip of land adjoining the site of the Schoolhouse. She was the widow of St. V. Beechey, a former Rector.

DEREHAM OR EAST DEREHAM (NORFOLK).

1703 A rent charge of £32 a year—free of all taxes—issuing out of a messuage, called "The Lodge" of East Dereham Park, and 234 acres, was bought with £800 belonging to the College, from H. Webster.

1802 The rent charge was sold for £800, invested in £1406. 11s. 11d. of 3 per cent. Consols to help to form a fund, with which to redeem the land taxes on various properties belonging to the College (*see* also HOCKWOLD and MORDEN).

DILHAM AND HONING (NORFOLK).

1634 Mr Matthew Stokys, Fellow, died and bequeathed to the College, by will dated July 20, 1631, the lease from the Bishop of Ely of the two Rectories of Dilham and Honing.

The annual rent paid to the Bishop was always (for 232 years) £13. 6s. 8d., and the lease was for 21 years: in 1661, when the lease was wholly run out, the College had to pay a fine of £500 for a renewal of the lease.

In 1799 the land tax, £9. 13s. 10d., was purchased for £355. 7s. 2¾d. Consols.

The lease was renewed from time to time, generally every seven years, until in 1866 the last lease was run out.

In 1868 the Ecclesiastical Commissioners purchased the land tax for £325 Consols—expense to the College £1. 1s. 0d.

The financial results of this Benefaction are interesting.

The fine paid to the Bishop every seven years for the renewal of the lease was at first (1641) £90, in 1669, £80. After that it sank till, in 1701, it was only £35. From that year it rose again till, in 1774, it reached £100, and there it remained till, in 1802, it was put at £200; in 1810 (8 years expired) at £500; in 1817 and at all following renewals, until the last in 1845, it was about either £1000 or £900.

In the earlier times, as the fines indicate (being then 1¼ years' value after the rent to his Lordship had been paid), the annual values did not vary much.

In 1776 the receipts were £105 as against £70, at which they had stood for many years. From this date the surplus rolled up till, in 1781, the College was able to buy £400 Consols (3 per cent.) for £224. 10s. 0d.

By 1791 the amount of Consols owned by the Benefaction was £1000, and the College, instead of letting the tithes to an intermediary, as heretofore, began to receive direct from the occupiers a composition of £114. 2s. 6d. for Dilham and £93. 9s. 3d. for Honing.

1799 The Benefaction contributed £250 " towards the £6000 and upwards lately expended in new College buildings and very expensive repairs " and "contributions for internal defence." *Gesta*, Oct. 30.

The compositions with the occupiers of land in the two parishes gradually rose, and finally, in 1814, were set at £297. 11s. 0d. and £229. 11s. 0d. respectively.

After the passing of the Tithe Commutation Act the apportionments of tithe rent charges were set at £315. 9s. 3d. for Dilham in 1842, and £283. 4s. 6d. for Honing in 1845.

Though the payments to the Fellow and Scholars provided for in Mr Stokys's will were considerably increased, the Benefaction still continued to buy Stock, and in 1861, when, under the new Statutes, this account began to be merged with the Bursar's College Account, the amount of Stock held was £7550 Consols and £500 Reduced Annuities, and the cash balance was £2047.

The account was kept open till 1868, when the lease had run out and the land tax had been purchased by the Commissioners.

By that time £4910 Consols and the £500 Reduced had been taken to form part of the new Reserve Fund, and £5086 Consols and £1780 cash had been taken to find the money for part of the cost of building the last five houses in Scroope Terrace and for the purchase of a leasehold in Trinity Street from Dr Whewell; also £800 had been taken (1854) to help to defray the cost of Hall, Kitchen, Library and Combination-room (*Gesta*, Nov. 1, 1854).

Ditton Hall and River

DITTON OR FEN DITTON (CAMBS).

For Poplar Hall Farm, *see* HORNINGSEA.

1904 For £4800 the College bought, from the devisees of J. W. Prior, Ditton Hall with 71 a. 2 r. 23 p.

Part of this estate is the pasture extending up the whole length of the Long Reach from the ʻPaddock, belonging to Ditton Rectory, to the Ditch immediately below the railway. The whole is freehold.

1905 A portion of this meadow, next the river, was fenced off to form an enclosure at the Boat Races.

The College spent £450 in 1906, £234 in 1907 and £110 in 1908 on the house and buildings.

DUXFORD (CAMBS).

1586 Mrs Joyce Frankland left (besides the Philip Lane property in London, which see) £1540 to buy lands of the yearly value of £70. 10s. 0d.

She was a benefactress of Brasenose College also.

1599 With the money was bought the reversion, after the death of Jane Middlemas, of the Manor of Dabernoons, in Duxford;

1606 and also—of R. Dunne—a tenement and 32 acres, copyhold of the Manor of Dabernoons.

1611 The above were conveyed to the College by the trustees under Mrs Frankland's will.

The annual income of the estate was then :

	£	s.	d.
Rent of farm	62	0	0
Customary and free rents of Manor	11	15	0

1648 The College bought, for £160, of Sir T. Symonds, two tenements, one croft and one acre of meadow.

The tenements (called Trope's and Malkin's) were turned into the farmhouse (in the village). *Gesta*, 1832, Feb. 25.

1677 May 18. The granary and dovecote were burned, owing to a fire in the Vicarage house adjoining, through no negligence or carelessness of the occupying tenant. Therefore the College in the next year paid £141. 15s. 7d. for the repairs, besides giving 120 oaks felled at Croxley (in Rickmansworth), for which the lessee paid the carriage.

1757 The farm consisted of 466 a. 2 r. 20 p., lying in 135 parcels, and common rights on upland commons and half-year lands for 300 sheep and great cattle.

1783 The College paid the beneficial leaseholder £40. 9s. 0d., being a quarter of his expenses in a (successful) lawsuit about our right to a sheep-walk.

1799 The College redeemed the land tax for the whole (of the then) estate, amounting to £17. 18s. 0d., by the transfer of £576. 3s. 0d. of 3 per cent. Consols.

1812 The extent of the farm was estimated at 457 a. 3 r. 32 p. and sheep-walk for 12 score sheep and common rights; but this acreage was thought to be incorrect and too small.

1823 The College bought two cottages and land (one acre) abutting on the farm called Hatch's, or Hitch's—for £216. 2s. 6d., copyhold of the Manor of Temple.

At the enclosure an allotment of 348 a. 3 r. 1 p. was made to the College, on 19 a. 1 r. 25 p. of which plantations were made.

1826   The acreage of the whole farm was 419 a. 2 r. 9 p.

1827   The College paid the beneficial leaseholder £140 for his interest in the land taken for plantations.

1823–32   The College spent between £1500 and £1600 for new buildings, plantations and other expenses connected with the enclosure. *Gesta,* 1832, Feb. 25.

1843   On the commutation of the tithe the share of the expense paid by the College was £25. 12s. 2d. (the beneficial leaseholder paying also £16. 11s. 5d.).

1845   The Eastern Counties Railway Company paid at the rate of £100 an acre for the 2 a. 1 r. 13 p. taken by them.   Of the proceeds our tenant received £90 and the remainder was invested in £152. 15s. 10d. Consols.

1867   The beneficial lease was run out and the farm was divided into two, viz. :
West Farm (The Allotment) 348 a. 3 r. 1 p.   Tithe, £109. 10s. 6d.   Rent, £394 ;
East Farm (in and around the village) 68 a. 1 r. 4 p.   Tithe, £25. 9s. 8d.   Rent, £116.

1868   A block of three cottages was built on the West Farm for £242. 17s. 6d.

1880   The College sold, to T. Holliday, for £6, 12 perches, formerly copyhold of the Manor and containing Rust's tenement.

1883   New buildings were erected on the West Farm at a cost of £305.

Frankland Book. Up to the year 1832 the receipts and expenditure on account of Mrs Frankland's Benefaction had been entered as part of the College Accounts in the Bursar's Book; but in this year it was decided that a separate account of them should be kept.   It was, however, found that, in consequence of the purchases of land, &c., subsequent to the original benefaction, and the improvements, which had been made with monies belonging to the College, one-seventh (in value) of the Farm belonged to the College.

Thus the then income of the new Book was made up of six-sevenths of the proceeds of the farm and all the proceeds of the rest of the Manor and of the London property.

By the year 1860, when the consolidation of the College Accounts took place, the Book had accumulated £1550 in Government securities, in addition to £150 Consols taken in 1854 to help to pay for the new hall, kitchens, &c.

The farm used to be let at a fixed annual rent of £62 on a lease for 20 years, which was renewed, generally, every seven years, for a fine.

This property presents a remarkable instance of the fixity of rents which formerly prevailed.   From the time it came into the hands of the College until the year 1867 the rent of the farm remained at £62, notwithstanding the additions made to it at different times and the improvements effected at the expense of the College.   The return for these would be the increase in the fine that would be paid every seven years for the renewal of the lease.

Thus an addition or an improvement to the farm was made at the expense of the Corporate Funds and the increased consideration paid every seventh year would, if the new Frankland Account and Book had not been started, have been considered to have been wholly the private property of the then Master and 12 Seniors.

The following are some of the fines paid for fresh leases at different times :

					£	s.	d.
1671	7	years expired	....		14	0	0
1687	9	,,	,,	....	35	0	0
1717	7	,,	,,	....	22	0	0
1750	20	,,	,,	....	66	4	0
1767	17	,,	,,	....	180	0	0

		£	s.	d.
1774	7 years expired	50	0	0
1797	7 ,, ,, ...	157	0	0
1804	7 ,, ,, ...	210	0	0
1812	7 ,, ,, ...	750	0	0
1819	7 ,, ,, ...	550	0	0
1826	For renewal of old lease, 7 years expired	726	8	0
	For new lease, for 20 years, of allotment for soil at recent enclosure	98	12	0
1833	7 years expired, total	684	0	0
1840	7 ,, ,, ,, ...	778	0	0
1847	7 ,, ,, ,, ...	800	0	0

After this the beneficial lease was not renewed.

According to the arrangement made in 1832 six-sevenths of the last three fines were entered in the new Account Book of the Frankland Benefaction; the remaining seventh being divided amongst the Master and (Senior) Fellows.

Petersfield Purchase.

1891 The College bought of the executors of J. Oslar the farmhouse in the High Street, with buildings and homestead (2 a. 3 r. 3 p.), copyhold of the Manor of Temple, together with 212 a. 2 r. 22 p. of arable land (partly copyhold), with frontages to the Ickleton and Duxford Grange Roads, for £3600, of which £3500 were the proceeds of the sale of land at Foulden to Lord Amherst.

	a.	r.	p.	
Of the 212 a. 2 r. 22 p.,	10	2	20	were freehold,
	130	3	10	copyhold of the Manor of Dabernoons,
	42	2	16	,, ,, ,, Temple,
	28	2	16	,, ,, ,, Lacey's.

The copyholds of the Manor of Temple were enfranchised at a total cost of £440. 7s. 8d.; the copyholds of Lacey's at £196. 15s. 2d. The money for these enfranchisements was provided from funds held by the Board of Agriculture on account of sales, &c., of other College lands.

A portion of what was copyhold of the Manor of Dabernoons is subject to the charge of distributing herrings to the poor of Duxford annually, now commuted for an annual payment of 15 shillings.

The apportionment of the tithe on our whole property in this parish is £210. 12s. 5d.

The total rental in 1875 was £524; in 1885, £435; in 1895 (after the above addition), £470, College paying tithe; in 1905, £511.

ELMHAM OR NORTH ELMHAM (NORFOLK).

1749 Bartholomew Wortley devised this amongst other estates (*see* ATHERINGTON) to the College. (He appears to have given £762 for the freehold portion.) 10 a. 2 r. are copyhold of the Manor of Nowers, the quit-rent being 17s. 2d.

1799 The land tax (£6. 4s.) was redeemed for £227. 6s. 8d. Consols.

Before the enclosure (1830) the estate consisted of 93 a. 1 r. 0 p. and common-rights for an unstinted number of cows. After the enclosure it contained 107 a. 2 r. 0 p., lying in two separate parcels.

1838 The tithe apportionment is £14. 9s. 0d.

1847 The Norfolk Railway Company took 3 a. 1 r. 3 p. and paid £550.

1848 The same Company took 1 a. 3 r. 25 p. and paid at the rate of £100 an acre.

1882 The G. E. R. Company took 4 a. 2 r. 12 p. and paid £900, invested in £825. 13s. 3d. Consols.

The rent in 1875 was £150; in 1885, £90; in 1895 (College paying tithe), £72; in 1905, £50.

FAKENHAM (NORFOLK).

1749 Bartholomew Wortley devised this amongst other estates (*see* ATHERING-TON) to the College. It was all copyhold, the acreage and quit rents being as follows:

Manor of Fakenham Lancaster, 47 a. 3 r. 20 p., quit rent 9s. 6d.
„ „ Rectory, 2 r. 0 p., „ „ 3d.

The fine in both Manors is 4s. an acre.

He had inherited 20 a. 1 r. 30 p. in the first-named Manor from his father, John Wortley.

He also left £1 a year to the poor of Fakenham to be paid by the College so long as the Churchwardens should keep in repair his father's tomb in the Churchyard—on the S. side of the Church—(*Caian* for 1905, Vol. XIV, p. 99).

1799 The land tax (£5. 19s.) was redeemed for £218. 3s. 4d. Consols.

1800 The Wortley Fund redeemed, for £48, from the proprietor of E. Barham Foldcourse his right of shackage over these lands (called the "half-year lands").

1807 The acreage was estimated at 50 a. 2 r. 30 p.

1856 The Wells and Fakenham Railway Company took 2 r. 19 p. and paid £150.

1861 The same Company sold to the Wortley Fund 1 r. 29 p. for £18. 0s. 0d., paying also £1. 7s. 2d. expenses.

1867 At the enclosure the College received an allotment of 1 acre, which was let for £1 annual rent.

The fields lie very scattered about the town.

The tithe apportionment upon the whole of the property is £23. 4s. 0d.

1908 The College enfranchised the whole of its copyhold land in the Manor of Fakenham Lancaster for £75. 2s. 2d. and £37. 7s. 3d. expenses.

The College also sold, for £420, 1½ a. of No. 133 on the Ordnance Map to the Norfolk County Council as the site for a school.

1910 For £123. 15s. we redeemed the tithe, apportioned at £4. 19s., on the 9 a. 3 r. 32 p. out of No. 133 retained after the sale in 1908.

FOULDEN (NORFOLK).
Advowson, Rectory and Vicarage.

1354 The College bought the advowsons of Foulden and Wilton from the Priory of Lewes, with the licenses of Lords Arundel and de Poynings, of whom "in capite tenebantur."

The Priory had been in receipt of pensions of £5 and £2. 10s. a year from the Churches of Foulden and Wilton respectively. The right to these was conveyed to the College upon the mediety of the Church of Walpoole being appropriated to the Priory, as compensation, by the Chapter of Norwich.

The Bishop (Bateman), with the consent of the Chapter, of Norwich, gave his license for the College to appropriate, after the next vacancy, the Church (*i.e.* the Rectory) of Foulden to the College, reserving for the Vicar £10 a year[1] and a suitable dwelling-house ("competens habitatio") and for the Bishop and his

[1] This, I suppose, meant that, besides the house to be provided, there should be reserved Vicarial glebe and tithe so much out of the glebes and tithes as would bring in an income of £10 a year.

successors £1 a year in lieu of firstfruits, and ordaining that at a vacancy
the College were to present two persons, of whom the Bishop was to choose one
and institute him as Vicar, and that the College might let the tithes and glebes,
but not for a period longer than five years.

We have no direct statement as to the acreage of the glebe lands. But a
survey by Dr Brady, made in 1661, puts the extent of all the land then owned
by the College at 112 a. 2 r. Deducting from this 25 a. 2 r., the amount of
the various lands acquired between 1354 and 1661, as stated below, we get
87 a. as the Rectorial glebe.

Part of it was a 3-acre piece, in which stood the Rectory House (called also
the Impropriation House) and the large barn.

The fixed rent of the glebe and tithes was £11. 13s. 4d., the tenant paying
all out-rents, such as the £1 to the Bishop and the £1. 6s. 8d. to Castle Acre
Priory mentioned below.

1362   The last Rector died and the College presented to the Vicarage, so that from
this date it enjoyed the Rectorial tithes and glebe. It then became necessary
to provide the suitable house required by Bishop Bateman.

1365   It was for this purpose that the College acquired (probably by purchase) from
W. Scheffol, at this time, an acre of pasture, with a tenement. It was conveyed
into the names of four feoffees, of whom one, R. Pulham, was a member, and
afterwards Master, of the College. We do not know that the other three were
members of the College, but the names of two appear as the transferees, about
this period, of other properties which afterwards passed into the possession of
the College.

In this year also the College agreed to pay a pension of £1. 6s. 8d. a year to
the Monastery of Castle Acre for two parts of the tithes due to the Monastery
out of the demesne lands, about 300 acres, of Robert Freville, of Foulden.
This pension was afterwards (at the dissolution of the Monasteries, I suppose)
paid to the Crown, and on Sept. 18, 1673, was granted out from the Crown,
and in 1753 belonged to T. Pyle, of whom it was then bought by the College
for £37

1386   Two feoffees of the Vicarage House released it to the other two, Wm. Pysale
and H. Thomson.

1391   In November an Act (15 Rich. II, cap. 5) required that, for all lands held
for the use of religious or spiritual bodies or for fraternities or guilds, the
King's license in mortmain should be obtained before Michaelmas, 1392, or
else the lands were to be alienated to other persons. *See* also MATTISHALL for
a similar series of licenses and transfers.

1392   (July) The King gave his license to the College to hold the Vicarage House
in mortmain and to H. Thomston and W. Preesehale to convey the same to
the College. (September) H. Thomson and W. Piecehale conveyed it to
John de Wilton and T. de Bodeney.

1393   (May) Wilton and Bodeney conveyed it (back) to Thomson and Pysale.
(June 26) The King again gave his license to the College to hold the house
in mortmain and to Piecehale and Tomston to convey it to the College. It is
stated that this second royal license was granted because the first was not
used at the proper time (and not, as stated in *Registrum Magnum*, because the
house was found to be *in alieno fœdo*).
(September) Thomson and Pysale gave the property to the College.

1411   Abp. Arundel confirmed the College in the possession of the Rectory of
Foulden (as well as those of Mutford, Wilton and Matsall).

1412   The Priory of Speney (or Spinney), near Soham (Cambs), released to the

College the 6 marks which it annually paid to the Priory for the above four rectories.

1479   Richard Powle, Vicar, devised by will to his successors his messuage, which he had bought of N. Blak, in lieu of the old Vicarage House, "in recompense of dilapidating and ruinating the said old Vicarage."

From this time the old Vicarage is let by the College with their Rectorial glebe and other property in the parish[1].

1651   When the *Registrum Magnum* was written it is stated that the Vicar enjoyed the house and an income of about £40 a year.

1653   The lease of the Rectory was renewed to Lady M. Button for 21 years, from Michaelmas, 1652, for a fine of £140.

1663   (July)   The College agreed to accept surrender of the lease granted in 1653 and grant a new lease (without a fine) for 21 years to feoffees for the benefit of the Vicars, and upon its expiration to grant leases for five years each, without fines, to successive Vicars, should they in each case remain Vicar so long.

1670   Mr Roberts, Vicar, gave notice to the College that the sub-tenant of their Impropriation at Foulden had let the houses of that Impropriation run into decay and that the barn was down (it was blown down in 1662) and the outhouses, and that the dwelling-house was ready to fall, and desired them to give leave that he might take down the house upon condition he repaired and built the Vicarage House as they should direct.   The Master and Fellows then agreed not to take any advantage of that clause and covenant in the lease which obligeth the tenant to keep the houses in repair and also to build them up in case they fall, and this was agreed upon the account that they had formerly obliged themselves to give all their Impropriations to the Vicar *pro tempore* without any fine, he only paying the old rent due to the College. *Gesta*, Dec. 7.

1761   The livings of Foulden and Oxburgh were consolidated.

1838   The Rectorial tithe was commuted for £268 and the Vicarial for £178. 3s. 6d.

1886   The Vicarial glebe is stated by the terrier to consist of the "scite" of the Vicarage House and 2 a. 3 r. 9 p., namely, Nos. 215, 216, 217, 303, 305 on the Tithe Map.

Nos. 215–17 surround the Vicarage House: Nos. 303 and 305 are near the river; they amount to "scarcely an acre," and were let (in 1900) for £1 a year.

Powle's Lands.

1479   R. Powle, Vicar, devised to the College 12 acres of arable land, namely:
(1)   3 acres, enclosed, in Payne's Croft.
(2)   6 acres, in one piece, in South Crofts.
(3)   3 acres, in pieces, in the town and fields of Foulden.

I have already mentioned his (nominal) bequest of the site of the old Vicarage.

We have a lease granted in 1496 by the College to J. Helver and J. Whitepayne, husbandmen, for five years ("except J. H. departeth this world") of the Rectorial glebes and tithes, Powle's Land, Drayton's House and the old Vicarage House, for the yearly rent of £12. 13s. 4d., namely, £4. 3s. 4d. at the Purification, £4. 3s. 4d. at Pentecost and £4. 6s. 8d. at the feast of S. Peter.

---

[1] He also devised to the College "the old Vicarage House"; but this, I take it, was *ultra vires*, as the legal estate had been in the College since 1393.   At any rate it expressed his opinion that that house would be no longer required for the use of the Vicars.

I suspect that the whole of the above property soon came to be considered as Rectorial glebe and was let in later years as "the Rectory"—at the yearly rent of £11. 13s. 4d.—at any rate all except Payne's Close.

The tenants paid, in addition, £1 for the pension payable to the Bishop of Norwich (p. 44), and the £1. 6s. 8d. originally payable to the monastery of Castle Acre.

1599 The rent of the Rectory (including the part of Powle's called Burnt Lane Close) was changed from £11. 13s. 4d. to £7. 15s. 6d., with 6 qrs. of wheat and 7 qrs. 5 bush. of malt.

In the terrier of 1661 there is an attempt, by notes in the margin, to indicate which were Powle's lands. These notes were added whilst T. Roberts was Vicar (1662–78). They succeed in pointing out four pieces, containing only 6 a. 2 r., as Powle's lands. Amongst them is the tenement with the "hempland[1]" of one rood, called Drayton's, apparently the cottage (rebuilt 1870) marked 345 in the present Tithe Map.

Payne's Close lay E. of Powle's new Vicarage House. It is uncertain whether Powle bought it (1475) and left it as his own to the College or whether it was bought with College money and transferred into the names of Powle and two others. In 1502 it was transferred to three persons, all Fellows. The *Registrum Magnum* says "it was bought for £40 from the Prioress of Thetford (Nunnery of S. George) and was vested in the Vicar (12d. a year being paid to the Prioress) but that, by the carelessness of R. Leader (Vicar 1519–40), the Prioress entered on it again and that it subsequently was redeemed and returned to the College by L. Mapted," whose brother Gregory was Vicar 1540–66.

Its annual rent was 6s. 8d. after it had been recovered for the College: this was changed, in 1610, to 6s. 8d. *with* 3 bush. of wheat and 1 bush. 1 peck of malt, and in 1626 to 4s. 4d. *with* 1½ bush. of wheat and 2 bush. of malt.

1609 J. Nunn released all his interest in it to the College, reserving the annual rent of 12½d. to his Manor of Foulden.

Mapted's Lands, including Nunne's Barn.

1557 L. Mapted, sometime Fellow of the College and afterwards Master of Corpus, devised by will to our College:
(1) His house in Foulden, called Shyllyngs, with a "hempland[1]."
(2) His lease of the ground containing Nunne's Barn, adjoining unto the said house.
(3) Nine acres of enclosed fen-land.
(4) Two acres of arable lying severally in the fields of Foulden.

Nunne's Barn, standing in 3 roods, was leased in 1522, with 6 acres, by the Prioress of Thetford to R. Hewar for 99 years. In 1546 Hewar leased it for 12d. a year for the remainder of the term to J. Mapted. After L. Mapted's death the lease was enjoyed by the College.

In 1663, to replace the Rectorial barn, blown down in 1662, the College bought, of R. Callibut, for £60, Nunne's Barn, with a yard and 3 roods of land—called also a barn and hempland. It was conveyed to J. Gostlin and others.

In 1705, T. Gostlin, as executor of J. Gostlin, conveyed it to the College. It lay to the W. of the (Powle's) Vicarage House and S. of the street.

Shortly before 1843 the barn was pulled down.

All the other three parcels of these lands had been bought—according to a note in the *Registrum Magnum*—with College money by L. Mapted. They

---

[1] A small piece of land set apart for growing flax for family use.—*English Dialect Dictionary.*

had been conveyed, apparently for convenience, to him or G. or J. Mapted. After the death of L. M. they were all conveyed to the College by G. or J. M. or both.

(1) Shyllings consisted of a messuage and 2 acres of hempland: to it belonged a right of commonage; it lay next Nunne's Barn, to the east.

(3) The nine acres were called at first Burr Croft, afterwards Norton Croft.

(4) The two acres consisted of two strips of ½ rood each in Towgate Field, one of 3 roods, and one of 2 roods in Burrough Field.

There was a free rent of 1s. 10d. due to the Manor of Foulden on some portion of these lands.

At first all "Mapted's Lands" were let (to E. Mapted) under the name of Shyllings, at the rent of 30s., changed in 1588 to 20s. with 1 qr. of wheat and 6 bush. of malt.

After the expiration of the 99 years' lease of Nunne's Barn at Michaelmas, 1621, the remaining three parcels (1), (3) and (4) were let for 14s. 8d. with 6 bush. of wheat and 4 bush. of malt.

1664   After Nunne's Barn came again into the possession of the College it was let to the Vicar for £3. 10s. a year.

He also had a lease of Shyllings for 10 years, if he so long continued Vicar. For it he used to pay a fine of £10 or £11 : once (1733) the fine was as much as 14 guineas.

No fine was paid for a new lease of lands bought after 1663, as they were supposed to be let at their full annual value.

1694   *Long's Land.* This (7½ a. pasture) was bought of C. Long for £110. Ives says it adjoined Nunne's Barn.

1695   *Hayes's tenements and 6 acres.* These were bought for £50 of F. and R. Hayes. The *Gesta Book* calls the property a messuage and *five* acres.

Ives says it adjoined Long's land. Part of it (3 acres) was copyhold of the Manor of Foulden, the quit rent being 6½d. On another part a quit rent of 2s. 2d. a year was payable to the Manor of Foulden; and on a third part one of 1s. 2d. to the Manor of Didlington.

The College let Long's and Hayes's lands to the Vicar for £10 a year.

1709   *The Two Roods.* For £8 the College acquired from W. Barber his interest in 2 roods of pasture held on a lease of 999 years from 1674, and let them to the Vicar for 10s. a year.

1734   *Horrex's Land.* The College bought, for £17, of E. Horrex 1 acre in Burrough Field, and let it to the Vicar for 17s. a year.

1754   The whole property owned by the College was found to consist of 79 different pieces, containing in all 118 a. 2 r.

1781   At the enclosure the Commissioners allotted to the College :
37 a. 2 r. 17 p. in Burrough Field, and
18 a. 0 r. 14 p. in Holme Field, of which 1 rood was copyhold of the Manor of Foulden Latimer and paid a quit rent of ¼d. a year.

The College also had the right of turning five head of cattle on three commons containing, in all, 306 a. 3 r. 29 p., paying therefor not more than 10s.

The property thus acquired was let to the Vicar for £5 a year.

The College also, under the Enclosure Award, had an exchange with Tyssen's devisees, taking in

	a.	r.	p.
Burrough Field	2	1	24,
	3	3	2,
	5	2	24;

and giving up

Great Tallants	6	1	24,
	1	3	0,
The Grove	3	1	37.

The arrangements for the Enclosure Act and of the subsequent enclosure seem to have given some little trouble. The College paid Mr J. White, the Vicar, £7. 2s. 9d., in 1781, for his expenses in appearing before a Committee of the House of Commons, and £7. 11s. 4d., in 1783, for the preparation of plans, &c., and £100, in 1785, for his trouble in the matter.

1801 By the transfer to the Government of £630. 13s. 4d. Consols the College redeemed a land tax of £8. 19s. 0d. on the Rectorial glebe and tithes, and land taxes amounting to £5. 5s. 0d. on its other lands, and purchased a tax of £3. 6s. 0d. payable out of the Vicarial glebe and tithes.

1839 The College gave 1 rood of land—part of No. 218 on the Tithe Map—for the site of a schoolroom. The conveyance was executed in 1871.

1884 The lands belonging to the College were let directly to the occupying tenants; and the College collected its own tithes directly, instead of letting them to the Vicar.

The total rack rents of the lands then amounted to £151.

1891 The College sold 101 a. 1 r. 37 p. to J. Mitford for £3500, retaining only the following pieces, all pasture, lying next the Vicarage House ·

	a.	r.	p.
No. 212 on Tithe Map, Homestall Piece, E. of Vicarage	1	3	14
No. 217 a, Pightle (formerly site of barn) S. of Vicarage	0	0	24
No. 218, Lower Homestall Piece, W. of Vicarage	1	1	13
Total	3	1	11

GRANTCHESTER (CAMBS). *Slegg's Closes.*

1782 For the purchase of these, with other property, *see* NEWNHAM (p. 29).

They were Lammas lands. The actual acreage was 3 a. 0 r. 27 p. and 3 a. 1 r. 23 p. At the Grantchester enclosure 3 r. 10 p. were taken from the latter and added to the former, and the remainder of the latter was assigned to King's College, by which our portion was freed from tithes and sheep-walk. Also two pieces of land in Barton, containing 3 r. 38 p. and 1 r. 25 p., were allotted to the College, for which *see* ELY TRUST.

1799 The land tax of 16s. was redeemed for £16. 8s. 6½d. money.

1872 The 3 a. 3 r. 37 p. was let for digging brick earth.

1899 The whole (then said to measure 3 a. 2 r. 38 p.) was sold to E. Bolton for £800.

HADDENHAM (CAMBS).

The property of the College in this parish previously belonged to the brothers W. and N. Buckenham, of whom W. B. was the Master of the College.

N. B. devised his lands to the College; but W. B. claimed them *jure cognationis*, and made good his claim [1].

1534   The College bought, for £200, of W. Buckenham (then Master), all his lands and houses in Haddenham and one of his three houses in Pease Market Hill, in Cambridge. They also paid him a further sum of £100 for securing this purchase in mortmain.

The £300 was (part of) the gift of Dr J. Baily for the foundation of the ninth fellowship.

The whole property then brought in £9. 12s. a year.

The Haddenham portion consisted of two tenancies.

(1) Madingley's, containing 157 a. 3 r., namely, 46 a. 1 r. 0 p. whole year lands and 111 a. 2 r. common field lands, of which 35 a. 3 r. were fen-land (20 a. 3 r. being in Grunty Fen), 7 a. 1 r. in Wentworth Fields and 3 roods in Sutton Fields, and having a fold course for 300 sheep. With it was let a marsh in Erith, called Mytfitter's, containing 2 roods. The rents were set at first at £8 and 4s. : these were afterwards (1603) altered, in accordance with the Corn Act of 1576, to £5. 9s. 4d., with 4 qrs. of wheat, 5 qrs. 5 bush. of malt and 4 wethers; and to 2s. 8d., with 1 bush. of wheat and 1 bush. of malt. Various out-rents for this farm amounted to 8s. 4d.

(2) Patrick's, consisting of a house and 54 acres, with Stevens', 25½ acres, for which a free rent of 2s. 11d. was paid to the Manor of Greyes. These farms lay in 99 different parcels and included 3 a. 2 r. 13 p. in Grunty Fen. The rents at first were set at £4 and £1. 3s. 0d. : these, in 1598 and 1617, were changed to £2. 13s. 4d., with 2 qrs. of wheat and 2 qrs. 5½ bush. of malt; and to 15s. 4d., with 2 qrs. of wheat and 6 bush. of malt ; also 4 capons.

1654   With the consent of the College the tenants of the farms exchanged 7 a. of Madingley's for 9 a. of Patrick's.

1657   In lieu of their right of commonage on Ewell Fen the College received from the Earl of Suffolk 2 acres in that fen, which were added to Madingley's.

1800   The fen-land is said to be daily improving from the last Drainage Act (passed within the preceding five years).

1843   Haddenham Enclosure Act was passed. Copies of portions of the map of this estate are annexed to show the minuteness of the subdivision into slips which prevailed before the Enclosure. The original, dated 1827, gives the highland parts, without the fen-land, consisting of 283 pieces and containing a total of 171 a. 0 r. 14 p. The second copy gives a smaller portion than the first, but on an enlarged scale to show more distinctly the area of each slip and the names of the adjoining owners.

The College share of the expenses of this enclosure was £84. 4s. 0d.

After it our acreage was as follows :

	a.	r.	p.	
Madingley's	132	1	27,	of which 84 a. 2 r. 35 p. were the allotments.
Patrick's..	65	2	8	
Ewell Fen	1	3	14	(tithe free).
In Wentworth	7	2	19	(tithe £2. 3s. 3d.).

Subsequently it was found that some land that should have come to the College under the Enclosure Award had been allotted to Lord Hardwicke. For this his Lordship paid compensation to the College. The actual amount I have not been able to find.

---

[1] As to the legality of this *see* HAGLO AND PULTON, p. 52.

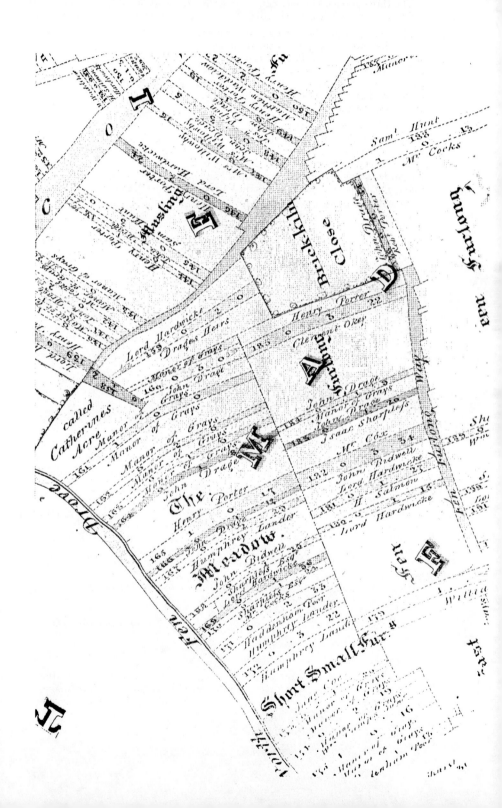

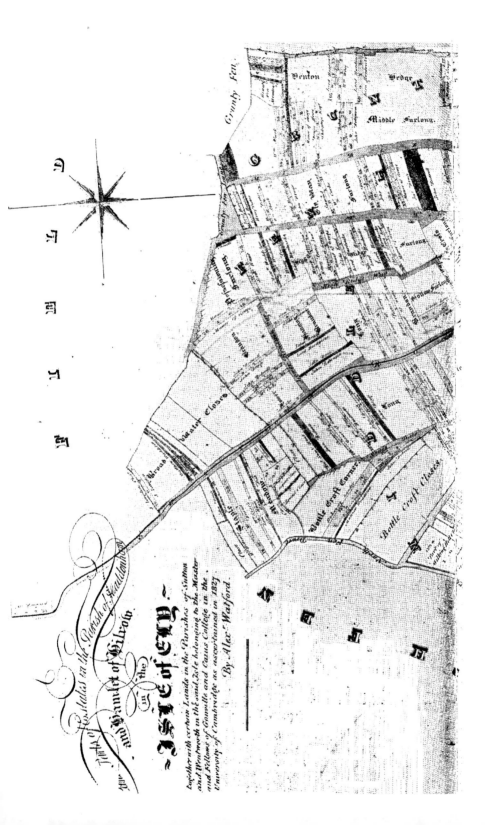

Plan of Fen Lands in the Parish of Haddenham and Hamlet of Hilrow in the

ISLE of ELY

together with certain Lands in the Parishes of Sutton and Wentworth in the said Isle belonging to the Master and Fellows of Gonville and Caius College in the University of Cambridge as ascertained in 1827

By Alexr. Watford

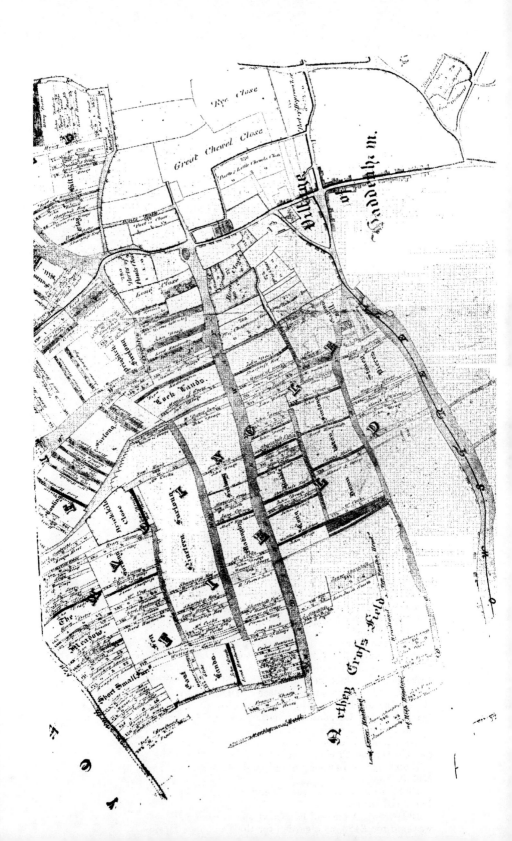

The land tax on Madingley's and Ewell Fen together was £5. 8s. 0d.

For three centuries these farms were let on leases for 20 years, which were renewed at intervals of, generally, seven years. The fines in the 17th and 18th centuries varied from £21 to £50 for Madingley's and from £12 to £35 for the other tenancies.

Some of the subsequent fines are given below.

Madingley's.

					£	s.	d.
In 1800	10	years	expired	....	361	0	0
1807	7	„	„	....	280	0	0
1827	20	„	„	....	1600	0	0
1834	7	„	„	....	280	0	0

In 1854, when the lease ran out, the farm was relet at a rack rent of £228.

In 1814, as the tenant did not take up a new lease, the Bursar's Book advanced £305. 5s., in lieu of the fine, for division amongst the Master and Fellows; and again, in 1821, £334.

In 1828, of the £1600 paid as a fine by the tenant on taking up his new lease, £885 was taken by the Bursar's Book as repayment for the advances in 1814 and 1821, and the remainder was divided amongst the Master and Fellows.

In 1841 and 1848 respectively £420 and £400 were paid by the Bursar's Book to the Registrary for division amongst the Master and 12 (Senior) Fellows in lieu of fines.

Patrick's and Stevens'.

					£	s.	d.
1802	7	years	expired	....	75	0	0
1809	7	„	„	....	126	0	0
1816	7	„	„	....	100	0	0
1837	7	„	„	....	110	0	0

In 1857, when the last 20 years' lease ran out, the farm was relet at a rack rent of £110.

In 1844 and again in 1851 the sum of £120 was paid out of the Bursar's Book for division amongst the Master and 12 Fellows in lieu of fines.

1861 Grunty Fen was enclosed and 14 a. 0 r. 9 p. were allotted to the College, of which 8 a. 2 r. 29 p. were added to Madingley's and 5 a. 1 r. 20 p. to Patrick's. The expense to the College was £108. 18s. 0d. The land is close to Wilburton Railway Station.

1866 The Railway Company took 1 a. 2 r. 9 p. and paid £108. 18s. 6d.

1867 A plot of ground adjoining Wilburton Station, containing 3 r. 2 p., was bought from the Railway Company for £53. 7s. 6d. and added to Madingley's.

1872 The land in Ewell Fen was sold to R. Camps for £150, which bought £161. 18s. 11d. Consols.

1892 The house was burned down and a new house was built at a cost of £528. 16s. 6d.

The apportionment of the tithe on the whole of our estate is £53. 2s. 5d.

In 1875 the rents amounted to £332; in 1885, £346; in 1895 (College paying tithe and Drainage Taxes), £100.

Note.—In the Registrum Magnum it is said that the College at one time owned 240 acres in Wickham and sold them (apparently in or just before Dr Caius's time) to J. Gudderell for 190 marks.

HAGLO AND PULTON (GLOUCESTERSHIRE).

Sir R. Willison, of Sugwas, in Herefordshire, formerly Fellow, devised by his will (proved 1575) to the College his customary lands in the Manor of Haglo and Pulton, in the parish of Awre, in the Forest of Dean, for the founding of two Scholarships.

He had during his lifetime leased these lands to various tenants for terms of 1000 years from 1568—the reserved rents amounting to £7. 1s. 4d.

But as, according to law, lands could not be passed to a Corporation by will, the widow, Anne, and John Skippe, the next heir, granted these lands to the College, the rents being enjoyed by the widow during her life.

1596   The widow died on August 4.

1859   These lands were sold to the Crown for £275, invested in £282. 15s. 6d. Consols.

HETHERSETT (NORFOLK).   *Advowson of the Rectory.*

1705   Dr J. Gostlin (*see* also SHALFORD) late President of the College and nephew of Dr Gostlin, at one time Master, died on Feb. 1, 1705, and devised to the College this advowson.

1723   Mr Morrant was presented to this living and to that of S. Clement, in Norwich (the advowson of which had been bought in 1705), and gave a bond that he would not resign one living without resigning the other. It was then intended that these two livings should always thus be held by the same Incumbent—one in the city and one in the county.

1787   The Rector (B. Edwards) exchanged 2 r. 1 p. of Glebe for three pieces, containing, in all, 1 a. 0 r. 4 p., belonging to J. L. Joslin. This exchange rendered the estates of both parties much more compact. Before it they had been inconveniently intermingled.

1860   Up to this year the presentation to the living had been in the gift of the Master. By the new Statutes, confirmed this year, the Master and Seniors had to present.

The tithe apportionment is £855 : and the Glebe contains 58 a.

HINTON OR CHERRY HINTON (CAMBS).

Willowes's Gift.

1503   Thomas Willowes, of Cambridge, glover, devised to the College the greater part of his lands in Hinton, Teversham (which see), Fulbourn and Ditton (part of which had been purchased of the executors of Lady Anne Scroope) for the term of 99 years ; and, if the College got them mortmained within that space, then for ever ; otherwise to sell the lands and with the money to maintain his donation.

The lands in Ditton and Fulbourn went with those in Teversham, to make up " Willowes's Farm " there.

The lands in Hinton (called Gaye's lands) contained 48 a. 1 r. They consisted of a close of pasture, containing 1 acre, in which a house formerly stood, 1½ roods of pasture in a close and 80 different strips, lying dispersedly in the eight unenclosed fields of Hinton.

The lands were held on a 20 years' lease.

The fine for a new lease when seven years had expired was about £8. 10s. (and when 20 years had expired £15) until 1796, when it was £33. 10s.

For some of these lands an out-rent of £1. 7s. was payable to the Manor of Netherhall.

1579 The "old rent" had been £2. In accordance with the Corn Act of 1576 this was changed into £1. 6s. 8d. of money and 2 quarters of wheat, to which was added 1 quarter of wheat in lieu of a boar formerly paid.

This was the first corn rent on any of our lands.

1611 This corn rent was changed to one of 2 quarters of wheat and 1 qr. 2 b. 3 p. of malt.

1752 The estimate of the acreage was 45 a. 1 r. 20 p. and a right of common.

Peters's Gift.

1708 W. Peters, Rector of Weeting, devised to the College his estate at Hinton.

It consisted of house, homestall, five closes and a large number of strips lying in the different fields. The acreage of the whole was 66 a. 3 r. A part of it was copyhold, for which a quit rent of 12s. was paid to the Manor of Netherhall.

It was always supposed to be rack rented.

At first the rent was £30.

1798 The land tax on Peters's farm, £3. 8s. 0d., was redeemed for £124. 13s. 4d. Consols.

The land tax on Gaye's (Willowes's) land was £1. 2s. 0d. It was redeemed with the land taxes on several of our other Cambs estates for one amount of Consols. The portion for Gaye's land would be £40. 6s. 8d.

1810 By the Enclosure Award (signed Dec. 18) the lands belonging to the College were completely changed for those of other owners; and the College thus obtained a very much more compact property.

The hedges, trees and underwoods on the old enclosures given up by the College were paid for to the College and those taken by the College were paid for to the persons giving them up.

The College received, in lieu of the whole of Willowes's land ·

One freehold allotment in Fendon Field,
   abutting on the Hills Road ....   22 a. 2 r. 16 p.

Besides the open field lands, the enclosures, originally part of Willowes's land and passed by the Award to other owners, are thus described:

One-half part (containing 1 r. 8 p.) of an old enclosure, No. 7, called the Pightle, awarded to T. S. Headley;

An old enclosure, No. 36, called L Close (containing 1 a. 0 r. 11 p.), awarded to J. Barrow;

Two parts of an old enclosure, called Bell Close, Nos. 150 and 152 (containing together 1 r. 33 p.), awarded to the Impropriators.

Besides the open field lands, the following enclosures, originally part of Peters's Farm, and at this time passed to other owners, are thus described in the Award:

One-half part, containing 1 r. 8 p., of an old enclosure, No. 27, called the Pightle, awarded to T. S. Headley;

An old enclosure, called Teversham Close, No. 27, containing 2 a. 3 r. 32 p., awarded to W. Pearce;

An old enclosure, called Pales' Close, No. 58, containing 1 r. 7 p., awarded to T. S. Headley.

After the enclosure, Peters's Farm was made up as follows:

	a.	r.	p.
One allotment, in Quarry Field, containing...	19	1	37
An allotment, called Moor Piece, containing..	7	0	26
An old enclosure, called Long Nuttings, No. 117, containing	2	1	31
A cottage and garden, late Window's, No. 118, containing	0	0	38
An old enclosure, late Window's, No. 119, containing		1	9
(The above three old enclosures belonged to T. S. Headley before the enclosure.)			
An old enclosure, No. 120, containing	2	0	25
An old enclosure, called Shepherds' Close, No. 121, containing	5	2	33
An old enclosure, called Shepherds' Close, No. 122, containing	0	3	32
(The above three belonged to W. Pearce, before the enclosure.)			
An allotment on the Common, containing ...	6	3	12,

copyhold of the Manor of Hinton Netherhall.

The College also purchased at this time of C. G. Brand and had conveyed to them by the Award all the following pieces:

		a.	r.	p.
No. 113	Cribb's Close	1	2	13
114	Orchard	0	3	32
115	Homestead..............................	1	0	27
116	Pightle	0	2	22
117	Collins' Croft	4	2	9
	Total	8	3	23

The sum of £126 was paid from the Peters Book to C. G. Brand, but this apparently (*Gesta*, April 29, 1809) was for No. 113 only. What was paid and whence the money was obtained for the rest of the purchase I cannot find. Possibly part of the sums paid to the Enclosure Commissioners, &c., mentioned below, may have been for this purchase.

The lands in the parish were freed from tithes.

The following are the payments to meet the expenses of this re-arrangement of our property:

From the Peters Book		£	s.	d.
1808	To Commissioners	169	4	3
	To Mr Ladds, for fencing	155	6	0
1809	To Commissioners	51	9	9
1810	,, ,, ...	33	16	10
From the Bursar's Book				
1808	To Commissioners	48	19	3
1810	To Ventris (tenant)......................	40	17	1
	To Commissioners	6	4	2

1810 Gaye's (Willowes's farm) land was let for a fine for the last time, namely, £40. 5s. 6d.

In 1817 and 1824, when under the old system the lease would have been renewed, the Bursar's Book advanced what would have been the fines, viz. £40 and £50, to the Master and Seniors, being recouped by the increase of rent, which was brought into it under the next lease, granted in 1830.

The rents of Peters's Farm about this time were as follows :

	£	s.	d.
Up to 1807	30	0	0
In 1812, &c. (after the enclosure and new purchases).......................................	65	0	0
In 1819, &c.	80	0	0
In 1827, &c.	86	0	0

1827–8 New buildings were put up at a cost of £308. 10s. 0d.

1830 A lease of all our land, 76 a. 1 r. 12 p., in Hinton, was granted to M. R. Ventris for eight years at a rent of £112, of which the College assigned £80 to the Peters Book and £32 to the Bursar's Book.
No mention is made of the old corn rents.

1845 In the lease for 12 years, granted this year, the rent is set at £120 and, in addition, the old corn rents are revived. Of the £120 the Peters Book received £93 and the Bursar's Book the remainder.

1860 When the accounts of all the College estates were consolidated into the Bursar's Book, the Peters Book had rolled up £1250 Consols, besides £150 Consols lent to the College in 1856 for the new hall. These amounts of Stock formed part of the Reserve Fund then established.

1871 The old corn rents were given up and the money rent set at £130.
Up to this year Peterhouse had paid us 10d. annually for one of their fields in Hinton. This they now commuted for £1. 6s. 8d. Possibly this was a quit rent of the Manor of Mortimer's.

1883 The College, for £1550, bought, of the executors of John Okes, 25 a. 2 r. 4 p., of which 20 a. 3 r. 4 p. are copyhold of the Manor of Netherhall (quit rent £1. 14s. 0d.). The pipes of the Cambridge Waterworks Company, between the reservoir and the town, are laid beneath this land.
The purchase money was provided partly by the sale of the following Consols :

£	s.	d.	
152	15	10	obtained from the Eastern Counties Railway Company for land taken at Duxford.
255	1	5	from the Lynn and Ely Railway Company for land taken at Denver.
897	15	2	from the Gt. Eastern Railway Company for land taken, in 1881, at Elmham.
196	15	2	from the sale of ½ acre at Croxley Green (Rickmansworth) in 1874.

The small remainder was obtained from money received for the sale of gravel and from enfranchisements of copyholds in Manors belonging to the College.

1900 Of the land purchased of C. G. Brand at the enclosure, part, namely 1 a. 2 r. 13 p., was copyhold and was enfranchised this year for £28. 7s. 5d.

1903 For £310 the College bought, of H. Willson and others, a spinney, called the Lime-kiln Close, containing 5 a. 3 r. 24 p. with a cottage, at the corner between the roads to Fulbourn and Shelford, copyhold of the Manor of Hinton Rectory. It was enfranchised in 1904 for £24. 4s. 3d. and £17. 18s. for expenses.
Also, for £2400, they bought, of G. and A. J. Keeble, 81 a. 3 r. 26 p. of freehold arable land, part of Uphall Farm (see 1906). This land adjoins our D'Engaynes Farm at Teversham.
In 1875 the total rental in Hinton was £130; in 1885, £189; in 1895, £120; in 1905, £240.

C IV 2   5

1906   For £916. 18s. 0d. the College bought, of Keeble's trustees, 18 acres of freehold pasture land (another portion of Uphall Farm, see 1903). This is
separated from the Churchyard by a narrow lane and lies to the E. of the
Church : it adjoins the other portion bought in 1903.

1908   For £72. 2s. 1d. the College enfranchised the whole of our land copyhold of
the Manor of Hinton Netherhall. The costs came to £3. 10s. 0d.

HINXTON (CAMBS).

William Gale, of Eye, in Suffolk, gave us (in addition to his Manor in
Cowling) his lands in Hinxton of the annual value of £4.

These were afterwards sold by John Skippe, Master, to Lord North (see
COWLING).

HOCKWOLD (see WILTON).

HORNINGSEA (CAMBS).

1904   For £3250 the College bought, of W. J. Abbott, Poplar Hall Farm,
containing 80 a. 2 r. 11 p., all freehold, in Horningsea and Ditton.

1905   After a fire the College spent £616 on the house and buildings, of which
£465 was repaid by the insurance office.

1906   The College spent £310 on the house and buildings.

KAISS, OR KEYSHO (BEDS).

1659   The College bought, of H. Peacocke, his farm at Keysho, of the annual
value of £50 and consisting of one house, two cottages and about 100 acres
of arable, pasture and closes, for the sum of £995. But the price was
afterwards settled at £981 as the land did not amount to so much as it was
represented to contain. The arable portion contained 68 acres.

This property was never fully conveyed to the College. It was held in
trust during the Commonwealth, and at the Restoration was sold again by
Dr Brady (for £730) just after he was made Master, for which, being for the
benefit of the College, he was indemnified under the common seal, December 26,
1661.

The rent is not entered in the Bursar's Book after Michaelmas, 1661.

In 1658, before it had been bought, though it was known that the value was
£50 a year, it was ordered that it should be let on lease for the yearly rent of
£20 for 20 years and a fine of £250.

1659   (October) It was agreed to abate £10 from this fine, and the lease was
granted to Merlin of Rickley or Donne (see WESTONING).

The rent of £20 was thus distributed :—£2 to the Master, £1 to each
Fellow and the remaining £6 to the College chest.

KETTLESTONE (NORFOLK).

1774   Dr Schuldham bequeathed a rent charge of £10. 0s. 0d. a year on Sir
Willoughby Jones's estate, for a piece of plate, to be given to the one deemed
most worthy of the incepting Bachelors.

Horn ngsea, Pop ar Hall and R ver

KIRSTEAD WITH LANGHALL (NORFOLK).

1811 The College bought on behalf of the Wortley Benefaction the advowson of this Rectory, for £2300, of the assignees of Sir R. Kerrison and Son.

The tithe commutation is :

	£	s.	d.
On lands in Kirstead	300	0	0
,, ,, ,, Brooke...........................	3	14	0
,, ,, ,, Seething	2	14	0
Total.................. £306		8	0

There are 40 acres of glebe.

KITTISFORD (SOMERSET).

1905 Mrs M. G. May, the wife of a member of the College and Rector, gave the advowson of the Rectory to the College.

The glebe contains 109 acres and the tithe rent charge is apportioned at £137.

LAVENHAM (SUFFOLK).

1713 The advowson of the Rectory was bought for the College by Mr Camborn's executors (*see* ASHDON and BLOFIELD) of Sir Symonds d'Ewes, Bart., for £710. 15s. 0d.

1799 A land tax of £48. 13s. 6d., payable out of the Rectory, was bought by the College for £1622. 10s. 0d. Consols.

The tithe apportionment is £894.   The glebe land contains 144 acres.

LONDON. *Charterhouse Square.*

1900 (May 4) The College bought, for £3900, of H. T. Tubbs, a piece of ground, with the building thereon—known as 40, Charterhouse Square—having a frontage of 22 ft. 4 in. to the Square and extending from it to the Aldersgate Station of the Metropolitan Railway.

The property formerly belonged to this Railway Company, who sold it subject to their right to re-enter and re-purchase it should it be required for the purposes of their railway within 21 years of the death of the last surviving grandchild of Queen Victoria who was alive on Aug. 4, 1880, and also subject to the condition that a narrow strip of it next the Aldersgate Street Station shall not be built on.

The lines and works of the Railway Company are beneath part of the premises and the Company may enter on them for the purpose of repairing these works, but compensating the owners and tenants for damage.

The College bought the property subject to a lease for 80 years from March 25, 1900, at an annual rent of £130.

Philip Lane.

1586 Mrs Joyce Frankland, widow (daughter of Robert and Johanna Trapps), devised to the College (besides the £1540 laid out on the Manor of Dabernoons in Duxford) her principal messuage and two tenements in Philip Lane, in the parish of Aldermanbury.

She says, "I value the 3 houses and will that they shall let after the rate of £33. 6s. 8d. by year and not under," "which rent I will not have abated, if so much may be made of the same, without any fine or income to be paid by any lessee or occupier of the same."

Until the Great Fire of London, the rent-roll of the estate, as shown by the Bursar's Book, remained as follows :

	£	s.	d.
Capital messuage in Philip Lane..................	20	0	0
Tenement next the above........	6	13	4
Corner house in Philip Lane	6	13	4

The corner is that between Philip Lane and Addle Street.

1669   After the Fire the ground whereon the houses lately stood was leased for
40 years, the rent to be £20. The tenant "will within 5 years erect so many
houses as he conveniently can, according to the Act for the rebuilding of the
City" and enters into a bond of £1500 for the performance of the covenants
of the lease.

1754   At Mr J. Smith's survey the plot was found to measure about 43 yards on the
west, along the Philip Lane front, 15 feet on the south, along Addle Street,
and 38 feet on the north. The houses were 8 in number. The Brewers' Hall
abuts on part of the east side.

Until 1864 the land was always let for £20 a year on a 40 years' lease.
The rent was paid with singular irregularity—sometimes as much as 7 years'
rents being paid at once. The lease was renewed at the following dates for
the fines mentioned below ·

		£	s.	d.
1694	7 years expired	60	0	0
1706		80	0	0
1735		273	0	0
1775	40 years expired	600	0	0·
1789		89	10	0
1824	35 years expired	1750	0	0
1839	14 years expired	325	0	0

The fines were shared between the Master and Seniors.

1864   A new lease for 25 years was granted to the sub-lessee, at a rent of £200,
he to expend at least £500 in improving the premises. He did this, apparently,
by rebuilding the corner house, which is now known as 22 Addle Street and
No. 1 Philip Lane.

1882   (December) At "the Wood Street Fire," Nos. 5–7 Philip Lane were
destroyed, Nos. 2–4 much injured.

1883   The lease was surrendered and the property relet from June 24, as follows ·
No. 1 Philip Lane and 22 Addle Street for 20¼ years, rent £110 for the
first 6¼ years and afterwards £200.
Nos. 2–5 Philip Lane, for 6¼ years at £110 and then for 53½ years at
£400.
Nos. 6 and 7 Philip Lane, for 2 years at £30, the next 4 years at £60 and
then for 53¾ years at £120.
Nos. 2–5 were rebuilt as 3 houses, a restaurant in the middle and show-
rooms for manufacturers' samples on each side.

1895   The lease of No. 1 Philip Lane and 22 Addle St. was abandoned and the
house was relet in three flats for rents amounting to £250, the College paying
rates and doing repairs. This house has an entrance in Philip Lane and at
the corner of Philip Lane and Addle Street, and is thus reckoned as being in
both streets.

MARSHWOOD (DORSET).

1900   The College bought, for £3300, of G. W. Dawes, two farms called Hackeridge
and Batts containing together 190 a. 2 r. 5 p.
The annual rent is £200, and the tithe apportionment £30. 14s. 10d.

1904–5   The College spent about £200 on the repairs and improvements of the
house and buildings.

MATTISHALL OR MATSALL (NORFOLK). *Advowson and Rectory.*

It is uncertain who was the benefactor who gave us this advowson—or whether it was bought by the College. Blomefield attributes the gift to Dame Pakenham.

The *Registrum Magnum*, following Caius's *Annals* and followed by the Commemoration Service, attributes it to Sir Ralph Heminghale, saying that he conveyed to the feoffees of the College both the (patronage) acre and the advowson.

The following is the course of events as shown by the documents.

1363 W. de Morlee conveys to R. de Hemenhall, R. de Walkessare, R. de Eccles the advowson and one acre with a certain tenement thereto belonging.

1370 (April 25) R. de Hemenhall and R. de Eccles convey the same to A. de Wykemer (Parson of Hockwold), W. de Aldeby, B. de Haddelie, H. de Tomston, W. de Herlyngg, S. de Hoghton, and R. de Pulham (afterwards Master).

(May 13) An agreement is made between Sir R. Hemenhale and the College. It recites that Sir R. H. had conveyed to A. de Wykemer, &c., the advowson and acre, in order that, when they had license from the King and all other feudal (*foedi*) lords for this purpose, they might convey the property to the College. The College is to celebrate annually a mass for Dame Pakenham and her son, Sir T. Pakenham, and pray for the health of Sir R. Hemenhale and his wife, and after their deaths shall solemnize their exequies every year in their chapel or the parish church; and, after that the Church of Mattishall shall be legally appropriated and acquired for their own use, the College shall provide three chaplains for this purpose. Sir R. Hemenhale also ordains that out of the proceeds of the Church of Mattishall the Master shall receive £1 a year and each of the Fellows (there were then three) 13s. 4d.

1389 R. de Pulham releases to H. de Thomson and W. de Harlyngg all his rights in the above property.

1390 (September) Andrew Dale (of Bathele), Rector, died. He had been Rector from 1358.

Thomas, son and heir of W. Morlee, presented one J. Pelle, but Thomson and Harling presented W. Rokehawe,

1391 who, in accordance with the order of the King's Courts, was instituted by the Bishop of Norwich.

It should be noted that, at any rate from 1321, the Rectors had been appointing Vicars.

In November was passed the Act (*see* Foulden Vicarage House) requiring that, for all lands held for fraternities, &c., the licenses in mortmain of the King and all mesne lords should be obtained before Michaelmas, 1392, or else the lands were to be alienated.

1392 (July) The King gives his license for the College to hold the advowson of Mattishall (and the Vicarage House at Foulden) in mortmain and to appropriate the Church at Mattishall. But this license could be used only after all mesne lords of the fee (if any) had had a sufficient time (6 months each, by 7 Ed. I, Stat. 3) in which to assert any claims they might have.

The Bishop of Ely claimed the Patronage (extensive possessions in Mattishall belonged to the See of Ely as late as the enclosure, in 1803). The College referred the case to Pope Boniface IX,

1392-3 who (Jan. 19) addressed a Bull to the Bishop of Coventry and Lichfield, directing him to enquire into the rights of the Bishop of Ely and to see that an adequate provision for the Vicars was being made out of the income of the Church. The Bull further gives leave for the College to take and retain possession of the parish Church and of all rights and appurtenances.

1393 (June 26) The King *again* gives his license for the advowson of Mattishall (and Vicarage House of Foulden) to be conveyed to, and held in mortmain by, the College, paying to the King, in addition to the former £10, a further sum of 10 marks for confirmation of his *former* license, as it had not been used at the proper time. The King further directed that the College should give yearly a sufficient sum to the poor of the parish and sufficiently endow the Vicarage according to the order which would be made by the Diocesan (*i.e.* in accordance with 15 Rich. II, c. 6, passed in 1391).

(July 30) The Bishop of Ely gives his license to the College to hold the advowson and one acre in mortmain, they being held of the Bishop in chief; the College paying yearly 1 lb. of frankincense at Fen Ditton, on the altar of the Bishop's chapel, as settled by the Bishop of Coventry and Lichfield.

(Sept. 22) The Prior and Chapter of Ely consent to the above arrangement.

(Oct. 6) The "littera executoria" of the Bishop of Coventry and Lichfield states that on enquiry he finds that the Vicarage, from of old, had been sufficiently endowed.

1393-4 The King—for 20s.—gives his license for the one acre at Mattishall (and a messuage in Cambridge) to be conveyed to, and held in mortmain by, the College.

1394 (May 1) Thomston and Herlyngg convey the advowson and acre to the College.

1395 (April 29) Rokehawe resigns the Rectory. The College presents A. Symond to the Vicarage.

(June 25) The Bishop of Norwich acknowledges to have received from the College 28 marks (£18. 13s. 4d.) as firstfruits of the Church.

Subsequently, it was arranged that the College should pay £1 a year to the Bishop of Norwich in lieu of firstfruits of the Church of Mattishall. I cannot find any deed settling this. It will be remembered that Bishop Bateman made a similar arrangement for Foulden, Mutford and Wilton when he appropriated the churches of those places to the College. Probably the Bishop made it for Mattishall when, in accordance with the Royal license of 1393 and 15 Rich. II, c. 6, he made order for provision for the Vicar and the poor. These four payments are still made annually by the College to the Ecclesiastical Commissioners.

1402 and 1407 The Pope's Nuncio in England gives his receipt for 20 marks as firstfruits of the Churches of Matsall and Wilton.

1411 Thomas de Arundel, Archbishop of Canterbury, confirms the College in the possession of the Churches of Mattishall, Foulden, Mutford and Wilton.

1412 The College redeemed the payment of 6 marks a year from Foulden, Wilton, Mattishall and Mutford to the convent of Spinney, near Soham (Cambs). I cannot find when or why this payment was imposed.

1622 Frederick, Lord of Pittinwenne, and his wife, surrendered to the College their right to the Parsonage, &c. The deed does not say if they received for this surrender any consideration; nor in what their right consisted.

Henceforth the College has remained in undisturbed possession of the advowson and Rectory without further confirmation.

All the College property in the parish (except the advowson and the trees) used to be let on one lease generally for 20 years : the rent was originally £14. In 1608 this was changed to £10 with 6 qrs. of wheat and 8 qrs. of malt.

In 1643 it began to be let to the Vicar, who undertook to pay all out-rents, to keep the chancel and other buildings in repair and to bring sufficient pea-straw into the Church at Christmas and Easter and strew it according to custom. No fine was paid for a new lease, which was to continue for 10 years, provided the lessee continued Vicar, and to terminate if within the 10 years he ceased to be Vicar.

In 1820 the rent was reset at £230 and in 1832 at £200.

1799   The land tax (£5) on the Rectory House, cottage, about 3 a. 2 r. of land and all the great tithes was acquired by transferring to the Government £183. 6s. 0d. Consols, which had been bought with £110. 2s. 3d. taken from the Wortley Book.

1803   The enclosure of the parish took place.

The College is stated to have owned before it :

      (1)   A messuage and barn,
      (2)   A parcel of land, 3 roods 10 poles,
      (3)   Another parcel, 2 a. 3 r. 9 p.,
      (4)   A cottage,

together with (5) rights of commonage, i.e. of cutting necessary fuel on commons and waste lands and of pasturing on the same the cattle *levant* and *couchant* on the premises (1)–(4).

By the Enclosure Award an allotment on Badeley Moor, containing 2 a. 1 r. 25 p., was assigned to the College in lieu of (5).

No. (1) was the old Rectory House (and is now divided into two tenements). No. (2) probably represents the one acre which is always referred to in the old conveyances and licenses, the possession of which seems to have been a necessary condition for the right of patronage, and was thus not part of the glebe.

The enclosure cost the College £1. 9s. 10d.

1838   The Tithe Award states the College property as follows :

		a.	r.	p.	
(1)	Allotment on Badeley Moor	2	1	25	arable
(2)	Barn and pasture	2	3	10	
(3)	House and yard	0	3	18	
(4)	Cottage and garden	0	17	38	

Of these (3) apparently consists of (1) and (2) of 1803 ; (4) is called Bashes in the old leases and is generally referred as something in addition to or separate from the Rectory.

The apportionment of the rectorial tithe is £488. 7s. 0d., including the tithes on the glebes.

1884   The system of leasing the land and tithes to the Vicar was given up ; the land and buildings were let directly to the occupiers for rents amounting to £23. 17s. ; and the College collected the tithes and repaired the chancel.

1905   For £35 the College sold to C. Norton a piece of land, viz. (4) of 1803 and 1838.

Vicar's Glebes.

1738 For the augmentation of the Vicarage the governors of Queen Anne's
Bounty, with £200 from the funds of a special charity left to them to be
administered for such purposes, and £200 from the general revenues of Queen
Anne's Bounty, bought a farm called Woodhouse, at Attleborough, containing :

a.	r.	p.	
2	3	0	of meadow,
3	1	30	of pasture,
and 22	1	36	of arable,

together with a dwelling house and farm buildings.

Four acres were copyhold of the Manor of "Attleborough on the Part of
the College" for which a quit rent of 5s. 9½d. is payable. The rent was then
£21. 10s. 0d.

At the enclosure of Attleborough parish in 1816 four pieces containing
5 a. 0 r. 3 p. were allotted to this farm.

1743 The Vicarage of Mattishall and the Rectory of Pattesley (which see) were
consolidated.

1784 According to the terrier made in this year, the Vicar's glebes were as follows :
The Vicarage House, standing on 940 feet and an outhouse standing on
250 feet ; and 28 pieces of land containing about 15 acres ; also a (valueless)
manor.

Two or three of the 28 pieces could not be identified and no rent was paid
for them.

The last six pieces lay in the parish of Mattishall Burgh and contained
1 a. 3 r. 20 p.

1795 The Vicarage House being unfit for the habitation of the minister and too
much out of repair to be put into repair by one year's income of the Vicarage,
Mr John Smith (then Vicar), for £50 and a rood of arable land, one of the
six pieces of Vicar's glebe lying in Mattishall Burgh, conveyed to the Vicar
and his successors (1) the house near the Church, which he was then occupying,
together with the right of commonage thereto belonging, (2) the yard and
garden adjoining the house and (3) an enclosure of pasture abutting on the
yard and garden.

The College advanced the £50 and were recouped out of the income of the
Vicarage by 20 annual instalments. The Bursar's Book for Michaelmas, 1799,
shows that the College paid the expenses of the conveyance (£7. 14s.).

1799 Mr John Smith redeemed the land tax of £5 on the Vicarage House (? that
acquired in 1795) and cottage (? the old Vicarage House) and about 15 a. 2 r.
of land and the small tithes.

1803 In a statement of the property belonging to the various owners in the parish,
drawn up for the use of the Enclosure Commissioners, that belonging to the
Vicar is said to be :
(1) Two messuages,
(2) 14 a. 1 r. 22 p. of glebe,
(3) Vicarage Manor,
(4) Rights of commonage, i.e. cutting necessary fuel on commons and
waste lands and of pasturing on the same the cattle levant and couchant on
the premises in (1). Of the open field land the Commissioners allotted to the
Vicar one triangular piece of land containing 2 a. 0 r. 7 p.

Of the commons and waste lands the Vicar was awarded 6 a. 3 r. 6 p. for
rights of common.

The Vicar (**Mr** J. Smith) also effected under the Award four exchanges tending greatly to the consolidation of his glebes.

He also effected a fifth, with himself in his private capacity. The Vicar gave up the old Vicarage House, outhouse, yard and garden and also two gardens, containing 2 r. 3 p. adjoining, and took 3 a. 1 r. 36 p. in Badeley Moor being the allotment of common and waste land to J. Smith in his private capacity.

1811 The enclosure of the parish of Mattishall Burgh took place.

The following is the description of the property belonging to the Vicar of Mattishall just previous to the enclosure:

It is said to consist of three tenancies, containing respectively 3 roods, 3 roods and 2 roods, together with a right of common of pasture for all his commonable cattle *levant* and *couchant* upon the same premises, in, over and upon all the common and waste lands in Mattishall Burgh at all times of the year.

In lieu of the above 1 a. 1 r. 25 p. was allotted to the Mattishall Vicarage.

1838 The Tithe Award states that the Vicar's glebe contains 28 a. 1 r. 28 p., including the Parsonage (2 r. 6 p.) and the meadow adjoining (1 r. 29 p.) and Churchyard (3 r. 25 p.).

The apportionment of Vicarial tithe is £296. 6s. 0d., including that on the Vicar's and College glebes.

1859 When the Rectorial barn was burned down the then Vicar—Mr Paddon—rebuilt it on the Vicarial glebe.

MELTON OR GREAT MELTON (NORFOLK).

1713 The advowson of the united Rectories of S. Mary and All Saints was bought by Mr Camborn's executors for £411. 7s. 3d., of E. Keene, who conveyed the advowson to the College.

1723 Mr Selth was presented to Melton and to S. Michael's, Coslany, and gave a bond to hold both or resign both together. It was at that time the intention of the College that these two benefices—one in the country and one in the city—should be held together, and that Hethersett and S. Clement's, Norwich, should also be held together: and this intention had the approbation of the Diocesan.

1799 The land tax of £3. 12s. on the Rectory was bought by the College for £132 Consols.

1839 The apportionment of Rectorial tithe was fixed at £753. 10s. 0d., including £5 on the glebe. The glebe contains 22 acres.

1896 The College exchanged, with the Rev. H. E. Lombe, the advowson of this benefice for that of Swanton Morley cum Worthing.

MEPAL (CAMBS)

1702 Mr J. Halman, Master of the College and Registrary of the University, bequeathed to the College his lease, from the Dean and Chapter of Ely, of the Manor Farm at Mepal, in the Isle of Ely,—at that time sub-leased for £85 a year—to pay an annuity of £10 to Mrs M. Lewis for her life and £1 a year to the Bursar for keeping a separate account of the benefaction; and the remainder of the yearly income to accumulate for five years for raising a fund to pay fines and other contingencies; after that to pay £2 a year to each of Dr Caius's 20 scholars and £2 a year to the College chest.

The farm consisted of 230 a. 3 r. 11 p. (about 100 a. being pasture) and two common rights and a sheep-walk for 300 sheep.

The lease from the Dean and Chapter was for 21 years and was renewed, generally, every 7 years for a fine, the reserved rent being

	£	s.	d.
2 quarters of wheat, or their value in money			
A brawn at Michaelmas, or	2	0	0
A calf at Easter, or....................................	0	10	0
And money	5	0	0

The last renewal was in 1866.

At various times the College spent money out of the accumulations of the benefaction on improvements to the farm, and about 1853 when the enclosure of the parish took place the College paid £320. 7s. 5d. towards the expenses of the enclosure and of fencing the portion allotted to the farm.

In 1868 the Ecclesiastical Commissioners succeeded to the property of the Dean and Chapter, and at Lady Day, 1871, bought the remainder of the lease and the land tax on the farm, which had been acquired by the College in 1799, by paying to the College £5500, invested in £5890. 4s. 6d. Consols.

The benefaction proved most valuable to the College, as shown by the following table:

	Rent paid by under-tenant	Fine, about	Paid for scholars	Paid to College chest
1710	£95	£70	£35. 10s.	No payment till 1732
1759	£90	£100	£39. 10s.	£2
1787	£125	£170	£38. 10s.	£2
1794	£125	£272	£37	£2
1808	£255	£420	£102[1]	£9
1839	£250	£630	£212[2]	£11
1845	£250	£800	£162. 10s.	£11
1866	£432. 10s.	£900	£245	

At Michaelmas, 1780, the balance belonging to the fund was £161.

In the following year (1781) the fund began to accumulate stock, buying £500 of the 3 p.c. Consols for about £280. After this, small purchases went on at short intervals, so that before the end of the century the fund owned £1000 Consols.

1799 £432. 1s. 1½d. Consols were used for the purchase of the land tax of £11. 15s. 8d. on the farm.

Also the fund made an extra cash payment of £200 to the College chest as a contribution towards the £6000 and upwards then lately expended in new College buildings and extensive repairs, and a contribution for the internal defence of the Kingdom (*Gesta*, 1799, Oct. 31).

In 1800 the fund again started buying Consols (giving £300 for £789. 15s. stock). The price of Consols being so low, the amount of stock resulting from the purchases, that went on almost every year, rapidly rose, till in 1817 it stood at £3680, at which it remained till 1835, when the cash balance having rolled up £1271, a further purchase of £600 stock was made for £553. 10s.

At the same time the fund effected a loan, from its cash balance, under "Gilbert's Act," for building the Hockwold Rectory House, which was paid off in 20 annual instalments.

[1] In 1802 the payment for each scholar was raised from £2 to £6.
[2] In 1819 this payment was raised to £10.

After 1852 no further purchases of Consols took place; but considerable improvements on the farm were paid for out of the income account, which in consequence became much overdrawn.

1856 £450 of the Consols were taken as a contribution towards the payments for the new Hall, Kitchen, Library and Combination-room.

1861 Under the (then) new Statutes £4650 Consols were transferred from this fund to the "Reserve Fund" of the College, which was then being formed.

It was also arranged that the excess of net income over £120 each year should be carried to the College Account (Bursar's Book) which now paid the scholars and the Bursar. Apparently it was considered that £120 a year would in time be sufficient to make up the adverse balance of £689. 6s. 8d. then existing and to provide for future renewals of the lease.

1865–6 The remaining £1100 Consols were sold, and the proceeds, £990, used in part payment for building the last five houses in Scroope Terrace.

1871 On the purchase of the remainder of the lease by the Ecclesiastical Commissioners, it was agreed that the remaining adverse balance, £459. 12s. 2d., should be paid off by 30 annual instalments from the corporate income of the College (Bursar's Book).

MILTON (CAMBS).

1660 Dr Batchcroft devised to the College his lands at Milton (Venn, Vol. III, p. 287).

They were called Rye Close, or Tempest's Close. Their area is 6 a. 1 r. 55 p. The rent has been as follows: 1661, £9; 1670, £7; 1751, £8; 1796, £9; 1818, £13.

The land was apparently always supposed to be rack-rented as I cannot find any mention of a fine.

1799 The land tax (£1. 4s. 0d.) was redeemed for £44. 2s. 0d. Consols.

1800 At the enclosure of the parish the College paid £43. 5s. 6d. to exonerate this land from tithe.

Latterly it has been let with our land at Chesterton.

In a lease of this land, dated 1768, we have the word *ear* as synonymous with plough, the tenant undertaking not to "plow, dig, break up, ear or convert into tillage."

STEEPLE MORDEN AND GUILDEN MORDEN (CAMBS), WITH ASHWELL (HERTS).

1539 J. Whitacre gave to the College his lands, containing a messuage—called Christmas's—with 5 a. of pasture and 147 a. of arable in the above parishes (Venn, III, p. 249).

For these lands there were paid as quit rents, £1. 5s. to the Manor of Steeple Morden and Browes, and 5s. to the Manor of Shengay.

Christmas's was at first let for £5. 3s. 6d. a year.

1556 N. Shaxton, Bishop of Salisbury, gave the sum of £20 (and other things) to buy lands of the annual value of 20s. This was used up; but in Dr Caius's time

1563 was restored, when, with £20, added by the College, 28 acres in Steeple Morden were bought of J. Sherman, close to our other land.

1572 Christmas's and Sherman's were let together for £10 a year.

1608   This rent was changed to £6. 13s. 4d., with 5 qrs. of wheat and 6 qrs. 5 bush. of malt.

1711   N. Parham bequeathed £200 for a scholarship.

1736   This sum was laid out in the purchase of 36 a. from S. Gundree, let at first for £8 to the tenant of our other lands until the renewal of the lease in 1768, when they were let under one lease with the other lands for £6. 13s. 4d. and 5 qrs. of wheat and 6 qrs. 5 bush. 2 pk. of malt.

The following are some of the fines paid for renewals of the lease ·

				£	s.	d.
1669	14	years expired		30	0	0
1734	8	„ „		13	4	0
1768	20	„ „		14	0	0
1777	8	„ „		7	0	0
1798	7	„ „		10	10	0

Thus neither in annual rents nor in renewal fines does the position of the College after 1768 appear to have been improved by the purchase in 1736.

1753   The whole property was said to contain 185 a. 3 r. lying in 165 parcels.

1799   The following is the schedule of the lands (by estimation):

	a.	r.	p.
Homestead, &c.	2	0	0
Pasture	4	0	0
Arable in Steeple Morden	175	0	0
„ „ Guilden Morden	10	2	0
„ „ Ashwell	6	2	0
Total	198	0	0

The annual value was put at £67 with £10 more for the sheep-walk for 120 sheep. The trees on the land were valued at £14. 14s.

The whole property was sold to Lord Hardwicke for £1485, which, with interest, was paid 17 April, 1801, when Consols were bought, with which to redeem the land taxes on our estates. *See* also SWAYCLIFFE, WILTON AND HOCKWOLD.

MUTFORD-CUM-BARNBY (SUFFOLK).

1354   Sir E. Hemegrave—with the license of the King—grants to the College the advowson of the Church of Mutford for a certain sum of ready money which they gave him.

About five weeks afterwards Bp. Bateman—with the consent of the Prior and Chapter of Norwich—appropriates the Church to the use of the College and gives them leave to enter upon the enjoyment of the revenues so soon as the then Rector vacates them—without the further license of anyone else; reserving to the Vicar a proper portion of the revenues, namely, 10 marks a year, and an appropriate dwelling. He further directs that the College may let the revenues, but not for a term longer than five years and only to an ecclesiastic (Proviso tamen quod Decime in solo ecclesiastico reponantur); and that in lieu of firstfruits the College shall pay to the Bishop of Norwich a pension of £1 a year. (This payment, to the Ecclesiastical Commissioners instead of to the Bishop, is still continued.)

1361   The College exercised for the first time the right of presenting a Vicar: so that from this year it has enjoyed the Rectorial revenues.

1409 There is in the College treasury a lease of this date—perhaps the oldest of our College leases extant—by which the College lets, to C. Chark, Rector of Hengrave, and Thomas Denny of Mutford, the Rectory of Mutford, except the advowson, for five years. The rent to be 10 marks (£6. 13s. 4d.) payable half-yearly.

In later leases the rent is £5. 6s. 8d., the lessee covenanting to pay also the £1 to the Bishop.

1411 T. Arundel, Archbishop of Canterbury, confirmed the College in the possession of the Churches of Foulden, Mutford, Wilton and Mattishall.

1412 The College redeemed the payment of 6 marks a year from the above four Churches to the Convent of Spinney, near Soham (Cambs). When or why this payment was first imposed I have been unable to find.

1414 There had been a dispute with the Rectors of Gyselham and Barnby as to the tithes of Hobebergh, and this year the Pope confirms the award of the Archbishop of Canterbury that they belonged to the Church of Mutford.

1431 The Bishop of Norwich gives leave for the union of Barnby with Mutford on certain conditions, which afterwards were varied by his successor.

1434 The Rectory of Barnby (which see) was consolidated with the Vicarage of Mutford.

1580 In accordance with the Corn Act of 1576 the rent of the Rectory, &c., was changed from £5. 6s. 8d. to £3. 11s. in money, together with 5 qrs. of wheat and 4 bushels of malt.

1598 At a survey held this year it appeared that the Rectorial glebes consisted of 47 acres.

1624 But at the survey held in 1624 it was found that these had been almost entirely lost, and that nothing of them remained, except the Parsonage House and the barn-yard on the north side of it.

1653 A lease of the impropriation was granted to one King for a fine of £70.

1654 *Subsequently* King is presented to Mutford-cum-Barnby and receives a lease of the impropriation for 21 years.

[Suckling makes no mention of King in his list of Vicars.]

1663 A lease, for five years (without fine), of the impropriation, lately seized into possession of the College for non-payment of rent, &c., is granted to T. Randall, Vicar, he to repair the barn and other houses and to satisfy the College for arrears of rent.

After this it was always leased to the Vicars (without fine) until 1880.

1789 The living of Wheatacre (which see) was consolidated with that of Mutford-cum-Barnby.

1800 Under the Enclosure Award for the two parishes there was allotted to the Rector one piece in Barnby, containing 3 a. 0 r. 22 p., for his rights of common and all commonable rights and interests over heaths, fens, and wastes in Barnby. He was exempted from any part of the costs of the enclosure, which amounted to £2547. 8s. 7d.

1801 The land tax of £2. 14s. 0d. on the Rectory of Mutford, and taxes of 11s. and £2. 4s. payable out of the Vicarage of Mutford and the Rectory of Barnby respectively, were bought by the College for £194. 6s. 8d. Consols (taken from the Wortley Book).

1847 The apportionments of the rent charges in lieu of tithes were as follows: Rectorial £251, Vicarial £113.

1856 Wheatacre was disunited from Mutford-cum-Barnby.

1859   An exchange of land was carried out between the Vicar and S. Robinson, by which the Vicar gave up six pieces, containing in all 6 a. 1 r. 25 p., and received three pieces, lying near the Church, containing 6 a. 1 r. 38 p.

1860   The rent paid by the Vicar for the impropriation was changed to one shilling.

1880   The College ceased to let the impropriation and took the tithes, repairing the chancel for itself and allowing the Vicar to have the use of the Parsonage House for the Curate.   It also endowed the Church (for the benefit of the Vicar) with a part of the Rectorial tithes to the apportioned value of £100.

The (Vicarial) glebe is 16 pieces and contains 28 a. 0 r. 8 p.   It is much mixed up with other people's land.

NORWICH.   *Advowson of S. Michael's, Coslany.*

1441   The patronage of this living and the Gonville half-acre (in Acle) was conveyed by Wm. Tweight to T. Attwood (then Master of the College) and others.

Tweight had been associated with others—probably as trustees—in holding the patronage and half-acre.   Whether these were a gift from Tweight to the College, or whether the College gave any consideration for them is not shown by the deeds.   It seems reasonable to suggest that, as the survivor of a succession of trustees, he did this with the view of the patronage &c. being ultimately transferred to the College as being able to hold them in perpetual trusteeship.

After the death of Attwood and some of his co-trustees the patronage and half-acre were conveyed by successive deeds to other sets of persons (obviously nominees of the College) until the year 1504 (20 Hen. VII).

The first Gonville-man who held the living was T. Drentall.   One of the trustees who presented him—in 1464—was Sir T. Boleyn (Master), who, Blomefield says, after much trouble got the advowson settled on the College. Although this may have been so, the old practice of conveying from one body of trustees to another was kept up—as mentioned above—till 1504.

This living was held by three masters of the College in succession, viz. by

Dr Barley, who built the Parsonage House from the ground ;

Dr E. Stubb, who bought the "backside of the Parsonage on the east side," and built the stable ; and

Dr W. Bokenham, who bought a little piece of ground to enlarge the yard.

To the Parsonage House belonged certain household stuff and books, of which two inventories, made in 1513 and 1540, are in the Treasury.   The successive parsons gave bonds to the College for the safe keeping of these goods and for the repair of the house.

1524   Robert Thorpe, Alderman of Norwich (who died 1501) obtained on Feb. 28, 1496-7, a royal license to found by himself or his executors a Chantry (cantarice) at S. Michael's, Coslany, and to endow it with lands to the annual value of £8.   This his executor, John Clerke, Alderman of Norwich, does by deed dated July 27, 1524.   He appoints R. Webber priest of the Chantry. He constitutes the Chantry priest a corporation sole—Gonville Hall to have the nomination of the said priest.   If any fellow of the College desires it, he shall have a preference.   The priest to hold no other benefice or cure. Here again it is suggested that he did this to obtain a perpetual trusteeship— thus obviating the difficulty of finding at intervals fresh persons to undertake it.

The lands, being vested in the Chantry priest, fell to the impropriator at the dissolution of the chantries under Edward VI (1547).

1563 Sir John Elwyn, parson and last Chantry priest, gave a tenement and parcel of ground adjoining the parsonage to be part of it, and also a piece of ground on the back side of the parsonage for the use of all future parsons.

1803 The College paid £100 to augment the value of the living.

To this living belonged some arable land at Wymondham, containing 33 a. 0 r. 7 p. and rented at £60.

1869 The advowson was sold for £100 to the Rev. E. Holland and others—the College paying the expenses, £21. 18s. 9d.

Houses in Norwich

1508 T. Symonds conveyed to E. Stubb, Master, and others a messuage, between the Church of S. Michael's, Coslany, and the Rectory House, together with a corner house and another lying adjacent to it.

The property was originally let as two leaseholds for 20 years.

(1) The messuage—divided into six or eight tenements—rent £2. 2s. 8d.

(2) Corner house and house adjacent—rent £1.

The two lessees had the joint use of the common yard and well.

1669 The same tenant held both leases. After this both portions were let on one lease.

The fines paid for the lease were as follows :

						£
1669	10	years of old lease expired				16
1750	20	,,	,,	,,	,,	90
1764	7	,,	,,	,,	,,	16
1771	7	,,	,,	,,	,,	32
1785	7	,,	,,	,,	,,	40
1827	7	,,	,,	,,	,,	100
1848	7	,,	,,	,,	,,	80

	£	s.	d.
In 1778 the annual value was reckoned at ...	47	8	0
, 1868 ,, ,, ,, ,, ...	66	18	0

The corner house had for some years been turned into a public-house, called the "Eight Ringers."

1868 The whole property was sold for £700 to Messrs Patterson and Steward.

Advowson of S. Clement's-on-the-Bridge.

1705 The College bought the advowson from Thomas Woode for £107. 10s. 0d., of which sum, £100 was the gift of Mr John Case.

1737 (about) The living was augmented by an estate of 34 a. 0 r. 3 p. at Brooke —let for £23 a year. The purchase money was provided by £200 from Q. A. B. and £200, the gift of the Rev. E. Brooke.

1802 The land tax (£3. 19s. 3d.) on the estate at Brooke was bought by the College for £132 Consols ; and that (£1. 19s, 6d.) on the Rectory for £49. 19s. 11d. Consols.

1843 The estate was exchanged for one of 42 a. 1 r. 15 p. in Rushall and Dickleburgh, and the new owner redeemed the land tax on it by paying £132 to the College.

1882 R. Rigg, the Rector of S. Clement's, bought the advowson of S. Edmund-at-Oak and united the two livings.

1887 He also bought a house (in which Opie lived at one time) and gave it to the united benefices as a parsonage house.

Various.

In the 16th century the College owned other properties as shown below. They cannot be further traced.

1537   R. Overy gives his receipt for £17, received from feoffees of the College, for a messuage and garden bought by him in the parish of S. Mary's " *Vnbrent.*"

Phil. and Mary   J. Goose sells to the College his house, &c., in the parish of S. Benedict's and the College covenants with him to restore this house in case he should pay them £80.

1562   There are acquittances for £120 paid by the College for the Hostelry (Diversorium) of the Swan over against S. Peter's, Mancroft. The annual rent was £5. 6s. 8d. It was bought incautiously, for it was soon after found to be in bad repair: it was then sold for £100.

OBORNE (DORSET).

1570   For purchase *see* BINCOMBE.
The Manor contained almost the whole of the parish and was divided into fifteen tenancies—or " livings "—held by copy of the Court Roll for three lives with widowhood.
The tenants paid fixed annual rents, of which the total was £14. 11s. 8d., and on the death of a tenant a heriot was received by the College. The heriot was generally the best beast or goods—in one case it was one ewe sheep, or 3s. 4d. In a few cases it was money, either 3s. 4d. or 5s. 4d. or £3. 13s. 4d. On the renewal of a tenancy a fine was paid. Upon one occasion (1753) the fine was £770. It was the general custom to carry these fines to the Bursar's Book as well as the similar fines obtained from Bincombe and the ordinary fines of manors in the east of England. Their accumulation provided the funds for the alteration of the College about 1750 and, partly, for the large College repairs at the end of the 18th century, and for the purchase of leaseholds of Oborne and Bincombe about the year 1825.

1629   The College bought a tenement and 19 acres of land from Ff. and J. Devonish for £110. Henceforth the College has owned practically the whole of the parish. This estate was called The Crofts. Its annual rent was, at first, £4. 10s., afterwards £7. Upon one occasion (1757) a fine of £10 was paid for the lease of it (for three lives).

1650   About this year the tenants exchanged lands with one another and enclosed all the fields and divided up the common. A terrier of 1656 speaks of the common as " lately enclosed." Such a method of enclosure, without the intervention of an Act of Parliament and Enclosure Commissioners, is, so far as I know, unique.

1750   About this year the College on the renewal of some of the tenancies substituted leases, still *for three lives*—under its seal—instead of copies of the Roll. It had been the intention of the College to have granted the leases for 99 years ; but they were advised by counsel that leases for years made them only chattels —and thus did not confer votes—whereas leases for lives were absolute freeholds.

1766   A survey drawn up this year put the acreage of the land belonging to the College at 555 statutable acres 3 roods 32 poles and at 671 customary acres 3 roods 9 poles (a statutable acre being to a customary one as 12·1 to 10 nearly).

1794 The acreage was put at 688 computed acres.

1826 The lease of one of the estates was bought up by the College for £1580, and the estate was let for £110.

1827 The lease of another estate (Grange Farm) was bought for £4845, and the estate was let for £340.

All the other leaseholds and the copyholds appear to have been run out. The College gave up 16 poles and 4½ poles for widening the Sherborne Turnpike Road.

1840 The College paid £61. 16s. 8d. as their share of the expense of apportioning the rent charge in lieu of tithe on their land. The apportionment was £160. 9s. 0d.

1856 The College bought 19 poles from B. Chant and another for £15. This parcel had been encroached from the roadside waste.

1858–60 Two new cottages and a chaise-house on the smaller farm were built for £320.

1861 The Salisbury and Yeovil Railway Company took 8 a. 3 r. 36 p. and paid £1154 (re-invested in the Trinity Street property bought of Dr Whewell). The College gave the site and £500 for the new Church.

1864 The road was diverted and the College gave £10 towards the expense.

1868 An old toll-house and garden were bought from the Turnpike Trustees for £30.

1870 A house and garden were bought from Miss Highmore for £400. They lie in the angle between the roads to Oborne village and Milborne Port. They had changed hands in 1766 for £20.

The expenses of this purchase and that in 1868 came to £22. 14s. 6d.

1874 The last life (Hull's) in the last leasehold ran out.

1876 The whole estate being now rack-rented, the rent roll was £1093.

The tithe apportionment was altered, £3. 12s. being settled on the land taken for the railway in 1861 and £159. 17s. left on the land owned by the College.

1878 Another old toll-house and garden, on the Bath Road, were bought, from the Trustees of the Sherborne Turnpike, for £70 on the abolition of the Trust. A new house for the Grange Farm cost £1510.

1889 A new riding-stable for the same farm cost £200.

1891 For this farm also an hydraulic ram was connected with the rivulet at a cost of £168.

1894 A garden on the waste of the manor was bought from G. Chant for £11 (expenses £2).

1895 The College bought a strip of garden ground by the roadside for £11.

1896 At the smaller farm the house was practically rebuilt for £420.

1898 A large tank was made on the hill on the E. side of the parish, to which water is pumped by a wind pump from the spring near the house, bought in 1870. From the tank are laid pipes, which supply the two farm-houses, the old farm-house of the Grange Farm and also two taps by the roadside for the use of the cottagers. The Rectory House was supplied later, for which service the Rector pays a rent under an agreement. The cost was about £280.

1899 The College bought, of the Rev. O. A. Benthall, for £120, a cottage (formerly two) on the S. of the road to Milborne Port.

The acreage of the parish is as follows :

	a.	r.	p.
College	560	2	14
Glebe and Church	8	0	3
Railway	13	3	5
Whole parish	582	1	22

The total rents from farms was in 1875, £1088; in 1885, £888; in 1895, £663; in 1905, £650. The College pays the tithe.

OXBURGH (NORFOLK). *Land—14 acres.*

1723 The feoffees of Hammond's Charity Lands (left for the benefit of the poor in 1679) gave a lease of them to Sir H. Bedingfield for 999 years from Lady Day at an annual rent of £2. 10s., this being above the rent previously obtained for them, and the rent was paid to the Rector for the benefit of the poor.

The lands then consisted of one messuage and a close of pasture, to which also appertained certain rights over the common.

1725 The Enclosure Commissioners allotted 3 acres of pasture and 8 of arable to this holding, which then consisted of 14 acres in all.

1726 Sir H. Bedingfield assigned the 14 acres to J. Meriton.

1733 J. Meriton for £100 sold to the College the remainder of the term of 999 years. The 14 acres were then let to the Rector for £6 a year, he or Sir H. Bedingfield paying also the £2. 10s. for the poor.

1839 The Commissioners for enquiring into charities under the Act of 59 Geo. III found that the property was worth more than the £2. 10s. a year, and in consequence the Attorney-General instituted a suit in Chancery and the lease of 1723 was annulled (Record Office, "Chancery Proceedings 1800–42, Nos. 3066 and 3174").

The College thus lost these lands.

Advowson of the Rectory.

1733 The advowson was bought, from J. Meriton, for £650. Mr Stephen Camborn's trustees advanced £550 of this sum and the College found the remaining £100.

1761 The livings of Oxburgh and Foulden were consolidated.

1801 By the transfer of £438. 3s. 4d. Consols to the Government the College (1) redeemed a land tax of 14s. on the 14 acres which it bought in 1733 and lost in 1839 and (2) bought a tax of £12. 7s. 6d. payable by the Rector out of the Rectorial glebe and tithes.

The glebe, including the Churchyard, contains 48 a. 1 r. 18 p. with house. The tithe rent charge is apportioned at £483. 14s. 4d.

PATTESLEY (NORFOLK).

1520 Dr Jeffrey Knight devised the Manor of Pattesley to Gonville Hall for the maintenance of two priests—excepting the advowson of the Rectory or Free Chapel of Pattesley, which he devised to Sir Christopher Heydon and Dame Katharine his wife. He also ordained that the manorial lands, called Stakecroft, shall for ever remain to the Chapel.

1521 This manor was exchanged for that of D'Engaynes in Teversham and Stow. Quy of the annual value of £21, its previous owner, Sir R. Townshend, receiving from the College £96 out of the money given by Dr Baily.

1576 Sir C. Heydon gave to the College the sinecure Rectory or Free Chapel of Pattesley, together with the perpetual advowson thereof.

1743 The Rectory of Pattesley and the Vicarage of Mattishall were consolidated.

		£
1741	The Governors of Queen Anne's Bounty gave	200
1743	Bishop Gooch lent	200
	The Governors of Q. A. B. again gave	200
	Total	£600

This sum was laid out in the purchase of a freehold farm at Standfield, consisting of messuage, barn, stable and cart-lodge with 40 a. of pasture, 2 a. of meadow and 23 a. of arable; these let for £30 a year.

It is within three miles of Pattesley. It is subject to the payment of quit rents of 9s. 3d. a year, and, as a relief, one year's quit rent on a change of owner.

The £200 lent by the Bishop (without interest) was gradually paid off by the incumbent, H. Goodall.

The 9s. 3d. quit rent was made up of 8s. 6d. due to the Manor of Grissenhall in N. Soken and 9d. due to the Manor of Butley in Brisley and Bilney. The tithe commutation on the farm is £23. 12s. 6d.

1788 The rent of the farm was at this time £42.

The tithe of Pattesley is represented by an annual payment of £8. 8s. made by the owner of the manor. At one time the payment was £10. 10s. 0d.

1798 The Rector (J. Smith) considered himself defrauded by this payment being so small and drew up long statements about it (copies of which are in the College Treasury and in the chest in Mattishall Church) and submitted them to various counsel, but apparently did not take the matter into court.

1816 At the enclosure of Standfield parish five pieces containing 10 a. 2 r. were allotted to the Standfield Farm, and also, by way of exchange in lieu of certain lands given up, three pieces containing 5 a. 1 r. 10 p.

1906 The farm at Standfield was sold for £775 to Mrs Case, and £56 was paid by the Rector (E. M. Madoc-Jones) on being thus relieved of dilapidations on the farm buildings.

PUTNEY (SURREY).

1896 The College bought, of Mr P. E. Lilley, for £9600, four houses and shops, being Nos. 138, 140, 142, 144 in High Street.

1897 The sum of £300 was laid out on the improvement of No. 144.

1907 The gross rental is £480.

RICKMANSWORTH (HERTS).

1557 Dr Caius gave to the College his manor of Croxley and Snellshall (at the same time as those of Runcton and Burnham Thorpe). It had formerly belonged to the Monastery of St Albans, and Dr Caius had bought it of the Crown (Philip and Mary) for £461, being 20 years' purchase of its then annual value.

The free and customary rents of the manor amounted to £12. 6s. 8d.

The manor contained three tracts of common land, viz. Croxley Green, the Common Moor and the common land at Cassiobridge.

From the earliest times payments, amounting usually to 4s. and called Haling Money, have been paid to the College by the free or, since 1618, the free and customary tenants of the manor. Some portions of these payments are for permission to turn cattle on to the Common Moor; other portions are commutations in money for services which had originally to be rendered to the lord.

This property has been peculiarly productive of lawsuits, of which the records are in the College Treasury (Venn, III, 129).

The demesne lands had been let for £15. 6s. 8d. on a lease from 1553 by Edward VI to one R. Lee. On the expiration of the lease Dr Caius gave a new lease, for 20 years, and raised the rent of the lands, with the under-wood, but without the timber, to £40, and directed in his statutes that it should so remain (or at £25 without the underwood).

The fines for the renewals of the lease of these lands (and of those of Runcton) he assigned to the Master on condition that he resided in College.

1597   The "old rent" of £15. 6s. 8d. was converted into a rent of £10. 4s. 4d. with 7½ quarters of wheat and 10½ quarters of malt, and to this was added the £24. 13s. 4d. by which the rent had been raised by Dr Caius, i.e. the money rent was £34. 17s. 8d.

The lease for 20 years was generally renewed after the expiration of 7 years. In 1812 the corn rent was raised to 13 quarters 6 bushels of wheat and 19 quarters 1 bushel of malt. I cannot find what was done with the increase of the corn rent till in 1832 and onwards it is stated to have been divided by the Master and Fellows.

The fines gradually increased from £124 in 1651, and £140 in 1677, to £424 in 1798.

The subsequent fines were as follows:

> £525 in 1805,
> £1860 in 1812,
> £1008 in 1819,
> £1865 in 1828 (9 years expired).

In 1835 the fine was set at £1400 but was not paid, and consequently the lease was not renewed. I have not found that anything was advanced from the Bursar's Book for division amongst the Master and 12 (Senior) Fellows.

In 1842 a new lease was granted for 20 years from 1835 and a fine of £1400 was paid. After this the beneficial lease was not renewed.

In 1849 £1400 was advanced in lieu of the fine.

In 1855 when the lease ran out the whole property was relet for £722 a year, wholly in money; and in 1868 for £900.

In 1856 the stipends of the Senior Fellows were increased by £24 each a year, in lieu of fines, in consequence of the increase of rents at Rickmansworth, Runcton and other places.

It will be seen that the whole property was let as one tenancy; but the lessee, no doubt, from the first, sublet different portions to different occupiers. Certainly he did in later times. In 1878 the property was broken up and let directly in different tenancies to the various occupiers at rents amounting to £1182.

1752   At the survey this year it was estimated that the meadow and arable lands contained together 479 acres 2 roods and the woods 91 acres; and that the full letting value (exclusive of timber) was £271. 12s. 0d.

The manor quit-rents then amounted to £11. 17s. 8d., and there was a free rent of £1 a year issuing out of Micklefield Hall.

BARN

At Croxley Hall Farm in Rickmansworth

1796 The Grand Junction Canal Company took 6 a. 1 r. 17 p.—exclusive of the land taken from the Common Moor—and paid £226. 17s. 6d. as compensation, of which £8. 3s. 0d. was paid to the tenant for his interest.

1799 The land tax, amounting to £23. 5s. 1½d., was redeemed for £852. 14s. 7¼d. Consols.

1800 The Canal Company took 30 poles of land and paid £6. 12s. 2¼d.

1828 The College conveyed to the Canal Company 1 a. 3 r. on the east side of the Common Moor—next Black Moor—and 3 roods, the remaining portion of Cashio Bridge Common on the west side of Cashio Bridge between the Canal and the River Gade, reserving a right of road over the latter. The Company paid for these two pieces £5. 7s. 0d. to the College and £75 to the Church-wardens. Also the Company covenanted to keep the reserved road in repair from Cashio Bridge.

By an Act of Parliament (9 Geo. IV *Private* c. 19) the College gave up to J. Dickenson—of Nash Mills in the parish of Abbots Langley—the following two pieces lying to the S.E. of the Canal:

	a.	r.	p.
Blackmoor	5	2	0;
Strip between Canal and River Gade	1	1	5; also
Another strip (part of Mallet Moor, on the E. of Cashio Bridge)	0	0	38;

and their rights, as Lords of the Manor, over the waters of the River Gade, excepting the fishing.

The College retained a right of way over a road to be made and maintained by J. Dickenson along the western side of the first strip.

And J. Dickenson gave up to the College the two parts, into which Lott Mead had been divided by the Grand Junction Canal (except a strip of the smaller part, 60 yds. by 12 yds. next the Canal). These parts contained respectively 10 a. 3 r. 31 p. and 3 a. 3 r. 10 p.

1829 Upon Black Moor J. Dickenson proceeded to build the paper mills and found subsequently that the arrangement for the road was inconvenient and so agreed to reconvey to the College the 38 p. and to maintain for the College another road, along which we were to have a right of way, partly on his and partly on our land.

Lott Mead was a meadow, partly freehold and partly copyhold of the manor, formerly owned by a number of persons, who mowed it every year, casting *lots* each year as to which portion each should mow. In order that the canal might be brought across it, the Company bought up the rights of the various owners and afterwards sold to J. Dickenson the two parts on either side which were not required for the purposes of the canal.

1843 The apportionments of the tithe rent charge were:

	£	s.	d.
In Rickmansworth	116	5	3
In Watford	7	10	6

1844 The Ordnance Survey gives our acreage as follows:

Arable	422·518
Pasture	104·110
Woods	100·143
Buildings and gardens	7·170
Watercress beds	8·108
Total	642·049

1860 Up to this year the College had been governed by Dr Caius's Statutes which prohibited the sale of any portions of this and of our other principal estates.

The new Statutes contained no such prohibition, and it will be seen below that in later years there have been frequent dealings with this estate.

1861 The Rickmansworth and Watford Railway Company took 3 a. 1 r. 1 p. of the demesne lands and 2 a. 1 r. 4 p. of the Common Moor, and paid to the College £500 for the former and £18 for their rights in the latter. The conveyance of the latter was sealed in 1862 and that of the former in 1881.

1874 The half-acre on Croxley Green, called Andrew's Plat, was sold to Mr T. H. Woods for £200.

1876 We sold to Mr Woods "Rhodes's Cottage" for £15, and a piece of land, 60 ft. by 40 ft, for £70.

1879 A triangular strip of land containing 20 poles above the chalk-pit on Scots Hill—next to the land of Mr R. Warwick—was sold to him for £20.

1880 An exchange of lands with Mr Woods was carried out. The College obtained 14 a. 8 r. 18 p. on S.E. of All Saints' Vicarage House, 1 r. 37 p. to the N. of the part of the Snellshall Field retained, and houses and homestead with 5 a. 2 r. 6 p. on N.W. of Croxley Green, through which the new road was carried in 1896; and gave up 23 a. 1 r. 37 p. in Great Snellshall Field, being the N.E. tip of the crescent in which our property lay.

The tithe rent charge was then apportioned on the above lands as follows :

	£	s.	d.
Land given up by College, Watford	1	3	3
„ „ „ „ Rickmansworth ...	3	13	1
Land taken by College, Rickmansworth	5	10	8

1885 The Metropolitan Railway Company took 10 a. 0 r. 30 p., part of the Croxley Hall Farm and 4 a. 2 r. 20 p. of the Common Moor and paid £4200 to the College.

1890 At Cassiobridge a pair of cottages was built for £460 ;

1891 and a pair on Croxley Hall Farm for £365.

Messrs Dickenson for £1500 bought 14·689 acres, a meadow S. of the River Gade (of which about 1 acre was watercress beds).

1895 Mr Woods bought 66 a. 3 r. 28 p. in Watford to the N. of Rouse Barn Lane and 35 a. 1 r. 27 p. in Rickmansworth to the N. of Baldwin Lane and paid £8146.

We bought, from Lord Essex, 3 r. 27 p. of watercress beds in Watford, in the angle between Rouse Barn Lane and the Canal, for £400.

1896 We effected an exchange with Mr Warwick, giving up 1 a. 2 r. 14 p. and taking 1 a. 2 r. 36 p. and paying £50 for equality of exchange. Over the land thus obtained we carried in 1906 the Copthorne Road, which starts from the foot of Scots Hill and ends at Croxley Green.

1897 Dickenson and Company bought 2 r. 30 p. for £200; and Mr Woods 3 a. 0 r. 6 p. on the E. side of the site of the present Copthorne Road for £759. 7s. 6d.

1899 The College bought 3 a. 3 r. 9 p. S. of Scots Hill from H. King for £1950 ; and three cottages, near Cassiobridge, from E. Moon's executors for £500.

1902 S. W. Greves for £7520 bought 44·365 acres containing Cassiobridge House, lying to the W. of the Canal and to the N. of Cassiobridge.

For £25 the Metropolitan Railway Company bought a strip of ground for a siding.

1905 W. J. Beasley bought for £300 an acre of land on a new road from Croxley Hall to Lavock Lane;

1906 and for a like sum another acre next to the former.

Copthorne Road was carried from Scots Hill to Croxley Green at a cost of about £2290.

A strip of ground on the W. side of this road, with a frontage of 1000 feet to it and a depth varying from 131 feet to 156 feet, was sold to various purchasers for a total sum of £2535.

For £15 (and £18. 16s. 0d. for expenses) the College bought of Lord Essex his watercress beds in Cassiobridge Common; and for £434. 9s. 7d. (and £12. 9s. 6d. for expenses) redeemed the tithe (£4. 2s. 6d. payable to the Vicar and £13. 15s. 2d. to the impropriator) on 7 pieces containing 68 a. 2 r. 17 p., of which the strip on the Copthorne Road, sold as above for £2535, formed part.

1907 The tithe, apportioned at £2. 7s. 3d. (viz. £1. 2s. 5d. payable to the Vicar and £1. 4s. 10d. to the impropriator) on 7 pieces on Scots Hill containing 8 a. 1 r. 22 p., was redeemed for £59. 1s. 3d. and £6. 18s. 9d. for expenses. The acreage of the portion in these pieces belonging to the College was 3 a. 3 r. 8 p. on which the tithes were 9s. 7d. and 11s. 6d., so that our share of the redemption money and expenses came to £29. 6s. 8d. This was the land bought of H. King in 1899.

The tithes on our property which still remained unredeemed were as follows·

	£	s.	d.
[1]Croxley Green	57	15	0
Rickmansworth (Vicar)	19	13	0
,, (Ecclesiastical Commissioners)	0	12	7
Watford (Rector)....................................	0	11	6
,, (Vicar)	1	2	1

1910 Within the last 10 years large quantities of gravel have been dug from this estate in the part adjoining the Metropolitan Railway.

The London and North Western Railway Company is taking 7 acres near Cassiobridge and paying £3000.

RUNCTON, OR RUNCTON HOLME (NORFOLK).

1557 Dr Caius gave to the College the three manors of Runcton, Burnham and Croxley, which he had bought of the Crown.

The manor of Runcton belonged to the Abbey of St Edmund's, Bury, till the dissolution of the Monasteries, and the Abbot, in October, 1522, had granted a lease of the demesne lands (and apparently the quit and free rents) for 60 years at the annual rent of £22.

Dr Caius bought the manor for £440, being 20 years' purchase of its then rentals. He ordained that the rent of the demesne lands should be raised to £40.

1582 This year a new lease of the demesne lands was granted at the rent of £36. 13s. 4d. with 5 quarters of wheat and 7 of malt.

Subsequently the rent of the estate stood in the Bursar's Book at £40, thus showing that, in accordance with the Corn· Act of 1576, £3. 6s. 8d. was the third of the "old rent," the whole of which must therefore have been £10.

1609 In this year, the first of the Bursar's Accounts still extant, the amount of quit and free rents collected was £8. 18s. 4d. Then, as now, the actual amounts collected in different years varied slightly (in 1665 the full amount of quit-rents is stated to be £9. 4s. 0d.).

[1] This parish was formed in 1872 of portions of Watford and of Rickmansworth.

In the seventeenth century the College made four additions to its property by purchase.

1666   (1) Of T. Hoogans, for £196. 10s. 0d., and £3. 5s. 0d. for expenses, a messuage, called Neal's, and 24 acres of land (partly copyhold) in 30 parcels. This was let at first for £12 a year, afterwards for £10, in 1747 for £6. 13s. 4d.

1678   (2) Of T. Poulter, for £60, and £1 expenses, a copyhold tenement, to which a right of commonage belonged, with 4½ a. of land. Let at first for £5, in 1747 for £3. 6s. 8d.

1680   (3) Of J. Boss, for £30, a copyhold tenement with 3 roods of land. Let at first for £3, in 1747 for £2.

1697   (4) Of J. and M. Lockart, for £100, a tenement with 36 a. 2 r. 20 p (in 31 parcels). Let for £11. A portion, 26 a. 3 r. 20 p., was copyhold of our manor. Two enclosures, containing 8 acres, are charged with a payment of £2 a year to the poor of Runcton and £2 a year to the poor of Holme, by the will of T. Taylor, dated March 22, 1621.

These four purchases were all let to the tenant of the demesne lands.

In the old leases of the demesne lands, in accordance with No. 93 of Caius's Statutes, there used to be a special covenant that the lessee would not alienate the property to the Lord of the Manor of Thorpland. The lessee also gave a bond for £1000 against breaking this covenant.

1751   A very careful survey of the manor was made by the Bursar, Mr John Smith. The demesne lands consisted of a messuage, 10½ acres of field lands (in eight pieces) and 23 enclosures, containing 231½ acres. The waste lands of the manor were put at 43½ acres. As lords of the manor, we had also the sole right of sheep-walk for 400 sheep, on the unsown fields of Runcton, from Michaelmas to Lady Day, and a right of keeping a flock on the commons of Runcton (about 400 acres) from Aug. 15 to Lady Day, and on the commons of Holme (about 500 or 600 acres) from Lady Day to Aug. 15.

The whole estate was valued at £149 a year.

It was noted that the owner of each tenement in Runcton had a right of keeping 60 sheep on the commons of Runcton and the owner of each tenement in Holme 60 sheep on the commons of Holme.

The quit rents and free rents of the manor amounted to £10. 18s. 3d.

The following are some of the fines paid for the renewal of the lease for 20 years, after 7 years had expired :

1655	£50, including Wiggenhall.
1684	£40 and £5 for Wiggenhall.
1761	£80
1789	£125
1796	£197. 10s.

After this it was not renewed and so ran out in 1816.

In 1803 £324. 17s. 6d. for Runcton and £114. 9s. 0d. for Wiggenhall, and in 1810 £485. 4s. 6d. and £167. 11s. 0d. were advanced from the Bursar's Book for division amongst the Master and 12 (Senior) Fellows in lieu of fines.

1801   The land tax £19. 15s. 0d. was redeemed for £724. 3s. 4d. Consols.

1803   The property was valued at £347 a year, and that in Wiggenhall at £104.

1815   The Act for the enclosure of the parish was passed. It provided
(1) that encroachments on commons, &c., within the previous 20 years were to be taken as parts of the commons, but to form parts of the final allotments to the parties in the possession of them, provided they did not exceed the amount of allotments to which such parties should be entitled ;

(2) that the allotments to the lords of the manors for the soil of the commons should be $\frac{1}{18}$th of the portion of the commons to be allotted to various owners of property in the parish.

(3) That, whereas the Commissioners were to sell as much land as would provide for the expenses of the enclosure to be borne by all the other owners, the College were empowered to pay for their portion of the expenses directly in money, so that no deduction was to be made by the Commissioners for this purpose from the lands to be allotted to the College.

1816   The following were allotted to the College

In South Runcton.

	a.	r.	p.
Six encroachments confirmed by Act	1	2	0
Old enclosure in exchange from Lee Warner's trustees	1	2	6
10 allotments in different parts	200	1	5

In Holme.

The College gave up to Sir M. B. Folkes an old enclosure of 5 a. 0 r. 36 p. and received

	a.	r.	p.
An old enclosure in lieu of the above from Sir M. B. Folkes	3	2	30
An old enclosure from the Rev. P. Bell	1	3	32
„ „ „ „ G. Vernon, Esq..........	4	0	19
Encroachment confirmed by Act..................	0	0	3
Allotment on the common	82	1	10

1816   The whole property (together with that at Wiggenhall) was let to W. Cambridge for £600 a year.

1817   The College paid £999. 19s. 6d. as their share of the expenses of the enclosure.   In this and the next five years we spent £3093 on the estate.

1823–31   "Haling Money," amounting to £3. 12s. 6d. a year, appears amongst the receipts in the Bursar's Book.   I have found no explanation of this entry.

1847   The College bought some cottages, copyhold of our manor, from — Goodall, for £355, of which £255 was the money paid by the Eastern Counties Railway Company for land taken at Shelford.

1867   The College exchanged with the Rector the site of an old cottage at Holme (probably Boss's) for 1 r. 7 p. in Vicar's Lane and paid £6. 6s. 0d. (£7. 15s., less half expenses) and further expenses £3. 3s. 0d.

1873   The sum of £353 was spent on repairing and rebuilding Goodall's cottages. The College bought of T. S. Cocks, for £6700, land, with cottages, containing 133 a. 3 r. 30 p.; and spent £343. 10s. on altering the cottages into three decent ones.

1874   A block of cottages was built on Cocks's land at a cost of £343. 10s. 0d.

1907   For £124. 10s. the College bought Carter's Pightle, containing $2\frac{1}{2}$ acres. It was added to the small farm.

The gross rental of the whole estate, with Wiggenhall, was in 1875, £1250, College paying drainage taxes; in 1885, £1070, College paying tithe and drainage taxes; in 1895, £520; in 1905, £524; in 1910, £593.

The apportionment of tithe rent charge on the whole of our property in Runcton is £214. 19s.

The drainage taxes amount to about £7 a year.

SHALFORD OR SHAWFORD (ESSEX).

1704   Dr John Gostlin, late President of the College and nephew to Dr Gostlin, formerly Master, gave £500 to the College, for augmenting the four scholarships founded by his uncle.

1708   The College with this money and £300 bought, from T. Dalton of Fulbourn, and Dorothy, his wife, a rent charge of £32 a year issuing out of their lands in Shalford.

SHELFORD OR GREAT SHELFORD (CAMBS).

1614   The College bought, for £2000, of the executors (selling under the will) of C. Rogers the Manor of Buristead (except the mansion and 10 acres) and the (King's) water mill.
The manor was held of the King's Manor of East Greenwich[1] " in fealty of free socage" and not " in chief or knight's service."
The mill was also held as a fee farm of the Manor of Greenwich by the rent of £6 a year.
The demesne lands at the time of the purchase were in the possession of J. W. Terry by right of two ancient leases from the Bishop of Ely, who owned the manor in the reigns of Henry VIII and Edward VI.   The first of these leases was granted in 1536 for 50 years and the second in 1553 for 60 years *after the expiration of the former lease*.   The rent was then £12 a year.
The quit and free rents of the manor amounted to £23. 10s. 7d. and thus were then nearly twice as valuable as the demesnes.   The rent of the mill was £38.

1627   The College bought for £21 of J. Gostlin, Fellow, a pasture-close adjoining the mill (Ives).   It was apparently let with the mill and referred to in the lease of 1628 and subsequent leases as the "new purchased close sometime Robert Weddes'."   The rent of the whole tenancy was set at £20.   It was generally let for 20 years and the lease was renewed every 7 years.

1635   The College bought, for £18, a little close adjoining the mills—called Charity's Close—and let it to the tenant of the mill for £1 a year.   This year the College paid £211. 10s. 5d. for repairing the mill.

1650   The College redeemed the £6 a year, payable for the mill, by paying £27 to the Exchequer and giving up the right to the £3 a year paid by the Exchequer for the site of Physwick's Hostel taken by Henry VIII for Trinity College.
"When the Crown returned to its rights" this redemption was held to be void and the two payments of £6 and £3 were renewed and the College lost its £27.

1674   F. Pattison's estate in our manor—both free and copyhold—escheated to the College.   The College let the free lands, called Hanchett's, for £4 a year and the copyhold lands and tenement for £13. 13s. 4d.
The expenses of seizing this land amounted to £1. 19s. 7d.   (Br. Bk. 1674.)

1702   T. Goldwell claimed "Hanchett's" as parcel of the Manor of Granham's (in Shelford).   Whatever his rights were he conveyed them to the College for £25.

1735   At a Manor Court, held on April 29, the College seized 2a. 1r. of copyhold land, late Tabram's, and let them for 14s. a year.

---

[1] A common form of grant from the Crown.   See "Manor of E. Greenwich" by E. P. Cheyney in Vol. XI of *American Historical Review*, pp. 29–35.

1754   At the survey made in this year our property was found to be as follows :

	a.	r.	a.	r.
Demesne lands—Arable land	284	0½		
Enclosed lands.........	32	1¼		
Common meadow......	6	3⅓		
			323	1⅓
Pattison's and Hanchett's			18	0⅔
Tabram's......................................			2	1
Mill lands			5	0
Total			348	3

Attached to the demesne lands was a right of keeping 400 sheep on the fields &c. of Great Shelford.

The following was the estimate of the then actual annual value of the demesnes :

Sheep-walk, £16
Arable land at 9s. an acre
Enclosed ,,   ,, 15s. ,,   } Total £169. 12s. 0d.
Meadow at 5s. an acre

Of the mill lands the most easternly is a small piece of 13 poles in the parish of Little Shelford. This was set out to us in the Enclosure Award of Little Shelford, 1815.

1783   A new copyhold tenant was admitted to Tabram's.

1799   The land tax on the manor (£27. 1s. 4d.) and that on the mills (£5. 8s. 0d.) were redeemed—together with the similar taxes on our other lands in Cambs by the transfer of £2554. 8s. 10¾d. Consols to the Government at the rate of £110 Consols for every £3 of taxes.

1815   The College bought of J. Nutter for £129. 2s. 0d. three pieces, containing 5½ a., copyhold of our manor and lying in Whitefield. They were let to the tenant of the demesnes for £5. 10s. 0d. a year.

1834   At the enclosure the tithe of the whole parish was redeemed by the allotment of certain lands to the tithe owners (Jesus College). Our College gave up 16 old enclosures containing 47 a. 0 r. 28 p. to the Commissioners for re-allotment.   We received

17 a. for our right and interest in the soil of the commons and waste lands ;

6 a. 3 r. 23 p. in two pieces, in lieu of open field lands and rights of common and sheep-walks ;

3 a. 1 r. 17 p., in three pieces, in lieu of freehold common rights and old enclosures ;

339 a. 1 r. 32 p., in four pieces, in lieu of freehold open field lands and rights of common and sheep-walk and foldage and old enclosures ;

24 a., in five pieces, for the enfranchisement of the copyhold lands held previously by five tenants of our manor.

Also 1 a. 0 r. 35 p. was added to the mill tenancy, which then contained 9 a. 2 r. 12 p.

The total cost of the enclosure to the College was £1810. 3s. 0d. (including £1. 7s. 5d. for moving the pound).

The greater part of the additional land, which we received at the enclosure, was let to the tenant of the demesnes for £21 : he paid also £37. 12s. 0d. as a percentage on the cost of enclosure.

After the enclosure our freehold property consisted of :

The farm, 386 a. 3 r. 22 p., let to the tenant who had previously held our demesnes ;

The mill and land around it containing 9 a. 2 r. 12 p. ;

Hanchett's, represented by 4 a. 3 r. 9 p. on the direct road from Great Shelford Church to Cambridge ;

Pattison's, represented by 2 a. 2 r. 38 p. at the angle near the railway station on the road from Great Shelford Church to the railway station. The two latter properties were then let for £15 a year.

1836 A new homestead was built for the farm at a cost of about £1800, for which we received an addition of £72 to the rent.

1846 The Eastern Counties Railway Company took 2 a. 1 r. 17 p. and paid £255.

1868 A barn and cartlodge at the farm were blown down by a whirlwind and the former was rebuilt at a cost of £170.

1890 The College bought, for £1275, of E. H. and A. T. Grain, 34 a. 0 r. 12 p. (freehold, tithe free and land tax redeemed) lying on the E. side of Hills Road—bounded on the N. by land belonging to the College and on the S. by a lime-pit (see 1897). This land was let to the tenant of the farm.
New buildings at the farm cost £170.
The mill was much altered at a cost of £3600.

1894 Two new cottages at the mill cost £250.

1897 The College bought for £1200, of A. Jones, 2·042 acres containing lime-pits and kiln, a public-house and buildings (land tax redeemed).

1899–1901 The golf links were formed partly on the Heath Farm in Stapleford and partly on the land purchased in 1890. The cost of forming them, including that of the pavilion and of the cottages, was about £1460.

1900 The College bought of Major de Freville, for £5570, a freehold farm of 160 a. 3 r. 6 p. It lies on the S.W. side of the road from Trumpington to Shelford. One portion, 150 a. 1 r. 32 p., lies next the Trumpington boundary, a short distance on this side of the railway to Harston, and the remainder, containing 10 a. 1 r. 14 p. of grass, with the buildings, lies immediately beyond this railway. This was originally copyhold of our manor and had been enfranchised in 1856.

1901 A house was built on the old farm at a cost of £1290.

1907 The sum of £170 was spent on new fencing at the golf links.

The College spent £563 on the house and buildings of the farm bought in 1900.

1907–8 We spent £1930 on the mill.

Letting of the Demesnes.

It has been stated that, when the manor was purchased by the College, the demesnes were let on a lease expiring 1646, under which the rent was £12.

However, the *Registrum Magnum* says that in 1635 E. Ventris had acquired this lease, and for no inconsiderable sum of money (" *ob summam numerorum haud contemnendam* "), *i.e.* a fine, obtained from the Masters and Fellows a new lease.

1635 This new lease was for 20 years and, in accordance with the Corn Act of 1576, one-third of the "old rent," namely £4, was changed into 7 qrs. 1 bush. of wheat and 6 qrs. 4 bush. of malt, keeping $\frac{2}{3}$rds, or £8, as a fixed annual payment. The following additions to the rent were made :—At Christmas a well-brawned boar or £2 ; at Easter (and also at Whitsuntide) two fat wethers or £1 ; also the tenant had to bring every Michaelmas a load of rye straw for the Master's horses.

The lease was renewed at intervals—generally at the end of seven years.

The following are some of the fines paid for renewals ·

		£			
1666	....	112			
1694	....	98			
1718	....	112			
1735	....	180			
1775	....	225	(at which they remained for several renewals)		
1819	....	630			
1826	....	550			
1835 (after the enclosure)		510	Money rent £144. 2s. 0d.		
1840	....	600	Rent	£199. 2s. 0d.	
1847	....	800	,,	£239. 2s. 0d.	
1854	....	800	,,	£285. 0s. 0d.	
1861	No fine.	Rent £404 to include all corn and other payments.			
1868	No fine.	Rent £485.			

This was the last beneficial lease of any of our agricultural lands.

The following are the particulars of some of the lettings of the mills :

				£
1778	Rent £20	Fine		40
1799	,, ,,	,,		120
1813	,, ,,			362
1820	,, £25			360
1827	,, ,,			700
1834	,, ,,	,,		550
1848	,, £30. 9s.	,,		800
1868	Rent £240, after considerable repairs. No fine.			

1904 6 The land—containing the cottage and now said to measure 2 a. 2 r. 16 p. referred to as Pattison's in the account of the enclosure in 1834, was sold to various purchasers for a total sum of £1195.

STAPLEFORD (CAMBS).

1896 The College bought the Heath Farm containing 231 acres, with a homestead, of Dr Collier, for £2750. It lies between our Farm at Shelford and the Gog Magog estate on the left-hand of the road from Cambridge to Linton.

1898 The land tax (£3) was redeemed for £90.

1899 For the Golf Links see SHELFORD.
As in several other parishes in the neighbourhood the land is tithe-free.

For STOCKPORT see Addenda on p. 114.

STOW-CUM-QUY (CAMBS).

1521 The College obtained the Manor of D'Engaynes and other lands in Stow-Quy and Teversham, of the then annual value of £21, in exchange for the Manor of Pattesley (q.v.), of the annual value of 20 marks, and £96. This money was part of Dr Baily's gift.

1604 The "old rent" of the lands belonging to us in Stow-Quy was £9, which by the Corn Act (of 1576) was changed into £6 and 4½ qrs. of wheat and 6 qrs. of malt; and this continued to be paid till 1821.

The tenant covenanted to repair the D'Engaynes dam and the banks of the river for about 148 poles on each side; and had the right of planting and cutting the trees growing on these banks.

The lands were as usual let on a lease for 20 years, renewed every few years for a fine.

1753 The acreage is estimated at 148¼ lying in 61 parcels in the fields, and it is stated that they are "subject to Mr Marten's flock of sheep." The value was put at 6s. 8d. an acre, giving a total annual value of £49. 9s. 2d.

1801 The land tax, £10, was redeemed for £366. 13s. 4d. Consols.

The following are some of the fines paid for the renewal of the 20 years' lease ·

	£	s.	d.
1670	49	0	0
1745	21	17	6
1780	50	0	0
1801	92	6	6; in this year the annual value was estimated at £109. 7s. 1d.

1823 The land was let at a rack rent of £100 on a lease for seven years.

1829 The acreage is stated to be as follows:

	a.	r.	p.
In Town Field	62	2	0
In Stow „	46	2	20
In Alder „	46	3	20;

but an acre probably did not contain more than 3 roods.

1838 The rent was now £138.

1839 The enclosure of the parish took place, and after it the schedule of our lands was as follows:

			a.	r.	p.
1.	Homestead		0	0	24
2.	Allotment		0	0	33
3.	„		3	0	32
4.			121	3	11
	Total		125	1	20

The College paid £111. 7s. 0d. as its share of the expenses of the enclosure. The tithe apportionment is £43. 7s. 1d.

1871 The annual value was estimated as £203. 10s. 0d.

1872 New buildings and a cottage cost £254. 18s. 6d., and the old homestead being Nos. 1 and 2 of the schedule after the enclosure—were sold for £200 to Mr C. Francis.

1880 The College gave 1 r. 3 p., being part of No. 3, to be added to the Churchyard.

The rent in 1875 was £193; in 1885, £200 (College paying tithe); in 1895, £120; in 1905, £120.

STRATTON S. MARY OR LONG STRATTON (SUFFOLK).

1725 The advowson was bought of J. Mallom, for £600 and legal expenses £39. 7s. 4d., part of the money left by Mr Stephen Camborn, Rector of Lawshall and sometime Fellow of the College.

He bequeathed the chief of the estate, amounting to about £3000, for the purchase of *a* living. The relatives tried to set aside the will; but the Court of Chancery decreed in favour of the College and allowed us to buy more livings than one. These were Ashdon, Lavenham, Melton, Stratton, Oxburgh and (in part) Blofield.

1799 The Vicar redeemed the land tax (£12), selling some detached bits of glebe for the purpose.

1839 Mr W. Walford, Incumbent of Stratton and formerly a Fellow, gave to the College a close called Camping Close, containing 1 a. 3 p.—situate between the Church and Parsonage House, in trust for the Rector.

The apportioned tithe rent charge is £436 and the glebe contains 39 acres.

SUDBURY (MIDDLESEX).

1895 The College bought the Hundred Elms Farm, containing 148 a. 0 r. 8 p. of pasture with homestead, for £14,500.

The rent was £330.

A plot containing 1773 sq. yds. was sold to the Harrow School Board for £150.

1898 The Ealing and Harrow Railway Company took 10 a. 1 r. 6 p. and paid £3005.

1899 The remainder of the estate was sold for £21,000.

SWANTON MORLEY CUM WORTHING (NORFOLK).

1896 The College acquired the advowson of this Rectory in the place of that of Great Melton by exchange with the Rev. H. E. Lombe.

The expenses paid by the College were £66. 6s. 0d.

The apportioned tithe rent charge is £1065: and the glebe contains 25 acres.

SWAYCLIFFE, OR SWALECLIFFE, AND WHITSTABLE (KENT).

1563 Joan Trapps—widow of R. Trapps, Goldsmith,—by her will directed her executors to settle lands on the College, of which the rent should provide four marks (£2. 13s. 4d.) for each of four poor scholars and 13s. 4d. to the College for extraordinary purposes (Venn, Vol. III, p. 227).

The executors—one of whom was Mrs Joyce Frankland, her daughter (subsequently our Benefactress)—for this purpose provided the following property in Swaycliffe and Whitstable:

A messuage, called Bodkin's, with barns, &c. ;
Seven closes of pasture and a barn ....about 34 acres ;
Two closes of pasture and arable .... „   2¾ „
Two great closes of pasture and arable ... „   21 „

called Sanderly and Knoll—(or Sunder Tye and Knowle). These two last were in Whitstable-near-the-Sea.

1669 Dr Brady found but one barn, somewhat ruinous, as also the dwelling-house.

1754 At the survey this year the property was found to contain 62½ acres. It was valued at 9s. an acre, except 3 acres of cliff, which were put at 3s. an acre, thus making the total valuation £27. 4s. 6d. a year.

1796 The land, except the 3 acres of cliff, was valued at 15s. an acre.

The rent always remained at £11. 6s. 8d. and does not seem to have been re-arranged in accordance with the Corn Act of 1576.

It was let on a lease for 20 years, renewed generally every 7 years. The fine was generally about £15; but in 1798, when 8 years were expired, it was £51.

1799   The whole property was sold to the tenant for £550, paid 5 July, 1801, and, with its interest, used in redeeming the land taxes on the various estates belonging to the College. (*See* also MORDEN and WILTON AND HOCKWOLD.)

TEVERSHAM (CAMBS).

1503   T. Willowes, glover, of Cambridge, devised to the College his lands in Teversham, Fulbourn, and Ditton—besides most of those in Hinton (*q.v.*).

1521   The College gave to Sir R. Townshend its Manor of Pattesley and £96 for his Manor of D'Engaynes in Teversham and Stow-cum-Quy (*q.v.*).
  There was a license from the Savoy for Sir R. Townshend to give and for the College to take the Manor of D'Engaynes, paying 4s. a year to the Lord of the Manor of Netherhall in Hinton, and 2s., at a change in the Mastership, as a relief.
  The quit rents of the manor amounted to £5. 10s. and so remained till 1860.

1799   The land taxes—£4. 12s. 0d. on the manor, and £11 on Willowes's lands— with those on our other estates in Cambs, were redeemed at the rate of £36. 13s. 4d. Consols per £1.

1808   The land (2 a. 0 r. 4 p.) allotted to the College at the Fulbourn Enclosure was exchanged with R. Walker for an equal quantity of land in Teversham.
  The exchange is recorded in the Award of Fulbourn Enclosure. For this enclosure the College paid £17. 8s. 0d.
  As no land was allotted to us at the Ditton Enclosure it may be inferred that, though Willowes's lands were described as lying in Teversham, Fulbourn and *Ditton*, when the boundaries of the parishes came to be traced accurately by the various Enclosure Commissioners, all the lands acquired from Willowes were found to lie in Teversham and (to a small extent) in Fulbourn.

1810   The enclosure of the parish of Teversham took place.
  The cost to the College, including payments to the Commissioners and those for fencing allotments, was £506. 16s. 0d.
  The College received seven allotments, containing 124 a. 2 r. 10 p., which were laid to the farm made up of the demesne lands of our manor, and two other allotments, containing 38 a. 2 r. 3 p. and 6 a. 2 r. 2 p., laid to Willowes's Farm.
  At this enclosure lands were allotted and money paid to the Rector in lieu of tithes, and thus all the lands in the parish were rendered tithe free.

Willowes's Farm.

This contained a house, barn, stables and orchard. The acreage was estimated at different times as follows:

		£	s.	d.
1753	Field land and common lays, 65 a. ½ r. 12 ft., annual value	21	8	2
	Enclosed land, 2 a. 2 r. 12 ft., annual value ...	1	0	0
	[Three roods were then taken as an acre.]			
1796	Field lands, 65 a., value	32	10	0
	Enclosed pastures, 2 a., value	3	0	0

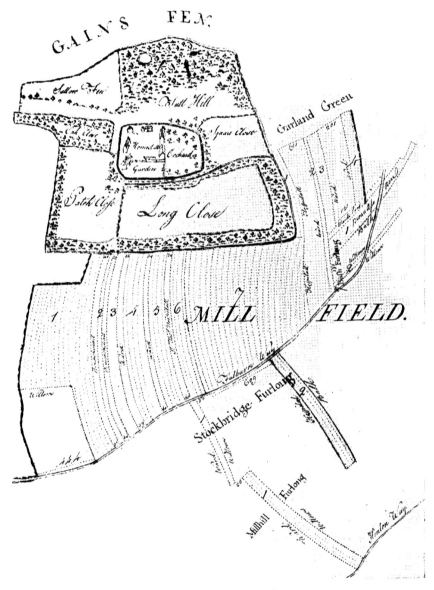

TEVERSHAM ESTATE

Plan showing the moat round the D'Engaynes Homestead
and the adjoining closes and arable strips

1811 [Immediately after the enclosure.]

	a.	r.	p.		£	s.	d.
Homestead and old enclosed land	8	2	8	value	21	7	6
Allotment	38	2	8	„	77	6	6

1812 The other allotment, of 6 a. 2 r. 2 p., was added to this farm.

The "old rent" had been apparently £4. In 1569 a new lease was granted at a rent of £4 for the first 10 years and £6 for the remaining 20 years, and yearly, on October 5, two couples of hens and one of capons, young, fat and great. In 1598 the rent was changed to £5. 6s. 8d. with 2 qrs. of wheat and 2 qrs. 6 bush. of malt.

1811 The money rent was raised by £10 after the enclosure.

1812 The rent was raised by £14. 14s. 0d. in consequence of the addition mentioned above.

Under the 20 years' lease, renewed about every seven years, the fine was generally about £17 ; in 1797, when eight years were expired, it was £32.

1818 The fine was set at £100 and the money rent at £30.

At subsequent renewals the fine was about £170.

1860 The lands bought at this time were added to Willowes's Farm and £91. 18s. 0d. to the rent.

1866 The beneficial lease expired and the farm was let at a rack rent of £214, the acreage then being 91 a. 0 r. 20 p.

1874 The cottages were burned down and rebuilt at a cost of £238. 10s.

1893 New stables were built and cost £78. 10s.

1894 A new granary cost £79.

1904 For new buildings the College paid £50.

1906 Another new granary cost £79. 5s.

D'Engaynes Farm.

By an agreement made in the sixth year of Edw. VI, a flock of 30 score sheep might be kept in the fields and commons of Teversham, of which nine score belonged to D'Engaynes Manor, 12 score to the Manor of the Savoy and nine score to the owners of other lands.

1557 This year a lease of the demesne lands for 40 years was granted at a yearly rent of £12. 10s. and 10s. towards a brawn to solace the company at home at Christmas yearly.

Apparently the "old rent" had been £7, for, in 1627, the rent was re-set at £4. 13s. 4d. in money, with 3½ qrs. of wheat and 4½ qrs. 2 bush. of malt, and, at Christmas, a brawn (or 30s.).

1753 By a private arrangement amongst the tenants the permissible flocks had been reduced by one-half.

	£	s.	d.
Our right (4½ score) was valued at	9	0	0
Field lands and common leys—138 a. 2½ r. at	46	4	2
Enclosed ground—23 a.	9	4	0
Total annual value..............£64		8	2

For this farm there were then paid, as out-rents, to the Manor of Nether-hall 4s. and to the Honor of Richmond 4s. 4d.

1777 The acreage was put at 139 a. 3 r. 27 p. and the annual value (including £3 for the sheep-walk) at £65. 18s. 4d.

1798 The acreage was again estimated as in 1753 and the annual value at £108. 19s. 6d. (including £12 for the grazing rights).

1812 After the enclosure the valuation was as follows:

	£	s.	d.
Homestall and 8 old enclosures, 23 a. 0 r. 31 p.	49	13	0
Seven allotments, 124 a. 2 r. 10 p.	301	10	9
	£351	3	9

1833 Total acreage 170 a. 3 r. 33 p.—annual value £244. 10s. 9d.

1873   ,,   ,,   171 a. 2 r. 31 p.   ,,   ,,   £402. 0s. 0d.

The lands were let on 20 years' leases renewed, generally, every 7 years for a fine.

Between 1677 and 1784 the fines varied between £28 and £50.
In 1798 (14 years expired) the fine was £260.
Between 1819 and 1854 the fines varied between £460 and £570.

1869 A block of three cottages was built for £318. 10s. 0d.
In 1812, after enclosure, the rent was increased by £23 and the fine was £65.

1874 The farm was let at a rack rent of £350.

1876 The buildings were burnt down.

1878 New buildings cost £1045.

1881 A new nag stable cost £57. 5s. 0d.

Further Purchases.

1860 The College bought, of S. and R. L. Walker,

    29 a. 1 r. 33 p. copyhold of our manor,
    1 a. 1 r. 28 p. copyhold of the Manor of Hinton Uphall,
    10 a. 1 r. 12 p. freehold.

The second portion was enfranchised.
Altogether the whole transaction cost the College £2246. 17s. 4d. and an annuity of £30 for a Mrs Webb, who died October 11, 1865.
The sum of £2246. 17s. 4d. was obtained from enfranchisements in our various manors.
The whole was added to Willowes's Farm.

1903 After the death of J. W. Tunwell the College bought, for £1355, of his trustees and others the following parcels of lands, which had been held by him, partly freehold and partly copyhold of our manor:

    (1) 3 a. 13 p. of which 3 r. 30 p. were freehold.
    (2) 4 a. 1 r. 12 p. of which 2 a. 3 r. 39 p. were freehold.
    (3) 11 a. 2 r. 25 p. of which 8 a. 3 r. 12 p. were freehold.
    (4) House and homestead, about 1 a., freehold.
    (5) Cottage and yard, &c., copyhold.
    (6) $3\frac{1}{4}$ a., freehold, containing four cottages.

The College spent in repairs and improvements on these parcels in

    1903, £201. 10s. 0d.
    1904, £70. 10s. 0d.
    1906, £144. 0s. 0d.

Altogether they were let for a total rental of £73.
The total rents from our whole property were in 1885, £474; in 1895, £320; in 1905, £484.

THORNHAM AND TITCHWELL (NORFOLK).

1504 John Carter, formerly a Fellow, gave to the College, partly in his lifetime and partly by will, his Manor of Thornham and his other lands in Thornham and Titchwell. The title was litigious and the recovery of the lands cost the College as much as they were worth.

No quit rents were payable by tenants of the manor.

Thornham Lands.

1753 The lands were found to contain 76 a. 2 r. lying very dispersedly in 57 separate parcels.

1776 The annual value was estimated at £43. 7s. 10d.

1797 At the enclosure 89 a. 2 r. 20 p. all in one piece were allotted to the College in lieu of all their rights in the parish. The annual value was then put at £71. 14s. 0d. I cannot find that the College paid anything towards the costs of this enclosure.

1811 The annual value was £134. 4s. 0d.

1838 The tithe apportionment was £27. 17s. 0d.

Titchwell Lands.

1753 The lands were found to contain 50 a. 2 r. in 28 different pieces.

1776 The annual value was put at £28. 6s. 7d.

1787 At the enclosure, in addition to the 1 r. 25 p. containing cottages, gardens and barn, the College had allotted to it two fields, one, adjoining the cottages, &c., containing 6 a. 1 r. 25 p. and one 12 a. 3 r. 24 p. The College paid £55. 1s. 3d. towards the expenses of the enclosure.

1796 The annual value was put at £30.

1811 The annual value was put at £38. 4s. 9d.

1838 The tithe was apportioned at £8. 5s. 0d.

1882 The cottages were pulled down.

Thornham and Titchwell Lettings.

Originally the two were let together under one lease for 20 years, renewed generally every 7 years.

The "old rent," £4, was converted in 1603 in accordance with the Corn Act of 1576 into £2. 13s. 4d. money and 2 quarters of wheat and 2 quarters 6 bushels of malt.

1670–1762 The fine on a renewal of the lease was about £40.

In 1769 it was £52 ; in 1776, £80 ; and in 1783, £100.

1797 The two properties were let on separate leases.

Thornham Separate Lettings.

1797 The rent was £1. 17s. 8d. in money, 1 qr. 3 b. 1 p. in wheat, and 1 qr. 7 b. in malt.

The fine for the new lease was £65.

In 1811 it was £302, and in 1818, £286.

1825 The tenant refused the offer of a fine at £310. In this year, and again, in 1832, £250 was advanced from the Bursar's Book for division amongst the Master and (12) Fellows in lieu of the fine.

1838 The land was let at a rack rent of £105 ; in 1860 at £117 ; in 1873, £140 ; 1885, £140 ; in 1895, £116 (College paying tithe) ; 1905, £67.

1909 New buildings were erected at a cost of £230, and the rent set at £90.

Titchwell Separate Lettings.

1797 The rent was 15s. 8d. in money with 4 b. 3 p. of wheat and 6 b. 2 p. of malt. The fine for the new lease was £35.
In 1804 it was £40. 10s. 0d. ; in 1811, £76. 10s. 0d. ; in 1837, £100.
After 1846 there was no renewal, and in 1853, and again in 1860, £100 was advanced from the Bursar's Book to the Master and Fellows in lieu of the fine.

1866 On the expiration of the beneficial lease the lands were let at a rack rent of £46.

TILBURY (ESSEX).

1560 William Cutting died March 4, 1560, and devised to the College a perpetual annual rent charge of £13. 6s. 8d. (20 marks) issuing out of his lands and tenements (called Alleyn's or Rumbold's) in the parishes of West Tilbury and Chadwell in Essex (Venn, Vol. III, p. 230).

1613 The College obtained a decree against one Stotteridge (the heir of W. Cutting) for the payment of this rent charge.
At present the lands out of which this rent charge issues are owned by the Corporation of Henley-on-Thames.

TITCHWELL (*see* THORNHAM AND TITCHWELL).

TRIPLOW (CAMBS).

1354 Bp. Bateman gave a letter of attorney to J. Princeger of Terlyngg to give possession of his Manor of Triplow to the Master and four Fellows (by name).
We may assume therefore that it was his intention to convey this manor to the College ; there is no further evidence that this was done and the College does not appear to have received license to hold it in mortmain.

TUTTINGTON (NORFOLK).

1487 Lady Elizabeth Clere gave all her lands and tenements in Tuttington and Burgh to the College. In the royal license for mortmain these are put at two messuages, 76 acres of arable land, six acres of meadow and six of pasture.
The "old rent" had been £4. 16s. 8d., and a lease at this rent was granted in 4 Edward VI for 61 years and again in 13 Elizabeth for 40 years.

1611 The rent was changed to £4. 8s. 10d. in money, 3 qrs. 5 b. 2 p. in wheat, and 4 qrs. in malt, and so remained for 240 years.

1725 The estate was visited and was reported to contain 145½ acres and ½ a rood, and to be worth £85 a year.

1753 The number of acres of arable land was put at 130½, worth 13s. an acre, it being whole-year-land and chiefly enclosed, which gave £84. 16s. 6d. as their annual value.

The meadow land contained 13 a. ½ r. valued at 8s. an acre—"it being but ordinary"—thus giving £5. 13s. 0d. as the annual value. Thus the total annual value was £90. 9s. 6d.

About 50 years before this the tenant had ploughed up the balks which separated our lands from his own lands and enclosed them together, so that it was difficult to distinguish them (see under 1858).

1801 The lands belonging to us and to our tenant being much intermixed they were carefully set out, by mutual consent, in a terrier and plan which were signed and sealed by both parties. The total acreage of the land belonging to the College is stated in the terrier to be 149 a. 3 r. 13 p.

1809 The annual value was put at £159. 5s. 0d.

1814–21 At the enclosure we had allotted to us three pieces in Burgh containing, in all, 6 a. 3 r. 25 p. and five in Tuttington amounting to 29 a. 3 r. 26 p.

We received also, in exchange with the Vicar and others, 12 pieces in Tuttington of different areas, varying from 22 p. to 1 a. 3 r. 13 p., and amounting to 10 a. 2 r. 32 p.

The farm used to be let on 20 years' leases, renewed every seven years.
From 1673 to 1708 the fines were about £65.
From 1739 to 1767 they were about £87.
Afterwards the following were some of the fines:

	£
1774	115
1795	140
1809	350
1823	300
1830	280
1844	400
1851	559 with an addition of £60 to the money rent.

1858 The College bought from our tenant 38 a. 1 r. 30 p. much intermixed with our own (see under 1753).

The College gave for this land £1980. 14s. 6d. arising from the sale of land at Bincombe to the Great Western Railway Company, and £300 from manorial enfranchisements; and £203. 4s. 1d. for legal expenses.

Of this purchase 6 a. 1 r. 38 p. are copyhold in the Manor of Aylsham Wood and 8 a. 3 r. 4 p. in that of Tuttington-with-Crackford, for which quit rents of £1. 0s. 10d. and 12s. 5d. are payable respectively. To the latter manor we also pay a free rent of 5s.

The tenant then received a lease (without a fine), for 20 years, of our whole property at a rent of £131. 8s. 10d. for the first 13 years and £287 for the last seven years, together with the same corn rent as before.

1878 The farm was re-let for £364. 9s. 6d.

The tithe apportionment on the whole farm is £58. 4s. 6d.

In 1885 the rent was £214; in 1895, £212 (College paying tithe); in 1905, £212.

WEETING (NORFOLK).

1632 The College bought, for £1900, of G. Fowler, the advowson of the rectories of S. Mary and All Saints and a rent charge of £100 issuing out of the Manor of Weeting.

Of the £1900, the sum of £400 was part of the donation of Dr Gostlin (see CAMBRIDGE, King's Parade) and £1500 was from the College chest.

A further sum of £20 was paid for the expenses of the purchase.

1671   The College bought, for £225, of Wm. and D. Peck, a tenement and piece of arable land adjoining, freehold ; and 14 acres copyhold—quit rent 1s. 1d.—of the Manor of Brandon ; and a tenement called Dowsing's, or Deway's, and 12 a. 3 r. copyhold—quit rent £1. 0s. 8d.—of the Manor of Weeting.

There was a charge of £2 on this estate, "for a light horse," payable to the Manor of Weeting.   This is still paid.

Of the £225, the sum of £100 had recently been left to the College by Mr Hobman.

These lands lay convenient for the Parsonage, and it was intended to let them to the Rector for £10 if he resided, and for £14 if he did not reside.

1672   T. Wright, Lord of the Manor of Brandon, enfranchised the above 14 acres in his manor for the enfranchisement of 2½ acres of pasture—quit rent 1s. 0½d.—copyhold of our Manor of Runcton Holme, to which E. Doughty had been admitted as tenant.

1678   The College bought, for £8, of A. and A. Fisher, 1½ acres.

Fisher's and Peck's lands were let to the Rector for £12. 10s.

Also the College paid £60 to Mr Tyrrell for the manumission of the copyhold lands in the Manor of Weeting bought in 1671, and for a fine supposed to be due to him for taking up these lands and also for sinking the quit rent of £1. 0s. 8d.   However, it turned out that he was not the Lord of the Manor and the manumission was void.

1747   The Rectories were consolidated at the cost of £10. 9s. 2d.

1775   The enclosure of the parish took place.   The College received an allotment of 10 acres, of which 6 a. 2 r. 20 p. were to be copyhold of the Manor of Weeting in lieu of 10 a. 3 r. previously held of the manor.

[The remainder of the copyhold land bought in 1671 and containing in all 12 a. 3 r. was made up as follows :—Deway's and three roods in Southgate Croft, one close containing 20 poles, and one acre near Claypits.   This is shown by the terms of the various admissions.]

The College paid £2. 12s. 4d. for the expense of the enclosure.

On the Rectory was settled the following allotments ·

a.	r.	p.	
5	0	27	
4	3	12	
20	2	7	(see 1859)
108	2	28	

1791   The terrier shows that the property belonging to the Rectory was as follows :

The Parsonage House, two barns, &c., garden with pightle adjoining, all containing 2 a.;

A close containing 3 a. and the above four allotments.

1837   The tithe apportionment of the parish was put at £517 ; that of our land at £3.

1859   Upon an exchange between the College and the Rector we received 20 a. 2 r. 7 p. lying adjacent to our allotment of 10 acres, and we gave up to the Rectory:

	a.	r.	p.
Pasture close and two lodges.....................	4	1	2
Do. Do.	2	1	8
Cottages and gardens	0	0	16
Total	6	2	26

all lying adjacent to the Rectory House.

This made up the whole of the land previously belonging to the College, except the allotment of 10 acres.

After this the 30 a. 2 r. 27 p. then belonging to the College were let to other tenants, but still at the rent, £12. 10s., for which the former possessions of the College had been let to the Rector.

1894 For £45 we enfranchised the 6 a. 2 r. 20 p. copyhold of the Manor of Weeting, together with the quit rent of £1. 0s. 8d. thereon.

WENTWORTH (CAMBS).

Part of our Haddenham property lay in Wentworth and Sutton Fields. It was always supposed that it was distributed as follows :

	a.	r.	p.
In Wentworth Field, 11 strips amounting in all to	6	1	6
In Sutton Field, three strips amounting to	0	2	39
Total......................	7	0	5

At the enclosure in lieu of this land an allotment of 7 a. 0 r. 9 p. in Wentworth parish was assigned to the College. After Lord Hardwicke's beneficial lease of the Haddenham estate had run out, this allotment was let to the tenant who had been holding under his lordship for £11. 10s. a year in addition to the payment of the tithe, the apportionment for which is £2. 3s. 3d.

WESTONING (BEDS).

1540 The Manor of Aynells was bought with the £300 paid to the College by Lord North for the Manor of Bansteds and certain other lands in Cowling and Cartling (q.v.).

1544 A lease of the demesne lands and of the quit rents was granted to Spicer, alias Helder, for 99 years at a rent of £14.

1570 About this time the College had to re-enter on the manor as the tenant had committed waste on the timber; but afterwards the disagreement was settled

1572 and a fresh lease was granted for seven years, i.e. it was terminable at the same time as the former one and on the same terms.

1634 Ten years before this lease expired a fresh lease was granted of the demesne lands above (without the quit rents).

In accordance with the Corn Act of 1576 the rent was set as follows :

Money, £9. 6s. 8d.
Wheat, 9 qrs.
Malt, 8 qrs.

The copyholds were then four in number, paying, respectively, quit rents of 1s., 6s., 5s. and 9s.

Subsequently the demesnes and these copyholds became the subject of a quarrel, during Dr Brady's Mastership, with William Dell, our Master during the Commonwealth.

It must be remembered that Dell was Master from 1649 till 1660 and that Dr Batchcroft returned in 1660 and was succeeded the same year by Dr Brady.

The following are the facts relating to this dispute so far as I can find them stated in our books and documents.

1653–4   On January 5, at a Manor Court, admission to the 22 acres, for which the quit rent was 6*s.*, was granted to J. Dunn, T. Gell and R. Glover.

On November 27 they executed a declaration that they held this parcel in trust for W. Dell, the surrender of it by the former tenant having been in consequence of money paid to him by W. Dell.

At the same court admission to the one acre, for which the quit rent was 5*s.*, was granted to W. Houghton, J. Houghton and W. Simonds; and in November they executed a similar declaration.

At the same court admission to the two acres, for which the quit rent was 9*s.*, was granted to L. Bynion, J. Pinkridge, senr., and J. Pinkridge, junr.; but who apparently did *not* execute a declaration such as the other nominees of W. Dell had made.

On February 27 a lease of (the demesnes of) Aynells for 20 years was granted to J. Guye, T. Rush and Houghton. No fine is mentioned.

In the Michaelmas accounts Houghton appears for the first time as paying the rent of the manor for the half-year and two of the quit rents (1*s.* and 6*s.*) for the year, to Michaelmas, 1654.

Also there is an entry in the Bursar's Book of £8 paid by Houghton for his copyhold land.

1659   The College sealed a deed of enfranchisement of some copyhold land for £40 to J. Donne.

The receipt of the £40 is entered in the Bursar's Michaelmas Account.

He was tenant for the lives of himself, T. Gell and R. Glover (all then living).

By the deed the yearly rent of 1*s.* is expressly reserved to the College, showing that this parcel is the first of the four copyholds.

There is a note in the lease book that for the security of this enfranchisement there were "tyed over" two closes of the new purchase in Caishoe (or Keysho, *q.v.*). This Donne was apparently the tenant of our then property at Keysho. This is the only connection between the two properties that I can find.

On October 22 an order was passed to "renew the lease of the manor for four years at £20 fine and register's fees."

No Date   The printed statement of the complaints of the College against Mr Dell, so far as it relates to Aynells, is as follows

(1)   That he had procured a lease of the manor for W. Houghton, a servant of his, in trust for him, without any considerable fine being paid to the College;

(2)   That he had wasted the manor by carrying off from it a barn and timber, which he had felled, and erecting therewith a barn and stable on his own land (at Harlington);

(3)   That he had procured the admission of his own trustees to the four copyholds without fines and had procured the enfranchisement of the most considerable one of these four copyholds for a consideration of only £40, there being at the time of this enfranchisement timber, the property of the lords, growing on the copyholds of over £200 in value.

In the end the matter was referred to two arbitrators,

1666   who settled that Mr Dell should pay to the College ·

For the barn	£40
"For fines of copyholds for three lives now in being"	£80
In all	£120 ;

and the College was to confirm or give a new grant for the lands at the choice of the tenant.

(April) The College allowed T. Raymond's name to be put into the lease of Aynells in place of Houghton's.

It must be remembered that T. Raymond was Dell's kinsman and legal adviser.

In the Bursar's Michaelmas Accounts T. Raymond appears for the first time as tenant of the manor and as paying the two quit rents of 1s. and 6s.

1666-7 (February) Mr Dell was abated £20 of the £120 he thus owed.

1667 The College agreed to give back £20 of the enfranchisement money (£40, paid in 1659) and confirm the lease to Raymond who was "to restore the copyholds to the condition they were in before 1658."

Thus, on balance, the College was to receive £80. This it received by instalments :

At Michaelmas, 1668, from Mr Dell	£20
„ 1671, „ Mrs Dell (widow).........	£30
„ 1672, „ „	£30

1668 In April, Mr Dell was allowed to renew his lease of Aynells, from Michaelmas, 1666, for seven years at £70 fine.

In the Michaelmas Accounts he appears for the first time as tenant of the demesnes and as owing the quit rents for three of the four copyholds, and, at Lady Day, 1669, as owing the rent of the remaining copyhold.

Soon after this the College disposed of a good deal of timber taken from this manor (demesnes and copyholds). The following receipts are acknowledged in the Bursar's Book :

		£	s.	d.
1669	Lady Day. For Timber..........................	80	0	0
	Michaelmas. „ „	184	13	10
1671	Lady Day. „ „	83	6	0

1670 Lady Day. *Mrs* Dell (widow) appears for the first time as tenant of the manor and as owing the quit rents for the copyholds.

1673 This year the College received £11 for quit rents for eleven years.

By this time the dispute may be assumed to have been closed. All through it seems to have been conducted without bitterness on either side.

1680 The College bought, for £500, of the widow and son of Wm. Dell and J. Ward their mortgagee, 18 a. 0 r. 20 p. freehold, and three tenements and 25 acres copyhold of our Manor of Aynells. This purchase included all the four copyhold parcels previously mentioned, and thus the manor was practically extinguished.

Apparently this purchase forms what was afterwards called Samsells.

In the Bursar's Accounts, at Lady Day, 1681, there is the entry of £500 paid to Mr Dell for his "freehold land."

In the same accounts there is a receipt from Mr Dell of £40 "for exchanging some copyhold lands in Westoning of the College from leases into lives."

I have not been able to find a satisfactory explanation of the two phrases quoted.

The whole of the purchase was added to J. Dell's holding and £25 was added to the money rent, making it in all £34. 6s. 8d.

He ceased in 1688 to be tenant of our land.

1799 The land tax upon the whole of our property, amounting to £28. 3s. 6d., was redeemed by the transfer of £1033. 1s. 8d. Consols to the Government.

1804 The whole estate was estimated to contain 217 a. 1 r. 23 p. and was valued at £243. 13s. 6d. a year.

1809 The estimated annual value was £334. 12s. 6d.

1826 The estimates are 222 a. 1 r. 17 p. and £228. 19s. 6d. a year.

The following are some of the fines paid at the renewals of the 20 years' lease ·

<pre>
1659, £20, when 2 years had expired.
1676, £150,   „   9   „   „
1695, £85,   „   8   „   „   (including Samsells)
1713, £180,   „ 11   „   „
1720, £130,   „   7   „   „
1776, £155,   „   7   „   „
1797, £184,   „   7   „   „
1804, £237,   „   7   „   „
</pre>

In 1811 the fine was set at £475, and in 1818 at £415 ; but these fines were refused by the tenant. Consequently the beneficial lease ran out in 1824.

In 1811 the Bursar's Book advanced £405, and in 1818 £385 for division amongst the Master and (12) Fellows in lieu of the fines.

1824 The property was let at rack rents in three annual tenancies, viz.

(1) Upper Samsells for £120 a year;

(2) Aynells—or Lower Samsells—for £107 (for which £100 was afterwards substituted) and the old corn rent ;

(3) A small holding for £8.

1838 (about) The apportionment for tithe rent charge on the whole estate was fixed at £83. 8s. 0d.

1842 At the enclosure of the parish the College received an allotment of 91 a. 1 r. 23 p. in the West Field. It received also a small allotment which it gave up to Mr J. Eagles in exchange for other lands (see below).

The College effected the following exchanges under the Award :

(1) With Mr Campion ; giving up

A cottage with garden and close, called Little Close (Nos. 146 and 147 on map), containing 1 a. 0 r. 1 p. ; and taking

Two ancient enclosures, called Sears' Spinney, with pightle (Nos. 11, 12a and 12b on map).

(2) With Mr Campion ; giving up

An ancient close, called Carter's Close (No. 108 on map) containing 1 a. 1 r. 2 p. ; and taking

2 r. 4 p. (part of No. 75 on map) and 1 a. 0 r. 10 p.

(3) With J. Eagles ; giving up

An ancient enclosure, called The Pightle (No. 15 on map) containing 1 a. 3 r. 27 p., and 1 a. 1 r. 0 p. ; and taking

An ancient enclosure called Four Acres (No. 7 on map) containing 4 a. 0 r. 14 p.

The Award gives a schedule of all the pieces of land in the parish after the enclosure belonging to each landowner. Ours amounted to 242 a. 0 r. 30 p.

1864 The Midland Railway Company took 4 a. 2 r. 32 p. and paid £800.

A fee farm rent of £1. 8s. 7d. payable to the manor of Young's was redeemed for £44. 0s. 4d. and expenses £6. 18s. 3d.

1865 A small exchange (21 p. given and taken on each side) was effected with Mr Campion for straightening a boundary fence.

1867 The Midland Railway Company took 1 a. 1 r. 34 p. and paid £150.

1868 New farm buildings were erected at (Upper) Samsells at a cost of £601. 0s. 2d.

1878 The old corn rent for Aynells was given up and the money rent fixed at £130.

1894 The Midland Railway Company took 23 poles and paid £19. 19s. 0d.
We sold 129 a. 1 r. 2 p. containing brick-earth to H. J. Forder for £8500.

WHEATACRE (NORFOLK).

1736 (January 25) J. Russel, for 5s., at the instance of Christopher Smear, conveyed to the College the advowson of the Rectory of All Saints, except the next presentation.
A few days before this the next presentation had been granted to C. Smear and L. Smear in trust to present C. Smear (the son of the aforesaid C. S.).
(February 16) The College presented C. S. (the son) to the livings of Mutford-c.-Barnby.

1758 The trustees presented the younger C. S. to Wheatacre.

1789 The livings of Mutford-c.-Barnby and Wheatacre were consolidated.
A new Parsonage House for Wheatacre was built.

1799 For £271. 6s. 8d. Consols the College bought the land tax of £8. 2s. 9d. on the Rectory of Wheatacre.

1812 The enclosure of the parish took place about this time, as well as that of the neighbouring parish of Aldeby, in which between 10 and 20 acres of the glebe of Wheatacre lie.
At these enclosures the situation and acreage of the glebe lands were very much altered, partly by allotment from the Common of 6 a. 0 r. 16 p., partly by exchange with other owners and partly by reckoning acreage by measure instead of by estimation.
The glebe now consists of about 73 acres.

1840 The tithe commutation was settled at £224, of which £16 is on glebe lands.
Also, for three tracts of marshes, moduses are paid amounting to 12s. 4d.

1856 The living of Wheatacre was disunited from those of Mutford-c.-Barnby.

WIGGENHALL S. GERMAN'S AND S. PETER'S (NORFOLK).

1618 Dr W. Branthwaite died. In his will he desired that land should be settled on the College worth 40 marks (£26. 13s. 4d.) a year.

1621 This was carried out by his executor, R. Branthwaite, conveying to the College 27 acres in Wiggenhall S. German's, called Gillings or Gillingore, and 37 acres in Wiggenhall S. Peter's. A lease had been granted of the two pieces together for four years as from the preceding Michaelmas at an annual rent of £30.

1660 On the expiration of the 40 years' lease the lands were again let together to the then tenant, at the same rent, on a lease for 20 years. In this case the provisions of the Corn Act of 1576 were not complied with, as no part of the rent was converted into a corn rent. Perhaps the Corn Act was held not to apply.
The rack rent was then considered to be 14s. an acre, and it was agreed that in setting the fines for renewals the College ought to take into consideration the fact that, under the lease, the tenant was put to a considerable expense in keeping up the banks of the river (Ouse). *See* 1752.

1670 The lease is said to have been renewed this year; but I cannot find the figure at which the fine was set.

1680 The lease was renewed for a fine of £10.

1684 The tenant of our Manor of Runcton appears to have acquired the lease of the Wiggenhall lands, as it was renewed to him for a fine of £5. After this the lease of these lands was renewed (about every seven years) concurrently with the lease of the Runcton Farm and to the same tenant. At first the fine was £5.

1752 In the survey taken this year it is stated that two lengths of river-banks were assigned to the College to keep in repair on account of 37 acres of these lands, namely, 4 r. 8 ft. 8 in. and 1 r. 6 ft. 7 in.; and 5 r. 10 ft. 6 in. and 0 r. 16 ft. 6 in. on account of 24 acres of them.

In 1775 the fine was set at £10; in 1789 at £15, and in 1796 at £72.

1801 The land taxes, £1. 16s. 0d. and £2. 9s. 4d., were redeemed for £66 and £90. 8s. 11d. Consols.

1816 On the expiration of the 20 years' leases of Runcton and these lands, the latter were let under the same lease as the Runcton Farm, and since then have always gone with it.

According to modern measurements the acreage is :

	a.	r.	p.
S. German's	22	0	4
S. Peter's	29	2	21

The tithe apportionments are £5. 15s. 0d. and £6. 8s. 6d.

A drainage tax for the Wiggenhall District is laid on these lands every few years at about 7d. an acre, and for the Ouse Bank, No. 1 District, every year at about 3s. an acre.

Wilton and Hockwold (Norfolk).

Advowsons and Rectory.

1354 The College (with its own money) bought, of the Monastery of S. Pancras at Lewes, the advowson and glebes of Wilton (and of Foulden and Mutford). The monastery also conveyed to the College the pension of £2. 10s. a year paid from the Church of Wilton. In return for giving up this pension and that of £5 from Foulden the monastery received on the next day (October 2) from the Bishop (Bateman) of Norwich, a mediety of the Church of Walpole.

The Earl of Arundel gives his license for the conveyance of Wilton (and Foulden) from the monastery to the College, these properties being held of him "*in capite*."

Lord de Poynings also gives his consent for the same, the properties being held of him "*in capite*."

Also the *royal* license was obtained for the mortmain and for the appropriation of Wilton (and Foulden) with the taxes and pensions.

The Bishop of Norwich grants leave to the College to appropriate the Rectory of Wilton, at the next vacancy; but reserves to the Vicar the dwelling-house and 10 marks a year.

(This house would be that in which the Vicar had previously lived, as the *Rectory* House passed to the College.)

Instead of firstfruits (payable to the Bishop) the Bishop directs that the College shall pay to himself and his successors £1 a year. (This annual payment is still made to the Ecclesiastical Commissioners.)

To this the Prior and Chapter of Norwich give their consent.

1386 The Rector died and the College presented W. Somersham (afterwards Master) to the living (probably the Rectory).

1393   Pope Boniface IX issues his Bull "*pro nova* incorporatione sive appropria-
tione" of the Church of Wilton.   We must suppose that this was earlier in
the year than the passing of the final "Statute of Provisors."   Apparently
the Bull was issued for the appropriation of both Wilton and Matsall.   For
it the firstfruits of the two Churches were to be paid to the Pope.

Later in the year Somersham resigned the living and the College appointed
a Vicar, so that certainly from this date (if not from 1386) the College has
enjoyed the profits of the Rectory.

1402   The College paid 20 marks to the Pope as firstfruits for Wilton and
Matsall, and obtained the receipt for the payment from the Pope's Nuncio.
A duplicate of this (and further confirmation) was given in 1407.

1411   The Archbishop of Canterbury confirms to the College the possession of
Wilton (as well as those of Mutford, Foulden and Matsall).

1412   The College redeemed the payment of six marks a year due from Foulden,
Wilton, Mutford and Matsall to the Convent of Spinney, near Soham in
Cambs.

1485-92   A dispute arose between the College and the Rector of Hockwold as to
the partition of the tithes payable to the two parties from the manor of Lord
de Gifford.   It was settled by an arrangement by which the Rector had half
these tithes and paid to the College £2. 6s. 8d. a year which the College
handed over to the Vicar of Wilton.

This payment ceased in 1664, when the College bought the advowson of the
Rectory of Hockwold and obtained the union of it with the Vicarage of
Wilton.

Originally the Rectory House, with some land, was let separately at the
annual rent of 10s.   In 1585 the rent was raised to 13s. 4d.

The Rectorial tithes and the remainder of the glebes were let together at
the annual rent of £11 at first, which was changed in 1574 to £14. 4s.

1596   In accordance with the Corn Act of 1576 the rent of tithes and glebe was
converted into £10. 10s. 8d., with 5 qrs. 4 bush. of wheat and 7 qrs. 3 bush.
of malt.

1646   A messuage or tenement with 3½ acres of arable (in Wilton and Hockwold)
was let away from the Rectory (*i.e.* Rectorial tithes and glebe) for 4s., the rent
of the Rectory remaining the same as in 1596.   This tenancy is always afterwards referred to as "Tindall's."

1664   Viscount Cullin, Sir T. Fanshaw, Sir R. Bankes and Lord R. C. Cornwallis
grant to the College the advowson of Hockwold, also 119 a. 3 r. in the fields
of H. and W. in exchange for 119 a. 1r. 3 p. of Wilton glebe lying in a variety
of pieces in the said fields ; also a portion of common (fen) of H. and W. for
our sheep-walk for 300 sheep.   Also 11 acres are specified to be given up to
the College if the Rector of Hockwold should demand the tithes of the lands
exchanged for Wilton glebe.

About this time the common fens of H. and W. were divided and enclosed
under the Act of 16 Charles II cap. 17 sect. 38.   Under the Enclosure Award
50 acres in two lots were assigned to the College, one in right of the Parsonage
(*i.e.* the Rectory of Wilton, apparently) and one for our sheep-walk for 300
wethers.   This last was, I suppose, in confirmation of a portion of the agreement of 1664.

The following are some of the fines paid for the renewal of the leases of the
Rectory for 20 years :   £

1653   40
1671   ....   70, seven years expired.
1676   ....   65, six   „   „

In 1683 the Rectory was let to the tenant of the demesnes of the Manor of Carles. He also hired the Rectory House and Tindall's, as well as "the 63 acres." (*See* below.)

The following are some of the fines paid for the renewals of the leases of the Rectory and Carles:

		£
1690	....	90, seven years expired.
1719	....	88, eight „ „
1764	....	112, seven „ „
1771	....	150 „ „ „

1771 Upon a survey made this year the Rectorial glebe was found to contain: in the fields, 123 a. 3 r.; in the "fennes" 50 a. 2 r.

This last had partly been allotted to the College upon the division of the Fens in right of the Parsonage, and the other part was the portion of the common acquired in 1664 in exchange for our sheep-walk.

It was now agreed that it would be to the advantage of the Incumbent, if the lease of the Rectory were granted to him. Consequently it was arranged that the lease should be run out; and that at the years, when it would under the former arrangement have been renewed, the College, out of the balance standing in the Bursar's Book, should advance to the Registrar, for division amongst the Master and (12) Fellows, the sums that would have been paid by the tenant as fines.

Thus in 1778 the Registrar received from the Bursar £177 in lieu of the fine, and £1. 14s. 6d. as his fees; in 1785, £177 and £1. 12s. 6d.; in 1791, £148. 15s. and £1. 10s. 10d. These sums are entered amongst the Extra-ordinary Expenditure in the Bursar's Book for the following Lady Days.

1791 Upon the expiration of the 20 years' lease, a lease of the Rectory (including the Rectorial tithes) was granted to E. White, the Vicar, for 10 years (if he remained Vicar so long) at the former rent in money and corn, together with an "additional rent" of £46. 13s., of which £25. 13s. was to indemnify the College for expending £641. 5s. for the purchase of the old lease (*i.e.* for paying the sums in lieu of the fines in 1778, 1785 and 1791), and £21 to supply future fines once in seven years.

This payment of £46. 13s. was entered in the Bursar's Book under "Extra-ordinary Receipts."

Mr White also hired the Rectory House for 13s. 4d. a year, and "Tindall's" for 4s.

The College obtained £154. 13s. 6d. from the old tenants for dilapidations on the manor, rectory and chancel, and allowed Mr White to draw on the Bursar from time to time to the extent of £154. 13s. 6d. for the repairs on the same tenancies, he having at the same time become the lessee of the manor (*q.v.*).

At every seventh year, up to and including 1827, the Bursar advanced £177 to the Registrar in lieu of the fine for the Rectory for division amongst the Master and Fellows.

1801 The College purchased the land tax of £10. 9s. a year on Hockwold Rectory and redeemed that of £8. 8s. 8d. on Wilton Rectory for £657. 11s. 2d. Consols.

1806 Upon Mr White's death his executors paid £143. 11s. 4d. for dilapidations of the Rectory, and the above holdings were let to the new Vicar, Mr Tilney, the Rectory, on a lease for 10 years (if he remained Vicar so long), the "*additional* rent" being set at £110.

1817 A fresh lease was granted to Mr Tilney: the former money rent and the additional rent were merged in one new money rent of £150, the corn rents remaining as before.

1818 The Enclosure Award was settled. It dealt with and redistributed the whole of the properties in the two parishes, except those lying in one portion. This portion was "the second" or Feltwell and Hockwold Drainage District as defined by two Acts of Parliament passed in the 13th and 42nd years of George III.

The method of allotment and redistribution was very intricate, and it is not always possible, in the absence of schedules of the three tenancies in which all the lands belonging to the College were previously let, namely, the Rectory, demesnes of Carles and Gathercole's (Sir J. Burrough's) (*see* below), to be sure to which tenancy the pieces given up, and in consequence to which tenancy the pieces taken in exchange, belonged. The lands of the Incumbent were also much re-arranged.

1820 The terrier of this date states that the glebes belonging to the Incumbent consisted of the Parsonage House and seven pieces, containing in all 86 a. 0 r. 5 p.

1827 In the new lease to Mr Tilney the corn rent was changed to 5 qrs. 4 bush. 2 pecks of wheat and 7 qrs. 4 bush. of malt, the money remaining as in 1817.

1834 (January) £200 having been added in 1831 to the annual stipend of the Master and £100 to that of each Senior Fellow in consequence of the increase of rents, the advance for the fine for Wilton Rectory was discontinued.

1835 A lease was granted to the then Vicar (Mr Hanson) for £100 money rent and the former corn rents.

1839 The tithes were commuted for the following rent charges:

	£	s.	d.
Hockwold	635	12	2
Wilton, Vicarial	91	4	6
Rectorial	180	12	0

The portions of these rent charges on lands belonging to the College and to the Incumbent are as follows ·

	£	s.	d.		a.	r.	p.
Hockwold, College....	26	0	3	on	217	3	15
" " (glebe) ...	8	0	0	"	49	0	2
" Rector	4	0	0	"	38	3	8
Wilton, College Vicarial ...	3	11	6	} "	59	2	27
Rectorial ...	3	16	3				
" " (glebe) Vicarial	6	5	0	} "	97	2	22
Rectorial ...	11	16	0				
" Vicar Vicarial	4	7	0.	} "	53	0	3
Rectorial	6	14	0				

1860 On the death of Mr Hanson the College let the Rectorial glebe directly to the occupiers and collected its own tithe rent charges.

1872 The terrier states that attached to the Vicarage is a wash-right in the Wilton Washes, extending to two head of stock; and that the other property of the Vicar consists of the Parsonage House with buildings and 91 a. 3 r. 11 p. in 10 parcels.

"*The 63 Acres.*"

1544   The College bought (apparently for £50), of Edm. ffrynd, 64½ acres (with a messuage and 5 roods) in Hockwold, Wilton and Feltwell.

As an instance of how property was then cut into small pieces, it may be noted that six acres of this lay in 66 pieces.

The land was at first held by L. Mapted and A. Deane as trustees for the College.

T. Tyndall, lord of Hockwold and Wilton, apparently in connection with this purchase, confirms to the College liberty of fouldage in Wilton.

1553   The trustees convey this land to the College.

The rent was at first £2 and was raised in 1575 to £2. 13s. 4d.   In accordance with the Corn Act of 1576 this was converted in 1594 into £2 money, with 1 qr. of wheat and 1 qr. 3 bush. of malt.

The following are some of the fines paid for the renewal of the 20 years' lease :

		£	s.	d.
1659	when 7 years were expired	10	0	0
1720	„ 7 „ „ „	12	0	0
1776	„ 7 „ „ „	24	0	0
1790	„ 14 „ „ „	90	0	0
1797	„ 7 „ „ „	41	18	0

1799   The property was sold to the tenant for £600, paid—with its interest, £52. 10s.—3 July, 1801, and used for the redemption of the land taxes on the estates of the College.   (*See* SWAYCLIFFE and MORDEN.)

Manor of Carles.

1681   The College bought the manor for £1000, of T. Blofield and H. Lestrange.

The demesnes were said to consist of the Manor House, 22 acres of home-stall and 184 acres chiefly fen.   The yearly extended rent was said to be £60.   The rent of all these actually paid by the tenant was £30.

They were let to the tenant of "the 63 acres," on a lease for 20 years, from Michaelmas, 1683, for a fine of £200.   He also hired the Rectory (*q.v.*).   The £200 was laid out in the purchase of Nossiter's estate at Bincombe.

1771   The demesnes were found to contain 190 acres.

1778   An attempt was made to survey our lands in Wilton, but the tenants would not show their lands.

1791   (Jan. 4)   Nineteen years of the old lease having expired, a concurrent lease for 20 years was granted for a fine of £300 to E. Lombe, who assigned it the same year to the Rev. E. White (Rector of Hockwold).

1798   Mr White paid a fine of £80 for the renewal of this lease.

1801   The land taxes of £5. 5s. 6d. on the demesnes and £3. 8s. 8d. on Sir J. Burrough's lands were redeemed for £319. 6s. 1d. Consols.

1806   Mr White died and his widow became the tenant of Carles.

1812   Mrs White not having renewed her lease, the sum of £355 was paid by the Bursar to the Registrar, for division amongst the Master and (Senior) Fellows in lieu of the fine.

1818   The Enclosure Award for the two parishes was settled and the College received an allotment containing 2 r. 3 p. for their share as lords of Carles in compensation for rights of pasturage on the commons and waste grounds attached to their messuage and cottages, being $\frac{1}{18}$th part of all such rights.

Three other allotments were made to the College in respect of their messuages, lands and grounds attached to their manor, amounting in all to 24 a. 1 r. 34 p. ; but part of these and several of the pieces formerly belonging to the manor were in a subsequent part of the Award exchanged for other pieces then received by the College and let to the tenant of the demesnes.

The College paid £9. 7s. 0d. for these exchanges and £66. 16s. 0d. for other expenses of the Enclosure Award.

This year Mrs White's lease expired and the demesnes were let for 12 years at £140.

1819   (January 13) The following order was passed : In consequence of the augmentation of the rent of the Manor of Carles to increase the annual stipend of the Master by £8 and of each Senior Fellow £4 from Michaelmas last (see p. x for the order of Oct. 30, 1816).

1827   The demesnes were found to contain 183 a. 0 r. 22 p.

1828   New buildings and repairs on the old buildings cost £457.

The manor and Sir J. Burrough's lands (q.v.) were then let together.

Sir J. Burrough's " Terrae et Tenementa."

1762   Sir J. Burrough (Master) devised to the College his estate at Wilton, containing 79 a. 1 r. 30 p. The tenement, barn, stables, &c., abutted on Wilton Church. There was also a blacksmith's shop standing in an acre.

The rent was £28. 10s. 0d. There was a quit rent of 9s. 7½d., payable out of these lands to the lord of the manor of Hockwold and one of 1s. to our Manor of Carles.

1792   A lease of these lands was granted to Denton, E. White and Gathercole for 10 years (should E. White so long continue Vicar) for the rent of £25, the tenants bearing all taxes and repairs.

1801   For redemption of land tax (£3. 8s. 8d.), see under Carles.

1802   The rent was raised to £35.

1812   ,,   ,,   ,,   ,,   ,, £80.

1818   For enclosure, see under Carles.

1821   The rent was reduced to £35.

1827   These lands are reported on as containing 88 a. 2 r. 27 p.

They were let to the tenant of Carles. The whole rent for the first year was £175, and afterwards £225.

1840   The College gave half an acre (with the blacksmith's shop) for a National School.

1860   After the death of the Vicar (Mr Hanson), when the College let the whole of their property directly to the occupiers, the following were the tenancies of the various lands and houses :

I.   College land in Hockwold, 217 a. 3 r. 15 p. ; tithe rent charge payable to Rector, £26. 0s. 3d. ; drainage tax at 5s. an acre on 182 a. 3 r. 8 p.

In Feltwell, 3 a. 1 r. 2 p. ; tithe rent charge payable to Rector, 15s. ; no drainage tax.

II.   Glebe (of Wilton) in Hockwold, belonging to the College, 49 a. 0 r. 2 p., tithe rent charge payable to the Rector, £8; drainage tax at 5s. on 24 a. 3 r. 38 p.

III.   Glebe in Wilton belonging to the College, 97 a. 2 r. 22 p., tithe rent charge payable to Vicar, £6. 5s. ; tithe rent charge payable to College, £11. 16s. ; drainage tax at 5s. on 11 a. 0 r. 16 p.

IV.   College land in Wilton, 59 a. 1 r. 23 p., tithe rent charge payable to Vicar, £3. 11s. 6d.; tithe rent charge payable to College, £3. 16s. 3d.; drainage tax at 5s. on 22 a. 2 r. 15 p.

1871   The tenancies were re-arranged without distinction as to how the different lands came into the hands of the College.

The field in Feltwell was let separately from the rest.

In all, the rents amounted to about £570, the College paying drainage taxes (about £70) and tithes and paying for the greater part of the repairs.

In 1875 the rents were £348; in 1885, £284; in 1895, £113; in 1905, £202.

WORLINGHAM (SUFFOLK).

Pain's Close.

This was secured to the College by an indenture between the College and T. Atkyn (Vicar of Mutford), dated 1539 and confirmed by his will. *See* Venn, Vol. III, p. 226.

The rent was £2 at first, changed in 1604, according to the Corn Act of 1576, into £1. 6s. 8d. in money with 1 qr. 6 bushels of wheat and 3 bushels of malt.

There was a rent charge out of it of 4d. a year, payable to the Parson of Worlingham.

The area was at first reputed to be 30 acres; but in 1645 at "a generall survey of ye whole towne," it was entered as 24 a. 3 r. 24½ p.

In 1778 the acreage was found to be 23 a. 2 r. 29 p.   The annual value was then reported to be £18. 18s. 11d. ; in 1813 it was thought to be £59.

The following are some of the fines paid for the renewal of the 20 years' lease ·

		£	s.	d.
1656	20 years expired	50	0	0
1670	14 „ „	21	0	0
1682	12 ,	17	10	0
1722	7 ,	13	0	0
1760	3 ,	4	15	0
1806	7 ,	30	0	0
1822	16 „ „	400	0	0
1836	7 „ „	60	0	0

In 1856 it was let to the Earl of Gosford for 11 years at the yearly rent of £33.

1867   The land was sold to Sir C. Clarke for £1200.   The acreage was then set at 22 a. 1 r. 17 p.

ELY TRUST.

Reginald Ely, of Cambridge, ffree-mason (*see* Willis and Clark's *Architectural History*, Vol. I, p. 419, note 2), by will dated Oct. 14, 1463, and proved July 17, 1471, amongst many legacies, left directions to his executors, viz. John Brokenshawe, his son-in-law, and John Melford, his apprentice, to provide a house for three poor people, each of whom was to receive 6s. 8d. a year out of the rents of his lands in Barton and Comberton.

1473 (March 25) The Master of Michael House conveyed a site for the alms-house in Michael (now Trinity) Lane to W. Malster, John Brokenshawe and others, for which they were to pay 9s. a year until lands of the same value were assigned to the House. When the property of Michael House was transferred by Henry VIII to Trinity College, the 9s. a year became payable to ⸳ new College, and was so paid until the site was sold in 1864 to Trinity College.

A conveyance, dated Aug. 29, 1476, of the adjoining property speaks of the newly-built almshouses called Reynoldes-ely-elmeshouses (Willis and Clark, Vol. II, p. 418). Thus the almshouses must have been built about 1474 or 1475.

Brokenshawe died in, apparently, 1479, and the executorship of R. Ely was passed on to others, until in 1493 it had devolved on W. Buckenham, Master of Gonville Hall 1514–36.

1516 W. Buckenham, John Ely and others, conveyed 24 acres in Barton and Grantchester to E. Croome, W. Medow, R. Hoare (Fellows of Gonville Hall) and others.

1539 W. Buckenham assigns the whole trust for the almshouse to Gonville Hall. He says that the almshouse had been built in Michael Lane, and that certain lands in Barton, Grantchester, Comberton and Chesterton of the clear annual value of 20s. had been bought "with the money and goodes" of R. Ely to maintain "the reparations" of the almshouse and to pay a yearly rent of 9s. He then assigns the management of the almshouse and lands to the Master and Fellows to receive the profit of the lands and thereout to keep the almshouse in repair and to pay the annual ground rent of 9s., "and with the overplus for to comefort and succour the pore people for the tyme being dwelling in the sayde almshouse so far as it will extend." He directs that the Master shall fill up vacancies amongst the poor people. He states that he has delivered to the Master and Fellows all the evidence belonging to the almshouse and lands, to be kept in their "counting house," and also the sum of £4. 12s. to be kept "in the common hutche" of the College for the repair of the almshouse. He further directs that one of the Fellows collect the rents, see to the repairs of the almshouse and keep the accounts, and that he receive 6s. 8d. a year for his pains, "if it may be borne."

1805 In this and in some later years the College paid £9. 10s. to the almsfolk; and in others 10s.

1864 The College exchanged the present site of the almshouse near S. Paul's Church for the old one in Trinity Lane—with the consent of the Charity Commissioners. The old site was subsequently sold to Trinity College for £200.

The College built the new almshouse, the expense of the exchange and building being £511. 6s. 7d.

1871 It was found that the income of the trust and its accumulation had repaid the College for its outlay, and since this date the surplus of the income, after paying for the repairs, has provided stipends for the almsfolk.

Lands.

It is difficult to make out exactly the particulars of the lands which came to the College when the management of the almshouse was handed over to it by W. Buckenham.

We have evidence of the following having been bought by Ely in his life-time :

    (1)   10 acres, in Barton, bought of J. Howson.
    (2)   2 acres, in Chesterton, bought of J. Aldrich.
    (3)   20 acres, in Comberton, bought of J. Attwood.

Also after Ely's death the executors bought the following :

    1469 (4) 6 acres, in Grantchester.
    1472 (5) 17 acres, in Barton.
    1492 (6) 2 acres, in Grantchester.
    1492 (7) 2 acres, in Barton.
    1493 (8) 7 acres, in Grantchester and Barton.

But there is nothing to show how much of all these were sold again by the executors before the remainder passed into the possession of the College.

In 1516—*i.e.* 23 years before he hands the almshouse over—W. Buckenham, as already stated, conveys 24 acres in the fields of Barton and Grantchester to three Fellows of the College and others.

Lands in Chesterton.

1506   E. Stubbe and W. Bokenham bought of J. Morice for £6. 10s. land in Chesterton, containing 6½ acres.

This must have been the land in Chesterton, which in 1539 Buckenham assigned to the College for the almshouses, as the land so assigned was always regarded as containing 6½ acres.

For 4½ acres of it a free rent of 1s. 6d. has always been paid to the lord of the manor of Chesterton Rectory. At first the Prior of Barnwell was the lord; subsequently it has been Trinity College.

The "old rent" of this land was 12s., converted in 1587—in accordance with the Corn Act of 1576—into 8s. with 4 bush. of wheat and 5 pecks of malt. This arrangement was continued till 1845 when the land was rack-rented.

It was let from 1671 under one lease to the same tenant who hired Sigo's land and an account of the fines and of the Enclosure Award will be found under Chesterton.

Lands in Barton, &c.

1655   D. Martin conveys to the College 1 a. 3 r. in Barton in lieu of so much of our land which he could not set out distinct from his own.

A lease of 1769 speaks of the lands as lying in the fields of Barton, Comberton and Grantchester; but the actual parish, in which each strip was, must have been uncertain, for one of the first pieces of business of the Comberton Enclosure Commissioners of 1840 was to define the boundary between Comberton and Barton and, as their Award does not speak of any land in Comberton as belonging to the College, it seems certain that when they had fixed the boundary they found that all our land lay on the Barton side of it.

At the Grantchester Enclosure the College received, for all the open field lands and rights of common in Grantchester, the following lands in the parish of Barton by agreement with their previous owners:

	r.	p.
2 lands in Brookfield—Newgate furlong	3	38
1 land ,, ,, —Bittersalt furlong	1	25

1754   The acreage of all the Barton land is put at 30 a. 1 r. 0 p.—in 35 parcels valued at 7s. an acre.

1797   The valuation is £16. 15s. 0d.

1799   The land tax of £1. 8s. 0d. was redeemed at the rate of £36. 13s. 4d. Consols per £1.

1811 The following is the acreage and valuation:

Old enclosures,	a.	r.	p.		£	s.	d.
Swallows' Close, pasture ...	3	0	0	value	6	0	0
Bulls' Close	1	2	0	,,	1	17	6
Common fields...................	9	3	0 ⎫				
	6	1	20 ⎬	,,	18	15	0
	8	3	20 ⎭				
Right of running ten sheep ...					1	5	0
Totals ...	29	2	0		£27	17	6

It is stated that the lands are supposed to be only 3 roods to the acre.

1840 In the Enclosure Award all the land belonging to the College is stated as follows, all freehold:

	a.	r.	p.	a.	r.	p.
First allotment,						
No. 21, Swallows' Close, from the University	0	1	20			
Pt. No. 23, Swallows' Close, from Anne Page	2	3	7			
				3	0	27
Second allotment, Brookfield				0	0	5
Third allotment, Hill Field				8	2	30
,, ,, in lieu of pt. of No. 17, Bulls' Close				1	1	32
Old enclosure, Swallows' Close, No. 22				2	1	17
				15	2	31

The College had given up the following enclosures to be allotted:

	a.	r.	p.
Part of the Bulls' Close, No. 17	1	0	26
,, ,, ,,	0	0	10
	1	0	36

The " old rent " was 18s. (lease of 1 Edw. VI) changed in 1569 to £2 and a good sound fat hog, and this latter in 1600 to 1 qr. of wheat and 1 qr. 11 bush. of malt.

In later times the money rent was £1. 6s. 8d. and the corn rent 1 qr. 4 bush. of wheat and 5 bush. 1 peck of malt. Also the tenant had to bring at Christmas a boar, or 6s. 8d., and two capons, or 3s. 4d.

The following are some of the fines paid for renewals of the 20 years' lease:

				£	s.	d.
1659	8 years expired	....		5	0	0
1677	7 ,, ,,	....		5	0	0
1693	16 ,, ,,	....		20	0	0
1740	7 ,, ,,	....		7	0	0
1797	7 ,, ,,	....		13	5	0
1811	7 ,, ,,	....		41	0	0
1825	7 ,, ,,	....		45	0	0

In 1832 this fine was set at £45 and in 1839 at £42; but not being paid by the tenant, the Bursar's Book advanced £42 on each occasion for division amongst the Master and (Senior) Fellows.

1845   The land was rack-rented and let at £22.

1874   The whole was sold to R. Holben for £1535 invested in £1666. 4s. 3d. Consols.

PERSE TRUST.

1615   Dr Perse died (Dr Venn, I, p. 57; III, pp. 218 and 231).

    The provisions of his will and the circumstances attending the discharge of its conditions are fully set out under this date in Cooper's *Annals of Cambridge*, and therefore need not be given here. It suffices to mention the principal points and those immediately connected with the College.

    He directed (1) that £5000 should be laid out so as to bring in £250 a year to be received by the Master and four Senior Fellows (called his Managers) and applied by them to a number of objects, amongst them being provision for certain Fellows and Scholars of Caius College and for a Master, Usher and Scholars of a Free Grammar School in the town of Cambridge and for six almswomen; (2) that £500 be laid out in building chambers in the College for his Fellows and Scholars; (3) he left his property in Lutburgh Lane, now called Free School Lane, to certain devisees and willed that on it should be built the Free Grammar School and the houses for his almswomen.

1617   The chambers were built this year (Willis-Clark, Vol. I, pp. 186 and 204).

    It is for this reason that the letters S. P. (for Stephen Perse) have been carved over the entrances to the present staircases Q to T; and a statue of Perse has been put up over the entrance to staircase S.

Cambridge—Free School Lane Property.

1621   A house was built on part of this land by the tenant, who held it on a 40 years' lease at an annual rent of £2. It was intended that this rent should provide for the repairs of the schoolhouse.

    It continued to be let for this rent, on leases for 40 years each, till 1858, when the last of these leases ran out, and the house was let at a rack rent of £60.

    The lease had been renewed at different times for very varying fines.

    Thus in 1722—when 22 years of the old lease were expired—the price was £12; in 1762—37 years expired—£100; in 1790—14 years expired—£21; in 1818—14 years—£135.

1623   By this year the schoolhouse and the almshouses had been built by the executors and the regulations for the school were then drawn up.

1810   The garden in front of the almshouses (between them and Pembroke Street) was taken on a lease from the Corporation of Cambridge, for 999 years, from Lady Day, at a rent of 5s.

1828–41   The large schoolroom was let at an annual rent of £50 to the trustees of the Fitzwilliam collection.

1829   The managers of the trust bought, of R. E. Kerrich (the tenant of the house built in 1621) for £1050 (and expenses £29), three houses and a small plot of garden, 16 feet square, all adjoining Free School Lane and the land left by Dr Perse.

    The three houses were let for £24, £14 and £13 a year. The small plot was let to Mr Kerrich, apparently without any rent, until 1858, when his lease of the house expired.

1842–4   The school and Master's houses were rebuilt at a cost of £2393. 2s. 1d.

1861   The almshouses were rebuilt on the plans of Mr Salvin at a cost of £1301. 15s. 7d.

1867 The leasehold garden of the almshouses was made freehold at a cost of £10.

1873 (Michaelmas) The school premises and the house built in 1621 were handed over to the new governing body of the school.

1874 (Michaelmas) The property bought in 1829 was sold to the University for £1520.

1885 The University acquired the site of the almshouses and their garden by conveying to the College the site at Newnham on which the almshouses now stand (having bought it for the purpose from Clare College) and by paying to the Charity Commissioners the sum of £2010 to defray the expense of taking down and re-erecting the almshouses and to increase the endowment of the almswomen. After the removal there remained £914. 9s. 0d. Consols, the interest on which has since been applied to the latter purpose.

Essex Property.

1618 Mr Martin Perse, the acting executor, for the purpose of providing the annual income of £250 bought, for £5000, of Sir T. Bendishe, the Manor of Frating with the following farms and woodlands in the same and adjoining parishes ·

    (1) 233 acres in Frating, Elmstead and Thorington.
    (2) 42 ,, ,, ,,
    (3) 128 ,, ,, ,, Great and Little Bentley, Elmstead and Thorington.
    (4) 84 ,, ,, Elmstead.
    (5) 160 ,, ,, Great and Little Bentley and Bromley.
    (6) 100 ,, ,, Frating and Thorington.
    (7) 55 ,, ,, some of the above parishe
    (8) 34 ,, ,, Great and Little Bentley.
The woodlands were:
120 acres in Great and Little Bentley, Much Bromley and Frating.
 46 ,, ,, Frating.

1627 A lease of this property for 66 years was granted to Martin Perse at the rent of £228. 18s. 0d. for the first year and £248. 18s. 0d. for each subsequent year; and a similar lease of the Bassingbourne property at the annual rent of £21. 2s. 0d. (see p. 7).

1797 In an exchange, with R. Manning, the managers gave up a driftway belonging to Frating Hall Farm measuring 13½ rods by 2 rods and took an alder carr 14 rods by 12½ rods.

1798 An exchange was made with the Rector of Frating of 2 r. 11 p. for an equal quantity of glebe.

1799–1802 The land tax of £33. 4s. 0d. on the then Essex property was redeemed by the payment of £1217. 6s. 0d. of the 3 per cent. Consols by 16 instalments.

1819 At the enclosure of Great Bentley, land was sold to defray the expenses of the Commissioners. The managers of the Trust paid £62. 17s. 4d. for their share of the expenses and received the following allotments:

	a.	r.	p.	
(1)	0	0	10	
(2)	0	1	8	
(3)	0	1	2	
(4)	0	0	35	
(5)	0	1	35	on Tye Common.
(6)	1	1	31	,, ,,
(7)	2	0	9	,, ,,

1830   The managers bought, of S. and H. Edenborough, for £1500, the tithes on 66 a. of woodland, 170 a. of arable and 8 a. of marshland in Great Bentley, part of the Crab Tree Farm.   These tithes at the commutation were commuted for £2. 10s. 0d. on the woodland and £55 on the arable.

1836   This year there was purchased, of O. Simons for £5250, the High Elms Farm, consisting of 150 a. in Alresford, Elmstead and Frating.

1843   In the Enclosure Award for Elmstead and Alresford no allotment was made to the Trust.

1844   Tithe amounting to £9 on 26 a. 3 r. 25 p. in Great Bentley, part of Pain's Farm, was bought for £212. 10s. 0d.
       In an exchange with the Rector of Frating the Managers gave up 5 a. 1 r. 2 p. (No. 86) and took tithes amounting to £13. 10s. 0d. on 107 a. 3 r. 21 p. in Hockley Farm—leaving the tithe on this farm at £16. 4s. 0d.

1845   For £270 were bought, of W. K. Dawson, 2 a. 3 r. 10 p. called Freighting Meadow in Elmstead.

1846   At the Bromley enclosure, land was sold to defray the expenses amounting to £2640. 11s. 11d. and the Trust received 1 r. 32 p. adjoining Bull's Green.

1860   The Managers bought, for £5. 5s. 0d., one rood of the waste of the Manor of Little Bentley next the road from Colchester to Thorpe.

1864   Tithe amounting to £4. 2s. 0d. on 12 a. 2 r. 20 p. of Great Bentley in the Dairy Farm was bought of Messrs Swain and Cross for £80.

1864–68   The Tendring Hundred Railway Company took 10 a. 1 r. 32 p. from High Elms and Hockley Farms, for which was paid first and last (£1250 + £395 + £30 =) £1675.

1869   The Managers gave 1600 sq. yds. adjoining the Churchyard of Frating as an addition to it.

1892   The Great Eastern Railway Company took further pieces amounting to 1 a. 1 r. 13 p. and paid £120.

1894   The 11 a. 0 r. 35 p. in Thorington severed by the railway from Hockley Farm was exchanged with A. K. Francis for 8 a. 1 r. 5$\frac{3}{4}$ p. on the N. side of the railway—he paying £25 for " equality of exchange."

1905   The following are the tithe apportionments on the estates in these various parishes retained for the Trust after the partition of the property in 1879 (see below):

	£	s.	d.
Great Bentley	18	10	3
Little Bentley	25	17	9
Great Bromley	5	8	9
Elmstead	17	14	9
Frating	36	9	8
Thorington	23	10	3
Alresford	28	8	6

Farm at S. Osyth.

1825   In the parish of S. Osyth a farm, consisting of a house and premises and 67 a. 2 r. 24 p., copyhold of the Manor of Chick S. Osyth, was bought by the Managers for £2600 of W. K. Dawson.   On this the land tax had been redeemed in 1798.

1841   The expense to the Trust of the tithe commutation was £7. 5s. 0d.

1859   A plot of 2 a. 1 r. 0 p. was bought, for £110, from J. T. Ambrose, executor of W. F. Nassau.

1865 At the enclosure 2 a. 1 r. of copyhold land on S. Osyth Heath was assigned to this farm. It cost £10. 12s. 0d. to fence it. The Commissioners sold land to defray their own expenses.

1905 The tithe apportionment on the whole farm is £23. 2s. 0d.

West Dereham (Norfolk) and Bassingbourne (Cambs).

1627 *Bassingbourne.* In consideration of the grant to Martin Perse to cut the woods and underwoods in Essex, he conveyed to feoffees for the College 77 acres in Bassingbourne of the annual value of £21. 2s. 0d. A lease of the property was granted to him for 66 years at the rent of £21. 2s. 0d.

This with the rent he paid for the Essex property made up the £250 a year which Dr Perse intended to secure to the Managers under his will.

1733 *West Dereham.* The 77 acres at Bassingbourne (then valued at £333. 6s. 8d.) and £739. 16s. 10d. in money were handed over to the College by the Perse Managers, who received in exchange all the lands at W. Dereham lately acquired by the College (*see* DENVER and BASSINGBOURNE).

Of these lands 22 a. 3 r. were copyhold of the Manor of Carples—fine 2s. an acre and quit-rent 7s. 4d. (of which 1s. 2d. was for eggs and hens); 35 a. 3 r. were copyhold of the Manor of Timworth—fine 2s. an acre, quit-rent 6s. 5d. (22 a. 2 r., out of the 35 a. 3 r., had been allotted at the enclosure in 1666.) Also there were 8 a. 2 r. copyhold of the Manor of W. Dereham, and 15 a. 2 r. were freehold. Of the freehold land 9 a. 2 r. had been allotted at the enclosure.

1799–1802 A land tax of £6. 12s. 0d. was redeemed by payment of £242 Consols in 11 instalments.

1873 The 8 a. 2 r. were enfranchised for £75.

1894 For £300 some arable land in four strips, containing 10 a. 2 r. 24 p., was bought of the executors of H. Aylmer. It was much intermixed with land belonging to the Trust.

Lawshall (Suffolk).

1733 The Managers bought, for £400, from the executor of Mr S. Camborn, a farm containing 16 a. 2 r. copyhold of the Manor of Lawshall and 22 a. 3 r. 8 p. freehold. (The executor handed the £400 over to the College as part payment of Mr C.'s legacy to the College of the chief part of his estate, amounting to £3000, for the purchase of advowsons.)

1795 The acreage was estimated at 33 a. and the annual value at £30. 7s. 0d.

1799–1802 The land tax, £3. 8s. 0d., with that on the Barningham Farm (£2. 16s. 0d.), was redeemed for £227. 6s. 8d. Consols. £124. 13s. 4d. was therefore the amount of Consols paid for the Lawshall land tax.

1810 The annual value was estimated at £40.

1864 Three roods, west of the house, were enclosed and added to the farm.

1875 The estate—then measuring 40 a. 0 r. 3 p.—was sold to the tenant for £1230.

Division of the Trust.

1837 41 It is unnecessary to give an account of the Chancery suit during these years. The results are fully set out in Cooper's *Annals of Cambridge* under this date.

By this time the Trust had accumulated £23,100 Consols and £2400 New South Sea Annuities.

1873   A new governing body for the school was appointed by order of the Charity Commissioners, and the Managers had to pay to the new governing body—as from Michaelmas 1873—a share of each annual net income which was to bear the same ratio to the net income that £626. 1s. 7d. bears to £2184. 7s. 6d.

1877   A careful valuation of the property of the Trust was effected—the timber being measured up—and a part was handed over to the governing body of the school. This part was:

		a.	r.	p.
(1)	Frating Hall Farm	379	1	1 ;
(2)	Part of Dairy Farm, Frating	15	3	33 ;
(3)	Woodlands	23	0	37 ;

(4) The Manor of Frating Hall in Frating, Bentley and Elmstead (except any rights over the land retained by the Managers);

(The above with the underwood and timber thereon were valued at £14,886.)

(5) Also £6228. 2s. 1d. of 3 per cent. Consols valued at £5932. 6s. 2d.

The portion retained by the Managers consisted of:

	a.	r.	p.
High Elms Farm	144	1	34
Hockley ,, ...	194	2	1
Part of Dairy Farm, Frating	68	3	9
Pain's Farm, Bentleys	117	1	34
Crab Tree Farm, Bentleys	236	1	31
Lamb's Farm, S. Osyth	71	3	34
Great Bromley Allotment.......................	0	1	35
Frating Rectory Allotment	5	1	12
Woodlands	92	2	29
West Dereham	79	3	4

(The above with underwood and timber thereon were valued at £38,981)

The value of the public stocks retained was £12,835. 5s. 2d.

The share of the expense attending this division paid by the Managers was £499. 7s. 7d.

This division of the property was sanctioned by the Charity Commissioners, Feb. 3, 1880, and took effect as from Michaelmas, 1879, and after that the property of the Trust was vested in the official trustee of charitable lands and funds.

Thenceforward the Managers of the Trust had no more to do with the finances of the school.

DAVY TRUST. *Heacham (Norfolk).*

1839   Dr Davy (Master) died and devised his estate in Heacham to the College for the use of the Master.

The estate then contained 200 a. 3 r. 3 p. with a residence (Heacham Lodge).

In the Lodge and Home Farm Miss E. Davy had a life interest.

Dr Davy also owned the Rectorial tithes (£25. 4s. 10d.) and left them to the College with the land.

Parts of the land were copyhold and held of three different manors.

1854   At the enclosure of the common the College received nine allotments containing 33 a. 3 r. 4 p., some of them copyhold of the Manor of Heacham.

A field containing 3 a. 3 r. 29 p. was bought for £300 of P. Sant.

1862   The Lynn and Hunstanton Railway Company took 1 a. 3 r. 35 p. and paid £170.

1868 For £99. 13*s.* 0*d.* the College enfranchised the quit-rents, &c., on the various copyholds, amounting to £2. 3*s.* 10*d.*

1869 Miss Davy died. From this time the Master has occupied the Lodge and enjoyed the rents of the Home Farm.

1875 For £347 the College bought, of W. Minns, 4 a. 0 r. 20 p., which he en-franchised before the conveyance was executed.

1893 For the consideration of £552. 10*s.* 0*d.* the College obtained the enfranchisements of 17 different parcels in the "Manor of Heacham with the Members" containing 76 a. 0 r. 36 p.
The rights reserved to Lords of Manor under Sec. 48 of the Copyhold Act 1852 were not enfranchised.

1898 The Rectorial tithes belonging to the College were merged in the land.

1900 For £650 a field, containing 4 a. 0 r. 4 p., was bought of R. Pull.

1901 The College bought, for £20, from Mr H. Ingleby, 485 square yards next the "Pit" (Pond) on the S. side of the road leading to the railway station. The rents (exclusive of that of the Home Farm) now amount to about £260.

DROSIER TRUST.

1889 Dr W. H. Drosier (Senior Fellow) died May 11 and devised his estate—after paying a few slight legacies—for the purpose of increasing the number of Fellowships; but subject to the payment of an annuity of £500 to his brother, Mr Charles Drosier, and of one or two quite small annuities.
The property consisted of
(1) Three cottages in Cambridge Place, in Cambridge, of which the annual rent amounted to £18. 18*s.* 0*d.* ;
(2) Land let on building leases for the following houses in Croydon (Surrey), viz. Nos. 1–8 Elton Villas and Nos. 1–10 Malvern Villas, all in Bensome Manor Road, of which the rents amounted to £152 ;
(3) Land let on building leases for 19 houses in Forest Gate (Essex), viz. Forest House, Malvern House and Nos. 1–17 Bolsena Road, of which the rents amounted to £85.
(4) Land let on building leases for 12 houses in Leytonstone (Essex), viz. Nos. 1–12 Elm Terrace, of which the rents amounted to £128.
(5) Two mortgages for £5900, on which the interest was £230.
(6) Cash and investments in railway stocks and Consols of which the value was £34,656.

1898 The site of the cottages in Cambridge Place was let on an agreement for a building lease for 99 years at a rent of £6 a year.

1899 A farm in Aldreth in the Isle of Ely, containing 146 a. 2 r. 16 p., was bought for £2500 of Major de Freville. It was partly copyhold of the Manor of Haddenham. The sum of £8. 17*s.* 6*d.* was paid for the timber and £76 for expenses. The rent was £160.
There was a land tax on the farm of £6. 7*s.* 0*d.* and a tithe apportioned at £39. 13*s.* 3*d.*
A house—divided into three tenements—in the Petty Cury in Cambridge was bought for £10,125 of Messrs Freeman, Hardy and Willis. The rents amounted to £425 and there was a land tax of £2. 2*s.* 0*d.* on the property. The expenses of the purchase were £126.

1901   The copyhold portion of the Aldreth property was enfranchised for £146.

1902   Bradfield's Farm, in Haddenham, adjoining the Aldreth Farm and containing 70 a. 1 r. 3 p., was bought, for £1200, of Mr E. Foster's trustees. Part of it was copyhold and was enfranchised for £35.
The expenses of the purchase were £37.
The rent was £70.   There was a land tax of £1. 17s. 4d. on the farm, and a drainage tax of about £14, and the tithe was apportioned at £17. 10s. 9d.

1905   Mr C. Drosier died.

1910   There are now six Fellowships on this Foundation.
The land tax on the property in Petty Cury has been redeemed for £63.

ADDENDA.

BINCOMBE.

1910   A ram was constructed at a cost of £404 to supply water from a spring behind the Royal Oak Inn to the West Farm and our houses in Ridgeway and Upwey.

CAXTON.

1910   The house &c. bought in 1824 was sold for £100.

DITTON.

1910   The College bought of G. Fletcher for £1050 (expenses £26) 10 a. 3 r. 33 p. lying E. of a footpath to Cambridge and N. of the railway to Mildenhall.

OBORNE.

1910   The College bought of W. H. C. Davey and others for £260 (expenses £12. 7s. 6d.) 4·996 a. of pasture in Castleton, lying W. of our property.

STOCKPORT (CHESHIRE).

1910   By the "S. Mary, Stockport, Rectory Act," promoted by Canon W. Symonds, Rector and Patron (Venn, II, 292), the Advowson of the Rectory, after the next presentation, will be vested in our College; and the stipend of future Rectors is fixed at £1250.
The Rector has considerable rights of patronage as regards District Churches in Stockport &c.

List of the Estates (omitting small additions), in the order in which they came into the possession of the College, with the names of the *donors* from whom, or with whose money, they were obtained :

1354	Capel
„	Foulden (Advowson)
„	Mutford „
„	Wilton „
1361	Mutford (Rectory)
1362	Foulden (Rectory)
1363	Mattishall (Advowson)
1386) or 1393)	} Wilton (Rectory)
1395	Mattishall (Rectory)
1431	Barnby
1441	Acle and Norwich (S. Michael's Coslany), *W. Tweight*
1478	Barningham, *S. Smith*
1479	Foulden (Land), *R. Powle*
1487	Tuttington, *Lady E. Clere*
1493	Causton, *Lady E. Clere*
1498	Cambridge (Mortimer's Manor), *Lady A. Scroope*
1503	Hinton and Teversham, *T. Willowes*
1504	Titchwell and Thornham, *J. Carter*
1505	Cowling (Bansteds)
1507	Chesterton, *W. Sigo*
1508	Norwich (Houses)
1520	Pattesley (Manor), *Dr J. Knight*
1521	Stow-cum-Quy and Teversham (D'Engaynes)
1534	Haddenham and Cambridge (Pease Market), *Dr J. Baily*
1539	Mordens, *J. Whitacre*
„	Barton and Chesterton, *R. Ely*
1540	Worlingham, *T. Atkyn*

1540	Cowling and Cartling, *T. Atkyn*
„	Westoning (Aynells)
1544	Wilton (The 63 Acres)
1557	Foulden (Lands), *Mapted*
1557	{ Rickmansworth (Croxley Manor) Runcton (Manor) Burnham „ } *Caius*
1560	Tilbury, *W. Cutting*
1563	Swaycliffe and Whitstable, *Mrs Joan Trapps*
1570	Haslingfield (see Barrington), *Dr T. Wendy*
„	Bincombe and Oborne, *Various*
1572	Burnham (The 16 Quarters), *N. Mynne*
1574	Caxton, *Caius*
1576	Pattesley (Rectory), *Sir C. Heydon*
1586	London (Philip Lane), *Mrs Joyce Frankland*
1596	Haglo and Pulton, *Sir R. Willison*
1599	Duxford (Dabernoons), *Mrs Joyce Frankland*
1609	Barrington
1614	Shelford (Manor and Mill)
1615 1618	*Perse* Estates
1621	Wiggenhall, *Dr W. Branthwaite*
1626	Cambridge (King's Parade), *Dr J. Gostlin* (Master)
1627	Bassingbourne, *Dr S. Perse*
1629	Dereham (West), *J. Lightwine*
1632	Weeting, *Dr J. Gostlin* (partly)
1634	Dilham and Honing, *M. Stokys*
1659	Keysho
1660	Milton, *Dr T. Batchcroft*

1664	Hockwold (Advowson)
1667	Bratton Fleming (Advowson), *G. Canham*
1669	Chilton Rentcharge, *Dr Cosin*
1680	Westoning (Samsells)
1681	Wilton (Carles)
1692	Cambridge, *Fairclough's* Holt
,,	Broadway, *Various*
1700	Denver (Land), *Dr Ro. Brady*
1702	Mepal, *J. Halman*
1703	Dereham (East)
1705	Norwich (S. Clement's), *J. Case*
,,	Hethersett, *Dr J. Gostlin* (President)
1708	Hinton, *W. Peters*
,,	Ashdon (Advowson), *S. Camborn*
,,	Shalford, *Dr J. Gostlin* (partly)
1712	Cowling Rentcharge
1713	Lavenham, *S. Camborn*
,,	Melton, *S. Camborn*
1716	Denver (Advowson), *Dr Ro. Brady*
1725	Stratton, *S. Camborn*
1728	Denver (Land), *N. White*
1729	W. Dereham, *J. Lightwine*
1733	Lawshall, *Dr S. Perse*
,,	Oxburgh, *S. Camborn* (partly)
1736	Wheatacre
,,	Blofield, *S. Camborn* (partly)
1749	Atherington, Bratton (Kippiscombe), Bray, Elmham, Fakenham, *B. Wortley*
1759	Ashdon (Mitchell's), *B. Wortley*
1762	Wilton (Farm), *Sir J. Burrough*
1774	Kettlestone, *Dr F. Schuldham*

1782	Cambridge (Trinity Street and Newnham), *B. Wortley*; Grantchester, *B. Wortley*
1810	Cambridge (Barnwell, part)
1811	Kirstead, *B. Wortley*
1818	Beachampton, *B. Wortley*
1825	S. Osyth, *Dr S. Perse*
1839	Heacham, *Dr M. Davy*
1852	Denver, *S. Coleby Smith*
1860	Teversham (Walker's Land)
1863	Ashdon (Street Farm)
1864	Cambridge (Gifford Place)
1873	Runcton (Cocks's Land)
1887	Cambridge (Rose Crescent)
1889	*Drosier* Estates
1891	Duxford (Petersfield)
1893	Cambridge (Trinity Street)
1895	Sudbury
1896	Swanton Morley
,,	Cambridge (Mill Lane)
,,	Stapleford
,,	Putney
1899	Aldreth, *Dr W. H. Drosier*
,,	Cambridge (Petty Cury), *Dr W. H. Drosier*
1900	Shelford (de Freville's Land)
,,	London (Charterhouse Square)
,,	Marshwood
1902	Haddenham, *Dr W. H. Drosier*
1903	Teversham (Tunwell's Land)
1904	Ditton (Hall)
,,	Horningsea
1905	Kittisford, *Mrs M. G. May*
1909	Chatteris
1910	Stockport, *W. Symonds*

INDEX

CAMBRIDGE: PRINTED BY JOHN CLAY, M.A. AT THE UNIVERSITY PRESS

Printed by BoD™in Norderstedt, Germany